Golf course communities are just one of the many growing populations of common area developments. Our golfer "Hubie"™ represents the Homeowner's Association lifestyle in just such a community!

The authors of this book want homeowner's association members to realize that condo management requires continuous attention to the:

(1) project improvements, and
(2) CC&Rs and Bylaws, as amended.

Homeowner's Association Management

Managing Common Interest Developments (CIDs)

First Edition

Walt Huber

Kim Tyler, JD

Educational Textbook Company, Inc.
P. O. Box 3597
Covina, California 91722
(626)339-7733
(626)332-4744 (Fax)
www.etcbooks.com

Library of Congress Cataloging-in-Publication Data

Homeowner's Association Management
Managing Common Interest Developments (CIDs) - Walt Huber and Kim Tyler

Summary: Covers all material in Homeowner's Association Management; Managing Common Interest Developments (CIDs) with special emphasis on California real estate and the Davis-Stirling Common Interest Development Act. Very clear and simple language, easy-to-read format with photographs, charts, and graphs. Includes glossary and index. Suitable for consumers, students, and teachers wishing information about personal real estate transactions. This textbook is designed to fulfill the course requirement necessary to take the California Real Estate Salesperson and Broker Exams.

ISBN 0-916772-46-2

Printed in the United States of America

Preface

California defines Common Interest Developments (CIDs) as:

1. condominium projects,
2. planned developments,
3. stock cooperatives, and
4. community apartment projects.

Although known by a variety of names in different states, all common interest developments allow homeowners to share in the use of common property and facilities, and provide a form a self-governance through a homeowner's association (HOA).

Homeowner Associations (HOAs) are made up of the homeowners in a development, who usually elect a board of directors from their membership to run the affairs of the association. As the number of CIDs and HOAs grows, so too does the need for professional property managers who specialize in this field.

The authors would like to thank the following educators for their input:

E. Denis Roden, MBA, Cabrillo College
Jay Mumford, CCIM, Chabot College
Bernie Mnichowicz, JD, Cosumnes River College
Dr. Donna Grogan, CPM, GRI, CRS, El Camino College
Sandra J. Vaughn, CPM, Fullerton College
Reynan L. Ledesma, MBS, JD, Glendale Community College
Patricia Moore, GRI, Los Medanos College
Ignacio Gonzalez, Real Estate Coordinator, Mendocino Community College
Ed Estes, Jr., JD, CRE, CCIM, GRI, Palomar College
M. Joel Carlson, GRI, CREC, DREI, Saddleback College and Santiago Canyon College
Norma Hurley, CRS, GRB, San Joaquin Delta College
Gary Goldberg, JD, Santa Barbara City College
Chris Grover, MBA, Department Chair, Victor Valley College
Jerome L. Fox, West Los Angeles College.

Authors Walt Huber and Kim Tyler would like to express our appreciation to the professionals who helped create this ground-breaking text. We couldn't have done it without the extraordinary efforts of Colleen Taber, our executive editor, and Rick Lee, our prepress and layout editor, as well as the editorial and proofreading skills of Shelley Geary, Linda Serra, and Andrea Adkins. We're also grateful for the talented contributions of art director Phillip Dockter, and cover artist Melinda Winters.

This book is dedicated to the authors' helpful and supportive wives:

Walt Huber, to his sweetie Debbie

&

Kim Tyler, to his darling Jenny

Table of Contents

Chapter 1: Introduction To Common Interest Developments: The Purchase and Sale 1

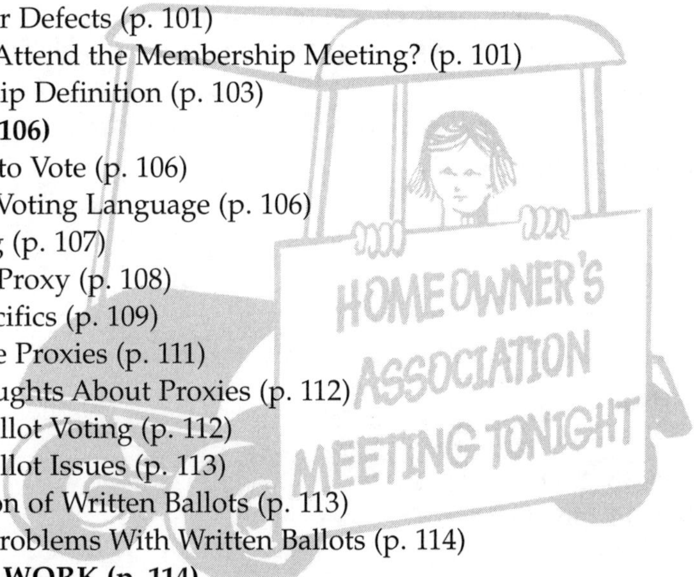
HOMEOWNER'S
ASSOCIATION
MEETING TONIGHT

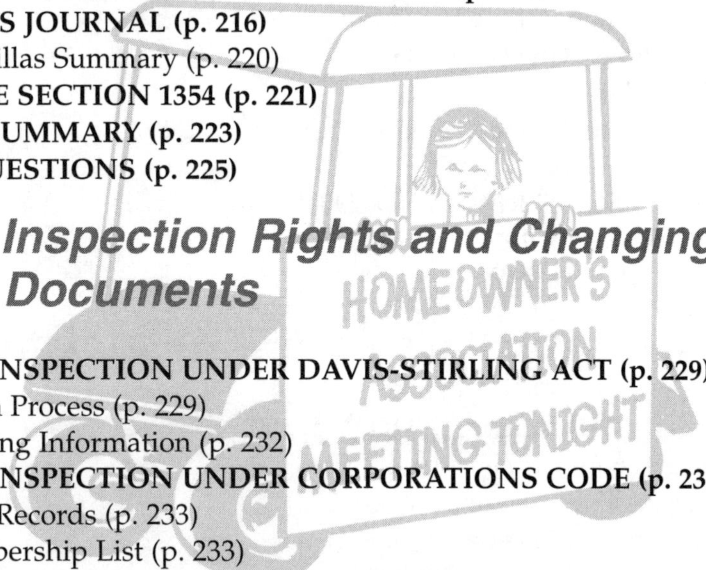
HOMEOWNER'S
ASSOCIATION
MEETING TONIGHT

Chapter 9: Financial Management of an HOA 263

Chapter 10: Assessments By the Association 297

HOME OWNER'S
ASSOCIATION
MEETING TONIGHT

HOMEOWNER'S
ASSOCIATION
MEETING TONIGHT

HOMEOWNER'S
ASSOCIATION
MEETING TONIGHT

Ocean Harbor
a condominium ft myers beac

CHAPTER 1

Introduction To Common Interest Developments: The Purchase and Sale

I. Hubie Highlands

It's a warm September morning and Gertrude is approaching the entrance to a large housing development. Gertrude has recently retired from thirty-three years of teaching at a community college. She wants to move to an area with a warmer climate and live in a development that provides activities and amenities that she would enjoy. She is excited about looking at a unit that one of the owners is selling in a development called Hubie Highlands. She was notified of the available unit by a former colleague of hers who retired in Hubie Highlands several years ago and has told her that it is a wonderful place for the active retiree.

As Gertrude approaches the entrance to Hubie Highlands, she is pleased to find that it is just like the photograph in the information her retired colleague had sent her about the property. As she enters, she notices that she is passing under a large arch way over the entrance with the name "Hubie Highlands" spelled out in wrought iron. Large red brick pillars hold up the arch way with decorative white lights and the property appears to be entirely fenced in stylish wrought iron fencing. There are several large palm trees on each side of the entrance with brilliant green grass and small colorful shrubs. As she drives down the entrance road, she sees rows of flowers in red, yellow, orange, and white, more tall palm trees on each side of the drive, attractive moguls of grass, and a wide sidewalk.

Chapter 1

CHAPTER OUTLINE

She notices that about a hundred yards in front of her, the road branches to the right and to the left, but if she continues straight, she enters into a parking lot for what appears to be an office/welcome facility with several lighted tennis courts behind it.

In front of the structure is a large Spanish-style fountain with water bubbling out of the top and cascading over into several basins before it spills into the large circular base of the fountain. The fountain is full of large colorful koi fish and water plants with large red and yellow flowers blooming. Gertrude decides to take the road to the right and she now notices the living units. All the living units are on her right and appear to be six-plexes with a ground floor and an upper floor, each containing three living units separated by a wide stairway. Every unit has decorative plants, flowers, grass, and a large sidewalk in front of it. The units each have a very distinctive door painted antique white, with stained glass of a beautiful desert scene with bright cactus flowers and desert plants.

Each unit has an enclosed two-stall garage between the six-plexes. Gertrude is certainly pleased with the southwestern architectural style of stucco and tile in a combination of desert colors of green, gold, yellow, and orange. Each building has an excellent view of the picturesque desert mountains in the distance. She counts twelve six-plexes and corresponding parking garages.

She notices that the road ahead is going to curve to the left and take her back to the entrance. At the top of the curve, there is a large single-story clubhouse, which is painted white with the same colorful tiles creating a walkway to the front double doors. Each door also has the stained glass desert scene. As the curve ends and the road straightens back to the entrance, she sees, on her left, the center section consisting of six lighted tennis courts with additional parking. The tennis courts are surrounded by a beautiful rose garden with every color of rose imaginable. Just past the tennis courts is a large grassy area with palm trees, several barbeque pits, numerous picnic tables, and a nice upscale children's playground. The playground has a desert theme to it with four large climbing structures that resemble a cactus. Each one is painted a different color, green, gold, yellow, and orange, just like the walkway tiles. This area is followed by a fenced swimming pool and Jacuzzi, complete with a cascading waterfall surrounded by colorful flowers and stone. The numerous lounge chairs, tables, and umbrellas are decorated using the same colors on the walkway in front of the clubhouse. The pool area has everything that would make a pool person like herself excited about living here.

Gertrude notices that there is some off-street parking at each of the venues and the entire center island is surrounded by a six-foot wide sidewalk. The sidewalk is decorated with colorful tiles that have different types of cactus flowers on each one. In the middle of the island, small bushes and shrubs are planted in rows with a different colored rose bush between each section of greenery. The roses were trimmed about three feet tall and each one has a wrought iron sign in front with the name of the particular rose. Tall, stylish light posts are placed about every twelve feet, making sure there is plenty of light. Gertrude thinks that this area would be an excellent place for her morning or evening walks.

Upon reaching the building by the entrance, she pulls into a visitor parking space and walks off in the dry desert air to find her friend's unit. She notes that a sign on the building says "Community Association Manager." During her walk, she remembered that her friend had written her that Hubie Highlands is a common interest development. Although vaguely familiar with the term "homeowner's association," she is unsure as to exactly what a "common interest development" means, and how they are related.

A. WHAT IS A COMMON INTEREST DEVELOPMENT (CID)?

A good place to start is with your state's Department of Real Estate website. In California, this can be found at **www.dre.gov.ca**. This site provides you with important information about common interest developments which can be accessed by clicking on "Subdivisions" and then clicking on "Living in a California Common Interest Development." To locate general information on this topic, there is a convenient question and answer format. For example:

What is a Common Interest Development (CID)?

A CID is descriptive not only of a certain type of real estate and form of home ownership, but also of a life-style that is becoming more and more common to the American way of life. To understand the concept, it is important to know that there is no one structural type, architectural style, or standard size for CIDs. They come in a variety of types and styles, such as single-family detached houses, two-story townhouses, garden-style units with shared "party walls," and apartment-like, multi-

(continued)

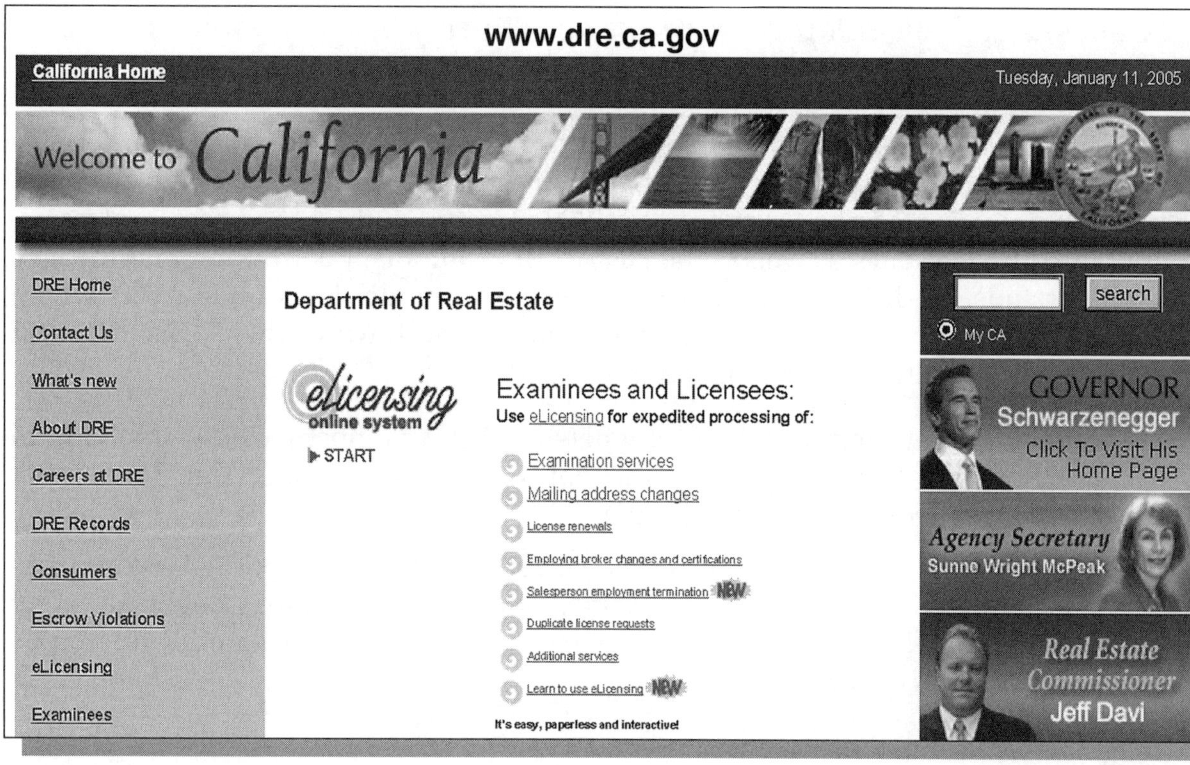

storied high rises. Currently in California, there are tens of thousands of CIDs which range in size from a simple two-unit development to a large complex having thousands of homes, many commonly-owned facilities, and multiple associations under the auspices of one overall master association.

Despite the wide range of differences that may exist among CIDs, all CIDs are similar in that they allow individual owners the use of common property and facilities and provide for a system of self-governance through an "association of the homeowners" within the CID.

The most common type of homeowner association (HOA) is the nonprofit mutual benefit corporation. This is a corporation in which the members of the corporation vote for a board of directors to run the affairs of the corporation. However, some associations, usually the older ones, are unincorporated associations. In many ways, unincorporated associations are treated the same as mutual benefit corporations under California law.

Some states have adopted uniform acts to regulate common interest developments.

States' uniform acts are prepared for state consideration by **The National Conference of Commissioners on Uniform State Laws**. According to information on its website, "The organization comprises more than 300 lawyers, judges, and law professors, appointed by the states as well as the District of Columbia, Puerto Rico, and the U.S. Virgin Islands, to draft proposals for uniform and model laws on subjects where uniformity is desirable and practicable and work toward their enactment in legislatures." Additionally, the site notes that:

1. The Uniform Common Interest Ownership Act was most recently amended in 1994 and has been adopted by the states of Alaska, Connecticut, Minnesota, Nevada, Vermont, and West Virginia.
2. The Uniform Condominium Act was most recently amended in 1980 and has been adopted by the states of Maine, Minnesota, Missouri, Nebraska, New Hampshire, New Mexico, North Carolina, Pennsylvania, Rhode Island, Texas, Virginia and Washington.

www.nccusi.org
The National Conference of Commissioners on Uniform State Laws

Many states, such as California, have state-specific legislation on common interest developments and/or condominiums, depending on that state's definition.

1. Specific CID Information

A common interest development, sometimes called a common interest community, has both a separate interest and a common interest.

The ***SEPARATE INTEREST*** *is the title or ownership interest acquired by a purchaser* and, along with that separate interest, the purchaser acquires an interest in the common area which consists of all of the remaining land and items upon that land which are not owned by those owning separate interest. So the ***COMMON AREA*** *in a common interest development is everything except the separate interests. In California, common interest developments are regulated by a variety of laws, but primarily by the* ***DAVIS-STIRLING COMMON INTEREST DEVELOPMENT ACT (The Act)***. The Act provides that a common interest development means any of the following:

1. A condominium project
2. A planned development

3. A stock cooperative
4. A community apartment project

Common Interest Developments are self-governed by Homeowner's Associations (HOAs). The term "Community Association" is used interchangeably with "Homeowner Association."

Gertrude is considering purchasing a unit in a condominium project. A **CONDOMINIUM** *consists of an undivided interest in common in a portion of the real property (common area) coupled with a separate interest in a space called a "unit."* The boundaries of the unit she is considering purchasing can typically be found in the condominium plan, which was recorded in the county recorder's office when the condominium project was built.

B. WHAT IS REAL PROPERTY?

In California, ***REAL PROPERTY*** *is generally thought of as the land, anything permanently attached to the land, anything appurtenant (something running with the land such as a recorded right-of-way to cross the land), and those things on the land which are considered to be immovable by law (such as a giant oak tree).* **PERSONAL PROPERTY** *is the other "property," and it can be viewed as all property which is not real property.*

C. BUYING A CONDOMINIUM UNIT

When Gertrude purchases the condominium unit, she will own a separate interest consisting of everything inside the edge of the four walls, bottom of the ceiling, and top of the floor. Gertrude will purchase air space plus an undivided 1/144 interest in the common area. Each of the 144 owners of a separate interest in the condominium project own an equal interest in the common areas. The common area will not only consist of the grounds and structures surrounding her unit in the six-plex, but also the walls, floors, ceilings, roof, and items contained therein and in each of the other six-plexes. All of the specifics are stated in detail in the "declaration."

D. WHAT IS A DECLARATION?

A **DECLARATION** *is the recorded document that states whether the common interest development is a community project apartment, condominium project, planned development, stock cooperative, or a combination thereof, and additionally, establishes enforceable restrictions on the use or enjoyment of any portion of the common interest development.* It also states the name of the association which will govern the development.

Declarations are also known as C&Rs (Covenants and Restrictions), CC&Rs (Covenants, Conditions, and Restrictions), or Declarations of Restrictions.

1. The Condominium

With regard to a condominium, unless the declaration provides otherwise, if walls, floors, or ceilings are designated as boundaries of a separate interest in a condominium, the interior surfaces of the perimeter walls, floors, ceilings, windows, doors, and outlets located on the edge of the separate interest are part of the separate interest. The remaining portions of the wall, floors, or ceilings are part of the common area.

In a California condominium project, some portion of the common area has to be owned by owners of the separate interest as tenants in common and the balance of the common area can be owned by the homeowner (community) association.

2. The Stock Cooperative

A ***STOCK COOPERATIVE*** *is a corporation which owns the entire development and each shareholder of the corporation has a separate interest which is the right to occupy a residential unit in the development.* An owner does not receive a deed to the property but owns a share of stock in the corporation which gives the owner the right to occupy a particular unit. The corporation will repair and maintain the property.

If the owner wants to sell a unit, the sale is accomplished with a transfer of ownership of a share of stock rather than transferring ownership by a deed.

3. The Community Apartment Project

A ***COMMUNITY APARTMENT PROJECT*** *is a development where the owners own the entire project and each owner gets the right to occupy one of the apartments.* So a 200-unit apartment building would be owned by 200 owners, each of whom have a separate interest, which is the right to occupy one of the units as provided in the deed that transferred title of the property to the owners.

The maintenance and operation of the community apartment project is handled by a board elected by the owners of the development.

4. The Planned Development

A ***PLANNED DEVELOPMENT*** *is a subdivision where the owner owns a lot as a separate interest and, typically, a homeowner (community) association owns the remaining common area rather than the lot owners.* Each lot owner automatically becomes a member of the homeowner association (HOA).

A common interest development may appear to be a typical subdivision, but it is not. Sometimes the homeowner (community)

association, rather than the local government, owns the streets, street lights, and utility lines, and has the obligation to maintain and repair those items.

Gertrude's friend mentioned she would be purchasing a separate interest.

E. WHAT INTERESTS ARE THERE IN A DEVELOPMENT?

1. The Separate Interest

A separate interest is what the purchaser is buying in a common interest development. It is sometimes referred to as "the property" or a "unit" or a "lot."

Separate Interest Meanings

According to the California Davis-Stirling Act, a separate interest has the following meanings:

1. In a condominium project, a separate interest means an individual unit.
2. In a planned development, a separate interest means a separately owned lot or parcel.
3. In a stock cooperative, a separate interest means the exclusive right to occupy a portion of the real property owned by the corporation by reason of the ownership of stock in the corporation.
4. In a community apartment project, a separate interest means the exclusive right to occupy an apartment.

2. The Common Area

In a condominium project, the ***COMMON AREA****, sometimes called the "common elements," can be owned in common by the owners of the separate interests, or some portion of the common area owned by the owners of separate interests and the balance of the common area owned by the homeowner (community) association.* Typically, the owners of the separate interest will own that part of the common area which provides them with the least risk for liability and expense and the risky and expensive areas will be owned by the homeowner or community association.

In a planned development, the common area is typically owned by the homeowner (community) association, but can be owned by the lot owners as tenants in common, however this is unlikely.

3. The Exclusive Use Common Area

Gertrude's friend also mentioned exclusive use areas for the condominium owners. What is that? In California, the ***EXCLUSIVE USE COMMON AREA*** *means that portion of the common area designated by the declaration for the exclusive use of a separate interest owner, rather than all the separate interest owners.* In Hubie Highlands, unless stated otherwise in the declaration, any shutters, awnings, window boxes, doorsteps, stoops, porches, balconies, patios, exterior doors, door frames and the hardware incident thereto, screens and windows, or other fixtures designed to serve a single separate interest, but located outside the boundaries of the separate interest, are exclusive use common areas allocated exclusively to the holder of that separate interest. Additionally, in California, external telephone wiring designed to serve a separate interest is an exclusive use common area.

A condominium buyer is purchasing the airspace within the finished walls, ceilings, floors, and those surfaces.

Additionally, a purchaser, such as Gertrude, will have an exclusive right to use a portion of the common area, including the items mentioned above, as well as the space in her parking garage, the space on her patio or balcony, and any other space designated in the declaration for the exclusive use of owners of separate interest. Gertrude needs to know that she is responsible for maintaining her separate interest in her unit, as well as the exclusive use common areas appurtenant to (running with or attached to) her separate interest.

When the owner of a separate interest sells that separate interest, the exclusive use common areas are also transferred to the new owner.

F. THE HOMEOWNER (COMMUNITY) ASSOCIATION (HOA)

Although "community association" is frequently used in California, the most commonly used term is "homeowner association" or "HOA." As such, this textbook uses the terms interchangeably.

Gertrude has been resting comfortably in her friend's condominium and has expressed her delight with the entire Hubie Highlands development, as well as the information her friend provided. She asks who maintains the common areas and keeps everything repaired and in such immaculate condition. Her friend, Luke, tells her that the condominium project is managed by an association incorporated under the non-profit mutual benefit laws of the state, and it is run by a board of directors elected by the association members, who are separate interest owners. The association does not have to be incorporated, but most associations are. The association is responsible for maintaining the common areas and does so through assessments paid by the members. A homeowner (community) association manager runs the development on a day-to-day basis as directed by the board.

G. STATE-BY-STATE LAWS GOVERNING HOAs

In California, the *Davis-Stirling Act* governs interest developments (including condominiums). Every state has different laws and regulations that govern these types of developments. Depending on the state in which you reside, you should consult one of the following websites to fully understand the community association laws.

www.megalaw.com/top/condo.php
MegaLaw.com

Alabama Code
www.legislature.state.al.us/CodeofAlabama/1975/coatoc.htm
Title 35, Chapter 8 - Condominium Ownership
Title 35, Chapter 8A - Alabama Uniform Condominium Act
Title 35, Chapter 8B - Community Development Districts
Alaska Horizontal Property Regimes Act
www.touchngo.com/lglcntr/akstats/Statutes/Title34/Chapter07.htm
Alaska Uniform Common Interest Ownership Act
www.touchngo.com/lglcntr/akstats/Statutes/Title34/Chapter08.htm
Arizona Condominium
www.azleg.state.az.us/ars/33/title33.htm
California Davis-Stirling Common Interest Development | [alt. source]
a http="/ca/cacodelink.php?codelink=http://www.leginfo.ca.gov/cgi-bin/waisgate?WAISdocID=31385012269+0+0+0&WAISaction=retrieve
Colorado Condominium Ownership Act
http://64.78.178.125/cgi-dos/statdspp.exe?LNP&doc=38-33-101
Colorado Common Interest Act
http://64.78.178.125/cgi-dos/statdspp.exe?LNP&doc=38-33.3-101
Connecticut Condominium Act
http://www.cga.state.ct.us/2001/pub/Chap825.htm
Connecticut Common Interest Ownership Act
http://www.cga.state.ct.us/2001/pub/Chap828.htm
Florida Condominium Act
/fl/flstatutes.php?App_mode=Display_Statute&codelink=URL=Ch0718/titl0718.htm@StatuteYear=2001@Title=%2D%3E2001%2D%3EChapter%20718
Georgia Condominium Act
www.ganet.state.ga.us/cgi-bin/pub/ocode/ocgsearch?docname=OCode/G/44/3/70
Hawaii Condominium Property Act
www.capitol.hawaii.gov/hrscurrent/Vol12/hrs514a

(continued)

Idaho Condominium Property Act
www.idwr.state.id.us/idstat/TOC/55015KTOC.html
Illinois Condominium Property Act | [alt. source]
www.legis.state.il.us/ilcs/ch765/ch765act605.htm
www.condolawyers.com/lawtext/law1.htm">[alt. source]
Indiana Horizontal Property Law
www.state.in.us/legislative/ic/code/title32/ar1/ch6.html
Iowa Horizontal Property Act
www2.legis.state.ia.us/IACODE/1999/499B
Kansas Apartment Ownership Act - Chapter 58, Articles 31 & 37
www.ink.org/public/legislative/statutes/statutes.cgi
Kentucky Horizontal Property Law (PDF format)
www.lrc.state.ky.us/KRS/381-00/CHAPTER.HTM
Maine Condominium Act
http://janus.state.me.us/legis/statutes/33/title33ch310sec0.html
Maryland Condominium Law
www.sos.state.md.us/sos/admin2/html/condoindex.html
Massachusetts Condominium Law
www.state.ma.us/legis/laws/mgl/gl-183A-toc.htm
Michigan Condominium Act
www.michiganlegislature.org/law/getObject.asp?objname=Act-59-of-1978&objType=statute
Minnesota Condominium Act
www.revisor.leg.state.mn.us/stats/515
Minnesota Uniform Condominium Act
www.revisor.leg.state.mn.us/stats/515A
Minnesota Common Interest Ownership Act
www.revisor.leg.state.mn.us/stats/515B
Mississippi Condominium Law
www.mscode.com/free/statutes/89/009/index.htm
Missouri Condominium Property Act
www.moga.state.mo.us/STATUTES/C448.HTM
Montana Unit Ownership Act
http://statedocs.msl.state.mt.us/cgi-bin/om_isapi.dll?clientID=2592&advquery=condominium&hitsperheading=on&infobase=MCA_97.NFO&record={4FA385}&softpage=Document&x=39&y=12
Nebraska (Search for 76-825 to 894)
http://statutes.unicam.state.ne.us/Statutes
Nevada Uniform Common-Interest Ownership Act
www.leg.state.nv.us/NRS/NRS-116.html

(continued)

Nevada Condominium Law
www.leg.state.nv.us/NRS/NRS-117.html
New Hampshire Condominium Act
http://sudoc.nhsl.lib.nh.us/rsa/356-B.htm
New Jersey Condominium Act
www.njleg.state.nj.us/html/statutes.htm
New Jersey Horizontal Property Act
www.njleg.state.nj.us/cgi-bin/om_isapi.dll?infobase=Statutes.nfo&dept
New Mexico Condominium Act
www.michie.com/resources1.html
New York Condominium Act
/ny/nycodetoc.php?QUERYDATA=@SLRPP0A9-B
North Carolina Condominium Act
www.ncga.state.nc.us/statutes/statutes_in_html/chp047c.html
North Carolina Unit Ownership Act
www.ncga.state.nc.us/statutes/statutes_in_html/chp047a.html
North Dakota Condominium Law - Section 47-04.1-01 (PDF format)
www.state.nd.us/lr/index.html
Ohio Condominium Law
http://onlinedocs.andersonpublishing.com/revisedcode/home3.cfm?GRDescription1=revised%20code&GRDescription2=title%2053&GRDescription3=&TextField=%3CJD%3A%225311%22%3ECHAPTER%205311%3A%20CONDOMINIUM%20PROPERTY&GRStructure1=5311&GRStructure2=
Oklahoma Condominium Law
http://oklegal.onenet.net/oklegal-cgi/get_statute?98/Title.60/60-501.html
Oregon Condominium Law
http://landru.leg.state.or.us/ors/100.html
Pennsylvania Condominium & Homeowner Laws - From PA Condo Law
www.pacondolaw.com/statutes_uca1.html
Rhode Island Condominium Ownership Act
www.rilin.state.ri.us/Statutes/TITLE34/34-36/INDEX.HTM
Rhode Island Condominium Act
www.rilin.state.ri.us/Statutes/TITLE34/34-36/INDEX.HTM
South Carolina Horizontal Property Act
www.lpitr.state.sc.us/code/t27c031.htm
South Dakota Condominium Law
www.michie.com/resources1.html
Tennessee Horizontal Property Act
www.michie.com/resources1.html

(continued)

Texas Property Code: Condominiums Created Before Adoption of Uniform Condominium Act
/tx/txcodefiles.php?file=http://www.capitol.state.tx.us/statutes/py/py008100toc.html
Texas Uniform Condominium Act
www.capitol.state.tx.us/statutes/py/py008200toc.html
Utah Condominium Ownership Act
www.le.state.ut.us/~code/TITLE57/57_07.htm
Vermont Condominium Ownership Act
www.leg.state.vt.us/statutes/title27/chap015.htm
Virginia Horizontal Property Act
http://leg1.state.va.us/cgi-bin/legp504.exe?000+cod+55-79.1
Virginia Condominium Act
http://leg1.state.va.us/cgi-bin/legp504.exe?000+cod+55-79.39
Washington Condominium Act
www.tenantsunion.org/ltlaw/rcw64_34.html
Wisconsin Condominium Ownership Act
http://folio.legis.state.wi.us/cgi-bin/om_isapi.dll?clientID=87640&infobase=stats.nfo&j1=703.01&jump=703.01&record={5257}
Wyoming Condominium Ownership Act
http://legisweb.state.wy.us/statutes/titles/title34/chapter20.htm

CONDOMINIUM LAW WEB SITES

ABA Section of Real Property, Probate and Trust Law
www.abanet.org/rppt/home.html
American Hotel & Lodging Association Condominium Committee
www.ahma.com/committees/view_committee.asp?mstr=39

II. Gertrude Buys Her Unit

A. DISCLOSURES BY A SELLER IN A COMMON INTEREST DEVELOPMENT (In California)

After looking at the unit she is interested in purchasing, Gertrude is now, more than ever, convinced that she wants to live in Hubie Highlands. Mr. and Mrs. Frank, the sellers of the unit, deliver to her, as required by California law, the following documents for her review, which are unique to common interest developments (CIDs).

1. Governing Documents

A copy of the governing documents of the common interest development is provided. These documents consist of the declaration, the homeowner (community) association's articles of incorporation, the association's corporation bylaws, and the operating rules and regulations of the association. If the association had not been incorporated, a statement to that effect would have been required.

2. Association Financial Statement and Collection Rights

Also provided is a copy of the most recent pro forma operating budget, the most recent review of the financial statement of the association by a licensed California board of accountancy professional (this is required since the gross income of the association exceeds $75,000 during the fiscal year), the association statement describing its policies and practices for enforcing lien rights or other legal remedies for delinquent payment of assessments by its members, and the summary of the association property, general liability, earthquake, flood, and fidelity insurance policies.

3. Assessment Notice and Unit Status

A true statement from the authorized representative of the association (in this case the association manager) must be delivered, disclosing the amount of the association's current regular and special assessments and fees, any assessments levied upon the seller's interest that are unpaid on the day of the statement, and any monetary fines or penalties levied upon the seller's interest and unpaid as of the date of the statement. The manager's statement also must include accurate information on late charges, interest, and cost of collection which, as of the date of the statement, are or may be made a lien upon the seller's interest in the development.

4. Discipline Notices

The sellers also deliver a copy or a summary of any notice previously sent to the sellers notifying the sellers of the board of director's meeting to consider imposing discipline upon the seller for any alleged violation of the governing documents that remains unresolved at this time.

5. Other Possible Disclosures

The following documents would also be provided to Gertrude if they are applicable at the time of the purchase of her unit:

a. A notice of any change in the association's current regular and special assessments and fees which have previously been approved by the association's board of directors that have yet to become due and payable.

b. Current legally enforceable age restrictions. State law allows common interest developments to restrict occupancy to seniors (discussed in a later chapter). If this is the case, Gertrude would learn the specifics in the declaration and receive a statement that such restrictions are only enforceable to the extent permitted by state law, plus a statement specifying the applicable provisions of the current law. This might cover situations where the age limitations in the declaration, which was recorded many years ago, are not valid under current state law.

c. The review of the financial statement of the association done by a CPA, if the gross income of the association is more than $75,000.

d. A copy of the preliminary list of construction defects and any agreement between the association and the builder with regard to a settlement of the defects. If no agreement has been reached, a statement that a final determination as to whether the list of defects is accurate and complete has not been made must be given to the purchaser.

The above information is provided to buyers of condominium units because it is the seller's legal obligation to do so.

Providing a condominium buyer with the appropriate disclosure requirements is the obligation of the seller, not the responsibility of the association.

If the seller willfully violates the obligation to provide a purchaser with the applicable documents, the seller is liable to the purchaser for any actual damages occasioned by the failure to deliver those documents and, in addition, must pay a civil penalty in an amount determined by the court not to exceed $500. In any lawsuit to enforce this liability, the prevailing party shall be awarded reasonable attorney's fees from the losing party as part of the judgment. The seller will also have to comply with transfer disclosure obligations applicable to sellers of California residential dwelling units, which will be listed later.

6. Airport Disclosure

If the common interest development in California is located within an airport-influenced area, a declaration, recorded after January 1, 2004, must contain the statement shown in **Figure 1-1**.

Figure 1-1

NOTICE OF AIRPORT IN VICINITY

This property is presently located in the vicinity of an airport, within what is known as an airport-influenced area. For that reason, the property may be subject to some of the annoyances or inconveniences associated with proximity to airport operations (for example: noise, vibration, or odors). Individual sensitivities to those annoyances can vary from person to person. You may wish to consider what airport annoyances, if any, are associated with the property before you complete your purchase and determine whether they are acceptable to you.

An ***AIRPORT-INFLUENCED AREA*** *(also known as an* ***airport referral area****) is the area in which current or future airport-related noise, over flight, safety, or airspace protection factors may significantly affect land uses or necessitate restrictions on those uses as determined by an airport land use commission.* Since this requirement was not in effect before January 1, 2004, it would certainly be in the best interest of a buyer of a separate interest in a common interest development to take the initiative and find out if there is an airport land use commission located in the general vicinity of the common interest development.

An airport vicinity notice in the declaration is not a defect, lien, or encumbrance on the title being purchased by the buyer.

7. First Sale Notice

As soon as practical before the transfer of title for the first sale of a unit, the owner/agent must deliver to the prospective buyer a written statement listing all substantial defects or malfunctions in the project. This applies to residential condominiums, community apartment complexes, or stock cooperatives which were converted from an existing dwelling. Also included should be a written statement which discloses any knowledge of a substantial defect or malfunction.

8. Blanket Encumbrance Disclosure

If a lot, parcel, or unit of a subdivision is subject to a blanket encumbrance, the subdivider, or the agent for the subdivider, shall not sell or lease the property for a term exceeding five years until the prospective buyer or tenant has been furnished with and has signed a copy of the following notice:

BUYER/LESSEE IS AWARE OF THE FACT THAT THE LOT, PARCEL, OR UNIT WHICH HE OR SHE IS PROPOSING TO PURCHASE OR LEASE IS SUBJECT TO A DEED OF TRUST, MORTGAGE, OR OTHER LIEN KNOWN AS A "BLANKET ENCUMBRANCE."

IF BUYER/LESSEE PURCHASES OR LEASES THIS LOT, PARCEL, OR UNIT, HE OR SHE COULD LOSE THAT INTEREST THROUGH FORECLOSURE OF THE BLANKET ENCUMBRANCE OR OTHER LEGAL PROCESSES EVEN THOUGH OUR LESSEE IS NOT DELINQUENT IN HIS OR HER PAYMENTS OR OTHER OBLIGATIONS UNDER THE MORTGAGE, DEED OF TRUST, OR LEASE. ____________DATE _________________________ SIGNATURE OF BUYER OR LESSEE.

B. A GENERAL DISCLOSURE

Some states require that the buyer receive a specific disclosure containing general information about purchasing in a common interest development. For example:

NEVADA REVISED STATUTES: CHAPTER 116

BEFORE YOU PURCHASE PROPERTY IN A COMMON INTEREST COMMUNITY DID YOU KNOW ...

1. YOU ARE AGREEING TO RESTRICTIONS ON HOW YOU CAN USE YOUR PROPERTY
These restrictions are contained in a document know as the Declaration of Covenants, Conditions and Restrictions (CC&Rs) that should be provided for your review before making your purchase. The CC&Rs become a part of the title to your property. They bind you and every future owner of the property whether or not you have read them or had them explained to you. The CC&Rs, together with other "governing documents" (such as association bylaws and rules and regulations), are intended to preserve the character and value of properties in the community, but may also restrict what you can do to improve or change your property and limit how you use and enjoy your property. By purchasing a property encumbered by CC&Rs, you are agreeing to limitations that could affect your lifestyle and freedom of choice. You should review the CC&Rs and other governing documents before purchasing to make sure that these limitations and controls are acceptable to you.

2. YOU WILL HAVE TO PAY OWNERS' ASSESSMENTS FOR AS LONG AS YOU OWN YOUR PROPERTY
As an owner in a common interest community, you are responsible for paying your share of expenses relating to the common elements, such as landscaping, shared amenities and the operation of any homeowner's association. The obligation to pay these assessments binds you and every future owner of the property. Owners' fees are usually assessed by the homeowner's association and due monthly. You have to pay dues whether or not you agree with the way the association is managing the property or spending the assessments.

(continued)

The executive board of the association may have the power to change and increase the amount of the assessment and to levy special assessments against your property to meet extraordinary expenses. In some communities, major components of the community such as roofs and private roads must be maintained and replaced by the association. If the association is not well managed or fails to maintain adequate reserves to repair, replace and restore common elements, you may be required to pay large, special assessments to accomplish these tasks.

3. IF YOU FAIL TO PAY OWNERS' ASSESSMENTS, YOU COULD LOSE YOUR HOME
If you do not pay these assessments when due, the association usually has the power to collect them by selling your property in a non-judicial foreclosure sale. If fees become delinquent, you may also be required to pay penalties and the association's costs and attorney's fees to become current. If you dispute the obligation or its amount, your only remedy to avoid the loss of your home may be to file a lawsuit and ask a court to intervene in the dispute.

4. YOU MAY BECOME A MEMBER OF A HOMEOWNER'S ASSOCIATION THAT HAS THE POWER TO AFFECT HOW YOU USE AND ENJOY YOUR PROPERTY
Many common interest communities have a homeowner's association. In a new development, the association will usually be controlled by the developer until a certain number of units have been sold. After the period of developer control, the association may be controlled by property owners like yourself who are elected by homeowners to sit on an executive board and other boards and committees formed by the association. The association, and its executive board, are responsible for assessing homeowners for the cost of operating the association and the common or shared elements of the community and for the day-to-day operation and management of the community. Because homeowners sitting on the executive board and other boards and committees of the association may not have the experience or professional background required to understand and carry out the responsibilities of the association properly, the association may hire professional managers to carry out these responsibilities. Homeowner's associations operate on democratic principles. Some decisions require all homeowners to vote, some decisions are made by the executive board or other boards or committees established by the association or governing documents. Although the actions of the association and its executive board are governed by state laws, the CC&Rs and other documents that govern the common interest community, decisions made by these persons will affect your use and enjoyment of your property, your lifestyle and freedom of choice, and your cost of living in the community. You may not agree with decisions made by the association or its governing bodies even though the decisions are ones which the association is authorized to make. Decisions may be made by a few persons on the executive board or governing bodies that do not necessarily reflect the view of the majority of homeowners in the community. If you do not agree with decisions made by the association, its executive board or other governing bodies, your remedy is typically to attempt to use the democratic processes of the association to seek the election of members of the executive board or other governing bodies that are more responsive to your needs. If persons controlling the association or its management are not complying with state laws or the governing documents, your remedy is typically to seek to mediate or arbitrate the dispute and, if mediation or arbitration is unsuccessful, file a lawsuit and ask a court to resolve the dispute. In addition to your personal cost in mediation or arbitration, or to prosecute a lawsuit, you may be responsible for paying your share of the association's cost in defending against your claim. There is no government agency in this state that investigates or intervenes to resolve disputes in homeowner's associations.

5. YOU ARE REQUIRED TO PROVIDE PROSPECTIVE BUYERS OF YOUR PROPERTY WITH INFORMATION ABOUT LIVING IN YOUR COMMON INTEREST COMMUNITY
The law requires you to provide to a prospective purchaser of your property, before you enter into a purchase agreement, a copy of the community's governing documents, including the CC&Rs, association bylaws, and rules and regulations, as well as a copy of this document.

(continued)

You are also required to provide a copy of the association's current financial statement, operating budget and information regarding the amount of the monthly assessment for common expenses, including the amount set aside as reserves for the repair, replacement, and restoration of common elements. You are also required to inform prospective purchasers of any outstanding judgments or lawsuits pending against the association of which you are aware. You are also required to provide a copy of the minutes from the most recent meeting of the homeowner's association or its executive board. For more information regarding these requirements, see Nevada Revised Statutes 116.4103.

6. YOU HAVE CERTAIN RIGHTS REGARDING OWNERSHIP IN A COMMON INTEREST COMMUNITY THAT ARE GUARANTEED YOU BY THE STATE

Pursuant to provisions of chapter 116 of Nevada Revised Statutes, you have the right:

(a) To be notified of all meetings of the association and its executive board, except in cases of emergency.

(b) To attend and speak at all meetings of the association and its executive board, except in some cases where the executive board is authorized to meet in closed, executive session.

(c) To request a special meeting of the association upon petition of at least 10 percent of the homeowners.

(d) To inspect, examine, photocopy and audit financial and other records of the association.

(e) To be notified of all changes in the community's rules and regulations and other actions by the association or board that affect you.

7. QUESTIONS?

Although they may be voluminous, you should take the time to read and understand the documents that will control your ownership of a property in a common interest community. You may wish to ask your real estate professional, lawyer or other person with experience to explain anything you do not understand. You may also request assistance from the ombudsman for owners in common interest communities, Nevada Real Estate Division, at 775-687-4280.

Buyer or prospective buyer's initials:_______________

Date: _______________________

C. PRACTICAL ISSUES FOR GERTRUDE'S CONSIDERATION

If Gertrude was buying a separate interest in a "planned development," she would be purchasing a lot and everything located on that lot. However, since she is purchasing a unit in a condominium, it is very important for Gertrude to understand exactly what her "unit" consists of.

The exact physical location of each unit must be described on a recorded final map, parcel map, or condominium plan in sufficient detail so as to locate the boundaries of each unit.

Additionally, in California, a declaration, recorded on or after January 1, 1986, must contain a legal description of a common interest development which will also contain a boundary description of a unit. Although the general concept of a "unit," as mentioned before, might be an easy concept to comprehend, the specifics of the unit's boundaries are incredibly important for each owner to be aware of. Gertrude may have been told her unit's location by her friend, however, she needs to read the recorded legal description to determine the accuracy of her friend's description. She will need to ascertain the following:

1. Since she is buying a unit on the second floor, and it includes a balcony, is the balcony part of the unit (separate interest) or assigned to the unit as an exclusive use of a common area?
2. How are the boundaries described with regard to walls surrounding her unit? She needs to determine if the description distinguishes different types of walls, such as perimeter walls which would surround her unit, perimeter walls may also be between units or between her unit and a common area such as a hallway, or the wall that leads to the outside air and environment. Is there a reference to structural walls that are load-bearing and support the building, versus non-structural walls that merely divide up room? Does the description tell her how much of each wall is part of a unit? Is it only the finished surface of the wall which would consist of wallpaper, paint, or paneling, or does the ownership extend deeper to include the finished surface of the wall which would typically be the wallboard or plaster on the unit's side of the wall? Does the unit consist of everything from the unit's side of the wall to the center of the framing of the wall, or does the unit consist of the entire wall?

Ownership of walls inside of the perimeter walls should be determined. Obviously, it's important to know what portion of a wall is owned by and is the responsibility of a unit owner and what portion of the wall, if any, is a common area or an area owned by another unit owner.

3. What portion of a floor or ceiling is included with a unit? Is it the entire floor or ceiling or only a portion of it? Like walls, does ownership include just the finished portion of a floor which would be carpet, tile, cork, linoleum, marble, etc.? The same question applies to the ceiling; does ownership stop with surface, which would consist of paint, stain, or ceiling tiles? If there are exposed beams on the ceiling, who owns those? Are the beams decorative or structural? Does ownership extend deeper into the floors and ceiling? Who owns the finished oak flooring, the plywood under the carpet, the plaster or sheet rock on the ceiling, the carpet pad, and the concrete floor? As with walls, Gertrude may find that there are different layers of ownership depending on whether the floor or ceiling is between her unit and another unit, a common area, or the outside.
4. The holes in the walls or ceiling can also present ownership issues. Does Gertrude own all or only a portion of the windows and doors to the unit? Does she own an entire door or just a portion of the door? Does she own all of the glass in a window or just a portion of the glass? Who owns the screens on the windows? Does it matter whether the door is an exterior door or a door completely within her unit? How much of a skylight or light tube is part of the unit?

5. Gertrude also needs to make sure she knows how much of the "stuff" located within the unit she owns. Who owns the kitchen appliances, cabinets, countertops, sinks, showers and tubs, toilets, ceiling fans, lights (especially recessed lighting), electrical switches and switch plates, electrical outlets and plates, disposal, built-in appliances, faucets, and fireplace or woodstove? Along this same line, what part of the following items, which are necessary for some of the "stuff" previously mentioned, are part of the unit: electrical wiring and circuit breakers; plumbing within the walls and exposed plumbing under the sink; the heating and air-conditioning system such as thermostat, duct work, filter, or the heating and air conditioning system which is wall or window mounted; the venting for the kitchen range or fireplace; and the security system, consisting of wiring, window and door sensors, motion detectors, and control panel, and the door bell or intercom system. Are there any other areas within the condominium project that are part of the unit such as separate ownership of a parking area, garage or a storage area? Exactly how are they described?

AN EXAMPLE - Minnesota Statute 515B. 2-102(b)

In a condominium or cooperative, except as the declaration otherwise provides, if the walls, floors, or ceiling of a unit are designated as its boundaries, then the boundaries shall be the interior, unfinished surfaces of the perimeter walls, floors, and ceilings of the unit. All paneling, tiles, wallpaper, paint, floor covering, and any other finishing materials applied to the interior surfaces of the perimeter walls, floors, or ceilings are a part of the unit, and all other portions of the walls, floors, or ceilings, including perimeter doors and windows, and their frames, are a part of the common elements.

Obviously, these would not be issues if Gertrude had purchased a lot with a structure on it as part of a planned development. Issues in that case might involve the ownership of items on the boundary line of a lot, such as trees, boulders, fences, or walls and easements (right-of-ways) allowing people to cross certain areas of the lot, as well as view easements and light easements. In any event, this is important information that you, as the homeowner (community) association manager, should also know.

III. Seller's Real Estate Agent

When Mr. and Mrs. Frank decided to sell their unit, they asked the association manager if there were any requirements regarding the use of a particular real estate broker or office when selling units in the development. Such a requirement may be possible in some locations.

In California, any attempt by the association to establish an exclusive relationship with a real estate broker for the sale or marketing of a separate interest in the development is void.

IV. Can the Association Charge a Fee When a Unit is Sold?

State laws may differ, but in California, the collection of fees by associations for selling units is very limited.

For example, in California, the community association may charge a fee for the preparation of the required documents that Mr. and Mrs. Frank legally must deliver to a purchaser. That fee cannot exceed the association's reasonable cost to prepare and reproduce those documents. Additionally, an association cannot impose or collect any assessment, penalty, or fee in connection with a transfer of title or any other interest except the association's actual cost to change its records. Therefore, the association cannot collect a percentage fee based on the selling price or a flat fee that would exceed its actual costs for record changing. As the association manager, you will have to establish the document preparation fee and the record changing fee. Obviously, the amount of time involved for such tasks will vary from sale to sale. A reasonable charge based on the wage of the preparer, divided by the time spent on the task, plus overhead for copies might be appropriate. You will have to be able to prove how the amount was calculated.

V. Additional Disclosures Made by Seller to Buyer

Some states have certain required disclosures that must be made to a real estate purchaser.

In California, the following disclosures and actions are required.

A. TRANSFER DISCLOSURE STATEMENT

The law requires sellers of residential property of from one-to-four units to provide prospective buyers with a Real Estate Transfer Disclosure Statement.

The ***REAL ESTATE TRANSFER DISCLOSURE STATEMENT*** *identifies items of value attached to the structure or land and states whether these items are operational.* It also asks the seller to identify any structural or material defects. This form provides an opportunity for the seller to completely disclose problems of any kind that might adversely affect

the value of the property. California law imposes the obligation to prepare and deliver the Transfer Disclosure Statement to the prospective buyer upon the seller and the seller's real estate broker if he or she has the property listed for sale with the broker.

The Real Estate Transfer Disclosure Statement is a form which was mandated and prepared by the legislature and is printed by and available from a variety of sources.

B. OCCUPANT'S DEATH

An occupant's death on the premises, whether from natural causes, suicide, murder, or age-related illness, can be a highly emotional issue. Therefore, the legislature requires the seller to disclose to the buyer the death of an occupant on the property when that death has occurred less than three years prior to the date the buyer offers to purchase the property. **The occupant's death, or manner of death, is not required to be disclosed if the death occurred more than three years prior to the offer to purchase.**

Additionally, the seller does not have to disclose to the purchaser that an occupant of the property was inflicted with or died from AIDS, even if it was during the three-year window. However, an intentional misrepresentation concerning an occupant's death on the property, in response to a direct inquiry, will subject the seller to liability for the misrepresentation. In other words, if the death occurred on the property four years ago, the seller would not have to make the disclosure to a prospective purchaser. However, if the purchaser has inquired as to whether there were any deaths on the property, then the seller must make the disclosure. Also, as the law only requires the disclosure of an occupant's death on the property during the three-year period, a potential issue is the definition of an "occupant."

C. NATURAL HAZARDS DISCLOSURE

If the property is located within one or more of the six specified natural hazard zones, the seller, or his or her agent, is required to provide prospective buyers with a revised **Natural Hazard Disclosure Statement**.

D. MELLO-ROOS BONDS AND TAXES

If the property is subject to a continuing lien securing the levy of special taxes to finance designated public facilities and services under the **Mello-Roos Community Facilities Act**, the seller must attempt to obtain a notice from an appropriate local agency disclosing details of the tax.

E. ORDNANCE LOCATION

The seller must give written knowledge of former state or federal ordnance locations within one mile of the property.

"Ordnances" are military material, such as weapons and ammunition, and may pose a threat of contamination or explosion.

F. WINDOW SECURITY BARS

The seller must disclose the existence of window security bars and safety release mechanisms.

G. EARTHQUAKE GUIDES

The seller and/or agent for the seller must provide the buyer with a copy of *The Homeowner's Guide to Earthquake Safety* from the Seismic Safety Commission. Additionally, disclosure must be made if the property is located in an earthquake zone.

H. SMOKE DETECTOR COMPLIANCE

The seller must provide the buyer with a written statement that the property complies with California Smoke Detector Law.

I. LEAD-BASED PAINT DISCLOSURE

The seller must disclose the presence of lead-based paint or a lead-based hazard and any other known information and reports, such as the location and condition of painted surfaces.

J. ENVIRONMENTAL HAZARD PAMPHLET

The Real Estate Transfer Disclosure Statement provided to the buyer by the seller must specify environmental hazards of which the seller is aware. If the buyer is given a pamphlet entitled *Environmental Hazards: A Guide for Homeowners, Buyers, Landlords, and Tenants,* neither the seller nor the seller's real estate agent is required to furnish any more information concerning such hazards, unless the seller or agent has actual knowledge of the existence of an environmental hazard on or affecting the property.

K. PEST INSPECTION

If required by the contract or by a lender, the seller and/or the seller's agent must deliver to the buyer, before the transfer of title, a report and written certification by a registered structural pest control company regarding the presence of wood-destroying organisms.

L. FOREIGN SELLERS

If the buyer knows that the seller is a "foreign person," then the buyer must withhold and send to the IRS 10% of the sales price of the property. See the IRS code for details.

M. SALES TAX WITHHOLDING

The buyer must withhold 3.33% of a total sales price as state income tax in certain transactions.

N. TITLE INSURANCE NOTICE

When no title insurance is to be used, the buyer must receive and sign or acknowledge a statutory notice regarding the advisability of obtaining title insurance with the close of escrow.

O. WATER HEATER SECURITY

A seller must certify in writing that the water heater has been braced, anchored, or strapped to resist movement due to earthquake motion.

P. REGISTERED SEX OFFENDERS

A statutorily defined notice regarding the existence of public access to database information regarding sex offenders is required.

Q. REAL ESTATE AGENCY RELATIONSHIPS

If a real estate agent is used by the seller, disclosures must be made. The ***DISCLOSURE REGARDING REAL ESTATE AGENCY RELATIONSHIPS*** *form states that an agent must disclose the nature of the agency relationship as soon as practical.*

An agent may represent a seller, a buyer, or both.

The law requires that both parties to the sales transaction be informed of the various options they have regarding real estate agent representation. Both the buyer and the seller must sign the form acknowledging they understand their rights and have received a copy of this disclosure. In addition, agency disclosure must again be confirmed by the **Residential Purchase Agreement** or on a separate form.

VI. Disclosure Litigation

The case of *Assilzadeh v. California Federal Bank* involves a dispute regarding the seller's obligation of disclosure.

Assilzadeh v. California Federal Bank

82 Cal.App.4th 399; 98 Cal.Rptr.2d 176 (App. 2 Dist. 2000)
Edited Excerpts From the Opinion of Judge Weisman

California Federal acquired title to the condominium unit in July, 1996, after a successful credit bid at a foreclosure sale. In April 1996, California Federal took possession of the unit and then on June 12, 1996 entered into an exclusive listing agreement with Fred Sands Realtors to market and sell the unit. Plaintiff Assilzadeh, who was a tenant living in another unit in the same condominium building, was interested in purchasing the particular unit owned by California Federal and being marketed by Sands. The final sale agreement provided the following: "Buyer to be aware that property was acquired through foreclosure and Seller is exempt from providing a property disclosure statement... No warranties expressed or implied are included in this sale. Subject property is being sold in its present "As Is" condition. Buyer will satisfy himself/herself as to the condition of said property,..."

Before the close of escrow, Sands disclosed in writing to Assilzadeh that the buyer should be aware that the homeowner's association of the condominium project where the unit was located had filed a lawsuit against the developer for construction defects and that the suit had recently been settled for $5.1 million. Assilzadeh was aware, prior to the close of escrow, that any improvements or alterations to the unit required prior submission to and approval by the architectural control committee of the homeowner's association. After the close of escrow, Assilzadeh's request to the homeowner's association for permission to install marble flooring in her unit was denied because the floor of her unit could not support the weight of the marble due to defective construction. Assilzadeh then filed suit against California Federal, Sands, and its agent based primarily on their failure to disclose in detail all of the specific defects alleged in the construction defect lawsuit.

As California Federal and Assilzadeh both point out, the exemption from statutory disclosure does not relieve a seller from its common law duty of disclosure. In the context of a real estate transaction, it is now settled in California that where the seller knows of facts materially affecting the value or desirability of the property and also knows that such facts are not known to, or within the reach of the diligent attention and observation of the buyer, the seller is under a duty to disclose them to the buyer. Undisclosed facts are material if they would have a significant and measurable effect on market value. The seller or his or her agent must have actual knowledge in order to be liable for failing to disclose a material fact.

Assilzadeh failed to present any evidence that California Federal or Sands knew the actual contents of the complaint filed in the construction defect litigation or had ever seen a copy of the court file or any document in the file. Thus, no duty existed on the part of California Federal to disclose all of the details of the suit since they were unaware of all the details. We conclude that California Federal satisfied its duty of disclosure by informing Assilzadeh of the existence of the construction defect litigation and its settlement. At that point, the details of the suit were certainly within the diligent attention of the buyer, who could have examined the file in its entirety to learn all the details of the suit and its settlement.

(continued)

We conclude that the material facts actually known to Sands and its agent were that a lawsuit had been filed and settled relating to alleged construction defect litigation, and that Sands and its agent satisfied their statutory duty to inspect and disclose when they disclosed the existence of the lawsuit to Assilzadeh. [The trial court judgment for the defendants is affirmed.]

California case law indicates that if a buyer knows of a settlement regarding construction defects, the buyer must take the responsibility to locate and read the settlement.

The California Department of Real Estate (DRE) Approved This Course!

California has approved this course as one of the statutorily required college-level courses for an applicant for the Real Estate Salesperson or Broker License. In addition, this course may also be taken for part of your four-year Continuing Education requirement.

It will be taught at many:

1. community colleges and universities;
2. private real estate schools; and
3. real estate or community associations.

This book and course must cover a minimum of 30 classroom hours to count towards the necessary "coursework" required to be **"Certified-Manager"** granted, after being tested by some of the following trade associations:

1. California Association of Community Managers (CACM)
2. Community Associations Institute (CAI)
3. Institute of Real Estate Management (IREM)
4. National Board for Certification of Community Association Managers (NBC-CAM)
5. Executive Council of Homeowners (ECHO)

Florida goes even further, requiring a license for Community Association Managers. There, an applicant must complete a course with a minimum of 18 classroom hours.

VII. CHAPTER SUMMARY

California, where the majority of homeowner's associations are for condominiums, uses the the all-inclusive ownership term Common Interest Developments (CIDs). CIDs include condominium projects, planned developments, stock cooperatives, and community apartment projects. All CIDs allow individual owners the use of common property and facilities and are governed by a homeowner's association (HOA). If you are a resident of another state, just substitute condominium for Common Interest Development.

CID's interests, like condominiums in other states, include: separate interest, common area interests, and exclusive use area interests.

The seller of a separate interest in a CID must deliver to the perspective buyer:

1. a copy of the governing documents;
2. the association's financial statements and collection rights;
3. a true statement of status of assessments and any additional fines, penalties, or charges against the seller; and
4. any disciplinary notices previously sent to the seller for alleged violations of the governing documents which are currently unresolved.

Sellers may be obligated to provide buyers with additional disclosures, if applicable, including changes in assessments and fees not yet due and payable, age restrictions, CPA review of association financial statement if gross income exceeds $75,000, and a preliminary list of construction defects or settlement with builder regarding such defects.

Homeowner Associations (HOAs) nationally are being replaced by the term Community Associations (CAs).

Airport influence, first sale notice, and blanket encumbrances may also be required.

Furthermore, buyers and community association managers need to be aware of boundary specifics, including "exclusive" versus "separate interests," where ownership of walls, ceilings and floors begin and end in a condo, and lot boundary lines or easements of a lot in a planned development.

In California, CIDs associations and/or managers cannot require the exclusive services of a real estate broker for the sale of units, and may only charge reasonable fees for the preparation and duplication of the required documents involved in the sale.

Selling a unit within a common interest development is subject to the same disclosure requirements as any other 1-4 unit residential property. In California, these include the transfer disclosure statement, occupant's death, natural hazards, Mello-Roos bonds and taxes, ordnance location, lead-based paint, and other disclosures.

VIII. REVIEW QUESTIONS

1. In California real estate, CIDs refers to:

   a. commission influenced deals.
   b. cooperative investment developments.
   c. common interest developments.
   d. none of the above.

2. All CIDs are similar in that they:

   a. have strict age restrictions.
   b. allow individual owners the use of common property and facilities.
   c. provide for self-governance through a homeowner's association (HOA).
   d. both b and c are correct answers.

3. Which of the following is not recognized as a common interest development in California?

   a. A stock co-operative
   b. A planned development
   c. A community tenant complex
   d. A community apartment project

4. In the sale of a separate interest in a stock co-operative, the seller conveys what document to the buyer?

   a. A share of stock in the corporation
   b. A quit claim deed
   c. A grant deed
   d. A 100-year lease

5. In a planned development, the separate interest purchased by a buyer is typically a:

   a. a unit.
   b. a lot or parcel.
   c. a share of stock in the corporation.
   d. a long-term lease.

6. Which of the following documents is the seller NOT required to give a buyer regarding a common interest development?

   a. The association's statement describing its policies and practices for enforcing lien rights or other collection tactics for delinquent assessments.
   b. The most recent pro forma operating budget.
   c. An association statement disclosing any unpaid assessments on the property.
   d. A copy of the current status of the seller's loan on the property being sold.

7. A notice in the declaration stating a common interest development is located in an airport-influenced area is considered:

   a. a defect.
   b. a lien.
   c. an encumbrance.
   d. none of the above.

8. Upon the sale of a member's separate interest, the board of directors of the Hubie Highlands Community Association is allowed to charge a fee:

   a. of no more than six percent of the sales price.
   b. to cover the reasonable cost to prepare and reproduce documents only.
   c. of $300 or less.
   d. none of the above.

9. Association member Nickelson decides to sell his unit nine months after an old college buddy died of a heart attack during a visit. Nickelson may not be required to disclose this death in California because:

   a. the death occurred within three years.
   b. the death did not occur of unnatural causes.
   c. only an occupant's death requires notification to the buyer.
   d. condominium developments are excluded from death notification disclosures.

10. In *Assilzadeh v. California Federal Bank*, the court held that:

   a. the seller had an obligation to disclose to the buyer the terms of the lawsuit settlement between the association and the developer.
   b. the seller had satisfied its obligation to disclose by informing the buyer of the existence of the construction defect litigation and its settlement.
   c. the seller had no obligation to disclose anything with regard to the construction defect litigation or the settlement to the buyer.
   d. the buyer could install marble flooring in the unit without approval of the architectural control committee.

ANSWERS: 1. c; 2. d; 3. c; 4. a; 5. b; 6. d; 7. d; 8. b; 9. c; 10. b

RESERVED
1

CHAPTER 2

Homeowner (Community) Association Management

I. Management of the Development

A. AN INTRODUCTION TO MANAGING THE DEVELOPMENT

The California Davis-Stirling Common Interest Development Act requires that a common interest development must be managed by a community association, also referred to as a homeowner association (HOA). The association can either be incorporated or unincorporated.

Since most community associations are incorporated as nonprofit mutual benefit corporations, we will cover only those. To become an incorporated community association, articles of incorporation must be filed with the Secretary of State. Gertrude learned this from her friend Luke, who told her he is on the board of directors for the community association of Hubie Highlands. A sample of a blank form that can be used for articles of incorporation for a nonprofit mutual benefit corporation and instructions for completion are contained in **Figure 2-1**. This form is found on the "forms" page of the Business Portal at the Secretary of State's website, and is called "Articles of Incorporation (Nonprofit Common Interest Development."

Chapter 2

CHAPTER OUTLINE

www.ss.ca.gov

If the managing association is unincorporated, it is granted most of the powers given to a nonprofit mutual benefit corporation.

This is to provide some structure to an unincorporated association by holding it to the same standards as a corporation. Therefore, whether incorporated or unincorporated, the association is governed by the particular requirements of your state law. This prevents unincorporated associations from making up their own rules and requirements for important issues regarding governance of the association.

As an association manager, you should review and become familiar with all documents relating to forming an incorporated or unincorporated association.

Hubie Highlands was completed and all units were sold several years ago. At that time, Luke became a member of the board of directors. The community association was formed as a nonprofit corporation under the California Nonprofit Mutual Benefit Corporation Law. The objective is a nonprofit association of members, who own separate interest in the development, that will be working toward the mutual benefit of each other by making a long-term commitment to the purpose of the Association, which is improving and maintaining the development. Since the Association is incorporated, it will undoubtedly have bylaws. The ***BYLAWS*** *govern the association's internal affairs (rules and procedures) and how it functions.* The bylaws need to conform to the requirements of the California Nonprofit Mutual Benefit

Figure 2-1

SAMPLE

ARTICLES OF INCORPORATION

I

The name of this corporation is ______*(NAME OF CORPORATION)*______.

II

A. This corporation is a nonprofit **MUTUAL BENEFIT CORPORATION** organized under the Nonprofit Mutual Benefit Corporation Law. The purpose of this corporation is to engage in any lawful act or activity, other than credit union business, for which a corporation may be organized under such law.

B. The specific purpose of this corporation is to ______________________________
____.

III

The name and address in the State of California of this corporation's initial agent for service of process is:

Name ____

Address ____

City ____________________ State **CALIFORNIA** Zip __________

IV

Notwithstanding any of the above statements of purposes and powers, this corporation shall not, except to an insubstantial degree, engage in any activities or exercise any powers that are not in furtherance of the specific purposes of this corporation.

V

This corporation is an association formed to manage a common interest development under the Davis - Stirling Common Interest Development Act.

VI

NOTE

Use only one of the two statements, ***if applicable.***

DO ***NOT*** *USE BOTH STATEMENTS*

The address of the business or corporate office of the association is __________
____________________________________ . This office is on site.

OR

The address of the business or corporate office of the association is __________
____________________. The nine-digit zip code of the common interest development is ____________. The front street and the nearest cross street to the common interest development are ______________________________
____.

Secretary of State ***Sample***
ARTS-MU-CID (Rev 07/2004)

Page 1 of 2

NOTE

*Use only **if applicable.***

VII

The name and address of the association's managing agent is ______________
____.

______*(Signature of Incorporator)*______
(Typed name of Incorporator), Incorporator

*Secretary of State **Sample***
ARTS-MU-CID (Rev 07/2004)

Page 2 of 2

Corporation Law, as well as regulations established by the California Department of Real Estate. Luke suggests that if Gertrude wants more particular information about the homeowner (community) association, she should talk with the association manager, LeeAnn, as she is at the office today. Gertrude walks across the development to LeeAnn's office which is behind the fountain at the main entrance.

B. WHAT A MANAGER SHOULD KNOW ABOUT THE COMMUNITY ASSOCIATION AND THE BOARD OF DIRECTORS

The board of directors of Hubie Highlands, of which Luke is a member, is charged with, among other things, the responsibility for making important decisions regarding the Association. Obviously, what is an "important" decision will vary with the size of the common interest development, both in terms of the number of members and the extent of the common areas it owns. Generally, the board is involved in three primary activities.

1. Financial Business

The board members are responsible for monitoring the financial and business affairs of the association to preserve and protect the interest of the members.

This can include topics such as resurfacing the tennis court, insurance coverage, roof replacement, retaining the services of a certified public accountant, and using a property manager.

2. Rules and Enforcement

The board members are responsible for knowing, enforcing, and revising the rules governing the common interest development.

This might involve the community association's bylaws, the recorded declaration, or the general rules regarding use of the common areas. Specifically, this might include collection of unpaid assessments from members, revising the regulations for guest parking, adopting a new regulation regarding pets, or holding a disciplinary hearing against a member for a major infraction of an association rule.

3. Community Association Goodwill

The board members must be respectful toward the issues and concerns of the members of the association which the board serves. Therefore, the board members must be good listeners, facilitators, mediators, and hopefully friends with the membership. The board must be receptive to new ideas and propose changes, be able to settle conflicts between members, and keep the membership informed about community association issues.

C. THE BOARD OF DIRECTORS

1. Board Members

The board of directors must act as a board, in other words, as a group, at a properly called meeting where a quorum is present. Exactly what does this mean? The ***BOARD MEMBERS*** *are individuals who are elected by the members of the association*. The ***MEMBERS OF THE ASSOCIATION*** *consist of the owners of the separate interests in the common interest development*. The procedure for the election will be discussed in another chapter. Unless the governing documents (i.e. the articles of incorporation, bylaws, regulations of the association, and declaration) or a state law or regulation states otherwise, there are no specific requirements as to who may become a director. As an association manager, you will probably find director eligibility requirements in the bylaws of the association. If particular requirements to be a director are desired, consider one or more of the following:

a. The director must be a member of the community association. It makes sense that if you want to be a member of a board making decisions regarding the membership of an association, you should have a vested interest in the association by owning a membership. On the other hand, this requirement would exclude residents in the development who are tenants of association members. If a tenant is on a long-term lease (assuming the renting of units is permissible), the tenant may have a genuine interest in the well-being of the association and be extremely knowledgeable about association issues to a larger extent than an absentee owner. This is particularly true if the absentee owner lives a significant distance from the development and only rarely visits the development.

   Another issue would be restricting board membership to resident members. Exactly what is a "resident" member? If a member only resides in the development for the months of January and February of each year, is two months out of twelve sufficient to make him or her a resident member?

Florida has condominium hotels in beach areas where the association rents out units to increase the owners' income.

b. The board member must be in "good standing" with the association. Typically, this means that the board member must be current on all payments, fees or assessments to the association and not have had membership privileges revoked at a disciplinary hearing because of a violation of an association rule. The theory here is that if the board member is not paying why should the member be entitled to spend the money paid by other association members? Additionally, if the member cannot follow the rules of the association, why would the member be allowed to enforce those rules as a director? An underlying issue here is whether the "good standing" requirement must be

met before the member is eligible to run for election to the board and what to do when a current board member who is in good standing at the time of election loses the status of good standing while serving on the board.

c. Before being eligible to run for a position on the board of directors, a member must own an interest or have resided in the development for a set period of time.

The theory here is that the members of the association are looking for familiarity with the issues that the association has encountered over time, which a new member might be unfamiliar with. This familiarity would, at least in theory, make the board member more productive and efficient. On the other hand, the association might be losing a new member who is an energetic, enthusiastic, devoted person who is a quick learner and is excited about the opportunity of enhancing the environment of the development. Why make that person wait for the established period of time (for example 18 months) before becoming eligible for a position on the board? Sometimes, the members who have held their interests longer than anyone else are the most apathetic members of the association.

2. Board Size and the Quorum

The size of the board is another item which is generally found in the association bylaws. Sometimes, the size of the board reflects the size of the development and the number of members. That is, the smaller the development and number of members, the smaller the size of the board and, conversely, the larger the development and number of members, the larger the number of members of the board of directors. Often times, the membership is set at either a board of five, six or seven directors.

As a general rule, the more members on the board of directors, the more difficult it is to resolve issues at board meetings. It is also more difficult to attract a significant number of candidates to run for board membership who are enthusiastic, confident, and committed to the best interest of the development.

Before a board can conduct business, a quorum must be present. Since a ***QUORUM*** *consists of a majority*, unless provided otherwise in the articles or bylaws, a small board can be a problem. For example, if you have a board of four, you need three members present in order to conduct business. Obviously, this is a problem if, through no fault of his or her own, a board member cannot make the meeting. Does that mean the other three must attend? Two members in non-attendance means the board would have to adjourn. It's possible that with a board of seven there is a greater likelihood that four of the seven will show up at the meeting.

You can now see why sometimes a board will be set at seven members rather than six, as there is a better likelihood of getting four of seven present to constitute a quorum than four of six members present. Also, it is sometimes thought that the board of directors should consist of an odd number of directors. This is because, assuming all members are in attendance, there is a better likelihood of passing or defeating motions since there is less chance for a tie vote than with an even number of board members.

Sometimes it's difficult, as a practical matter, to get enough directors to attend a board meeting to constitute a quorum. If a quorum is not present, no business can be conducted. Therefore, legislation may allow the articles or bylaws to provide for a quorum of less than a majority of the directors.

Unless provided otherwise by legislation, a decision made by a majority of the directors present at a meeting, at which a quorum is present, is an act of the board. The articles or bylaws of the corporation may require a higher percentage than a majority to constitute an action of the board; however, this is unlikely due to the sometime sporadic attendance at board meetings by the members. For example, if the authorized number of board members is seven, it will take four members to be present in order to constitute a quorum. If a quorum of four is present, then three members of the board voting for or against a proposal constitutes an action of the board. Obviously, if all seven members are present at the meeting, then four is the majority necessary for board action.

In California, the articles or bylaws may not provide that a lesser vote than a majority of the directors present at a meeting constitute an act of the board.

AN EXAMPLE - California Corporations Code § 7211(a)(7)

The articles or bylaws may not provide that a quorum shall be less than one-fifth the number of directors authorized in the articles or bylaws, or less than two, whichever is larger, unless the number of directors authorized in the articles or bylaws is one, in which case one director constitutes a quorum.

If a quorum is not present at the board meeting, the majority of the directors present may adjourn the meeting to another time and place. This can present the practical problem of notifying members who were not in attendance of the rescheduled meeting. In California, if the meeting is adjourned for more than twenty-four hours, notice of any adjournment to another time and place must be given prior to the time of the rescheduled meeting to the directors who were not present at the time of the adjournment. As a practical matter, the new meeting should be scheduled at a time far enough in advance so that the required four-day notice, set by California civil code, to members of the association and board members can be satisfied.

3. Length of Term

The term a member may serve on the board will probably be limited by state law or regulation, the articles of incorporation, or the bylaws of the association.

The term "restriction" should be examined carefully to see whether it limits a director from being elected for a consecutive term. For example, a board member is elected for a term of two years. Is there anything that appears to be a "term limit" which would prevent the director from running for a second two-year term? Also, there might be a limit of the maximum term for which a person can be elected as a director. This would prevent directors from being elected to a board for life.

Sometimes there is a provision providing for the election of members to serve on a board of directors for staggered terms. For example, each board member is elected to a term of three years. If you have a board of five members and they are all elected at the same time, then three years later five new people will be elected to the board. If the staggered terms are used, two directors could be elected for a three-year term; one year later two more directors are elected for a three-year term; and one year later a single director will be elected to a three-year term. This would mean that, in the following year, two directors will be elected to fill the vacancies of the two directors whose three-year terms just expired.

Staggered terms are an effective way to keep experienced individuals on a board while new members gain experience. It also allows a degree of continuity amongst existing board members, which may be beneficial.

4. Nominations

Typically, the bylaws, or perhaps one of the other governing documents, specifies a procedure for nominating members to run for election to the board of directors. This nomination procedure is usually done by one or more of the following:

a. The appointment of a nominating committee which will follow the established procedure and timelines to recruit qualified members to run for election to the board.

b. The nomination of a member to run for the board of directors which will be done at a membership meeting.

c. Nomination of a member by a petition signed by the required number of members.

5. When the Board Meets

Generally, the governing documents or a state law or regulation will set the requirements for how often a board must meet. The requirement might be for a monthly meeting, quarterly meeting, semi-annual meeting, or an annual meeting.

As the association manager, you need to be aware of when the meetings will take place and generally will have the responsibility to send out the notices and make the proper arrangements for the meeting.

AN EXAMPLE - California Civil Code § 1365.5

Unless the governing documents impose more stringent standards, the board of directors of the association must meet at least quarterly to review the current reconciliation of the association's operating accounts, a current reconciliation of the association's reserve accounts, the current year's actual reserve revenues and expenses compared to the current year's budget, review an income and expense statement for the association's operating and reserve accounts, and review the latest account statements prepared by the financial institution where the association has its operating and reserve accounts.

6. Notice of Board Meetings

Once again, the bylaws will normally provide for giving notice to association members of a board meeting. Usually, a written notice must be given, and there is some time period attached to the notice. It is very important to follow the notice procedure exactly as it is stated so that there is no problem with an issue of a defective notice and perhaps an invalid board meeting. As you can imagine, board members and/or association members might get very upset with the individual who gave the defective notice.

Unless otherwise specified, the California Civil Code requires notification at least four days prior to the meeting.

Accompanying the notice of the meeting should be a meeting agenda. The bylaws will probably also contain directions for calling an emergency meeting of the board when the customary time for the notice is unworkable. There may be a situation in which the bylaws or other governing documents of the association do not provide for regularly scheduled meetings and/or the specifics for giving notice of a meeting. If that's the case, a state law or a regulation may work as a default rule in the absence of a homeowner (community) association's regulations, or the board should consider establishing specific notice requirements.

AN EXAMPLE - California Civil Code § 1363.05(f)-(h)

Unless the time and place of the meeting is fixed by the bylaws, or unless the bylaws provide for a longer period of notice, members shall be given notice of the time and place of a meeting, except for an emergency meeting, at least **four days prior to the meeting**. A meeting includes any congregation of a majority of the members of the board at the same time and place to hear, discuss, or deliberate upon any item of business scheduled to be heard by the board, except those matters that may be discussed in executive session. Notice shall be given by posting the notice in a prominent place or places within the common area and by mail to any owner who had requested notification of board meetings by mail, at the address requested by the owner.

Notice may also be given by mail or delivery of the notice to each unit in the development or by newsletter or by similar means of communication.

An emergency meeting of the board may be called by the president of the association, or by any two members of the governing body other than the president, if there are circumstances that could not have been reasonably foreseen which require immediate attention and possible action by the board, and which of necessity make it impracticable to provide notice as required by the section.

Note in the above example, the notice of the board meeting was given to members of the association. This notice would only have to be given to members if the time and place of the board meeting was not fixed in the bylaws. Also, if a longer notice period is required in the bylaws the bylaws will control. Posting a notice and the agenda, or putting it in a newsletter, would seem to be an appropriate and cost effective way of getting the word out to the membership.

In California, the above legislation is part of the ***COMMON INTEREST DEVELOPMENT OPEN MEETING ACT***, *enacted to make certain that members of the association/corporation will receive notice of board meetings and have an opportunity to attend and to speak at the meetings*. This should eliminate complaints about a board of directors taking actions that the members of the association were unable to address. Recall that a meeting includes "any congregation of a majority of the members of the board at the same time and place to hear, discuss, or deliberate upon any item of business scheduled to be heard by the board, except those matters that may be discussed in executive session." This rules out any pre-board meeting gatherings to work on items away from the membership. Apparently, a pre-board meeting is allowed if it is attended by less than a majority of the board members.

The only time when members are not entitled to be present is when the board of directors meets in executive session to consider litigation, matters relating to the formation of contracts with third parties, member discipline, personnel matters, or to meet with a member, upon the member's request, regarding the payment of assessments. Additionally, the board must meet in executive session if it is requested to do so by a member who may be subject to a fine, penalty, or other form of discipline, and the member is entitled to attend the executive session.

Members of the association must be permitted to speak at any meeting of the association or board of directors other than the executive sessions.

The board of directors must establish a reasonable time limit for all members of the association to speak to the board or speak before a meeting of the association. Because members are entitled to attend and speak at board meetings, the opportunity for the board of directors to meet by conference telephone or by video conference may be limited.

7. Preparing for the Board Meeting

Because the association is incorporated, the activities and affairs of the corporation must be conducted, and all corporate powers must be exercised, by or under the direction of the board of directors.

The board may delegate the management of activities of the association to others, provided that the activities and affairs are managed and all corporate powers are exercised under the ultimate direction of the board. The legislation which controls the running of a corporation will provide numerous rules regarding how the association's corporation will operate. In addition, the corporation bylaws will help in the day-to-day running of the community association's affairs through the operation of the corporation. Regular meetings of the board may be established in the governing documents of the association. Legislation or governing documents typically provide that non-scheduled meetings can also take place.

AN EXAMPLE - California Corporations Code § 7211(a)(2)

Meetings of the board may be called by the chair of the board or the president or any vice-president or the secretary or any two directors.

As the association manager, you should send meeting notices, as a reminder to each board member, along with the agenda, prior meeting minutes, and any supporting materials or documents the board members will need in preparation for the meeting. You, the manager, will probably be working closely with the board president and/or secretary on the preparation of these items.

Regular meetings of the board are held at the time and place fixed in the bylaws or established by the board.

Special meetings of the board must be held upon 4-days' notice to directors by first-class mail, or 48-hours' notice delivered personally or by telephone, including a voice messaging system or other system or technology designed to record and communicate messages, telegraph, fax, electronic mail (e-mail), or other electronic means.

Therefore, the notice requirement to board members is different than members of the association. Obviously, if all directors are members of the association, then no notice needs to be given if the meeting is a "regular meeting" established in the bylaws. If the meeting is a special meeting, the board member may receive as little as a 48-hour notice or receive the standard 4-day notice given to the membership. For consistency purposes, it might be advisable to give a 4-day notice to both association members and board members. If the meeting is an **emergency meeting**, it may be impractical to provide notices within the above timelines.

Once the time for an emergency meeting is set, a posted notice to the membership is advisable.

If, as the association manager, you have sent out the notices for the board meeting, you should also prepare the place for the meeting. Hopefully, there is a convenient and adequate meeting room on the development's site. Prior to the meeting, you should make certain that the heating and air-conditioning system, as well as the plumbing, are working adequately.

Enough seats should be set up to meet reasonably anticipated attendance. It might be advisable to set up one-and-a-half times the number of seats believed necessary to meet the number anticipated at the meeting. It is better to have more seats than not enough seats. If there are not enough seats, then those attending either have to stand or bring out more seats from a storage room or other meeting room which is inconvenient, noisy, and distracting. This is particularly true when done by the individuals who are late in coming to the meeting. It is also going to create an impression that you weren't "thinking clearly" in preparing for the board meeting. Additionally, some people who are unable to find a seat might be discouraged and leave the meeting.

A round table will work best for the board members, as each member can see the other members during conversation.

This may not be practical if there will be a large audience. The board may wish to have other members seated at the table, such as the attorney for the association, officers of the association, the accountant for the association, and you, the community association manager. It might be a good idea to have name cards placed in front of each person seated at the table as well as pitchers of water and drinking glasses. You should have extra agendas and supporting documents for the members who forgot theirs. Leaving them at the back of the room is a good idea as they can be picked up when entering.

8. Functioning of the Board at the Meeting

Once the chairman of the board determines that a quorum is present, the chairman, or whoever is considered to be the "presiding officer" of the meeting, should call the meeting to order. From this point on some form of parliamentary procedure will govern the conduct at the meeting. How formal or informal the procedure is usually varies according to the number of those in attendance. Everything that follows at the meeting will usually be in the order listed on the agenda that you, as the association manager, will provide (see **Figure 2-2**).

The person who customarily takes the minutes of the meeting must do so or the task needs to be assigned to another person. Typically, this would be the secretary or the assistant to the secretary of the association. Large associations may hire a professional for this task. If at all possible, neither board members nor the association manager should take minutes as it is a task that may distract from the important business at hand.

The next item that may take place is an introduction of those in attendance at the board meeting. This can be limited to board members or also include those in "special" attendance because they are part of agenda items or act in an advisory capacity. If your meeting is attended by members of the association, they may also be introduced, but this will not be practical if a large number of members are present. A sign-in list might work better in that regard. Any corrections or changes in addresses, phone numbers, e-mails, or other pertinent information about the board members should be done at this time.

The next item on the agenda is typically the approval of the minutes of the previous meeting. Those minutes would have been sent out with the notice of this meeting and the agendas so that each board member has an opportunity to peruse the minutes prior to this meeting.

Figure 2-2

**HUBIE HIGHLANDS COMMUNITY ASSOCIATION MONTHLY
BOARD OF DIRECTORS MEETING**

6:30 p.m. August 21, 20XX
Association Clubhouse

AGENDA

1. Call to order 6:30 p.m.
2. Roll call; Verify quorum present; Proof of Notice of Meeting
3. Roster review/corrections
4. Introductions
5. Minutes of preceding meeting
   a. Review/correction of minutes of July 19, 20XX meeting
   b. Approval of minutes
6. Members address the Board-4 minutes per member
7. Reports
   a. President's report
   b. Financial officer's report
   c. Manager's report
   d. Committee reports
      1. Energy reduction committee
      2. Playground safety committee
8. Unfinished business
   a. Changing lawn/grounds maintenance provider
   b. Resealing swimming pool
9. New business
   a. Excessive noise concerns
   b. Lawsuit by Eagle Pools for alleged unpaid pool service
   c. Improving the lighting in the common area
   d. Other
10. Next meeting date, location and time
11. Adjournment 8:30 p.m.

Board members may need to make corrections to the minutes of the previous meeting.

If there is a significant time period between meetings, the current meeting minutes should be sent to board members as soon as possible after the meeting is adjourned so that the items remain fresh in each board member's mind for any corrections to the minutes. Another set of minutes can be sent out with the notice of the current meeting for those members who did not read or misplaced the minutes that were previously sent to them. Any matter discussed in executive session must be generally noted in the minutes for the board meeting immediately following. Obviously, since the executive session is a closed meeting, only the general topic discussed in the executive session needs to be noted in the minutes.

AN EXAMPLE

The board adjourned to executive session to discuss the lawsuit by Eagle Pools against the association for alleged unpaid pool services. Following a discussion of the lawsuit, the board, through its president, will have the association attorney file a response for the association.

At an open board meeting, the board should have an established procedure which allows the members to address the board members before the board starts action on agenda items. This can either take place after the reading of the minutes, or before each item on the agenda is acted upon by the board.

A reasonable time limit for all members to speak must be established by the board.

AN EXAMPLE - California Civil Code § 1363.05(d)

In an effort to keep the members informed of the actions of the board, the minutes, or draft or summary minutes, of the board meeting, other than an executive session, must be made available to members within 30 days of the meeting. They must be distributed to any member of the association upon request and upon reimbursement of the association's cost for making that distribution. It would be advisable for a member to make the request in writing as well as the association manager to keep that written request on file.

If the person presiding at the meeting is having difficulty keeping board members on task with agenda items, it may be necessary for you, as the association manager, to assist in trying to move matters along and keep things focused. The object is not to have a board meeting that drags on and on as an excessive amount of time spent unproductively will cause frustration for some board members. That may lead to absenteeism or a withdrawal from board activities at a meeting.

Unless the board has serious objections, it is important to follow the established agenda. Sometimes the agenda has time allocations for each item. This serves as a reminder to board members that only so much time can be spent on each item and that time should be productive. Whether or not the board continues to focus on an item after the time has expired is up to the discretion of the board. The board can decide that items not finished within the allowed time will be tabled for the next meeting. However, time limits help the board conduct its affairs in a timely manner. Meetings should take 1-2 hours.

Meetings that last longer than two hours will probably be unproductive, as members lose interest.

The person in charge of taking the minutes needs to remember that minutes are a summary of the action taken by the board of directors. Discussion, arguments for and against, and conversational items should not be contained in the minutes. Sometimes a tape recorder is used to record the board meeting for accuracy in the minutes. Recording may make a speaker nervous and should not be done without advanced approval.

9. How the Manager Can Help at a Board Meeting

If you are the manager, you should consider sitting next to the person presiding at the meeting for quick assistance. If the board is looking to you as the association manager to facilitate a board meeting, you must pay careful attention to:

a. discussions which go off of the topic;
b. discussions which tend to get bogged down;
c. discussions which tend to focus on personal issues rather than the topic;
d. discussions which are excessive in time;
e. discussions which appear to be heading in a direction that would violate association bylaws or association regulations; and
f. items which were resolved at a prior board meeting.

In your role as manager, sometimes it may be important for you to:

a. try and pull the board together by offering a summary of the progress so far;
b. clarify a particular issue or direction;
c. suggest that the board entertain a motion to resolve a particular issue;
d. ask questions of board members to make sure that you understand exactly what is going on; and
e. remind the board if a proposal or a motion is consistent with previous actions taken by the board on similar topics.

It may be necessary for you, the manager, to act as a facilitator to actively involve a board member in a discussion when it appears that, for whatever reason, he or she is not actively engaged.

Direct questions will hopefully cause the board member to open up and discuss the item or offer an explanation for non-discussion. Sometimes the easiest way to handle a board meeting is to go around the table seeking discussion from each board member on the topic before moving on to the next board member. In this manner, all board members feel comfortable with the opportunity to talk. This is particularly useful when you have certain board members that tend to dominate the discussion or are intimidating.

Additionally, watch out for temper problems at the meeting. Sometimes members are very adamant about a particular proposal and tempers may start to flare up. If necessary, suggest a "time out" or, if appropriate, a postponement of the meeting. You will probably discover that there are individuals on the board who are very active, "get it done" type of people and those who are not. Some board members may be real active with discussion and carefully thought out motions, but are not participatory when it comes to putting things down on paper or researching for additional information. You should try to get a "read" on all the board members to determine those with whom you can expect to create a productive and efficient working relationship.

The board members may have to be reminded that they are there to make decisions.

Usually found as an agenda item is the ***MANAGER'S REPORT****, which is your opportunity, as manager, to inform the members about the daily operation of the development since the last meeting*. This may consist of any new sales or leases of units, citations for violation of association rules, fines imposed, scheduled hearings with members, important correspondence, recent purchases (if not covered in the financial report), and current status of items motioned and approved at prior board meetings.

You should anticipate the areas of the manager's report that will generate questions from board members and prepare responses prior to the meeting.

Bring supporting materials to distribute to members if necessary, as well as manager-invited guests who can give the board a professional opinion on a topic outside of your expertise. As a manager, you should be careful not to answer questions or give opinions in unfamiliar areas. You should review the minutes of the last several meetings and bring them to the meeting, because board members will sometimes forget what took place, but will expect you to remember. Hopefully, the secretary can locate any past minutes from the minutes book. Consider having a scanner and printer nearby to duplicate items quickly.

Other reports on the agenda will usually include a financial report by you or the treasurer, and any committee reports, such as the annual Hubie Highlands' picnic committee or the playground improvement committee. Items discussed at the previous meeting, but not acted upon or postponed to the next meeting, will be listed as **Unfinished Business,** and new items for the meeting will be listed as **New Business**.

10. Post-Meeting Manager Activities

Make sure the minutes, any draft of minutes proposed for adoption, or any summary of the minutes of the board meeting are available to the members within 30 days after the meeting. The items available to members must be distributed to any member on request and on reimbursement of the association's cost incurred in making that distribution. The cost reimbursed might consist of duplication, envelopes, postage, and employee time. Good communication with the association's secretary who took the minutes is important here.

As soon as possible after the meeting, follow through on items the board directed you, as the manager, to do. You should also meet with the board president to set an agenda for the next board meeting.

D. EFFECTIVE PARLIAMENTARY PROCEDURE

When the board of directors is progressing through various agenda items, it may be necessary for the board to make a decision on a particular topic. For example, the agenda item might be consideration of the purchase and installation for a cover for the swimming pool. The board members will probably discuss the advantages and disadvantages of using a pool cover. At some point in time, it will be necessary for a board member to make a motion regarding the purchase of the pool cover.

A"motion" is a call for action that is used to get a group to make a decision on a particular topic.

Most motions are either a "main motion" or a "secondary motion." Secondary motions are those which typically deal with the main motion.

1. Making a Motion

As the homeowner (community) association manager, you should be very knowledgeable of the specific requirements in the bylaws of the association regarding conduct of the board at a board meeting. If the bylaws require a certain format or procedure, then that is exactly how the board must conduct its affairs. The following is a useful and simple example of how to effectively use parliamentary procedure at a board meeting.

In order to make a motion, the maker must be recognized by the person conducting the meeting, which will usually be the chairperson of the board of

> directors. Once recognized by the chairperson, the maker states "I move that . . ." For example, "I move that the Hubie Highlands community association purchase the Black Moon model 3366 solar pool cover, including installation, with a price of $7,850."

This motion will then need a **second** by another board member, which backs up or approves the motion. The reason for a second is that it prevents spending a lot of board member time on a motion which raises an issue that is of interest to only the person making the motion. If no second is made, the motion will die. If there is a second, the motion is opened for discussion. It is advisable for the person taking the minutes of the meeting to note the name of the person making the motion as well as the name of the person who seconded the motion. When the discussion begins, the person who made the motion has the right to speak first about the motion. It is advisable for the chairperson to recognize each board member by name before that person speaks to the motion. It is also advisable for the chairperson to make sure that the discussion stays directly related to the motion, and that other board members not be allowed to interrupt a recognized speaker and interject or steal discussion time.

Upon recognition from the chair, a **secondary motion** can be made to amend the motion being discussed. This motion also needs a second, and then it is open for discussion. It will be necessary for the board to vote on the motion to amend prior to voting on the original motion.

If the discussion of a motion is wandering, meeting time is running out, or for any other reason, a vote on the current motion can be called for. If it appears that it will be necessary to continue discussion of a motion, a board member may ask that the motion be tabled. A **motion to table** also requires a second, and normally postpones an immediate vote. In other words, the motion to table cannot be amended and debate or discussion is not allowed. A motion may state that the tabling (postponement) is for an indefinite period or, in the alternative, it may table the motion for a specific date for reconsideration.

There is also a **motion for reconsideration**. This motion allows reconsideration of a postponed motion that was tabled at a previous time. A motion for reconsideration requires a second, is not subject to amendment, is not open for discussion or debate, and will move immediately to a vote.

When motions are made, they should be stated in clear and concise language.

This is particularly important for the person who is taking the minutes of the meeting, as well as for those who at some future point in time will have forgotten the exact language of the motion. It makes good practical sense to have the minute secretary read back the motion as written to make sure that it is exactly as it was stated.

2. Voting on a Motion

There a several methods for indicating a vote on a motion. The bylaws should be checked to see whether they require a particular type of vote. If the bylaws state such a method, it must be followed.

One of the most common methods of voting is for the chairperson to ask those in favor of the motion to say "Aye" and those opposed to say "No." By listening to the votes, the chairperson will state whether the motion passes or was defeated. Unless the bylaws or governing document require otherwise, a majority of votes decides the motion. The bylaws may indicate situations where either a two-thirds vote or three-quarters vote is required in order to pass a resolution. If it is deemed necessary, a board member may ask for an exact count of the votes, rather than relying on apparent "volume" of the voters.

Another way of voting is by a ***SECRET BALLOT***, *a written vote without a person's name on the vote*. This method of voting is used when board members desire that their vote be kept secret.

Sometimes a ***ROLL CALL VOTE*** *is used whereby the chairperson calls out the name of each individual member, and that member either answers with a "Yes" or "No" on the motion as the person's name is called*. The minute secretary will write down the name of each board member and how they voted on the motion.

In the alternative, a vote can be by a show of hands or raising of arms. Those in favor of the motion raise their arms signifying "Aye," and those opposed to the motion raise their arms signifying "No." This is easier than the voice vote for determining accuracy. All the chairperson has to do is count the number of arms raised for and the number of arms raised against passage of the motion.

Another way of voting is to vote by **general consent**. Typically, the chairperson will say something like "If there is no objection, then . . ." If none of the board members object, then their silence indicates approval and the motion passes. Obviously, if a member objects, the motion will have to be voted on by one of the alternate methods previously discussed.

As a practical matter, the "general consent" motion may make sense for a large membership meeting, but not for a small board of directors meeting.

A roll call vote will generally serve a useful purpose when compared to the other voting methods. The reason for this preference is that something in the future could happen whereby it will be necessary to read the minutes to see how each member voted on a particular motion. Unless there is a roll call vote, several board members could claim they voted one way, when in fact they did not.

A roll call vote is a kind of "paper trail" in case there are future disagreements as to how board members previously voted.

The ***FINAL MOTION*** *would be a motion to adjourn the meeting.* This motion also requires a second, cannot be amended or changed, is not open for debate or discussion, and requires an immediate vote. After the board has passed a motion to adjourn, the minute taker must note the time of the adjournment.

It is very important to be consistent when using a method of parliamentary procedure.

If used in a fair, reasonable, and equitable manner, the board members, as well as the association membership, will be respectful of the procedure. As an association manager, if you notice that a very hotly contested and important motion is coming up for a vote, it is probably advisable that the vote be taken by secret ballot, and you may want to offer this suggestion to the chairperson. This will eliminate any form of intimidation or harassment accompanying the vote.

E. CORPORATE OFFICERS

If the association is incorporated, the corporation not only needs a chairman of the board of directors, but officers as well. The corporation should have a president, a secretary, and a chief financial officer, as well as any other officers that may be required in the bylaws or determined necessary by the board. Unless the articles or bylaws provide otherwise, any number of offices may be held by the same person. The president, or if there is no president, the chairman of the board, is the general manager and chief executive officer of the corporation. Officers are chosen by the board and serve at the pleasure of the board subject to any rights the officer may have under a contract of employment with the association.

It is important to note that when a contract is signed by the chairman of the board, the president or any vice-president, secretary or any assistant secretary, the chief financial officer, or any assistant treasurer of the corporation, it is binding on the corporation unless the other party to the contract knew the person signing on behalf of the corporation had no authority to do so.

II. MANAGER'S JOURNAL

The most important obligation for you, as the manager, is to become well-versed in how the board of directors and the officers function in regards to managing the homeowner (community) association.

The source of management authority will typically be in the bylaws of the nonprofit corporation. Board members may rely on you, as the manager, for the exact details of the functioning of the board. It would be advisable for you to always carry a copy of the articles of incorporation and the corporation bylaws to each board meeting for reference purposes.

An additional area of concern for you, as the manager, is how formal the board of directors would like the meeting to be. Hopefully, the board is looking for "rules of order" for board meetings that are not extremely complex. Once again, the board may rely on you to provide simple rules of order for board meetings.

Punctuality and accuracy are extremely important when dealing with the board. Additionally, the board will rely on you, as the manager, for organizing, giving notice, and basically "running" the board meeting. Some boards want the manager to handle most of the running of the meeting, while other boards would prefer to have the president run the meeting with "support" from the manager. This may vary from election to election depending on who is the incoming chairman of the board of directors.

A key quality that will make the relationship with the board run as smooth as possible is your ability to get along with the diverse personalities of each board member. Being able to observe and guide those personalities through a successful board meeting and to adjournment is a major task for you as the association manager.

III. CHAPTER SUMMARY

In California, the Davis-Stirling Common Interest Development Act requires that a common interest development (CID) must be managed by a community or homeowner's association (HOA), which can be incorporated or unincorporated. Incorporated community associations must file articles of incorporation with the Secretary of State.

Most community associations are incorporated as nonprofit mutual benefit corporations, the objective of which is to bring together an association of members who own separate interest in the development, working not to make a profit, but toward the mutual benefit of each other by making a long-term commitment to improving and maintaining the development.

The bylaws of the corporation govern the association's internal affairs (rules and procedures) and how it functions. Members of the homeowner's association consist of the owners of the separate interests in the CID. They elect a board of directors, who are responsible for monitoring the financial and business affairs of the association, knowing, enforcing, and revising the rules governing the common interest development, and maintaining goodwill with the association members. Board members must normally be members of and in good standing with the community association.

The size of the board is generally found in the association bylaws. According to California law, before a board can conduct business, a quorum must be present, meaning a majority of the board members. The length of term, procedures for nominating board members, frequency of board meetings, and notice of board meetings requirements will usually be found in the governing documents or set by state law or regulation. In California, for example, the Common Interest Development Open Meeting Act requires that members be notified at least four days prior to a board meeting.

Regular board meetings are open to all members of the association. Executive sessions may be limited to board members to consider litigation, contracts with third parties, member discipline, personnel matters or, upon a member's request, to discuss his or her payment of assessments, fines, penalties or other forms of discipline.

Parliamentary procedures should be followed in board meetings, with the details recorded in the minutes of the meeting. The board should establish a reasonable time limit for all members to speak at a meeting. The manager's report is usually on the agenda at a board meeting, detailing the daily operations of the development since the last meeting.

To make a decision on a particular topic, a motion must be made, then seconded (backed up) by another board member. A secondary motion amends the original motion, a motion to table, which must also be seconded, postpones an immediate vote. A motion for reconsideration, which must be seconded, calls for an immediate vote on a previously tabled (postponed) motion.

If methods for voting on motions are set forth in the bylaws, they must be followed. Voting methods include the "aye or nay" vote, the secret ballot, the roll call vote, and the general consent vote. The motion to adjourn the meeting is called the final motion.

As a corporation, an association board should have a chairman of the board, a president, a secretary, and a chief financial officer, as well as other officers as required in the bylaws. When these officers, including the vice-president, assistant secretary, and assistant treasurer, sign a contract on behalf of a corporation, that contract is binding on the corporation unless the other party knew that person did not have the authority to do so.

IV. REVIEW QUESTIONS

1. Which of the following requires that common interest developments in California be managed by an association?

   a. The Davis-Stirling Act
   b. The David Starling Act
   c. The HOA Statute Act
   d. None of the above

2. In California, the association that manages a common interest development:

   a. must be nonprofit.
   b. must be incorporated.
   c. must be unincorporated.
   d. can be either incorporated or unincorporated.

3. In order to officially create an incorporated homeowner (community) association, which of the following documents must be filed with the California Secretary of State?

   a. Articles of Incorporation
   b. Corporation Bylaws
   c. The Declaration
   d. The Master Deed

4. Which of the following is a general activity of the board of directors of a common interest development?

a. Enacting and enforcing rules and regulations within the development.
b. Monitoring the financial and business affairs of the association.
c. Operating the association with goodwill toward the members.
d. All of the above are correct answers.

5. In order to act as a board, which of the following must be present at a board of director's meeting?

a. The chairman of the board of directors
b. The community association manager
c. A quorum
d. All board members

6. The number of members on the board of directors is usually determined by:

a. the association bylaws.
b. the articles of incorporation for the association.
c. the declaration.
d. the members at the first annual membership meeting.

7. To be a board member, a person must be in "good standing" with the association. What does "good standing" mean?

a. Properly elected by the membership
b. Properly appointed by the board of directors
c. Current on all payments, fees, or assessments to the association
d. Have the respect of the other members of the board

8. If the board consists of seven members, how many must be present to constitute a quorum?

a. Two
b. Three
c. Four
d. Seven

9. With regard to board meetings, "executive session" means:

   a. the board members and the membership meet to discuss the budget for the next fiscal year.
   b. the membership in attendance at a board meeting can require the board to take a pause in its activities while the membership meets behind closed doors to discuss what the board is doing.
   c. the membership has an opportunity to address the board about any and all items felt necessary to bring to the board's attention.
   d. the board members meet in private to discuss personnel or contract issues.

10. Depending on the bylaws of the association, members may vote on a motion by:

   a. secret ballot.
   b. roll call vote.
   c. general consent.
   d. all of the above.

ANSWERS: 1. *a*; 2. *d*; 3. *a*; 4. *d*; 5. *c*; 6. *a*; 7. *c*; 8. *c*; 9. *d*; 10. *d*

Sell Your Home
FASTER
with Feng Shui
SOLD

CHAPTER 3

The Board of Directors

I. Authority and Responsibility of the Board of Directors

A. SOURCE OF AUTHORITY

Whenever the homeowner (community) association's board of directors (in some states the "executive board") conducts business, it must make sure that it is acting within the authority given by:

1. the articles of incorporation forming the corporation that runs the development;
2. the bylaws for that corporation or association;
3. any state laws or government regulations applicable to common interest developments; and
4. the governing documents (the declaration or master deed).

It is important for you, as the the association manager, to have an adequate working knowledge of each of these areas, since some board members may not be well-versed in running and managing a common interest development.

Chapter 3

CHAPTER OUTLINE

If there is a conflict between governing documents and legislation or agency regulations, it should be handled by the attorney for the association.

Most of the time, if the governing documents are more restrictive than the applicable legislation or government regulations, the more restrictive rules will apply. However, this is not always the case, so it may be better to invest the money for an attorney's advice on the matter.

The term "association" refers to a homeowner association, often called a community association.

B. BOARD RESPONSIBILITY TO THE ASSOCIATION

When the board conducts business on behalf of the association it represents, board members collectively and individually owe the highest duty of loyalty and good faith to the corporation that they serve.

This means that each member must act with reasonable care and diligence to the association/corporation that they serve, always placing the interest of the association/corporation above any personal interest. The general legal term that covers this duty is "fiduciary duty." The board of directors is solely responsible for its own decisions in managing the affairs of the association. The board can delegate the task of researching and making recommendations to subcommittees, the general manager, board officers, or other professionals. However, the board is ultimately responsible for making final decisions and implementing those decisions.

Generally, the board's responsibility is to "preserve and improve the value of the common areas," which equates to preserving and improving the value of a member's individual ownership interest in the development.

Obviously, the membership will not be happy with deterioration in the common areas, which will lead to a decrease in the value of the owner's interest in the development. In order to fulfill the obligation to the association, the board of directors will take responsibility for the following items on behalf of the association:

1. Proper fiscal management accomplished through budgeting and assessments.
2. The maintenance and improvement of the common areas.
3. Using risk management to preserve, protect, and replace components of the common area.

4. Using board authority to pass and enforce rules and regulations for the benefit of the membership.
5. Using human resource management skills to maintain professionals, employees, and volunteers who will carry out the board's policy to preserve and increase the common areas and quality of life in the development.

Once the board of directors has made its policy a decision, that decision needs to be implemented within the development.

This implementation will depend largely on the size of the common interest development. In a small development, all owners may be on the board of directors, occupy officer positions, and collectively implement board decisions. The implementation is relatively simple because each owner is aware of the reason behind the board's decision and exactly how it will be carried out. In large common interest developments, the members who serve on the board of directors may represent a very small percentage of the total number of members within the development. In large developments, the management or implementation of board policy may be handled by a contract between the association and an outside management company, or a person hired directly as an association manager. Each of these forms of management will be discussed in detail in a later chapter.

C. BOARD RESPONSIBILITY TO THE PUBLIC/STATE

In California, one of the formal responsibilities of the board of directors is to make sure that the "general public and the state" are given information concerning the details of the organization running the common interest development.

This information is important for determining who is in charge of the organization and how the organization may be served with important documents or lawsuit papers. Certain documents are required to be filed with the Secretary of State's office in Sacramento. A California nonprofit common interest development corporation must file both **Form SI-100** (Statement of Information - **Figure 3-1**) and **Form SI-CID** (Statement By Common Interest Development Association - **Figure 3-2**). An unincorporated association must file Form SI-CID.

The Statement by Common Interest Development Association (SI-CID) must be accompanied by a $15 filing fee. If a nonprofit corporation is filing the form, it must be filed within 90 days after the filing of the original Articles of Incorporation and biannually thereafter at the same time the corporation files its Statement of Information form (SI-100).

Although unincorporated associations are not required to register with the Secretary of State's office, they must file the SI-100 form biannually in the month of July.

Figure 3-1

State of California
Kevin Shelley
Secretary of State
STATEMENT OF INFORMATION
(Domestic Nonprofit Corporation)

Filing Fee $20.00 — If amendment, see instructions.

IMPORTANT — READ INSTRUCTIONS BEFORE COMPLETING THIS FORM

1. CORPORATE NAME: (Please do not alter if name is preprinted.)

This Space For Filing Use Only

COMPLETE ADDRESSES FOR THE FOLLOWING (Do not abbreviate the name of the city. Item 2 cannot be a PO Box.)

2. STREET ADDRESS OF PRINCIPAL OFFICE IN CALIFORNIA, IF ANY (If none, complete Item 3.)	CITY	STATE CA	ZIP CODE
3. MAILING ADDRESS	CITY AND STATE		ZIP CODE

NAMES AND COMPLETE ADDRESSES OF THE FOLLOWING OFFICERS (The corporation must have these three officers. A comparable title for the specific officer may be added; however, the preprinted titles on this statement must not be altered.)

4. CHIEF EXECUTIVE OFFICER/	ADDRESS	CITY AND STATE	ZIP CODE
5. SECRETARY/	ADDRESS	CITY AND STATE	ZIP CODE
6. CHIEF FINANCIAL OFFICER/	ADDRESS	CITY AND STATE	ZIP CODE

AGENT FOR SERVICE OF PROCESS

- If an individual, the agent must reside in California and Item 8 must be completed with a California address.
- If another corporation, the agent must have on file with the California Secretary of State a certificate pursuant to Corporations Code section 1505 and Item 8 must be left blank.

7. NAME OF AGENT FOR SERVICE OF PROCESS

8. ADDRESS OF AGENT FOR SERVICE OF PROCESS IN CALIFORNIA, IF AN INDIVIDUAL	CITY	STATE CA	ZIP CODE

DAVIS-STIRLING COMMON INTEREST DEVELOPMENT ACT (California Civil Code section 1350, et seq.)

9. ☐ CHECK HERE IF THE CORPORATION IS AN ASSOCIATION FORMED TO MANAGE A COMMON INTEREST DEVELOPMENT UNDER THE DAVIS-STIRLING COMMON INTEREST DEVELOPMENT ACT AND PROCEED TO ITEMS 10, 11 AND 12.

NOTE: CORPORATIONS FORMED TO MANAGE A COMMON INTEREST DEVELOPMENT MUST ALSO FILE A STATEMENT BY COMMON INTEREST DEVELOPMENT ASSOCIATION (FORM SI-CID) AS REQUIRED BY CALIFORNIA CIVIL CODE SECTION 1363.6. PLEASE SEE INSTRUCTIONS ON THE REVERSE SIDE OF THIS FORM.

10. ADDRESS OF BUSINESS OR CORPORATE OFFICE OF THE ASSOCIATION, IF ANY	CITY	STATE	ZIP CODE
11. FRONT STREET AND NEAREST CROSS STREET FOR THE PHYSICAL LOCATION OF THE COMMON INTEREST DEVELOPMENT (Complete if the business or corporate office is not on the site of the common interest development.)			9-DIGIT ZIP CODE
12. NAME AND ADDRESS OF ASSOCIATION'S MANAGING AGENT, IF ANY	CITY	STATE	ZIP CODE

13. THE INFORMATION CONTAINED HEREIN IS TRUE AND CORRECT.

TYPE OR PRINT NAME OF OFFICER OR AGENT	SIGNATURE	TITLE	DATE

SI-100 (REV 08/2003) APPROVED BY SECRETARY OF STATE

Clear Form | Save Form | Print Form

Figure 3-2

State of California
Kevin Shelley
Secretary of State

STATEMENT BY COMMON INTEREST DEVELOPMENT ASSOCIATION

(California Civil Code section 1363.6)

Filing Fee $15.00 — If amendment, see instructions.

IMPORTANT — READ INSTRUCTIONS BEFORE COMPLETING THIS FORM

1. NAME OF ASSOCIATION

This Space For Filing Use Only

2. THE ABOVE NAMED ASSOCIATION IS FORMED TO MANAGE A COMMON INTEREST DEVELOPMENT UNDER THE CALIFORNIA DAVIS-STIRLING COMMON INTEREST DEVELOPMENT ACT. (This statement is required by Civil Code section 1363.6(a)(1) and must not be altered.)

3. THIS ASSOCIATION IS ☐ INCORPORATED ☐ UNINCORPORATED

STREET ADDRESS OF ASSOCIATION'S ONSITE OFFICE OR, IF NONE, THE ADDRESS OF THE ASSOCIATION'S RESPONSIBLE OFFICER OR MANAGING AGENT (Please do not abbreviate the name of the city. Item 4 cannot be a PO Box.)

4. STREET ADDRESS	CITY	STATE	ZIP CODE

NAME, ADDRESS AND EITHER THE DAYTIME TELEPHONE NUMBER OR E-MAIL ADDRESS OF THE PRESIDENT OF THE ASSOCIATION (This information **must be different** from the name, address, telephone number, or e-mail address of the association's onsite office or managing agent. Please see instructions for additional information.)

5. NAME			PHONE NUMBER OR E-MAIL ADDRESS
ADDRESS	CITY	STATE	ZIP CODE

NAME, COMPLETE STREET ADDRESS, AND DAYTIME TELEPHONE NUMBER OF THE ASSOCIATION'S MANAGING AGENT, IF ANY (Please do not abbreviate the name of the city. Item 6 cannot be a PO Box.)

6. NAME			PHONE NUMBER
STREET ADDRESS	CITY	STATE	ZIP CODE

PHYSICAL LOCATION OF THE DEVELOPMENT (Please see instructions for additional information.)

7. COUNTY OR COUNTIES	7A. CITY (If in an unincorporated area, enter the city closest in proximity.)

8. FRONT STREET	NEAREST CROSS STREET	NINE-DIGIT ZIP CODE

TYPE OF COMMON INTEREST DEVELOPMENT MANAGED BY THE ASSOCIATION (At least one of the types listed must be checked. Refer to Civil Code section 1351 for definitions.)

9. CHECK THE APPLICABLE BOX

- ☐ A COMMUNITY APARTMENT PROJECT
- ☐ A CONDOMINIUM PROJECT
- ☐ A PLANNED DEVELOPMENT
- ☐ A STOCK COOPERATIVE

SEPARATE INTERESTS (Please note, "Zero" or "none" is not acceptable.)

10. THE NUMBER OF SEPARATE INTERESTS IN THE DEVELOPMENT

11. THE INFORMATION CONTAINED HEREIN IS TRUE AND CORRECT.

TYPE OR PRINT NAME OF OFFICER OR AGENT	SIGNATURE	TITLE	DATE

SI-CID (REV 11/2003) APPROVED BY SECRETARY OF STATE

The Statement of Information form (SI-100) also has a filing fee and must be filed within 90 days after filing the original Articles of Incorporation and biannually thereafter during the applicable filing period. The applicable filing period for a corporation is the end of the calendar month during which its original Articles of Incorporation were filed and the immediately preceding five calendar months.

A California association shall notify the Secretary of State of any change in the street address of the association's onsite office or of the responsible officer or managing agent of the association on a form from the office of the Secretary of State within 60 days of the change.

II. Director Protection From Liability

A. BUSINESS JUDGMENT RULE

Most of the time, the members of the board of directors of the homeowner (community) association serve without compensation.

Board members make decisions about what is in the best interest of the association currently, as well as in the future. A director, however, does not guarantee that every decision made will be the best decision. The success of the association comes from the hard work of the directors, but those directors do not guarantee that success. The ***BUSINESS JUDGMENT RULE*** *acknowledges that directors sometimes make very difficult decisions on behalf of the association and those decisions should not be second-guessed by a court or a jury as long as the director acted in good faith, and with an eye toward the best interest of the association as any reasonably prudent person would do.*

Remember that the board of directors is ultimately responsible for running the association. Of course, decisions made by the board that turn out to be mistakes will undoubtedly upset some of the association members who want to point the finger of blame at the board of directors and, perhaps, attempt to hold each of the board members financially responsible for the mistakes.

Fortunately for the directors, they are protected against personal liability for mistakes in judgment by the "business judgment rule."

Generally, the business judgment rule also protects corporate officers from individual liability for mistakes of judgment. Consider the following legislation stating the business judgment rule.

A director, such as Gertrude's friend Luke, is protected against personal liability by basing a decision on the information or opinion from another whom the director

AN EXAMPLE - California Corporations Code Section 7231(a),(b)

A director shall perform the duties of a director, including duties as a member of any committee of the board upon which the director may serve, in good faith, in a manner such director believes to be in the best interest of the corporation and with such care, including reasonable inquiry, as an ordinarily prudent person in a like position would use under similar circumstances.

In performing the duties of a director, a director shall be entitled to rely on information, opinions, reports or statements, including financial statements and other financial data, in each case prepared or presented by: (1) one or more officers or employees of the corporation with whom the director believes to be reliable and competent in the manners presented; (2) counsel, independent accountants, or other persons as to matters which the director believes to be within such person's professional or expert competence; or (3) a committee of the board upon which the director does not serve, as to matters within its designated authority, which committee the director believes to merit competence, so long as, in any such case, the director acts in good faith, after reasonable inquiry when the need therefore is indicated by the circumstances and without knowledge that would cause such reliance to be unwarranted.

AN EXAMPLE - Nevada Revised Statutes 116.3101

1. Except as otherwise provided in the declaration, the bylaws, this section or other provisions of this chapter, the executive board may act in all instances on behalf of the association. In the performance of their duties, the officers and members of the executive board are fiduciaries. The members of the executive board are required to exercise the ordinary and reasonable care of directors of a corporation, subject to the business judgment rule.

believes is competent and reliable. A director is responsible for making reasonable inquiry. Therefore, if Luke becomes aware of facts, information, circumstances, or conditions which in some way relate to or affect the community association and the common development, he should start further inquiry about the particular issue, if that is what an ordinarily prudent person would do.

The smart director, wishing to avoid liability, quickly learns that "when in doubt-check it out."

The director does not want to be personally liable to pay for association losses because he or she didn't feel comfortable in investigating the problem when it surfaced.

B. INSURANCE PROTECTION

If an officer or director causes injury to another person or property, the following California Civil Code Section will protect the officer or director from personally paying for the harm caused.

AN EXAMPLE - California Civil Code Section 1365.7

A volunteer officer or director of the community association is not personally liable for an amount in excess of the insurance coverage in (4) below, to any person who suffers injury, including, but not limited to, bodily injury, emotional distress, wrongful death, or property damage or a loss as a result of the tortuous act or omission of the director when: (1) The common interest development is exclusively residential. (2) The act was performed within the scope of the duties of the association. (3) The act was not willful, wanton, or grossly negligent. (4) And at the time of the act, the association had insurance that covered the general liability of the association and individual liability of officers and directors for negligent acts or omissions in the minimum amount of $500,000, if the development consists of 100 or fewer separate interests, or $1,000,000, if the development has more than 100 separate interests. (5) The officer or director has to be a volunteer, i.e., receiving no compensation for services rendered, however payment of actual expenses occurred does not affect the volunteer status. (6) An officer or director who at the time of the act was a person who signed the declaration of restrictions for the development or who received compensation as an employee of the declarant, compensation from a financial institution that purchased a separate interest at a foreclosure sale is not a volunteer. (7) The limitation of liability applies only to a volunteer officer or director who is a tenant of a separate interest in the common development or who owns no more than two separate interests. (8) The association's liability for its own negligent acts is not limited.

Notice the protection extends only to claims for bodily injury, wrongful death, emotional distress, or property damage. Liability is not limited for a claim of breach of contract. Obviously, the director or officer wants to make sure that the association is always current with its insurance coverage in the proper amounts.

The director or officer is only protected if the association has the proper insurance.

Additionally, the protection is for liability in excess of that insurance, not an immunity from a lawsuit. If a lawsuit is filed, it must still be defended with all the

appropriate expenses. Officers or directors may want to make sure that the insurance coverage in effect requires the insurance company to pay the cost and expenses of a defense. The exposure to litigation expenses may, even with an unwarranted lawsuit, be just enough to discourage members from serving on the board of directors or becoming an officer of the community association. Thus, if during a 10 minute break at a board meeting, Luke accidentally trips a member causing her to break her hip, leg, and pelvis, he is not personally liable for her injuries.

C. THE STATUTE OF LIMITATIONS

The remaining area of liability protection involves the statute of limitations. The ***STATUTE OF LIMITATIONS*** *is the period of time within which a person must file a lawsuit against a defendant.* If the lawsuit is not filed within that period, the court can dismiss the case. Therefore, expiration of the statute of limitations will protect the officer or director.

AN EXAMPLE - Statute of Limitations in California:

An action for injury to real property must be brought within 3 years of the injury.
An action for injury to another must be brought within 1 year from the injury.
An action against a director to enforce the director's duty to the corporation must be brought within 3 years from the discovery of the act.

D. PROTECTION TIPS

Here is a list of tips that can help protect the member who becomes an officer or director of a homeowner (community) association from having personal liability:

1. Follow all legislation, rules, and regulations of the governing documents with regard to the authority of a director or officer.
2. Follow the standard of the business judgment rule.
3. Make certain that your community association carries and maintains adequate insurance coverage. The fact that the association carries the minimum of insurance required by any legislation may not be enough. Sometimes, it's advisable to have more insurance coverage than a required minimum. This would certainly show that the board is acting in the best interest of the association and protecting not only itself, but individual officers and directors from potential liability. It also gives some personal comfort in knowing that an injured party was covered by adequate insurance rather than only a portion of the injury or claim being paid by minimum insurance.
4. Ask appropriate questions and rely on the advice of the association's accountant, attorney, insurance agent, or anyone else with expertise such as a contractor,

swimming pool maintenance person, tennis court maintenance person, landscape architect, pest control provider, electrician, and government official.

5. As mentioned earlier with board minutes, if you think the majority of the board is doing something against the best interest of the community association and its members, make certain to vote the opposite and have your express reason for that vote saved in the minutes of the board meeting.

III. Liability of the Homeowner (Community) Association for Injury or Property Damage

The homeowner association, also called the community association, has potential liability for personal injury or property damage caused by its negligence. ***NEGLIGENCE*** *can be defined as conduct that falls below the standard of care that a reasonable person (in this case, a reasonable community association) would exercise under the circumstances; sometimes called carelessness or recklessness.* As mentioned previously, the community association may be incorporated or unincorporated. The actions of the association are controlled by a board of directors. The homeowner (community) association most likely owns and certainly controls the common areas of the development. Therefore, the community association is responsible for injuries caused by its negligence in operating and maintaining those areas. This is important to the members of the association, since these members own separate interests in the development, as well as the common areas controlled by the association.

Successful claims against the homeowner (community) association ultimately means monetary losses for the members.

A. FAILURE TO MAINTAIN THE COMMON AREA

A claim for liability against the community association is brought either by the owner of a separate interest or a non-owner. Non-owners would consist of individuals like employees of the association, guests of owners, visitors, and outside individuals on the development to perform various activities.

AN EXAMPLE - California Civil Code Section 1364(a)

Unless otherwise provided in the declaration of a common interest development, the association is responsible for repairing, replacing, or maintaining the common areas, other than exclusive use common areas, and the owner of each separate interest is responsible for maintaining that separate interest and any exclusive use common area appurtenant (attached to) to the separate interest.

To recover for a personal injury or for property damage caused by an association, the injured individual must prove that the association owed a duty to the individual, breached that duty, that the individual or the individual's property was injured or damaged and to what extent, and that the association's breach of duty was a proximate cause of the injury.

Most injury claims involve the failure to maintain the community association's common areas.

For example, a claim could be for a personal injury on a slip and fall because of a leaky water sprinkler causing a slippery surface on a sidewalk or because of an uneven sidewalk due to weather cracking or root cracking, or a loose stair or step. It could also involve property damage for the failure to trim dead tree limbs which ultimately fell and damaged a member's vehicle.

The association owes a duty of reasonable care to protect people against a foreseeable risk of injury by repairing or warning members and non-members of the situation that could cause injury.

If there is a sprinkler head that is not retracting and it is reasonably foreseeable that a person might trip over it, the association must make the area safe from harm. This can be done by either taping it off or in some way fencing it or guarding it to fulfill the obligation to warn a person or, in the alternative, to repair or replace the sprinkler head. The association owes a duty to properly maintain common areas, and it can breach that duty by failing to make the sprinkler area safe or warn people of potential danger. If the association's breach was the proximate cause of the injury to an individual who tripped over the sprinkler head while taking a late evening walk, the association must pay for the injury. This is a primary example of why the community association maintains adequate insurance covering this type of injury.

King v. Magnolia Homeowner's Association

205 Cal. App. 3d 1312; 253 Cal. Rptr. 140; (App. 2 Dist. 1988)
Edited Excerpts From the Opinion of Justice Ashby

FACTS AND ISSUES

Harold King, an independent contractor, came to the 10-unit condominium complex managed by the Magnolia Homeowner's Association to fix a roof-mounted air conditioner on an unscheduled service call based on a complaint the air conditioner was not working. King successfully went up and down a 30-foot ladder affixed to the building to see what was wrong with the air conditioner.

(continued)

During his initial trip straight up and down the ladder, he noticed that the ladder seemed "too close" to the building for him to climb comfortably. He had to bend his knees outward, and when he placed his feet on the rungs his toes would touch the building. After the initial trip up and down, King went to the Association manager and complained that he thought the ladder was unsafe, and he asked the manager if there was any other way to get to the roof. The manager told him there was no other way and "There's nothing to it, I go up there all the time myself." King told the manager, "Well, I guess if you can do it, I can do it."

King ascended the ladder again and serviced the air conditioner. The accident occurred on his way back down, when he was 3 or 4 steps down from the top. He was carrying some tools strapped to his shoulder, but both his hands were free. King fell when he thought he had a good hand grip on the rung of the ladder but was mistaken and when he tried to re-grip he had released his other hand and lost his balance falling backward.

King based his case primarily on the assertion that the ladder did not comply with a provision of the City of Los Angeles Mechanical Code. The code section, which relates to access to rooftop heating equipment by a ladder, states that the ladder shall "have a minimum 3½ inch toe space." After the accident, the ladder was examined and it was found that the toe space measured 2½ inches. King's expert witness opined that inadequate toe space made it more difficult for King to save himself because "once he missed his hand hold and lost his balance, there was no chance for him to regain his hold or balance by exerting a righting torque with his ankles."

Prior to this accident, the Homeowner's Association had never received any notice that the ladder was dangerous or defective or in need of repair. The ladder was the only access to the roof and had been used frequently without prior complaints. The trial court decided the case in favor of the Magnolia Homeowner's Association and King appealed.

DECISION AND REASONS

As the trial court concluded, the claimed inadequate toe space in the ladder was obvious to King upon King's initial trip up and down the ladder. King discussed the ladder with the manager then told her, ". . . if you can do it, I can do it." King, already having succeeded in climbing the ladder, assumed the risk that he could do it again. He had knowledge and appreciation of the specific risk involved, and he voluntarily exposed himself to the danger.

King produced no evidence that he was free to refuse to service the air conditioner after discovering the risk in the ladder. Instead, the evidence shows that King elected to assume the risk. In the particular circumstances of this case, the trial court properly found assumption of the risk to be applicable. The judgment for the Magnolia Homeowner's Association is affirmed.

The learning point of this case is that the Magnolia Homeowner's Association might have incurred liability if they knew the 30-foot ladder was in violation of the local code or if it was aware of previous problems encountered by those who went up and down the ladder. The following case explores association liability for injuries on non-association property.

Alpert v. Villa Romano Homeowner's Association

81 Cal. App. 4th 1320, 96 Cal. Rptr. 2d 364 (App. 2 Dist. 2000)
Edited Excerpts From the Opinion of Justice Goodman

FACTS AND ISSUES:

On July 27, 1992, Alpert, then 69 and in good health, took her dog for a walk. Alpert's walk ended when one of her feet came in contact with an upturned, jagged piece of sidewalk, causing her to lose her balance and fall, face first to the sidewalk. The fall knocked the wind out of her. In the fall, Alpert fractured her right wrist, fractured and lacerated her left knee, broke her fourth and fifth ribs, and sustained a large hematoma in the area of her right breast. She sought medical attention for her injuries, eventually having surgery to repair her left knee. At the time of trial, she was unable to walk for more than a block without pain, and was using a wheelchair to go longer distances.

The fall occurred on the sidewalk in front of the Villa Romano Homeowner's Association (VRHA) condominium property. At trial, Alpert showed that the gardener for twenty years employed by VRHA had been aware of the break in the sidewalk for a few years before Alpert's fall. A concrete expert measured the difference in elevation caused by the break in the sidewalk at the scene of the fall at between three-fourths of an inch and one inch. Another expert witness testified that the sidewalk defect had existed for years prior to the fall and had been caused by the progressive growth of a subterranean tree root under the sidewalk.

In his opinion, the root that caused the uplifting came from a tree growing on the lawn of the VRHA as the root sought moisture. It was also his opinion that the growth of the tree and the root system had been enhanced by the fertilizing, watering, and the trimming of the tree, which VRHA had done on its property.

VRHA had large pine trees growing on the condominium side of the sidewalk and bottle bush trees growing in the parkway between the sidewalk and the street. Both areas were watered by VRHA and attended to by its gardener.

The person in charge of the gardening committee for VRHA inspected the property shortly after becoming chairman of the committee in the summer of 1992. She had been aware for some time of the existence of cracks in the sidewalk in the area in which Alpert fell and of other cracks in the sidewalk which ran along the property. According to the former president of VRHA, the City of Los Angeles controlled the sidewalks and all VRHA needed to do was keep the sidewalks clean.

(continued)

At the conclusion of the presentation of Alpert's case, VRHA made a motion for nonsuit. The trial court granted the motion concluding that the owner and possessor of property owes no duty to warn or protect pedestrians from dangerous conditions known to be present on a public sidewalk. Alpert appealed.

DECISION AND REASONS

The fundamental legal issue raised by the judgment of nonsuit is whether VRHA as landowner and party in possession and control owed a duty to pedestrians such as Alpert to either warn them of a dangerous condition of the premises or repair it. From a previous California Supreme Court decision, a landowner or possessor of land has a duty to take reasonable measures to protect persons from dangerous conditions on adjoining land when the landowner or possessor exercises possession or control over the land. The facts of this case reveal that VRHA had planted and maintained all of the trees and vegetation in the area, on both sides of the sidewalk, had installed sprinklers on both sides of that walkway, and watered and trimmed the trees which grew the roots which caused the sidewalk to be uplifted and cracked, presenting the danger which befell Alpert. Further, VRHA had known for approximately two years prior to Alpert's fall of the condition of the sidewalk at the location of the fall and elsewhere along that path. VRHA exercised control over the sidewalk and the area between the sidewalk and the curb.

There is enough evidence to overcome the motion for nonsuit. The judgment of nonsuit is reversed. The matter is remanded to the trial court for further proceedings.

The above case certainly emphasizes the importance of the association manager or other appropriate association officials to conduct periodic inspections of the premises to find dangerous conditions and make those conditions safe or warn others of the danger. Even though the assumption is that the responsibility to warn and repair fell upon the city, it would have been prudent, upon the discovery of a possible dangerous condition, to immediately notify an officer of the association, and it would have been advisable to seek further legal opinion.

B. CRIMINAL ACTIVITIES

An additional, and perhaps more remote concern involves the liability of a community association for criminal activities which cause harm to individuals or property on the premises. For example, suppose that several of the members' vehicles have been vandalized or that one evening a member was beaten up and robbed while walking from the tennis courts back to his residential unit. Is the association going to be liable for damages? If that type of criminal activity and damage is reasonably foreseeable, a community association could be liable for its failure to make the premises safe for its members. After all, the association maintains the common areas over which the members have little or no control.

The general issue surrounding association liability for criminal activity is whether that particular activity should have been foreseeable on the premises.

In some jurisdictions, the criminal activity is not foreseeable unless previous acts were committed on the premises. In other jurisdictions, for example California, foreseeability of the criminal activity may be shown even though previous similar criminal activities did not take place on the premises. Most directors are members of the association and have an intimate knowledge of what has taken place on the premises. This knowledge gives the board of directors an opportunity to investigate or fix the dangerous situation. Obviously, something that requires immediate attention would be given directly to the association manager so that members could be protected as soon as possible. For example, fixing or warning of the dangerous sprinkler head. As the manager, you can respond quicker than the board, as they typically only meet periodically or by calling a special meeting. If there is a risk of injury or property damage because of criminal conduct, once again, as the association manager, you can handle this quickly, where a board meeting will take some time.

The homeowner (community) association is not a protector and will not be held liable for all damage due to criminal conduct. Liability exists only if the criminal conduct was foreseeable and the association didn't take reasonable steps to protect its members.

If the robbery of the member walking back to the unit from the tennis court was not foreseeable, there is no association liability. Obviously, if this type of conduct, or something similar to it, had taken place on the premises on prior occasions, that conduct became foreseeable and the association should either warn its members and/or take steps to attempt to prevent that situation from occurring in the future. However, where there is a will, there is a way, meaning that there are some occurrences that cannot be protected against even though the association has instituted a reasonable security system, but nevertheless, the unfortunate incident occurred anyway. Additionally, the fact that there has been some vandalism to a member's car probably is not sufficient to make it foreseeable that an individual would break into a member's unit and rob and rape the member.

However, if these types of crimes have become very frequent in the neighborhood of adjoining properties to the development, it may be foreseeable that it might occur on the association premises. If that is the case, it may be necessary for the board or you, as the property manager, to increase the wattage of the security lights, perhaps install new security lighting in darker areas on the premises and cut down or trim vegetation back to allow the light to penetrate into areas that in the past would offer a place for a criminal to hide in the darkness.

Warning the members and taking steps to deter foreseeable criminal conduct in the common areas will help protect the association from liability.

C. PREVENTIVE PROGRAMS

If the homeowner association has advertised that it provides security on the premises or, if because of a change in circumstance, the association has decided to provide security, the association may have potential issues of concern. For example, if certain types of security are advertised, then that type of security will need to be provided and maintained unless the members agree to reduce the level of security. If the association had a locked gate and the gate is broken, the association needs to repair and maintain that security or it may be liable for damages to members for the failure to keep the gate locked. If the association hires an employee as a security guard, the association needs to make certain that the person is properly trained and also that it has conducted a reasonable investigation of the employee's background. It may be better to hire a security service rather than an employee.

The question then becomes whether security guards are protectors of the safety of individual members and their property or are they observers and deterers of criminal conduct? The association and the membership need to make it crystal clear exactly what the job description and the expectation is with regard to the services of a security guard. In fact, it may be beneficial to refer to the individual as "security" rather than "security guard," or perhaps "patrol person," "surveillance person," "front gate monitor," or something that shows the person is to observe and report unusual, unsafe, or suspicious situations to appropriate personnel, whether that be you, the association manager, or the local law enforcement official, rather than engage in correcting the situation.

D. MEMBER PROTECTION

If the association is incorporated and held liable for the injury to person or property that occurred in the common areas, the members are not personally responsible financially for that injury.

The members are protected from personal liability to the same extent that shareholders are protected from personal liability for the corporations that they own. The injured party must look to the assets of the corporation and not the assets of the individual members for compensation. Obviously, this is a good reason to incorporate your community association and to make sure the community association has adequate insurance to pay injury claims.

ECC Construction, Inc. v. Ganson

82 Cal. App. 4th 572; 98 Cal. Rptr. 2d 292 (App. 2 Dist. 2000)
Edited Excerpts From the Opinion of Justice Masterson

FACTS AND ISSUES

The Oak Park Calabasas condominium complex was damaged in the 1994 Northridge earthquake. The Homeowner's Association signed a contract with ECC Construction, Inc., to repair the common areas and the individual units. None of the homeowners were signatories to the contract. A dispute arose as to the amount due ECC Construction under the contract. In July 1995, ECC Construction filed a lawsuit against the Association and the homeowners (approximately 300 in number), seeking to recover over $2 million allegedly due under the contract.

The homeowners moved for summary judgment on the ground that they were not parties to the contract. The trial court granted the motion, leaving the Association as the sole defendant. ECC Construction appealed.

DECISION AND REASON

The Homeowner's Association is a California nonprofit mutual benefit corporation. Such corporations are formed principally for the mutual benefit of their members. A member of such a corporation is not, as such, personally liable for the debts, liabilities, or obligations of the corporation (California Corporations Code Section 7350[a]). Members of mutual benefit corporations, like shareholders, have no personal liability for the debts of the corporation. The owners were not parties to the construction contract, and they are not liable for the Association's debts or liabilities. Nevertheless, ECC Construction argues that the homeowners may be personally liable where the Association acts as their agent or for their benefit. Not so. By definition, the Association acts for the benefit of the owners.

The Association may also act as their agent. Thus, under ECC Construction's scenario, the owners would always be liable for the Association's debts and liabilities, and the immunity granted the owners by the Corporation's Code would be rendered meaningless—a result we are not willing to accept.

In sum, the Corporations Code contemplates that third parties such as ECC Construction will recover damages, if at all, from the Association. In turn, the Association will look to its members, if necessary, to pay its debts. Accordingly, the homeowners are not liable to ECC Construction for any wrongful conduct related to the payments due under the construction contract.

The judgment of the trial court is affirmed.

The lesson here is that for ECC Construction to receive a judgment against each of the homeowners, it would have been necessary for it to have gotten each homeowner's signature agreeing to the terms of the contract. Therefore, a homeowner as a party to the contract would have liability. In the alternative, ECC Construction will receive a judgment against the Homeowner's Association, and then the Homeowner's Association will have to use a special or emergency assessment in order to pay off the judgment.

AN EXAMPLE - California Civil Code Section 1365.9

Any cause of action in tort (such as negligence) against any owner of a separate interest arising solely by reason of an ownership interest as a tenant in common in the common area of a common interest development shall be brought only against the association and not against the individual owners of a separate interest, as long as the association has general liability insurance of at least $2,000,000, if the common interest consists of 100 or fewer separate interests, or $3,000,000, if the common interest has more than 100 separate interest.

Obviously, the association wants to make sure that the insurance coverage meets the minimum obligation and, perhaps, may wish to have a higher dollar limit. One reason for a higher dollar limit is that the above legislation doesn't provide for what happens if the judgment for the injured party exceeds the minimum amount of insurance coverage, assuming the association carries the minimum amount. For example, if the development has 85 separate interests and the association is held liable for $2.75 million, who pays the $2.75 million? Is it an association/member obligation that will probably require an assessment to pay? It would seem that incorporating the community association, and covering the common areas with adequate insurance would be in the best interest of the members.

IV. Board Members Want to Protect Personal Assets

Any person seeking to become a member on the board of directors will probably want to know what happens if the board and the individual director are threatened with litigation or actually sued in an attempt to hold the director personally responsible for some sort of loss. The director will be looking for something in the operating documents, legislation, or insurance policy which will cover the litigation expenses, as well as a judgment or settlement against the director. Legislation may solve the problem in many states, including the following California example.

AN EXAMPLE - California Corporations Code Section 7237

A corporation has the power to indemnify (to compensate or reimburse) any of its directors, officers, employees, or other agents against expenses, judgments, fines, settlements and other amounts actually and reasonable incurred in connection with an actual lawsuit or a threatened lawsuit against them. When the association indemnifies a director, that means the director is protected against personal monetary liability for the claim because the corporation will compensate the director for the expenses or liability to the person making the claim. Indemnification can only take place if the corporation's agent acted in good faith and in a manner that was reasonably believed to be in the best interest of the corporation and, in the case of a criminal proceeding, the agent had no reasonable cause to believe the conduct was unlawful. This makes it possible for payment of attorney's fees, litigation expenses, judgments, fines, and settlements by the corporation to the corporation's agent.

When a member of the association sues a director, officer, or other agent on behalf of the association, the association has the power to indemnify its agent for expenses actually and reasonably incurred regarding the defense or settlement of the claim, if the agent acted in good faith in a manner believed to be in the best interest of the corporation including reasonable inquiry. However, indemnification cannot be made: (1) if the agent has been held liable to the corporation by the court, unless and only to the extent that the court determines the person is fairly and reasonably entitled to indemnification or expenses; (2) for amounts paid by the person in settling or otherwise disposing of a threatened or pending action, with or without court approval; or (3) for expenses incurred in defending the action which was settled without court approval.

The indemnification mentioned in the previous two paragraphs can only be made by the corporation by: (1) a majority vote of a quorum consisting of directors who are not parties to the proceedings; (2) approval of the members of the association without allowing the person seeking indemnification to vote; or (3) the court in which the proceeding is pending.

On the other hand, if the agent has been successful in the defense of any claim, the agent shall be indemnified by the association against expenses actually and reasonably incurred in connection with the defense.

Expenses in defending a proceeding may be advanced by the corporation before final disposition of the proceeding if the person receiving the advance provides an undertaking (bond) to the corporation to repay the amount, unless it is determined ultimately that the agent is entitled to indemnification. No provision in any governing documents of the corporation to indemnify its agents is valid unless it is consistent with the above.

(continued)

The typical place for the indemnification provisions to be located would be in the bylaws of the corporation. If the association manager is considered an agent of the corporation, the indemnification provision mentioned above will protect the manager. If there is nothing in the bylaws giving the association manager protection, the manager should insist on the board of directors agreeing in the employment contract to provide the manager with indemnification for specific activities.

Unless the person seeking indemnification was successful in the defense of the claim, the court in which the action was pending will not order indemnification or an advance when it appears that it would be inconsistent with the governing documents of the association.

A. PURCHASE INSURANCE

Obviously, the association needs to purchase adequate insurance to cover against any liability asserted against or incurred by an agent of the association acting on behalf of the association, whether or not the corporation would have the power to indemnify the agent as provided above.

Liability insurance makes sense because the insurance company has to cover the indemnification or handle the legal defense for the agent.

The association, as mentioned above, can pay the indemnification of its agent, but this is a payment directly from the association out of the association's revenues.

B. FIND AND FIX

To protect board members from liability, the board should periodically require maintenance checks of the common areas, either done by board members or the association manager.

Additionally, you, as the association manager, or the board, needs to respond within a reasonable amount of time to complaints lodged with you or an individual board member about unsafe conditions on the premises. If it is an area that is a separate interest of a member or under the exclusive control of a member, the member should be given notice to remedy the situation. Additionally, the directors need periodic reports from you, as the association manager, listing the time and date of the noticed or complained about unsafe or dangerous condition and the time and date you remedied the situation, or gave a warning of the condition prior to remedy.

Since the board has, to a certain extent, delegated the responsibility to maintain the common areas to you, as the association manager, the board is ultimately responsible for the repairs and maintenance under your care. Problems can arise if the association doesn't have enough money to repair a condition or maintain the common areas. If that's the case, the board should consider an assessment to remedy the situation. While seeking funding, it is important that you, as the association manager, inform the members of the situation which might be unsafe and dangerous to members. The board always has the option of a special assessment in the event of an emergency, and this will be discussed in the chapter on assessments. If you or the board members are not individually competent to inspect the property looking for potential unsafe and dangerous conditions, it may be necessary to retain the services of an outside expert to conduct an inspection. You and the board should be careful about hiring individuals who obviously want you to retain their services to repair the conditions that are discovered.

It is in the best interest of the association to find an expert who reports on the conditions but doesn't actually remedy them.

Additionally, as the association manager, you should ask for the members to report any unsafe condition regarding the physical property or security of the premises. Obviously, you don't want to be flooded by notifications from members of trivial conditions which then have to be addressed. However, this is a good way to keep informed about the perceived condition of the premises.

Local law enforcement may be a good source to evaluate the security and safety of the premises.

Board members must remember that once they are informed of a dangerous condition, they have the duty to inquire and investigate the situation and take some sort of reasonable action.

Board members will not each be personally liable for their conduct unless the conduct is determined to be clearly unreasonable under the circumstances that existed at the time of the board action.

V. A Director's Conflict of Interest with the Association

A conflict of interest occurs when an individual's private interest differs from his or her professional obligations.

A conflict of interest can arise when a board member, or members, desire to personally contract with the association. Typically, the contract is going to involve either the board member selling goods or services to the association, or the board member wanting to buy something the association has for sale. For example, a board member may own an office supply store and wishes to sell or lease office machines to the association. A business owner typically wants to get the highest price for products or services sold. However, the board member, owing a fiduciary duty to the corporation of highest loyalty, must attempt to get the office machinery at the lowest price to benefit the corporation and its members. This is the conflict of interest. The opposite would be true when the board member is desiring to purchase something the association wishes to sell. Obviously, the association would like to get the highest price for the item and the individual who is the board member would like to pay the lowest price.

Conflicts of interest are often regulated by state or government legislation.

AN EXAMPLE - California Corporations Code Section 7233(a)

No contract or other transaction between a corporation and one or more of its directors, who have a material financial interest, is either void or voidable because such director or directors are present at the meeting of the board which authorizes, approves or ratifies the contract or transaction if: (1) the material (important) facts regarding the transaction and the director's interest are fully disclosed or known to the members of the association and the contract or transaction is approved by the members in good faith not counting the interested director's vote; or (2) the material facts regarding the transaction and the director's interest are fully disclosed or known to the board of directors and the board approves the contract or transaction in good faith without counting any vote from the interested director and, the contract or transaction is just and reasonable as to the corporation at the time of its approval.

If the contract or transaction of the interested director or directors was not approved as provided above, then it becomes the burden of the director or directors to prove the contract was just and reasonable to the corporation at the time it was authorized, approved or ratified.

Full disclosure by the interested director to the association members or the board of directors for a vote, not counting a vote by the interested director, gives the members or the board an opportunity to assess the contract or transaction and determine its fairness to the corporation.

In a case where fairness to the corporation is a close call, or if you cannot get a disinterested number of directors to constitute a quorum or a majority vote, it would be in the best interest of the board to have the members vote on the contract or transaction. Obviously, it is much more difficult for a member to complain about the contract or transaction after the member has been fully informed and a majority of the members, not counting the interested members, voted for approval. On the other hand, the interested

director can go ahead and contract with the association, say through the association manager, and worry about approval at a later date, should it be questioned by a member. Then the director must prove the transaction was fair and reasonable to the corporation. A director would only have to realize that burden if a member sued the director in court. If there is little likelihood of that, the director may just as soon contract with the association and worry about the burden of proof at a later date.

VI. MANAGER'S JOURNAL

It is important for you, as the manager, to remember that decisions regarding policy for the association are made by the board of directors. In this regard, it can be anticipated that the board will lean heavily upon you for recommendations and suggestions as well as exact language for resolutions in order to accomplish board objectives. The ultimate decision and responsibility for that decision rests with board members and it may be necessary for you to remind board members of this. You may discover that board members will tend to blame you for a board resolution that turned out to be unpopular with the association members. Therefore, as a practical matter, you should insist upon written instructions from the board or board members specifying exactly what you are to accomplish for the board. Building a paper trail may be a way of not "taking a fall" for unpopular board decisions.

As the manager, you should make certain that the articles of incorporation, bylaws, appropriate government laws, and governing documents for the association have been reviewed in detail to make an accurate determination of the exact authority of the board. Members of the board may think they have authority to accomplish certain tasks but it may be necessary for you to point out that they may not.

If the board has insurance protecting the board members and officers from liability, you need to make certain that the insurance premiums are paid on time so the policy will always be active.

Remember, the board will rely heavily on you for information about conditions within the common interest development that require board action. Therefore, a regular visual inspection or walk through the development is imperative to assess any problem areas that need to be brought to the attention of the board.

VII. CHAPTER SUMMARY

The board of directors of an HOA must act within the authority given to it by the articles of incorporation, the bylaws, any state laws or government regulations applicable to CIDs, and the governing documents (the declaration or master deed). If there is a conflict between governing documents and legislation or agency regulations, an attorney for the association should be called in.

Board members owe the highest duty of loyalty and good faith to the corporation that they serve. It is their responsibility to preserve and improve the value of the common areas which equates to preserving and improving the value of a member's individual ownership interest in the development. In California, the board of directors is responsible for making sure that the general public and the state are given information concerning the details of the organization running the CID.

Although unincorporated associations are not required to register with the Secretary of State's office, they must file the SI-100 form, biannually, in the month of July. In California, an association must notify the Secretary of State of any changes in the street address of the association's onsite office, responsible officer or managing agent of the association, within 60 days of the change.

The business judgment rule protects directors against personal liability for mistakes in judgment. The director or officer is only protected from liability for bodily injury, wrongful death, emotional distress or property damage, only if the association has the proper insurance.

The statute of limitations is the period of time within which a person must file a lawsuit against a defendant. In California, an action for injury to real property must be brought within three years of the injury, injury to another person must be brought within one year of the injury, and action against a director to enforce a director's duty to the corporation must be brought within three years from the discovery of the act.

Negligence is conduct that falls below the standard of care that a reasonable person would exercise under the circumstances, also referred to as carelessness or recklessness. Most injury claims against an association involve the failure to maintain the community association's common areas. The association owes a duty of reasonable care to protect people against a foreseeable risk of injury by repairing or warning them of the situation that could cause injury. Therefore, it is important for association managers, or appropriate association officials to conduct periodic inspections of the premises.

The general issue surrounding association liability for criminal activity is whether the particular activity should have been foreseeable on the premises. An association will only be held liable if the criminal conduct was foreseeable and didn't take reasonable steps to protect its members.

If the association is incorporated and held liable for the injury to person or property that occurred in the common areas, the members are not personally responsible financially for that injury.

A conflict of interest occurs when an individual private interest differs from his or her professional obligations. Conflicts of interest are often regulated by state or government legislation. Full disclosure by the interested director must be presented to the association members or the board of directors for a vote. This gives them the opportunity to access the contract and determine its fairness to the corporation.

VIII. REVIEW QUESTIONS

1. The authority for a board of directors to act comes from:

a. the bylaws of the association.
b. the articles of incorporation.
c. state law.
d. all of the above.

2. Wells, a board member, voted with the entire board on a financial proposal which was based on the report of the corporation treasurer. The report was an intentional deception, costing the association a large financial loss, which ultimately must be reimbursed by the association members. The membership sues Wells and the other board members for personal reimbursement for the loss.

a. Wells is not liable if Wells reasonably relied on the report of the treasurer.
b. Wells is liable because directors are always responsible for bad financial decisions.
c. Wells is liable because Wells should have conducted an independent investigation of the report before voting on the proposal.
d. None of the above.

3. In California, the statute of limitations for bringing an action against a director to enforce the director's duty to the corporation must be brought within:

a. one year from the discovery of the act.
b. two years from the discovery of the act.
c. three years the discovery of the act.
d. none of the above.

4. The board of directors has scheduled a meeting for tomorrow night to discuss a problem discovered by the association's manager today. The manager believes a large tree is starting to lean over the parking lot and therefore notified each board member. The manager marked the area with no parking signs and waited for the board meeting. Five minutes after children took the signs away, a guest of a member parked a car in one of the parking spots, the tree fell, and the car was damaged. Most likely:

a. every member of the association will be personally responsible for the damage.
b. the manager is clearly liable for the damage.
c. each board member is personally responsible for the damage.
d. none of the above are correct answers.

5. A board member owns an insurance company. If the board member wants to personally sell insurance to the association, this may present a problem because of:

a. a conflict of interest.
b. a statute of limitations problem.
c. a personality conflict.
d. none of the above.

6. A board member wants to purchase the used garden tractor the association is selling for the asking price.

a. This type of transaction is illegal.
b. This transaction is valid if approved by a majority of the board members, not counting the purchasing board member's vote.
c. This transaction must be approved by a majority of the members of the association, including the purchasing board member's vote.
d. None of the above.

7. A criminal act, such as vandalism, is committed in a common area of an association. Under what circumstances would the association be held liable?

a. If it is proved that the board of directors could have reasonably foreseen the event occurring.
b. If the association is incorporated.
c. If the board of directors has liability insurance.
d. The association is always liable for any criminal act that occurs in a common area.

8. As a volunteer director for Hubie Highlands, you cannot be held liable for an amount in excess of insurance coverage if the association maintains a minimum amount of coverage for negligence by an officer or director. If Hubie Highlands consists of 144 units, the minimum amount of the coverage would be:

a. $100,000.
b. $300,000.
c. $500,000.
d. $1,000,000.

9. A maintenance employee of the association forgot to lower the rock guard on the association's lawnmower. As a result, while mowing grass in the common area, a rock was thrown by the lawnmower causing injury to a member's knee. The association has refused to pay for any of the medical bills associated with the knee injury. The member must file a lawsuit against the association to recover for damages to the knee within:

a. six months from the date of the injury.
b. one year from the date of the injury.
c. three years from the date of the injury.
d. there is no time limit in which to file the lawsuit.

10. If a board member believes the board is about to vote for a resolution which could be extremely risky for the association's membership in the long-term, the director should do which of the following?

a. Cast a vote along with the majority, as the majority typically knows what is in the best interest of the association.
b. Cast a vote that is identical with the vote of the chairman of the board of directors.
c. Cast a vote against the resolution and have the reasons for the vote placed in the board minutes by the board secretary.
d. Walk out of the meeting, and refuse to vote.

ANSWERS: 1. *d*; 2. *a*; 3. *c*; 4. *d*; 5. *a*; 6. *b*; 7. *a*; 8. *d*; 9. *b*; 10. *c*

CHAPTER 4

Association Meetings

I. Rights of the Membership

When Gertrude purchases a unit (separate interest) in Hubie Highlands, she automatically becomes a member of the Hubie Highlands Homeowner's Association (the Association). As a member of the Association, she acquires the rights that all other members have and which are normally found in the governing documents in the Association. Once again, those documents will consist of the recorded Declaration and bylaws of the incorporated Association and the rules and regulations of the Association. Looking at the Association in the big picture, Gertrude understands that the Association members will periodically have meetings to discuss and vote on various topics, including the election of the board of directors who will be making the major policy decisions for the Association on behalf of the membership.

Unless the articles of incorporation, its bylaws, or California law provide that certain activities and affairs are reserved for membership approval, all corporate power is exercised by the "board of directors."

Chapter 4

CHAPTER OUTLINE

A. MEMBERSHIP MEETINGS – INTRODUCTION

In most instances, the governing documents set the requirements for calling and conducting membership meetings.

Obviously, Gertrude will need to read these documents carefully to assess her rights and responsibilities as a member. Most likely she will find that the governing documents will set the time for an annual membership meeting, or other fixed meetings throughout the year, as well as the meeting designated for the election of the board members. Typically, the bylaws of the Association will contain this information. Gertrude may discover that some of the meetings set forth in the bylaws are located outside of the state.

If no place is designated in the bylaws for the location of meetings, the meetings must be held at the association's principle office.

Since the Hubie Highlands manager's office is inadequate for a membership meeting, the meeting will take place in the Association's meeting facility. As an interesting aside, unless prohibited in the Articles of Incorporation or the bylaws of the Hubie Highlands Association, any action which may be taken at any regular or special meeting of the members may be taken without a meeting, if the Association distributes a written ballot to every member entitled to vote on the matter. This will be discussed in more detail later. This is probably not a wise idea, because it is good for the membership to get together at meetings, discuss issues, and get to know each other better. The Association also has the ability to call a **special meeting**.

A written ballot may make sense for voting as it would be particularly useful for members who do not live in their units and are located a considerable distance from the development.

B. GERTRUDE'S FIRST MEETING

As luck would have it, the first meeting that Gertrude attends is the Hubie Highlands Association annual membership meeting at which the board of directors is elected.

California law requires that meetings of the membership must be conducted in accordance with a recognized system of parliamentary procedure or any parliamentary procedures the association may adopt.

There are any number of books available for parliamentary procedure at meetings, including the standard **"Robert's Rules of Order,"** which would fall under the "recognized system" of parliamentary procedure. However, the board may adopt its own parliamentary procedure. Since those procedures need to be adopted by the board, if the board does not wish to follow a recognized parliamentary procedure, it will be necessary for the board of directors to establish a detailed parliamentary procedure and have it adopted by a board resolution or placed in the bylaws of the association.

The one thing Gertrude has to remember is that there is a difference between being a member of the Hubie Highlands Association, because she has purchased a unit, and her membership in the Hubie Highlands Association, which is a nonprofit mutual benefit corporation formed under California law. As a corporation, a number of the activities of the members are governed by California corporation law. Like California, all states have their own corporate regulation. Regular meetings of the membership are held according to the provisions of the bylaws of the association. In any event, in each year in which directors are to be elected there must be a membership meeting for that purpose and to transact any other proper business which may be brought before the membership at the meeting.

C. FAILURE TO HOLD MEETINGS

California law provides that if the association fails to hold a required meeting and **sixty days** pass, or, if no date for a meeting has been designated and a period of **fifteen months** has passed since its last regular meeting, a member can ask the superior court of that county to order a meeting to be held, as long as the association was given proper notice of the member's application and given an opportunity to be heard in court. Obviously, this forces the association members to follow the bylaws regarding meetings or consider conducting an annual meeting.

D. SPECIAL MEETINGS

A "special meeting" of the members may be called for any lawful purpose by the board of directors, the chairman of the board, the president, or such other persons, if any, as are specified in the bylaws, or by "five percent" or more of the members.

Since the term "lawful purpose" is not specifically defined, the assumption is that it means a purpose which is not illegal, and a purpose or activity that a nonprofit mutual benefit corporation can legally do.

II. Notice of Meetings

A. NOTICE OF REGULAR MEETINGS

A written notice of meetings must be given not less than 10, nor more than 90 days, before the date of the meeting.

The notice is given to each member who is entitled to vote at the meeting. The bylaws may provide, or, in the absence of such provision, the board may fix in advance a date as the record date for purpose of determining the members entitled to receive notice of any meeting. Members on the association's record on that date receive the notice. The record date cannot be more than 90, or less than 10, days before the meeting date.

If a date is selected, the date is the business day before the notice is to be given. The notice must state the place, date, and time of the meeting. If the notice is for a special meeting, the general nature of the business to be transacted at the special meeting must be stated, and no other business must be transacted at the special meeting. If the notice is for a regular meeting, those matters which the board of directors intends to present for action by the members, and any other proper matter, may be presented at the meeting for action by the membership. If the meeting is one in which directors are to be elected, the notice must include the names of all who are nominees at the time the notice is given to the members.

The notice of the meeting must be given personally, by mail, or by other means of written communication, addressed to the member at the address appearing on association records, or an address given by the member to the association for the purpose of notice.

If no address is available, the notice can be given at the place where the principle office of the association is located, or it may be published at least once in a newspaper of general circulation in the county where the principle office is located. If the notice is given by mail and by means other than first class, registered, or certified mail, that notice shall be given not less than twenty days before the meeting. It would seem rather unlikely that a mailed notice would be by means other than those specified.

Additionally, as the manager, you need to know if a notice or report addressed to a member is returned by the postal services indicating that it was undeliverable to the member at the address. All future notices or reports shall be deemed duly given without further mailing, if they are available for the member upon written demand from the member at the principle office of the association for a period of one year from the date of the giving of the notice or report to all other members. In other words, as the manager, you can continue to incur the cost of each mailing or just hold the mailings for a year after the first one was returned and wait for a written demand from the member.

B. CERTAIN ACTIONS MUST BE IN NOTICE OF MEETING

Action at a membership meeting is valid only if the general nature of the action so approved was stated in the notice of the meeting or in any written waiver of notice. The following such actions are then allowed:

1. Any action to remove any or all directors without cause.
2. An action to fill vacancies on the board of directors when a membership vote is required.
3. Any contract or other transaction between the corporation and one or more of its directors who has a material financial interest in the contract or transaction.
4. Any action to amend the Articles of Incorporation for the Association.

5. Any proposal by the association to voluntarily line up and dissolve the corporation.
6. Any plan of distribution after the process of lining up the corporation which is not in accordance with the existing liquidation rights of any class of membership.

C. NOTICE OF SPECIAL MEETINGS

If the chairman of the board of the association, president, vice president, or secretary receives a written request for a special meeting for a lawful purpose from five percent or more of the members, the officer receiving the request must cause notice of the special meeting to be given to the members entitled to vote at that meeting. You may find that the notice for the special meeting has been delegated to the manager. As the manager, what do you need to know?

A "special meeting" must be held at a time fixed by the board not less than 35 nor more than 90 days after the receipt of the written request.

If the notice of the meeting is not given within 20 days after the receipt of the request, those members who called the special meeting may give their own notice of the meeting or petition the superior court to order the board to give the notice after the association is given notice of an opportunity to be heard in court. Obviously, if the membership is small in number, the easiest way to handle the board's lack of notice would be for the members who requested the special meeting to give their own notice of the meeting. If the membership is small in number, it is most likely that those requesting the special meeting can incur the expense of preparing the notice and mailing it to the other members.

On the other hand, if the membership is large, it may be that the cost of notice preparation and mailing is significant enough that it might be easier for the members calling the special meeting to petition the superior court for a hearing, seeking a court order requiring the board to give notice of the special meeting. If the membership seeks the court order, the board must be given an opportunity to be heard by the court, so it can offer an explanation as to why it was unable to meet the twenty-day deadline. Depending on the reason given by the board, the court may issue orders as it deems appropriate, designating a time and place of the meeting, the form of the notice, how it will be distributed, etc.

The twenty-day limitation after a request is received is to be used for verification of the proper number of members requesting the special meeting. Once the number of members is verified, the twenty-day limit allows the time necessary to prepare and duplicate a notice of the meeting.

It should be noted that the board fixes the time for the meeting, not the requesting members. Also, remember that it must be held no more than 90 days after receipt of the written request for the special meeting.

III. The Meeting

A. QUORUM

In California, the number of voting members necessary to "constitute a quorum" for a membership meeting may be set by a bylaw of the association. Absent that, one-third of the voting power, represented in person or by proxy, shall constitute a quorum at a meeting of the membership.

If a quorum is present at the membership meeting, the affirmative vote of a majority of the voting power present at the meeting, and entitled to vote, shall be the act of the members unless the vote of a greater number is required by law or the articles or bylaws of the association.

Any "bylaw amendment" to increase the quorum may be adopted by approval of the members.

Where a bylaw authorizes the association to conduct a meeting with a quorum of less than one-third, the only matters that may be voted upon at any regular meeting, actually attended in person or by proxy by less than one-third of the voting power, are matters of a general nature which were contained in the notice of the general meeting. If the membership does not have a quorum, the meeting may be adjourned by a vote of the majority of the members present either in person or by proxy, but no other business may be transacted at the meeting. Remember that it is not necessary to have the quorum set at one-third of the voting members. The quorum can be established at a higher number. Additionally, the bylaws could provide for a higher percentage for approval than the majority of the voting power represented at the meeting.

Also, remember that if you do not have the number of members present to constitute a quorum, that doesn't mean the meeting cannot take place. The meeting can take place with lively discussion, voicing of concerns, questions, and answers. The members are prevented, however, from taking any formal votes or actions on any matter or topic.

When a members' meeting is adjourned to another time or place, unless the bylaws require otherwise, notice need not be given of the adjourned meeting if the time and place thereof are announced at the meeting at which the adjournment was taken.

No member meeting may be adjourned for more than 45 days.

At the adjourned meeting, the association may transact any business which might have been transacted at the original meeting. If a meeting is adjourned for lack of a quorum and there is no announcement of adjournment to a new meeting date, when a new date and time is set, notice must be given to the membership in the same manner as the notice given for the regular meeting which was adjourned.

B. ALTERNATIVE TO ACTUAL MEETING – WRITTEN BALLOT

Unless it is prohibited in the articles or bylaws, any action which may be taken at any regular or special meeting of the members may be taken without a meeting if the association distributes a written ballot to every member entitled to vote on the matter.

A written ballot must state the proposed action, provide an opportunity to specify approval or disapproval of any proposal, and provide a reasonable time to return the ballot to the association.

This approval by ballot is valid only when the number of votes cast within the time period specified equals or exceeds the quorum requirement to present at a meeting authorizing the action. The number of approvals must equal or exceed the number of votes that would be required for approval at an actual meeting at which the total number of votes cast was the same as the number of votes cast by ballot. This is useful if it is unlikely that the number of members physically attending a meeting, or holding proxies for the meeting, will be sufficient to constitute a quorum.

Absentee owners may be more likely to fill out a written ballot than physically attend a meeting.

The ballot solicitations must indicate the number of responses needed to meet the quorum requirement and, with respect to ballots other than for the election of directors, must state the percentage of approvals necessary to pass the measure submitted on the ballot. Additionally, they must specify the time the ballot must be received in order to be counted. A written ballot may not be revoked unless it is provided otherwise in the articles or bylaws. Directors may be elected by written ballot if authorized by the articles or bylaws, unless the directors are elected by cumulative voting, which will be discussed later.

If you, as the manager, are going to be in charge of ballot preparation, it is important to know if and when the directors are to be elected by written ballot and if the articles or bylaws prescribe a nomination procedure. The procedure may provide for a date for the close of nominations prior to the printing of the distribution of the written ballots. Consequently, Gertrude needs to review the bylaws of the Hubie Highlands

Association to see whether she would be voting on Association matters by written ballot and not attending an Association meeting.

C. WAIVERS FOR DEFECTS

The transactions that took place at any meeting of the members, however called and noticed, are as valid as though they had taken place at a meeting duly held after a proper notice was sent out. If a quorum was present either in person or by proxy, each of the persons entitled to vote could sign in person or by proxy a written waiver of notice or consent to the holding of the meeting or an approval of the minutes of the meeting. Any such waivers have to be filed with the association records or made a part of the minutes of the meeting.

Any waiver allows a problem with a defective notice to be overlooked if those who were not in attendance agreed to the actions taken at the meeting, as long as a quorum was in attendance. If some of those not present at the meeting refuse to sign a waiver, it could be anticipated that a new meeting will have to be held on proper notice. This emphasizes the importance of checking the notice very carefully before it is distributed to the membership. Members may tend to get cranky when a defective notice requires a subsequent meeting.

Those in attendance at a meeting, which was held on the basis of a defective notice, cannot later complain that the actions at the meeting were invalid, because their attendance at the meeting constitutes a waiver of the notice.

This, of course, would not be true if a member attended the meeting for the purpose of objecting to a defective notice and that meeting was improperly called. Obviously, it is important for you, as the association manager, if you handle notices of meetings, to make sure that the notice is correct and also make sure that the notice covers any topics for membership voting. This is especially important when the topics deal with the members of the board of directors, the corporation itself, the Articles of Incorporation, any assessment issues, or any actions to change fundamental documents, such as the declaration or changes in the common areas. Therefore, to be on the safe side, any action that is going to require the approval of the membership should be specifically mentioned in the notice. Trying to get waiver, consent, or minute approvals from all members who do not attend may be next to impossible.

D. WHO CAN ATTEND THE MEMBERSHIP MEETING?

Obviously, the members of an association can attend a membership meeting. The question that occasionally comes up is whether a non-member, such as a visiting relative, fiancée, tenant, attorney, or accountant for a member has a legal right to attend the meeting. Since there is no legislation or other requirement that a membership meeting has to be opened to the public, the association can probably require that only individuals who are members of the association attend the meeting. Additionally, if voting by proxy is permitted in the association, whomever is designated as the proxy holder of the non-attending member would be allowed to attend the meeting.

It is important for you, as the manager, to research whether proxies are allowed, and if proxies can only be held by other members or by any member of the public.

Recall that the homeowner (community) association's governing documents, typically the declaration, will probably define the "members" as those people who are the owners of the separate interest within the community development. Therefore, one acquires a membership by owning a separate interest in the community development. It is also important to note that the declaration probably states that the membership is tied to, or "appurtenant" to, the separate interest and cannot be transferred separately from the separate interest. So the governing documents will probably provide for situations where one person, for example, owns four units in a condominium. Does that person now have four memberships in the association, or in the alternative, only one membership in the association? Additionally, does that member have one vote for each separate interest owned or one membership with one vote?

California law provides that a person who owns four separate units in a condominium development has four separate memberships in the association.

Another problem may arise when one unit in a condominium is owned by six individuals. The unit acquires a single membership in the association. The governing documents will provide how the co-owners will cast their single vote. Since six individuals own the condominium, does that mean all six individuals hold a "membership" in the association for the use and enjoyment of the common areas? For example, can all six co-owners use the tennis courts or the swimming pools? If one unit was owned by 33 co-owners, how would the association handle the "membership" issue and the "membership" voting issue?

AN EXAMPLE

Section11.22 "Member" shall mean any party holding a membership in the association.

Section 11.38 "Owner" shall mean person or persons holding fee simple interest of record to, or the real estate contract purchaser of, any lot or dwelling unit which is a part of the property.

(continued)

Section 33.22 When more than one person holds an interest in any lot, all such persons shall be members. Members shall be entitled to one vote for each lot owned. In no event shall more than one vote be cast with respect to any lot.

Section 33.23 Vote-distribution. Members shall be entitled to one vote for each lot owned. When more than one person has an interest in any lot ("co-owner"), all such co-owners shall be members and may attend any meeting of the association, but only one such co-owner shall be entitled to exercise the vote to which the lot is entitled. Such co-owners may from time to time designate in writing one of their number to vote. Fractional votes shall not be allowed, and the vote for each lot shall be exercised, if at all, as a unit. Where no voting co-owner is designated or if such designation has been revoked, the vote for such lot shall be exercised as a majority of the co-owners of the lot mutually agreed. Unless the board receives a written objection from a co-owner, it shall be presumed that the voting co-owner is acting with the consent of his or her co-owners. No vote shall be cast for any lot where the majority of the co-owners present in person or by proxy in representing such lot cannot agree to said vote or other action.

The non-voting co-owner or co-owners shall be jointly or severally responsible for all of the obligations imposed upon the jointly owned lot and shall be entitled to all other benefits of ownership.

All agreements and determinations lawfully made by the association in accordance with the voting percentages established herein, or in the bylaws, shall be deemed to be binding on all owners, their successors and assigned. Said voting rights shall be subject to the restrictions and limitations provided in this Declaration, the Articles and bylaws...

The association is governed by the Corporations Code, which provides the following:

> "If a membership stands of record in the names of two or more persons, ...unless the secretary of the corporation is given written notice to the contrary and is furnished with a copy of the instrument or order appointing them or creating the relationship wherein it is so provided, Their acts with respect to voting shall have the following effect: (a) If only one votes, such act binds all; or (b) If more than one vote, the act of the majority so voting binds all."

E. MEMBERSHIP DEFINITION

Another potential problem is that membership in the association and membership in the corporation may have slightly different meanings. For example, under California corporation law, "member" means any person who, (1) pursuant to a specific provision in a corporation's articles or bylaws, has the right to vote for the election of a director or directors or (2) vote on a disposition of all or substantially all of the assets of the corporation or (3) vote on a merger or dissolution. "Member" also means (4) any person designated in the articles or bylaws who has the right to vote on changes in the articles or bylaws. Therefore, if a person does not have one of the voting powers mentioned above, that person may not vote because that person is not considered to be a "member" under California law.

An additional issue involving ownership and membership will occur when a married couple acquires title to the unit and does so only in the name of one spouse. Once again, there will be a problem with the governing documents if they speak in terms of rights given to "owners of record" and only one spouse appears as owner of record. Is the owner of record the only person entitled to a "membership" in the community association? Or, in the alternative, do both a husband and wife receive membership privileges even though the title to the separate property interest is held in the name of only one spouse?

It is vitally important for you, as the association manager, to research the qualifications for membership voting rights in the association.

Hopefully, a crystal clear bylaw provision will handle the situation. If the membership and voting issue appears to be confusing, it is in the best interest of the association that the confusion be eliminated by modification or substitution of a provision that clearly states voting rights and membership privileges. The association's attorney can be useful here.

The following case illustrates how big the problem can be with language.

King v. Oakmoore Highlands Association

195 Cal. App. 3rd 779; 241 Cal. Rptr. 140 (App. 1 Dist. 1987)
Edited Excerpts From the Opinion of Justice White

FACTS AND ISSUES

The 443 lots at Oakmoor Highlands Association in Oakland were subject to a "Declaration of Restrictions," which provides that it could be extended for periods not exceeding twenty years "by the assent, evidenced by appropriate agreement entitled to record, entered into by the owners of record of not less than sixty-five (65) per cent in the area of said property,..." A resolution recorded on December 31, 1980, extended the Declaration of Restrictions for an additional twenty years. Of those voting to extend, all owners of 287 lots signed the agreement; one or more but not all owners of 14 lots signed the agreement, as to 9 lots, one owner, separated or divorced from the other owner, signed, and the non-resident spouse did not sign. Property owners King and Cadigan contested the validity of the vote.

(continued)

King and Cadigan contend that the extension was invalid because they failed to achieve the necessary sixty-five percent of all of the members' vote. The contention is based on the many non-voting members who were either joint tenants or tenants in common with voting members. Their position is that under the bylaws, the votes of the owners of a particular lot could not be applied toward fulfilling the sixty-five percent requirement where the votes of the co-tenants of such owners were not reported. The issue is whether the co-tenant's vote may bind a non-voting co-tenant. The trial court found the vote valid. King and Cadigan appealed.

DECISION AND REASONS

We base our decision on the interpretation of an association bylaw, and find our interpretation to be consistent with the principles of co-tenancy. The bylaw provides: "When a building site is owned of record in joint tenancy or tenancy in common, the membership as to such building site shall be joint, and the rights of such membership (including the voting power arising there from) shall be exercised only by the joint action of all owners of such building site."

The key phrase of the bylaw is "joint action." The most reasonable interpretation of the joint action requirement is that for a vote to be valid, it must reflect the joint action of all co-tenants of the property, and joint action means that each and every lot owner's position must be reflected, either by that person's actual vote or by authorization of a co-tenant to vote as his or her representative. If there is division among the co-tenants, the vote is not valid. If there are non-voting co-tenants, the voting co-tenant's vote should count as one full vote as long as the non-voting co-tenant authorizes such vote on his or her behalf; if the non-voting co-tenant has not so authorized such vote, the voting co-tenant's vote does not reflect "joint action of all owners," and should not be considered a valid vote under the bylaw.

In this case, there was no evidence that the co-tenants who cast votes were acting jointly with their non-voting co-tenants. We cannot infer that joint action existed merely for the presence of a single co-tenant's signature. Indeed, that all owner's of a large portion of the lots signed the signature sheets may indicate a general recognition that a joint action, as evidenced by the signatures of all co-tenants, was required. Our holding is consistent with the laws relating to co-tenancy, in particular, case law which has constantly held that one joint tenant has not by reason of the relationship any authority to bind its co-tenant with respect to the latter's interest in the common property. We find the general rule limiting a co-tenant's power to encumber property without the co-tenant's consent applicable here. The judgment of the trial court is reversed.

Once again, it is important for the board of directors and the association manager to research the recorded governing documents of the homeowner (community) association, particularly the Articles of Incorporation, more particularly the bylaws, to determine if problems such as the one in the case above exist and, if so, propose a remedy. Does the previous "AN EXAMPLE" language remedy the problem in the King case above? If the association needs to remedy a voting problem, undoubtedly a member will come up with the idea of fractional votes. This is probably not a good idea, as it can be a mess to keep track of. Consideration can be given to the language in the "AN EXAMPLE" or to the earlier section which mentions how the California Corporations Code handles voting when a membership stands of record in the names of two or more persons.

IV. Voting

A. ELIGIBILITY TO VOTE

Assume that the voting problem has been solved, as a membership in which two or more persons have an ownership interest will be treated as one membership for voting purposes, but that all members can attend the meeting. Now it may be necessary for the secretary of the association to be given proof of the membership interests to make sure those in attendance are really members of the association. Additionally, if the governing documents or bylaws allow only members in good standing to vote at a membership meeting, does this mean the member not in good standing can attend the meeting but cannot vote? Either way, the governing documents should be checked to make sure when a member is not in good standing.

Typically, the governing documents provide that, to be in good standing, the member must be current in the payment of all assessments against the member's interest. They may also provide for a loss of voting power for some other disciplinary action.

B. CHOOSING VOTING LANGUAGE

If, as the manager, your research uncovers the term "approved by the members," this means that the proposal must be approved by a vote of a majority of the members represented either by proxy or in person, voting at a properly noticed meeting, where a quorum is present. In other words, the approval votes must equal the majority of votes present at the meeting, provided a quorum has been established. For example, assume that the association's requirement for a quorum is a majority of the members present. If the total membership is 400, and 300 members attend the meeting, a quorum has been established because all that is required is 201 members physically present or present by proxy to constitute a quorum. With 300 members either physically present or present by proxy, a majority of 151 votes must be affirmatively cast for a resolution to pass.

If your research uncovers the term "approved by a majority of all members," then the proposal must be approved by a majority of the votes of all members entitled to vote. For example, if the community association has 400 members, 201 votes must be cast for approval. Therefore, if 230 members show up at the meeting, and a majority constitutes a quorum, we have a quorum for the meeting. Out of the 230 members present at the meeting, 201 must vote for passage of a resolution.

If your research uncovers the term "voting power," prepare to be confused. For example, if "a majority of the voting power" is required, it is necessary to determine who has the power to vote at the meeting. For example, if the member has lost the power to vote because of a disciplinary action, that number does not count toward the "voting power." This term is in the California Commercial Code and was encountered earlier in:

> "One-third of the voting power, represented in person or by proxy, shall constitute a quorum at a meeting of members, but, ... a bylaw may set a different quorum."

***VOTING POWER** is defined under the corporation law to mean "the power to vote for the election of the directors at the time any determination of voting power is made and does not include the right to vote upon the happening of some condition or event which has not yet occurred."* In other words, the determination must be made as to which of the members have the power to vote in an election of directors, and that determination establishes the identity of the voting power in the association. Since this can be a time consuming project, it might be advisable to remove the term "voting power" to the extent permissible by law. Otherwise, considerable time will be spent on determining who is in the class of "voting power."

If your research discovers a term which specifies a particular number or percentage of members or owners, that should not be too difficult to determine. For example, the wording might be "...and it must be passed by a vote of 70% of the membership." If the community association has 400 members, and 310 are present in person or by proxy at a meeting, obviously a quorum has been established, and the affirmative votes necessary to pass the resolution must equal 280. Obviously, you may have a quorum established for a meeting but not be able to vote on a proposal because you cannot obtain the required number of votes.

C. THE VOTING

Under California law, the governing documents prepared by the developer of the common interest development must authorize the use of cumulative voting in the selection of directors for all elections in which two or more positions are filled.

Usually, after the transition of control from the developer, the association's bylaws are amended to discontinue cumulative voting. Cumulative voting is used only for the election of directors under the nonprofit mutual benefit corporation laws.

With the elimination of cumulative voting for directors, voting by the members for directors is now the same as voting for all other proposals, which is one vote per membership. For example, if the membership is voting on whether to add a tennis

court, each member would vote once either in the affirmative or the negative for the proposal. However, the "one vote per membership" approach does have some concerns that need to be resolved by the association. For example, suppose there are three openings on the board of directors and the membership is voting to fill the vacancies from a slate of individuals running for the director positions. The question is whether a member has one vote and can vote for any candidate desired to fill that position or, in the alternative, does the member have three votes to vote for three individuals to fill the three vacancies? Hopefully, as the manager, you can find specific language in the governing documents that will resolve this issue.

AN EXAMPLE - California Corporations Code Section 7615

(a) If the articles or bylaws authorize cumulative voting, but not otherwise, every member entitled to vote at any election of directors may cumulate the members' votes and give one candidate a number of votes equal to the number of directors to be elected multiplied by the number of votes to which the member is entitled, or distribute the members' votes on the same principle among as many candidates as the member thinks fit. ...

...

(c) In any election of directors by cumulative voting, the candidates receiving the highest numbers of votes are elected, ...

...

(e) Elections for directors need not be by ballot unless a member demands election by ballot at the meeting and before the voting begins or unless the bylaws so require.

D. VOTING BY PROXY

A proxy is the authority or written authorization to act for another.

In California, any member of a nonprofit mutual benefit corporation may authorize another person to "act by proxy" with respect to such membership, although this right may be limited or withdrawn by the articles or bylaws.

In other words, members have the ability to vote by proxy unless it has been limited or taken away. Some limitations countered might be, (1) allowing the use of a proxy only for counting the necessary members present for a quorum, or (2) allowing proxy voting only for particular matters up for the vote of the membership. Of course, any amendment of the articles or bylaws of the corporation which involve proxy rights must be approved by the members. From our previous discussion we know that "approval by the members" means a vote by a majority of the members present at a meeting which was properly noticed and where a quorum is present. Recall, however, that the governing documents may require a higher percentage for this type of vote.

The object behind proxy voting is to permit members of the association an opportunity to vote on issues presented at a properly called meeting, in which a quorum is present, when a member is unable to attend.

This is particularly useful if you have members who are a significant geographic distance from the development. One negative for proxies is that members who receive the proxy may tend to vote on a issue without hearing the debate or discussion on that issue that would take place at the membership meeting. Therefore, the member is voting by proxy prior to discussion of the issue at the meeting. Another issue that is presented by proxy voting is whether the member cast the vote either affirmatively or negatively for the issue or whether the member gives a fellow member or, perhaps another person, a ***BLANK PROXY****, which allows the person to vote for the absent member however the person chooses to do so.* Yet another problem with proxy voting is that the board of directors may solicit proxies from the membership, the cost of which is paid by the association. Obviously, the board wants to stay in power and the members are seeking votes to that effect from those who will not attend the meeting. Additionally, the board may be seeking a particular vote on a issue and the solicitation will hopefully be returned the way the board desires.

If a member returns a blank proxy in response to the board's solicitation, then the board can vote that proxy however it desires.

E. PROXY SPECIFICS

Each state has its own rules regarding voting by proxy.

What follows is a look at California's proxy rules.

A ***PROXY*** *is a written authorization, signed by a member or the member's attorney in fact, giving another person or persons power to vote on behalf of such member.* **SIGNED** *means the placing of the member's name on the proxy (whether by manual signature, typewriting, telegraphing transmission, or otherwise) by the member or such member's attorney in fact.* Obviously, the ***PROXY HOLDER*** *is the person or persons to whom the proxy is given.*

No proxy is valid after the expiration of eleven months from the date of the proxy, unless otherwise provided in the proxy, although the maximum term of any proxy is three years from the date of signing.

A proxy remains in effect until it is revoked by the person signing it prior to being voted. **Revocation** can take place by delivering a written revocation to the corporation (association) or by a subsequent proxy executed by the same person who signed the previous proxy and presented at the meeting, or by the person who signed the original proxy attending the meeting and voting in person.

The death or incapacity of the person who signed the proxy will terminate the proxy only if written notice of the death or incapacity is received by the association before the proxy vote is counted.

AN EXAMPLE - Corporation Code Section 5034

"Approval by (or approval of) the members" means approved or ratified by the affirmative vote of a majority of the votes represented and voting at a duly held meeting at which a quorum is present (which affirmative votes also constitute a majority of the required quorum)...

To make things slightly more complicated for the association using proxies, any revocable proxy is not valid, meaning it cannot be voted unless the proxy states the general nature of the matter to be voted on if the matter is one of the following:

1. An amendment of the articles or bylaws repealing, restricting, creating, or expanding proxy rights.
2. Removal of a director without cause.
3. Filling a vacancy on the board of directors when that vacancy is being filled by a vote of the members.
4. The approval of a contract or transaction in which one or more of the association directors has a material financial interest.
5. Approval of amendments of the Articles of Incorporation.
6. Approval of a sale of all or substantially all of the assets of the corporation approved by the members either before or after approval by the board of directors and before or after the transaction.
7. Approval of a merger with another corporation as well as any amendment to the merger agreement.
8. A proposal to wind up and dissolve the corporation.
9. If the corporation is in the process of winding up any plan for distribution that is not in accordance with the current liquidation rights of any class of memberships.

As a reminder, if the membership is to vote on any of the above listed items, a ***REVOCABLE PROXY*** *may vote on the item only if the proxy form set forth the general nature of that item.* Even though the requirement is for the "general nature of the matter to be voted on," it may be in the best interest of the association to be more specific in the proxy.

Any form of proxy distributed to ten or more members within an association with 100 or more members must provide the opportunity on the proxy to specify a choice between approval and disapproval of each matter or group of related matters intended, at the time the proxy is distributed, to be acted upon at the meeting for which the proxy is solicited. The proxy must also provide, subject to reasonable specified conditions, where the person solicited specifies a choice with respect to any matter, the vote shall be cast in accordance with that choice.

Additionally, in an election of directors, and any form of proxy in which the directors to be voted on are named as candidates and the member marks "withhold" on the proxy or otherwise marks it in a matter indicating that the authority to vote for the election of directors is withheld, is not considered a vote for or against the election or director. If there is a failure to comply with the above notices to be stated on a proxy, it does not invalidate any election, but it may be the basis for challenging any proxy at the meeting, and a superior court may compel compliance with the proxy rules if a member brings a lawsuit.

F. IRREVOCABLE PROXIES

Unless it is otherwise provided in the articles or bylaws, if a proxy states it is ***IRREVOCABLE***, *it cannot be recalled or withdrawn for the period specified in the proxy* when it is held by any of the following:

1. A person who purchased or who has agreed to purchased the membership;
2. A creditor of the corporation or member who received credit in consideration of the giving of the proxy to the creditor;
3. A person who has contracted to perform services as an employee of the corporation, if the proxy is required by the employment contract and it states that it was given in consideration of the contract, the name of the employee, and the period of employment.

Notwithstanding the period of irrevocability mentioned above, the proxy becomes revocable when the agreement to purchase a membership is terminated, the debt of the proxy giver is paid to the creditor, or the period of the employment contract has terminated. Additionally, a proxy can be made irrevocable if it is given to secure performance of a duty or protect a title until a happening of an event which, by its terms, discharges the obligation secured by the proxy.

Even though the proxy states it is irrevocable, it may be revoked by a person acquiring a membership without knowledge of the existence of the irrevocable proxy, unless the irrevocability appears on a certificate representing the membership.

G. SOME THOUGHTS ABOUT PROXIES

An association has to decide whether using proxies is a good idea or not.

The association may already be bound to proxies because it is provided in the governing documents of the association. If not, an association may consider the use of proxies by amending the governing documents to provide for proxies. Another alternative would be for the association to make some changes in the current proxy rules for the association. Voting by proxy can be eliminated in the articles or bylaws by a vote of the association. Depending on the association, elimination of proxies may make it difficult to conduct business at a membership meeting without proxies present to constitute a quorum.

The proxy gives a person who is unable, for whatever reason, to attend a membership meeting an opportunity to vote a particular way on an action to be presented at the meeting.

Without proxies, it may be that only the most active of the members may have a block significant enough to form a quorum or to pass or block resolutions presented at the meeting. Additionally, with proxies, the board of directors can solicit, at association expense, proxies which support the board's position. Members who are not familiar with the issues may blindly follow the solicitation of the board, thinking the board knows what is in the best interest of the association, and send the board a blank proxy giving the board, or perhaps the secretary of the board, the power to vote it as the secretary or board sees fit.

Sometimes an association might have proxies only for determining if a quorum is present. Other associations may allow the proxies to vote for only specified actions and not others. For example, the association may limit the voting by proxy only to the election of the board of directors and any changes in the governing documents. Another approach would be to allow an officer of the corporation, perhaps the secretary, to have any proxies put in the name of the secretary as the proxy holder to be voted in accordance with the wishes of proxy giver as expressed on the proxy. If the proxy giver has not expressed a choice of the matters on the proxy, it cannot be voted, and could only count toward the formation of a quorum.

H. WRITTEN BALLOT VOTING

Unless prohibited in the articles or bylaws, any action which may take place at a regular or special meeting of the members may be taken without a meeting if the association distributes a written ballot to every member entitled to vote on the matter. Such ballot must, 1) set forth the proposed action; 2) provide an opportunity to specify approval or disapproval of the action; and 3) provide a reasonable time in which to return the ballot to the corporation.

I. WRITTEN BALLOT ISSUES

The association needs some way of determining who is voting by written ballot.

In other words, how does the association know that the member voted the ballot unless there is some sort of identification number, signature, or other means validating that this is the member's vote? Obviously, this makes the secret ballot somewhat un-secret. For checking on a signature of a person to work, you need something in the association records which represents an accurate signature of each member entitled to vote by written ballot.

If the association wants to keep the vote as secret as possible, it can use the double envelope method. With this method, the voting member returns a ballot in a envelope which is placed anonymously inside another envelope that is signed by the member. This would appear to be a means to keep the ballot secret. Alternatively, sometimes all ballots are sent to a neutral third party, such as the association's accountant or attorney, and that person receives and counts all of the ballots. Additionally, the regulations of the California Real Estate Commissioner provide that "Voting for the governing body shall be by secret written ballot." Other than that, Gertrude may find that the voting at the meeting is conducted by a raising of hands or arms which certainly doesn't make the voting secret.

A vote by written ballot would imply some degree of secrecy, which is not available when a vote is conducted by raising arms.

J. DISTRIBUTION OF WRITTEN BALLOTS

The bylaws may provide or, in the absence of such a provision, the board may fix, in advance, a date as the "record date" (of the owners as of that date) for the purpose of determining the members entitled to cast written ballots. The record date cannot be more than 60 days before the date on which the first written ballot is mailed or solicited. If no record date is fixed, members on the day the first written ballot is mailed or solicited are entitled to cast their written ballots.

As in giving a notice of a meeting, the written ballot can either be personally delivered, delivered by mail, or other means of written communication.

Additionally, as with a proxy, if the ballot is distributed to ten or more members in an association with 100 or more members, it must be specifically stated, on the written ballot, the choice between approval or disapproval of each matter, or group of matters, intended to be acted upon for which the written ballot is being sent. Note that such a specific ballot is not required if, in the unlikely event, it is distributed to nine or less members out of an association of 100 or more. The specific language on the ballot appears not to be required if the ballot is distributed to ten or more members if the association membership is under 100.

Additionally, as with the proxy, if the written ballot is for the election of directors, the member can indicate the withholding of a vote showing the intention not to vote either for or against the election of a particular person. The association must follow the member's vote as cast on the ballot. If the association fails to hold a written ballot for a period of 60 days after the date designated for it, then the superior court may order the ballot to be conducted on an application to the court by a member of the association after notice to the association giving it an opportunity to be heard.

K. PRACTICAL PROBLEMS WITH WRITTEN BALLOTS

The object behind the association using a written ballot is to avoid the apathy of the members who will not attend a membership meeting.

Lack of attendance at the membership meeting may prevent a quorum from being established and prevent the membership from conducting business. The thought is that more members will return a written ballot than will attend an actual meeting. Even with a written ballot solicitation, it may be necessary for the association to consider extending the deadline for return of the written ballot in order to get enough ballots returned to make the vote valid. The association may consider conducting an actual meeting along with the written ballot solicitation. This will allow members to cast their written ballots at the membership meeting, assuming they did not already return their ballots to the association. This can create a practical problem for the association in determining whether a member is voting again at the membership meeting having previously voted by written ballot. Voting by written ballot solicitation is common, and unless otherwise provided in the articles or bylaws, the vote is irrevocable. It might be advisable for the association to have a membership meeting at which it can announce the results of the written ballot and introduce the directors elected or the method for carrying out a matter that passed by written vote.

If an association is going to use a written vote solicitation as well as voting by written ballot at an association meeting, it is important that some mechanism be established to prevent membership voting fraud.

V. Making It Work

A. INSPECTORS OF ELECTION

In advance of any meeting of members, the board may appoint either one or three inspectors of election to act at a meeting and any adjournment thereof.

If no inspectors are appointed or they fail to appear or refuse to act, the chairman of the meeting may, and if requested by a member or proxy, shall, appoint inspectors of election at the meeting. The number of inspectors must be either one or three. If the appointment is at the request of a member or a member's proxy, the majority of members present in person or by proxy shall vote for a determination of one or three inspectors to be appointed. Inspectors of election may also be appointed in a case of actions taken by written ballot.

The inspectors determine the number of memberships and the voting power of each, the number represented at the meeting, the existence of a quorum, and the validity of proxies. They also receive votes, hear and determine all challenges and questions in connection with the right to vote, count and tabulate all votes, determine when the polls shall close, determine the result, and do acts as may be proper to conduct the election or vote with fairness to all members.

The inspectors must perform their duties impartially, in good faith, to the best of their ability, and as expeditiously as practical.

If three inspectors are appointed, the majority controls.

B. COURT ENFORCEMENT

California law provides that if for any reason it is impractical or unduly difficult for the association to call or conduct a meeting of its members, directors, or otherwise obtain their consent, in the manner prescribed in its articles or bylaws, or according to the law, then a petition can be brought before the local county superior court. This petition can be brought by a director, officer, or member requesting that a meeting be called or a written ballot or other form of obtaining the vote of the members or the directors be authorized in a manner which is fair and equitable under the circumstances. The court may so order, and if so, it must provide a method of notice reasonably designed to give actual notice to all parties who would be entitled to notice of a meeting. The court may also determine who the members or directors are. The court's order may dispense with any requirement relating to the holding of and voting at meetings and obtaining votes, including any requirement as to quorums or as to the number or percentage of votes needed for approval, that otherwise are imposed on the association.

Whenever practical, the court's order must limit the subject matter of the meetings or other forms of consent to authorized items, including amendments to the articles or bylaws, the resolution of which will or may enable the association to continue managing its affairs without further resort to court action. Further, the court's order may also authorize the obtaining of whatever votes and approvals are necessary for the dissolution, merger, sale of assets, or reorganization of the association. A meeting or other method of obtaining votes of the members or directors which is conducted

pursuant to the court's order is considered a valid meeting or vote, and has the same force or effect as if it complied with every requirement imposed by the articles, bylaws, or state law. Obviously, a major issue for the superior court is finding whether it is "impractical" or "unduly difficult" for the corporation to conduct its business in the manner prescribed by its articles or bylaws, or by state law.

C. ENCOURAGING MEMBERS TO ATTEND MEETINGS

A practical problem is how to get members involved in the association's activities. Some sort of enticement to get them to a membership meeting might be appropriate. It has been said "Give them food, and they will come." For example, if the association meets once a month, consideration should be given to having a food or beverage theme for that month's meeting. Some ideas might be sampling different coffees from around the world, or having members bring various desserts for everyone to sample, a burger and potato salad theme, or something as simple as pizza night. Obviously, the food and beverage could be more elaborate. With a very large association, payment to a caterer might be appropriate. Careful consideration should be given to the serving of alcoholic beverages. Margarita night might be somewhat different than a wine sampling night. In other words, intoxicated members would probably mean obnoxious members. A drawing for a prize of some sort might be useful. Or, perhaps a twenty minute presentation by the attorney for the association regarding enforcement of the new parking regulations might be enough to increase attendance.

VI. MANAGER'S JOURNAL

Obviously, it is important to have an enthusiastic membership that is involved in the decision making process of the association. Apathy is common and it is difficult to get a quorum for membership meetings. As the association manager, you need to be familiar with the requirements for notices, attendance, voting, and everything else previously mentioned in the chapter. Mistakes can be very costly, both in terms of time and money and may cause some members to lack confidence in your abilities as the association manager. Sometimes the board of directors will handle many of the membership meeting tasks through its own actions, through the action of its secretary, or through the action of an appointed committee. This does not alleviate your responsibility for making sure the actions follow the rules established in the corporation's articles or bylaws, or any other governing documents or the laws of the state in which the community association is located.

Depending on the size and makeup of the association, the use of **inspectors of the election** may be a great idea to eliminate controversy regarding voting by the members. Even if all of the members do not understand or have knowledge of the specific rules governing the conduct of membership meetings, it is important that you, as the association manager do. Certainly, any questions raised by you research can be answered by the attorney for the association. Preventing problems from occurring is certainly well worth the cost, rather than trying to fix the problem after it has occurred, especially if it leads to litigation.

Additionally, it is important for you, as the manager of the association, to learn who the "players" are in the association. Typically, there will be a core of members who are extremely active in membership issues. Learn who these people are and, if you can, learn a little bit about their typical positions on membership issues. These people can be very helpful in keeping the membership functioning and assisting with membership tasks. Volunteers are always useful, assuming they are good volunteers. Also, try to learn who the members are that are apathetic toward membership activities. Make a special effort to reach out to these members with friendly encouragement to help the association become a better functioning organization. Ask and encourage the apathetic members to become more active. Be careful not to push them too hard or upset them. Graciously take "no" for an answer if that is what is required.

VII. CHAPTER SUMMARY

All corporate power is exercised by the board of directors, unless the articles of incorporation, association bylaws, or California law provides that certain activities and affairs are reserved for membership approval. In most instances, the governing documents set the requirements for calling and conducting membership meetings. If no place is designated in the bylaws for the location of meetings, the meetings must be held at the association's principle office.

California law requires that meetings of the membership must be conducted in accordance with a recognized system of parliamentary procedure or any parliamentary procedures the association may adopt. If the association fails to hold a required meeting and sixty days passes, or fifteen months has passed since the last regular meeting, a member can ask the superior court to order a meeting be held.

A "special meeting" of the members may be called for any lawful purpose by the board of directors, the chairman of the board, the president, or such other persons, if any are specified in the bylaws, or by five percent or more of the members.

A written notice of regular meetings must be given not less than 10, nor more than 90, days before the date of the meeting. The notice must be given personally, by mail, or by other means of written communication, addressed to the member of the address appearing on association records, or at the address given by the member to the association for the purpose of notice.

Special meetings must be held at a time fixed by the board (not the requesting members) not less than 35, nor more than 90, days after the receipt of the written request.

In California, the number of voting members necessary to constitute a quorum for a membership meeting may be set by a bylaw of the association. Absent that, one-third of the voting power, represented in person or by proxy, shall constitute a quorum at a meeting of the membership. Any bylaw amendment to increase the quorum may be adopted by the approval of the members. No member meeting may be adjourned for more than 45 days.

A written ballot must state the proposed action, provide an opportunity to specify approval or disapproval of any proposal, and provide a reasonable time to return the ballot to the association. Absentee owners may be more likely to fill out a written ballot than physically attend a meeting.

The members in attendance at a meeting held on the basis of a defective notice cannot later complain that the actions at the meeting were invalid, because their attendance constitutes a waiver of the notice.

California law provides that a person who owns four separate units in a condominium development has four separate memberships in the association.

Typically, the governing documents provide that, to be in good standing, the member must be current in the payment of all assessments against the member's interest. They may also provide for a loss of voting power for some other disciplinary action.

Voting power is defined under the corporation law to mean "the power to vote for the election of the directors at the time any determination of voting power is made and does not include the right to vote upon the happening of some condition or event which has not yet occurred." Under California law, the governing documents prepared by the developer of the CID must authorize the use of cumulative voting in the selection of directors for all elections in which two or more positions are filled.

Each state has its own rules regarding voting by proxy. A proxy is the authority or written authorization to act for another. In California, any member of a nonprofit mutual benefit corporation may authorize another person too "act by proxy" with respect to such membership, although this right may be withdrawn by the articles or bylaws. The object is to permit members of the association an opportunity to vote on issues presented at a properly called meeting, in which a quorum is present, when a member is unable to attend.

A blank proxy allows the person to vote for the absent member however the person chooses to do so.

A proxy may be revocable or irrevocable (meaning it cannot be recalled or withdrawn for the period specified in the proxy). An irrevocable proxy may still be revoked if a member did not have knowledge of the existence of the irrevocable proxy, unless it is so stated on a certificate representing membership.

Voting may take place by written ballot. The written ballot can either be personally delivered, delivered by mail, or other means of written communication. If the association is going to use a written vote solicitation as well as voting by written ballot at an association meeting, it is important that some mechanism be established to prevent membership voting fraud. In advance of any meeting of members, the board may appoint either one or three inspectors of election to act at a meeting and any adjournment thereof. If three inspectors are appointed, the majority controls.

VIII. REVIEW QUESTIONS

1. Primary responsibility for making decisions regarding the running of the association rests with the:

a. board of directors.
b. association members.
c. community association manager.
d. secretary of the association.

2. Any action which may be taken at a regular or special meeting of the members may be taken without a meeting if the association:

a. allows voting by proxy.
b. distributes a ballot to every member.
c. holds a secret meeting.
d. all of the above.

3. The Hubie Highlands Community Association had a scheduled meeting on June 1, but it failed to hold the meeting or reschedule it. An association member can ask the superior court to order that the meeting be held provided that how many days have passed since June 1?

a. 15
b. 30
c. 60
d. 90

4. A special meeting can be called by the members of the association provided they represent:

a. 5% or more of the members.
b. 10% or more of the members.
c. 15% or more of the members.
d. 20% or more of the members.

5. A written notice of meetings must be given not less than 10, nor more than:

a. 60 days before the date of the meeting.
b. 90 days before the date of the meeting.
c. 120 days before the date of the meeting.
d. none of the above.

6. A quorum is:

a. a form of subdivision.
b. the total number of members in the association.
c. the total number of votes necessary to discuss association business casually.
d. the number of voting members necessary to conduct business at a membership meeting.

7. Under California law, how many memberships in an association does a person who owns four separate units in a condominium development have?

a. 4
b. 2
c. 1
d. None of the above.

8. Under California law, if a membership stands of record in the name of two or more persons, which of the following is true?

a. The vote of the owners must be unanimous to constitute a valid vote.
b. All members must cast a vote for it to be valid, and the majority so voting binds the other members.
c. The first owner to vote binds the others.
d. If one owner votes, it binds the others, or if more than one votes, the act of the majority binds the others.

9. "Approved by the members" means:

   a. the proposal must be approved by a vote of a majority of the members represented at a properly noticed meeting where a quorum is present.
   b. the proposal must be approved by a all of the members.
   c. a proposal must be approved by a majority vote of the board of directors.
   d. none of the above.

10. The term "blank proxy" typically means:

   a. a proxy distributed to the membership was defective because information required was left off of the proxy, therefore it was "blank."
   b. the member voted the proxy by guessing rather than reading and trying to understand the proposals open for voting.
   c. the person returning the proxy did so without marking any votes on it which means it is a "blank proxy" and, since there is no vote, the proxy cannot be voted and it must be destroyed.
   d. it allows the person to vote for the absent member, however the person who holds the "blank proxy" chooses to do so.

ANSWERS: 1. *a*; 2. *b*; 3. *c*; 4. *a*; 5. *b*; 6. *d*; 7. *a*; 8. *d*; 9. *a*; 10. *d*

JobsiteRules
OSHA/SWPP
Regulations Strictly Enforced
Hard hats required.
All visitors must be accompanied by a home counselor. All others, check in with superintendent.
ABSOLUTELY NO: eating, drinking, smoking in houses, animals, children, drugs or loud music.
Please do not park your vehicle in driveways or garages.
Construction parking in designated areas only.
No alcohol or drug use.
All accidents are to be reported to project superintendent immediately.
Prohibido el uso de drogas y alcohol.
Todo accidente debe ser reportado inmediatamente al superintendente.
John Laing Homes
Hand crafted since 1848
SpeedLimit
5

CHAPTER 5

Homeowner (Community) Association Restrictions: Part 1

I. Restrictions Imposed by Homeowner (Community) Associations

Restrictions are generally used in a common interest development for the following:

1. To ensure consistency in architectural style;
2. For consistency in use of member owned property; and
3. For consistent use of the property owned in common.

These restrictions are often the reason individuals choose to buy in a common interest development (CID). Owners in a CID know that there is a degree of consistency and predictability that can be enforced by the homeowner (community) association or association members.

The authority the association has to establish and enforce restrictions can come from one or more of the following sources:

1. State or federal law;
2. The governing documents of the development consisting of the declaration and/or CC&Rs;

Chapter 5

CHAPTER OUTLINE

3. Rules established by the board of directors of the community association; and
4. Court decisions.

If the homeowner (community) association does not have the authority to impose restrictions, or change existing restrictions, or it exceeds its authority, then the actions of the association are unenforceable.

A. AUTHORITY TO REGULATE

In a common interest development (CID), members may wish to alter their property. Obviously, this can be a problem in a planned development where the member owns the structure and the lot, which, nevertheless, falls under certain association restrictions about the appearance and modification of the property. There are common issues involving condominiums, stock cooperatives, and community apartment projects. For example, a member may wish to add a satellite dish, a patio cover, an awning, a fence, stained glass window, a fireplace and chimney, plant certain trees or vegetation, hang a large flower basket, put in several skylights, install outdoor lighting or patio lighting, and the list can go on and on. Whether the member can do so depends on the existence or known existence of architectural restrictions.

Sometimes the member will submit a proposal to an "architectural committee" that may accept or reject the proposal, or work with the member on modifications to reach a reasonable compromise.

If there is no architectural committee, the proposal may be submitted directly to the board of directors of the community association, which will make the ultimate decision. Problems arise when the member's request is denied and the member feels there was no rational basis for the denial, bias or prejudice against the member caused the denial, or the proposal was denied, but previous members had similar proposals approved.

For a better understanding of the material regarding restrictions on the property, it is necessary to mention the following concepts.

1. Covenants Running With the Land

A ***COVENANT*** *can be defined as an agreement between two landowners regarding a promise of one landowner to either do or not do something with regard to the property owned by that landowner.* This promise, or covenant, benefits the other property owner and places a burden on the owner of the servient property.

If the covenant states that it will bind subsequent owners of the land to that same promise, the covenant "runs with the land."

In most states, as in California, legislation sets out the requirement to have a covenant which will run with the land. In California, **Civil Code §1468** provides, in essence:

1. The covenant must be in writing and recorded in the county where the land is located:
2. The land affected by the covenant and the land to benefit from the covenant are particularly described in the writing;
3. The writing expressly states that successive owners of the land are to be bound by the covenant; and
4. The covenant must relate some way to the use of the land itself.

2. Equitable Servitude

If, for one reason or another, a covenant does not run with the land because it fails to meet the necessary requirements, the covenant may still be enforceable if it would be "equitable" (fair and just) to do so.

For example, if the covenant was never recorded but the new purchaser had full knowledge of the covenant, it would be inequitable to allow the new purchaser to escape the obligations of the covenant merely because the document wasn't recorded.

Equitable servitude allows the covenant to be a burden on the land, binding successive owners if they have knowledge of it.

3. Reasons for Regulations

Justice Kennard, in writing the opinion of the Supreme Court of California in the case of *Nahrstedt v. Lakeside Village Condominium Association, Inc.*, does an excellent job of providing background information concerning ability to regulate the use of property. The following is an edited portion of the opinion:

> Today, condominiums, cooperatives, and planned-unit developments with homeowners have become a widely accepted form of real property ownerships. These ownership arrangements are known as "common interest" developments....the owner not only enjoys many of the traditional advantages associated with individual ownership of real property, but also acquires an interest in common with others in the amenities and facilities included in the project. It is this hybrid nature of property rights that largely accounts for the popularity of these new and innovative forms of ownership in the twentieth century....
>
> The term "condominium," which is used to describe a system of ownership as well as an individually owned unit in a multi-unit development, is Latin in origin and means "joint dominion" or "co-ownership"....

...The declaration, which is the operative document for the creation of any common interest development, is the collection of covenants, conditions, and servitudes that govern the project....Typically the declaration describes the real property and any structures on the property, delineates the common areas within the project as well as the individually held lots and units, and sets forth restrictions pertaining to the use of property....

Use restrictions are an inherit part of any common interest development and are crucial to the stable, planned environment of any shared ownership arrangement....

The restrictions on the use of property of any common interest development may limit activities conducted in the common areas as well as the confines of the home itself....Commonly, "use restrictions" preclude alterations of building exteriors, limit the number of persons who can occupy each unit, and place limitations on—or prohibit altogether—the keeping of pets....

Restrictions on property use are not the only characteristics of common interest ownership. Ordinarily, such ownership also entails mandatory membership in an owner's association, which, through an elected board of directors, is empowered to enforce any use restrictions contained in the project's declaration or master deed and to enact new rules governing the use and occupancy of the property within the project....Because of its considerable power in managing and regulating a common interest development, the governing board of an owner's association must guard against the potential for abuse of that power....Therefore, anyone who buys a unit in a common interest development with knowledge of its owner's association's discretionary power accepts "the risk that the power may be used in a way that benefits the commonality but harms the individual." Generally, courts will uphold decisions made by the governing board of an owner's association so long as they represent good faith efforts to further the purposes of the common interest development, are consistent with the development's governing documents, and comply with public policy. The power to regulate pertains to a "wide spectrum of activities."

Thus, subordination of individual property rights to the collective judgment of the owner's association together with restrictions on the use of real property comprise the chief attributes of owning property in a common interest development....

Notwithstanding the limitations on personal autonomy that are inherent in the concept of shared ownership of residential property, common interest developments have increased in popularity in recent years, in part because they generally provide a more affordable alternative to ownership of a single-family home....

> One significant factor in the continued popularity of the common interest form of property ownership is the ability of homeowners to enforce restrictive CC&Rs against other owners (including future purchasers) of project units....Generally, however, such enforcement is possible only if the restriction that is sought to be enforced meets the requirements of equitable servitudes or of covenants running with the land....
>
> Restrictive covenants will run with the land, and thus bind successive owners, if the deed or other instrument containing the restrictive covenant particularly describes the land to be benefited and burdened by the restriction and expressly provides the successors and interest of the covenantor's land will be bound for the benefit of the convenantee's land. Moreover, restrictions must relate to the use, repair, maintenance, or improvement of the property, or to the payment of taxes or assessments, and the instrument containing the restrictions must be recorded....Restrictions that do not meet the requirements of covenants running with the land may be enforceable as equitable servitude provided the person bound by the restrictions had notice of their existence.
>
> When restrictions limiting the use of property within a common interest development satisfy the requirements of covenants running with the land or of equitable servitudes, what standard or test governs their enforceability? In California,...our legislature has made common interest development use restrictions contained in a project's recorded declaration "enforceable...*unless unreasonable.*"

In states lacking such legislative guidance, some courts have adopted a standard under which a common interest development's recorded use restrictions will be enforceable so long as they are "reasonable."

In *Hidden Harbour Estates v. Basso,* (Fla.Dist.Ct.App. 1991) 393 So.2d 637, the Florida court distinguished two categories of use restrictions, including:

1. Use restrictions set forth in the declaration or master deed of the condominium project itself, or
2. Rules promulgated (made public) by the governing board of the condominium owner's association or the board's interpretation of a rule.

The latter category of use restrictions, the court said, should be subject to a "reasonableness" test, so as to "somewhat fetter the discretion of the board of directors." Such a standard, the court explained, best assures that governing boards will "enact rules and make decisions that are reasonably related to the promotion of health, happiness, and peace of mind" of the project owners, considered collectively.

In Florida, restrictions promulgated (made public) by a condo association's governing board are subject to a "reasonable " test.

By contrast, restrictions contained in the declaration or master deed of the condominium complex, the Florida court concluded, should not be evaluated under a "reasonableness" standard.... Rather, such use restrictions are "clothed with a very strong presumption of validity" and should be upheld even if they exhibit some degree of unreasonableness. Non-enforcement would be proper only if such restrictions were arbitrary or in violation of public policy or some fundamental constitutional right.... Indeed, given difference to use restrictions contained in a condominium project's originating documents protects the general expectations of condominium owners "that restrictions in place at the time they purchase their units will be enforceable."...This in turn encourages the development of shared ownership housing—generally a less costly alternative to single-dwelling ownership—by attracting buyers who prefer a stable, planned environment. It also protects buyers who have paid a premium for condominium units in reliance on a particular restrictive scheme.

In Florida, use restrictions set forth in the master deed or declaration are generally enforceable as long as they are not arbitrary or in violation of public policy, or some fundamental constitutional right.

B. RESTRICTIONS ON PETS

Restriction on pet ownership is obviously a bigger problem in a condominium or similar development such as a stock cooperative or community apartment project than it would be with a planned development.

However, a planned development may also have a restriction regarding animals or pets on the properties owned by the members.

Condominiums, or similar developments, have the unique problem of owners being in close proximity to each other. Here also, pets can become an issue which is significantly more important that the pets in a planned development. The following examples are typical pet restrictions.

AN EXAMPLE - IDAHO CONDOMINIUM

Pets. Domestic household pets, such as dogs and cats, may be kept by Unit Owners, provided that the keeping of pets shall be subject to such reasonable rules and regulations as the Board may from time to time adopt.

(continued)

The Board may require the removal of any animal which the Board, in the exercise of reasonable discretion, finds disturbing other Unit Owners unreasonably, and may exercise this authority for specific animals, even though other animals are permitted to remain.

Pets will not be allowed on any Common Elements (or Limited Common Elements allocated for the use of more than one Unit) unless they are on a leash or being carried and are being walked to or from the Unit to a public walk or street.

At all times the Common Elements shall be free of any pet debris, including food and fecal matter. At no time is pet feces to be deposited in garbage. No livestock, poultry, rabbits, or other animals whatsoever shall be allowed or kept in any part of the Condominium, nor may any animal be bred or used therein for any commercial purpose. Any outside facility for pets must be kept clean on a daily basis and no waste products or food left in either the facility or on the Property.

AN EXAMPLE - PLANNED DEVELOPMENT

Animal Restrictions. No insects, reptiles, poultry, or animals of any kind shall be raised, bred, or kept in or on any Lot, Dwelling, Unit, Commercial Unit, or the Common Areas, except that usual and ordinary dogs, cats, fish, birds, and other household pets (excluding, without limitations, equine, bovine, sheep, swine, and goats) may be kept within the Units, provided that they are not kept, bred, or maintained for commercial purposes or in unreasonable quantities, nor in violation of the rules and regulations adopted by the Association as provided in the bylaws or the applicable ordinances of the City of Post Falls, Idaho. As used in this Declaration, "unreasonable quantities" shall ordinarily mean more than one (1) small pet per household; provided however, that the Association (or the Board or such other person as the Association may from time to time designate) may determine that a reasonable number in any instance may be more or less.

The Association, acting through the Board of Directors, shall have the right to prohibit maintenance of any animal which constitutes, in the opinion of the Board, a nuisance to any other owner or guest thereof. Animals belonging to Owners, occupants, or their licensees, tenants, or invitees within the Property must be kept either within an enclosure or on a leash being held by a person capable of controlling the animal. Furthermore, any Owner shall be absolutely liable to each and all remaining Owners, their families, guests, tenants, and invitees, for any unreasonable noise or damage to person or property caused by any animals brought or kept upon the property by an Owner or by members of his family, his tenants, or his guests, and it shall be the absolute duty and responsibility of each such Owner of an animal to clean up after such animals which have used any portion of the Common Areas, Lots, and/or Dwelling Units. Absolutely no dog runs or kennels will be allowed anywhere on the Property.

On occasion, owners end up with pets in their unit in alleged violation of the restrictions against pet ownership. As a result, litigation will follow involving the enforceability of a pet restriction. The following case concerns that problem.

Nahrstedt v. Lakeside Village Condominium Association, Inc.

8 Cal.4th 361, 878 P.2d 1275, 33Cal.Rptr.2d 63 (1994)
Edited Excerpts From the Opinion of Kennard, J.

FACTS AND ISSUES

Lakeside Village is a large condominium development in Culver City, Los Angeles County. It consists of 530 units spread throughout 12 separate 3-story buildings. Residents share common lobbies and hallways, in addition to laundry and trash facilities. The Lakeside Village project is subject to certain covenants, conditions and restrictions (herein after CC&Rs) that were included in the developer's declaration recorded with the Los Angeles County recorder on April 17, 1978, at the inception of the development project. Ownership of a unit includes membership in the project's homeowner's association, the Lakeside Village Condominium Association (herein after Association), the body that enforces the project CC&Rs, including the pet restrictions, which provides in relative part: "No animals (which shall mean dogs and cats), livestock, reptiles or poultry shall be kept in any unit." However, owners can keep "domestic fish and birds."

In January 1988, plaintiff Natore Nahrstedt purchased a Lakeside Village condominium and moved in with her three cats. When the Association learned of the cats' presence, it demanded their removal and assessed fines against Nahrstedt for each successive month that she remained in violation of the condominium project's pet restriction.

Nahrstedt then brought this lawsuit against the Association, its officers, and two of its employees asking the trial court to invalidate the assessments, to enjoin future assessments,...and to declare the pet restriction "unreasonable" as applied to indoor cats (such as hers) that are not allowed free run of the project's common areas. Nahrstedt also alleged that she did not know of the pet restriction when she bought her condominium. The Association argued that the pet restriction furthers the collective "health, happiness and peace of mind" of persons living in close proximity within the Lakeside Village Condominium development, and therefore is reasonable as a matter of law. The trial court agreed and dismissed Nahrstedt's complaint. Nahrstedt appealed.

DECISION AND REASONS

A divided Court of Appeal reversed the trial court's judgment of dismissal. According to the majority, whether a condominium use restriction is "reasonable," as that term is used in Civil Code Section1354 hinges on the facts of a particular homeowner's case. Thus, the majority reason Nahrstedt would be entitled to...relief if application of the pet restriction in her case would not be reasonable.

(continued)

As we have mentioned..., Civil Code Section1354 states that covenants and restrictions appearing in the recorded declaration of a common interest development are "enforceable equitable servitudes, unless unreasonable."...

Thus, when enforcing equitable servitudes, courts are generally disinclined to question the wisdom of agreed-to restrictions....An equitable servitude will be enforced unless it violates public policy; it bears no rational relationship to the protection, preservation, operation or purpose of the affected land; or it otherwise imposes burdens on the affected land that are so disproportionate to the restriction's beneficial effects that the restriction should not be enforced....When courts accord presumption of validity to all such recorded use restrictions...It discourages lawsuits by the owners of individual units seeking personal exemptions from such restrictions. This also promotes stability and predictability in two ways. It provides substantial assurance to perspective condominium purchasers that they may rely with confidence on the promises embodied in the project's recorded CC&Rs. And it protects all owners in the planned development of unanticipated increases and association fees to fund the defense of legal challenges to recorded restrictions....Of course when an association determines that a unit owner has violated a use restriction, the association must do so in good faith, not in an arbitrary or capricious manner, and its enforcement procedures must be fair and applied uniformly.

Refusing to enforce the CC&Rs contained in a recorded declaration, or enforcing them only after protractive litigation that would require justification of their application on a case-by-case basis, would impose great strain on the social fabric of the common interest development. It would frustrate owners who had purchased their units in the reliance on the CC&Rs. It would put the owners and the homeowner's association in a difficult and divisive position of deciding whether particular CC&Rs should be applied to a particular owner. Here, for example, deciding whether a particular animal is "confined to an owner's unit and creates no noise, odor, or nuisance" is a fact-intensive determination that can only be made by examining in detail the behavior of the particular animal and the behavior of the particular owner.

Homeowner associations are ill-equipped to make such investigations, and any decision they might make in a particular case could be divisive or subject to claims of partiality.

When, as here, a restriction is contained in the declaration of a common interest development, and it is recorded with the county recorder, the restriction is presumed to be reasonable and will be enforced uniformly against all residents of the common interest development...Accordingly, here Nahrstedt could prevent enforcement of the Lakeside Village pet restriction by proving that the restriction is arbitrary, that it is substantially more burdensome than beneficial to the affected properties, or that it violates a fundamental policy. Nahrstedt's complaint fails to adequately allege any of the three grounds of unreasonableness. We conclude, as a matter of law, that the recorded pet restriction of the Lakeside Village Condominium development prohibiting cats or dogs but allowing some other pets is not arbitrary, but is rationally related to health, sanitation and noise concerns legitimately held by residence of a high density condominium project such as Lakeside Village, which includes 530 units and 12 separate three-story buildings.

1. Nahrstedt Summary

From the *Nahrstedt* case in California, we can conclude that recorded restrictions are:

1. Presumed valid unless the complaining party can prove the restrictions are unreasonable.
2. The restriction is unreasonable if:
   a) it violates public policy;
   b) there is not a rational relationship to the protection, preservation, operation, or purpose of the affected land; or
   c) it imposes burdens on the affected land that are so disproportionate to the restriction's beneficial effects that the restriction should not be enforced.

The burden of proof is on the complaining owner to prove the unreasonableness of a recorded restriction.

The restriction cannot be proved as unreasonable by the owner by showing how the restriction affects the owner or that the owner's conduct is exemplary, even though it violates the restriction. Therefore, the owner has a heavy burden of proof to show that the restriction is unreasonable under one of the three grounds mentioned above. Although excised for brevity in the *Nahrstedt* case, the court stated that "those of us who have cats or dogs can attest to their wonderful companionship and affection. Not surprisingly, studies have confirmed this affect. But the issue before us is not whether, in the abstract, pets can have a beneficial effect on humans. Rather, the narrow issue is whether a pet restriction as contained in the recorded declaration of a condominium complex is enforceable or gets the challenge of a homeowner." The fact that the burden is now on the property owner rather than the association will certainly discourage litigation.

2. Pet Legislation

As a result of the "pets versus no pets" controversy, California passed laws regarding pets in a common interest development. That legislation is contained in **Civil Code Section 1360.5** and states the following:

a) No governing documents shall prohibit the owner of a separate interest within a common interest development from keeping at least one pet within the common interest development, subject to reasonable rules and regulations of the association. This section may not be construed to affect any other rights provided by law to an owner of a separate interest to keep a pet within the development.

b) For purposes of this section, "pet" means any domesticated bird, cat, dog, aquatic animal kept within an aquarium, or other animal as agreed to between the association and the homeowner.

c) If the association implements a rule or regulation restricting the number of pets an owner may keep, the new rule or regulation shall not apply to prohibit an owner from continuing to keep any pet that the owner currently keeps in his or her separate interest if the pet otherwise conforms with the previous rules or regulations relating to pets.

d) For the purposes of this section, "governing documents" shall include, but are not limited to, the conditions, covenants, and restrictions of the common interest development, and the bylaws, rules, and regulations of the association.

e) This section shall become operative on January 1, 2001, and shall only apply to governing documents entered into, amended, or otherwise modified on or after that date.

The key points of this legislation are as follows:

1. The owner can keep at least one pet;
2. The keeping of a pet is subject to reasonable rules and regulations of the association;
3. Since a pet is a domesticated bird, cat, dog, aquatic animal kept within an aquarium, a rabbit or a python could only be considered a pet if it was agreed to between the homeowner and the association;
4. The association can restrict the number of pets an owner may keep but an enacted restriction is not allowed to be retroactive;
5. The restrictions on pets does not have to exclusively be in the recorded declaration. However, for the unrecorded regulation to be effective against the homeowner, the association must be sure that the homeowners are given a copy of the unrecorded regulations regarding pets prior to purchase of a unit;
6. This legislation became operative on January 1, 2001. The legislation does not work backwards. In other words, it only applies to governing documents entered into, amended, or otherwise modified on or after January 1, 2001. Owners who are subject to governing documents restricting pets which were in existence prior to January 1, 2001 are still subject to those restrictions. If a significant number of owners are unhappy with the existing pet restrictions, they should attempt to amend or delete the restrictions.

California law also provides that individuals using the services of a guide dog, signal dog, or service dog are allowed to keep the dog on the premises.

The association can establish rules that would reasonably regulate the presence of guide dogs, signal dogs, or service dogs on the premises of the development. The association would need to make sure that the regulations are reasonable.

Additionally, the owner with the dog is liable for any damages proved to have been caused by the dog. Also, those authorized to train signal dogs, guide dogs, and service dogs, are allowed to do so on the property. Further, the owner or trainer of the dog is not required to pay an extra charge or security deposit for the guide dog, signal dog, or service dog.

C. ARCHITECTURAL, LANDSCAPE, AND APPEARANCE RESTRICTIONS

The declarations for most common interest developments have restrictions that limit what an owner can do regarding structural and landscape changes or improvements on the premises.

Once again, the governing documents provide the authority of the community association to enforce the restrictions contained therein. Some sample restrictions follow.

Restrictions For a Condominium Development

18 Alteration of Units. Each Owner shall have the right, at his sole cost and expense, to:

19 Non-Structural. Make any improvements or alterations to the Owner's unit that do not affect the structural integrity or mechanical or electrical systems or lessen the support of any portion of the Condominium, including the right to construct, alter, maintain, repair, paint, paper, panel, plaster, tile, and finish: the windows; window frames; doors; door frames and trims; interior non-load bearing partitions; and the interior surfaces of the ceiling, floors, and the perimeter walls of the unit and the surfaces of the bearing and non-bearing walls located within the unit; provided that the Owner or his assignee, contractors, or other agents or representative shall not paint or in any manner cover the original sprinkler heads installed anywhere in a unit.

20 Finished surfaces. Substitute new finished surfaces for the finished surfaces then existing on said ceilings, floors, and walls; provided that, hard surface flooring shall only be installed in units in accordance with the following: (a) By the declarant at any time, either before, during, or after purchase and occupancy by the Owner; (b) As part of original construction of the unit; (c) By the Owner of the unit only after securing prior written consent of the unit Owner below, if any (but such consent will not be required to merely replace existing hard surface flooring with substantially identical flooring). In the event that an Owner is given permission to install hard surface flooring, including but not limited to hardwood, marble, granite, slate or other like surface, the design, construction, and installation of such hard surface flooring shall meet the impact sound transmission and insulation Class II C standards as measured in accordance to ASTM designation E492-77, Standard Method of Laboratory Measurement of Impact Sound Transmission through the floor/ceiling assemblies using a "tapping machine" or other equivalent standard and measurement device as of the date of the proposed installation.

(continued)

21 Area Carpets. Where hardwood surface flooring is installed in a unit, area carpets shall be used to convey normal foot traffic and areas of the unit located immediately above another unit except area carpets are not required where such hard surface flooring is installed in the front entryway, kitchen or kitchen nook, or bathroom(s) by the Declarant at any time, as part of original construction..

22 Common Elements. May not change the appearance of the Common Elements or the exterior appearance of a unit without permission of the Association.

Regarding a planned development:

Section 38d Approval by the Board. No buildings, fence, wall, or other structures shall be commenced, erected, or maintained upon the property, nor shall an exterior addition to or change or alteration therein be made until the plan and specifications showing the nature, kind, shape, height, materials, and location of the same shall have been submitted to and approved in writing as to the quality of materials, harmony of external design, and location in relation to surrounding structures and topography by the Board of Directors or designated agent thereof.

The common issues that can arise on a daily basis can be as complex or as simple as one can imagine. As the community association manager, how would you handle the following situations?

In a condominium:

1. Mr. and Mrs. Fernandez have submitted a written request to install a canvas awning over their patio doors in their condominium unit because the westward facing unit receives too much hot afternoon sun to enjoy sitting on the balcony, and without any shade, the heat penetrates the windows.
2. Mr. Ahkoi has hung several large and extremely colorful flower baskets from the balcony of the condominium unit above his patio.
3. Mr. and Mrs. Johnson have planted two yucca plants in the common area alongside their unit.
4. The Saelees and the Silvermans have each submitted requests to install a television satellite reception dish on the eaves of their units.

In a planned development (house and lot owned separately—other areas owned in common):

1. The Glotzbachs are replacing the wood fence surrounding their unit with a new vinyl fence.
2. Several lot owners have complained that the Kramermans are installing solar panels on the rear house roof and rear patio roof.

3. Mr. and Mrs. Hattree have submitted a request and accompanying plans to build a chain linked fenced dog run in their backyard.

Typically, the community association has standards and procedures for reviewing requests to alter structures set forth in its governing documents. A dispute involving enforcement of association standards for structural improvement, landscape changes, and general appearance may end up in the court room. Relying on the standards set forth in the *Nahrstedt* case mentioned above regarding pets, consider the following case:

Dolan-King v. Rancho Santa Fe Association

81 Cal.App.4th 965, 97 Cal.Rptr.2d 280 (App. 4 Dist. 2000)
Edited Excerpts From the Opinion of Justice O'Rourke

FACTS AND ISSUES

In 1969, Dolan-King purchased a home on an approximately 3-acre lot in the residential community of Rancho Santa Fe. Development in Rancho Santa Fe is subject to the Rancho Santa Fe protective Covenant. The Covenant states that "Rancho Santa Fe is unusually attractive and valuable as a high class place of residence because of the rare quality of its landscape, trees and shrubs and the fine architecture and other improvements established by its property owners."

The Covenant recognizes the Rancho Santa Fe property owners' desire of "preserving, continuing, and maintaining the character of community and rare landscape features and of upholding the quality of all future architecture and improvements, and of restricting the use, height and bulk of buildings..." To that end, the Covenant not only contains expressed restrictions on such things as height requirements and building set backs, but it also requires the property improvements and structures to be approved by the Association with the written advice of the Rancho Santa Fe Art Jury "so as to ensure a uniform and reasonably high standard of artistic result and attractiveness in exterior and physical appearance of said property and improvements." The Covenant charges the Association and the Art Jury with power to interpret and enforce its provisions. The Board of Directors adopted and published unrecorded Guidelines containing numerous specific examples and pictures of design principles that "increase the probability" of application approval by the Art Jury and Board of Directors.

Dolan-King was aware of the Covenant's existence and had "read over it" before she agreed to purchase the house. However, she desired to make some changes and through architects Dolan-King submitted to the Art Jury plans for a new perimeter fence as well as "turret-style" additions to her living and family room. In place of the original three-rail corral-type fence on her property when she purchased it, she proposed a fence composed of stucco columns joined by horizontal wood beams. The proposed room addition structures were designed with large windows and French doors wrapped around their upper and lower levels to provide increased natural lighting as well as views north and east of her house.

(continued)

The Art Jury denied Dolan-King's applications. They found her proposed fence design inconsistent with the Rancho Santa Fe Residential Design Guidelines, the desired rural community character, and the existing neighborhood character. The Art Jury stated the turret-style additions would be acceptable if Dolan-King decreased the proportion of window to stucco mass in a manner similar to examples presented to them by her architect and suggested she reevaluate that as well as the thickness of the walls and size and quantity of the windows. The parties stipulated the provisions of the Covenant controlled over those contained in the Guidelines. The Covenant vests the Board with authority to modify the Art Jury's decisions in cases where 4/5ths of the Board find the Art Jury's decision "works at undue hardship" on the petitioner; modification of the Art Jury's decision "will not tend unduly to lower the standards of attractiveness of the surrounding property or depreciate the neighborhood"; or there was "biased or prejudice on the party of one or more of the Art Jury as to said decision or ruling." The Board unanimously upheld the Art Jury's decision. Dolan-King filed suit against the Association, its Board of Directors, and the Art Jury seeking a judicial determination of the validity and enforceability of the Guidelines and Criteria and restrictions used by the Art Jury to reject her applications. The trial court entered a judgment for Dolan-King. It awarded Dolan-King attorney's fees in the amount of $187,677.

DECISION AND REASONS

The California Supreme Court has made it clear that restrictions on the use of property contained in covenants recorded with the county recorder are presumed to be reasonable and will be enforced uniformly against all residents of the common interest development unless the restriction is arbitrary, imposes burdens on the use of lands it affects that substantially outweigh the restriction's benefits to the development's residents, or violates a fundamental public policy. Such deference to the originating covenants, conditions and restrictions protects the general expectations of condominium owners that restrictions in place at the time they purchase their units will be enforced. Restrictions are evaluated for reasonableness in light of the restriction's effect on the project as a whole, not from the perspective of the individual homeowner. Accordingly, courts do not conduct a case-by-case analysis of restrictions to determine the effect on an individual homeowner; we must consider the reasonableness of the restrictions by looking at the goals and concerns of the entire development.

Enforcement of the Guidelines. There is no evidence Dolan-King had notice of the unrecorded guidelines at the time she purchased her property. Restrictions that do not meet the requirements of covenants running with the land may be enforced as equitable servitude provided the person bound by the restrictions had notice of their existence. In Nahrstedt, the court suggested that such unrecorded restrictions are not accorded a presumption of reasonableness, but are viewed under a straight reasonableness test so as to somewhat fetter the discretion of the board of directors. The Guidelines themselves do not purport to be strict restrictions on improvements or land use. They state: "These are general guidelines, and the Art Jury and Association Board may exercise the full breadth of their discretion in considering any land use proposal. The Association has the expressed right under the Protective Covenant to evaluate the land use and building applications by standards other than those contained herein."

(continued)

The guidelines are the Association's attempt to give property owners guidance, by way of detailed examples and explanation, on the criteria used by the Art Jury and Board in reviewing proposed improvements and exercising their broad discretion under the Covenant.

Where the record indicates the Art Jury and Board acted within the authority granted to it by the Covenant, pursuant to a reasonable investigation, in the best interest of the community and not an arbitrary manner, we will respect and uphold their decision. Having sought the declaration that the Art Jury and Board imposed restrictions unreasonably and arbitrarily, it was Dolan-King's burden at trial to make that showing before the court which she did not do.

The Room Addition Proposal.

The Art Jury's decision to reject Dolan-King's room addition proposal was well within the scope of its authority under the Covenant, and, based on its investigation and the stated reasoning, it was a reasonable and good faith effort to maintain architectural consistency with the remainder of her home as well as the neighborhood. Dolan-King did not meet her burden to show otherwise. While Dolan-King pointed out several commercial buildings and homes with turret-shaped rooms in Rancho Santa Fe in our view they did not reflect the kind of inconsistency between the addition and the original structure as the Art Jury noted with regard to Dolan-King's proposals. The Boards action of upholding the Art Jury's decision was also well within its discretion and authority.

The Fence Proposal.

The Covenant's designation of architectural types is not only imprecise, but application of architectural restriction is further "subject to the discretion of the Art Jury." The trial court's findings and conclusions did not establish that either the Art Jury or Board acted arbitrarily, without reasonable investigation or in bad faith in denying Dolan-King's fence application. While Dolan-King demonstrated homes in Rancho Santa Fe have a mix of fences and walls ranging from solid stucco, wrought iron rail, combined brick and wrought iron, and layered stone, the mere existence of varying fence styles within Rancho Santa Fe does not establish arbitrary action under the Covenant, which contains no specific design criteria or limitations for perimeter walls and fences. Dolan-King did not demonstrate that those homes with more formal fence styles were surrounded by others having pasture-rail fences or no fences at all.

We recognize the law requiring even-handed application of use restrictions creates some tension with the discretionary authority granted to the Art Jury and Board. While aesthetic considerations have their place in the Covenant and there are no absolute standards to guide an Art Jury's judgment and taste, we must point out that if the evidence had shown the perimeter fences and walls within Dolan-King's immediate neighborhood lacked consistency, Dolan-King's proposed fence design would not be inappropriate because it would not be out of harmony with them. On the record before us, however, we cannot find Dolan-King proved she was subjected to the Board's selective and arbitrary exercise of discretion with respect to her fence proposal.

(continued)

Attorney Fee Award and Disposition.

The judgment and order awarding attorney's fees are reversed and the matter remanded for the superior court to enter judgment for the Association and determine entitlement to attorney's fees.

1. Dolan-King Summary

a. Recorded restrictions are presumed to be reasonable.

b. Unrecorded restrictions, when attempted to be enforced, are viewed as to whether or not they are reasonable under the circumstances.

c. Judicial deference places limits on how an architectural committee or board may exercise discretion in approving or rejecting improvement plans based on subjective aesthetic judgment:

1. The association's action must be within an authority granted to it by the recorded restrictions.
2. There has been a reasonable investigation.
3. The actions are in the best interest of the community.
4. The actions are not done in an arbitrary manner.

There is an obvious problem with unrecorded guidelines, regulations, or restrictions.

The owner is not bound by unrecorded restrictions, unless the owner has actual knowledge of them. "Actual knowledge" can be accomplished by recording the restrictions or making sure that the owner receives a copy of them prior to purchasing a unit.

Therefore, it would be in your best interest, as the community manager, to obtain some type of receipt signed by a perspective purchaser that he or she has received a copy of the restrictions. In the alternative, the escrow documents could serve as evidence of receipt of the restrictions assuming they have been delivered by the seller of the unit or lot.

In the *Dolan-King* case above, the Association, its Board of Directors, and the Art Jury were all sued by Dolan-King. It may be difficult to find members who want to sit on a board of directors or on an architectural or other committee if there is a risk of litigation and potential liability. The following case addresses that issue.

Lamden v. La Jolla Shores Club Condominium Homeowner's Association

21 Cal.4th 249, 980 P.2d 940, 87Cal.Rptr.2d 237 (1999)
Edited Excerpts From the Opinion of Justice Werdegar

FACTS AND ISSUES

Plaintiff Gertrude M. Lamden owns a condominium unit in one of three buildings comprising the La Jolla Shores Club Condominium Development. Lamden remodeled the interior of her condominium in 1990. At that time, the Association's manager arranged for a termite extermination company to spot-treat areas where Lamden had encountered termites. The following year, both Lamden and the Association obtained termite inspection reports recommending fumigation, but the Association's Board decided against that approach. The Board based its decision not to fumigate on concerns about the cost of fumigation, logistical problems with temporarily relocating residents, concern that fumigation residue could affect resident's health and safety, awareness that upcoming walkway renovations would include replacement of damaged areas, pet moving expenses, anticipated breakage by the termite company, lost rental income, and the likelihood that termite infestation would reoccur even if primary treatment were utilized. The Board decided to continue to rely on secondary treatment until a more widespread problem was demonstrated.

Lamden sued and stated numerous causes of actions based on the Association's refusal to fumigate for termites, naming as defendants certain individual members of the Board as well as the Association.

Lamden alleged that, as a proximate result of the Association's breaching its responsibilities, she had suffered diminution in the value of her condominium unit, repair expenses, and fees and costs in connection with this litigation.

As to the causes of the Development's termite infestation, the trial court concluded that the "key problem came about from what you might say is a poor design" and the resulting "water intrusion." In short, the trial court stated "The real culprit is not so much the Board, but it's poor design and water damage that is conducive to bringing the termites in." As to the Association's actions, the trial court stated, "The Board did take appropriate action." The court noted the Board "did come up with a plan," to engage a pest control service to "come out and spot-treat termite infestation when it was found." The trial judge opined he might, "from a personal relation standpoint," have acted sooner or differently under the circumstances than did the Association, but nevertheless concluded "The Board did have a rational bases for their decision to reject fumigation, and to do what it did." Ultimately the court gave judgment for the Association applying what it called a "business judgment test." Lamden appealed.

The Court of Appeals agreed with Lamden that the trial court had applied the wrong standard of care in assessing the Association's actions. In the Court of Appeals' view, relative statutes, the governing Declaration, and principles of common law imposed on the Association an objective duty of reasonable care in repairing and maintaining the Development's common areas near Lamden's unit as occasioned by the presence of termites.

(continued)

The court also concluded that, had the court analyzed the Association's actions under an objective standard of reasonableness, an outcome more favorable to Lamden likely would have resulted. Accordingly, the Court of Appeals reversed the judgment of the trial court.

DECISION AND REASONS

Contrary to the Court of Appeals, we conclude the trial court was correct to defer to the Board's decision. We hold that, where a duly constituted community association board, upon reasonable investigation, in good faith and with regard for the best interest of the community association and its members, exercises discretion within the scope of its authority under relevant statutes, covenants, and restrictions to select among means for discharging an obligation to maintain and repair a development's common areas, courts should defer to the board's authority and presume expertise. The formulation we have articulated affords homeowners, community associations, courts, and advocates a clear standard for judicial review of discretionary economic decisions by community association boards, mandating a degree of difference to the latter's business judgments sufficient to discourage meritless litigation, yet, at the same time, without either eviscerating the long-established duty to guard against unreasonable risk to residents' personal safety owed by associations that function as landlords in maintaining the common areas or modifying the enforceability of a common interest development's CC&Rs.

Common sense suggests that judicial deference in such cases as this is appropriate, in view of the relative competence over that of the courts, possessed by owners and directors of common interest developments to make the detailed and peculiar economic decisions necessary in maintenance of those developments. A differential standard will, by minimizing the likelihood of unproductive litigation over their governing association's discretionary economic decisions, foster stability, certainty, and predictability in the governance and maintenance of common interest developments. Beneficial corollaries include enhancement of the incentives for essential voluntary owner participation in common interest development governance and conservation of scarce judicial recourses. The judgment of the Court of Appeals is reversed.

2. Lamden Summary

The decision of a community board of directors is valid if:

1. The board is acting officially in accordance with governing documents.
2. The board is acting in good faith.
3. The board is acting upon a reasonable investigation.
4. The board is exercising its discretion within the scope of its authority under relevant statutes, covenants, and restrictions to elect alternatives for discharging an obligation to maintain and repair a development's common areas.
5. A court defers to the board's authority and presumed expertise.

The courts have upheld that a restriction needs some rational relationship to the enhancement or preservation of the community development.

In other words, the restriction cannot be completely arbitrary or lack a rational relationship to the development. It is important that those who will make the decision on an application or a proposal study it in detail to see if it protects and preserves the community development and, if possible, review the property and surrounding neighborhood for conformity. If appropriate, as was done in the *Dolan-King* case, the decision-makers should meet with the applicant and the applicant's architect to see if a reasonable modification or compromise can be reached. Additionally, a detailed explanation to the applicant for a rejection should remove suspicions of arbitrariness or favoritism. Upon rejection of the application, the owner will now have to commence litigation and prove that the community association acted in an arbitrary or an unreasonable manner in rejecting the owner's application.

II. What About Solar Collectors?

Solar energy may or may not be a viable alternative to traditional energy sources, depending on where the property is located in the United States.

In California, the legislature has addressed the issue of solar energy specifically, stating that "It is the policy of the state to promote and encourage the use of solar energy systems and to remove obstacles thereto." Solar energy systems may have an appearance which many owners in the planned development find objectionable. Due to the nature of solar energy systems, most areas of concern will be in planned developments, as opposed to condominiums or other community housing.

A. DEFINING THE TERMS

In California, any CC&R contained in any deed, contract, or other instrument affecting the transfer or sale of, or any interest in, real property that effectively prohibits or restricts the installation or use of a solar energy system is void and unenforceable.

A solar energy system can be:

1. Any solar collector or other solar energy device whose primary purpose is to provide for the collection, storage, and distribution of solar energy for space heating, space cooling, electric generation, or water heating; or

2. Any structure design feature of a building, whose primary purpose is to provide for the collection, storage, and distribution of solar energy for electricity generation, space heating, or cooling or for water heating.

Solar collectors must meet applicable standards and requirements imposed by state or local authorities. Additionally, solar energy systems must be certified by the **Solar Rating Certification Corporation** or other nationally recognized certification agencies. Certification is for the entire solar energy system as well as the installation of the system. The solar energy system must also meet all applicable safety and performance standards established by national, state, or local agencies, utility commissions, and accredited by testing laboratories where applicable.

B. REASONABLE RESTRICTIONS

California law allows for reasonable restrictions to be placed on solar energy systems. Reasonable restrictions are those restrictions that:

1. Do not significantly increase the cost of the system or significantly decrease its efficiency or specified performance; or
2. Allow an alternative system of comparable costs, efficiency, and energy conservation benefits. With regard to number 1 above, "significantly" means an amount exceeding 20% of the cost of the system or decreasing the efficiency of the solar energy system by an amount exceeding 20%, as originally specified and proposed. Therefore, the community association can impose restrictions on the solar energy system as long as those restrictions do not "significantly" impact the system. This might mean that, for aesthetic purposes, the association would like to have the owner install a different style of system that is less visible. Apparently, as long as the alternative system is of comparable cost, efficiency and energy conservation benefit and does not increase the owner's cost by more than 20% it is an appropriate restriction and the owner would have to purchase the alternate system.

Whenever approval by the homeowner (community) association board or architectural committee is required for the installation or use of the solar energy system, the application for approval must be processed and approved in the same manner as an application for approval of an architectural modification to the property.

Also, the application cannot be willfully avoided or delayed. If the board or committee willfully violates this section, it shall be liable to the applicant for any actual damages caused by the delay and must pay a civil penalty to the applicant not to exceed $1,000. Additionally, if the applicant has to bring a lawsuit to enforce compliance, the prevailing party in the lawsuit shall be awarded reasonable attorney's fees paid by the losing party.

1. Restriction Summary

The community association may impose reasonable provisions which:

1. Restrict the installation of solar energy systems installed in common areas to systems approved by the association.
2. Require the owner of a separate interest to obtain approval of the association for the installation of a solar energy system in a separate interest owned by another.
3. Provide for the maintenance, repair, or replacement of roofs or other building components.
4. Require installers of solar energy systems to indemnify or reimburse the association or its members for loss or damage caused by the installation, maintenance, or use of the solar energy system.

The following case deals with the problem of a homeowner who installed a solar system and the homeowner's association that objected.

Palos Verdes Homes Association v. Rodman

182 Cal.App.3d 324, 227 Cal.Rptr.81 (App. 2 Dist. 1986)
Edited Excerpts From the Opinion of Justice Hastings

FACTS AND ISSUES

Defendant Stacey Rodman resides on the Palos Verdes Peninsula in an area governed by conditions, covenants, and restrictions recorded by the plaintiff Palos Verdes Homes Association. The CC&Rs include a provision which requires prior approval by the Association of plans and specifications for any works of improvement to be done on any of the covered properties. When an owner seeks to install a solar unit, he or she must comply with the requirements of the solar unit guidelines formulated by the Association's Art Jury.

Co-defendant Servamatic Solar System contracted with Rodman to install a passive solar water heating unit on the roof of the Rodman home. Servamatic sought approval of the Association for this installation; approval was denied. When the Association discovered that Servamatic had installed the system, it sent a letter to Rodman notifying him that the property was in a condition of non-compliance with the CC&Rs and enclosed a copy of its solar unit guidelines. The Association subsequently filed its complaint for relief against Rodman and Servamatic. The trial court entered a judgment for the Association which provided:

1. That defendants are enjoined from maintaining the solar units on the property;
2. That defendants are required to comply with the requirements of the Art Jury within 90 days of entry of the judgment;
3. If defendants do not comply with the requirements of the Art Jury within 90 days they are ordered to remove the solar units;

(continued)

4. The restrictions of the Palos Verdes Homes Association on solar energy systems installed by defendants are reasonable and meet the standards set forth in California law.

Rodman and Servamatic appeal from this judgment.

DECISIONS AND REASONS

In support of their appeal, they cite the testimony regarding three types of solar systems allowed by the California State Energy Commission; active (or flat-paneled); passive (integral Collector System [ICS]); and thermosyphan (a combination of both). Rodman and Servamatic assert that the guidelines allow installation of active systems, but effectively preclude installation of the ICS, the only type Servamatic installs, because it sits 18 inches on top the roof, is painted black, and looks like an upside-down bathtub; and that the guidelines would require the ICS to be set in the roof adding between $1,400 to $1,800 to the cost of the installation.

The evidence presented at the court trial included testimony by William Nelson Rowley, Ph.D. a mechanical engineer. Based on his study comparing 26 systems installed on the Palos Verdes Peninsula with the Rodman-Servamatic ICS, he concluded the solar units permitted by the Association guidelines were comparable to the ICS in performance and cost. Given this evidence and the facts that the Rodman-Servamatic witness agreed that the various solar systems discussed by Dr. Rowley were compatible, we cannot say as a matter of law the trial court erred. The judgment is affirmed.

2. Palos Verdes Summary

The court in *Palos Verdes* determined that the solar unit guidelines were reasonable. The following guidelines were contained in the court decision:

1. Solar Units not on the roof should be maintained a minimum of 5 feet from the property line and concealed from the neighboring view, and a fence or wall of sufficient height to accomplish the same may be appropriate.
2. Solar Units on a roof should be within the wall line of the structure. However, the Art Jury may require more roof area between the solar unit and roof edge if the roof overhang is minimal.
3. All aluminum trim should be bronze anodized or otherwise color treated.
4. Solar Units should be in or below the plane of roofing material.
5. Solar Unit should be constructed of rigid materials (units may not be of flexible material).
6. All plumbing lines should be concealed and the method of installation shown and detailed.
7. Panel material should be dark in color.
8. Sample of the proposed solar unit should be submitted with application.
9. Professionally drawn construction details which apply to specific installation should be provided. They should be drawn to scale and should

clearly show all elevations, assembly, the attachment to the roof structure and proposed location on the lot or building.

10. Calculations should be provided verifying the number and/or area of panels required.
11. Photographs should be submitted showing the location of the proposed solar units and their visibility from neighboring structures, street, or streets.
12. A cover plate or the glazing should be either transparent or white to reduce the reflectance of light. Cover material, if flammable, should be self-extinguishing.

The Art Jury may ask for alternative combinations in smaller groupings when large areas of group solar panels are found not to be aesthetically satisfactory.

3. Solar Easement

Once a member has installed a solar collector, a future concern will be something that blocks all or part of the necessary sunlight. Vegetation grows and structures are built. California allows solar easements to receive sunlight on or over land in Civil Code Section 801.5 which provides in part:

(a) The right of receiving sunlight . . . shall be referred to as a solar easement.

"Solar easement" means the right of receiving sunlight across real property of another for any solar energy system.

As used in this section, "solar energy system" means either of the following:

(1) Any solar collector, or other solar energy device, whose primary purpose is to provide for the collection, storage, and distribution of solar energy for space heating, space cooling, electric generation, or water heating.

(2) Any structural design feature of a building, whose primary purpose is to provide for the collection, storage, and distribution of solar energy for electricity generation, space heating or cooling, or for water heating.

(b) Any instrument creating a solar easement shall include, at a minimum, all of the following:

(1) A description of the dimensions of the easement expressed in measurable terms, such as vertical or horizontal angles measured in degrees, or the hours of the day on specified dates during which direct sunlight to a specified surface of a solar collector, device, or structural design feature may not be obstructed, or a combination of these descriptions.

(2) The restrictions placed upon vegetation, structures, and other objects that would impair or obstruct the passage of sunlight through the easement.
(3) The terms or conditions, if any, under which the easement may be revised or terminated.

If an owner with a solar system asks the community manager for a solar easement, the matter must be handled by the association board and its attorney.

III. MANAGER'S JOURNAL

As a manager, you need to be aware of the rules and regulations governing conduct of the members of the common interest development. At one end of the spectrum will be the United States Constitution, federal laws, federal court decisions, and federal administrative agency regulations. Next, would be a state constitution, state laws, state court decisions, and administrative agency regulations for that state. For example, we have certainly discovered that the California legislature has demonstrated its intent to micro-manage common interest developments. Next in order of priority would be county laws, regulations, and court decisions followed by municipal ordinances and regulations.

Perhaps the most important document regarding rules and their enforcement would be the Declaration (sometimes referred to as the **Master Deed** or **CC&Rs**) or an Ownership Occupancy Agreement or Member Lease. Additionally, you need to be aware of the Articles of Incorporation if the association is incorporated and the bylaws which govern the detailed workings of the association. Also of great importance are the resolutions passed by the board of directors for the community association. These resolutions probably contain rules applicable to the members of the association. Normally, the resolutions can be found in the minute book of the board of directors or a separate book of resolutions.

The important thing to note is that association rules, regulations, or guidelines are at the bottom of the list. In other words, a conflict with anything above will be resolved in favor of the higher authority. Obviously, a provision of a state constitution controls over a rule passed by an association board. A board resolution is not valid if it conflicts with a provision in the declaration.

Suppose the board of the association has requested that you, as the manager, develop a rule regarding traffic flow, safety, and guest parking or perhaps a rule regarding specific times for pool and Jacuzzi use by different categories of members. You may consider using the following steps in formulating a response:

1. Determine exactly why the board is making the request. Normally, rules are not necessary unless there is some problem, activity, or issue which requires a rule

to change conduct. Locating the perceived problem or issue that needs to be addressed is an important first step.

2. Conduct an investigation to see if there are any rules or regulations from a source of higher authority. Are there any local laws or regulations governing traffic flow, speed limits, stop signs, and duration of parking that take precedence over any association rules? Are there any local rules or regulations to deal with swimming pool operation, such as maximum number of individuals occupying the pool, necessity of a lifeguard, or hours of operation?

   It would be very embarrassing to propose a rule and then discover that it conflicts with a municipal ordinance. Additionally, the manager needs to check all previous rules and board resolutions as well as by-laws and governing documents for the community development to see if this topic, or something similar to it, has been addressed in the past. Further, it must be determined that the declaration or master deed gives the association the authority to regulate this particular topic. Board members are going to want to know if they have the authority to pass the resolution implementing the rule as, once again, it would be embarrassing to pass a rule where the board had no authority to act.

3. In preparing the rule, as the manager, you must always keep in mind the problem to be solved or corrected and try to identify those who will be affected by the rule. Some members could care less about the rule, yet for other members this rule may have a significant impact. Those who use the swimming pool will certainly be more affected by a new rule than those who do not. Traffic flow and parking may directly affect each member.

4. If the board is requesting a draft of rule or regulation, it is probably because members have brought that issue to the board's attention at a board meeting, or through direct conversations, or by other means of communication. Before spending a lot of time on the language of a rule, it might be important to make the members aware that the board is considering adopting a rule on that particular topic. In making the members aware of the proposed rule, it would be a good idea to set up a time period where the members can offer their comments or input regarding the situation and a proposed rule. This gets the members involved in the rule making process and you will not have to listen to the "well, why didn't you ask me, I had some good ideas" statements from the membership.

5. Remember that rules will tend to be ignored if there is no penalty. In other words, as the manager, you will have to establish a penalty that is severe enough that the rule will not be ignored by the membership, yet not so severe that membership will contemplate a mutiny. Additionally, there has to be some procedure for enforcement of the rule. How do we know when a person violates the rule; is it necessary to develop some sort of proof or evidence; is there a verbal warning or written citation; and how is the penalty enforced if it is ignored?

6. In choosing the wording of the rules, use clarity and brevity if at all possible. Choose words that are simple, specific, and easily understood. Rules tend to be stated more in terms of "thou shall nots" rather than "thou shall." Also keep in mind whether the rule will be completely black and white or whether there is some desired flexibility in the rule. In other words, there is a difference between a rule and a guideline.

   Guidelines tend to be statements which are specific enough so that there is a general understanding of what is required, yet general enough that they can be interpreted in a given situation. Guidelines are merely an attempt to guide or assist in reaching a result. For example, architectural review committees generally must interpret building guidelines.

7. When a violator has been notified of the violation a procedure of "due process" should be established unless the association has one in existence. This means that the member has the right to dispute the alleged violation, in what is typically a hearing, with the ultimate decision coming from the board or whomever has been properly designated by the board for conducting hearings.

8. Once the rule has reached its final draft, if at all possible, as the manager, you should give careful consideration to notify the membership that the proposed rule is coming up for adoption at the next board meeting. Once again, this gives the membership an opportunity to make comments at the board meeting before the board votes to either adopt the proposed rule or not. It might be necessary, or advisable, to work with a board member or a member committee in preparing the language of the rule. Additionally, it may be advisable for the attorney for the association to review the rule and its enforcement prior to the board considering the adoption of it.

9. Once the board has adopted the rule and the date it will go into effect, a notice needs to be given to association members and/or occupants to ensure the membership will be aware of the new rule. The notice can be posted at one or more conspicuous places on the property, sent to each member by first-class mail or personal delivery, sent to each member as an inclusion in the monthly assessment statement, or reproduced in the association's newsletter.

10. It is possible that sometime in the future a member who has been notified of a violation of the rule may decide to contest the rule's enforcement in court. From the previous material in this chapter it was noted that board decisions will be upheld if:

    a. it furthers the purpose of the common interest development;
    b. it is consistent with the governing documents of the common interest development; and
    c. it does not violate public policy.

If the court is asked to enforce a restriction in the declaration, it will be enforced if:

a. exact language of the restriction has been recorded in the county recorder's office;
b. it describes the land benefited and burdened by the restriction;
c. the restriction specifically states that it is binding on its successors (new owners) of the property; and
d. the restriction relates to the use, repair, maintenance, or improvement of the property or payment of taxes or assessments.

If the association is seeking to enforce a rule or regulation that is not recorded, it is considered an equitable servitude and is enforceable only if the member has notice of its existence. The rule or regulation has no presumption of reasonableness. Therefore, if litigation ensues, the court will determine whether the rule and its enforcement was reasonable under the circumstances that are being contested. Here, the court will consider the following:

a. Has the association acted according to and with the authority of provisions in the governing documents which allow such enforcement?
b. Is the association acting with the best interest of the community in mind?
c. Are the actions of the association consistent? This means the board is not acting in an arbitrary manner, not showing favoritism, and enforcement of the rule has been consistent even though membership on the board has changed since adoption of the rule.
d. Did the association conduct a reasonable investigation by itself or through an appropriate committee in which the situation was viewed in a neutral manner, key people were spoken with, and the association made every attempt to discover the facts and issues involved?

IV. CHAPTER SUMMARY

Common interest developments (CIDs) usually impose restrictions to maintain consistency in architectural style, use of member owned property, and use of property owned in common. This consistency allows owners a degree of predictability.

A **covenant** is an agreement between two landowners, when one landowner promises to do or not do something with regard to the property. A covenant that "runs with the land" binds subsequent (later) owners of the land to the same promise. If a covenant is not recorded, it may still be enforceable under the rule of "equitable servitude" if the successive owners had knowledge of the covenant.

"Use restrictions" are either set forth in the governing documents or determined and declared by the association board. Use restrictions promulgated by the board are subject to a "reasonableness" test, whereas CC&R restrictions are not held to that standard, unless obviously arbitrary in nature.

Pet restrictions may be dictated by a homeowner (community) association, although due to space constraints, it is generally a bigger issue in a condominium development than it is in a planned development. In the *Nahrstedt* case, the owner with three cats failed to prove that the Association's pet restriction was arbitrary or unreasonable. California law allows CID owners to keep at least one pet, and service dogs to be kept on the premises. It also defines a pet as a domesticated bird, cat, dog, or aquatic animal, unless otherwise agreed to by the owner and the association.

Most CIDs have restrictions limiting structural and landscape changes or improvements that can be made by an owner. In the *Dolan-King* case, the court found that even though the architectural guidelines were unrecorded, the owner did not prove that the Board acted unreasonably or arbitrarily in denying permission to build a particular type of fence and turret-style room additions.

Guidelines, regulations, and restrictions can be enforced if an owner has "actual knowledge" of them. This can be accomplished by recording them, or ensuring that the owner receives a copy of them prior to purchasing a unit.

In the *Lamden* case, the court ultimately ruled against owner Lamden and upheld the HOA board's right to spot-treat for termites rather than fumigate. If a restriction is not clearly arbitrary and doesn't lack a rational relationship to the enhancement or preservation of a development, then the courts should defer to the board's authority and presumed expertise.

Solar energy systems provide for the collection, storage, and distribution of solar energy for electricity space heating or cooling, or for water heating. In California, CC&Rs that restrict or prohibit the installation or use of solar energy systems are void and unenforceable, although the law does provide for some reasonable association restrictions and provisions.

In the *Palos Verdes* case, the court ultimately ruled in the Association's favor. It determined that the solar units permitted by the Association were comparable to the unit installed by the defendant, Rodman, therefore the guidelines were not unreasonable, and Rodman was obligated to comply with them.

In California, a **solar easement** gives a solar energy system owner the right to receive sunlight across the real property of another. An owner's request for a solar easement must be handled by the association board and its attorney.

V. REVIEW QUESTIONS

1. A property owner has agreed with the neighbor not to plant any trees along their common boundary because it would block the neighbor's view. A new buyer purchases the burdened property and plants a row of trees obstructing the view. To be an enforceable equitable servitude, the complaining property owner must show:

a. that the original agreement was in writing.
b. that the original agreement was in writing, signed by the property owners, and notarized.
c. that the new purchaser was aware of the specifics regarding the promise not to plant trees.
d. none of the above.

2. In the Florida case of *Hidden Harbor Estates v. Basso*, the court distinguished between:

a. covenants running with the land and equitable servitude.
b. restrictions set forth in the declaration or master deed and rules adopted by the governing board and the board's interpretation of those rules.
c. lawful restrictions and unlawful restrictions.
d. good taste and bad taste.

3. The case of *Nahrstedt v. Lakeside Village Condominium Association, Inc.* involved a dispute regarding:

a. the owner's right to build a fence.
b. the owner's three cats.
c. the owner's dog.
d. the condition of the owner's property.

4. In a common interest development, restrictions are generally imposed to maintain consistency in the:

a. architectural style.
b. use of member-owned property.
c. use of property owned in common.
d. all of the above.

5. In the case of *Nahrstedt v. Lakeside Village Condominium Association, Inc.*, the court concluded that:

a. all pet restrictions within a common interest development are unenforceable.
b. the pet restriction in that case was unenforceable because it was unreasonable under the circumstances.
c. if a pet restriction is contained in a recorded declaration for the development, it is presumed to be reasonable and will be uniformly enforced against all members.
d. the pet restriction was enforceable because Nahrstedt's pet was obnoxious and an annoying nuisance to other members.

6. California's legislation regarding pets allows an owner of a separate interest within a common interest development, under the right circumstances, to keep a pet. According to the legislation, a pet means all of the following except:

a. a rotweiler.
b. a parrot.
c. ten piranha kept in an aquarium.
d. a rabbit.

7. In the case of *Dolan-King v. Rancho Santa Fe Association* involving architectural restrictions:

a. Dolan-King won on both of her requests to install the new perimeter fence and the turret-style additions to the house.
b. Dolan-King won on the installation of the perimeter fence but lost on the request for the turret-style additions to the house.
c. Dolan-King won on the ability to install turret-style additions to the house but lost on the ability to install the new perimeter fence.
d. Dolan-King lost on both the ability to install the new perimeter fence as well as the turret-style additions to the house.

8. In the case of *Lamden v. La Jolla Shores Club Condominium Homeowner's Association*, the court concluded that:

a. since the pet restriction was recorded in the declaration for the development, it is presumed reasonable and enforceable.
b. the board of directors acted properly in making its decision to spot-treat termite infestation rather than fumigation.
c. the board acted properly when it concluded that it should fumigate termite infestation rather than spot-treat the problem.
d. the board lacked authority and acted improperly with its decision regarding treating termite infestation.

9. California law provides that:

a. a restriction in a declaration that prohibits the installation of solar energy is enforceable.
b. solar energy systems can be allowed in a common interest development as long as it is stated in the recorded declaration.
c. any recorded restrictions prohibiting solar energy systems are unenforceable.
d. California does not have any legislation regarding solar energy systems.

10. "Actual knowledge" of restrictions can be accomplished by:

a. recording the restrictions.
b. making sure the owner receives a copy of the restrictions prior to purchase.
c. both a and b are correct.
d. neither a nor b are correct.

ANSWERS: 1. c; 2. b; 3. b; 4. d; 5. c; 6. d; 7. d; 8. b; 9. c; 10. c

Welcome to the
Ballona Freshwater Marsh
To help us care for this fragile habitat, please observe the following:
♦ Remain on the public trail.
♦ Leash your pets (and clean up after them).
♦ Properly dispose of or recycle waste.
♦ Do not feed or harass the wildlife.
♦ Refrain from picking wildflowers or plants.
For your safety and that of others, be advised that:
♦ Minors should be under direct adult supervision at all times.
♦ The trail is closed from dusk until dawn.
♦ Bicycles and skateboards are not allowed on the trail.
♦ Slippery marsh shores can pose a danger of injury or drowning—please stay outside the fenced area.
♦ Water at the marsh is not suitable for human consumption.
♦ Raccoons and other wildlife are natural members of the marsh community. Please leave all wildlife alone as their behavior can be unpredictable and dangerous.
Docent tours are available through Friends of Ballona Wetlands. For more information on tours, local wetlands, wildlife, and volunteer opportunities, visit the following websites:
Friends of Ballona Wetlands
www.ballonafriends.org
Audubon California
www.ca.audubon.org
Experience Ballona
www.experienceballona.lmu.edu

CHAPTER 6

Homeowner (Community) Association Restrictions: Part 2

I. Traffic Enforcement

Any common interest development will have some type of vehicle traffic in the common areas. The smaller developments may find vehicle traffic is limited to a driveway and parking lot and large planned developments may have an extensive roadway system.

In a development that is beyond driveways and parking lots, the question becomes who owns the roadways? A planned development may find the roadways are owned by the local municipal government and, along with that ownership, comes the obligation to maintain and enforce traffic rules. On the other hand, the community association may own the roadways along with the obligation to maintain them. But what about traffic enforcement on the private roadways? Association members may complain that other members are driving too fast on the roadways or in a careless manner.

In order for the association to regulate traffic, it must have the authority to do so. This authority may be found in the governing documents, most likely in the declaration, or perhaps, in the bylaws of the association.

Chapter 6

CHAPTER OUTLINE

The rules and regulations passed by the association to govern activities in the development are derived from the authority given to the association to regulate that area. If the association does not have the authority in the governing documents to regulate that area, then the rules and regulations passed by the association are not enforceable. An additional source for authority to regulate traffic would be any law passed in your state allowing common interest developments to do so.

In California, the Vehicle Code provides a way for community associations to regulate traffic on private roads within the development.

The California Vehicle Code allows a city or county, by ordinance or resolution, to find and declare that there are privately owned and maintained roads that are not generally held open for use of the public but, by reason of their proximity to or connection with highways, the interest of residents residing along the roads and the motoring public would best be served by applying public traffic regulations to those private roads. **In order to accomplish this, a petition must be filed requesting it by a majority of the owners of any privately owned and maintained road, or by at least a majority of the board of directors of a common interest development that is responsible for maintaining the road**. A public hearing will be held on the request with a ten-day prior written notice to all owners of the road or all of the owners in the development.

If the city ordinance is enacted, the traffic rules of the state Vehicle Code will apply to the privately owned and maintained road if appropriate signs are erected at the entrance to the road of the size, shape, and color as to be readily legible during daylight hours from a distance of 100 feet, to the effect that the road is subject to the provisions of the Vehicle Code. The city or county may impose reasonable conditions and may authorize the owners, or board of directors of the common interest development, to erect traffic signs, signals, markings, and devices which conform to the uniform standards and specifications adopted by the California Department of Transportation.

However, it appears that the Department of the California Highway Patrol is not required to provide patrol or enforcement of the Vehicle Code on any privately owned and maintained road. **Whether or not the local city or county will provide law enforcement of Vehicle Code provisions within a common interest development will be a decision that is made locally, as it is not mandated under state law**. Consequently, it may be necessary for you, as the community association manager, or representatives from the board of directors to try and convince local authorities to provide enforcement of Vehicle Code provisions within the common interest development. The California Vehicle Code provides for an almost identical process for making the Vehicle Code applicable to privately owned and maintained roads that are generally held open for use by the public for vehicle travel such that the public cannot determine that the roads are not highways.

If the community association decides to regulate traffic through the provisions of the Vehicle Code, as the community association manager, you need to remember:

1. The community association must find the authority in the governing documents to regulate traffic;
2. The association needs to follow the established procedures in the Vehicle Code to subject the private roadways of the development to regulations by applying provisions of the Vehicle Code; and
3. Law enforcement agencies are not required to patrol or enforce the Vehicle Code on the private roadways unless they choose to do so.

Additionally, the association may adopt its own traffic rules and regulations for the private roadways owned by the community, place signs on the roadways giving the members notice, and set up a procedure for enforcement of the traffic restrictions. Once again, the authority to regulate the traffic must be found in the governing documents of the association. Members must be made aware of the rules and regulations applicable to traffic on the premises. And the members and the association must understand the mechanism for enforcing infractions.

The association can only enforce infractions against the members and NOT against members of the public who happen to be on a roadway owned by the association.

A major issue is how the infractions will be enforced. Will the association hire a private security company to give citations to members for traffic violations; will the association appoint members charged with the responsibility of enforcing vehicle regulations by citing other members for violations; and who will make the ultimate decision regarding the citation if the member contests it? What are the penalties? Does the association collect a "traffic fine"? Can the association bar a member from driving on the private roadways? Does the association post a "wanted for speeding" poster of the member in order to shame the member and others from driving incorrectly? Will the local court system enforce community association fines for Vehicle Code violations?

II. How Does the Association Regulate Parking?

Similar to traffic regulation by the state, the community association can adopt its own rules and regulations regarding parking, as authorized under the governing documents and/or adopt Vehicle Code provisions governing parking. If the community association used the Vehicle Code provisions to make the Vehicle Code applicable to traffic regulation on privately owned and maintained roads, that procedure also makes applicable Vehicle Code provisions regarding parking on those roadways.

For example, the Vehicle Code contains restrictions about parking on a crosswalk, parking in front of a public or private driveway, parking on any portion of a sidewalk, parking in a designated fire lane, parking in front of or upon that portion of the curb that has been cut down to provide wheelchair assess ability to the sidewalk, parking in excess of 18 inches from the right hand curb, (if adopted by local ordinance) restricting parking on certain streets between the hours of 2 a.m. and 6 a.m., restricting parking of commercial vehicles exceeding a gross vehicle rating of 10,000 pounds or more, parking a vehicle in a disabled persons parking spot, parking for snow removal, and parking within 15 feet of a fire hydrant or within 7.5 feet of the nearest rail of a railroad.

In addition, or in the alternative, most governing documents of a common interest development contain some type of parking restrictions or allow the association to adopt such restrictions.

Many associations adopt rules and regulations regarding parking which bind the members of the association, but not members of the public visiting on the premises. Once again, the issue becomes how to handle a parking violation. Are citations issued? Is there a schedule of fines for different infractions? How does the homeowner pay the fines? What happens if the homeowner does not pay? Can parking privileges be revoked for non-payment of a fine? What does the association do when a member disputes the citation?

A. REMOVAL OF IMPROPERLY PARKED VEHICLES

The California Vehicle Code allows a community association to remove a vehicle parked on that property to the nearest public garage if all the following requirements are satisfied:

1. A sign not less than 17 x 22 inches in size with lettering not less than 1 inch in height appears at each entrance to the common interest development and contains the following:
   a. A statement that public parking is prohibited and all vehicles not authorized to park on the common interest development will be removed at the owner's expense.
   b. The telephone number of the local traffic law enforcement agency.
   c. The sign may also indicate that a citation may be issued for the violation.

2. If the identity of the registered owner of the vehicle is known or readily ascertainable, the president of the association or designee shall, within a reasonable time, notify the owner of the removal by first-class mail. If the identity of the owner is not known or ascertainable and the vehicle is not returned to the owner within 120 hours, the president or designee must immediately send a written report of the removal by mail to the Department of Justice Stolen Vehicle System in Sacramento. Further, the president or designee shall file a copy of the notice with the proprietor of any public garage in which the vehicle may be stored. The report must be made on a form furnished by the Department of Justice and must include a complete description of the vehicle, the date, time, and place from which the vehicle was removed, and the amount of mileage on the vehicle at the time of removal, the grounds for removal, and the name of the garage or place where the vehicle is stored.

3. The president of the association or designee must give notice of the removal to the local traffic law enforcement agency immediately after the vehicle has been removed. The notice must include a description of the vehicle, the license plate number, and the address from where the vehicle was removed.

Additionally, the association may remove a vehicle without notice if it is parked in a marked fire lane, within 15 feet of a fire hydrant, in a parking space designated for the handicapped without proper authority, or in a manner which interferes with entrance to, or exit from, the common interest development or any separate interest contained therein.

The association is not liable for any damages incurred by the vehicle owner (such as taxi fare) because of the removal of the vehicle as long as the association was within compliance with the law. Nor is it liable for any damage to the vehicle (such as a paint scratch) caused by the removal. However, the owner of the removed vehicle may recover for any damage to the vehicle resulting from any intentional or negligent act of the association or any person causing the removal of the vehicle.

If the community association fails to post the required sign or to state the grounds for the removal of the vehicle if requested by the legal or registered owner of the vehicle, it is liable for double the storage or towing charges.

Obviously, if the association receives a request by the legal or registered owner of the vehicle, it needs to state the grounds for removal of the vehicle.

III. Manager's Enforcement of Traffic Issues

It's important for you, as the homeowner (community) association manager, to understand how to enforce the traffic and parking issues within the development. The following summary should help:

1. Check to verify that the association has the authority to regulate traffic and/or parking. Authority should be contained in the governing documents for the development.
2. Locate and review any traffic and/or parking regulations that the members are obligated to follow. This information might be found in the rules and regulations passed by the board of directors of the community association.
3. Verify if the members are aware of applicable traffic or parking rules and if signs are necessary.
4. See if the local municipality has passed an ordinance making state traffic laws enforceable on the streets of the development. Additionally, determine if local law enforcement has agreed to enforce state traffic laws on the streets of the development.

5. Determine if traffic laws and/or parking rules have been enforced in the development in the past. If so, determine how they were enforced and the role of the community association manager with regard to enforcements.
6. Make certain that any appropriate signs and notices have been given regarding traffic rules and parking enforcement. Keep in mind that under certain circumstances members of the public are not subject to association enforced traffic rules and parking rules. Make certain that if vehicles are to be towed for parking violations a determination has been made whether it is a vehicle owned by a member of the public or by a member of the association.

IV. Homeowner (Community) Association Use Restrictions

As the homeowner (community) association manager, you need to know if all of the lots or units are restricted to "residential use" only. That restriction will normally be found in the recorded declaration for the common interest development.

Sometimes the declaration will give a detailed definition of "residential use." In the alternative, there may be no definition provided for "residential use," which works on the assumption that people know what residential use is and what it isn't. If the term residential use is unclear, then it may be up to the courts to determine what is and what is not residential use. Obviously, the court will try to enforce the intentions of the parties at the time the document was recorded. However, litigation is time consuming and expensive.

Suppose it comes to your attention as the Hubie Highland's Community Association Manager that Martin Lee is suspected of conducting a profitable business from his unit, buying and selling certain merchandise over the Internet while, very seldom if ever, taking possession of any of the items. Kim Whitetree appears to be running a cosmetic business out of the unit since Whitetree's vehicle has several bumper stickers that say "See me for (cosmetic company name)," indicating that she must be doing business out of her unit. Carl Chambers is day trading stocks out of his unit. Gladys Crosby has taken her placemat and napkin making hobby and turned it into a profitable venture. She takes the items that she makes in her unit and displays them at craft fairs throughout the local area. Maggie Carpenter spends most of her time in her unit writing short stories and books which she sells over the Internet using the services of a publish-on-demand print shop. San Saelee often burns the lights into the wee hours of the morning doing some of his restaurant's business at home. And the list can go on and on.

When **"doing business"** complaints are lodged with you, the community association manager, how do you approach the "residential only" restriction? The first place to look for guidance would be the governing documents, more specifically the recorded declaration. The following represents two samples of such restrictions.

EXAMPLE 1

All real property within the property shall be held, used and enjoyed subject to the following limitations and restrictions,...

22.A – Single-Family Dwelling Units; Leases. Each Dwelling Unit shall be used as a residence for a single family and for no other purpose. No unit shall be leased or rented for less than six (6) months, without prior written approval by the Association Board of Directors.

22.B – Business or Commercial Activity. No part of the Property shall ever be used or caused to be used or allowed or authorized an any way, directly or indirectly, for any commercial, manufacturing, mercantile, retail, wholesale, storage, vending, or other business purposes; except Grantor, its successor, or assignees, may use any portion of the Property for model home sites, and display a sales office during the construction and/or sale period.

EXAMPLE 2

8. – Residential Units. The Units shall be used:

8.1 – For Residential Purposes only, including sleeping, eating, food preparation for on-site consumption by occupants and guests, entertaining by occupants of personal guests, and similar activities commonly conducted within a residential dwelling, without regard to whether the Unit Owner or occupant resides in the Unit as a primary or secondary personal residence, on an ownership, rental, lease, or invitee basis;

8.2 – For such other reasonable ancillary purposes commonly associated with residential dwellings and otherwise in compliance with the Declaration and applicable law in residential dwellings (including without limitation a home/professional business office). The owners shall use their respective properties in such a manner so as not to offend or detract from other owners' enjoyment of their own respective properties. All owners shall use their property solely and exclusively for private single-family residences. Conduct of a private business shall be permitted on the condition that: (1) the equivalent of not more than one full-time nonresident is employed at the business location; (2) business visits to the home do not average more than ten per day; and (3) the owner complies with all applicable governmental regulations and codes applicable to such use. The providing of on-site health and mental care services to a Unit resident shall not constitute a private business so long as otherwise in compliance with the Declaration and applicable law.

Hopefully, the declaration contains language that is specific enough to make a determination whether and what kind of in-the-home businesses are or are not allowed in the development. If the particular type of business is not covered specifically in the declaration, a second step would be to check the local zoning ordinances to see whether this type of business is allowed in a residential area. Some declarations will allow for mixed uses; for example, in an urban setting, the bottom floors of a large high-rise might be for the exclusive use of stores and offices, while the remaining upper floors are for the exclusive use as residential dwellings.

There will undoubtedly be situations in today's economy where, because of computers and the Internet, more people can conduct business out of their residences. Also, some businesses encourage people to do a portion of their normal work at home rather than at the office. There will also be situations where an individual association member believes that the activities being conducted in the residence are perfectly proper, whereas other members, the board of directors, or you, as the association manager, might think to the contrary. If a compromise cannot be reached, it may be up to the courts to determine whether or not the activity is permissible. The following cases illustrate how several courts have approached this dilemma.

Biagini v. Hyde

3 Cal.App.3d 877;83 Cal.Rptr. 875 (App. 1 Dist. 1970)
Edited Excerpts From the Opinion of Justice Christian

FACTS AND ISSUES

Prior to the Hyde's purchase of the home, the developers of the subdivision had recorded a declaration of restrictions upon all the property in the subdivision. The restriction reads: "A-1. Land Use and Building Type. No lot shall be used except for residential purposes. No building shall be erected, altered, placed, or permitted to remain on any lot other than the one detached single-family dwelling not to exceed 2½ stories in height and a private garage for not more than 2 cars."

Mrs. Hyde is licensed as a cosmetologist. Prior to purchasing her home, she discussed with the subdivider her desire to provide limited beautician services in her residence. She was informed that "...if the City of Sunnyvale said this was a legal use in the City, we felt there would be no objection to it because we had no objections to it. If it was legal within the City, it was legal as far as we're concerned." We do not hold that this expression was binding on other owners, who might otherwise be entitled to enforce equitably the terms of the recorded restrictions. The Hyde's received notice that other owners in the subdivision objected to her intended use as a violation of a covenant and that should she proceed with her plans, they would bring suit against her. She nevertheless commenced the activity and the other residents sued to stop the activity.

(continued)

Mrs. Hyde did not advertise in any way, no external evidence of her activities could be seen, and no inconvenience to the neighbors was caused. But she admitted that she saw as many as six customers a day, and she was sufficiently active in the cosmetology business to produce a revenue of about $5,000 a year. The trial court found that the described activities constituted a "commercial use" detrimental to the other owners, carried on in violation of the restriction quoted above; and the court entered a judgment against Mrs. Hyde prohibiting her activities. Hyde appealed.

DECISIONS AND REASONS

Despite the existence of a restrictive covenant limiting the use of the property to residential purposes, incidental use of the property for commercial purposes has been allowed by courts in other states. These court cases have developed no precise test of incidental use, but such factors have been considered as to whether the use is casual or infrequent, results in no appreciable damage to other owners in the area, create no inconvenience or annoyance to neighboring residents, and is in substantial harmony with the purpose of the parties in establishing the restriction.

Restrictive covenants will be construed strictly against persons seeking to enforce them, and in favor of the unencumbered use of property. We are not persuaded that to allow a general exemption for vaguely defined "incidental" commercial uses would assist in the construction of such covenants. We conclude that the trial court was correct in determining that Mrs. Hyde's activities violated the requirement that "no lot shall be used except for residential purposes." The evidence reasonably supports an inference that the use complained of was detrimental to the plaintiffs in appreciably detracting from the residential character of the neighborhood. The judgment is affirmed.

Houck v. Rivers

316 S.C. 414; 450 S.E.2d 106 (South Carolina Court of Appeals 1994)
Edited Excerpts From the Opinion of the Court

FACTS AND ISSUES

Houck sued Rivers to stop her operation of a bed and breakfast inn in her home contrary to the Master Deed and Bylaws of the Horizontal Property Regime. Houck also sued for attorney's fees. The trial court found River's bed and breakfast operation was a use consistent with the language of the Master Deed and denied relief. Houck appealed.

DECISION AND REASONS

The Master Deed provides, in pertinent part:

EASEMENTS, COVENANTS, USES, AND RESTRICTIONS

(continued)

Section 21: each dwelling unit, together with its percentage interest in the common elements and limited common elements, shall, for all purposes, constitute a separate parcel of real property. Each dwelling unit shall be occupied and used by the respective owner only as private residential dwellings for the owner, his family, his servants, tenants, and social guests and for no other purpose. Each unit may be used for office or studio purposes in connection with customary home occupations.

It is undisputed that Rivers is using her unit as a bed and breakfast operation. She provides rooms and occasional breakfast meals to guests who stay overnight at a cost of $75 to $110 per night. It is clear that River's customers are not "social guests," or "tenants" in a usual sense these terms are employed. Rivers argues that under the City of Charleston's Zoning Ordinance, her bed and breakfast operation is considered a "home occupation" and, thus, under Section 21 of the Master Deed she is permitted to operate a bed and breakfast operation as a "customary home occupation." We disagree. Under this interpretation of Section 21, Rivers could operate any business out of her home as long as it qualified as a home occupation under the City Zoning Ordinance. If that were the intent of the drafter of the covenants, the covenants could easily have permitted all "customary home occupations" instead of limiting use of a property for "office or studio purposes in connection with customary home occupation." Therefore, even if River's use is a "customary home occupation," as she claims, the particular use of her home as a bed and breakfast operation is not permitted by the Master Deed because it is not being used for office or studio purposes.

We find River's use of her property clearly violative of both the Master Deed and the Bylaws of the Horizontal Property Regime. As a general rule, a restrictive covenant will be enforced irrespective of the amount of damage which will result from the breach, and even though there is no substantial monetary damage to the complainant by reason of the violation. Our review of the Master Deed and Bylaws does not reveal authorization for the awarding of attorney's fees. We affirm the trial court's denial of attorney's fees and reverse the denial of injunctive relief. We hereby order Rivers restrained and enjoined from using her property for a bed and breakfast operation.

Gerber v. Hamilton

276 Ill. App. 3d 1091, 659 N.E.2d 443 (Appellate Court of Illinois, 1995)
Edited Excerpts From the Opinion of Justice Welch

FACTS AND ISSUES

Property owners sued seeking to enjoin the defendant from continuing the operation of a beauty salon in her home. The plaintiffs, neighbors of the defendant, alleged that defendants' operation of a beauty salon violates the restrictive covenants incorporated into the deed of the lots within their subdivision, Whispering Oaks. The trial court held the defendants' operation of a beauty salon did not violate the restrictive covenants. The plaintiffs appealed.

(continued)

DECISIONS AND REASONS

Two restrictive covenants for the subdivision provide as follows:

1. Said restricted lots shall be used for residential purposes only for the construction thereon of not more than one single-family dwelling house not to exceed two stories in height and private garage, if any, must be attached to the house.

6. No person shall use or occupy any lot in such a manner as to create a nuisance to the other lot owners or in a manner which would tend to make the neighborhood undesirable for residential purposes. No advertising signs shall be displayed on the premises except for sale or rent of the property, or for advertising display homes. No business, trade, or other commercial enterprise shall be set up on any lot. Nothing herein shall prevent any owner from doing professional work in his own home provided that there are no signs to that effect placed upon the premises or other advertising to that effect.

The defendants' house is located on a cul-de-sac with six other homes, all of similar size and value. Lana Hamilton, a defendant, testified she owns and operates "Lana's Place," a beauty salon business, out of her residence. Lana's Place is open 3½ days a week and averages between 10 and 15 customers a day, and approximately 35-40 cars driven by customers arrive at the house each week. Plaintiff Debra Gerber testified that once the Hamiltons moved into the subdivision, she began hearing the constant sound of car doors opening and closing, the sound of hair dryers blowing, and the sound of people talking loudly to be heard above the noise of the hair dryers, and she began noticing an increase in traffic in the neighborhood. Plaintiff Alberta Gallay, who lives directly next door to the defendants, testified as to the same disturbances but further added that on a few occasions people had mistaken her house for that of the defendant's. Harold Blasters, the developer of the subdivision, who had the covenants and restrictions drafted, testified that he did not want the subdivision to turn into a commercial venture but that he also knew people were doing various things in their homes. He never directly affirmed or denied the proposition that defendants' operation of a beauty salon is prohibited by the restrictive covenants he drafted.

The trial court found that at the current level of activity there was no nuisance, that defendants' business is a professional business, that the primary use of the home was residential, and that the current use of the premises is consistent with the restrictions in the covenants.

DECISIONS AND REASONS

The specific language of a restrictive covenant in the deed for the Whispering Oaks subdivision prohibits the setting up of a business, trade, or commercial enterprise. "No business, trade, or other commercial enterprise shall be set up on any lot." There is no dispute that "Lana's Place" is a business. During the testimony of defendant Lana Hamilton, she referred to her beauty salon as a "business" more than a half a dozen times. This establishment of a business is in direct violation of the specific language of this restrictive covenant.

(continued)

Defendant argues that her beauty salon falls under a professional work exception in a covenant which states, "Nothing herein shall prevent any owner from doing professional work in his own home provided that there are no signs to that effect placed upon the premises or other advertising to that effect." We disagree. When viewing the specific language of this deed and the circumstances surrounding its execution, there is a distinction between allowing an individual to engage in professional work at home and allowing an individual to establish and operate a business at home. The former is allowed, the latter is prohibited. Defendant has gone beyond the mere engaging in professional work at home and have set up a business. Clients come to the defendants' home, all business calls are received at the defendant's home, noises related to the business can be heard coming from the defendants' home, and all the work relating to Lana's beauty salon business is performed at the defendants' home. This violates the intent of the restrictive covenant in the deed.

The judgment is reversed and remanded with directions to enter an injunction prohibiting defendant from conducting her cosmetology business out of her home.

Robins v. Walter

670 So. 2d 971 (Court of Appeal of Florida, 1995)
Edited Excerpts From the Opinion of Justice Wolf

FACTS AND ISSUES

The Robins appeal from a judgment which precluded them from running a bed and breakfast on their property in the Highlands Subdivision. Certain restrictive covenants, located in the public records, bind the property owners of Highland. The restriction states the following in relevant part:

2. No structure shall be erected, altered, placed, or permitted to remain on any residential building lot other than one detached single-family dwelling unit with attached or detached garage, with quarters for domestics attached to the garage.
3. No structure of any said lot shall be used for business or commercial purposes provided, however, the renting of the premises in whole or in part shall not be construed to be a business or commercial operation.

Defendants purchased a lot designated as a residential building lot, and had actual and constructive knowledge of the restrictive covenants binding property owners. Defendants obtained a building permit which allowed them to construct a residential home with detached garage and mother-in-law apartment above the garage. According to the floor plans, defendants built a five-bedroom main house and then a "carriage house" above the garage. Each bedroom had a separate entrance to the outside. Defendants received a certificate of registration to collect sales and use tax for "A Highland House" from the Florida Apartment of Revenue. Defendants also attached two signs outside the structure, one stating, "A Highland House" and the other, "Bed and Breakfast Inn."

(continued)

The plaintiffs are property owners of lots located within the Highlands. After a non-jury trial, the court entered a written order of final judgment. The order enjoined defendants from (1) renting out the "carriage house"; (2) renting out portions of their property as "A Highlands House Bed and Breakfast" to any persons other than single families at any one time for residential use; (3) selling food from their property, whether charged separately or included as part of the rental.

DECISIONS AND REASONS

This court has specifically found that, when interpreting covenants, one must look at the document as a whole to determine the intent of the parties. In addition, while we are aware that restrictive covenants should be narrowly construed, they should never be construed in a manner that would defeat the plain and obvious purpose and intent of the restriction. A bed and breakfast inn is an ongoing business or commercial use of property which would violate the intent of the Highlands covenant.

The defendants assert that the exception that provides that "the renting of premises in whole or in part shall not be construed to be a business or commercial operation," would allow the operation of a bed and breakfast inn. We find that this is a strained interpretation of the general understanding of the term "rental." The rental of a residence in the context of the deed restrictions in the instant case and under common understanding involves the rental as a residence rather than just a facility serving temporary or transient guests from the general public. We, therefore, find that all of the restrictions concerning the use of the premises as a bed and breakfast inn were properly imposed by the trial court. We do, however, find that in light of the language in the restrictions, which exempts rentals from being designated commercial, the judgment on the rental of the "carriage house" was overly broad and must be stricken.

A. SUMMARY OF CASES

The above cases offer the following observations:

1. In *Biagini*, a 1970 case, the restriction was a very simple "No lot shall be used except for residential purposes." The court, however, noted that some courts have decided that the incidental use of a dwelling for business or professional purposes does not necessarily constitute a violation of a recorded covenant restricting the use of the property to residential purposes. Whether it is or is not a violation depends on the extent or the manner of the incidental use. So, despite the existence of the restrictive covenant, incidental use of a dwelling has been allowed after considering whether or not the use is casual or infrequent, whether the use results in no appreciable damage to other owners in the area, whether it creates an inconvenience or annoyance to the neighbors, and whether it is in substantial harmony with the intent of the restriction.

In the Biagini case, the Hyde's operation of a cosmetology business clearly violated the restriction prohibiting any use other than for residential purposes.

2. In the 1995 *Gerber* case, the beauty salon appeared again and the court considered all of the factors mentioned in the *Biagini* case, and also determined that the beauty salon violated the restrictions on the property. However, this case involves restrictions which were more contemporary by allowing professional work to be conducted in the home provided there were no signs or advertising to that effect. The court then used the facts to determine that the beauty salon was the operation of a business at home and not the engaging in professional work at home. Additionally, in both *Biagini* and *Gerber*, there was an issue involving what the developer told the purchaser of the lot. Obviously, some developers may be overly anxious to sell lots and tell the purchaser whatever is necessary to make the sale. This can present a problem later on. Obviously, purchasers need to know that they are bound by the recorded restrictions and the declaration which they should have read carefully before concluding their purchase.

3. In *Robins*, the court considered the "renting of the premises in whole or in part" and concluded that a bed and breakfast was inappropriate, but renting the carriage house was acceptable under those restrictions. The bed and breakfast was an ongoing business, but renting the carriage house was allowed. The *Houck* case followed the same line of thinking and concluded that "Each unit may be used for office or studio purposes in connection or with customary home occupation" was not broad enough to cover the operation of a bed and breakfast.

In summary, if the community development has some kind of residential use restriction on the property, the board of directors or the association members should discuss their views concerning those restrictions and, if necessary, consider creating clear restrictions that would permit home business which would not interfere with the residential character of the development.

In the contemporary marketplace, conducting a business by using computers, phone lines, and satellite links within a dwelling would appear to have no impact on the neighbors or the development.

Since businesses are, to a certain degree, headed in that direction, it seems as though amending the restriction to allow such a limited, specific change would be appropriate. Establishing specific activities which would be allowed in the amended restrictions, whether by name or by activity, as well as those which would not be allowed, would hopefully be enough to keep the association and its members out of the courtroom. Litigation is expensive, time consuming, and emotional. If a dispute over the conducting of some sort of business in a residence is not resolved under the language of the restrictions, every effort should be taken to find a workable compromise for all parties concerned.

B. RESIDENCES USED AS FAMILY DAYCARE

In today's society, more and more married couples with small children are finding it necessary that both parents must work to provide an income stream sufficient to pay obligations. It is then necessary for parents to find suitable care for the small children during the absence of the parents during the day. This is also true for the single parent with children.

We often hear that the child is at "daycare." Daycare facilities are popping up in residences throughout the United States. In some areas of the country, the government is involved in licensing and regulating daycare facilities more so than in other areas, or maybe not at all. The problem with daycare facilities in common interest communities often falls back on the "for residential use only" or "no businesses can be conducted in any residences" language contained in the declaration or regulations of the community development. Although recognizing the problems of income mentioned above, residents of a development are often leery of allowing a daycare facility because of the increase in traffic and the possibility of increased noise from more children playing outside or utilizing playground facilities in the development. Obviously, the closer the residences are to each other in the development, the larger the concerns about operating a daycare facility.

1. Government Regulations

Some states have felt the need to pass laws or regulations covering daycare facilities in residences of common interest developments. For example, consider the following from California:

> "It is the intent of the legislature that family daycare homes for children should be situated in normal residential surroundings so as to give children the calm environment which is conducive to healthy and safe development. It is the public policy of this state to provide children in a family daycare home the same home environment as provided in a traditional family setting.
>
> The legislature declared this policy to be of statewide concern, with the purpose of occupying the field to the exclusion of municipal zoning, building, and fire codes and regulations governing the use or occupancy of family daycare homes for children, except as specifically provided for in this chapter, and to prohibit any restrictions relating to the use of single-family residences for family daycare homes for children except as provided for by this chapter.
>
> Except as provided in subdivision (d), every restriction or prohibition entered into, whether by way of covenant, condition upon use or occupancy, or upon transfer of title to real property, which restricts or prohibits directly, or indirectly limits, the acquisition, use, or occupancy of such property for a family daycare home for children is void."

The intent of the California legislature appears to be that restrictive covenants, community association rules and regulations, or local governmental laws or ordinances cannot prevent family daycare in residences. But exactly what type of family daycare did the legislature have in mind? The following information on the California law might be of interest to the board of directors, you, as the association manager, or those living close to a daycare site.

1. It will be difficult for those opposed to daycare facilities to argue that it fundamentally changes the nature of the community. The legislature has stated: "Family daycare homes operated under the standards of state law constitute accessory uses of residentially zoned and occupied properties and do not fundamentally alter the nature of the underlying residential uses. Family daycare homes draw clients and vehicles to their sites during a limited time of day and do not require the attendance of a large number of employees and equipment."
2. The legislature has classified family daycare facilities as either "small" or "large," with specific requirements and conditions on the operation of each. A ***FAMILY DAYCARE HOME*** *is one that regularly provides care, protection, and supervision for 14 or fewer children, in the provider's own home, for periods of less than 24 hours per day, while the parents or guardian are away.* A ***LARGE FAMILY DAYCARE HOME*** *is one that provides family daycare for 7-14 children, inclusive, including children under the age of 10 years who reside at the home.* A ***SMALL FAMILY DAYCARE HOME*** *is one that provides family daycare for 8 or fewer children, including children under the age of 10 who reside at the home.*
3. California law provides that all family daycare homes must maintain liability insurance covering injury to clients and guests in the amount of at least $100,000 per occurrence and $300,000 in the total annual aggregate, sustained on the account of the negligence of the licensee or its employees, or post a bond in the amount of $300,000.

Instead of buying insurance or posting a bond, the family daycare can have each parent sign an affidavit that states that the parent has been informed that the family daycare home does not carry liability insurance nor has it posted a bond.

Therefore, because of potential liability for the association, as the association manager, you should make sure that the insurance provider for the development knows that the daycare facility is operating within the development and that the association is covered by adequate insurance. Upon the determination of you and the insurance agent, adequate insurance may be in an amount higher than that required of the daycare provider. A copy of the **Affidavit Regarding Liability Insurance For Family Child Care Home** is shown in **Figure 6-1**.

Figure 6-1

STATE OF CALIFORNIA - HEALTH AND HUMAN SERVICES AGENCY

CALIFORNIA DEPARTMENT OF SOCIAL SERVICES

AFFIDAVIT REGARDING LIABILITY INSURANCE FOR FAMILY CHILD CARE HOME

SECTION A:

I/We, the parent(s)/guardian(s) of ______________________________,
(Child's Name)

acknowledge that ______________________________,
(Licensee'sName)

the licensee of ______________________________,
(Name of Family Child Care Home)

has informed me/us that this facility does not carry liability insurance or a bond in accordance with standards established by Family Child Care statute.

SECTION B: To be completed only if licensee does not own premises or the licensee is a member of a condominium or Homeowner's Association.

I/We, the parent(s)/guardian(s) of ______________________________,
(Child's Name)

acknowledge that ______________________________,
(Licensee's Name)

the licensee of ______________________________,
(Name of Family Child Care Home)

has informed me/us that she/he does not own the premises or is a member of a condominium or Homeowner's Association, and the liability insurance, if any, of the owner/Homeowners' Association may not provide coverage for losses arising out of, or in connection with, the operation of the family child care home, except to the extent that the losses are caused by, or result from, an action or omission by the owner/Homeowners' Association, for which the owner/Homeowners' Association would otherwise be liable under the law.

______________________________ ______________
Signature of Parent(s)/Guardian(s) Date

NOTE: The law requires Family Child Care providers to carry liability insurance or bond in the amount of $300,000 annually or to maintain this signed statement in the facility file. Lack of a bond or insurance does not effect the right of parents to bring legal action against the facility.

LIC 282 (ENG/SP) (6/99)

The additional and detailed requirements for the operation of the daycare facility is something that you, the community association manager, should become familiar with for the protection of the use and enjoyment of those residences effected by the daycare facility. In other words, you should verify that the daycare facility is in full compliance with the law to ensure that it will not adversely effect the interests of surrounding property owners or the association.

Since daycare, under the law, is stated to be a residential use and a single-family use of property, neither the board of directors nor the recorded declaration can prohibit the operation of a daycare. **If the community development is located in an area where no legislation on daycare verses residential use has been enacted, the determination on whether daycare is an appropriate use of residential property will be left for the courts.**

The following two cases are not bound by California law, and therefore represent different opinions on how restrictive covenants in other states affect the use of the home as a daycare facility.

Metzner v. Wojodyla

Supreme Court of Washington
125 Wn.2d 445,886 P.2d 154 (1994)
Edited Excerpts From the Opinion of Justice Smith

The Metzners purchased a home in the housing development located in Bellingham Washington in January 1989. The Wojdylas purchased a home in the development in October 1990. The Metzner's property and Wojodyla's property are separated by a corner lot at an intersection and their property abuts in a short corner of their backyards. The properties are subject to the following restrictive covenant:

1. Said property shall be used for residential purposes only. No building shall be erected, placed, altered, or permitted to remain on any lot other than one detached single-family dwelling with a private garage for not more than three cars...

Both parties were aware of the restriction when they purchased their parcels. Wojdyla obtained a family daycare home license from the Department of Social and Health Services. After the Wojdylas started providing daycare services, the Metzners began to complain about excessive noise from the children. Ultimately the Metzners sued to enjoin the Wojdylas from using their property as a daycare facility. The trial court issued a permanent injunction against the Wojdylas. The Wojdylas appealed. The Court of Appeals reversed the trial court, holding that the Wojodyla's use of the property did not violate the restrictive covenant. The Metzners appealed.

DECISIONS AND REASONS

Some states have held that operation of a residential childcare facility violates covenants restricting use of premises to residential purposes only. **(continued)**

However, other states have held the use of a private residence for a child daycare facility does not violate covenants restricting use of property to residential purposes only.

Restrictive covenants are designed to make residential subdivisions more attractive for residential purposes, and are enforced by injunctive relief without showing substantial damage from the violation. The restriction in the covenant in this case relates only to whether the premises are used for residential purposes only. It is beyond question that the Wojdylas are indeed operating a business. The child daycare operated by the Wojdylas accepts money in exchange for the care of persons (in this instance, children) not related to them. The operator of a licensed child daycare facility in a residence in a subdivision violates a restrictive covenant which provides that the "property shall be used for residential purposes only". Respondents Wojodyla's operations of a licensed daycare facility in their residence constitutes operation of a business and is thus in violation of the restrictive covenant. We reverse the Court of Appeals.

Stewart v. Jackson

Court of Appeals of Indiana 635 N.E. 2d 186 (1994)
Edited Excerpts From the Opinion of Justice Baker

The Stewart's and the Jacksons are next-door neighbors in an Evansville, Indiana, subdivision. Leigh Jackson operates a home daycare for remuneration and maintains a state license to care for 10 children in her home. The restrictive covenants governing the neighborhood require lots to be used solely for residential purposes and specifically exclude any commercial business, trade, or activity. The Stewart's filed suit against the Jacksons seeking injunctive relief to prohibit the Jacksons from operating a daycare in their home.

At the trial, the Jacksons provided evidence that, in addition to four other daycare homes in the neighborhood, a salesman worked out of his home, a woman taught piano lessons, another woman sold crafts from her home, and another man ran a part-time computer consulting business in his home. In addition, the Stewart's had incorporated a toy business, "The Idea People," and had operated as a toy manufacturer and wholesaler from their home. More recently, Kenneth Stewart had operated a contracting construction company called "First City Builders" from the home. Neighbors, other than the Stewart's, claimed that the Jackson's daycare was an asset to the neighborhood and that it enhanced their relationships. The trial court determined the Jacksons had not violated their restrictive covenants, finding that a home daycare is not a commercial business, trade or activity. The trial court further held that the restrictive covenants prohibiting home daycare are void and against public policy.

DECISIONS AND REASONS

At the time of the trial and judgment, Leigh cared for fewer than 6 children in her home; thus, she was not statutorily required to be licensed.

(continued)

Therefore, we limit our discussion to the consideration of unlicensed home daycare. We do not address the broader issue whether licensed home daycare is a residential use. In Indiana, restrictive covenants are not favored by the law, but will be enforced if the restrictions are unambiguous and do not violate public policy.

The plain and ordinary meeting of "residential purpose" is: One in which people reside or dwell, or in which they make their homes. Residential use is distinguishable from commercial or business use. The language of the restriction is concerned with the physical activity carried on upon the premises, and not with the presence or absence of a profit-making motive on the part of the landowner. Leigh receives a total of $245 per week for her services. Leigh's receipt of compensation for caring for children does not render her home daycare a business. Leigh compared her home daycare to having a relative watch one's children. Most often, the children play indoors but occasionally they play outside in the backyard.

The Stewart's complained primarily about traffic flow incidental to the daycare. Two of the five children live across the street from Leigh and walk to the daycare. The three remaining children are dropped off in the morning at Leigh's and picked up in the evening by their parents in a car. Although the traffic at times of the children's arrival and departure slightly increased, the activities are substantially residential in nature. We cannot find the slight departure from residential use renders a licensed home daycare to be a commercial use of property even considering the income aspect. We note that these particular restrictive covenants became effective in 1978 when many mothers did not work outside the home and cared for their children in their own homes. Because it could not be foreseen that care homes would become so prevalent in light of the significant increase in the number of two working-parent households, they cannot find that these restrictive covenants contemplated the exclusion of unlicensed daycare homes as commercial businesses.

Weighing the minimal obtrusiveness and the public policy supporting homecare against the legal meaning of the residential use covenant here, we find that unlicensed homecare is a residential use and that Leigh's home daycare did not violate the restrictive covenant. We, as judges, are not required to forget what we know from human experience. Our observations have been that neighborhoods bustle from the hustle of parents heeding their children's needs and attending to their extra-curricular schedules. Were our decisions otherwise, it would reflect poorly upon our commitment to one of society's most prized possessions, our children. Even if the home daycare were determined to be a commercial activity in violation of the restrictive covenants, the Stewart's were not entitled to injunctive relief because they acquiesced to similar daycare homes in the neighborhood.

C. RESIDENTIAL CARE FACILITIES

Certain types of **community care facilities** might seek to locate within the common interest community. Once again, this would fall under the declaration for the development stating the property can be used for residential purposes only and no businesses may be conducted in those dwellings. As was previously noted, with daycare homes, either legislation is going to permit residential care facilities to exist within the development or court decisions interpreting the recorded covenants will probably be the deciding factor on whether the facility can operate within the development.

In California, the legislature addressed this topic with the **Community Care Facilities Act**. A ***COMMUNITY CARE FACILITY*** *is any facility, place, or building that is maintained and operated to provide non-medical residential care, day treatment, adult daycare, or foster family agency services for children, adults, or children and adults, including, but not limited to, the physically handicapped, mentally impaired, incompetent persons, and abused and neglected children*. The following are examples of community care facilities.

1. Residential Facility

A ***RESIDENTIAL FACILITY*** *is any family home, group care facility, or similar facility for 24-hour non-medical care of persons in need of personal services, supervision, or assistance essential for sustaining the activities of daily living or for the protection of the individual.* The law further provides that for the purposes of any contract, deed, or covenant for the transfer of real property executed on or after January 1, 1979, a residential facility which serves 6 or fewer persons shall be considered a residential use of property and a use of property by a single family. Therefore, the members of the association, the board of directors, and you, as the property manager, need to understand that as long as 6 or fewer persons are served under the umbrella of a residential facility, it is considered a residential use of property as well as the use of the property by a single family.

What kind of residential facilities are there? Any of the following constitute a residential facility, the activity of which must be allowed as long as there are 6 or fewer persons.

a. Foster Family Home

A ***FOSTER FAMILY HOME*** *provides 24-hour care for six or fewer foster children and is the residence of the foster parent or parents, including their family, and in whose care the foster children have been placed.*

b. Small Family Home

A ***SMALL FAMILY HOME*** *provides 24-hour care in the licensee's home for six or fewer foster children who have mental disorders or developmental or physical disabilities and who require special care and supervision as a result of their disabilities.*

c. Social Rehabilitation Facility

A ***SOCIAL REHABILITATION FACILITY*** *provides social rehabilitation services for no longer than 18 months in a group setting to adults recovering from mental illness who temporarily need assistance, guidance, or counseling.*

d. Community Treatment Facility

A *COMMUNITY TREATMENT FACILITY provides mental health treatment services to children in a group setting and has the capacity to provide secure containment.*

e. Transitional Shelter Care Facility

A *TRANSITIONAL SHELTER CARE FACILITY means any group care facility that provides for 24-hour non-medical care of persons under 18 years of age in need of personal services, supervision, or assistance essential for sustaining the activities of daily living or for the protection of the individual for up to 90 days.*

f. Transitional Housing Placement Facility

A *TRANSITIONAL HOUSING PLACEMENT FACILITY is licensed to provide transitional housing opportunities to persons at least 16 years old and not more than 18 years old who are in out-of-home placement under county social services or probation supervision and are participating in an independent living program.*

g. Adult Day Program

An *ADULT DAY PROGRAM is any community-based facility or program that provides care to persons 18 years of age or older in need of personal services, supervision, or assistance essential for sustaining the activities of daily living or for the protection of these individuals on less than a 24-hour basis.*

h. Therapeutic Day Services

A *THERAPEUTIC DAY SERVICE provides non-medical care, counseling, education or vocational support, or social rehabilitation services on less than a 24-hour basis to persons under 18 years of age who would otherwise be placed in foster care or are returning to families from foster care.*

i. Facility For Persons With Life Threatening Illnesses

A *RESIDENTIAL CARE FACILITY provides for persons with "chronic life-threatening illness" which serves six or fewer persons who are 18 or older, emancipated minors, or family units is considered a residential use of the property and the use of property by a single family.* "Chronic, life-threatening illness" means HIV disease or AIDS.

j. Elderly Residential Care Facility

An *ELDERLY RESIDENTIAL CARE FACILITY is a housing arrangement chosen voluntarily by persons 60 years or older where varying levels and intensities of care are provided based on varying needs.* The facility provides for 6 or fewer persons, with each considered a residential use of the property and a use of the property as a single-family residence. Persons under 60 years with compatible needs and supervision may be admitted.

Timing is important, as any restriction to the contrary in the recorded declaration, if it was recorded after January 1, 1979, comes under the above mentioned requirements. The state legislation does not affect restrictive covenants which existed prior to January 1, 1979. Therefore, those covenants are still enforceable and the above mentioned activities would be most likely considered non-residential, non-single-family, or commercial.

V. MANAGER'S JOURNAL

As a manager, you should become familiar with the language regarding any use restrictions in the governing documents. You should analyze whether the restrictions are rather general or extremely specific. This will guide you in how to respond when a complaint is received regarding the use of a unit. Keeping track of recent court decisions, state legislation, and attending workshops or programs on recent developments in community associations would be a wise idea. Additionally, becoming familiar with the legislation on family daycare and residential care facilities is essential when members either seek to establish such a use within a unit or complain about an established use within another unit. It might be useful to reproduce the legislation to pass out among the members so that they can answer their own questions. If there is a concern it may be necessary to seek the advice of the association's attorney.

VI. CHAPTER SUMMARY

The authority for an association to regulate traffic may be found in the governing documents, usually in the declaration or the bylaws. Authority may also be granted by state law.

The California Vehicle Code allows cities or counties to pass ordinances or resolutions applying public traffic regulations to private roads. This can be accomplished if a majority of the owners of the privately owned and maintained roads, or at least a majority of the board of directors of a CID responsible for maintaining the roads, files a petition requesting it. The traffic rules of the state Vehicle Code will only apply, however, if appropriate signs are erected at the entrances to the privately owned roads.

Because it is not mandated by state law, the decision as to whether or not the local city or county will provide law enforcement of the Vehicle Code within a CID is made locally.

If the association adopts its own traffic rules and regulations, it can only enforce infractions against its members and not against members of the public.

Most CID's governing documents allow the association to create and enforce parking restrictions. The association can tow a vehicle as long as proper signage is posted, the registered owner (if known) is notified in a reasonable time by first-class mail, and the local traffic law enforcement agency is notified immediately upon removal. If the required sign is not posted, or a request by the vehicle's owner to state the grounds for removal is not fulfilled, the association is liable for double the storage or towing charges.

Many community associations have a "residential use only" restriction in their recorded declarations. Sometimes the declaration gives a detailed definition of "residential use," but when the term is unclear, it is subject to interpretation, often by the courts.

In the *Biagini v. Hyde* case, the California court ruled that the operation of a cosmetology business clearly violated the restrictive covenant prohibiting any use other than for residential purposes and interfered with the residential character of the neighborhood.

In the *Gerber v. Hamilton* case, the Illinois court ruled that the operation of a beauty salon was a business and not a profession, and therefore was in violation of the association's "residential use" restriction.

In the *Robins v. Walter* and *Houck v. Rivers* cases, both the Florida and South Carolina courts ruled that the operation of a bed and breakfast was not consistent with the customary definition of "residential use."

Modern phone, computer, and satellite technologies allow homeowners to conduct business at home without impacting neighbors or the residential quality of a neighborhood. As such, it may be appropriate to amend the "residential use" restriction to reflect this fact.

Although legislation differs from state-to-state, in California, neither restrictive CC&Rs nor local laws or ordinances can prevent the operation of family daycare facilities in residences. A family daycare home provides care, protection, and supervision for 14 or fewer children, in the provider's own home, for periods of less than 24 hours per day, while the parents or guardians are away. A large family daycare home provides for 7 to 14 children, and a small family daycare home for 8 or fewer children.

California law requires family daycare homes to maintain $300,000 in total aggregate liability insurance or posted as a bond. Otherwise, each parent must sign an affidavit affirming that they have been informed of the lack thereof.

A community care facility is any facility, place, or building that is maintained and operated to provide non-medical residential care, day treatment, adult daycare, or foster family agency services for children, adults, or both, including, but not limited to the physically handicapped, mentally impaired, incompetent persons, and abused and neglected children.

Residential facilities are considered community care facilities, which include foster family homes, small family homes, social rehabilitation facilities, community treatment facilities, transitional shelter care facilities, transitional housing placement facilities, adult daycare programs, therapeutic day services, life threatening illness facilities, and elderly residential care facilities.

VII. REVIEW QUESTIONS

1. According to the California Vehicle Code, the request to apply public traffic regulations to privately owned and maintained roads must come from a majority of the:

a. city council members.
b. owners of the private roadways.
c. the board of directors of a development responsible for maintaining the roads.
d. both b and c are correct.

2. Once a city or county has adopted an ordinance to apply public traffic regulations to private roadways in a CID, enforcement of those laws is:

a. mandated by state law.
b. always the responsibility of the California Highway Patrol.
c. locally determined, as it is not mandated by state law.
d. both a and b are correct.

3. On roadways owned by an association, the association can enforce infractions against:

a. members of the public only.
b. members of the association only.
c. both members of the public and the association.
d. none of the above.

4. Under the California Vehicle Code, which of the following is not a requirement for a community association to remove a parked vehicle?

a. The president of the association or designee must give notice of the removal of the vehicle to the local traffic law enforcement agency immediately after the vehicle has been removed.
b. If the identity of the registered owner is known notify the owner by first-class mail within a reasonable period of time after the removal.
c. A sign containing required statement regarding removal of a parked vehicle must appear at each entrance to the development.
d. Only a tow truck owned and operated by the association may remove the vehicle.

5. If the community association did not post the required sign and nevertheless tows a vehicle:

a. the association is liable for a minimum of $300 to the owner of the towed vehicle.
b. the association is liable for a maximum of $100 to the owner of the towed vehicle.
c. the association is liable to the owner of the towed vehicle for double the amount of the storage or towing charges.
d. the association is not liable to the owner of the vehicle for anything.

6. Often the governing documents limit a unit owner's use of the property for "residential purposes only." What activities are considered"residential" has been made crystal clear by:

a. a United States Supreme Court decision.
b. a California Supreme Court decision.
c. the Legislature.
d. none of the above.

7. In the California case of *Biagini v. Hyde*, regarding a "residential purpose" restriction, the court decided:

a. Mrs. Hyde's activities as a cosmetologist violated the restriction.
b. Mrs. Hyde's activities as a cosmetologist did not violate the restriction.
c. Mrs. Hyde's activities as a cosmetologist did not fit the definition of a business.
d. the restriction was illegal, therefore did not apply.

8. Which of the following is true regarding the use of property in a common interest development as a daycare facility?

a. It has been expressly disallowed by a California Supreme Court decision.
b. The California legislature has declared that any restriction prohibiting a family daycare home in a common interest development is void.
c. Whether daycare facilities are allowed in a common interest development is subject to local city or county ordinances.
d. The United States Congress has passed legislation specifically allowing daycare facilities in common interest developments throughout the United States.

9. In the case of *Metzner v. Wojdyla*, the Supreme Court of Washington held that the operation of a licensed daycare facility in a residence:

a. constituted the operation of a business in violation of a restrictive covenant for the in the declaration.
b. did not constitute the operation of a business, so was not in violation of the development's restrictive covenant.
c. was allowed by federal legislation which superceded the development's restriction.
d. was not in violation of the restrictive covenant since because other residences were allowed operate daycare facilities.

10. Which of the following is not considered a Community Care Facility under California legislation?

a. Foster family home
b. Adult day program
c. Youth hostel
d. Transitional shelter care facility

ANSWERS: 1. d; 2. c; 3. b; 4. d; 5. c; 6. d; 7. a; 8. b; 9. a; 10. c

Homeowner (Community) Association Restrictions: Part 2

CHAPTER 7

Enforcement of Covenants and Restrictions

I. Introduction

A. THE GOVERNING DOCUMENTS

The recorded declaration will undoubtedly include covenants and restrictions applicable to the members in the community. Unless the restrictions are unreasonable, they are enforceable as equitable servitudes and benefit and bind all of the separate interests in the development. As discussed in Chapter 5, Homeowner *(Community) Association Restrictions: Part 1,* ***EQUITABLE SERVITUDE*** *is a covenant or restriction that is enforceable against another if the other person had knowledge of it, even though it wasn't recorded.* In other words, since you knew of the restriction it would only be equitable for you to abide by the restriction. Note that, if the restriction is unreasonable, it cannot be enforced as an equitable servitude. Obviously, whether a restriction is reasonable is subject to debate and may ultimately have to be decided by a court. Additionally, unless the declaration states otherwise, the servitudes may be enforced by any owner of a separate interest or by the association, or by both.

Chapter 7

CHAPTER OUTLINE

When there is a potential issue regarding a restriction and its enforcement, it is in your best interest, as the association manager, to check the recorded declaration to see how the restriction can be enforced.

AN EXAMPLE - CONDOMINIUM

6.1 Enforcement.

Each Owner shall comply strictly with the provisions of this Declaration, the bylaws and administrative rules and regulations passed hereunder, as the same may be lawfully amended from time to time, and with all decisions adopted pursuant to this Declaration, the bylaws and administrative rules and regulations. Failure to comply shall be grounds for an action to recover sums due for damages, or injunctive relief, or both, maintainable by the Board (acting through its officers on behalf of the Owners), or by the aggrieved Owner on his own against the party (including an Owner or the Association) failing to comply.

6.2 No Waiver Of Strict Performance.

The failure of the Board in any one or more instances to insist upon the strict performance of the Declaration, of the bylaws, or to exercise any right or option contained in such documents, or to serve any notice or to institute any action, shall not be construed as a waiver or a relinquishment for the future enforcement of such term, covenant, condition, or restriction but such term, covenant, condition, or restriction shall remain in full force and effect. The receipt by the Board of any assessment from an Owner with knowledge of any such breach shall not be deemed a waiver of such breach, and no waiver by the Board of any provision hereof shall be deemed to have been made unless expressed in writing and signed by the Board.

FOR EXAMPLE - LOT OWNERS
17A.

Breach of any of the covenants, conditions, and restrictions contained in the Declaration or the bylaws and the continuation of any such breach may be enjoined, abated, or remedied by appropriate legal proceedings by an Owner or by the Association.

(continued)

Any judgment rendered in any action or proceeding pursuant hereto shall include the sum for attorney's fees in an amount as the Court may deem reasonable, interest thereon, cost of collection, and court cost.

17.b

The failure of the Association or any Owner to enforce any of the covenants, conditions, or restrictions contained in this Declaration or in the bylaws shall not constitute a waiver of the right to enforce the same thereafter.

Notice that in each of the above examples, both the association and an owner are given the opportunity to enforce a restriction. The waiver provision is important because it gives the association the opportunity to make a judgment call, as well as an owner, in determining if there might be a breach of a restriction worth pursuing.

If the association or an owner or owners choose not to pursue a possible breach of a restriction against another owner, this conduct in no way condones the same conduct in the future.

The community does not want a situation where one person broke a restriction (usually a minor breach) and no one complained about it, therefore similar breaches are permissible today.

Additionally, the association has to have some latitude in making decisions whether to pursue a violation of any of the governing documents. It may be that the board decides that minor violations would be pursued by **letters and other forms of friendly persuasion** in order to gain compliance with the restriction. It may be that the violation is minor enough that the board may not want to incur the cost of enforcement in court, except possibly through small claims court. In making the decision on how to remedy the violation, the association has to balance various factors. Ultimately, the decision might be to let the violation go under the circumstances and fall back on the "no waiver" provision if subsequent parties see the violation and to attempt to do the same thing.

Normally, individual members will not pursue enforcement on their own. Litigation is very expensive. Typically, for a member to pursue enforcement, either the member has the financial backing to do so, is an attorney, or the violation is significant and cannot be allowed. If it is the latter, the association should take action, instead of the member, or risk that the member will sue the breaching party as well as the association. That puts the association at risk for a breach of fiduciary duty claim for damages as in the *Posey* case (page 192).

B. THE LAW

California law also gives the association the legal standing to bring proceedings, such as administrative proceedings, arbitration, mediation, or litigation, in its own name regarding the following matters:

1. Enforcement of governing documents.
2. Damage to the common areas.
3. Damage to the separate interest which the association is obligated to maintain or repair.
4. Damage to the separate interest which arises out of, or is integrally related to, number 1 or 2 above.

In the event the association maintains an action to collect for number 2, 3, or 4 above, the amount of any damages recovered by the association must be reduced by the amount of damages representing the association's percentage of fault, based upon the principles of comparable fault.

Comparable fault (assessed damage) can be pleaded only as a defense to a claim by the association where the only damage was sustained by the association or its members.

For example, the association pursues litigation against a member for damage to an association riding lawn tractor. The claim is for $1,700 to pay to repair the tractor when the member negligently backed a minivan into it while it was parked. The member's affirmative defense is that the association, through its employee, was careless in leaving the unattended lawn tractor in that location, so close to the area where members back their vehicles out of the tennis court parking. Therefore, the member is raising an affirmative defense to the association lawsuit claiming the association was also careless in leaving the tractor in that location. The court may conclude that the damage to the lawn mower was 80% the fault of the member and 20% the fault of the association. Therefore, the association's damage claim would be reduced by 20%, and it would receive a judgment for the balance.

II. To Enforce or Not to Enforce – That is the Question

Most often, an association board must decide whether or not to initiate enforcement action.

Taking action will involve expenditures of time and money, especially if the dispute ends up in the court, as well as upsetting some of the membership. Not taking any action may appear to be the easy way out, but is it?

Posey v. Leavitt

229 Cal. App. 3d 1236, 280 Cal. Rptr. 568 (App. 4 Dist. 1991)
Edited Excerpts From the Opinion of Justice Hollenhorst

FACTS AND ISSUES

Plaintiff Posey, owner of a condominium at Lake Arrowhead, filed this action against Mr. and Mrs. Leavitt, owners of another condominium in the same development. Posey contended that the Leavitts built a deck extension on the side of their condominium that encroached the common area and obstructed his view. Posey is suing for willful trespass and nuisance seeking a **mandatory injunction** requiring removal of the deck extension and damages. Additionally, Posey sued the condominium Association for breach of fiduciary duty for approving the deck extension, and not requiring its removal. He is seeking damages against the Association.

The Leavitts contend that, under real estate and corporate law principles, the homeowner's Association (HOA) owned the common area, and that the board of directors therefore had the power to sell, transfer, or in this case, authorize an encroachment into the common area. The articles of the association empower it to "sell, lease, transfer, dedicate for public use, or otherwise dispose of real or personal property in connection with the affairs of the Association." The Leavitts contend that the power to sell must include the lesser power to consent to an encroachment. Additionally, the Leavitts contend that the board of directors approved of the deck extension by ratification, when it chose not to restrict the extension into the common area.

The jury decided that the Leavitts did not obtain the required written consent of the board of directors at the meeting on June 25, 1981, but that the board subsequently ratified the deck construction and the chairman of the board led the Leavitts to reasonably believe they had board approval. The parties here focused on a section of the declaration which states: "No owner shall, without first obtaining written consent of the board, make or permit to be made any structural alteration or structural improvement in or to his Lot or in or to any other part of the Project. No owner shall take any action or permit any action to be taken that will impair the structural soundness or safety or any building or structure in the Project or impair any easement or right or personal property which is part of the Project without the written consent of all Owners." The Leavitts argued that, having obtained written consent required by the first sentence, their Project met the requirements of the declaration, even though it was not approved by the other homeowners.

The trial court entered a judgment in favor of the Leavitts and against Posey. However, the jury awarded Posey $30,000 damages against the Association.

DECISION AND REASONS

We disagree. Under the second sentence, an encroachment into the common area impairs the easements of all other owners over the common area, and thus requires the consent of all homeowners.

(continued)

Under well-accepted principles of condominium law, a homeowner can sue the association for damages and an injunction to compel the association to enforce the provisions of the declaration. More importantly here, the homeowner can sue directly to enforce the declaration. Posey's cause of action against the Association was for breach of fiduciary duty. Although Posey claimed a diminishment in value of approximately $50,000, it is not clear that damages were awarded for that diminishment. The jury may well have awarded the $30,000 to Mr. Posey, payable by the Association, to compensate him for the cost of bringing an action that the Association should have brought. Damages were the legal remedy for the breach of fiduciary duty.

The judgment is reversed and the case is remanded with instructions to the trial court to exercise its discretion to decide whether or not to issue an injunction. In making this determination, the trial court should consider whether or not the encroachment by the Leavitts was innocently made, whether Mr. Posey will suffer irreparable injury if the injunction is not issued, and the relative hardships to the parties caused by granting or denying the injunction. The $30,000 judgement against the Association is affirmed, Posey to recover costs on the appeal.

In Posey v. Leavitt, the court decided that the HOA breached its fiduciary duty to the member by failing to enforce the governing documents regarding encroachment onto the common areas.

This mistake cost the association $30,000. The problem is the trial court's decision does not indicate exactly what the $30,000 was for. Nevertheless, the award was upheld by the appellate court and gives fair warning to an association that it needs to carefully consider the requirements set out in the governing documents of the association in terms of how they will be enforced, if they will be enforced, and be extremely careful about an appearance of ratification (later approval) of an action violating a restriction after it has taken place.

III. If an Association Loses a Lawsuit

On occasion, an association will bring a lawsuit to remedy an alleged breach of a restriction only to find that the association's position was incorrect. This may expose the association to the payment of attorney's fees, court costs, and other appropriate costs incurred by the member in defending the lawsuit.

AN EXAMPLE - California Civil Code Section 1354(f)

In any action ... to enforce the governing documents, the prevailing party shall be awarded reasonable attorney's fees and costs. Upon motion by any party for attorney's fees and costs to be awarded to the prevailing party in these actions, the court, in determining the amount of the award, may consider a party's refusal to participate in alternative dispute resolution prior to the filing of the action.

IV. Court Standards to Enforce Restrictions

The enforcement of restrictions is permissible as long as the restrictions are not unreasonable. Whether a restriction is reasonable or not is usually determined by a court.

Normally, this is because one person's idea of what is reasonable is not the same as another person's. The standard for reasonableness for a restriction was covered in detail in the court cases in the Chapter 5. These standards are important to remember because sometimes the defendant wants to challenge the restriction as being unreasonable. If it is ultimately determined to be unreasonable, then it cannot be enforced.

To help understand the requirements of the court when enforcing restrictions, review the following summaries from three important cases in Chapter 5.

A. NAHRSTEDT SUMMARY

From the *Nahrstedt* case in California, recorded restrictions are:

1. Presumed valid unless the complaining party can prove the restrictions are unreasonable.
2. Considered unreasonable if:
    a. they violate public policy;
    b. there is no rational relationship to the protection, preservation, operation, or purpose of the affected land;
    c. they impose burdens on the affected land that are so disproportionate to the restrictions' beneficial effects that the restrictions should not be enforced.

B. LAMDEN SUMMARY

From the *Lamden* case, the decision of a community board of directors is valid if:

1. The board is acting officially in accordance with governing documents.
2. The board is acting in good faith.
3. The board is acting upon a reasonable investigation.
4. The board is exercising its discretion within the scope of its authority under relevant statutes, covenants, and restrictions to elect alternatives for discharging an obligation to maintain and repair a development's common areas.
5. The court defers to the board's authority and presumed expertise.

C. DOLAN-KING SUMMARY

1. Recorded restrictions are presumed to be reasonable.
2. Unrecorded restrictions, when attempted to be enforced, are viewed as to whether or not they are reasonable under the circumstances.
3. Judicial deference places limits on how an architectural committee or board may exercise discretion in approving or rejecting improvement plans, based on subjective aesthetic judgment, if:

    a. the association's action is within the authority granted to it by the recorded restrictions;
    b. there has been a reasonable investigation;
    c. the actions are in the best interest of the community; and
    d. the actions are not done in an arbitrary manner.

V. Follow Established Procedure

A. NO ARBITRARY DECISIONS

Consider the following case involving a lawsuit by members of the association against the association.

Cohen v. Kite Hill Community Association

142 Cal. App. 3d 642, 191 Cal. Rptr. 209 (App. 4 Dist. 1983)
Edited Excerpts From the Opinion of Justice McDaniel

FACTS AND ISSUES

Plaintiffs, Mr. and Mrs. Cohen, purchased a lot in Kite Hill which afforded a panoramic view of the surrounding countryside. They paid a premium for this view. Kite Hill is a residential community in Rolling Hills in southern Orange County run by an association as a nonprofit corporation.

Shortly after the Cohens purchased their home, they submitted to the Association's architectural committee plans for certain improvements and landscaping in their front and rear yards. The Declaration requires that such plans be submitted to the Committee in writing and be approved before any construction can begin. One part of the plan approved by the Committee was a slump stone and wrought iron fence (a two-foot slump stone base topped by a three-foot iron fence). This is the type of fence designated by the Declaration for use in a lot such as the Cohen's; i.e., a side yard with a view. Shortly thereafter, Cohen's neighbors, the Ehles, received approval from the Committee to construct a solid slump stone fence immediately adjacent to the Cohen's slump stone and wrought iron fence. The Ehle's is the type of fence designated in the Declaration for side yard without a view.

(continued)

Plaintiffs objected to the installation of the non-conforming fence because they believed it would materially obstruct their view. However, their efforts to persuade the Ehles and the Association to modify or prevent the construction were unsuccessful.

The Cohens initiated this lawsuit against the Ehles and the Association and sought a restraining order to prevent the Ehles from completing construction on the fence. The Cohens also sought damages and a mandatory injunction to compel the Association to take certain steps to force the Ehles to comply with the architectural standards set forth in the Declaration. The trial court granted the Association's demurrer and dismissed it from the lawsuit.

DECISION AND REASONS

It is a settled rule of law that a homeowners' association must exercise its authority to approve or disapprove an individual homeowner's construction or improvement plans in conformity with the declaration of covenants and restrictions, and in good faith. The converse should likewise be true, that the power to approve plans must not be exercised capriciously or arbitrarily. We conclude that the courts must be available to protect neighboring property interests from arbitrary actions by homeowner associations.

The trial court must review the Association's decision approving the Ehle's fence to assure that it was neither arbitrary nor in violation of the restriction in the Declaration. The Declaration expressly provides that the Committee's approval of improvements "shall be based, among other things, on the effect of location and use of improvements and landscaping on neighboring property, improvements, landscaping, operations, and uses..."

Plaintiffs' suit here turns on the good faith and lack of arbitrariness of the Committee's approval, assessed in the light of all of the provisions of the Declaration. It appears from the record that the fence in question was not in conformity with the provisions of the Declaration. Although the Declaration vests "sole discretion" in the Committee and allows for reasonable variances, their decisions must be in keeping with the general plan for the improvement and development of the Project, and of course, they must be made in good faith and not be arbitrary. These are clearly questions of fact for a jury. Accordingly, the Association was a proper defendant in the action, and dismissing it from the action was error by the trial court. We hold that the Association, in reviewing the Ehle's improvement plan, owed a fiduciary duty to the Cohens to act in good faith and avoid arbitrary action. These are questions of fact raised by the pleadings and are to be determined by a jury. As a consequence, the demurrer was improperly sustained and the lower court judgment is reversed with instructions for the court to determine whether the Association's decision of proving the Ehle's wall was arbitrary.

Obviously, as the association manager, you need to insure that, if there are established procedures for approving homeowner projects, those procedures are followed, and some sort of documentation is provided, proving that they were followed. A good paper trail will show the fairness and reasonableness of the procedure. With a reasonable procedure that the members are aware of, as well as a paper trail of actions that took place, the association should be able to defeat any claim of arbitrariness. If the determination is made that the association followed its reasonable procedure, it also must be proved that the association's action was not contrary to public policy or capricious.

B. NECESSARY DOCUMENTATION

Ironwood Owner's Association IX v. Solomon

178 Cal. App. 3d 766, 224 Cal. Rptr. 18 (App. 4 Dist. 1986)
Edited Excerpts From the Opinion of Justice Kaufman

FACTS AND ISSUES

The Solomons purchased a residential lot in the Ironwood Country Club, a planned unit development. The date palm trees in question were planted somewhere around four years later and continued to remain there. The Solomons have admitted they did not file a plan regarding the palm trees with the Association's architectural control committee and accordingly never received a permit or approval for the landscaping addition. The Association filed the lawsuit seeking a mandatory objection compelling removal of the trees. The trial court agreed with the Association. The Solomons appealed.

REASONS AND DECISION

We have concluded that the court ruled that the CC&Rs required the submission of a plan to the architectural control committee for substantial landscape changes such as the planting of eight tall date palm trees.

According to the CC&Rs, the Association is governed by a board of directors, but there is nothing in the record showing any decision with respect to this matter by the Association's board of directors. Secondly, the record does not document, and the parties do not indicate, that the architectural control committee ever met to consider whether or not the Solomons' palm trees violated the standards set forth in the Declaration and the reason upon which the disapproval of the palm trees was based. The record indicates no evidence that either the board or the architectural control committee made any findings, formal or informal.

Despite the Association's being correct in its contention the Solomons violated the CC&Rs by failing to submit a plan, more was required to establish its right to enforce the CC&Rs by mandatory injunction. When a homeowner's association seeks to enforce a provision of its CC&Rs to compel an act by one of its member owners, it is incumbent upon it to show that it followed its own standards and procedures prior to pursuing such a remedy, that those procedures were fair and reasonable, and that its decision was made in good faith, and is reasonable, not arbitrary or capricious.

(continued)

The criteria for testing the reasonableness of an exercise of power by an homeowner's association is: 1) Whether the reason for withholding approval is rationally related to the protection, preservation, or proper operation of the property in the purposes of the association as set forth in its governing documents; and 2) Whether the power was exercised in a fair and nondiscriminatory manner.

The palm tree matter was apparently discussed at several meetings, members of the board communicated in writing and over the phone with Solomon, and at least two "polls" were conducted to illicit community opinion. However, these acts on the part of the Association, without appropriate decision by the governing board or the proper committee did not constitute a reasonable application of the CC&Rs to the palm tree dispute.

The CC&Rs carefully and thoroughly provide for the establishment of an architectural control committee and impose upon it specifically defined duties, procedures, and standards in the consideration of such matters. The record discloses a manifest disregard for these provisions: whatever decision was made does not appear to be that of the governing body or the committee designated to make the decision; no findings of any sort bridge the gap between facts and the conclusions of the decision maker, whoever that was; and the record provides no means for ascertaining what standard was employed in the decision making process.

Having failed to establish that its actions were regular, fair and reasonable, the Association was not entitled to a **mandatory injunction** and the trial court erred in granting that relief.

What that case shows is that the court is aware that the members violated the established procedure in not applying for permission from the architectural committee when doing landscaping, but that does not give the association the ability to remove the trees if the association hasn't followed its own procedures.

A written paper trail of what was done at each step is critical for association success.

VI. Manager's Journal - Establishing and Following Association Procedures

An association should have a clear yet simple process for handling alleged violations of the governing documents of the association.

Consider something as simple as the following.

A. PUT IT IN WRITING

When there is an alleged violation of the governing documents of the association, that violation needs to be put in writing.

Whether it's a complaint by an association member or members, the association manager, a board member, or a committee member, it must be put in written form. The written complaint needs to specify exactly which restriction is alleged to have been violated and exactly how it has been violated.

B. INVESTIGATION

The board of directors, or enforcement committee if there is one, needs to review the written complaint, and conduct a reasonable investigation based on it.

That investigation consists of researching the governing documents and the facts of the situation. This could be done by a board member, a committee of the board, or you, as the association manager. Obviously, the quest is to determine if there is a possible violation. After reviewing the written complaint, it may be determined that the complaint is insufficient, unclear, or lacks enough information to conduct an investigation. If so, the complaint needs to be returned with a written statement as to why it is being returned and guidelines as to what would be required to properly prepare it for an investigation.

C. DECISION AND RESPONSE

After a reasonable investigation is completed, a determination needs to be made whether there is a violation, an appearance that there might be a violation, or there is no violation.

If it is determined that there is no violation, a letter stating that, and the reason why, should be sent to the person who filed the complaint. If that person is an individual association member, this places the burden on the member to decide whether to pursue what he or she deems to be a violation. Most members will not pursue a remedy to the courts because it is too expensive.

If the determination is that there may or may not be a violation, but it's just not clear after a reasonable investigation, the board will either conduct another investigation or decide that it's not worth the effort to pursue something that isn't a crystal clear violation. In other words, the board "does not think" that there is a violation after its reasonable investigation, but it is not totally convinced of that. In all likelihood, the board will not pursue the matter further, leaving that up to the complaining association member.

The third alternative is that the board's investigation shows an obvious violation. If that is the case, whoever is in charge of handling complaints, whether that be the board, the manager, or a committee, needs to contact the alleged violator in order to solve the problem.

Effective human relation skills call for the alleged violator to be contacted in person to point out the violation and try and reach an agreeable conclusion through negotiation.

There will be times when the violator is unaware of the restriction or its violation. Hopefully, the violator will agree to correct the situation. Building a proper paper trail may mean sending a confirmation letter to the violator in a positive manner stating that the parties have met and what exactly was agreed to. In reaching an agreement with a violator, it is important to set out a time frame to remedy the violation.

Whether it is immediate, a matter of days, or a matter of weeks, some time frame needs to be established so that a violator has a deadline to comply with the restriction.

If the alleged violator is unavailable for a personal visit or refuses to remedy the situation, then a letter needs to be sent to the alleged violator specifically stating the violation, enclosing a copy of the restriction violated, and demanding the violator remedy the situation within a specific time period. Obviously, a specific time period may not be appropriate if the urgency of the situation requires immediate stopping of the violation. Hopefully, this will conclude the problem to everyone's satisfaction.

D. IN-HOUSE ENFORCEMENT

If personal resolution fails to remedy the violation, then the association needs to follow its in-house procedure for enforcement. Recall that the board of directors has the ultimate responsibility for decisions on behalf of the association.

In California, when the board is to meet to consider or impose discipline upon a member, it must notify the member in writing, either by personal delivery or by first-class mail, at least ten days prior to the meeting.

The notification must contain, at the minimum, the following:

1. The date, time, and place of the meeting;
2. The nature of the alleged violation for which the member may be disciplined; and
3. A statement that the member has a right to attend and may address the board at the meeting.

If the board fails to fulfill the notice requirements, any disciplinary action is not effective against a member.

If the board decides against the member, the board must provide the member with a written notification of the disciplinary action by either personal delivery or by first-class mail, within fifteen days following the action.

As a practical suggestion, either the in-house procedure or the notification of the meeting might offer an opportunity to either diffuse the situation or solidify the member's position. It is always good to know exactly where the opponent stands. Therefore, consideration should be given to providing a deadline by which the member can provide the board with a written statement or documentation why he or she does not believe there is a violation. The deadline for receipt of this response should give enough time to duplicate the response, get it to members of the board, and consider it prior to the meeting. This helps prevent surprises when the member meets with the board, helps the board clarify its position, and perhaps will even generate a solution prior to the board meeting.

The in-house procedure should also allow the member access to what the reasonable investigation of the association revealed. In other words, he or she should have the opportunity to inspect and copy any written reports generated by the investigation, any written statements from other association members, any photographs or videotapes prepared during the investigation, and the names and addresses of any individuals the board intends to call for the hearing. Obviously, the association needs to make this information available to the member within a reasonable amount of time prior to the hearing so that the member can prepare for the hearing.

One important person who must appear at the hearing is the person who filed the original written complaint. This is easy if it is a committee member or the association manager. However, there may be some reluctance on the part of the association member or members who filed the written complaint to appear at a formal hearing.

Somewhere in the governing documents of the association, it needs to make an appearance at a hearing mandatory for the complaining member.

In other words, if it is important enough to file a written complaint, it's important enough to confront the alleged violator in person. If the complaining member refuses to appear, the board should have the discretion to continue with the enforcement or dismiss it. The requirement of a mandatory appearance by the complaining member at the hearing might be enough to discourage members from filing written complaints for technical violations at the drop of a hat, with the hope of hiding behind the board's enforcement. Confronting an accuser is an important part of our

legal culture to provide due process to the accused. On the other hand, the ultimate decision lies with the board.

If the complaining member pointed out a very serious violation of a restriction, which the investigation also confirmed, the association needs to go forward with the disciplinary hearing even if the complaining member refuses to testify at a hearing.

1. The Hearing

The association should have, at the minimum, some very simple rules on how hearings will take place.

Typically, the hearing will follow a court trial in very general terms. In other words, someone with authority, perhaps the president of the board, will explain the procedure to the participants. Normally, each party is given an opportunity to make an opening statement, with the complaining party starting first. Next, each party is given an opportunity to present evidence in support of their position. Again, the complaining party should start first. This evidence may consist of testimony from others, photographs, documents or reports of others, portions of the governing documents, and the testimony of the party involved. Additionally, each party should have the opportunity to ask questions of (cross examine) the other party and of any person making a statement at the hearing. Finally, the hearing should end with a closing statement made by each party with the alleged violator making the final statement. In a large association, this entire process might be handled by a disciplinary committee assigned that function by the board of directors.

2. Hearing Concludes

At the conclusion of the hearing, the decision may be made immediately or taken for further consideration. Obviously, the determination needs to be made as quickly as possible. If the matter is taken for consideration, there should be a time limit for the decision to be made. Any decision must be in writing and also include any factual findings that were made. For example, say the board determined that "the antenna reached a height of 26 feet 11 inches"; "the eight date palm trees have been planted"; or that "a 75 foot wall is being erected made out of solid slump stone and 6 feet of the wall was completed as of 5 p.m. April 16."

A failure to make the factual findings resulting from the hearing can be a procedural defect that will invalidate the decision.

The written decision and the factual findings need to be delivered to each party at the hearing and the board of directors if the decision was made by a committee. If the decision was made by more than one person, the procedure should require that the majority rules. If the person bringing the written complaint is a member of the board of directors or enforcement committee, that member should not participate in the decision. If the decision was made by an enforcement committee, association rules should provide that the decision may be appealed to the board of directors. The board will then decide whether to review the decision itself and either confirm or adjust it, or decide to hold a new hearing. Obviously, if there are a large number of complaints, the board may want the decision made by an enforcement committee to spare the board members the time of doing it themselves. On the other hand, if the board handles the hearing itself, then there will be no duplication of effort if there is an appeal. If the board does conduct a separate hearing and the result is the same, that's "two strikes," and the likelihood of the losing party filing litigation is certainly minimized. It is probably better to spend the time in hearings than in the courtroom.

E. A REMEDY

The authority for appropriate remedies may rest with state law or the governing documents. Obviously, the remedy that's sought depends on the situation.

1. Money Payment

California law provides that the association cannot impose or collect an assessment or fee that exceeds the amount necessary to defray the cost for which it is levied.

It needs to be assumed that a fine or penalty is the equivalent of an assessment or fee.

Additionally, if the association adopts, or has adopted, a policy imposing any monetary penalty, including any fee, on a member for a violation of the governing documents or association rules, including a monetary penalty relating to the activities of a guest or invitee of the member, the board of directors must adopt and distribute to each member a schedule of monetary penalties that may be imposed for those violations. Distribution to each member must be made by personal delivery or first-class mail. Any penalty or fee must be in accordance with an authorization for member discipline found in the governing documents. The board of directors must distribute a new schedule of monetary penalties if there are changes from the schedule that was adopted and distributed to the members previously.

Notice that the situation where the association "adopts or has adopted" a **penalty schedule** is addressed. What happens if the association has not adopted a penalty schedule? The governing documents will have to be researched to see if the association has the authority to impose a schedule of penalties. Additionally, what is the effect of an adopted schedule or an amended schedule which was not distributed to the membership as required? Does that mean that no penalties or fines can be

collected without such a distribution? How specific does the final penalty have to be? In other words, does it need to be a set amount, for example, $25 for a parking violation? Or can the fee vary? For example, the board has the authority to levy a parking fine not exceeding $50. If that's the case, it's very important that the board be consistent in imposing fines for the same type of violation.

Remember that a monetary penalty, imposed by the association as a disciplinary measure for a failure of a member to comply with the governing instruments, cannot be characterized or treated as an assessment that can become a lien against the member's separate interest.

What happens if the association has imposed a fine on a member and the member refuses to pay? The association will then have to decide how it chooses to collect the unpaid fine. Additionally, say it is determined that the eight palm trees were planted without association approval and the association followed its in-house rules and regulations and documented the procedure in writing, so as to satisfy procedural concerns. As such, the member is ordered to remove the trees and refuses to do so. How are these situations handled? They will be discussed later in the chapter.

2. Suspension of Privileges

An alternative remedy to a fine would be the elimination of some membership right as the penalty for the violation.

Membership rights usually consist of the following:

1. The right of use and enjoyment of the common area.
2. The right to vote as a member at membership meetings.
3. The right to be a board member or be a member of a committee.

3. Expulsion, Suspension, or Termination of Membership

The removal of membership rights is governed under California law.

Since membership is automatic with the purchase of a separate interest, the legislature felt it was important enough for legislation. The following is a summary of that legislation.

California Legislation Summary Regarding Removal of Association Membership Rights

No member may be expelled or suspended, and no membership may be terminated or suspended, except according to the following procedures. And expulsion, termination or suspension not following these procedures is void.

1. Any expulsion, suspension, or termination must be done in good faith and in a fair and reasonable manner. A procedure is fair and reasonable when:
   a. The provisions of the procedure have been set forth in the articles or bylaws, or copies of such provisions are sent annually to all the members as required by the articles or bylaws;
   b. It provides the giving of fifteen days' prior notice of the expulsion, suspension or termination and the reasons therefore; and it provides an opportunity for the member to be heard, orally or in writing, not less than five days before the effective date of the expulsion, suspension or termination by a person or body authorized to decide that the proposed expulsion, termination or suspension not take place.

A court may also find that other procedures are fair and reasonable when the full circumstances of the suspension, termination, or expulsion are considered. Probably, the smart move for the association would be to follow the California law and not be second-guessed about whether its procedure will be considered fair and reasonable under the circumstances. Also, it is important to note that the terms "expulsion, suspension, or termination" are not specifically defined. Notice that the member has an opportunity to be heard not less than five days before the effective day of the expulsion, suspension, or termination. Obviously, the decision has already been made to do so and now the member receiving the notice has an opportunity to try and stop that action from taking place. The required notice may be given by any method reasonably calculated to provide actual notice. A notice given by mail must be given by first-class or registered mail sent to the last address of the member shown on the association's records.

A member may challenge the expulsion, suspension, or termination of the membership, including a claim alleging defective notice, but the action must be commenced within one year of the date of the expulsion, suspension, or termination. If the action is successful, the court may order any relief, including reinstatement, that it finds equitable under the circumstances. However, no vote of the members can be set aside solely because the person was at the time of the vote wrongfully excluded, unless the court finds that the expulsion, suspension, or termination was wrongful and in bad faith and for the purpose, and with the effect of wrongfully excluding the member from the vote.

These legal requirements govern only the procedures for expulsion, suspension, or termination and not the substantive grounds therefore. An expulsion, suspension, or termination based upon substantive grounds which violate contractual or other rights of the member, or are otherwise unlawful, is not made valid by merely complying with the above procedure. The member who is expelled, suspended, or whose membership has terminated is liable for any charges incurred, services or benefits actually rendered, dues, assessment, or fees incurred before the expulsion, suspension or termination or arising from contract, or otherwise.

Most governing documents for an association will contain the specific situations for loss or suspension of a membership.

Those situations may be challenged in court. However, if the association follows the stated procedure and the situations for loss of membership are reasonable, the association should prevail.

Since the procedure allows for the member to be heard, orally or in writing, it would seem to be in the best interest of the association to allow the member the choice. Obviously, a member living some distance from the property may prefer to be heard in writing, or a member on the premises to be heard orally. Also, when the board of directors is to meet to consider or impose discipline upon a member, the board must meet in executive session if requested by the member being disciplined. If you recall, "executive session" means the board meets outside of the ears of the membership. The member being heard can be there through the entire executive session and the board must follow its standard procedure for meeting in executive session. An additional issue is whether the member being heard in writing can require an executive session for the discussion of the membership issue. It would seem that the board must meet in executive session even though the member is not present, as the member may not want certain things discussed in front of the general membership. It is doubtful that the association could permanently remove a member from the premises on a rule violation.

Removal may be accomplished if the expelled member refuses to pay any assessments due the association and the association chooses to foreclose on the separate interest of the member.

4. Suspending Privileges

Suspending privileges of a member is different than expulsion, suspension, or termination of a membership interest.

Hubie Highlands may choose to suspend a member's privileges to use the swimming pool or the tennis courts. The governing documents will probably contain situations where privileges can be suspended, the specifics of which might be stated in the association rules. It would seem that such a suspension should follow the previously mentioned procedure for the ten-day notice of the board hearing on disciplinary actions.

VII. Arbitration Before Litigation

Recall that, in California, covenants and restrictions in the declaration, unless unreasonable, are enforceable by any owner of a separate interest or by the association or by both. However, when a civil action is filed in court by either party solely for declaratory relief or injunctive relief either independently or in conjunction with a claim for money damages not in excess of $5,000 related to the enforcement of the governing documents, the plaintiff must file with the complaint a certificate stating that alternative dispute resolution (ADR) has been completed in compliance with the law regarding such claims.

The failure to file an ADR certificate may cause the case to be thrown out of court.

A. WHAT IS THE ALTERNATIVE DISPUTE RESOLUTION PROCEDURE?

Before the filing of the lawsuit seeking the relief mentioned above, the parties "shall endeavor" to submit their dispute to a forum for alternative dispute resolutions such as mediation or arbitration. (Chapter 15 covers alternative dispute resolution.) Therefore, the parties get a choice of mediation or arbitration. Additionally, the choice is whether it be binding or non-binding at the option of the parties (**mediation is not binding**). Any party to the dispute initiates the process by serving on the other party a **Request for Resolution**. The Request for Resolution must contain:

1. a brief description of the dispute between the parties;
2. a request for alternative dispute resolution; and
3. a notice that the party receiving the request is required to respond within 30 days or it will be deemed rejected.

The request must be served in the same manner as a small claims court action. Small claims court service will be covered in Chapter 14. The party receiving the request has 30 days following the receipt to accept or reject the proposal. If the receiving party does nothing, it will be deemed rejected at the end of 30 days. If it is accepted, the alternative dispute resolution must be completed within 90 days of receipt of the acceptance by the party who sent out the request, unless the parties agree by written stipulation to extend the time. The cost of the alternative dispute resolution, whether mediation or arbitration, is borne by the parties. Therefore, the Request for Resolution will usually indicate whether the initiating party is seeking mediation or is seeking arbitration.

B. IMPORTANT CONSIDERATIONS

There are numerous factors to consider when determining the appropriateness of alternative dispute resolution. They include the following:

1. The alternative dispute resolution process is not required if the statute of limitations for the type of lawsuit being brought would expire within 120 days. In other words, there is no need to tie up time in ADR and then discover the statute of limitations ran out while you were engaged in that process and you are now prevented from bringing a lawsuit.
2. Apparently, the alternative dispute resolution process is not applicable to lawsuits collecting association assessments, even though they are less than $5,000.
3. Once the legal action has been filed, the parties can enter into a written stipulation to refer the matter to alternative dispute resolution and agree to suspend the litigation pending the ADR process.
4. Unless all parties consent in writing, evidence of anything said or admitted, or any documents prepared for the alternative dispute resolution, cannot be admitted into evidence for any civil litigation. If the matter ends up in litigation, the prevailing party shall be awarded reasonable attorney's fees and costs. In determining the amount of the award, the court may consider a party's refusal to participate in ADR prior to filing the lawsuit.
5. It's not necessary to file the completion certificate if:
   a. the party filing the lawsuit certifies in writing that the other party refused alternative dispute resolution;
   b. preliminary or temporary injunctive relief is necessary;
   c. the alternative dispute resolution is not required because the action is seeking a different recovery;
   d. the limitation period for bringing the action would have run within the 120-day period following the filing of the action; or
   e. a court finds that dismissal of the action for failure to use alternative dispute resolution would result in substantial prejudice to one of the parties.

C. ANNUAL NOTICE

Members of the association must annually be provided with a summary of the process for litigation regarding enforcement of covenants and restrictions and the prerequisites of alternative dispute resolution.

The summary must include the following language:

> "Failure by any member of the association to comply with the pre-filing requirements of Section 1354 of the Civil Code (see page 221) may result in the loss of your rights to sue the association or another member of the association regarding enforcements of the governing documents."

This summary must be provided either at the time the pro forma budget is distributed, or if mailed or delivered to members at the address appearing in the association books or as part of a newsletter, magazine, or other documents regularly sent to members.

D. LEGISLATION REQUIREMENT

Any Request for Resolution sent to the owner of a separate interest must include a copy of Civil Code Section 1354.

A copy of Civil Code Section 1354 is provided on page 221.

VIII. Litigation Issues

The process involved in a lawsuit is discussed in Chapter 14. The following topics are legal issues that might be uncovered in a lawsuit involving enforcement of restrictions.

A. TYPICAL REMEDIES FOR RESTRICTION DISPUTES

1. Injunction

The association, or a member seeking to enforce a restriction, will probably file a lawsuit for injunctive relief to stop a member from violating a restriction. Generally, money is not the issue, but stopping conduct is. If money damages would not provide adequate relief, the court may look at issuing an injunction under appropriate circumstances. An ***INJUNCTION*** *is a court order that either stops conduct (**PROHIBITORY INJUNCTION**) or requires conduct (**MANDATORY INJUNCTION**).*

The first step is often a temporary restraining order issued by the court pending a hearing on whether or not the plaintiff is entitled to a preliminary injunction. The ***TEMPORARY RESTRAINING ORDER****, freezing the status of the situation,* is served on the defendant, and the parties will appear at the hearing. If the court grants a ***PRELIMINARY INJUNCTION*** *at the hearing, that injunction keeps the situation from changing pending the possible issuance of a* ***PERMANENT INJUNCTION*** *(final injunction) after a trial.* On the other hand, a mandatory injunction will also require a court hearing to see if the court will order a person to do or not do an act which is the subject of the lawsuit.

The proper place to file a lawsuit seeking an injunction is with the county superior court.

The remedy for an injunction is an equitable remedy, and it will be filed as an unlimited jurisdiction action. Before the court can act on the plaintiff's request for an injunction, the court will need personal jurisdiction over the defendant.

2. Declaratory Relief

***DECLARATORY RELIEF** is a remedy-seeking statement from the court declaring the rights and/or duties contained in a written instrument or contract which can include a determination of the validity of all or part of the instrument or contract or a question of construction or interpretation of the document.* For example, an association member is considering building a specific type of fence and believes that it does not violate the association's restriction on fences. However, the fence is questionable, as other members have indicated that the fence could possibly violate the restriction. Rather than buy the materials and start constructing the fence, only to have it stopped by a prohibitory injunction for an alleged violation of the restriction or, alternatively, build the entire fence and risk having to tear it down under a mandatory injunction for violation of the restriction, the member may seek a declaratory relief option.

A member may bring an action in superior court for "declaratory relief" asking the court to "declare" whether a restriction has been violated.

With the member and the association present, the court can interpret the contract, and then the parties can act accordingly. Also, the association or one of its members, may bring an action for declaratory relief seeking the court's declaration regarding the restriction. Now the court can make its interpretation, and if it is determined that the fence violates the restriction, at least the member does not needlessly incur additional expenses in completing it.

B. STATUTE OF LIMITATIONS

Legal action for a violation of a restriction must be commenced within five years from the time the party seeking to enforce the restriction discovered, or, through the exercise of reasonable diligence, should have discovered the violation.

What this tells you as the property manager is to be vigilant and become familiar with the restrictions and take a periodic walk through of the complete community in order to see if there are any possible violations. Obviously, the goal is to fix the restriction violation by using the resolution techniques. In any event, if those techniques do not work and the problem results in litigation, it is important to keep track of the timeline to make sure the lawsuit is filed within the five-year period. Remember, if you, as the association manager, or someone else with authority in the association, such as one of the members of the board of directors, through reasonable diligence, should have discovered the violation, the time period starts from when you should have discovered it.

C. WAIVER DEFENSE

Sometimes the lawsuit to enforce the restriction may fail because of the waiver defense. The ***WAIVER DEFENSE*** *means that the person initiating the litigation to enforce the restriction has not sought enforcement of the restriction for previous violations with other persons and that lack of enforcement has led this person to believe that the restriction in this lawsuit is no longer being enforced.* For example, the palm tree restriction has not been enforced for years, and as a result, ten percent of the association members have planted palm trees in violation of a no palm tree restriction and this is common knowledge to you, the association manager, and board members. The question is, why is it being enforced against the defendant at this point in time. It would seem obvious to the defendant that the ability to enforce the restriction has been waived by the association and the other members of the association.

Another possible defense is called "estoppel," which is illustrated in the following case.

Deane Gardenhome Association v. Denktas

13 Cal. App. 4th 1394, 16 Cal. Rptr. 2nd 816 (App. 4 Dist. 1993)
Edited Excerpts From the Opinion of Justice Wallin

FACTS AND ISSUES

Dean Gardenhome Association (Association) filed suit against Haluk and Mary Denktas for injunctive relief and damages after the Denktases allegedly painted their house in violation of the Association's restrictive covenants encumbering the Denktases' property. The CC&Rs contained an attorney's fees provision. The trial court entered judgment in favor of the Denktases, but denied their request for attorney's fees. The Denktases appealed.

The Denktases were homeowners in a Huntington Beach development governed by the Association and covered by recorded CC&Rs. The CC&Rs required homeowners to obtain approval of the Association's architectural review committee before painting the exterior of the house and restricted the color choices to those approved by the Association. The Denktases hired a painter to paint their house pink and green. The painter took paint samples to the Association's president to obtain his approval of the colors. The president approved the green shade but admonished the painter to "tone down" the pink shade. The painter returned with a different shade of pink which was approved by the president.

After the Denktases painted their house, the Association advised them that the colors were unacceptable and the house would have to be repainted. The Association denied that its president had approved the selected colors. Haluk Denktas responded with a letter to the Association stating he would not repaint his house. He warned the Association by telling it in a letter that he hoped it did not attempt to do a foolish thing like repaint any of the walls as such an encroachment on his property was not within the provisions of the CC&Rs and would be considered as a trespass and dealt with swiftly and with extreme prejudice. The cost of repainting the house would have been between $1,500 and $1,800.

(continued)

The Association filed its complaint seeking injunctive relief, damages, cost, and attorney's fees, provided for in the CC&Rs. The Association stated it was seeking $16,708 in attorney's fees incurred up to the time of trial.

DECISION AND REASONS

The trial court ruled in favor of the Denktases, concluding the Association's president had approved the color choice. The Association did not appeal.

The ***DOCTRINE OF ESTOPPEL*** *is a defense used to prohibit someone from recanting a previous statement, approval, or position.* In the example above, estoppel was used to prevent the association from alleging a breach of the CC&Rs, when, in fact, the president had previously authorized the color selection. If the president of the association approved the color selection for the house, what other approval would have been needed? After all, this is the "president" of the association that approved the color choice. The president knew and approved of the colors for the painting of the house, the president knew that the Denktases would be relying on the president's color selection and that they would paint their house according to the president's approval, and the Denktases relied on the president's approval to the detriment of the amount of money paid the painter to paint the house. The homeowners may have concluded that the most important person to talk to would be the association president and do what the president said. The president misled the Denktases into believing that this color choice was acceptable to the association and, therefore, the association is estopped from enforcing the restriction for an architectural committee approval.

Waivers arise because others have been allowed to or have gotten away with it. Estoppel takes place because the defendant was told the conduct would be acceptable, the party saying so knew the defendant would rely on what was said, and the defendant relied on it to the defendant 's detriment.

D. MANAGER'S JOURNAL

If it is discovered that someone from the association represented that the member could go ahead and do something which is in violation of an association restriction, and it comes to the attention of the board or the association manager, it is very important that the party breaking the restriction be notified immediately to stop and, if done verbally, to follow it up with a written confirmation letter. The person so informing the member should do so in a calm and understanding manner, and needs to find out exactly what caused the member to believe the restriction violation was acceptable. In other words, is the member's situation one of estoppel or waiver?

E. THE DOCTRINE OF LACHES

Although similar to a statute of limitations, ***LACHES*** *is the legal doctrine that a legal right or claim will not be enforced or allowed if a long delay in asserting the right or claim has prejudiced the adverse party (hurt the opponent) as a sort of "legal ambush."* What this means is that the complaining party has waited too long to issue the complaint or bring the lawsuit and, as a result, the other party has been prejudiced by the delay. In other words, if you know the neighbor is violating the CC&Rs by painting a house pink and green without the approval of the architectural committee, it would be important to let your neighbor know at the time the painting commences that architectural committee approval is required. It is unfair for the complaining neighbor to see what is taking place and allow the complete painting of the house only to bring up the problem at a later date. If that is the case, the complaining neighbor is guilty of laches by unreasonably delaying the notification of the violation to the neighbor to the prejudice of the neighbor in paying for the painting of the house.

F. RATIFICATION

If the house was painted pink and green without the knowledge of an association board member, the association manager, or any other agent of the association, the association could not be guilty of laches because it neither knew, nor should have known, that the house was painted without architectural committee approval. By the time the board finds out, the house has already been painted. The issue now becomes **ratification**. *RATIFICATION is the confirmation or adoption of a previous act done either by the party himself or by another.* If the board allows the house to remain painted in violation of the restriction, it can be argued that the board has ratified the conduct of the member and approved the color scheme of the house. The issue would be when the board received notice of the violation of the restriction and how much time has passed without any action by the board regarding the painting. Obviously, the longer the time passes knowing of the violation, the more likely it is that the board approved (ratified) the improper painting.

Since it is more likely that you, as the manager, will learn of restriction violations before board members, it is important to inform the board immediately and, hopefully, the board will take action (reflected in the minutes) to pursue remedying the violation.

Such a statement in the minutes should be able to stop the notion that the restriction violation was ratified in any way by the board.

IX. Limits on Association Enforcement

The following case involves an association attempting to enforce its covenants, conditions, and restrictions (CC&Rs) which provide the following:

1. **Article XIII states:** "The owners shall maintain the interiors of their residential units and garages, including the interior walls, ceilings, floors, and permanent fixtures and appurtenances in a clean, sanitary, and attractive condition, reserving to each owner, however, complete discretion as to choice of furniture, furnishings, and interior decorating and interior landscaping."
2. **Article XIV states:** "The Board as agents may enter any unit when necessary in connection with maintenance, landscaping, or construction for which the Board is responsible. Such entry shall be made with as little inconvenience to the owners as practicable, and any damage caused thereby shall be repaired by the Board, at the expense of the maintenance fund."

The above would appear to be typical of provisions in a community development. The following case concerns how the association interpreted the above restrictions and sought to enforce them.

Fountain Valley Chateau Blanc Homeowner's Association v. Department of Veterans Affairs

67 Cal. App. 4th 743, 79 Cal. Rptr. 2d 248 (App. 4 Dist. 1998)
Edited Excerpts From the Opinion of Justice Sills

FACTS AND ISSUES

Cunningham bought an attached home subject to the restrictions of the Fountain Valley Chateau Blanc Homeowner's Association. He is a senior citizen who suffers from Hodgkin's disease. In September, a roofing contractor hired by the Association complained he could not maneuver his equipment in Cunningham's backyard due to "debris" there. That, and some previous complaints by neighbors, generated a letter from the Association lawyers demanding Cunningham not only clear his patio, but also open up the interior of his unit because there had been reports of fire hazards inside. Cunningham allowed Association representatives to inspect his home under the threat of litigation. After the inspection, he removed a number of personal items from the house.

In December, the Association conducted another inspection and decided he still had not removed enough of his belongings. This generated another letter threatening litigation. In March, litigation started based on alleged fire and safety hazards arising from the junk and paper stored in and about his home.

In May, housing code and fire inspectors found no hazardous conditions on the property. Subsequently, he received a letter from the attorneys detailing inadequacies in his housekeeping and demanding that he do the following with regard to the interior of his home:

(continued)

Clear his bed of all paper and books; remove paper, cardboard boxes, and books from the floor area around his bed and dresser; remove all boxes and papers not currently in use in the living room and dining room because they increase the risk of fire; clear all objects, including cardboard boxes, from his interior stairs and stairwells to allow passage; not use his downstairs bathroom for storage; and maintain a functioning electrical light in his downstair's bathroom.

Additionally, the letter stated "the Association suggests that all outdated clothing that has not been worn in the last five years be removed and/or donated to the Salvation Army or similar organization. This would allow the upstair's bathroom to be used for what [that was] designed for. The other remaining clothes could be stored in a walk-in closet." It further stated that "Books that are currently on book shelves, which are considered standard reading material, can remain in place." The letter ended by reminding him that the Association's attorney's fees had reached over $34,000 and were continuing.

The Association filed a lawsuit against Cunningham. Cunningham found an attorney who filed a cross-complaint against the Association for, among other things, violations of the right of privacy and trespass, seeking monetary damages.

This case involves complex legal issues and maneuvering but the important result was that the jury returned a verdict in favor of Cunningham on the liability issue, having specifically found that the Association had acted unreasonably. The trial judge stated that he believed the Association acted "totally reasonably" and the issue was ultimately appealed.

DECISION AND REASONS

We begin with the now established fact that there was no actual fire danger that a reasonable person would perceive—the relevant city departments had, after all, found no fire hazard. Further, the Association did not have a good faith, albeit mistaken, belief in that danger. The jury resolved these questions against the Association.

In light of the facts, it is virtually impossible to say the Association acted reasonably. The two sections of the CC&Rs cannot reasonably be read to allow an association to dictate the amount of clutter in which a person chooses to live; one man's old piece of junk is another man's art. The Association's rather high-handed attempt to micro-manage Cunningham's personal housekeeping—telling him how he could and could not use the interior rooms of his own house—clearly crossed the line and was beyond the purview of any legitimate interest it had in preventing undesirable external effects or maintaining property values.

Particularly galling to us—and clearly to the jury as well—was the presumptuous attempt to lecture Cunningham about getting rid of his old clothes, the way he kept his own bedroom, and the kind of "reading material" he could have.

(continued)

To obtain some perspective here, we have the spectacle of a homeowner's association telling a senior citizen suffering from Hodgkin's disease that, in effect, he could not read in his own bed! When Cunningham bought his unit, we seriously doubt that he contemplated the Association would ever tell him to clean up his own bedroom like some parent nagging an errant teenager. If it is indeed true that a homeowner's association can often function "as a second municipal government," then we have a clear cut case of a "nanny state"—nanny in almost a literal sense—going too far. The jury could thus find that the Association did not act reasonably under the circumstances.

The case is returned to proceed with the issue of the amount of damages. Cunningham is to recover his costs. Because the trial judge predetermined that Cunningham was to lose, we direct the presiding judge of the superior court to reassign the case to another judge for further proceedings.

Obviously, the jury and the appellate court decided that there are limits to enforcement of CC&Rs. A reasonable interpretation of the intent behind the association restrictions, which all members agree to abide by, plus a common sense approach to getting the members to obey the restrictions, is what is necessary to prevail. In this case, the appellate court sent the matter back to the trial court in order to ascertain damages and how much money the association is going to pay Cunningham for its conduct. It is curious that the law firm representing the association could not see the lawsuit by Cunningham on the horizon when the attorneys wrote letters to Cunningham on behalf of the association. And, in any event, after reviewing the history of the relationship with Cunningham, why would the attorneys and the association decide to pursue litigation against an eccentric association member with Hodgkin's disease?

X. MANAGER'S JOURNAL

The following case will tie together a variety of issues previously raised in this and other chapters, and demonstrate the complexity of the law and how the appellate court will weave the decisions on a variety of issues to ultimately resolve the case. This case should serve as an excellent review of legal issues, as well as a reminder of practical steps that you, as the association manager, will find helpful when handling enforcement of restrictions.

Cabrini Villas Homeowner's Association v. Haghberdian

111 Cal. App. 4th 683, 4 Cal. Rptr. 3d 192 (App. 2 Dist. 2003)
Edited Excerpts From the Opinion of Justice Rubin

FACTS AND ISSUES

Cabrini Villas is a common interest development of 863 townhomes (units) located on 77 acres in Burbank. It is governed by CC&Rs which, among other things, provide the following:

1. Homeowners are prevented from making any alterations effecting the structural integrity of the unit without the prior written approval of the Architectural Committee, and;
2. that no machines, equipment, or similar objects or unsightly objects of any kind shall be allowed on the exterior of the buildings, nor shall any such objects be allowed to protrude the walls of any building.

Defendant owns a unit that has central air conditioning. Defendant installed a 20-inch wide wall-mounted air conditioning unit through an exterior wall in her unit to air condition her closet. Defendant did not obtain prior written approval for the installation. The general manager of the Association and an engineer noticed the air conditioning unit and were concerned the installation may have compromised the structural integrity of the load-bearing wall and/or the water tightness of the building. That day, the general manager wrote to the board of directors informing them of the air conditioner installed without prior approval.

The manager invited the defendant to discuss the matter of the air conditioner at a meeting of the Association's judicial committee. Defendant claimed she did not receive the correspondence and did not attend the meeting. The judicial committee concluded the air conditioner must be removed. A recommended fine was imposed of $50 if she failed to remove the air conditioner within 30 days, an additional $100 if she failed to do so within 60 days, and an additional $150 if she failed to do so within 90 days. The committee recommended reviewing the matter after 90 days. The unit was not removed and the board of directors unanimously decided to file a lawsuit against the defendant. The lawsuit:

1. alleged breach of the CC&Rs arising out of installation of an air conditioning unit without prior consent;
2. sought declaratory relief regarding the respective rights and duties of the defendant and the Association under the CC&Rs and;
3. sought an injunction compelling the defendant to remove the air conditioning unit and repair the wall.

The defendant demurred to the complaint based on the Association's alleged failure to file a certificate that the Association had complied with alternative dispute resolution as required by Civil Code Section 1354. The Association's attorney submitted a sworn statement that the law firm sent defendant a letter requesting ADR by regular and certified mail.

(continued)

Since the defendant failed to respond to the letter within the statutory 30-day time period, the law firm filed this lawsuit. The trial court ruled in favor of the Association. The defendant appealed.

DECISION AND REASONS

1. Defendant contends that the trial court did not have jurisdiction over the dispute because the Association failed to properly serve a request for ADR.

Civil Code Section 1354 provides that service of a request for ADR "shall be in the same manner as prescribed for service in a small claims action ..." One way a small claims court action can be served is that the "Clerk may cause a copy of the claim and order to be mailed to the defendant by any form of mail providing for a return receipt." Service is deemed complete on the date the defendant signs the mailed return receipt. Unfortunately, the Association does not have a signed return receipt, however, evidence indicates it would be reasonable to infer that the defendant did, in fact, receive the Association's letter by regular mail if not by certified mail.

Two issues are presented by this evidence: First, was it significant that the Association, rather than a court clerk, served the defendant, and second was the defendant's failure to sign the return receipt faithful to the Association's compliance with the statute.

The legislative purpose behind Section 1354 is to encourage parties in a condominium CC&Rs dispute, involving minimal monetary damages, to resolve their differences by ADR. Accordingly, the law requires the parties to "endeavor" to submit their dispute to ADR prior to the filing of the action. Because no action has yet been filed at the time of the request for ADR it is required to be served, there is no clerk involved who could serve the request in the manner provided by the law. We recognize, by allowing a party to effect service under the statute, we necessarily ignore the word "clerk" in the statute. We conclude that the legislature intended to allow a party to an action to enforce CC&Rs pursuant to the statute to serve a request for ADR by the more informal, yet still reliable, method of service-namely service by any form of mail requiring a return receipt-prescribed by the statute. Accordingly, the Association complied with the statute when it served the request for ADR in that manner. This, however, does not end our inquiry. The question remains that a service was completed despite the fact that the defendant did not sign the mail return receipt.

Here, it is undisputed that the defendant did not sign the return receipt. Accordingly, service of the ADR request was not completed pursuant to the statute. However, we find that the defendant has waived this error by raising it for the first time in her reply brief here in the appellate court and failing to raise it in the trial court below. An appellate court will not consider procedural defects or erroneous rulings where an objection could have been, but was not, raised in the court below. It is unfair to the trial judge and to the adverse party to take advantage of an alleged error on appeal where it could easily had been corrected at trial. If the defendant had raised the objection at the trial the trial court could have, among other things, dismissed the lawsuit which would leave the Association to properly serve the request for ADR and start all over again.

(continued)

2. The Defendant contends that the Association failed to follow its own procedures and policies because the Architectural Committee did not review the air conditioner to determine whether it was "unsightly"; the board had no information concerning whether installation of the air conditioner lessened the structural integrity of the building; and the Association did not exercise its authority in a fair and non-discriminatory way. We disagree.

Defendant is incorrect in her assertion that there was no evidence the Architectural Committee ever considered defendant's air conditioner. The Association CC&Rs provide that the Architectural Committee "shall be composed of the Board of Directors of the Association or of three or more representatives appointed by the board." The president of the five-member board, Gina Phelps, testified that the board acted as the architectural review committee. After discussing the defendant's air conditioner with the manager, the board concluded installation of it constituted a violation of the Association's architectural restrictions. Thus, there was evidence that the board acting in this case as the architectural committee and considered defendant's air conditioner.

Phelps testified that the board considers maintaining the aesthetic value of the buildings at Cabrini Villas as essential to protecting the financial future of the community. To maintain the architectural integrity of the property, the board determines how best to remedy violations of the CC&Rs. Before defendant installed her air conditioner, Phelps testified, on two prior occasions residents had been required to remove room air conditioning units they had installed in windows because such installation was found to be a violation of the CC&Rs. This was because the board found these air conditioners to be "unsightly."

The board also had evidence that the installation of the air conditioner lessened the structural integrity of the building. In order to install her air conditioner it was necessary to cut a stud in the wall. The engineer testified that to some extent the integrity of the lateral load resisting system had been diminished although not to a great extent. The Association spent 2 million dollars on applying a product that made the stucco building water tight. Now a hole has been cut in the wall. It can be reasonably inferred that both the general manager and the engineer informed the board of their concerns that installation of the air conditioner diminished the structural integrity and water tightness of the building.

We are also not persuaded by defendant's assertion that the Association discriminated against her based upon her disability in violation of the Unruh Civil Rights Act. She alleges the board had been advised of her health condition and ignored her disability in attempting to remove the air conditioning unit. The evidence was to the contrary. The evidence established the condominium had central air conditioning. The wall-mounted air conditioner was in a walk-in closet for the purpose of alleviating heat in the closet, which she believed was having an adverse effect on the things she stored there. The wall air conditioner did not affect any of the living areas. There was no evidence the air conditioner in any way improved her health problems. Thus, there is no evidence that the Association's decision to remove the air conditioner was somehow discriminatory.

(continued)

The defendant argues that the Association had an adequate remedy at law, such as the imposition of a fine for the defendant's violation of the CC&Rs, and allowing the air conditioner to remain. Under the circumstances, defendant has failed to establish that the imposition of a fine was an adequate remedy at law. A monetary penalty would not cure the unsightliness of the air conditioner, nor would it bolster the structural integrity or water tightness of the building.

The court of appeals affirms the trial court's order issuing an injunction to the owner to remove the air conditioner and repair the wall.

A. CABRINI VILLAS SUMMARY

1. Even though the CC&Rs did not specifically prohibit wall air conditioners, the Association's policy and the CC&Rs expressly prohibited alterations effecting the structural integrity of the unit without prior written approval of the Architectural Committee. The evidence from the testimony of the engineer was that the air conditioner compromised the structural integrity and water tightness of the building.

2. The CC&Rs prohibit unsightly objects from protruding through exterior walls. The air conditioner could be seen from other units as well as the common area and was determined by the Architectural Committee to be "unsightly."

3. The Association did not discriminate against the defendant because of her health condition since the air conditioner was used to cool only the closet, not any other living area.

4. In a dispute involving violation of restriction, the Association must file a certificate that it complied with alternative dispute resolution. The Association may properly serve a Request for Resolution by mail providing for a return receipt. If the return receipt is not signed the request will have to be served by another manner. The Association was lucky because the defendant did not raise the issue of the unsigned receipt at the trial court. Therefore, the defendant could not raise the issue at the appellate court. The Association won on a technicality.

5. The Association followed a fair and reasonable procedure to resolve the air conditioning issue. The CC&Rs were not arbitrarily applied against the defendant. On two prior occasions the board had window air conditioning units removed as violating the restrictions.

6. This case demonstrates the use by the court of a mandatory injunction (removal of the air conditioner) and declaratory relief (the court issued an interpretation of the restrictions).

7. Monetary damages paid by the defendant to the Association would not be an adequate remedy for the installation of the air conditioning unit.

XI. CIVIL CODE SECTION 1354

1354. (a) The covenants and restrictions in the declaration shall be enforceable equitable servitudes, unless unreasonable, and shall inure to the benefit of and bind all owners of separate interests in the development. Unless the declaration states otherwise, these servitudes may be enforced by any owner of a separate interest or by the association, or by both.

(b) Unless the applicable time limitation for commencing the action would run within 120 days, prior to the filing of a civil action by either an association or an owner or a member of a common interest development solely for declaratory relief or injunctive relief, or for declaratory relief or injunctive relief in conjunction with a claim for monetary damages, other than association assessments, not in excess of five thousand dollars ($5,000), related to the enforcement of the governing documents, the parties shall endeavor, as provided in this subdivision, to submit their dispute to a form of alternative dispute resolution such as mediation or arbitration. The form of alternative dispute resolution chosen may be binding or non-binding at the option of the parties. Any party to such a dispute may initiate this process by serving on another party to the dispute a Request for Resolution. The Request for Resolution shall include (1) a brief description of the dispute between the parties, (2) a request for alternative dispute resolution, and (3) a notice that the party receiving the Request for Resolution is required to respond thereto within 30 days of receipt or it will be deemed rejected. Service of the Request for Resolution shall be in the same manner as prescribed for service in a small claims action as provided in Section 116.340 of the Code of Civil Procedure. Parties receiving a Request for Resolution shall have 30 days following service of the Request for Resolution to accept or reject alternative dispute resolution and, if not accepted within the 30-day period by a party, shall be deemed rejected by that party. If alternative dispute resolution is accepted by the party upon whom the Request for Resolution is served, the alternative dispute resolution shall be completed within 90 days of receipt of the acceptance by the party initiating the Request for Resolution, unless extended by written stipulation signed by both parties. The costs of the alternative dispute resolution shall be borne by the parties.

(c) At the time of filing a civil action by either an association or an owner or a member of a common interest development solely for declaratory relief or injunctive relief, or for declaratory relief or injunctive relief in conjunction with a claim for monetary damages not in excess of five thousand dollars ($5,000), related to the enforcement of the governing documents, the party filing the action shall file with the complaint a certificate stating that alternative dispute resolution has been completed in compliance with subdivision (b). The failure to file a certificate as required by subdivision (b) shall be grounds for a demurrer pursuant to Section 430.10 of the Code of Civil Procedure or a motion to strike pursuant to Section 435 of the Code of

(continued)

Civil Procedure unless the filing party certifies in writing that one of the other parties to the dispute refused alternative dispute resolution prior to the filing of the complaint, that preliminary or temporary injunctive relief is necessary, or that alternative dispute resolution is not required by subdivision (b), because the limitation period for bringing the action would have run within the 120-day period next following the filing of the action, or the court finds that dismissal of the action for failure to comply with subdivision (b) would result in substantial prejudice to one of the parties.

(d) Once a civil action specified in subdivision (a) to enforce the governing documents has been filed by either an association or an owner or member of a common interest development, upon written stipulation of the parties the matter may be referred to alternative dispute resolution and stayed. The costs of the alternative dispute resolution shall be borne by the parties. During this referral, the action shall not be subject to the rules implementing subdivision (c) of Section 68603 of the Government Code.

(e) The requirements of subdivisions (b) and (c) shall not apply to the filing of a cross-complaint.

(f) In any action specified in subdivision (a) to enforce the governing documents, the prevailing party shall be awarded reasonable attorney's fees and costs. Upon motion by any party for attorney's fees and costs to be awarded to the prevailing party in these actions, the court, in determining the amount of the award, may consider a party's refusal to participate in alternative dispute resolution prior to the filing of the action.

(g) Unless consented to by both parties to alternative dispute resolution that is initiated by a Request for Resolution under subdivision (b), evidence of anything said or of admissions made in the course of the alternative dispute resolution process shall not be admissible in evidence, and testimony or disclosure of such a statement or admission may not be compelled, in any civil action in which, pursuant to law, testimony can be compelled to be given.

(h) Unless consented to by both parties to alternative dispute resolution that is initiated by a Request for Resolution under subdivision (b), documents prepared for the purpose or in the course of, or pursuant to, the alternative dispute resolution shall not be admissible in evidence, and disclosure of these documents may not be compelled, in any civil action in which, pursuant to law, testimony can be compelled to be given.

(i) Members of the association shall annually be provided a summary of the provisions of this section, which specifically references this section. The summary shall include the following language:

> "Failure by any member of the association to comply with the pre-filing requirements of Section 1354 of the Civil Code may result in the loss of your rights to sue the association or another member of the association regarding enforcement of the governing documents."

(continued)

The summary shall be provided either at the time the pro forma budget required by Section 1365 is distributed or in the manner specified in Section 5016 of the Corporations Code.

(j) Any Request for Resolution sent to the owner of a separate interest pursuant to subdivision (b) shall include a copy of this section.

XII. CHAPTER SUMMARY

The recorded declaration will contain covenants, conditions, and restrictions (CC&Rs) governing the members of a homeowner's association (HOA). The owners and the association are given the opportunity to enforce a restriction, but not pursuing a breach in no way condones the same conduct in the future. Damages collected by the association may be reduced when comparable fault (shared fault) is pleaded as a defense, and determined by a judge or jury. Most of the time it is up to the association board to decide whether to take enforcement action or not.

In the *Posey v. Leavitt* case, the court decided that the association breached its fiduciary duty to the member by failing to enforce the governing documents regarding encroachment onto the common areas. If an association loses a lawsuit, it may have to pay attorney's fees, court costs, and other appropriate costs incurred by the member in defending the lawsuit.

A restriction may be enforced only if it is reasonable, which is usually a determination made by a court. The association manager must insure that established procedures for approving homeowner projects are followed and a paper trail is established. When there is an alleged violation of governing documents, the violation needs to be put in writing. The board of directors or enforcement committee needs to review the written complaint and conduct a reasonable investigation based on it. After the reasonable investigation is completed, a determination needs to be made as to whether a violation took place. A time frame then needs to be established for the violator to comply with the restriction.

In California, when a board meets to consider imposing discipline upon a member, it must notify the member in writing, either by personal delivery or by first-class mail, at least ten days prior to the meeting. The notification must contain the date, time, and place of the meeting, the nature of the alleged violation, and a statement that the member has a right to attend and address the board at the meeting. If the board decides against the member, he or she must be notified by personal delivery or first-class mail within fifteen days of the disciplinary action decided upon.

The governing documents of an HOA should make a hearing appearance mandatory for a complaining member. If the complaining member refuses to testify, but the board investigation has shown a serious restriction violation has occurred, it must go forward with the disciplinary hearing.

If, after a hearing, a monetary remedy is imposed against a violator, as in an assessment fee, that amount cannot exceed the amount necessary to defray the cost for which it is imposed. An alternative to a fine is to eliminate some membership right as the penalty for a violation. The removal of membership rights is governed by law in California. Removal may be accomplished if the expelled member refuses to pay an assessment due the association and the association chooses to foreclose the separate interest of the member.

Suspending privileges of a member is different than expulsion, suspension, or termination of a membership interest.

Alternative Dispute Resolution (ADR) is initiated by either party filing a Request for Resolution. The party receiving the request has 30 days to reject or accept the proposal. If accepted, the ADR must be completed within 90 days. The Request for Resolution will usually indicate whether the initiating party is seeking mediation or arbitration.

"Estoppel" is a defense used to prohibit someone from recanting a previous statement, approval, or position.

"Laches" is the unreasonable delaying of notifying a party that he or she is in violation of a restriction to the prejudice of that member (i.e., the cost of painting a house).

"Ratification" occurs when an association becomes aware of a violation, but does not act upon it within a reasonable time, thereby approving it.

"Declaratory relief" is an action brought in superior court asking for the court to determine (declare) whether a restriction has been violated before a member continues a project that is allegedly a violation of the CC&Rs.

The "Statute of Limitations" requires that legal action for a violation of a restriction must be commenced within five years from the time the party seeking enforcement discovered, or should have discovered, the violation.

XIII. REVIEW QUESTIONS

1. In the case of *Posey v. Leavitt*, the plaintiff Posey complained about a deck that the Leavitts built as an extension to their condominium. One of the remedies sought by plaintiff Posey was a:

   a. prohibitory injunction.
   b. mandatory injunction.
   c. preliminary injunction.
   d. temporary injunction.

2. In the case of *Ironwood Owner's Association IX v. Solomon*, the Solomons:

   a. did not file a plan regarding the palm tree planting with the architectural control committee.
   b. filed a plan with the architectural committee for the palm trees, which the committee denied, and planted the trees anyway.
   c. argued the palm trees did not violate any of the Association's architectural standards.
   d. removed the objectionable palm trees and sued the Association for money damages.

3. When the association manager hears of a complaint about an alleged violation of the association restrictions, the first thing he or she should do is:

   a. inform the board of directors.
   b. conduct an investigation of the complaint.
   c. have the complaining party put the complaint in writing.
   d. wait and see if the complaint surfaces a second time and then investigate it.

4. If the board of directors is going to meet to consider imposing discipline on a member for violation of a restriction, how many days prior to the meeting must it notify the member?

   a. 5 days
   b. 10 days
   c. 15 days
   d. 30 days

5. If the board of directors is considering expulsion, suspension, or termination of an owner's membership, a notice, including the reason therefore, must be given to the owner how many days prior to that action?

   a. 5 days
   b. 10 days
   c. 15 days
   d. 30 days

6. Any party to a dispute regarding restrictions should first initiate alternative dispute resolution by serving on the other party a:

   a. summons.
   b. complaint.
   c. request for resolution.
   d. temporary restraining order.

7. Once a lawsuit is filed and served on the parties:

   a. the parties can no longer enter into alternative dispute resolution.
   b. the parties can only enter into mediation.
   c. the parties may now only enter into arbitration.
   d. the parties can enter into a written stipulation to use alternative dispute resolution, or be ordered by the court to use alternate dispute resolution.

8. The statute of limitation for bringing legal action for violation of a restriction is:

   a. one year.
   b. two years.
   c. five years.
   d. non-existent; the lawsuit can be brought at any time.

9. An important lesson to be learned from the case of *Deane Gardenhome Association v. Denktas* is:

   a. only an association's architectural review committee can authorize the colors for a house.
   b. the association manager had authority to authorize the colors for the house painting.
   c. since the Denktases did not receive architectural review committee approval before painting the house, they must repaint the house in a suitable color.
   d. the president of the association has the authority to approve house painting colors.

10. In the case of *Cabrini Villas Homeowner's Association v. Haghberdian*:

   a. because the air conditioning unit was so small, it did not interfere at all with the structural integrity of the wall in which it was inserted.
   b. the wall-mounted air conditioner was not visible from the common area.
   c. as long as the owner paid the fine assessed by the board of directors, the air conditioning unit could stay in place.
   d. the court ordered the air conditioning unit removed.

ANSWERS: 1. b; 2. a; 3. c; 4. b; 5. c; 6. c; 7. d; 8. c; 9. d; 10. d

Enforcement of Covenants and Restrictions

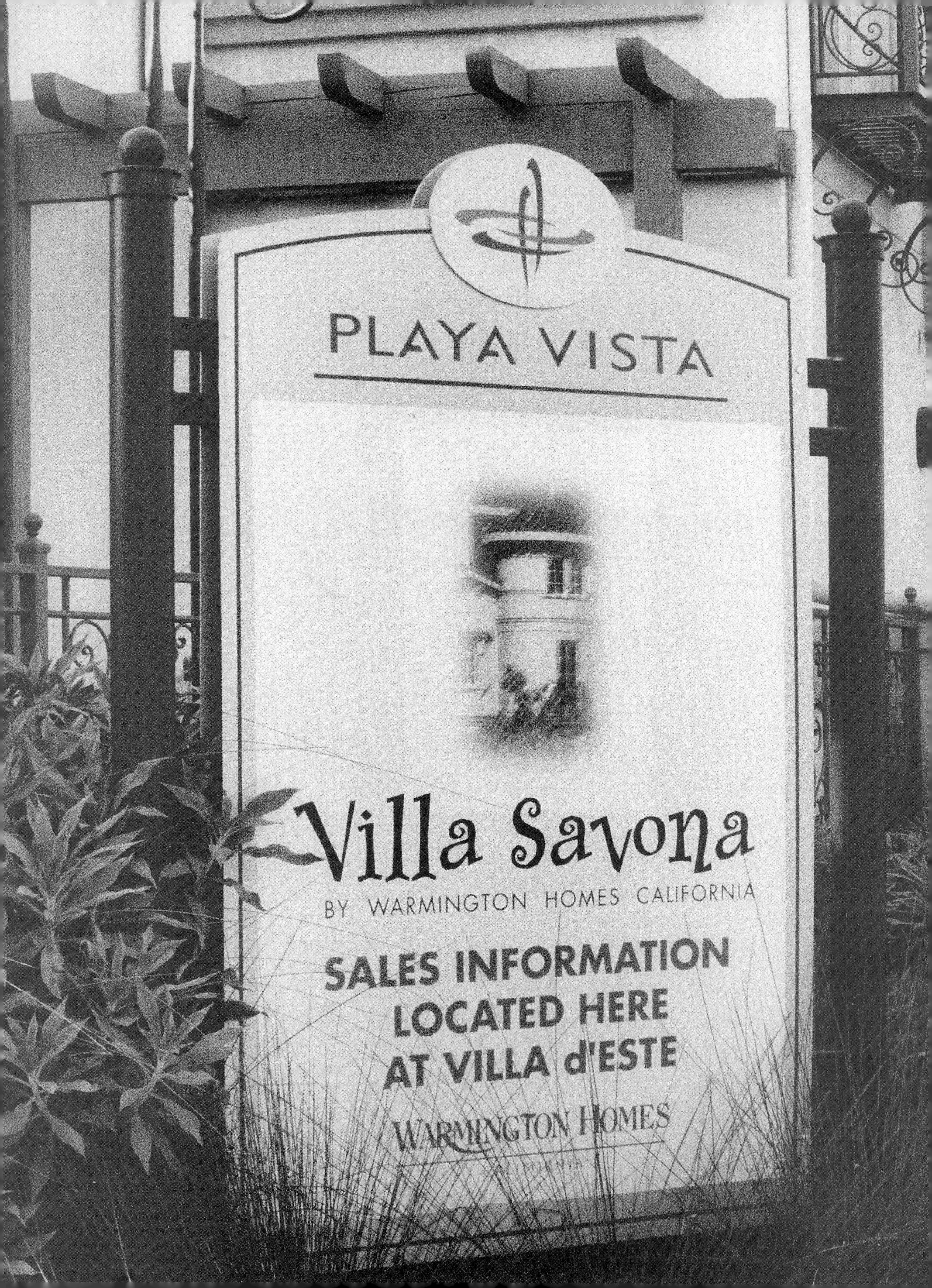
PLAYA VISTA
Villa Savona
BY WARMINGTON HOMES CALIFORNIA
SALES INFORMATION
LOCATED HERE
AT VILLA d'ESTE
WARMINGTON HOMES

CHAPTER 8

Inspection Rights and Changing Governing Documents

I. Right of Inspection Under Davis-Stirling Act

Occasionally, members of Hubie Highlands may wish to inspect the Association books and records. The reasons may vary. A member or members may be warranted in seeing how the assessments are computed, how much the pool maintenance contract is costing, why the grounds committee removed a row of palm trees, or to find data to support an amendment to the declaration. Each state may approach this differently.

In California, the ***DAVIS-STIRLING COMMON INTEREST DEVELOPMENT ACT*** *(Davis-Stirling Act) provides for inspection rights for members. It requires that the association must make the accounting books and records, and the minutes of proceedings of the association, available for inspection and copying by a member of the association or the member's designated representative.* If the member chooses to designate a representative, the member must make this designation in writing. So it is important for you, the association manager, to correctly handle a request for inspection by a member.

A. INSPECTION PROCESS

The association must make the accounting books and records, and the minutes, available for inspection and copying in the association's business office within the common interest development. If the association doesn't have a business office within

Chapter 8

CHAPTER OUTLINE

the development, it must make the items available for inspection and copying at a place agreed upon between the member and the association. If no agreement can be reached, or if the member submits a written request directly to the association for copies, the association may make the documents available for inspection and copying by mailing copies of the requested documents to the member by first-class mail within 10 days of receiving the request. To compensate the association for this task, it may bill the requesting member for its actual, reasonable cost for copying and mailing the requested documents. However, the association must inform the member of the amount of the copying and mailing cost before sending the requested documents.

The association may not withhold or redact (cross-out) information concerning the compensation paid to employees, vendors, or contractors. Compensation information for individual employees must be set forth by job classification or title, and not by the employees name, social security number, or other personal information. Obviously, this does not in any way infringe on the attorney-client privilege. Consider the following case.

Smith v. Laguna Sur Villas Community Association

79 Cal. App. 4th 639, 94 Cal. Rptr. 2d 321 (App. 4 Dist. 2000)
Edited Excerpts From the Opinion of Justice Crosby

FACTS AND ISSUES

The defendants brought a construction defect lawsuit involving a 253-unit condominium project in the Laguna Sur Development in the City of Laguna Nigel. The project was governed by the Laguna Sur Villas Community Association. Another group, the Laguna Sur Community Association, owned the development's open space. Both Associations jointly retained the law firm of Duke, Gerstel, Shearer, & Bretantd (Duke) to sue the developer. They split the legal fees and shared expenses.

The litigation proved to be more costly than anticipated and the fees exceeded $450,000. The Villas' board of directors adopted an emergency assessment of $2,000 per unit. The assessment was imposed without polling the members. The Villas' board thereafter recommended an additional special assessment of $4,000 per unit. This new assessment was ratified by a membership vote. Dissident residents sued the Villas' directors to recover the amount of the assessments. They demanded to review Duke's work product and legal bills. Duke objected on the grounds of attorney-client and work product privileges. The trial court found the special assessment was valid and the Villas held an attorney-client privilege. The dissident plaintiffs appealed.

(continued)

DECISION AND REASONS

Villas brought the construction defect litigation on its behalf. California law expressly permits a mutual benefit nonprofit corporation to "institute, defend, settle, or intervene in litigation. ...in its own name as the real party in interest and without joining with it the individual owners" in actions for damage to the common areas or for separate areas which must be repaired or maintained. Corporations have a separate legal identity and enjoy the benefit of the attorney/client privilege. Although plaintiffs, as condominium owners, were members of Villas, they were not individually named as plaintiffs in the construction defect litigation. Because they did not consult with or retain the Duke firm, they are not joint-clients with the Villas. The plaintiffs did not individually arrange to pay their proportionate fees of the Duke legal fees; instead, the fees were billed to and paid by Villas, which drew its funds from the member assessments. Such indirect payments do not suffice to create an attorney-client relationship between the plaintiffs and the Duke firm to give them access to the work product and legal bills.

Unlike directors, the residents owe no fiduciary duties to one another and may have been willing to waive or breach the attorney-client privilege for some reasons unrelated to the best interest of the Association. As Villas points out, "One can only imagine the sleepless nights an attorney and the Board of Directors may incur if privileged information is placed in the hands of hundreds of homeowners who may not all have the same goals in mind." With the privilege restricted to an Association's board of directors, this is one worry, at least, that their lawyers can put to rest.

The judgment, including the fee award to Villas as the prevailing party, is affirmed. Cost on appeal, including reasonable attorney fees to be assessed by the superior court, are awarded to Villas.

B. WITHHOLDING INFORMATION

The association may withhold or redact information from the accounting books and records and the minutes of proceedings for any of the following reasons:

1. The release of information has a reasonable chance of leading to identity theft. This means the unauthorized use of another person's personal identifying information to obtain credit, goods, services, money, or property.
2. The release of the information is reasonably likely to lead to fraud in connection with the association.
3. The information is privileged under law.

The accounting books and records, the minutes, and any information from them may not be sold, used for a commercial purpose, or used for any other purpose not reasonably related to the member's interest as a member. The association can file a lawsuit against any person who violates this rule for an injunction to stop the violation and for actual damages to the association caused by the violation. The association is entitled to recover reasonable costs and expenses, including reasonable attorney's fees, in a successful action to enforce the above mentioned rights. In the alternative, a member may bring an action to enforce the right to inspect and copy the accounting books and minutes.

If a court finds an association unreasonably withheld access, the court shall award the member reasonable costs and expenses, including attorney's fees, and may assess a civil penalty of up to $500 for each violation.

II. Right of Inspection Under Corporations Code

The Davis-Stirling Act also provides that members of the association have the right of access to association records in accordance with the California Corporations Code.

The members are given the same access to operating rules of the association that they have to the accounting books and records of the association. Most of the Corporations Code's provisions were somewhat duplicated in the Davis-Stirling Act (mentioned above).

A. REQUIRED RECORDS

Under the Corporations Code, the association is required to keep the following:

1. Adequate and correct books and records of account.
2. Minutes of the proceedings of its members, board, and committees of the board.
3. A record of its members, giving their names and addresses and the class and membership held by each.
4. Articles of incorporation and bylaws, as amended to date.

Minutes must be kept in written form. Other books and records must be kept either in written form or in any other form capable of being converted into written form. Notice that the books and records of account and the minutes of meetings were made available under the Davis-Stirling Act, but the above section also allows the members access to the membership list.

B. THE MEMBERSHIP LIST

1. Who Can Inspect?

Either a member or an authorized number of members (discussed later in the chapter) can inspect and copy the membership list. A member can:

1. Inspect and copy the record of all members' names, addresses, and voting rights, at reasonable times, upon five business days' prior written demand upon the association. The demand must state the purpose for which the inspection rights are requested; or
2. Obtain from the secretary of the association, upon written demand and payment of a reasonable charge, a list of the names, addresses and voting rights of those members entitled to vote for the election of directors. This demand must also state the purpose for which the list is requested. The association must make the list available for ten business days after the demand is received or after the date specified in the request as the date as of which the list is to be compiled, whichever is later.

2. Denying Inspection

This right is available to any member for a purpose reasonably related to the person's interest as a member. The inspection rights can also be exercised by an authorized member for a purpose reasonably related to a group of members' interest. The association may deny member access to the list for the following reasons:

1. Where it reasonably believes that the information will be used for another purpose; or
2. Within ten business days after receiving the demand, deliver to the person a written offer of an alternative method of achieving the purpose of the demand without providing access to or a copy of the membership list. Any rejection of the association's offer shall be in writing and must indicate the reasons the alternative proposed does not meet the proper purpose of the demand made by the member.

3. The Alternative Offer

Naturally, the association is concerned with, after providing a copy of the membership list, finding out the list was used for improper, undesirable, or unacceptable purposes toward some or all of the members listed. Because of this concern, the association is provided with the option of giving the member a written alternative offer for achieving the purpose stated in the member's demand without giving the member the membership list. The association has ten days to prepare this offer. For example, if the member wished to communicate with other members regarding a particular issue to be voted on at the annual membership meeting, the association might offer to mail the information to the other members, which should achieve the desired result without exposure of the membership list. Depending on the size of the association, the association might want reimbursement for the cost of mailing or duplication cost.

4. Litigation

In any lawsuit brought by a member, the court must enforce the rights of inspection of the membership list, unless the association proves:

1. that the member will allow the use of the information for purposes unrelated to the person's interest as a member; or
2. that the alternative method reasonably achieves the proper purpose set forth in the demand. Here, it is the association that has the burden of proof. In the alternative, the association can petition the superior court for a court order setting aside the demand of the member if it can meet this burden of proof.

The court may, in its discretion, order an alternative mechanism for achieving the proper purposes of the requesting parties, or impose just and proper conditions or limitations on the use of the membership list which reasonably assures compliance with the association's disclosure requirement. This can happen where such limitation or restriction is necessary to protect the rights of any member under the Constitution of the United States or the Constitution of the State of California. Such a protective order, insofar as possible, must provide an alternative mechanism by which the person seeking the inspection rights of the membership list may communicate with members for a purpose reasonably related to their interest as members. The court must also award reasonable cost and expenses, including reasonable attorney's fees, to requesting parties who successfully opposed any petition or application filed to block the inspection. Also, the corporation has the right to obtain damages for any misuse of the membership list or to obtain an injunction restraining misuse of the membership list. Once again, the corporation should be entitled to recover reasonable costs and expenses, as well as reasonable attorney's fees, included in its successful litigation.

5. The Member's Proper Purpose

Recall that a member's demand to inspect documents must state a reason that is reasonably related to the member's interest as a member of the association. Since the membership list is a corporate asset, it may not be disclosed to a member without board consent, if it is for a purpose not reasonably related to the member's interest as a member. Without the consent of the board of directors, a membership list or any part thereof may not be:

1. Used to solicit money or property unless such property would be used solely to solicit the vote of members in an election to be held by their corporation.
2. Used for any purpose which the user does not reasonably and in good faith believe will benefit the association.
3. Used for any commercial purpose or purpose in competition with the association.

4. Sold to or purchased by any person.

Any person who violates the above is liable for any damage such violation caused the association and must account for and pay to the association any profit derived as a result of the violation. Additionally, the court, in its discretion, may award exemplary damages for a fraudulent or malicious violation in the use of the membership list. The exemplary damages are in addition to an award to the association of reasonable cost and expenses, including reasonable attorney's fees, in connection with the litigation.

6. The "Authorized Number" of Members

Occasionally, the law bestows certain rights upon the members if the members constitute the "authorized number" of members. For example, inspection and copying the membership list may be exercised by:

1. Any member, for a purpose reasonably related to such person's interest as a member (covered above); or
2. The authorized number of members for a purpose reasonably related to the members' interest as members (covered now).

Most of the time, "authorized number" of members means five percent of the voting power of the membership.

In the alternative, however:

1. If the total number of votes entitled to be cast for a director is 1,000 or more, or less than 5,000, the authorized number shall be 2.5 % of the voting power, but not less than 50 members.
2. If the total number of votes entitled to be cast for a director is 5,000 or more, the authorized number shall be one-twentieth of one percent of the voting power, but not less than 125 members.

We have learned that if a member seeks the membership list and the association reasonably believes the information will be used for a purpose not reasonably related to the member's interest as a member or if it chooses to provide a reasonable alternative to the request, it may deny the member access to the list. This places the burden on the member to initiate a superior court action to gain access to the membership list.

However, where the association, in good faith, and with substantial basis, believes that the membership list demanded by the "authorized number" will be used for a purpose that is not reasonably related to the interest as members or provides a reasonable alternative offer to the membership, which is rejected, the association may petition the superior court for an order setting aside the demand. In this case, the initiation of the petition is made by the association. If the association fails to file a petition within the legal time limit, then the association must comply with the demand and the association is barred from any further legal action.

The association has ten business days after the demand is received to file its petition with the superior court or ten business days after the association receives a written rejection of its alternative, whichever is later.

The association may file a petition more than ten business days after the demand or rejection of the alternative, but only upon showing the delay was caused by excusable neglect. In no event, however, may any petition be considered if filed more than thirty days after the requesting parties' demand or rejection, whichever is later. Additionally, the association's petition must be accompanied by an application for a hearing on the petition. The court must set the hearing not more than twenty days from the filing of the petition. The court must also issue a protective order stopping production of the list demanded until the hearing is concluded.

The superior court must issue the final order setting aside the demand only if the association proves that:

1. there is a reasonable probability that the requesting parties will permit use of the membership list for a purpose unrelated to their interest as members; or
2. the method offered by the corporation is a reasonable alternative to achieve the proper purpose set forth in the demand.

The court, in its discretion, may order an alternative mechanism for achieving the proper purpose of the requesting parties, or impose just and proper conditions on the use of the membership list.

The court must award reasonable costs and expenses, including reasonable attorney's fees, to requesting parties who successfully oppose any petition or filed application. Further, if the association did not comply with time limits for the demand made by the "authorized number" or obtain a protective order from the court stopping production of the list, or a final order setting aside the demand for the list, the parties requesting the demand may petition the superior court for an order compelling the association to comply with the demand. No inquiry may be made in this proceeding into the use for which the "authorized number" seek the list. Basically, the association refused the demand and did nothing thereafter. If successful, the demanding parties shall be awarded reasonable costs and expenses, including reasonable attorney's fees.

C. INSPECTION OF ACCOUNTING RECORDS AND MINUTES

As mentioned, the accounting books and records and minutes of proceedings of members, the board, and committees of the board are also open to inspection upon the written demand to the association, by any member at any reasonable time, for a purpose reasonably related to such person's interest as a member.

Upon the association's refusal of a lawful demand of inspection of a membership list or the books and records of account, or minutes of proceedings, the court may enforce the demand or right of inspection with just and proper conditions. In the alternative, the court, for good cause shown, may appoint one or more competent inspectors or independent accountants to audit the financial statements and investigate the property, funds, and affairs of the corporation and to report in such manner as the court may direct. Additionally, all officers and agents of the corporation must produce, to the inspectors and accountants so appointed, all books and documents in their custody and power, under penalty for contempt of court. All expenses of investigations or audit shall be defrayed by the person demanding inspection, unless the court orders payment to be paid or shared by the corporation. Obviously, this allows the court to give access to more information than the production of the membership list, books of account, and minutes of proceedings would ever have allowed.

All expenses of the investigation or audit are paid by the applicant unless the court orders them to be paid by, or shared with, the association.

D. INSPECTION OF ARTICLES AND BYLAWS

The association (corporation) must keep at its principal office the current articles and bylaws which are open to inspection by the members at all reasonable times during office hours.

E. INSPECTION RIGHTS OF DIRECTORS

The law provides that every director shall have the absolute right, at any reasonable time, to inspect and copy all books, records, and documents of every kind and to inspect the physical properties of the association of which such person is a director. The director does not have to make the demand in writing, although a written demand is probably a good idea, and the director need not include a statement regarding the director's purpose for the inspection. Additionally, the director is not required to disclose how the inspection rights are being exercised for a purpose reasonably related to the director's interest as a member of the board of directors of the association. This certainly gives the appearance that the director has enormous power for inspecting documents which may contain information that could be used for the director's own personal benefit. Obviously, a board member wants to be careful not to breach the "fiduciary duty" that the director owes to the association. This duty generally means that the director places the interest of the association above any personal interest or, if not, may face legal liability. Is the director's "absolute right" of inspection always absolute? Consider the following case.

Chantiles v. Lake Forest II Master Homeowner's Association

37 Cal. App. 4th 914, 45 Cal. Rptr. 2nd 1(App. 4 Dist. 1995)
Edited Excerpts From the Opinion of Justice Wallin

FACTS AND ISSUES

Chantiles was elected a member of the board of directors of the Lake Forest II Master Homeowner's Association (Association). Voting was done by proxy ballot. The proxy ballots are mailed to each member. The ballot gives the members several options. He or she first designates a person as that member's voting proxy holder. If no person is named, by default, the chair of the Association's election committee is designated proxy holder. The proxy holder is authorized to cast the member's votes. The member may indicate on the ballot how those votes are to be cast, i.e., he or she may directly vote for the candidates listed on the ballot. If no direction is made, the proxy holder has discretion to cast the votes in whatever way he or she chooses. The member may indicate on the ballot that the proxy designation is solely for the purpose of achieving a quorum and no votes may be cast for any candidate.

Chantiles ran for a tenth term in 1992 and was re-elected, apparently as a member of a minority faction. Believing that he had been shorted by 800 to 1,300 proxy votes, which he presumably would have cast for other candidates from his faction, Chantiles demanded the Association allow him to inspect and copy all of the ballots cast in the 1992 annual election. Citing its concern for presuming the privacy of individual voting members, the Association refused.

Eventually, Chantiles filed a petition to compel the Association to permit the inspection and copying of the ballots under Corporations Code Section 8334 which gives directors of nonprofit corporations the right to inspect and copy corporate records. The Association argued that unfettered access to the ballots would violate its members' expectations that their votes were private. It submitted declarations from 120 members who stated they believed their ballots to have been secret when they cast them, and they did not wish the ballots to be divulged to Chantiles.

The trial court ordered the Association to make available to Chantiles' attorney all ballots cast in the 1992 election. Council for the Association, or another representative, could be present during the inspection. Chantiles' attorney could take notes while inspecting, but those notes could not contain the names of the voting members, only the names of their designated proxy holders. He could not disclose to anyone the names of the persons who voted, or how any individual voted, without further order of the court. Rather than conduct the inspection authorized by the court, Chantiles filed an appeal.

(continued)

DECISION AND REASONS

Chantiles argues that Section 8334 confirms an absolute right to inspect and copy all corporate books, records, and property, and the ballots or documents to which the director has a right of access. Chantiles begins by assuming that the homeowner members of the Association have no legitimate expectation of privacy in their voting decisions because the voting is done by proxy. A proxy, by its very nature, connotes revealing to another person one's voting choice.

Furthermore, the homeowners must certainly realize that their votes would be revealed to the inspector of elections, who is charged with tabulating proxy votes, again negating any expectation of privacy.

Article I, Section 1 of the California Constitution provides: "All people are by nature free and independent and have inalienable rights. Among these are enjoying and defending life and liberty, acquiring, possessing, and protecting property, and pursuing and obtaining safety, happiness, and privacy."

We reject Chantiles' assertion that there is no expectation of privacy in a written proxy ballot. In choosing any of the proxy options, a member has an expectation of privacy. The trial court correctly concluded that homeowner's association voting was a class of information in which members have a reasonable expectation of privacy. The Association submitted declarations of 120 members stating they believed their ballots were private and they did not want them to be divulged. As the trial court stated, "Homeowner Association elections may raise emotions as high or higher than those involved in political elections. Under these circumstances, a degree of privacy afforded to the electors in such elections appears to be desirable. Neighbors may cease to speak to each other if it became publicly known that certain votes were cast. Voters may be intimidated to vote in a certain way should their ballots be subject to public scrutiny. Under these circumstances, the expectation of privacy to which many of the voters certified in their declarations gains credibility."

We hold that the Homeowner's Association members have a constitutional privacy right in their voting decisions, even when conducted by proxy ballot. A homeowner's association director's statutory right to inspect the records of an association must be balanced against this privacy right. Chantiles wanted to compare the votes he believed he had been promised to the votes he actually received. We can conceive of no greater violation of the privacy of the Association's members. Any member may well have told Chantiles he would receive his or her proxy votes, but actually cast his or her votes otherwise. To now give Chantiles personal access to the names of those voting and how they voted certainly violates well-established social norms.

The trial court offered a reasonable resolution. Chantiles refused this resolution, which strongly suggests his motive was not simply to check the math, but to find out how his neighbors actually voted. The trial court's order was appropriate.

III. Changing the Governing Documents

A. INTRODUCTION

In Hubie Highlands, the development construction is complete and all units have been sold to buyers for several years. Usually, after all the units have been sold, the association members, the association board of directors, and the association attorneys will review the governing documents and "clean house" by revising, changing, deleting, and amending the existing documents to eliminate provisions that were weighted toward control of the association by the developer. These extensive changes, as well as problems with construction defects involving the developer, are not discussed herein. What is discussed is the normal day-to-day operation of Hubie Highlands when it may become necessary to amend the governing documents to reflect a recent change in legislation, to conform the documents to a recent court decision, or to reflect a change in circumstance, prevailing attitude, or philosophy of the members. Governing documents from the past may not accurately reflect current lifestyles. Additionally, a change may be necessary because of current financial issues plaguing an association.

B. CHANGING THE ARTICLES AND BYLAWS

Since the Hubie Highlands Homeowner's Association is a corporation created under state law, state law will govern the changes to the articles and bylaws. The following represents California's approach.

1. Changing the Articles of Incorporation

An association (corporation) may amend its articles, so long as its articles, as amended, contain only such provisions as it would be lawful to insert in the original articles filed at the same time as the amendment.

Therefore, it doesn't matter whether the provision contained in the amendment was permissible at the time of the original incorporation, it is only important whether it is lawful at the time the amendment is filed. Amendments to the articles may be adopted, if approved by the board of directors (a majority of a quorum), approved by the members (a majority of a quorum), and approved by such other person or persons as required by the articles. In determining the amount of approval necessary for an amendment, if the articles require a larger proportion of the directors, members, or votes than required under the law, the provision in the existing articles controls.

a. Officer's Certificate

Upon adoption of an amendment, the association shall file a Certificate of Amendment with the Secretary of State, which shall consist of an officer's certificate stating:

1. The wording of the amendment;
2. The amendment has been approved by the board;
3. If the amendment is one for which the approval of the members or the approval of 100% of the voting power is required, that the amendment was approved by the required vote of the members;
4. If the amendment is one which may be adopted with approval by the board alone, a statement of the facts entitling the board alone to adopt the amendment; and
5. If the amendment is one for which the approval of a person other than the incorporators, directors or members is required, that the approval of such person or persons has been obtained.

b. Certificate of Amendment

The Certificate of Amendment must establish the wording of the amendment or amended articles by one or more of the following means:

1. By stating that the article shall be amended to read as herein set forth in full.
2. By stating that any provision of the articles, which shall be identified by the numerical or other designation given it in the articles or by stating the words thereof, shall be stricken from the articles or shall be amended to read as set forth in the certificate.
3. By stating that the provision set forth herein shall be added to the articles.

Upon the filing of the certificate of amendment, the articles are amended in accordance with the certificate and a copy of the certificate, certified by the Secretary of State, is evidence of the performance of the conditions necessary to adopt the amendment.

Sometimes the development contains different classes of memberships. The development might have some residential members and some retail or commercial members. The development might also have different classes of memberships if it contains a different composition of residences. For example, there may be large houses on large acreages and a series of condominiums. Any amendment must be approved by a majority vote of a quorum of the members of any class, or a larger number if required in the articles, whether or not the class is entitled to vote thereon if the amendment would:

1. materially and adversely affect the rights, privileges, preferences, restrictions, or conditions of that class as to voting, dissolution, redemption, or transfer in a manner different than such action affects another class;
2. materially and adversely affect such class as to voting, dissolution, redemption, or transfer by changing the rights, privileges, preferences, restrictions, or conditions of another class;
3. increase or decrease the number of memberships authorized for such class or increase the number of memberships authorized for another class; or
4. authorize a new class of memberships; or effect an exchange, reclassification or cancellation of all or part of the memberships of such class.

A "quorum" consists of 50% of the owners who own no more than two separate interests in a development.

These rules make sure that, if the amendment is going to affect the members of a class, the members of the class are entitled to vote on the amendment, with passage being a minimum of the majority of a quorum, or a higher percentage as might be provided in the articles, even if the articles do not entitle that class to a vote.

Generally speaking, a class of members has the right to approve, by a specific number of votes, any amendments that may significantly affect their rights or standing as members.

2. Changing the Bylaws

The board of directors may adopt, amend, or repeal bylaws, unless the action would do any of the following:

1. Materially and adversely affect the rights of members as to voting, dissolution, redemption, or transfer;
2. Increase or decrease the number of members authorized in total or for any class;
3. Effect and exchange, reclassify, or cancel all or part of the memberships;
4. Authorize a new class of memberships;
5. Change the number of directors on the board of directors;
6. Go against the articles or bylaws which have restricted or eliminated the power of the board to adopt, amend, or repeal any or all bylaws;
7. Extend the term of a director beyond that for which the director was elected or increasing the terms of directors;

8. Allow the board of directors to fill a vacancy on the board by reason of the removal of a director (unless the articles or bylaws approved by the members allow the board to do so);
9. Change a provision in the bylaws requiring a greater vote than required by law;
10. Increase the percentage of members necessary to constitute a quorum at a membership meeting;
11. Appeal, restrict, create or expand proxy rights; or
12. Repeal or amend a provision authorizing cumulative voting.

In summary, other than the items listed above, the board may amend the bylaws. Most of the above, however, will require membership approval.

As sort of an oddball provision in the law, you, as the manager, should look for a bylaw that provides for the repeal or amendment of bylaws that may occur only with the approval, in writing, of a specified person or persons other than the board members. Here is a bylaw provision that will need immediate amendment if the person whose approval is required is deceased.

Once the bylaws are amended, it is not necessary to file the amendment with the Secretary of State, with whom the original bylaws were not filed. California law provides that, if for any reason it is impractical or unduly difficult for a corporation to call or conduct a meeting of its members or directors, or otherwise obtain their consent, then the superior court may order such a meeting be called, or that a written ballot or other form of obtaining a vote of the members be authorized in a manner the court finds fair and equitable under the circumstances. The court has considerable latitude on: 1) how to give notice to those entitled to notice; 2) dispensing with requirements related to holding and voting at meetings, requirements of quorums, or percentages of votes needed for approval; or 3) limiting the subject matter of the meetings in order to enable the corporation to continue managing its affairs without further resort to court interference.

C. AMENDING THE DECLARATION

Recall that the declaration is the recorded document that contains the legal description of the common interest development, which of the four types of common interest development it is, the name of the association, the restrictions on the use or enjoyment of any portion of the development that are intended to be enforced as equitable servitude, and any other matters deemed appropriate. Over time, and for a variety of reasons, it may be necessary to amend the declaration. There are several ways to accomplish this.

1. California Civil Code Section 1355(a)

The declaration may be amended pursuant to the governing documents or Civil Code Section 1355(a). To be an effective amendment, the following is required:

1. The approval of the percentage of owners required by the governing documents;
2. The fact has been certified in writing, executed and acknowledged by the officer designated in the declaration or by the association for that purpose, or, if no one is designated, by the president of the association; and
3. The writing has been recorded in each county in which a portion of the common interest development is located.

2. As Provided in the Declaration

Amendments and supplements must be recorded in the county where the development is located.

Amendment of the declaration can be accomplished by following the provisions in the declaration that provide for amendments or changes in the document itself. It is most likely that the amendment process in the declaration will refer to votes by the "owners." This is common because the declaration will usually refer to the owners of the separate interest in the development. Of particular concern will be an amendment provision in the declaration that requires approval of the members.

The term "members" is used most commonly when dealing with an unincorporated association and the requirements under California law dealing with the voting of members in a nonprofit mutual benefit corporation.

The voting by members is more regulated than the voting by owners. As noted above, the amendment must be in recordable form and recorded in each county where the development is located.

FOR EXAMPLE

Amendments.

This declaration may be amended only by the affirmative vote or written consent of not less than 75% of the voting power of each class of members. Any supplement or amendment to this declaration must be signed by at least two officers of the association, indicating that the requisite approvals have been obtained, and such amendment or supplement must be recorded in the office of the county auditor.

3. Amendment By Court Order

If the declaration requires the owners to have more than 50% of the votes in favor of an amendment, the association, or any owner of a separate interest, may petition the superior court of the county in which the development is located for an order reducing the percentage of affirmative votes necessary to approve the amendment. This is useful if it is not possible, for whatever reason, to get the necessary votes. The petition must describe the effort that has been made to solicit approval of the association members in the manner provided by the declaration, the number of affirmative and negative votes actually received, the number or percentage of affirmative votes required to effect the amendment in accordance with the declaration, and other matters the petitioner considers relevant to the court's determination. The petition must also contain, as attached exhibits, copies of the following:

1. The governing document;
2. A complete text of the amendment;
3. Copies of any notice and solicitation materials utilized in the solicitation of owner approvals;
4. A short explanation of the reason for the amendment; and
5. Any other documentation relevant to the court's determination.

If more than 50% of the owners' votes are required to pass an amendment, a petition to reduce that percentage may be filed with the county superior court.

Undoubtedly, the petition would be drafted by an attorney. However, it is important to know the process involved in this rather complex method of amending a declaration. Once the petition is filed, the court must set the matter for a hearing and issue an order setting forth the manner in which notice of the hearing shall be given.

The court may, but is not required to, grant a petition if it finds all of the following:

1. The petitioner has given not less than 15 days' written notice of the court hearing to all members of the association, and any lender or government that is entitled to notice under the terms of the declaration.
2. Voting on the proposed amendment was conducted in accordance with the provisions of the governing documents.
3. A reasonably diligent effort was made to permit all eligible members to vote on the proposed amendment.
4. Owners having more than 50% of the votes, voted in favor of the amendment.

5. The amendment is reasonable.
6. The amendment will not do any of the following:
   a. Change provisions in the declaration requiring approval of owners having more than 50% of the votes unless owners having more than 50% of the votes approved the amendment.
   b. Eliminate any special rights, preferences, or privileges designated in the declaration as to belonging to the declarant, without the consent of the declarant.
   c. Impair the security interest of a mortgagee or beneficiary of a deed of trust without the approval of the percentage of the mortgagees and beneficiaries specified in the declaration, if the declaration so requires.

If the court makes the above findings, any order issued is a valid amendment of the declaration approved on the basis of the affirmative votes actually received during the balloting. Or the order may dispense with any requirement relating to quorums or to the number or percentage of votes needed for approval of the amendment that would otherwise exist under the governing documents.

An amendment to a declaration is not effective until the court order and amendment is recorded in the counties where the development is located.

Once recorded, the amendment is effective. Finally, within a reasonable time after the amendment is recorded, the association must mail a copy of the amendment to each member of the association, together with the statement that it has been recorded.

The purpose of the court proceeding is to acquire an amendment to a declaration which is critical to the functioning of the association, but under the rules of the declaration, the required percentage of votes for the amendment is not possible. For example, suppose that the number of owners who cast ballots during the initial vote on the amendment was 59%, with the remaining owners voting against the amendment change. If the declaration requires 75% of the owners voting for a change in the declaration, the proposed amendment to the declaration failed to receive approval. However, owners with more than 50% of the votes in the association (59%) voted for the amendment to the declaration. This information may allow the court to make an appropriate adjustment in the percentage required for approval of an amendment to the declaration.

Greenback Townhomes Homeowner's Association v. Rizan

166 Cal. App. 3d 843, 212 Cal. Rptr. 678 (App. 3 Dist. 1985)
Edited Excerpts From the Opinion of Justice Sims

FACTS AND ISSUES:

Greenback Townhomes Homeowner's Association (Association) is a nonprofit, mutual benefit corporation. It owns and maintains the common area facilities within a planned development known as Greenback Townhomes.

The Association enforces certain covenants, conditions, and restrictions which regulate its affairs. Rizan is a homeowner in Greenback Townhomes. The Association's board of directors decided to revise its bylaws and restrictions to conform to recent changes in state law. These revisions required a vote of 75% of all members. After the Association totaled up the ballot vote, 121 members of the Association's total membership of 155 voted, with 94 members in favor of adopting the revisions and 27 members opposed.

Subsequently, a petition was brought in the name of the Association, by its president, in superior court under the California Corporations Code section which provides that "If for any reason it is impractical or possible for any corporation to call or conduct a meeting of its members, delegates, or directors, or otherwise obtain their consent in the manner prescribed by its articles or bylaws, or this part, then the superior court of the proper county, upon a petition of a director, officer, delegate or member, may order that such a meeting be called, or that a written ballot or other form of obtaining the vote of members, delegates, or directors be authorized in such a manner as a court finds fair and equitable under the circumstances."

The court ordered a modification of the voting requirement so as to allow approval of amendments by a written ballot of 75% of those voting, so long as the total ballots cast represent at least the majority of the total membership. All members of the Association, including Rizan, received notice that the petition had been brought. No one opposed the petition before it was granted. Rizan filed a motion to vacate the order granting the petition on the basis that the trial court had no subject matter jurisdiction. The motion was denied and Rizan appealed.

DECISION AND REASONS:

Rizan asserts that, because the Association was the only party petitioning the court, and because no director, officer, delegate, or member was a party, no proper party brought the action and the court had no jurisdiction to grant relief. The Association, as the corporation affected by the petition, was the real party in interest and the proper party to petition the court. Since the petition was signed by an officer of the Association (its president), the petition satisfied the provision of the law. The court, therefore, had jurisdiction to adjudicate the petition and issue its order. Consequently, Rizan's motion to set aside the judgment was properly denied.

You, the association manager, may be involved in preparing and signing a sworn statement that the numerous requirements listed above have been accomplished in order for the courts to consider granting the petition. For example, the superior court judge doesn't know if the notices of the court hearing were given not less than 15 days before the hearing, or whether balloting on the amendment was conducted in accordance with the governing documents. It then becomes important for you, the association manager, to assist in the success of the petition request.

4. Deletion of Developer Provisions

Regardless of what it says in the governing documents, the board of directors may adopt amendments deleting any provision which is unequivocally designed and intended, or which, by its nature, can only have been designed and intended to facilitate the developer in completing the construction or marketing of the development. The board can only do this if the developer has completed construction of the development, has terminated construction activities, and has terminated marketing activities regarding separate interests within the development.

The provisions which may be deleted by the board are limited to those which provide for access by the developer over or across the common area for the purposes of completion of construction of the development, and erection, construction, or maintenance of structures, or other facilities, designed to complete construction or marketing of separate interests.

At least 30 days prior to the board taking this action, it must mail to all owners of a separate interest, by first-class mail:

1. a copy of all amendments to the governing documents proposed; and
2. a notice of the time, date, and place that the board will consider adoption of the amendments.

Deleting developer provisions can only be done at a meeting which is open to all owners of separate interests within the development, and those owners must be given an opportunity to make comments.

Additionally, all deliberations of the board regarding the amendments must be conducted in an open meeting.

Finally, the board of directors may not amend the governing documents without the approval of the owners. This must be a majority of the votes at a meeting or election of the association constituting a quorum (meaning more than 50% of the owners who own no more than two separate interests in the development). In other words, the board cannot delete the developer provisions from the declaration by amendment without first obtaining the approval of the owners.

5. Amending the Declaration With No Provision to Do So

A declaration may be amended at any time, unless it provides, in express terms, that it cannot be amended, in whole or part, at all times during its existence.

The amendment is only effective after:

1. the proposed amendment has been distributed to all of the owners of separate interests in the development by first-class mail, postage prepaid, or personal delivery, not less than 15 days, and not more than 60 days, prior to any approval being solicited;
2. the approval of owners representing more than 50%, or any higher required percentage, of the separate interest in the development has been given, and that fact has been certified in writing, executed, and acknowledged by an officer of the association; and
3. the amendment has been recorded in each county in which a portion of the common interest development is located. Further, a copy of the adopted amendment must be distributed, by first-class mail, postage prepaid or personal delivery, to all of the owners of separate interest immediately upon its recordation.

6. Extending the Term of the Declaration

In California, the legislature found that the deed restrictions of some common interest developments do not provide a means for the property owners to extend the term of declaration. Therefore, it is in the public interest to provide a vehicle for extending the term of a declaration if the owners, having more than 50% of the votes in the association, choose to do so.

A declaration which states a termination date, but contains no provision for extension of that date, may be extended by the approval of the owners having more than 50% of the votes in the association or any greater percentage specified in the declaration for an amendment thereto.

If necessary, the term may be extended by petition and court order, as mentioned above, regarding amendments to the declaration. No single extension of the terms of the declaration shall exceed the initial term of the declaration or 20 years, whichever is less. However, more than one extension may occur under this provision of the law.

An extension becomes effective upon its recording in the county where the development is located.

AN EXAMPLE - Section 17.

The covenants, conditions, and restrictions of this declaration shall run with and bind the property, and shall ensure to the benefit of, and be enforceable by, the association and the owners of any land subject to this declaration, their respective legal representatives, heirs, successive owners, and assigns, for a term of 25 years from the date this declaration is recorded, after which time such covenants, conditions, restrictions, reservation of easements, and equitable servitudes shall automatically be extended, for successive periods of ten years, unless an amendment to this declaration has been recorded, agreeing to change or terminate said covenants and restrictions in whole or in part.

D. ADOPTING AND CHANGING OPERATING RULES

1. Introduction

The California legislature found it necessary to assist common interest developments with the passing of association rules by the board of directors and with rule changes. An ***OPERATING RULE*** *is a regulation adopted by the board of directors that applies generally to management and operation of the development for the conduct of the business and affairs of the association.* A ***RULE CHANGE*** *means the adoption, amendment, or repeal of an operating rule by the board of directors.*

2. Valid Rules

An operating rule is valid and enforceable only if all of the following requirements are satisfied:

1. The rule is in writing;
2. The rule is within the authority of the board of directors conferred by law, or by the declaration, articles of incorporation, or association, or bylaws of the association;
3. The rule is not inconsistent with governing law, and the declaration, articles, and bylaws of the association;
4. The rule is adopted, amended, or repealed in good faith and in substantial compliance with the requirements of this legislation; and
5. The rule is reasonable.

3. Notice of Rule Change

The board of directors must provide written notice of a proposed rule change to the members at least 30 days before making it.

The notice must include the text of the proposed change and a description of the purpose and effect of the change. Notices are not required if the board determines that an immediate rule change is necessary to address an imminent threat to public health or safety, or imminent risk of substantial economic loss to the association.

A decision on the proposed rule change must be made at a meeting of the board of directors, after consideration of any comments made by association members. As soon as possible after making a rule change, but not more than 15 days after making the change, the board must deliver a notice of the change to each association member. If the change was an emergency change the notice shall include the text of the rule change, a description of the purpose and effect of the rule change, and the date the rule change expires.

If the board determines that an immediate rule change is required, it may make an emergency rule change and no notice is required.

An emergency rule change is effective for 120 days, unless it provides for a shorter effective period. An emergency rule change may not be readopted.

4. Reversing a Rule Change

Members of the association, owning 5% or more of the separate interests, may call a special meeting of the members to reverse a rule change.

This is done by delivering a written request to the president or secretary of the board. The written request may not be delivered more than 30 days after the members are notified of the rule change. The board must now deliver the notice of the meeting to the association's members and hold the meeting in conformity with California Corporations Law. The notice of the special meeting must be given at least 10 days, and not more than 90 days, before the special meeting. The notice must include the date, time, place, and specific subject matter of the special meeting and state that no other business will be done at the meeting. The board has to set the meeting date not less than 35 days, nor more than 90 days, after receiving the request for the special meeting. If the board does not send out the notice of the meeting within 20 days of receiving the request the members may send out the notice.

Members are notified of a rule change by delivery of notice of the rule change, or enforcement of the rule, whichever is sooner.

A demand to inspect and copy the names and addresses of voting members to collect signatures needed to call a special meeting is considered a purpose reasonably related to the interest of the members of the association. Therefore, the association may not deny such an inspection.

The rule change is reversed by an affirmative vote of a majority of the votes present and voting at a duly held meeting at which a quorum is present, or by a greater vote if required by the declaration or bylaws. In the alternative, distribution and voting by written ballot is permissible. Unless provided otherwise in the declaration or bylaws, a member may cast one vote per separate interest owned.

If a rule change is reversed, it may not be readopted for one year after the date of the meeting reversing the rule.

Nothing, however, precludes the board from adopting a different rule on the same subject as the rule change that has been reversed. As soon as possible after the close of voting, but not more than 15 days after the close, the board must provide notice of the results to every association member. Notice must be delivered according to the section "Delivery of a Document," which follows shortly. However, there can be no reversal of an emergency rule change.

5. Limitations on Rule Changes and Their Reversal

The notice of rule change and reversing a rule change topics discussed above only apply to operating rules that relate to one or more of the following subjects:

1. Use of the common area or of an exclusive use common area.
2. Use of a separate interest, including any aesthetic or architectural standards that govern alteration of a separate interest.
3. Member discipline, including any schedule of monetary penalties for violation of the governing documents and any procedure for the imposition of penalties.
4. Any standards for delinquent assessment payment plans.
5. Any procedures adopted by the association for resolution of assessment disputes.

The conditions regulating the notice and reversal of rule changes do not apply to the following actions by the board:

1. A decision regarding maintenance of the common area.
2. A decision on a specific matter that is not intended to apply generally.
3. A decision setting the amount of a regular or special assessment.
4. A rule change that is required by law, if the board of directors has no discretion as to the substantive effect of the rule change.
5. Issuance of a document that merely repeats existing law or the governing documents.

E. DELIVERY OF A DOCUMENT

On occasion it is necessary for the association or manager to deliver a document to the members. This document could consist of a notice for a special meeting of the members of the association, a notice of a change in the parking regulations or swimming pool hours, or any common type of notice given by associations. Is it sufficient for you, as the association manager, to post the notice on the association membership bulletin board or must it be mailed to each member? There are, in fact, several alternative ways the association may use to deliver a document when made applicable or required by provisions of the Davis-Stirling Act, such as the previous section on rule changes. The following is a list of alternative choices:

1. Personal delivery of the document to a member.
2. First-class mail, postage pre-paid, addressed to a member at the address last shown on the books of the association or otherwise provided by the member.

Delivery is deemed to be complete on deposit into the United States mail.

What this means is that the delivery of the document is completed at the time of mailing, regardless of the fact that the member may not receive it for several days, or that it may not be received at all.

3. E-mail, fax, or other electronic means, if the recipient has agreed to that method of delivery.

If the association chooses to deliver a document by electronic means, it is a prerequisite to get the consent of the recipient/member agreeing to such a delivery.

Conceivably, this permission could be acquired at the time a member purchases an interest in the community. Obviously, a prudent manager would get the member to agree to the method of delivery in writing and have it signed by the member. Additionally, if the document is delivered by electronic means, delivery is completed at the time of transmission.

4. By publication in a periodical that is circulated primarily to members of the association. This alternative means appears to suggest that publishing the document in the membership newsletter would be sufficient. The question is how many times must it be published in the newsletter? The answer depends on how frequently the newsletter is published. Generally, the more infrequent the publication, the more likely that one notice would be sufficient. If the newsletter is published regularly, say, for example, each week, then it may need to be published in more than one issue. Also, the frequency of publication depends on the urgency behind the notice. It should be anticipated, however, that the notice will be deemed to have been delivered once the periodical has been delivered to the member.

5. Using a method of delivery provided in a recorded provision in the governing documents. In other words, if the recorded declaration contains a provision on how documents are to be delivered, that is an acceptable way of delivering them. The recorded provision, for example, may allow the posting of a notice on a bulletin board as a means to notify the membership. A question may arise, however, if it is known that only a small percentage of the members actually read the bulletin board.
6. If the association broadcasts television programming for the purpose of distributing information to its members regarding association business, the document may be included in the programming. Here the question is at what time, and how often during the program, must the notification be made to say "the document has been delivered."
7. Any method of delivery, other than the above, is permissible, provided that the recipient has agreed to that method of delivery. This is a method association managers may consider using. Once again, even if the membership agreed to receive notice documents by posting the notices on the manager's bulletin board, it must be determined whether or not it is a sufficient method of notification.
8. Additionally, a document may be included in, or delivered with, a billing statement, newsletter, or other documentation that is delivered by one of the methods provided above.

An unrecorded provision in the governing documents (such as a bylaw), which provides for a particular method of delivery, does not constitute agreement by a member of the association to that method of delivery.

IV. Manager's Journal

Since you, as the manager, will, in all likelihood, be the person who receives a demand for inspection rights or is asked how to change governing documents, the following summaries are useful.

A. INSPECTION RIGHTS SUMMARY

1. Under the Davis-Stirling Act, the association must make the accounting books and records, and the minutes, available for inspection and copying at the business office within the development. If there is no office, and an agreement cannot be reached on a location, or if the member requests copies, the association can mail copies to the member within 10 days of receiving the request. The member may pay reasonable cost for copying and mailing, if informed of the amount in advance.
2. Members are entitled to compensation information on contracts, including employees, but only by job classification or title.

3. The association may withhold or redact information if disclosure is reasonably likely to lead to identity theft, fraud with the association, or is privileged.
4. Under the Corporations Code, members can inspect and copy the membership list upon a five business days' prior written demand. The demand must include the reason for the inspection. Or, upon written demand and payment of reasonable charge, the secretary of the association can send the list.
5. Inspection may be denied if it is reasonably believed that the information will be used for a purpose other than indicated. Within 10 days after receiving the demand, the association may propose a written alternative method to achieve the purpose of the demand. A member's rejection of the alternative must be in writing and include the reasons why.
6. If a demand is refused by the association, a member can bring a lawsuit for inspection. The court has discretion to order an alternative procedure for achieving the purpose.
7. A member cannot use membership to solicit money or property, or any other purpose not in good faith with the association, any commercial purpose or for the purpose of competition with the association, or sell the list. A member may be liable for damages in court.
8. If an "authorized number" of members seeks inspection and copying, and if the association believes the purpose is not reasonably related to membership interest, or provides an alternative which is rejected, the association may petition the court for an order denying the demand. If the association doesn't bring the lawsuit within 10 business days after the demand, the association, absent an extension of time, may lose its ability to object.
9. Accounting records and minutes are also available for inspection, upon written demand, for a proper purpose. The member pays the cost for inspection or investigation. Association denial can lead to court action to compel inspection.
10. The articles of incorporation and the bylaws are available for inspection at the association's principle place of business.
11. The directors have an absolute right, at any reasonable time, to inspect and copy association documents, but must remember the fiduciary duty to the association.

B. CHANGING DOCUMENTS SUMMARY

1. Changing the articles can occur with approval of a majority of a quorum of the board or the members, or any other person required, or by a larger amount if the articles so require.
2. A certificate of amendment must be filed with the Secretary of State. It must include an officer's certificate stating: the wording of the amendment; it was approved by the requisite number of board members and association members; if it was only approved by the board, a statement indicating how that was possible; and the approval of any other person required.

3. The certificate of amendment can state any one of the following: 1) The articles are amended to read as follows; 2) The specific part of the articles by designation or exact words that are stricken from the articles or amended to read as follows; or 3) By stating the provision wording that is being added to the articles.
4. Except for the items listed in the chapter, the board of directors may adopt, amend, or repeal bylaws as it deems necessary. The exceptions listed in the chapter normally require membership approval.
5. Amending the declaration can be accomplished as provided by state law, as provided by the declaration itself, or by court order.
6. The board of directors may adopt amendments to the declaration which delete provisions designed and intended to facilitate the developer in construction or marketing of the development.
7. State law allows the declaration to be amended when it fails to include a provision. Therefore, a notice by mail or personal delivery must be given to each owner not less than 15 days, nor more than 60 days, prior to approval being solicited. The amendment is effective with the approval of a majority of the owners, or a higher percentage, as required in the declaration. The change is then mailed to the owners.
8. The law provides for an extension of the term of the declaration if the declaration does not provide thereof. Approval requires more than 50% of the owners voting in favor thereof, or a greater percentage specified in the declaration. A single extension cannot exceed the initial term of the declaration, or twenty years, whichever is less. More than one extension can occur.

C. ADOPTING AND CHANGING RULES SUMMARY

1. A valid rule must be: 1) in writing; 2) within board's authority; 3) consistent with governing documents and law; 4) acted on in good faith and legally; and 5) reasonable.
2. Only certain subject areas for rules must follow these notice requirements.
3. Notice of proposed adoption or change must be: 1) in writing; 2) given to members at least 30 days before action; and 3) an emergency rule exception.
4. After action: 1) notice of change to members within 15 days of action, including emergency rule; 2) emergency rule maximum 120 days; and 3) cannot be readopted.
5. Reverse rule action: needs 5% + of separate interest; call special meeting; must be less than 30 days from action or enforcement; by majority of quorum; board has maximum of 15 days from vote to notify members.
6. All above notices must be delivered by specific requirements applicable to: personal delivery, mail, electronic means, publication, recorded governing documents, broadcast, members agreed to, or included with other documents delivered as previously listed.

V. CHAPTER SUMMARY

The Davis-Stirling Common Interest Development Act provides for inspection rights for members. It requires the association to make the accounting books and records, and the minutes or proceedings of the association, available for inspection and copying by a member of the association or his or her designated representative. If the court finds the association unreasonably withheld access, the court shall award the member reasonable cost and expenses, including attorney's fees, and may assess a civil penalty of up to $500 for each violation.

Under the Davis-Stirling Act, members of the association have the right to access association records in accordance with the California Corporations Code. This right is available to any member for a purpose reasonably related to the person's interest as a member. It can be denied where it reasonably believes the information will be used for another purpose, or within ten business days after receiving the demand, deliver notice to the association that they have an alternative method of achieving the purpose of the demand.

The member's proper purpose for demanding to inspect documents must not be to solicit money or property unless it is used solely to solicit the vote of members in an election to be held by their corporation. It also cannot be used for any purpose which the user does not reasonably and in good faith believe will benefit the association, used for any commercial purpose or purpose in competition with the association, nor sold to or purchased by any person.

If denied access to the membership list, the member may initiate a superior court action to gain access to the list. The court may order an alternative mechanism for achieving the proper purpose of the requesting parties, or impose just and proper conditions on the use of the membership list.

All the expenses of the investigation or audit are paid by the applicant unless the court orders them to be paid by or shared with the association.

An association (corporation) may amend its articles, so long as they contain only such provisions as it would be lawful to insert in the original articles filed at the same time as the amendment. When an amendment is adopted, the association must file a certificate of amendment with the Secretary of State. Generally speaking, a class of members has the right to approve, by a specific number of votes, any amendments that may significantly affect their rights or standing as members.

Under the proper circumstances, a board of directors may adopt, amend, or repeal bylaws. The declaration of a CID may be amended pursuant to the Civil Code, as provided in the declaration, or by court order. An amendment to the declaration is not effective until the court order and amendment have been recorded in the county where the development is located.

Provisions in the governing documents for access by the developer over or across the common area for purpose of completion of construction, erection, or maintenance may be deleted only if the developer has completed construction.

This must be done at a meeting which is open to all owners of separate interests within the development and the owners must be given an opportunity to make comments. Amendments cannot be amended if the declaration provides in express terms that they cannot be amended in whole or part at all times during their existence.

The terms of a declaration may be extended, effective upon its recording in the county where the development is located.

An operating rule is a regulation adopted by the board of directors that applies generally to management and operation of the development for the conduct of the business and affairs of the association. A rule change means the adoption, amendment, or repeal of an operating rule by the board of directors. The board of directors must provide written notice of a proposed rule change to the members at least 30 days before making it. Rules may be changed in an emergency with no notice required.

Members of the association, owning 5% or more of the separate interests, may call a special meeting of the members to reverse a rule change. Members are notified of a rule change by delivery of notice of the rule change, or enforcement of the rule, whichever is sooner. If a rule change is reversed, it may not be readopted for one year after the date of the meeting reversing the rule.

Delivery of a document is deemed to be complete on deposit into the United States mail. To deliver a document by e-mail, fax, or other electronic means, the recipient has to agree to that method of delivery. An unrecorded provision in the governing documents, which provides for a particular method of delivery, does not constitute agreement by a member to that method of delivery.

VI. REVIEW QUESTIONS

1. If the association does not have a business office within the development to make the documents available for inspection by the member, then:

   a. the member is required to inspect and copy the documents at a place designated by the association.
   b. the member is unable to inspect and copy the documents.
   c. the member and the association will try and reach an agreement for a place for inspection and copying.
   d. none of the above.

2. The association may withhold information from inspection by a member if:
   a. the information is privileged under law.
   b. the release of the information is reasonably likely to lead to fraud in connection with the association.
   c. the release of information is reasonably likely to lead to identity theft.
   d. all of the above.

3. The right of inspection of the association membership list by a member is:
   a. not available to a member unless the president and secretary of the association agree to it.
   b. available to any member for a purpose reasonably related to the interest of the member.
   c. available to any member for any purpose.
   d. never allowed.

4. Within how many days after receiving a demand for inspection can the association deliver a written offer of an alternative method of achieving the purpose of the demand without providing access or a copy of the membership list?
   a. 5 business days
   b. 10 business days
   c. 15 business days
   d. None of the above.

5. Regarding the inspection of the documents under the Corporations Code, if a member rejects the association's alternative offer:
   a. the rejection may be verbal or in writing.
   b. the rejection must be in writing and need contain nothing more than a rejection of the alternative offer.
   c. the rejection must be in writing and must indicate the reasons the alternative proposed does not meet the proper purpose of the demand.
   d. none of the above.

6. Which of the following is a reason for considering changing the governing documents?
   a. To reflect a change in the philosophy of the membership.
   b. To update the documents to reflect a recent change in state law.
   c. To accommodate a recent change in the financial condition of the association.
   d. All of the above answers are possible reasons.

7. Upon the adoption of an amendment changing the Articles of Incorporation, the association must file a certificate of amendment with:

a. the County Recorder's office.
b. the Secretary of State's office.
c. the State Attorney General's office.
d. all of the above.

8. The board of directors may amend a bylaw of the association to do which of the following?

a. Lengthen the terms the directors hold office.
b. Change the number of directors on the board of directors.
c. Increase the number of board of director meetings.
d. None of the above.

9. When the board of directors has successfully amended the bylaws, that amendment:

a. must be filed with the Secretary of State.
b. must be recorded in the county recorder of deeds office.
c. must be filed with the county clerk.
d. none of the above are correct answers.

10. Which of the following is a method allowed to amend the declaration?

a. The declaration may be amended pursuant to the provisions regarding amendment contained in the declaration.
b. The declaration may be amended by following the provisions of state law which provide for amendments.
c. The declaration may be amended by petitioning the court for a procedure established by the court for an amendment.
d. All of the above are correct procedures to amend the declaration.

ANSWERS: 1. c; 2. d; 3. b; 4. b; 5. c; 6. d; 7. b; 8. c; 9. d; 10. d

NEW LOFTS
FOR SALE
(213) 741-2124
grandlofts.com
PCL
CONSTRUCTION LEAD
ONE WAY
POST
NO
BILL
POST
NO
BILL
WARNING
SIDEWALK CLOSED

CHAPTER 9

Financial Management of an HOA

I. Financial Disclosure Requirements of the Association

A. INTRODUCTION

The members of the Hubie Highlands Homeowner's Association need to be kept informed of the financial condition of their association. Since the association has the responsibility to repair and maintain the common areas, the association needs the funds to do so. These funds are generally received through monthly assessments whereby each member of the association pays money to the association for its expenses. Without disclosure statements given to the membership by the association, the members will have no specific information regarding the income and expenditures of their homeowner's (community) association. The governing documents, legislation, or government regulations may require the type of disclosure to be given to the membership.

Chapter 9

CHAPTER OUTLINE

AN EXAMPLE - California Civil Code Section 1365

Unless the governing documents impose more stringent standards, the association shall prepare and distribute to all of its members the following documents:

1. A pro forma operating budget.
2. A review of the financial statement of the association, if required.
3. A statement describing the association's policies and practices in enforcing lien rights for assessment defaults.
4. A summary of the association's property, general liability, and earthquake and flood and fidelity insurance policies.

The California requirements are comprehensive and the listed documents could be a valuable resource for any HOA in any state. Notice the listed documents are the minimum disclosure documents every homeowner (community) association must prepare.

B. PREPARATION

Who is going to prepare and distribute the financial papers of an HOA? It could be done by the corporation treasurer, a finance committee appointed by the board of directors, the accountant for the corporation, the community association manager, or some combination of these individuals. The documents are important because they give the members an opportunity to assess the financial condition of the association, anticipate the magnitude of future expenses, and offer the opportunity to see how the association is doing, compared with previously distributed financial papers.

The California approach establishes four important documents related to the financial management of the homeowner (community) association. The first one is a ***PRO FORMA OPERATING BUDGET***, *which gives the HOA board an idea of current estimates for future expenditures*. The second document is the ***CURRENT FINANCIAL STATEMENT*** *of the HOA, showing assets and liabilities the association currently has and year-to-date revenues and expenses*. Consideration of this document can help the board plan for the future. The third document is the HOA's ***POLICIES AND PROCEDURES FOR COLLECTING DELINQUENT ASSESSMENTS***. *This document is a basic reminder to the members of the association of what can happen if they do not pay*

their assessments when due. Assessments are discussed in Chapter 10. The fourth document, involving the **insurance policies of the HOA**, is useful to members in analyzing whether the association has enough insurance to protect itself from serious financial difficulty. Insurance is discussed in Chapter 12.

C. THE HOA PRO FORMA OPERATING BUDGET

1. Requirements

*"**BUDGETING** is the process of identifying, gathering, summarizing, and communicating financial and non-financial information about an organization's future activities.* The budgeting process provides managers with the opportunity to carefully match the goals of the organization with the resources necessary to accomplish those goals." (*Financial & Managerial Accounting*, Needles, Powers, Mills, and Anderson, 5th Edition, Houghton & Mifflin, 1999, page 903.) The budget is the physical document that is the action plan for meeting the organizational goals. What does the term "pro forma" add to this definition? The term ***PRO FORMA STATEMENT*** *is defined as "A carefully formulated expression of predicted results."* (*An Introduction To Financial Accounting*, Horngren, Sundem, Elliott 7th edition Prentice Hall, 1999 page G7.) Therefore, we are going to use the budget to predict the financial condition of the association for a given time in the future. According to California law (and good financial policy for any state), this budget must contain all of the following.

a. HOA Revenue and Expense Estimates

The homeowner association must estimate revenue and expenses on an accrual basis. *"In **ACCRUAL BASIS ACCOUNTING**, an accountant records the impact of a business event as it occurs. When the business performs a service, makes a sale, or incurs an expense, the accountant enters the transaction onto the books, whether or not cash has been received or paid."* (*Accounting*, Horngren, Harrison, 4th edition, 1999, Prentice Hall page 92.) Therefore, the budget will list estimated revenue and expense entries showing when they are expected.

b. HOA Reserve Summary

A summary of the homeowner association's reserves is based upon the most recent review or study, which must be printed in bold faced type and include:

1. The current estimated repair costs, estimated remaining life, and estimated useful life of each major component.
2. As of the end of the fiscal year for which the study is prepared:
   a. The current estimate of the amount of cash revenues necessary to repair, replace, restore, or maintain the major components.
   b. The current amount of accumulated cash reserves actually set aside to repair, replace, restore, or maintain the major components.

c. If applicable, the amount of funds received from either a compensatory damage award or settlement for injuries to property arising out of construction or design defects and the expenditure for the cost of repairing those defects.

3. A percentage of the current amount of accumulated cash reserves set aside for major components compared to the current estimate of the amount of cash reserves necessary for those components.

c. HOA Special Assessments

A statement from the board of directors as to whether it has determined or anticipates a special assessment will be required to maintain major components or to provide reserves therefore.

d. HOA Reserve Calculations

A general statement of the procedures used for the calculation and establishment of those reserves for major components.

The point of reserve calculations is to predict how much money must be collected in advance to pay for the replacement of major items when needed.

2. Distribution

A copy of the HOA's operating budget must be distributed annually, not less than 45 days, nor more than 60 days, prior to the beginning of the association's fiscal year.

The ***FISCAL YEAR*** *is the chosen or established year for accounting purposes. If the year ends on December 31, it would be commonly referred to as a* ***CALENDAR YEAR***. The fiscal year can start and stop on the dates chosen by the association and it will always start or stop on those specific days. For example, the fiscal year can end on June 30 if that's what the board chose or that is what was required in the bylaws of the corporation. The subsequent fiscal year would start on July 1.

In lieu of the distribution of the pro forma operating budget, the board of directors may elect to distribute a summary of this budget to all of its members with a written notice that the entire budget is in the association's business office or at another location within the development, and that copies will be provided upon request at the expense of the homeowner association. If a member requests that a copy of the budget be mailed to the member, the association must, at its expense, copy and mail the copy to the member by first-class mail and it must be delivered within five days. This written notice to the membership regarding acquiring a copy of the budget must be in at least 10-point bold-faced type on the front page of the summary of the budget. It might be advisable for you, as the association manager, to consider this "in lieu of" approach because:

1. It should save time and money.
2. Too much information to the membership may invite too many questions. Most members will be happy with a summary.

The four items in the pro forma operating budget required in California consist of excellent financial documents that could easily be used in any area of the country to assist the board of directors and the members with financial planning for the common interest development.

As an association manager, you need to keep current on financial disclosures required by your state law or required by the governing documents.

Additional consideration will now be given to each of the four elements.

II. Estimated Revenue and Expenses on an Accrual Basis

Accrual accounting puts the revenue (earned) and expenses (incurred) into the proper month in which they occurred, not in the month they were received or paid.

Since most common interest developments are either planned developments or condominiums, coverage will be limited to these. Additionally, regarding condominiums, the discussion will be limited to the condominium development of Hubie Highlands. Obviously, this eliminates high-rise condominiums which would have some particular and specific financial requirements different than those of Hubie Highlands. In the preparation of estimated revenue and expenses, it is probably best to start with a list of all expenses which might be incurred by the community association. Expenses are directly related to the duty of the association to maintain the common areas. It would be wise to check governing documents to make sure the exact nature of the common area is known, as well as any specific duties of the association with regard to it. Since the estimated expenses are for the coming fiscal year, it would probably be wise to list the expenses as either fixed expenses or variable expenses.

A. HOA OPERATING EXPENSES

Operating expenses may consist of the following for Hubie Highlands Homeowner's Association.

1. Insurance

The homeowner (community) association needs to cover the common areas with fire and liability insurance.

The cost of this insurance is normally fixed by the insurance company for the policy period, which is usually annually. In a planned development, the fire insurance, as well as liability insurance, is usually, although not always, the responsibility of the lot owner. The association has the burden of covering the common areas with fire and liability insurance. Fire coverage in a condominium development is more complex.

Typically, the association obtains a blanket fire insurance policy that covers the common areas as well as the separate interests of all the owners.

This coverage is largely driven by the lenders financing condominium purchases who need insurance to cover the loan. Obviously, the members, as well as any perspective buyers, should check the blanket fire insurance policy to make sure they are comfortable with the coverage and that it would satisfy a lender for the purchase or refinancing of a unit.

Fire insurance on the personal property inside the unit is the responsibility of the unit owner.

A policy of liability insurance will cover the homeowner association's obligations for personal injury claims occurring in the common areas. Also, the association may choose to insure individual board members against liability for mistakes with **errors and omissions insurance**. Adequate insurance is certainly an incentive for individuals to run for a position on the board of directors. **Director liability** was previously discussed in the section on the business judgment rule.

Workmen's compensation insurance and fidelity insurance might be necessary if the HOA hires employees and some of those employees have access to association funds.

Because of the board's fiduciary obligation to the association, it may be necessary for the board to periodically search for proposals from different insurance carriers for good value coverage, although it is to be assumed that, once the association has a good relationship with an insurance carrier or broker, it may not be interested in changing coverage. Sometimes this good working relationship, particularly for the payment of claims, may override a slightly cheaper policy. Additionally, since most insurance claims have a **deductible**, the homeowner (community) association should make sure the amount of the deductible is set aside in a specific fund. **Insurance coverage for flood and or earthquake may or may not be appropriate under the circumstances.**

2. Real Property Taxes

Depending on the state and county where the property is located, real property taxes will be a fixed amount for the next year. If real property taxes are appropriate, how those taxes are assessed depends on local law. The common area real property taxes in a planned development might be assessed at a total value of the project, which is then split amongst the individual lot owners so that lot owners pay a property tax on their lot as well as their proportion of the common area.

In some areas, the assessment may be on the value of the common area and, if the HOA holds title to that property, the property tax bill is an obligation of the association. These same problems occur with assessing the common areas and the units in condominiums. Certainly, the history of the payment of taxes in the development or an inquiry at the assessor's office will explain to you, as the association manager, how the property taxes appropriate to the association are determined. The tax amount then becomes an expense in the budget.

3. Labor Expense

The wages, salaries, and payroll taxes of employees of the association could be an estimated expense. If the association is employing an independent contractor to run the physical affairs of the development and/or the financial affairs of the development, that fee for the next year will be a known expense.

4. License Fees

Local authorities may require payment of a fee for a **license permit** for items like inspection of the swimming pool/spa, restrooms, cooking areas, elevators, and motor vehicles.

5. Corporation Fees

If the homeowner (community) association is incorporated, it may have to pay an annual fee and/or file a periodic tax return with the appropriate state and local government authorities.

6. Electricity

The expense for electricity will vary depending on the amount of usage and the appropriate rate at the time of usage.

One way to estimate future electrical expenses would be to look at the past expenses.

Past performance can show the amount of electricity used as well as the most recent cost for the electricity. The electricity provider can give current rate information and perhaps an idea of rates for the budget period.

It may be necessary to break down the electricity consumption of the association into specific areas rather than one bill for the common area of the development. In order to do this, an inventory of electrical equipment should be conducted. This inventory is probably a good idea in any event since replacement of the electrical equipment will probably fall under the reserve inventory. In Hubie Highlands, the homeowner association's electrical expenses would include the air conditioning system for the office, the lights in the common area of the development such as walkways, parking lots, tennis courts, swimming pool area, as well as decorative lights. The circulating pump on the swimming pool and Jacuzzi are also electrical expenses.

Normally, in a planned development, each lot owner (and in a condominium each unit owner) will have a separate meter for individual electrical consumption.

It might be appropriate for the board to have an energy audit conducted so that the board knows an approximate amount for operating each cost center with electricity. For example, the air conditioning unit at the association office might be consuming a tremendous amount of the electricity each month. Therefore, with this knowledge, the board might consider saving electrical expenses by replacing the existing unit with a more energy efficient unit. The energy audit will consider the horsepower of electrical motors and the operating hours for each, along with the current charge for electricity, to provide a more accurate estimate of the sources of electrical consumption. Lighting will also be analyzed.

7. Gas Consumption for Pool Area

Once again, past history can be a reasonable predictor of gas expenses for the current budget, assuming the amount of consumption and the rate stay about the same. In Hubie Highlands, the major HOA expense for gas is heating water for the swimming pool and spa. The utility company or an energy audit can provide a formula for approximating the gas consumption to keep the pool heated. This is particularly important if the association does not know how much of the gas bill goes for heating the water. Obviously, this expense will vary depending on the climate of the area where the pool is located, the desired temperature of the water, whether the pool is covered when it is not being used, whether the pool is kept at a constant temperature or the water is re-heated to the desired temperature after it has dropped during a non-use period, and whether the pool is drained during portions of the budget year. The same analysis could be used for the spa/Jacuzzi.

8. Hot Water

In Hubie Highlands, hot water is used in the kitchen area of the recreational hall, the washing machine in the Homeowner's Association office, and the restroom facilities in the development. Once again, an energy audit can estimate the cost associated with each area of gas consumption for hot water. In Hubie Highlands, each unit owner has a separate hot water heater which is individually metered. Sometimes, however, hot water is supplied by an association to the individual unit and it becomes a large association expense with complex issues involving how much each owner should pay.

9. Heating Air

In Hubie Highlands, gas is used to heat the recreational building and the Association office. An energy audit can estimate the cost for heating the space in those facilities considering the size of the heating unit, and the estimated hours of operation of the unit based on the desired temperature. Obviously, the cost will be related to the climate and weather conditions, as well as the degree of insulation in the structure. In Hubie Highlands, the clothes dryer in the office area is also heated by gas.

10. Waste Disposal

Garbage disposal may be supplied by the association through a contract with an independent contractor or supplied by the local municipality. In planned developments, garbage is usually picked up by the can, and is either billed to the individual lot owner as part of the utility service for that lot, or is paid for under a blanket contract for garbage pickup by the association. In condominiums, garbage pickup is typically in large bins rather than individual cans. It would be more common for the association to pay for the garbage service rather than each unit owner. The charge may vary with the quantity and frequency of pickup. With regard to the common areas, the association will have either individual can pickup or bin pickup. Additionally, there may be imposed special local requirements for recycling which may be an additional cost to the association.

11. Water

The Hubie Highlands Homeowner's Association typically uses water for irrigation purposes for the common areas consisting of lawn, shrubbery, plants, and trees. Additionally, water is supplied for a swimming pool and spa. Also included is the restroom and sink areas for the office facility and recreational building. The cost for water consumption may be either a **fixed amount** (by the month), or **variable amount** (by quantity used), or a combination of both (fixed rate up to a certain quantity and variable for the excess).

12. Sewage

In a planned development, the lot owner is generally responsible for the sewage charge as with the other previously mentioned utilities. Sometimes the charge is a flat rate per lot or a fee determined by the quantity of the water consumed. In a condominium, if individual units are on separate water meters, each unit could be billed for sewage according to a water use formula. Or each unit could be billed a flat rate for sewage or perhaps a charge per occupant. If the units are not on a separate water meter, then, if the HOA is supplying the water, the association may be charged for the sewage disposal and will have to include a portion in each member's assessment.

13. Maintenance

Keeping the Hubie Highlands property in a clean and attractive condition is beneficial to the members because it helps each member's unit maintain or increase its value.

a. Landscape

The budget expense for maintenance may be determined by looking at the history of how maintenance has been provided in the development. If the homeowner's association has full or part-time employees who provide maintenance services, the cost of each person's services can be determined by anticipating the number of hours that person will work multiplied by the wage and adding associated employment expenses.

On the other hand, the association may be paying for landscape maintenance by hiring an independent contractor. If the contract is a yearly contract or a monthly contract, that amount can be included in the budget as a fixed expense. This is an area which is very price competitive and it might be in the best interest of the board to compare the cost of reputable landscape maintenance services on an annual basis in order to get the best bargain for the membership. This annual review is a project that either you, the association manager, or a member committee could complete.

Usually, members provide a great source of feedback on how the landscape maintenance personnel are completing their assigned tasks. Typically, landscape maintenance is divided between care for trees and shrubs, care for the grass, and care for flower beds. Additional expenses will be incurred for replacement or new planting of flowers, shrubs, and grass. The board can decide which of these items is the most costly and adjust the estimated expenses accordingly.

If the homeowner (community) association is using its own employees for landscape maintenance, estimated expenses will also have to cover supplies for that service. These supplies can consist of fertilizer, weed killers, hoses, sprinklers, trimming equipment, mowers, sprinkler repairs, and possibly some way to move equipment, debris, and waste. There may be a further cost for debris disposal.

It may be necessary to explore whether there are any environmentally sensitive areas on the property which require specific preservation or maintenance.

An additional area of maintenance would involve the sweeping of sidewalks, streets, tennis courts, parking lots, etc. In a large planned development, an independent contractor with a street sweeper might be employed to periodically clean the streets and parking lots. The same may be true of a condominium complex depending on the extent of the streets. Sometimes maintenance personnel will blow the sidewalks clear of debris. Significant additional maintenance costs can be associated with the running of a golf course by the association and, to a lesser extent, jogging, equestrian trails, picnic areas, or playgrounds.

b. Pool Maintenance

Hubie Highlands, and many other common interest developments (CIDs), have swimming pools and spas. These require regular maintenance and typically an outside pool service will provide that maintenance. This is another item of expense for the HOA budget which might be a fixed (monthly) or variable (per visit) amount.

c. Janitorial

This is an additional maintenance expense for keeping the HOA manager's office facility and the recreational area cleaned. This could be a job responsibility for a person working there which would be included in the wage, salary, or payroll tax budget. On the other hand, this expense could be incurred by hiring an independent outside custodial service to periodically clean the premises. This amount could also be a fixed expense or a variable expense.

d. Tennis Court

For the Hubie Highlands' tennis court to be useful for the members it must be swept clean of debris. Once again, this may be within the job description of an employee of the HOA, handled by an outside independent contractor, or handled by the members who play tennis on a voluntary or as-needed basis.

e. Pest Control

Pest control is a bigger problem for condominium HOAs than for planned development HOAs.

In planned developments, each lot owner is generally responsible for pest control. Pest control in the common areas of a planned development, as well as in condominiums, is an expense for the association. Since the HOA is responsible for the control and maintenance of the common areas, it is important that periodic inspections be conducted to look for and prevent termite infestation. A periodic pest control service can also handle problems with ants, spiders and other insects. This service can be a particular benefit in condominiums where the common area plays an important part of the members' enjoyment of hallways, walkways, areas immediately surrounding decks and patios, garages, or carports. Once again, pest control could be a fixed and/or variable amount.

f. Window Service

The homeowner (community) association may retain a window service to periodically clean the inside and outside windows of property on the common area. In a condominium, it may be the association's obligation to clean the outside surfaces of the unit windows.

g. Elevators

Although Hubie Highlands does not have elevators, elevators are typically maintained under a long-term service contract provided by the manufacturer, installer, or an independent elevator service provider. Additionally, state or local law may require periodic elevator inspections which may have a cost attached for a fee or license.

h. Development Security

Expenses associated with security could consist of maintaining perimeter fencing or walls, the wages and expenses incurred in hiring and providing entry gate security, and having a regularly scheduled security patrol service provided by an independent contractor. Security expenses may also include maintaining any motorized security gates, padlocks and chains, intercom systems, closed-circuit surveillance systems, alarms, etc.

i. Regular Repairs

This variable expense needs to cover a variety of (hopefully) anticipated expenses for items such as service contracts for maintaining the heating and air conditioning systems under the responsibility of the association. In Hubie Highlands, this would involve the association manager's office and the

recreational building. Depending on the type of construction for condominiums, it may be that the association owns and must maintain a central heating and air conditioning system for the individual units. Typical minor repairs for common areas include:

1. Broken glass, light bulb replacement, roof patches or fallen tree removal.
2. Maintenance of office equipment, telephone charges, postage charges.
3. Expenses for office supplies such as computer paper, Internet service provider, and copy machine.
4. Graffiti removal and vandalism repairs.
5. Common parking area repairs such as garage doors, openers, etc.
6. Any other of the dozens of unanticipated things that will break, need fixing, or replacement.

j. Snow Removal

In certain areas, snow removal will be a problem. This expense can, and usually is, handled by an independent contractor for the association. Occasionally, the association will use its own employee and/or equipment for the removal.

14. Professional Services

Expenses here include the usual and customary expenses for an outside accounting or bookkeeping service handling the homeowner association's books and records, unless the association management provides this service. An additional cost may be a periodic compilation, review, or audit by a certified public accountant. An estimate for legal services can be added on as an expense. If the financial services for the association and the management services are handled by independent contractors, those expenses will be listed. If the association handles disputes with members by using alternative dispute resolution procedures any necessary expenses for a mediator or arbitrator can be added on as an expense.

15. Fire Prevention

Fire prevention expenses for an HOA include the costs for maintaining extinguishers and alarms.

16. Contingency Expense

Sometimes the budget will include a dollar amount for a contingency fund established for unanticipated expenses which occur during the budget year. No one likes budget surprises. This could cover an unanticipated expense for removal of hazardous waste, problems with an Americans With Disability access cost, or unanticipated professional fees.

B. IMPROVEMENT EXPENSES

Unlike the typical operating expenses listed above, improvement expenses are not required to keep the association functional. ***IMPROVEMENT EXPENSES** are for new items which will enhance the living environment and increase the value of the units.* However, these items are generally discretionary expenses, that is, they are not required, but would be nice to have. Possible examples could be:

1. a new van for transporting members;
2. adding a sauna and steam bath to the pool area;
3. adding a workout room to the recreation center; and
4. purchasing new playground equipment.

Since improvement items tend to be motivated by special interest groups, they can be controversial and will probably become a priority issue for the membership.

Should the HOA expand the playground (younger family members) or purchase another shuttle van (older members) becomes the priority question if the association cannot afford both. Here, it becomes obvious that a budget is a tool for managing the desires of the association members.

III. Summary of the HOA's Reserves

Because the homeowner's association, through its board of directors, has the legal obligation to repair and maintain the common areas, the board needs the funds to accomplish this task. Members of the association must understand that maintaining the common areas as well as the repair, replacement, and upgrading of components within the common area benefit the homeowners by providing an attractive and functional place to live. Additionally, good maintenance will help increase property values for the separate interest of the members.

The legal definition for **reserve accounts** can have two meanings. The first one is monies that the homeowner (community) association's board of directors has identified for use to defray the future repair or replacement of, or additions to, those major components which the association is obligated to maintain. Therefore, the objective of a reserve is to set aside enough funds in advance so that when a major component needs to be replaced, the funds will be there. These reserve funds are estimates based on assumptions about the HOA's current maintenance and repair program and the expenses needed for items in the program.

The second meaning of reserve accounts refers to funds received and not yet expended from a damage award or supplement to the homeowner (community) association for any injuries or damage arising from construction or design defects. These funds have to

be separately itemized from the usual reserve account funds dealing with major components mentioned above.

Recall that the operating expenses previously mentioned are funded through regular (monthly) assessments paid by individual members. Reserve expenses are paid for through a replacement reserve account which has been established and also usually funded as a part of the regular member assessment. ***RESERVE EXPENSES*** *deal with replacement of major components and* ***OPERATING EXPENSES*** *deal with the normal day-to-day operation of the association.* The association is, therefore, responsible for maintenance, both short- and long-term, and the replacement or upgrading of common area major components as those components end their useful lives. The Hubie Highlands Homeowner's Association board of directors has planned for replacement well in advance. To prepare the summary of the association's reserves, it must be based upon the most recent review or study of reserve requirements.

> *A "reserve study" is an important planning document which will help the board in preparing for the financial longevity and success of the development.*

In California, the board has to conduct a reasonably competent and diligent visual inspection of the accessible areas of the major components which the association is obligated to repair, replace, restore, or maintain as a part of a study of the reserve account requirements.

> *The board must conduct an inspection of the major components at least once every three years and has the option of doing it more frequently.*

The inspection is not required if the homeowner association does not have a common area or if the current replacement value of the major components is less than one half of the gross budget of the association, excluding the association's reserve account for that period.

Obviously, a reserve study cannot be prepared without an adequate and thorough study of the major components which fall under the obligation of the board. The board must review the study annually and must consider and implement necessary adjustments to the reserve accounts as a result of that review. The required reserve study must include at least the following:

1. Identification of the major components which the HOA is obligated to repair, replace, restore, or maintain which, as of the date of the study, have a **remaining useful life of less than 30 years**.
2. Identification of the probable remaining useful life of the major components as of the date of the study.

3. An estimate of the cost of repair, replacement, restoration, or maintenance of the major components during and at the end of their useful life.
4. An estimate of the total annual contribution necessary to defray the cost to repair, replace, restore, or maintain the major components during and at the end of their useful life after subtracting total reserve funds as of the date of the study. In order to provide a summary of the association's reserves, it is necessary to have a reserve study.

How to Prepare an HOA Reserve Study

The first step in preparing your reserve study is to do a complete major component analysis. The steps for the major component analysis include the following:

1. Inventory the major components that have a remaining useful life of less than 30 years.
2. Estimate the remaining useful life of the inventoried major components.
3. Prepare an estimate of the cost of repair, replacement, restoration, or maintenance of the major components during and at the end of their useful life.
4. Determine annual contribution necessary to accomplish 3 above.

A. CONDUCTING THE MAJOR COMPONENT ANALYSIS

The HOA board of directors will meet to develop a plan for conducting the analysis of the major components. The first issue will be deciding which components to include in the study and which components to exclude. In a planned development, individual lot owners must maintain their property according to the governing documents, most particularly the declaration. Exclusive use common areas are the responsibility of owners, while maintaining the components of the common areas is a responsibility of the association. However, for the reserve study, only "major" components with a remaining life of less than 30 years are included. With no legal definition of what is a major component, the board must use its own insight or rely on experts to determine what is a major component and what is not. The inventory of major component items should remain fairly constant during each budget year.

The condition of the major component, its remaining useful life, and the cost to replace it will change annually. Additionally, any new major components added will require a new and separate listing.

1. Who Will Do the Study?

The board must develop a plan to determine which items are the major components, analyze the current condition of each inventoried item, make a determination of its remaining useful life, and then estimate the amounts required as a reserve for each item.

In a small common interest development, the board may want to conduct the survey itself. Perhaps there are board members or other members of the association that have expertise in specific areas required in the study and are willing to participate.

The larger the common interest development, the more complex the survey will be and the board will probably be less interested in preparing the survey itself.

The fiduciary obligation of the board to do what is in the best interest of the association may make the board members uncomfortable with personal preparation of the reserve study. Typically, the reserve study will require expertise beyond the capacity of the members of the association board. The board may consider getting advice about each major component from an expert in the use of that component. For example, a heating and air conditioning specialist might be retained to analyze the current condition, remaining life, and estimate a reserve for that particular major component. A swimming pool contractor, a tennis court specialist, or a paving contractor could all provide useful data for the reserve study. In the alternative, if the development has contracted with an outside service provider for financial services, the provider may have the expertise to prepare the reserve survey or recommend someone who can.

It is important for board members to remember that they are entitled to rely on information, opinions, and reports prepared by attorneys, independent accountants, or other persons as to matters which the director of the board believes to be within such person's professional or expert competence.

This shows reasonableness and is a way of maintaining protection from claims by members that there was a breach of the fiduciary obligation of the board member to the association. For this protection to exist, the director must believe the subject matter is within the provider's professional or expert competence. Therefore, board members are probably on notice to inquire as to the person's competence. This will involve a check into the background of a prospective provider with regard to education, experience, references, and industry association credentials.

The board must make a confident decision as to what is a major component and what is not.

It may not be as simple as a light bulb versus an air conditioning system. One issue would be whether major components are exclusively mechanical in nature. Are the row of palm trees along the entrance way, or the metal windmill that is the showpiece of the front entrance to the development, or the large mosaic tile fountain with its twenty-seven koi fish in front of the office considered to be major components?

Everything that is listed in the declaration as a maintenance responsibility of the association is not going to be considered a major component for the reserve study.

If the association has the responsibility for maintenance and repair of the exclusive use common areas, such as decks, patios, and balconies, these items should be included in a list of major components. The board should make a list of the items not included as major items for the reserve study with the reason why they are not included and any supporting documentation for that decision. These remaining items will be inventoried as line items on the reserve study. The reasoning behind listing or not listing a component as "major" might be as simple as listing items which cost over a certain amount, for example $500, to replace. Or the board might determine an item is major if it has an estimated remaining life longer than a certain period of time; for example, longer than three years. Or the board could consider the combination of both time and money. For example, an item is a major component if it has a remaining life of longer than four years and would cost more than $600 to replace. Once again, problems can be minimized by hiring a company that specializes in reserve studies.

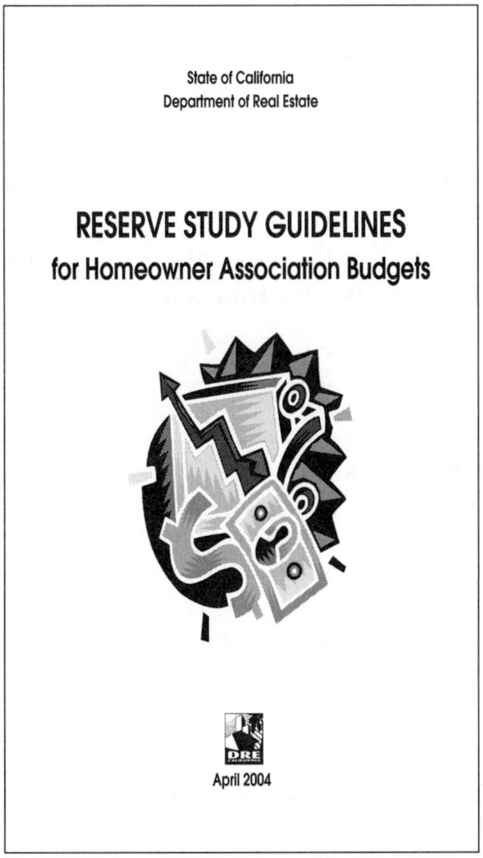
State of California
Department of Real Estate

RESERVE STUDY GUIDELINES
for Homeowner Association Budgets

April 2004

The State of California Department of Real Estate has prepared a helpful publication to assist in preparing reserve studies. It is called *Reserve Study Guidelines for Homeowner Association Budgets*. It contains two appendices which provide an excellent check list approach for what are commonly considered major components and major components which are frequently overlooked. This publication also provides a useful "Interview Guide for Physical Analyst Preparers" and an "Interview Guide for Funding Analyst Preparers."

Once the major components have been identified, it is also necessary to give a specific description of each item, as well as the quantities. It is necessary, for example, to compute the square footage for parking lots, roadways, roofs, and walls. Linear footage is necessary to measure fences and some types of decking. It is also important to remember that there are incidental items that would be necessary in replacement of the obvious item. For example, when replacing a wood fence, not only do you need the fence posts, braces, and the "fencing," but you also need nails or screws, cement, paint or stain, and hinges and latches for any gates. The description of the inventory items should also include their grade or quality. For example, the fence might be redwood or Douglas fir, the screws to hold the fencing together might be regular or rust resistance, and the stain might be a long-lasting stain or a lesser quality.

B. THE REMAINING (USEFUL) LIFE OF THE MAJOR COMPONENT

Having determined the exact nature of each major component, it is now time to determine the remaining life of each item. Usually the first step is to determine the entire useful life of the item by finding the date it was constructed or installed. Next, past records of maintenance and repair, if available, for each item as well as a current inspection of the item will help determine if the useful life of the item will be as anticipated.

If there are no records of past maintenance or that maintenance has been sub-standard or deficient, the useful life of the component will be shorter than if proper maintenance had been provided.

Sometimes, the manufacturer's warranty for a component indicates its useful life. However, the warranty usually expires well before the useful life of the component since the manufacturer doesn't want to be responsible for the cost of repairing or replacing an item in its final years of service. Additionally, the following websites may be helpful.

www.marshallswift.com **(Marshall & Swift)**
www.saylor.com **(Saylor Publications, Inc.)**
www.dodgeconstruction.com **(McGraw Hill Construction Dodge)**
www.rsmeans.com **(RSMeans)**
www.dre.ca.gov/pdf_docs/re8.pdf
(DRE - California - Operating Costs Manual For Homeowner Associations)

Determining the remaining useful life of an item or major component can sometimes be a difficult task, even for an experienced appraiser.

In using any guides for estimating useful life, it is important to consider unique characteristics of the particular location of the common interest development, particularly the weather.

Once the ***REMAINING LIFE**, which is the anticipated number of years the major component will continue to exist and serve its purpose,* has been determined the next step is to determine the cost of replacement for that item.

C. DETERMINING REPLACEMENT COSTS

The replacement cost can be determined by a board doing its own reserve survey, by contacting manufacturers, suppliers, repair, or service shops, or contracting licensed contractors to obtain replacement cost estimates. Additional costs to be considered would be disposal costs, removal costs, as well as installation costs and any costs incurred in a maintenance service contract or extended warranty. Once again, the board needs to make sure that it is receiving the opinion of an "expert" by checking the qualifications of the cost preparer. Additionally, if the board is using any of the above reference manuals for cost information, the board needs to note the year the cost was determined. Obviously, the older the cost guideline in a manual, the less accurate it would be in today's marketplace. Additionally, the board needs to consider the possibility of replacing the item with something different than the existing one. Perhaps it will be necessary to determine the replacement cost of a more efficient unit, or perhaps a higher quality, or even lower quality major component. For example, replacing copper tubing with plastic tubing may save the association money. Finally, the board might consider not replacing the major component at all once its useful life has expired. Justification for this decision needs to be in the reserve survey.

Additionally, the survey must include an estimate of the cost of repair, replacement, restoration, or maintenance of each major component not only at the end of its useful life but during its useful life. That would mean that the survey must include the replacement cost for the component in the given budget year as well as maintenance cost during the current budget year and through the life expectancy of the component.

Maintenance for non-major components is usually an annual expense item which is normally found in the estimate of revenue and expenses previously discussed.

Finally, replacement is not the only option for an item which has lost its useful life. Repair or restoration is also a cost that should be considered.

D. ACQUIRING RESERVE FUNDS (Contributions)

A reserve survey must contain an estimate of the total annual contribution necessary to defray the cost to replace major components at the end of their useful life after subtracting the total reserve funds on hand as of the date of the study.

The members of the association need to pay an annual dollar amount for maintenance of the common areas (operating expenses) as well as an annual dollar amount for the reserve for replacement of the major components. The board can decide how to raise the needed reserve funds.

Reserve funds can be raised by regular assessments each year and/or raised by special assessments.

The object is for the board to establish a reserve account so that the current amount in the account equals the estimated value of the wear and tear on all major components at the current point in time. In other words, if 60% of the life of the major component has expired, there should be at least 60% of the replacement cost for that component in a reserve account. At that current point in time, 60% of the life of the component has expired due to ordinary wear and tear.

When the board considers the reserve survey, it will be looking at the current replacement cost for each major component. The current cost will then be divided by the useful life of the component to determine the cost per year that should be in a reserve account each year to replace the item when its useful life expires. The board will then look at the age of the item and take that age times the reserve amount per year and that should be the balance that is in the reserve account for that particular item. Consider **Figure 9-1**.

Figure 9-1

Major Component	Replacement Cost	Total Useful Life	Current Age	Reserve Balance Needed
Fence	$22,000.00	11 Years	3 Years	$6,000.00
Parking Lot	$64,000.00	16 Years	8 Years	$32,000.00
Total Reserve Balance Needed				$38,000.00
Current Cash Reserves				$30,000.00
Reserve Deficiency				$8,000.00
Percentage Funded				79%

The above example shows that the association's reserve account is not 100% currently funded. Only 79% of what it needs is currently in the account. To bring the account current, the preparer would divide the $8,000 deficiency by the numbers of the association, which will show how much each member must contribute to bring the reserve account to 100%. Somehow, this balance will have to be made up or the association will not have the reserve balances necessary to cover replacement costs as they become due. **It may be necessary to charge the members with a special assessment to bring the reserve account to 100%. This could be a lump sum special assessment or an assessment that is spread out over a period of time**. Members should be informed of the problem in running a **deficient reserve** (less than the amount of money required) should he or she decide to sell a unit. A prudent buyer will reduce the purchase price by the amount of unfunded reserve for that particular unit. The association board should be using the reserve survey to finance the reserve account through regular assessments. Most members will appreciate this, as it will spread the reserve cost over a period of time rather than being tagged with a large one-time special assessment. However, some associations would prefer to set aside little, if any, reserves and fund replacements with special assessments.

In the above example, if the board is going to use the current cost to determine the reserve account, it must update the current replacement cost for each item annually.

Updating the current replacement cost annually will avoid the problem of adhering to a general inflation rate, which may or may not be applicable to each particular item in the inventory.

Remember, when the summary of the association's reserves is placed in the official pro forma budget, it must be printed in **boldface type**.

E. WHAT ABOUT THE INFLATION RATE?

***INFLATION** can be defined as the annual rise in the general price level of goods and services.* ***DEFLATION** would be just the opposite.* To see whether there has been an inflation of prices, the board only has to look at the price per fifty-pound bag of lawn fertilizer from one year ago and compare that with the current price. If the price is higher this year than last year, there has been an inflation of the price of lawn fertilizer. The board can do this with each and every item listed as an expense on last year's budget and compare it with the current price of each item. Some prices may have decreased, others may have stayed the same, but many prices may have increased over the last year. Since the board is doing a budget for the expenses for the next twelve months, what inflation factor should the board use? As previously mentioned, the board can figure the percentage increase in the price of each item of expense on the budget from last year compared to this year and increase the budget for next year by the same percentage for that item. If the lawn fertilizer increased 4.7% from a year ago, so the board might anticipate a 4.7% increase for the lawn fertilizer for the upcoming

budget year. Natural gas might have averaged a 1.9% increase for this year, therefore, the board can factor in an estimate of 1.9% for the increase of the price of natural gas for next year.

An alternative (shortcut) approach would be to take each expense item and increase it by the annual inflation rate. What is the annual inflation rate (percentage) and how is it determined? The ***BUREAU OF LABOR STATISTICS*** *is the federal agency that computes the* ***CONSUMER PRICE INDEX****, which is defined as "a measure of the average change over time in the prices paid by urban consumers for a market basket of consumer goods and services."* It is a comparison between index numbers that give us points in time that can be used to compute the inflation rate. One problem using the index is that it represents goods and services purchased for consumption as determined from periodic family surveys. The market basket of goods and services includes general categories of food and beverages, housing, apparel, transportation, medical care, recreation, education and communication, and a general category of other goods and services. Obviously, there are numerous items in the categories of goods and services which the association is not purchasing.

The current base year for the index is 1994. Here is an example to show how the index works.

> Suppose in 1994, a particular tire costs $100. That same tire today costs $136. The index is given the number 100 for 1994 and 136 for today. Obviously, the index increased 36 points, so we need to convert this to an inflation rate. We divide the 36 points by the base year of 100 and that equals .36 or 36%. This tells us that there has been a 36% increase in the price of that tire since 1994. Obviously, the items listed as expenses for the board will probably be similar in nature to items listed as expenses in similar common interest developments around the country. However, prices will vary from location to location. The price of electricity in one location is not necessarily the same halfway across the United States. Fortunately, the Bureau of Labor Statistics surveys the market basket of goods and services in different geographic locations. For example, there is a **western urban price index** for all states from the Rocky Mountains and all states west, including Alaska and Hawaii. There are also more regionally specific areas. The board of directors for Hubie Highlands Homeowner's Association uses the consumer price index for all urban consumers in the Los Angeles-Riverside-Orange County area. A copy of that index for the last ten years as computed monthly, including the annual average, is shown in **Figure 9-2**.

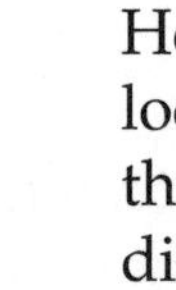

www.bls.gov
U.S. Bureau of Labor Statistics

If the board of directors met in May of 2003 to prepare a budget for the next fiscal year, which was the same thing that was done in May of 2002, the board could compute an

Figure 9-2

Consumer Price Index - All Urban Consumers

Series Id: CUURA421SA0,CUUSA421SA0
Not Seasonally Adjusted
Area: Los Angeles-Riverside-Orange County, CA
Item: All items
Base Period:

Year	Jan	Feb	Mar	Apr	May	Jun	Jul	Aug	Sep	Oct	Nov	Dec	Annual	HALF1	HALF2
1994	152.2	152.2	152.5	152.0	151.4	151.3	151.7	152.0	152.7	153.4	152.9	153.4	152.3	151.9	152.7
1995	154.3	154.5	154.6	154.7	155.1	154.8	154.5	154.4	154.6	155.2	154.4	154.6	154.6	154.7	154.6
1996	155.7	156.2	157.3	157.7	157.5	156.7	157.6	157.3	158.2	158.8	158.4	158.3	157.5	156.9	158.1
1997	159.1	159.2	159.8	159.9	159.5	159.4	159.5	159.7	160.5	161.1	160.7	161.2	160.0	159.5	160.5
1998	161.0	161.1	161.4	161.8	162.3	162.2	162.1	162.6	162.6	163.2	163.4	163.5	162.3	161.6	162.9
1999	164.2	164.6	165.0	166.6	166.2	165.4	165.8	166.3	167.2	167.2	167.1	167.3	166.1	165.3	166.8
2000	167.9	169.3	170.7	170.6	171.1	171.0	171.7	172.2	173.3	173.8	173.5	173.5	171.6	170.1	173.0
2001	174.2	175.4	176.2	176.6	177.5	178.9	178.3	178.4	178.8	178.3	178.1	177.1	177.3	176.5	178.2
2002	178.9	180.1	181.1	182.2	182.6	181.9	182.2	183.0	183.4	183.7	184.0	183.7	182.2	181.1	183.3
2003	185.2	186.5	188.2	187.6	186.4	186.3	186.3	186.9	188.2	187.8	187.1	187.0	187.0	186.7	187.2
2004	188.5	190.1	191.5	191.9	193.3	193.7	193.4	193.1	194.5					191.5	

overall inflation rate between those two points in time. The board would have taken the consumer price index of 186.4 for May of 2003 and subtracted 182.6 from one year before. The difference was 3.8. Divide 3.8 by the May 2002 figure of 182.6 and that equals .0208. Move the decimal place two points to the right and the inflation rate at that time, compared with one year before, was 2.08%. The board estimated that all expenses for the budgeted year of May 2003 - May 2004 would increase by 2.08%. This approach was not as accurate as figuring the percentage price increases for each line item as an expense in the budget from the previous year, but on average it equalled out about the same and it certainly was a lot less work. Additionally, the inflation rate can be used to determine the replacement cost of an item for the upcoming fiscal year. You take the cost for replacement from the last fiscal year budget and increase it by the inflation rate to determine the cost necessary to replace the item for the next fiscal year.

FOR EXAMPLE

Inflationary Increase in Dollar Amounts. Any dollar amounts specified in this declaration in connection with any proposed action or decision of the board of directors or the homeowner association, may, in the discretion of the board of directors, be increased proportionately by the increase in the consumer price index for the City of ________ for All Urban Consumers prepared by the United States Department of Labor for the base period, January 1, of the calendar year following the year in which this declaration was recorded, to adjust for any inflation or deflation in the value of the dollar.

IV. Spending Reserve Funds

The board of directors cannot expend reserve funds for any purpose other than the repair, restoration, replacement, or maintenance of, or litigation involving repair, restoration, replacement, or maintenance of major components for which the association was obligated to establish a reserve fund.

Recall earlier that the reserve account is to be segregated into one category for the usual reserve contributions and another category for reserve funds contributed because of payment for claims for defective design or construction.

The board of directors may authorize the temporary transfer of money from a reserve fund to the association's general operating fund to meet short-term cash-flow requirements or other expenses.

The transferred funds must be restored to the reserve fund within one year of the date of the initial transfer. However, the board of directors may, upon making a finding supported by documentation, determine that a temporary delay would be in the best interest of the common interest development, and temporarily delay the restoration.

The board of directors must exercise prudent fiscal management in maintaining the integrity of the reserve account and must, if necessary, levy a special assessment to recover the full amount of the expended funds within the restoration time limit.

When the board of directors has made a decision to use reserve funds or temporarily transfer money from the reserve fund to pay for litigation, the association must notify the members of that decision in the next available mailing to all members and advise the members of the availability of an accounting of those expenses.

Unless the governing documents require a more frequent standard, the association must make an accounting of expenses related to litigation at least quarterly.

The accounting must also be available for inspection by association members in the homeowner association's office. The mailing of the notice can take the form of an inclusion in a regularly sent newsletter to the membership which would minimize mailing costs.

V. Estimated Revenue

A. DETERMINING ASSESSMENT INCOME FROM EXPENSES

Once the estimated expenses (operation and improvement plus reserve) are totaled, it can be as simple as dividing the total expenses by the number of units or lots and that will equal the assessment amount for each member for the year. Divide that by twelve to determine the monthly assessment for each member.

The estimated revenue gets more complex if each member's separate interest is not equal to every other member's separate interest.

The theory here is that those with larger units may have a larger demand on the common areas. Therefore, the percentage of the total expenses may be divided up on the basis of a percentage of the square footage of each member's interest. In other words, total the square footage of the entire separate interest and divide that into the square footage of each member's separate interest and that figure represents the proportionate interest of the member in the total separate interest. Take that figure times the total expenses and that equals the annual assessment for the member. Members are legally obligated to pay the assessment to the association. If, for some reason, the expenses exceed the maximum allowed for regular assessment, the expenses must be cut or a special assessment used to make up the difference, or the members will vote on an assessment increase. Assessments are covered in Chapter 10.

AN EXAMPLE

OPERATION/IMPROVEMENT EXPENSES	$8,560	.8861
RESERVE EXPENSES	$1,100	.1139
	$9,660	1.0000

UNIT	SQUARE FOOTAGE	EXPENSE ALLOCATION	REGULAR ASSESSMENT	MONTHLY
A	794	.1665	1598.73	133.23
B	804	.1675	1618.05	134.84
C	1065	.2219	2143.55	178.63
D	1069	.2228	2152.25	179.35
E	1067	.2223	2147.42	178.95
	4799	1.0000	$9660.00	

B. OTHER ASSOCIATION INCOME

The association will have an operating account at a financial institution which is filled with the regular assessments paid by the members and used to pay expenses. The association will also have a reserve account where payments by members will accumulate for future expenditures. One or both of the accounts could earn interest income for the association. The estimated interest rate can be determined by looking at current bank rates or certificate of deposit rates and may tend to be more stable and, hence, more predictable, than the inflation rate.

The interest income from operating and reserve accounts is taxable to the association.

After the deduction for payment of taxes, the after tax interest for each account can be listed. Additionally, small sources of income will come from payment of fines, user fees, interest on delinquent amounts, lost key or card fees, etc.

VI. Financial Statement Review

Like other states, California has specific accounting standards.

In addition to the annual operating budget, a homeowner association may be required to provide members with a review of its financial statement. In California, this review must be prepared in accordance with generally accepted accounting principles by a licensed accountant (CPA) with the California Board of Accountancy and is only required if gross income to the association exceeds $75,000. A copy of the review must be distributed within 120 days after the close of each fiscal year. This allows the members to note how well the association did during the last fiscal year compared to the budget for that year. If it can afford to do so, it is prudent financial practice for each homeowner (community) association to do a review of the financial statement every year, even if not required.

According to California law, a nonprofit benefit corporation with gross revenues over $10,000 must prepare a current financial report and notify all members of their right to receive that report, and furnish a copy of it upon request.

The financial report must be prepared not later than 120 days after the close of the corporation's fiscal year and must contain:

1. End of the fiscal year balance sheet, income statement, and statement of changes in financial position for that year.
2. A statement of the place where the names and addresses of the current members is located.
3. A statement of a "covered transaction":
    a. A covered transaction is one between the corporation and a director or officer or any holder of more than 10% of the voting power of the corporation.
    b. In general, the parties to the transaction and their relationship to the corporation must be disclosed if transactions involved more than $50,000 (excluding director or officer compensation) or involved any loans, guaranties, indemnifications, or advances totaling more than $10,000.
    c. Approval of the transaction by the members with an affirmative vote of a majority of the votes at a meeting at which a quorum is present or by appropriate written ballot will remove the transaction from this required disclosure.

This financial report must be accompanied by any report thereon by independent accountants or the certification of an authorized officer that the statements were prepared without audit from the books and records of the corporation.

A financial report does not have to be prepared if the gross revenues were less than $10,000.

Additionally, the board of directors is required by law to, at least quarterly, review the following:

1. The current reconciliation of the association's operating accounts;
2. A current reconciliation of the association's reserve accounts;
3. The current year's actual reserve revenues and expenses compared to the current year's budget; and
4. An income and expense statement for the association's operating and reserve accounts.

Additionally, the board must review the latest account's statements prepared by the financial institutions where the association has its operating and reserve accounts.

VII. CHAPTER SUMMARY

As the HOA manager, you must always keep in mind that unless the governing documents require more, the association is to annually distribute to its members the following four documents:

1. A pro forma operating budget.
2. A review of the financial statement of the association.
3. A summary of the association's insurance policies.
4. A statement of the association's policies and practices in enforcing lien rights for assessment defaults.

These are not documents that can be prepared at the last moment. Depending on the size of the association, the operating budget and the financial statement review could take a considerable amount of work. Enforcement of lien rights will usually remain consistent from year to year. The insurance summary may vary depending upon changes in the coverage. As an association manager, you may be delegated the responsibility to prepare the financial documents, which probably would necessitate some accounting background. On the other hand, the association may have an outside contractor, for example a common interest development management firm, prepare the documents. Perhaps there are one or two accountants who are members of the association that are willing to do this work for the board. In any event, if you, as the association manager, are not preparing the documents, those who are will rely on your information about operating expenses and income to help with the preparation. Organization of the data and accuracy regarding amounts is critical.

As the association manager, you must make sure that the operating budget, or its summary, must be distributed to the association members not less than 45 days, nor more than 60 days, before the start of the next fiscal year. This gives the membership the opportunity to review the budget or, if sent a summary, the opportunity to acquire a copy of the complete budget well before the start of the next fiscal year.

Putting aside of reserve funds is based on expectations of the lifetime of major components within the development. As the association manager, you need the necessary skills to identify the major components and acquire information regarding the life expectancy of each major component. Additionally, it will be necessary to determine the estimated cost of repair or replacement of the major components at the end of their useful lives.

You need to be aware of which major components have a remaining life of more than thirty years. Once these components hit the thirty-year barrier, they need to be factored into reserve study.

To help in preparation of the reserve study, as the manager, you need to remember the study must include at least the following:

1. Identification of the major components which the association is obligated to repair, replace, restore or maintain which have, as of the date of the study, a remaining useful life of less than thirty years.
2. Identification of the probable remaining useful life of the major component as of the date of the study.
3. An estimate of the cost of the repair, replacement, restoration or maintenance of the major component at the end of its useful life.
4. An estimate of the total annual contributions necessary to defray those costs during and at the end of each major component's useful life after subtracting the amount of currently held reserves.

Since, in all likelihood, the board of directors will conduct the inspection once every three years (as required by California law), it is important for you, as the manager, to keep an accurate list of new major components which will now enter the thirty-year barrier, as well as the existing major components which have deteriorated significantly or required extensive repairs during the three-year period. Significant changes in the condition of major components may require an adjustment to a shorter useful life.

It might be advisable for you, as the manager, to make sure that reserve funds are placed in a separate interest-bearing account, rather than the normal operating account. You might be able to get a higher interest rate for the reserve account since it will have fewer transactions out of it during a year than the operating account.

The association has to provide the members with the review of its financial statement. In California, if the gross income of the association exceeds $75,000 for a physical year, the review must be prepared by a licensed California accountant. As the manager, you may be involved in assisting with the financial statement review if you are responsible for preparing the association's balance sheet, income statement, and other financial items that are included in the financial review.

VIII. REVIEW QUESTIONS

1. In California, unless the governing documents require more, the association must distribute to each of its members all of the following documents, except:

   a. a summary of the association's insurance policies.
   b. a review of the financial statement of the association.
   c. the details of the management contract with the association manager.
   d. the association's procedure for enforcing lien rights for delinquent assessments.

2. In California, the budget of the association must contain which of the following?

   a. Statement of reserve calculations.
   b. A summary of the association's reserves.
   c. A statement regarding special assessments.
   d. All of the above are correct answers.

3. When preparing a budget, the cost of the annual premium for fire insurance coverage of HOA common areas is a:

   a. variable expense.
   b. service expense.
   c. hidden expense.
   d. fixed expense.

4. A high-rise condominium association must pay each year for a permit to operate its elevators, which involves a safety inspection by a government official. This expense would be listed in the budget as a:

   a. fixed expense.
   b. variable expense.
   c. special assessment expense.
   d. none of the above.

5. In preparing a budget, the cost to an HOA for utilities necessary to heat the water in the swimming pool and Jacuzzi should be listed as:

   a. a fixed expense.
   b. a variable expense.
   c. an optional expense.
   d. the amount is unknown, so it cannot be listed as an expense.

6. For the purpose of a reserve study, only "major" components are included with a remaining life of less than:

   a. ten years.
   b. fifteen years.
   c. twenty years.
   d. thirty years.

7. Although it has the option of doing it more frequently, the board of directors must conduct a visible inspection of the major components at least once every:

a. year.
b. two years.
c. three years.
d. five years.

8. A measure of the average change over time in the prices paid by urban consumers for a market basket of consumer goods and services is a definition for the:

a. inflation rate.
b. consumer price index—all urban consumers.
c. consumer price index—all rural consumers.
d. none of the above.

9. The association has a bank account that contains accumulated reserves and earns interest. The interest earned is:

a. always equal to the inflation rate.
b. not taxable to the association since the association is a nonprofit corporation.
c. taxable to the association.
d. none of the above.

10. In a reserve study, at the end of the useful life of the major component, which of the following costs must be determined?

a. The cost to replace the item.
b. The cost to restore the item.
c. The cost to repair the item.
d. All of the above are correct answers.

ANSWERS: 1. *c*; 2. *d*; 3. *d*; 4. *a*; 5. *b*; 6. *d*; 7. *c*; 8. *b*; 9. *c*; 10. *d*

NOW
SELLING
FROM
$600,000
415

CHAPTER 10

Assessments By the Association

I. Assessments By the Association

One of the major advantages of owning a unit or a lot in a common interest development is the benefit received from using the common areas. In Hubie Highlands, the members have the beneficial use and enjoyment of the swimming pool and Jacuzzi, tennis courts, clubhouse facility, manager's office, additional parking, and beautiful grounds. But along with the beneficial use of these items, the members understand that they must individually pay for those benefits. The payments from members for operating expenses, as well as reserves for future replacements, is sometimes controlled by the governing documents of the development, regulations imposed on developments through a state agency, or requirements imposed directly by a state law.

Stating assessment authority in the governing documents makes it very clear to prospective purchasers exactly what is each member's financial obligation to the association when purchasing a unit.

It is then up to the perspective purchaser to decide whether the governing documents propose adequate funding for future maintenance and replacement. If the perspective member is comfortable with the potential financial obligations of the association and its ability to maintain the common areas, then the buyer can purchase a unit. If the buyer is

Chapter 10

CHAPTER OUTLINE

not satisfied with the adequacy of future funding, then the buyer can purchase somewhere else. At this stage, unit purchasers are probably not expecting that in the future a state agency or the legislature will attempt to "change the rules" and impose obligations not bargained for at the time of contracting. Why would the legislature or a government agency be given the power to regulate assessments when the members already have a contract with the association for regulation?

> *Problems develop when the original governing documents imposed assessment amounts which were either fixed or could be raised only in small increments, and now expenditures threaten to out strip association income.*

It is possible that the original governing documents set the assessment at a low amount to encourage sales in the development to buyers who might be concerned about purchasing in a development where assessments could be raised to a level that would be a burden on the member. Some members like to have the use of all of the advantages offered in the common areas but want to pay the absolute minimum for providing those services. Usually, these members have no idea what it costs to run the association's common areas. This is why there are significant disclosures required in California and other states regarding the financial condition of the association. Sometimes, developers were interested initially in subsidizing the association expenses associated with the common areas so they were in top notch condition, which encouraged perspective purchasers to buy a lot or a unit. Once the development was sold out, the developer walked away from it, stopping the subsidized funding and left the association to pick up the slack. If the governing documents fixed an assessment at an unrealistic amount, the association could not maintain the quality of the common areas. Members became unhappy and property values suffered.

Funding problems can develop with significant increases in insurance premiums, breakage of high-dollar major components with inadequate funds for repair or replacement, or members subsequently discover that the common areas were willfully undersized to meet the current demands of members. If enough of these problems exist, members will complain to their legislative representatives and the end result may be government regulation of common interest developments.

> *In California, a portion of the Davis-Stirling Common Interest Development Act regulates the ability of the association to levy and increase assessments on the members notwithstanding more restrictive limitations placed on the board of directors by the existing governing documents.*

Certainly, there are those members who think the association's assessment is too high given the circumstances and other members who would argue the assessment is too low under the circumstances. When enough of these situations occur, the government may step in to regulate the area of assessments, as it has done in California.

A. INCREASING REGULAR ASSESSMENTS

As the association manager, you must become familiar with the section of the governing documents providing for member assessments and any applicable agency regulation or state law. This is important because there may or may not be limits placed on assessment increases. For example, the California law requires that the association levy regular assessments (for normal routine operating expenses) and special assessments (to repair, replace, or restore any major component or provide adequate reserves therefore) sufficient to perform its obligations under the governing documents and the law. One legal limitation involves annual increases in regular assessments by the board.

The board may not impose a regular assessment that is more than 20% greater than the regular assessment for the association's preceding fiscal year, unless the board has obtained the approval of the owners at a meeting or election of the association.

A ***QUORUM***, *which is generally more than 50% of the owners of the association,* must have been present at the meeting and the assessment must have received a majority of the votes at the meeting.

The 20% maximum increase prevails over a more restrictive limitation in the governing documents. For example, if the declaration provides that the board cannot increase regular assessments by more than 10% of the previous year's assessment, that restriction is invalid since the state law allows a larger increase. The board can increase an assessment by 20% or less by complying with the financial disclosure distribution (discussed in Chapter 9) followed by a board of directors meeting or by obtaining the same membership vote required for a more than 20% increase. California law also provides that the voting does not have to take place at a membership meeting, it can take place without the meeting if a written ballot has been distributed to each member. Approval by written ballot will take place only when the number of votes cast by ballot equals or exceeds the quorum number required to be present at a meeting, and the number of approvals equals or exceeds the number or votes required for approval had there been a meeting.

B. SETTING SPECIAL ASSESSMENT AMOUNTS

In California, the board may not impose special assessments totaling more than 5% of the budgeted gross expenses of the association for that fiscal year without approval of the owners. Once again, the meeting or election of the members must have more than 50% of the owners of the association present and a majority vote in favor of the special assessment.

Approval by a written ballot can take place only when the number of votes cast by ballot equals or exceeds the quorum number required to be present at a meeting, and the number of approvals equals or exceeds the number of votes required for approval at the meeting.

In making its determination, the board will total the amount of the special assessment to see if it exceeds 5% of the budgeted gross expenses for that fiscal year. If the total assessment is 5% or less, the board does not need member approval provided the financial disclosure documents were distributed. Although not defined, "budgeted" probably refers to the pro forma budget and "gross expenses" probably refers to the total expenses of the association budgeted for that fiscal year which would include both fixed and variable expenses, as well as reserve expenses. The special assessment may be imposed by the board during its budget process or during the year.

C. EMERGENCY (SPECIAL) ASSESSMENTS

The board may impose an emergency assessment (a type of special assessment) without membership approval when it is necessary for emergency situations.

In California, an emergency situation is defined as an extraordinary expense:

1. Required by court order; or
2. Necessary to repair or maintain the common interest development or any part of it for which the association is responsible where a threat to personal safety on the property is discovered; or
3. Necessary to repair or maintain the common interest development or any part of it for which the association is responsible that could not have been reasonably foreseen by the board in preparing and distributing the pro forma operating budget. However, prior to the imposition or collection of the assessment, the board must pass a resolution containing written findings as to the necessity of the extraordinary expense involved and why the expense was not or could not have been reasonably foreseen in the budgeting process. Additionally, the resolution must be distributed to members with the notice of the emergency assessment.

Other than a court order, the emergency expenses typically deal with repairing or maintaining the common areas. Arguably, repair and maintenance is not the same as building improvements or adding to the common areas. An emergency assessment might involve attorney fees to pay for an unexpected lawsuit or the removal of many large trees currently presenting a safety hazard resulting from a massive wind storm.

In some areas of the country, as the association manager, you may find that an owner's vote is required for special assessments/emergency assessments or for assessment increases.

D. NOTICE OF ASSESSMENT INCREASES

How are the members notified that their assessments have increased and at what point the increases become due? In California, the association must provide a written notice by first-class mail to the owners of any increase in regular or special assessments not less than 30, nor more than 60 days, prior to the increase becoming due. Since the board has been looking at the previous fiscal year budget in preparation of the pro forma operating budget for the next fiscal year, as well as the regular and special assessments for the upcoming fiscal year, the board might as well give notice of the increase in assessments when it distributes the pro forma operating budget. Recall that the operating budget has to be distributed not less than 45, nor more than 60 days, prior to the beginning of the association's fiscal year. For example, you, the association manager, could distribute the pro forma operating budget 50 days before the beginning of the next fiscal year and include a 50-day notice to the members of the increase and the assessments. The distribution might also include a notice of a special board of director's meeting or of a special meeting of the association membership. Obviously, the increased assessment amounts are considered in the operating budget for the next fiscal year anyway. Since the increase in assessment notice must be mailed, this would necessitate the board mailing its pro forma operating budget. Giving the notice along with the budget also necessitates a board planning ahead in order to conclude any necessary voting on the increase prior to mailing.

E. DELINQUENT ASSESSMENTS

In California, regular and special assessments are delinquent 15 days after they become due, unless the declaration provides a longer time period, in which case the longer time period applies. When an assessment becomes delinquent, the association may recover from the member, in addition to the amount of the delinquent assessment, all of the following:

1. Reasonable cost incurred in collecting the delinquent assessment, including reasonable attorney's fees;
2. A late charge not exceeding 10% of the delinquent assessment or $10, whichever is greater, unless the declaration specifies a smaller late charge, in which case the smaller amount prevails;
3. Interest at an annual rate not to exceed 12% on the total of the delinquent assessment, reasonable fees and costs of collection, and reasonable attorney's fees starting 30 days after the assessment becomes due, unless the declaration provides for a lower interest rate, in which case the lower rate shall prevail.

F. ASSESSMENTS PROTECTED FROM JUDGMENT CREDITORS OF THE ASSOCIATION

In California, regular assessments imposed or collected to perform the obligations of an association under the governing documents or the law are exempt from execution by a judgment creditor of the association only to the extent necessary for the association to perform essential services, such as paying for utilities or insurance. For example, assume the association failed to pay the full contract price for a band that played at the association's New Year's party. The contract provider sued the association and won a judgment for $2,650. The association refused to pay the court judgment, so the contract provider, now a creditor of the association with a judgment, has decided to use the appropriate legal procedure to take the amount of the judgment plus accruing interest from the association's bank account. The association claims that the money in the account is exempt because it needs to be used for payment of essential services. A court hearing will probably be necessary where the court must insure that only essential services are protected and any remaining funds are available to the judgment creditor. The exemption (protection) from taking by the judgment creditor does not apply to any of the following:

1. A judgment creditor whose judgment resulted from any consensual pledge, lien, or encumbrance that was approved by the owners of the association at a meeting or election where a quorum was present and a majority of the votes at the meeting were cast in favor of it;
2. Any state tax lien;
3. Any lien for labor or materials supplied to the common area, (which usually involves construction).

It should be noted that regular assessments have the exemption from execution. The legislation does not state that the exemption also applies to special assessments or emergency assessments.

II. How the Association Can Collect Assessments

Every common interest development association has concerns about collecting the assessments necessary to maintain and restore the common areas for the benefit of all members.

Each association needs to carefully establish and periodically review a "crystal clear" collection policy understandable by the members and consistently enforce the policy.

In California, a statement (see **Figure 10-1**) describing the association's policy and practices in enforcing lien rights or other legal remedies for default in payment of its assessments against its members must be delivered annually to the members during the 60-day period immediately preceding the beginning of the association's fiscal year. Read this notice carefully. Every association must have a policy and practice for enforcing

liens. This legal requirement ensures that each member gets a least an annual statement of association remedies for a default in payment of an assessment.

Obviously, the association wants to make sure that all payments are made on time. However, this is not always the case. Sometimes it will be necessary for the person responsible for collecting assessments, whether that be the association treasurer, you, as the association manager, or someone else, to handle delinquent payments. It may be important for this person to find out why the payment is delinquent. Perhaps the reason will allow for an easy and speedy remedy of the situation.

Aggressive collection programs can be very unpopular with the members.

On the other hand, collection tactics which are courteous, respectful, polite, yet consistent and firm may achieve better results. This is especially true when the association uses an outside third party or service to collect the delinquencies.

Figure 10-1

NOTICE
ASSESSMENTS AND FORECLOSURE
(California Only)

This notice outlines some of the rights and responsibilities of owners of property in common interest developments and the associations that manage them. Please refer to the sections of the Civil Code indicated for further information. A portion of the information in this notice applies only to liens recorded on or after January 1, 2003. You may wish to consult a lawyer if you dispute an assessment.

ASSESSMENTS AND NONJUDICIAL FORECLOSURE

The failure to pay association assessments may result in the loss of an owner's property without court action, often referred to as nonjudicial foreclosure. When using nonjudicial foreclosure, the association records a lien on the owner's property. The owner's property may be sold to satisfy the lien if the lien is not paid. Assessments become delinquent 15 days after they are due, unless the governing documents of the association provide for a longer time. (Sections 1366 and 1367.1 of the Civil Code)

In a nonjudicial foreclosure, the association may recover assessments, reasonable costs of collection, reasonable attorney's fees, late charges, and interest. The association may not use nonjudicial foreclosure to collect fines or penalties, except for costs to repair common areas damaged by a member or a member's guests, if the governing documents provide for this. (Sections 1366 and 1367.1 of the Civil Code)

(continued)

The association must comply with the requirements of Section 1367.1 of the Civil Code when collecting delinquent assessments. If the association fails to follow these requirements, it may not record a lien on the owner's property until it has satisfied those requirements. Any additional costs that result from satisfying the requirements are the responsibility of the association. (Section 1367.1 of the Civil Code)

At least 30 days prior to recording a lien on an owner's separate interest, the association must provide the owner of record with certain documents by certified mail. Among these documents, the association must send a description of its collection and lien enforcement procedures and the method of calculating the amount. It must also provide an itemized statement of the charges owed by the owner. An owner has a right to review the association's records to verify the debt. (Section 1367.1 of the Civil Code)

If a lien is recorded against an owner's property in error, the person who recorded the lien is required to record a lien release within 21 days, and to provide an owner certain documents in this regard. (Section 1367.1 of the Civil Code)

The collection practices of the association may be governed by state and federal laws regarding fair debt collection. Penalties can be imposed for debt collection practices that violate these laws.

PAYMENTS

When an owner makes a payment, he or she may request a receipt, and the association is required to provide it. On the receipt, the association must indicate the date of payment and the person who received it. The association must inform owners of a mailing address for overnight payments. (Sections 1367.1 and 1367.1 of the Civil Code)

An owner may dispute an assessment debt by giving the board of the association a written explanation, and the board must respond within 15 days if certain conditions are met. An owner may pay assessments that are in dispute in full under protest, and then request alternative dispute resolution. (Sections 1366.3 and 1367.1 of the Civil Code)

An owner is not liable for charges, interest, and costs of collection, if it is established that the assessment was paid properly on time. (Section 1367.1 of the Civil Code)

MEETINGS AND PAYMENT PLANS

An owner of a separate interest that is not a time-share may request the association to consider a payment plan to satisfy a delinquent assessment. The association must inform owners of the standards for payment plans, if any exist. (Section 1367.1 of the Civil Code)

The board of the directors must meet with an owner who makes a proper written request for a meeting to discuss a payment plan when the owner has received a notice of a delinquent assessment. These payment plans must conform with the payment plan standards of the association, if they exist. (Section 1367.1 of the Civil Code)

A. ASSOCIATION RECORDS STATEMENT TO HELP OWNERS PAY

In order to facilitate the collection of regular assessments, special assessments, transfer fees, and similar charges, the board is authorized to record a statement or amended statement in the county recorder's office identifying relevant information about the association. The board is not required to record this statement but it may assist the members in making payments. The statement may include any or all of the following:

1. The name of the association as shown in the declaration or the current name if it is different.
2. The name and address of a managing agent or treasurer of the association, or other individual or entity authorized to receive payments of assessments and fees imposed by the association, and a daytime telephone number of this individual if it is available.
3. A list of separate interests subject to assessment by the association, showing the assessor's parcel number or legal description, or both, of the separate interest.
4. The recording information identifying the declaration governing the association.
5. If this is an amended statement being recorded, the recording information identifying the prior statement or statements which this amendment is superceding.

Remember that this recording is optional by the board of directors and its purpose is to provide a central source for information that might be of interest to separate property owners.

Some of the recorded information may change over time, which will require an amended information statement be recorded. This fact alone may discourage the association from recording this statement since it may end up paying recording fees for changes in a phone number or an address.

B. WHEN ASSESSMENTS ARE DUE

The board of directors must determine when regular and/or special assessments will be due and payable.

Assessments may be due monthly, every two months, quarterly, semi-annually, or annually. If cash flow is important to the association, then the board may use a monthly assessment date and will probably send a monthly assessment bill to each member, which should arrive several days before the assessment is due. In a large common interest development, this monthly mailing may involve considerable time and effort, as well as expense, in its preparation and mailing. Perhaps the easiest collection method is to have the members make arrangements with their financial institution to have the assessment automatically deducted from their account each month and paid to the association. A monthly statement/invoice should be sent to members who do not pay automatically.

The billing statement/invoice should remind the member that the assessment payment is delinquent 15 days after it is due.

If there is a later date when the payment becomes delinquent stated in the declaration, that later date must be used. Remembering that consistency is important, the board needs to have an established policy regarding what happens when the payment is delinquent. Should the delinquent member immediately be assessed a late charge? Should members be allowed an additional grace period before a late charge is imposed? Should the member be notified in writing or personally that the payment is now delinquent? Recall that the late charge cannot exceed 10% of the delinquent assessment or $10, whichever is greater, unless the declaration specifies the late charge of a smaller amount.

III. Enforcing Assessment Liens

A. THE PRE-LIEN NOTICE

Liens are used in many states as a way of collecting unpaid assessments. In California, if the association wishes to place a ***LIEN*** *(a recorded document against the owner's property which makes the property security for the amount owed)* upon the separate interest of the owner of the unit or lot in order to collect the past due assessment and any applicable fees and costs of collection, reasonable attorney fees, late charges and any interest, the association has to send a notice to the owner in writing by certified mail at least 30 days prior to recording the lien. The pre-lien notice must contain the following:

1. The method of calculation of the amount due the association.
2. A general description of the collection and lien enforcement procedures of the association.
3. A statement that the owner has the right to inspect the association records pursuant to Corporations Code §8333.
4. A statement in 14-point bold faced type, if printed, or in capital letters, if typed stating: "IMPORTANT NOTICE: IF YOUR SEPARATE INTEREST IS PLACED IN FORECLOSURE BECAUSE YOU ARE BEHIND IN YOUR ASSESSMENT, IT MAY BE SOLD WITHOUT COURT ACTION."
5. An itemized statement of the charges owed by the owner, including items on the statement which indicate the amount of any delinquent assessments, the fees and reasonable costs of collection, reasonable attorney's fees, any late charges, and interest, if any.
6. A statement that the owner is not liable to pay the charges, interest, and costs of collection, if it is determined the assessment was paid on time to the association.
7. A statement notifying the owner that the owner can request a meeting with the board of directors to dispute this debt notice.

1. Important Considerations Regarding the Pre-Lien Notice

The association cannot record a lien against the owner's interest until 30 days after the certified mailing of the notice described above.

The notice must contain an itemized statement of the charges owed by the owner. The statement of the amount of any delinquent assessments should be broken down into the amount of a special assessment as well as the amount of a regular assessment. The fees and reasonable cost of collection need to be listed. For example, if an attorney is being used, the reasonable attorney's fee would be included, along with a late charge and interest. **The association can charge interest at the rate of 12% a year, unless the declaration specifies a lower rate of interest, and interest starts 30 days after the assessment becomes due**. Therefore, unless this pre-lien notice covers an assessment that is more than 30 days delinquent, an interest charge will not appear on it. It is very important that the "reasonable" cost of collection and attorney's fees be reasonable and provable if necessary. For example, is there a flat rate for the preparation of every pre-lien notice? Or, is the cost used in preparation of the notice determined at a specific rate per hour or per minute increment of time? Obviously, the certified mailing cost is an appropriate charge.

Along with the general description of the collection policies and lien enforcement procedures of the association, also included is the method of calculation of the amount claim to be owed to the association. The method of calculation probably refers to the necessary expenses in the pro forma budget for the existing fiscal year and/or the reserve expenses divided by the increments of payment (for example monthly) by members. This computation demonstrates how the assessment amount was calculated.

With regard to the right of the owner to inspect association records, Corporations Code §8333 provides that "The accounting books and records and minutes of proceeding of the members of the board and committees of the board shall be open to inspection upon the written demand of the corporation of any member at any reasonable time, for a purpose reasonably related to such person's interest as a member." Therefore, a written demand from the owner related to the determination of the amount the owner owes the association requires that the accounting books and records be open to inspection at a reasonable time.

The right of the owner to request a meeting of the board is for the owner to dispute the debt stated in the pre-lien notice.

The pre-lien notice must advise the owner that the owner may submit to the board a written explanation of the reasons for the dispute. The board must respond in writing to the owner within 15 days of the date of the postmark of the explanation, or presumably, if the explanation was delivered in person, within 15 days of the delivery.

As the pre-lien notice stated, the owner may submit a written request to meet with the board to discuss a payment plan for the debt stated in the notice. The association must provide the owner with the standards for payment plans, if any exist. Therefore, the board is not required to have a payment plan, but if it allows payments over a period of time, there must be a set standard for doing so. The board must meet with the owner in executive session within 45 days of the postmark of the request, provided the request for a meeting was mailed within 15 days of the date of the postmark of the pre-lien notice. If there is no regularly scheduled board meeting within that period, the board may designate a committee of one or more members to meet with the owner. One thing the board should keep in mind is if the members find out that the board is receptive to payment plans, there may be a flood of members requesting deferred payments. This can create an obvious cash flow problem for the board. Therefore, a board should give serious consideration to the ramifications of adopting a standard payment plan before doing so. It may be in the best interest of the association to deny a request for payment plans.

The pre-lien notice should be signed by the appropriate person who handles collection of assessments.

2. Owner's Response to Pre-Lien Notice

Upon receipt of the pre-lien notice, the owner will typically do one of the following:

1. Pay all or part of the amount of the delinquent assessment(s) and the other amounts stated in the pre-lien notice.
2. Dispute the debt stated in the notice.
3. Request a meeting of the board to discuss a payment plan. The owner must make sure that the written request for the meeting is mailed within 15 days of the date of the postmark of the pre-lien notice.

Any payments made by the owner toward the debt as stated in the pre-lien notice must first be applied to the assessment owed, and, only after the assessments owed are paid in full shall the payments be applied to the fees and costs of collection, attorney's fees, late charges, or interest.

If the owner requests a receipt at the time of payment, the association must provide one. This receipt must indicate the date of payment and the person who received it. Additionally, the association must provide a mailing address for overnight payment of assessments by the members.

B. THE ASSOCIATION RECORDS A NOTICE OF DELINQUENT ASSESSMENT

Thirty days or more following the mailing of the pre-lien notice to the owner, the association may record a **Notice of Delinquent Assessment**. This notice is recorded at the county recorders office in the county where the common interest development is located.

The purpose of recording a Notice of Delinquent Assessment is to create a lien against the owner's separate interest in the development.

The amount of the lien consists of the amount of the assessment, plus any cost of collection, late charges, and interest assessed. Recall that the lien means that the association has a security interest in the owner's separate interest and can sell the separate interest and use the proceeds to pay off the money the association is entitled to. If the association failed to comply with any of the above procedures it must, prior to recording a lien, re-commence the required notice process. Any cost associated with re-commencing the notice process must be paid by the association and not the owner of the separate interest.

It is very important for you, as the association manager, or whomever is handling collection of delinquent assessments, to comply exactly with the legal requirements.

Obviously, it is a waste of time and money if a mistake is made and the process has to be started all over again from the beginning.

1. The Lien Document

The actual Notice of Delinquent Assessment document must contain the following:

1. The amount of the assessment and other sums mentioned above that the association is legally entitled to.
2. A legal description of the owner's interest in the common interest development. This would be the legal description that is on the title that the owner received at the time of purchase.
3. The name of the recorded owner of the separate interest.
4. In order for the lien to be enforced by nonjudicial foreclosure, the Notice of Delinquent Assessment must state the name and address of the trustee authorized by the association to enforce the lien by sale of the separate interest.
5. The Notice of Delinquent Assessment must be signed by the person designated in the declaration or by the association for that purpose, or, if no one is designated, then by the president of the association.

6. A copy of this recorded notice must be mailed by registered or certified mail to the owner of the separate interest within 10 days after it was recorded.

Once the owner receives a copy of the recorded Notice of Delinquent Assessment, he or she knows that the property can now be sold to satisfy the amount owed as stated in the notice. Typically, the owner will now pay the association the amount owed rather than risk loss of his or her separate interest. The recording of the notice of delinquent assessment is evidence to the owner that the association is serious about collecting fees owed to the association.

Within 21 days of payment of the sum stated in the Notice of Delinquent Assessment, the association must cause a lien release or notice of rescission to be recorded, which will give the public notice that there is no longer a lien on the owner's separate interest.

Additionally, the owner must be provided with a copy of the recorded lien release or notice of rescission stating that the delinquent assessment has been satisfied. Also, if it is determined that a previously recorded lien was recorded in error, the association must, within 21 days, cause a lien release or notice of rescission to be recorded and provide the owner with a declaration (sworn statement) that the recording was in error, and also provide a copy of the recorded lien release or notice of rescission.

C. THE COMMON AREA DAMAGE LIEN

Sometimes a member, or the member's guest or tenants, cause damage to the common areas. Examples are driving over the grass, knocking over a pedestrian light pole, throwing baseballs and breaking a window, cutting down an inconvenient bush or tree, and any number of other situations. The damage could be caused intentionally or because of negligence. In any event, a monetary charge can be imposed by the association as a means of reimbursing it for the cost incurred because of the member, guest, or tenants who are responsible. If this charge is not paid, the amount may become a lien against the member's separate interest, provided the authority to impose a lien is set forth in the governing documents of the development.

To collect the damage amount, a written pre-lien notice similar to the one for delinquent assessments could be used as well as a recorded notice of delinquency similar to the notice of delinquent assessment.

D. LIEN LIMITS

1. Only Two Liens

There are only two recorded liens that can be used against an owner's separate property.

One is the delinquent assessment plus the legally allowed amounts for collection fees, attorney's fees, a late charge, and interest (previously discussed). The second one is the lien for damage to the common areas by a member, guest, or tenants. (mentioned above) The damage lien, although probably occurring less often than the assessment lien, would be handled in the same way. If the association has a claim against a member for something other than assessments or damages, another type of collection procedure must be used. Other collection tactics, such as litigation, will be discussed in a later chapter.

2. Limited Assignment

An association may not voluntarily assign or pledge the association's right to collect payments or assessments or to enforce or foreclose a lien to a third party, except when the assessment or pledge is made to a financial institution or lender as security for a loan obtained by the association.

However, this does not restrict the right or the ability of the association to assign any unpaid obligations of a former member to a third party for collection or to use a trustee for a foreclosure as long as 30 days has passed since the recording of the lien.

E. THE LIEN IS RECORDED: WHAT NOW?

In California, thirty days after the recording of the lien it may be enforced in any manner permitted by the law, including a sale by the court, a sale by the trustee designated in the notice of delinquent assessment, or a trustee substituted for the designated trustee.

The sale will be held in the same manner as a typical foreclosure sale under a deed of trust when a property owner stops making payments. Trustee fees for such sales are established by law. After the sale costs and fees are taken from the proceeds of the sale to the highest bidder, the amount of the lien is paid and any remaining funds are given to the former owner.

F. DEED IN LIEU OF FORECLOSURE

Sometimes, although probably not very often, an owner would prefer to end a possible foreclosure and deed the owner's interest to the association as a settlement in full of the owner's indebtedness to the association. The association takes the deed to the owner's property instead of foreclosing on it and eliminates the debt. This is not a likely scenario, however, since it is rare that delinquent assessments for common area repair obligations would not be exceeded by the owner's equity in the property.

G. OWNER DISPUTES AMOUNT AND PAYS LIEN AMOUNT UNDER PROTEST

Within 30 days from the recording of a notice of delinquent assessment, the owner may pay the association, under protest, the full amount of the disputed assessment, late charges, interest, and all reasonable fees and costs associated with the preparation and recording of a notice of delinquent assessment, including all mailing costs, plus reasonable attorney's fees not to exceed $425. The protest must be in writing and sent with the full payment by certified mail. Upon receipt of the protest payment, the association must inform the owner that the owner may resolve the dispute through alternative dispute resolution, civil court action, and any other procedures that may be available to the association.

H. RESOLVING DISPUTE THROUGH ALTERNATIVE DISPUTE RESOLUTION (ADR)

Assume the owner of the separate interest decided to pay to the association the proper amount under protest. Upon receipt of the protest payment, the association must inform the owner that the owner may resolve the dispute through alternative dispute resolution as set forth in California Civil Code §1354, by civil court action, and any other procedure to resolve the dispute that might be available through the association. The alternative dispute resolution (see Chapter 15) may be binding or nonbinding at the option of the parties. If both parties choose nonbinding arbitration, the decision of the arbitrator can either be performed or ignored. If the parties choose binding arbitration, the parties agree that the decision of the arbitrator is final.

Under the law, alternative dispute resolution may not be exercised more than two times in any single calendar year, and not more than three times within any five calendar years.

However, if the owner and the association mutually agree, they can enter into alternative dispute resolution more than the maximum number of times.

If the owner shows an error in the notice or recordation process, the owner will receive a refund of the amounts paid under protest plus interest on those amounts. The association will then have to either re-compute the amounts and start the process again or, if the whole thing was started in error in the first place, determine why it occurred and prevent a similar situation from occurring in the future. On the other hand, if the association prevails in the alternative dispute resolution process, then the association presumably can keep the payment and release the lien.

Either the property owner or the association may initiate the alternative dispute resolution process by serving on the other party to the dispute a "Request for Resolution."

The Request for Resolution must include the following:

1. A brief description of the dispute between the parties;
2. A request for alternative dispute resolution; and
3. A notice that the party receiving the Request for Resolution is required to respond to it within 30 days of receipt or it will deem to be rejected.

1. Service of the Request for Resolution

In California, service for Request for Resolution must be made in the same manner prescribed for service of a small claims action under Code of Civil Procedure §116.340.

There are alternative ways to accomplish service of a small claims action that would appear to be inappropriate for the service of Request for Resolution, leaving the remaining methods below as the most appropriate:

1. Either party (the separate interest owner or the association) may obtain service by mailing the Request for Resolution to the other party by any form of mail providing for a return receipt. Service shall be deemed complete on the day the party signed the mail return receipt.
2. Either party may cause the physical delivery of the Request for Resolution to the other party in person. Service shall be deemed complete on the date the person was personally served. This physical delivery should be done by someone other than the member, who should note in writing the time, place, and person the Request was delivered to.

Either alternative above would seem the most appropriate for serving the Request for Resolution. Obviously, it will not be difficult for the property owner to accomplish a service on the association, however, it may be more difficult for the association to accomplish service on the property owner. If the property owner is absent from the dwelling, no service can be accomplished by mail or in person. If the property owner is an absentee owner and rents the unit out, it is very important that the association keep accurate records of the current addresses of all owners.

Service on the association can be accomplished by mailing the Request for Resolution to the agent for service of process stated in the Articles of Incorporation or the Statement of Information (SI-100) filed by a domestic nonprofit corporation.

The Statement of Information has to be filed every two years and was discussed in an earlier chapter. Additionally, service information might be found in an amendment to the statement of information filed during the two-year period.

In the alternative, service information could be acquired from the most recent Statement by Common Interest Development Association.

The statements must be filed every two years or upon address changes of the on-site office, responsible officer, or managing agent. If the association is not incorporated, the property owner can look to the Statement by Common Interest Development Association which has to be filed by every unincorporated association formed to manage a common interest development every two years in the month of July or upon changes in the address of the on-site office, responsible officer, or managing agent. The statement by Common Interest Development contains the name and address of the association's managing agent if any, the street address of the association's on-site office or, if none, the address of the association's responsible officer or managing agent, or the address of the president of the association. These addresses can be used for personal service or service by mail of the Request for Resolution.

As a practical matter, it is doubtful that there will be any problem with service of the Request for Resolution by either the property owner or the association. More complex service problems will be discussed in a later chapter. The important point is that one party must initiate the alternative dispute resolution process. Typically, it would be assumed that the payment and protest letter of the property owner would include the Request for Resolution. If not included, the property owner will soon acquire the information on what to do next because the association must inform the owner of the rights the owner has to resolve the dispute, and alternative dispute resolution is one of those rights. However, the notice doesn't mention the procedure (Request for Resolution) for doing so. The board of directors should develop a standard policy for the association that establishes who initiates the request for alternative dispute resolution and a deadline for doing so. Instead of waiting for the owner to act, the association can start the alternative dispute resolution with a service of the Request for Resolution, but probably has little incentive to do so since it has now been paid in full although under protest. Therefore, if the association desires, it can wait for the owner to either serve a Request for Resolution or file a civil lawsuit to resolve the protest. If the owner files a civil lawsuit, the court will resolve the protest.

If the owner serves the Request for Resolution, the protest will be resolved through arbitration.

2. After the Request for Resolution Has Been Served

Assuming the Request for Resolution has been properly served, the party receiving the request has 30 days following the service of the request to accept or reject it.

If the request is not accepted within the 30-day period by the receiving party, it is deemed rejected by the receiving party and court action may be the next step. If the receiving party accepts the request, the alternative dispute resolution must be completed within 90 days of the receipt of the acceptance by the party who initiated the Request for Resolution. However, both parties can agree in writing to extend the 90-day completion time. Obviously, if the recipient chooses to accept the request for alternative dispute resolution, some affirmative act of acceptance is necessary. Although no formality for the acceptance is required, a written notice of acceptance would be advisable, as well as some means of confirmation that the acceptance has been received by the person initiating the request.

I. UNRESOLVED AREAS OF CONCERN FOR MANAGEMENT

1. Even though a Notice of Delinquent Assessment has been recorded, recall that the Pre-Lien Notice to the owner provided that the owner had the right to dispute the debt in the notice by submitting to the board of directors a written explanation of the reasons for the dispute. Since there is no time limit on the owner's right to provide this written explanation to the board, it is conceivable that the written explanation may now surface. Recall that the board of directors has 15 days from the date of the postmark of the owner's explanation if it was mailed or 15 days from receipt if it was delivered to respond in writing to the explanation. Assuming the computations in the Pre-Lien Notice are correct and the board has responded within the time period, the owner's written dispute may have caused a small delay in the association's collection of the delinquency.

2. If the owner paid the appropriate amounts under protest by certified mail within the 30-day time limit, recall that the association must advise the owner of the owner's right to resolve the amount paid under protest. However, there is no time period or specific manner provided on how the association must inform the owner of the owner's options. The suggestion here would be a written notice as soon as possible after receipt of the protest payment with a confirmation of its receipt by the owner. Unfortunately, there is no timeline for a response to the association's notice by the owner. Therefore, in all likelihood, unless the association has some need to initiate alternative dispute resolution by serving a Request for Resolution, the association has the paid under protest amount and is now in the foggy zone trying to figure out what to do next. Since the association must record a release of the lien within 21 days of payment, must the association do so even though the payment was under protest? Additionally, if enough time has expired it is likely that the owners now are at least another month behind in assessment payments. It may be time to start the cycle of collection again.

3. In order to try and resolve the above problems, recall that the notice the association must send the owner who pays under protest must inform the owner that he or she may resolve the dispute through alternative dispute resolution as set forth in

California Civil Code §1354, by civil action, and any other procedures to resolve the dispute that may be available through the association.

Perhaps it is advisable to take the "may be available through the association" language and provide a mechanism in the association's assessment collection policy that clarifies the rights and obligations of the owner and the association to resolve the above mentioned problems.

For example, the collection policy may inform all owners that if they pay under protest the owner is obligated to also include a Request for Resolution by alternative dispute resolution with the payment. Also, the Request must indicate whether the owner is seeking mediation or arbitration and, if it is arbitration, whether the owner requests binding or nonbinding arbitration. In the alternative, the owner would be required to provide a written explanation of the reasons for the payment under protest and at that time must indicate if the owner wants to appear before the board of directors to resolve the dispute. If the owner does not include the Request for Resolution or the written explanation of the reasons for the payment under protest with a request for a board hearing, the association should include in the policy a presumption that the owner by default chooses the appearance before the board of directors. The owner will be notified of the hearing time and location. In this manner, the association is establishing a policy which does everything possible to offer an opportunity for the owner to resolve the delinquencies and in a reasonable manner attempt to close the issue.

Keep in mind, however, that the owner can still bring a civil action to resolve the protested amount. Due to the cost of litigation, a lawsuit by a disgruntled owner is probably unlikely. This is especially true since in any civil litigation to enforce the governing documents which contain the obligation to pay assessments, the prevailing party is awarded reasonable attorney's fees and costs. Additionally, when the court determines the award of attorney's fees and costs to the prevailing party, the court might consider the refusal by a party to participate in alternative dispute resolution prior to filing the civil action. The owner had the opportunity to resolve the protest amount by alternative dispute resolution but chose to litigate instead. Once again, it cannot be emphasized enough that the accuracy in determining the exact amount owed by an owner is extremely important by the person who is doing the computation for the association. The details involved in arbitration and mediation are discussed in Chapter 15.

J. NONJUDICIAL FORECLOSURE

Assuming that the association has heard nothing from the owner and the Notice of Delinquent Assessment has been recorded in the county where the property is located, what happens next? The recording of the Notice of Delinquent Assessment places a lien on the owner's property which can be enforced through a trustee's sale, which does not involve any court action or supervision provided the sale is conducted according to the law.

The law permits the trustee who was identified by name and address in the Notice of Delinquent Assessment to sell the delinquent owner's property in order to obtain proceeds to pay off the owner's delinquencies.

K. FORECLOSURE OF THE ASSESSMENT LIEN

If the association chooses to foreclose under its previously recorded Notice of Delinquent Assessment, the association will contact the trustee stated in the notice that the association desires to have the owner's property sold. Typically, the association has a working relationship with the trustee so that the trustee knows exactly how to proceed with the foreclosure. If the trustee chooses not to proceed with the foreclosure when requested by the association, it will be necessary for the association to substitute another trustee who will do the foreclosure stated in the notice. The trustee being substituted will prepare the necessary paperwork and record a notice in the county recorders office of being substituted in place of the trustee mentioned in the Notice of Delinquent Assessment. Once again, the association needs to make sure the trustee is familiar with foreclosures on delinquent assessment liens as this is not your typical foreclosure on a delinquent real estate loan. The sale by the trustee will undoubtedly be what is known as a private sale. With a ***PRIVATE SALE****, it is not necessary for the association to file any court papers in order to sell the owner's property*. In the alternative, the law provides that there can be a ***JUDICIAL FORECLOSURE****, which means that the sale of the property results from the filing of court papers and is a court supervised sale.*

1. Notice of Default

The first step in the foreclosure process by the trustee is to record a Notice of Default. This seems somewhat redundant because the recorded Notice of Delinquent Assessment already states that the property owner is in default and sums that are owed.

Within ten business days after the Notice of Default is recorded, the trustee must mail a copy to the owner by certified or registered mail.

In addition, a second copy must be sent to the owner by first-class mail and the trustee has to execute an affidavit (sworn statement) of its mailing. In the same ten business day period, the trustee must also send a copy of the Notice of Default, by certified or registered mail, to everyone who has recorded a request for a Notice of Default. For example, if the owner borrowed money to purchase the owner's interest in the development and gave the lender a security interest in the property being purchased, the lender may want to know that the borrower is delinquent in paying the assessments on the property the lender has financed.

2. Notice of Sale

The trustee's next step is to issue a Notice of Sale.

The Notice of Sale cannot be issued until at least three months after the Notice of Default was recorded.

This Notice of Sale states the time and place that the trustee's sale will be held. It gives the name, address, and phone number of the trustee conducting the sale and it identifies the debtor and the property to be sold. It also states the amount that is due to the association plus an estimate of the costs and expenses of the sale. A warning to the property owner is included in the notice:

"UNLESS YOU TAKE ACTION TO PROTECT YOUR PROPERTY, IT MAY BE SOLD AT A PUBLIC SALE. IF YOU NEED AN EXPLANATION OF THE NATURE OF THE PROCEEDING AGAINST YOU, YOU SHOULD CONTACT A LAWYER."

To "issue" the Notice of Sale, the trustee must do all of the following, at least 20 days before the sale:

1. Post a copy of the notice at a public place (such as the courthouse) in the city or judicial district where the property is located;
2. Begin publishing a notice once a week in a newspaper of general circulation in the city or judicial district where the property is located;
3. Post a copy in a conspicuous place on the property to be sold (the notice should be on the front door, if possible); and
4. Send the property owner one copy by registered or certified mail and another copy by first-class mail; and send a copy to each of the parties that requested and were sent a Notice of Default.

In addition, at least 14 days before the sale, the trustee must record a copy of the Notice of Sale in the county where the property is located.

Up until the date of sale, the law also provides that the property owner can stop the sales process.

One way to do so would be to give the association a deed in lieu of foreclosure. This was mentioned before and is an unlikely occurrence. Another way that it is possible the foreclosure sale will not take place is if the property owner decides to pay the delinquent amounts and the accumulation of interest, fees, and costs. This payment is now being handled by the trustee and not the association. Therefore, the association is looking to the trustee for collecting all amounts the association is legally entitled to. Obviously, several months have passed since the recording

of the Notice of Delinquent Assessment. The owner of the property is probably delinquent in paying assessments that have become due since the recording of the notice. Most likely, these newer delinquent assessments would be called "reoccurring obligations" which would also have to be paid by the property owner in order to stop the sale of the property.

3. The Trustee Sale

A trustee's sale is a public auction; the foreclosed property is sold to the highest bidder.

The sale must be held during ordinary business hours, in the county where the property is located. The trustee's role is to conduct the sale in a fair and open manner, and to protect all interested parties which include the association and the property owner. The property is then sold to the highest bidder with the proceeds of the sale paying the amount owed to the association after paying the cost of the sale.

The association can credit bid at the sale. With ***CREDIT BIDDING****, the amount owed to it as of the date of the sale can be bid thereby insuring that if there is another bidder for the property, the association will be certain to get all amounts that it is owed to date.* In the alternative, the association may wish to acquire title to the delinquent owner's property. If the association is the highest bidder, it will own the property. Keep in mind, however, that purchasing the property means that the new owner, whether that is the association or someone else, will be purchasing the property subject to any other security interests in that property that were recorded prior to the recording of foreclosure documents. This priority may vary from state-to-state, and is something you, as the association manager, should know.

If the delinquent owner initially financed the purchase of the property, the new owners will be purchasing the property with that previous loan recorded against it, whether it is current or not, and will have to keep that loan current or risk foreclosure by that lender.

An additional problem is that the lender who loaned money to the property owner to purchase the property may, upon receiving a Notice of Default mailed by the trustee, declare its loan in default for failure to pay assessments and start the foreclosure process (see case on the next page).

4. The Trustee's Deed

The purchaser at the trustee sale receives title to the property immediately. The purchaser is given a trustee's deed.

The former property owner has no further right to recover the property. If the former property owner is still in possession of the property, that person can be evicted by the new owner.

Thaler v. Household Finance Corporation

80 Cal. App. 4th 1093; 95 Cal. Rptr. 2d 779 (App. 1 Dist. 2000)
Edited Excerpts From the Opinion of Justice Stevens

FACTS AND ISSUES

In 1998, Thaler purchased a condominium at a nonjudicial foreclosure sale held pursuant to an assessment lien that had been recorded on the property in 1997. Also in the record of title was a second deed of trust recorded in 1992 by the predecessor of Household Finance Corporation. The amended CC&Rs of the Heritage Commons Homeowner's Association were recorded in 1985 and provided in part that an assessment lien shall be subordinate to any recorded first mortgage or first deed of trust, but they are otherwise silent with respect to their priority over other recorded documents. Thaler alleged that the foreclosure of the assessment lien extinguished Household's security interest in the property. The trial court concluded that Thaler's interest in the property was subject to Household's second deed of trust. Thaler appealed.

DECISION AND REASONS

California follows the "first in time, first in right" system of lien priorities. With respect to real property, a conveyance recorded first generally has priority over any latter-recorded conveyance. A properly recorded conveyance of real property also serves as constructive notice of its contents to all subsequent purchasers and encumbrances.

An assessment lien under California law is a debt of the condominium owner and it constitutes a lien on the owner's interest upon the recording of a notice of delinquent assessment. After a thirty-day period following the recording of the assessment lien, the lien may be enforced in any manner permitted by law, including by nonjudicial foreclosure sale. Civil Code Section 1367(d) provides: "A lien created pursuant to subdivision (b) shall be prior to all other liens recorded subsequent to the notice of assessment, except that the declaration may provide for the subordination thereof to any other liens and encumbrances." Consequently, this section follows the first in time, first in right concept of lien priorities. Although Section 1367 does not mention conveyances filed before the assessment lien, there is no reason to believe the Legislature intended to deviate from the system of first in time, first in right. We need look no further than the plain, unambiguous language of Section 1367 to determine its meaning. The order of the trial court is affirmed.

5. Foreclosure Summary

In comparing the amount of the delinquent assessment(s) to the equity that would generally be found in the owners' property, it is unlikely that the assessment lien foreclosure will actually go to sale. Usually, the delinquency will be paid. The association may reach the point after it records a Notice of Delinquent Assessment to lien the property when it will shift to the small claims court to seek a judgment that might be easier to collect. The association must remember that once it collects payment, it needs to record a release of the lien. Collection by litigation will be discussed in another chapter.

L. JUDICIAL FORECLOSURE

As an alternative to the private sale by a trustee of the owner's property to pay the delinquent assessment, the association can file a foreclosure suit with the superior court.

Obviously, the association would use the services of an attorney for this complex and time-consuming procedure. Precisely for those reasons, the judicial foreclosure is not a viable alternative. In essence, the lawsuit and the complex procedure will ultimately result in a sheriff's sale of the property and the purchaser will receive a sheriff's deed immediately after the sale.

Problems with the judicial foreclosure involve the expense and time of using the court and attorneys, and the possible ability of the property owner to reclaim the property within a period from three months to one year after the sale.

IV. Property Owner in Bankruptcy

It is important that the association be a secured creditor at the time a property owner files bankruptcy. The association can become a secured creditor by recording its lien for delinquent assessments. This means that the association, assuming there is equity in the property owner's real estate, at some point in time will find that the bankruptcy court will issue an order granting relief from the automatic stay which allows the association to continue its foreclosure on the property. The entire matter is being handled by the bankruptcy court and the automatic stay is a court order that creditors must stop collection and wait for bankruptcy court action. There are penalties for violations.

There is a problem if the property owner is delinquent on the loan for the purchase of the property. That lender-recorded security interest takes priority over the assessment lien in California.

In other words, if the recorded purchase loan on the property was recorded prior to the association's assessment lien, and it is in foreclosure, there is a risk that the association may not receive any funds from its lien. The association's lien for assessments will be extinguished unless the sale of the property generates a surplus of money over and above the amount necessary to pay off the foreclosing party (lender). If such a surplus exists, it will be distributed to the subsequently recorded lien (association) or other liens in the order that they were recorded. Therefore, if there is a surplus and the association's lien was the next lien to be recorded after the lender's lien being foreclosed, those proceeds will go to pay off the assessment lien to the extent there are proceeds.

California Considerations (Assessments)

1. Board limited to 20% or less increase in regular assessments over previous year without owner approval.
2. Board limited on increase in special assessments to 5% or less of budgeted gross expenses for that fiscal year without owner approval.
3. Board not limited in amount for emergency assessment, only the requirements for an emergency.
4. Notices of regular or special assessment increases not less than 30 nor more than 60 days prior to starting.
5. Assessments are delinquent 15 days after due.
6. Consider use of common area damage lien.
7. If amount not paid, send a pre-lien notice containing required statements, or turn the entire matter over to the association's attorney.
8. Await owner's response to pre-lien notice and respond accordingly:
   a. Owner may pay in full-say "thank you."
   b. Owner may make partial payment, continue with collection, or wait for remainder.
   c. Owner may dispute amount-arrange for board hearing or alternative dispute resolution.
   d. Owner may want to meet with the board-make arrangements.
   e. Owner may want to inspect association records-make arrangements.
9. Recordation of the Notice of Delinquent Assessment no sooner than 30 days following the mailing of the pre-lien notice.
10. Use a professional for foreclosure or do it yourself.
11. Record a Notice of Default.
12. Record and serve a Notice of Sale after 90 days from recording the Notice of Default.
13. Sale is conducted.
14. Distribution of sale proceeds.
15. May litigate instead of foreclosing after recording the Notice of Delinquent Assessment.
16. Record a release of the lien after member pays in full.

V. MANAGER'S JOURNAL

The following items are important areas for investigation, knowledge and action by you, as a community association manager:

1. Develop a working knowledge of how the association can increase assessments. Are there any regulations in the governing documents or in state law which limit the ability to increase assessments? Additionally, become familiar with the exact procedure for the association to increase assessments.
2. Become familiar with the definition of and procedure for creating a special assessment. Additionally, become aware of the procedure for increasing the amount of the special assessment and whether there are any limitations on the amount of the increase.
3. Become familiar with the procedure for the association to impose an emergency assessment. Is there a definition of an "emergency"? Are there any limitations on the amount of an emergency assessment or the frequency with which an emergency can be declared?
4. Since, as the manager, you might be responsible for initiating a collection procedure, you must know exactly when an assessment becomes delinquent.
5. As the association manager, you need to know the procedure to be used when a creditor of the association is attempting to collect a money judgment against the association. In all likelihood, this matter should be immediately turned over to the attorney for the association.
6. With regard to a delinquent assessment, at this point you, the association manager, have either turned the matter over to an attorney for collection or are personally sending out the necessary delinquent notice and otherwise doing the things necessary to place a lien on the owner's property. Usually, the board of directors has previously instructed you on how to handle this situation.
7. Once a lien has been placed upon the owner's property, the decision must be made whether to continue with the foreclosure of that lien or, in the alternative, try and collect the amount that is owed through litigation. Additionally, as the manager, you will need to have a response ready if the owner makes a partial payment or wishes to meet with the board to establish a reasonable payment plan.
8. If the owner disputes the amount, you must verify the accuracy of the delinquent amount, as well as the interest and cost that have accumulated since the delinquency.
9. You will then need to request instructions from the board, probably the treasurer, whether to proceed with a foreclosure of the lien or start litigation to collect the delinquent amount. Additionally, as the manager, you need to know whether to turn the foreclosure over to a professional, personally continue the process, or whether to assist a board member in bringing the litigation by following the procedures of state law.

10. If a member files bankruptcy, the matter should be turned over to the association's attorney.

VI. CHAPTER SUMMARY

Each member's financial obligation to the association is clearly detailed in the assessment authority granted in the association's governing documents. In California, a portion of the Davis-Stirling Act regulates the ability of the association to levy and increase assessments notwithstanding more restrictive limitations by the governing documents.

The board may not impose a regular assessment that is more than 20% greater than the regular assessment for the association's preceding fiscal year without the approval of the owners at a meeting or election. In California, the board may not impose special assessments totaling more than 5% of the budgeted gross expenses of the association for that fiscal year without approval of the owners.

A quorum, which is more than 50% of the owners of the association, must be present at the meeting and the assessment must have received a majority of the votes at the meeting. Approval by a written ballot can take place only when the number of votes cast by ballot equals or exceeds the quorum and number required to be present and approve the vote.

In California, the association must provide a written notice by first-class mail to the owners of any increase in regular or special assessments not less than 30, nor more than 60 days, prior to the increase becoming due. They become delinquent 15 days after they become due, unless the declaration provides a longer time period. In California, but not in all states, during emergency situations, the board may impose an emergency (special) assessment without membership approval.

Each association must establish, review and consistently enforce a "crystal clear" collection policy that is understandable by the members.

The board of directors must determine when regular and/or special assessments will be due and payable. The billing statement/invoice should remind the member that the assessment payment is delinquent 15 days after it is due.

Liens are used in many states as a way of collecting unpaid assessments.

In California, before the association can place a lien against the separate interest of the owner in order to collect the past due assessment and applicable fees and costs of collection, reasonable attorney fees, late charges, and any interest, they must send a pre-lien notice to the owner by certified mail at least 30 days prior to recording the lien.

Any payments made toward the debt must be applied to the assessment owed first. The owner may dispute the debt stated in the pre-lien notice by requesting a meeting of the board. The association's accounting books and records must be open to inspection by the owner at any reasonable time.

Thirty days or more after the mailing of the pre-lien notice, a notice of delinquent assessment may be recorded. This creates a lien against the owner's separate interest in the development. An association may not assign or pledge their right to collect payments or assessments or to enforce or foreclose a lien to a third party, unless the assessment or pledge is made to a financial institution or lender as security for a loan obtained by the association.

In California, 30 days after recording the lien, it may be enforced in any manner permitted by law, including a sale by the court, a sale by the trustee designated in the notice of delinquent assessment, or a substituted trustee.

Occasionally, an owner will end a possible foreclosure by deeding his or her interest to the association.

An owner may also choose to pay the association the full amount owed under protest. If so, the association must notify the owner of the possibility of resolving the dispute through alternative dispute resolution (ADR). Either party may initiate the ADR process by serving a Request for Resolution on the other party to the dispute. If the owner serves the Request for Resolution, the protest will be resolved through arbitration.

Under the law, ADR may not be exercised more than two times in any single calendar year, and not more than three times within any five calendar years.

Once the Request for Resolution has been properly served, the party receiving the request has 30 days to accept or reject it. The lien can be enforced through a trustee's sale, which does not involve any court action. With a private sale, it is not necessary for the association to file any court papers in order to sell the owner's property. With a judicial foreclosure, the sale of the property results from the filing of court papers and is a court-supervised sale.

The first step in the foreclosure process by the trustee is to record a Notice of Default. Within 10 business days after the notice is recorded, the trustee must mail a copy to the owner by certified or registered mail.

The next step is to issue a Notice of Sale, which cannot be issued until at least three months after the Notice of Default was recorded. The property owner can stop the sales process up until the date of sale.

The trustee's sale is a public auction, where the foreclosed property is sold to the highest bidder. The association can utilize credit bidding, meaning the amount owed to it as of the date of sale can be bid, thereby insuring that if there is another bidder, the association will get all the money it's owed. The buyer at the trustee sale receives title to the property immediately, and is given a trustee's deed.

As an alternative to the private sale by the trustee, the association can file a foreclosure suit with the superior court, which is more expensive and time consuming. Also, the owner can reclaim the property within a period from three months to one year after the sale.

In California, if a property owner is delinquent on the loan for the purchase of the property, the lender-recorded security interest takes priority over the assessment lien.

VII. REVIEW QUESTIONS

1. Limitations on the total amount of an annual assessment or on the amount of increase in an annual assessment from the previous year may be:

   a. limited by state law.
   b. limited by the declaration or master deed.
   c. limited by the association bylaws if the association is incorporated.
   d. all of the above are correct answers.

2. In California, unless the board of directors has obtained approval from the association members, the board cannot impose a regular assessment that is ______ greater than the regular assessment for the association's preceding fiscal year.

   a. 2%
   b. 5%
   c. 20%
   d. None of the above are correct answers.

3. A special assessment may be imposed by the board of directors:

   a. only at the time the board adopts the association budget for the coming fiscal year.
   b. at any time during the next fiscal year.
   c. only with approval of 75% of the members of the association.
   d. for the regular payment of the association phone bill.

4. The maximum amount of increase in an emergency assessment is:

   a. 5% of the most recent emergency assessment.
   b. 20% of the most recent emergency assessment.
   c. 5% of the current fiscal year's total amount for regular assessments.
   d. The law does not place a limitation on the amount of an emergency assessment.

5. In California, the association members must receive a notice of any increase in regular or special assessments:

   a. not less than 30, nor more than 60 days, prior to the increase becoming due.
   b. not less than 30, nor more than 60 days, prior to the board meeting where the assessment increase will be voted on.
   c. not less than 45 days prior to the increase becoming due.
   d. no notice is required to be sent to the membership for an increase in regular or special assessments.

6. What is the major advantage of using a lien to collect a delinquent assessment?

   a. Once a lien has been recorded against the owner's interest, the lien allows a foreclosure sale of the member's interest which could generate enough proceeds to pay off the delinquent assessment.
   b. Once the lien is recorded against the member's ownership interest, the association can immediately physically evict the owner from the property and list the property for sale.
   c. Once a lien has been recorded against the member's ownership interest, the member must pay the lien within 90 days or be placed in the county jail until the amount is paid.
   d. There is no advantage.

7. When does an assessment become delinquent?

   a. If it is unpaid on the date it is due.
   b. 15 days after it is due, unless stated otherwise in the declaration.
   c. If the declaration for the development says that assessments are delinquent 28 days after they are due, then the assessment is delinquent 28 days after it is due.
   d. b and c are both correct answers.

8. In California, what interest rate can be charged on a delinquent assessment?

   a. The association is not entitled to interest on a delinquent assessment.
   b. An annual rate of 10%.
   c. An annual rate of 12%.
   d. None of the above.

9. With regard to an incorporated association, each member has the right to inspect which of the following documents?

   a. Accounting books and records
   b. Minutes of the board meetings and committee meetings
   c. Both a and b are correct answers
   d. None of the above answers are correct as members have no legal right to inspect any records of the corporation

10. In California, if a member pays the delinquent assessment after a lien has been recorded against the owner's property, the association must record a lien release within:

a. 10 days of the payment.
b. 3 days of the payment.
c. 21 days of the payment.
d. none of the above.

ANSWERS: 1. d; 2. c; 3. b; 4. d; 5. a; 6. a; 7. d; 8. c; 9. c; 10. c

LIBRARY of
NEW HOMES &
CONDOMINIUMS
John Gee
REALTORS
& Company
2807

Chapter 11

Agency, Contracting With Others, and Discrimination

Homeowner (community) associations frequently enter into contracts. Typical contracts would include:

1. hiring employees;
2. retaining management services;
3. using an accountant or attorney;
4. buying patio furniture, tennis nets, flowers, and plants;
5. purchasing a computer system and a lawn mower;
6. agreeing with independent contractors for pool service, lawn maintenance, road resurfacing, and tree removal.

To begin, this chapter will cover the requirements for a binding contract. Next, those who have the agency power to contract for the association will be covered. Finally, the discussion will turn to discrimination issues in employment contracts.

Chapter 11

CHAPTER OUTLINE

I. Association Contracts

A. THE CONCEPT

People entering into a contract generally focus on expectations.

If two parties form a contract, the expectation is that both parties will perform their obligations. Without some procedure for enforcing these obligations, parties would be free to change their minds at any time, break the promise, and have no further obligation for the results of the broken promise. In the business world, this would be totally unacceptable. People and businesses depend on the promises of others. Therefore, our society has developed a legal system that enforces contracts, realizing that contracts are an essential part of the market economy. The following material represents a small portion of California contract law. It was selected for applicability and usefulness to those of you involved in managing a common interest development (CID), or a homeowner's association (HOA).

If, at any time, you think you may have a legal problem, it is wise to consult a real estate attorney.

B. TERMS AND DEFINITIONS

1. Express Contract

An ***EXPRESS CONTRACT*** *is one in which the terms are stated in written or spoken words*. You, as the Hubie Highlands Association manager, and a pruner agree that the pruner will remove the dead fronds from the palm trees around the development, in return for which the Association will pay $450. This contract can be verbal or, preferably, put in written words and signed by each party.

2. Implied Contract

An ***IMPLIED CONTRACT*** *is one in which the existence and terms are based on conduct*. In other words, there are no written or spoken words. When an office supply salesperson stops in the Hubie Highlands Association office you, the association manager, are on the phone. The office supply person raises a case of photocopy paper for you to see. You point to the case of paper and signify two. The salesperson places two cases of photocopy paper on the counter at the office and leaves. The conduct of the parties created an implied contract for the purchase and sale of two cases of photocopy paper. When the invoice is sent, the Hubie Highlands Association must pay.

3. Quasi Contract

A ***QUASI CONTRACT*** *is one that is imposed by the courts to prevent unjust enrichment when the technical requirements of a contract have not been met*. It arises when the plaintiff sues a defendant to recover for a benefit conferred on the defendant, when no express or implied contract exists between the two parties. If the court agrees that it would be unjust for the defendant to retain the benefit conferred without compensating the plaintiff, the court creates a quasi contract, and awards the plaintiff the value of the conferred benefit. For the plaintiff to win the lawsuit, he or she must show that:

1. a benefit was conferred on the defendant;
2. the benefit was conferred with the expectation of payment not as a gratuity; and
3. it would be unjust for the defendant to keep the benefit without paying its value.

For example, Gertrude is walking to her car in the tennis parking lot and discovers that a local glass company has just replaced her chipped windshield. This is an obvious mistake, since she did not request the replacement and she certainly does not intend on paying for it. It turns out that the company employees made a mistake and confused her vehicle with a similar one which was to have its windshield replaced. If the glass company sues, is Gertrude obligated to pay? No, she did receive a benefit, it was conferred expecting that it would be paid for, but it would not be just to force Gertrude to pay for another person's mistake. Gertrude has not been "unjustly enriched" at the glass company's expense. However, if she was approaching her car from a distance and witnessed that the glass company was about to start removing her old windshield and replace it with a new one, and did nothing to prevent this from taking place, she is guilty of receiving unjust enrichment and would have to pay for the windshield. Obviously, this is a big proof issue. The glass company would have to prove that she knew in advance that her windshield was to be replaced and she deliberately avoided stopping the activity in order to acquire a new windshield for free. This would be unjust enrichment for Gertrude.

4. The Offeror

The ***OFFEROR*** *is the party who makes the offer to an offeree.*

5. The Offeree

The ***OFFEREE*** *is the party who receives an offer from the offeror.*

6. Acceptance

ACCEPTANCE *is the indication by the offeree of agreement to the terms of the offer, thereby forming a contract.*

7. Executed Contract

If a contract has been fully performed by both parties, it is an ***EXECUTED CONTRACT***. The palm trees have been pruned, for example, and the association has paid the pruner.

8. Executory Contract

An ***EXECUTORY CONTRACT*** *is one in which performance remains to be completed by either one or both parties*. The pruner has pruned the palm trees, for example, but the association has not yet paid the bill.

9. Bilateral Contract

A *BILATERAL CONTRACT is one in which a promise is exchanged for another promise.* Therefore, there are two promises. The pruner promised you, the association manager, that the palm trees would be pruned.

10. Unilateral Contract

"Uni" means "one," and a *UNILATERAL CONTRACT represents a promise made by the promisor, given in exchange, not for another promise (bilateral), but for the performance of an act.* As the association manager, you tell the pruner "If you can prune all of the dead fronds off of our palm trees before 5 p.m. on Friday, I will pay you $750." This is a promise given in exchange for an act. The pruner does not have to prune the palm trees because no promise was made to do so. If the pruner completes the act by 5 p.m. on Friday, the pruner has performed the requested act (accepted the offer) and can collect the money. If the pruner does not choose to prune the palm trees, there is no breach of a promise by the pruner to do so.

11. The Offer

The first step in forming a contract is for an offeror to make an offer to an offeree.

The offeror will indicate to the offeree that he or she wishes to enter into a contract. The offer will contain the terms upon which the offeror is willing to contract. This offer must:

1. show a present intention to enter into a contract;
2. be definite in its terms; and
3. be communicated to the offeree.

An example of an offer can be found in the bilateral contract and unilateral contract offer examples above.

C. TERMINATION OF THE OFFER

An offeree has the power to accept an offer and form a contract, unless the offer was terminated prior to acceptance.

1. Revocation

The offeror may revoke an offer at any time prior to acceptance by the offeree.

For example, in your capacity as the association manager, you mailed a written offer to the tree pruner to prune the palm trees. You can revoke this offer at any time before acceptance. The revocation can take place by:

1. calling the tree pruner and revoking the offer made (which the tree pruner has probably not yet received);
2. e-mail;
3. fax;
4. messenger;
5. in person; or
6. mail.

In California, revocations are generally effective to terminate offers when they are sent. In other states, revocations are effective to terminate offers when they have been received by the offeree.

Therefore, in California, the moment in time that you put the revocation through the mail slot at the post office, or the mail carrier picks it up at the association office, it has been sent and the offer is officially revoked.

2. Rejection

When an offeree rejects the offer, the rejection terminates the offer.

Rejections are effective to terminate offers when they are received by the offeror. For example, the tree pruner receives your written offer to prune the palm trees. The pruner calls you and says "I'm sorry, I will not be trimming your palm trees. That price is unacceptable." The offer is now terminated. Termination can also take place through e-mail, fax, personal conversation, mail, or messenger.

3. Lapse of Time

An offer will terminate after the stated time period has expired. The offer is gone.

If your tree pruning offer states that it will expire at noon on Saturday, March 13, then at that moment in time the offer terminates. If the tree pruner tenders an attempted acceptance at 1 p.m. on Saturday, there is no contract. If the offer does not state a period of time for acceptance, the offer is terminated after the lapse of a "reasonable period of time." What is a reasonable period of time varies with the circumstances. One person's idea of reasonable may not be the same as another's. Therefore, it is very important to set a specific point in time for the offer to expire. Generally, in a face-to-face conversation, the offer will terminate at the end of the conversation.

4. Death or Incompetence of Either Party

The offer is terminated by the death or insanity of either the offeror or the offeree prior to acceptance of the offer.

5. Destruction of the Subject Matter of the Offer

If the subject matter of the offer is destroyed prior to communication of the acceptance, the offer terminates immediately upon that destruction, even though neither the offeror or offeree is aware of it.

6. Change of Law

If, after an offer has been made to the offeree, a court decision or legislation makes the subject matter of that offer illegal, the offer is immediately terminated.

D. ACCEPTANCE OF CONTRACT OFFERS

The offeror is the master of the offer and can designate whomever he or she desires to be the intended offeree.

Only the intended offeree can accept the offer. Since a unilateral contract offer is a promise for the performance of an act, full completion of the act (pruning the palm trees) will constitute the acceptance and form the unilateral contract.

The acceptance of an offer must be unqualified, unequivocal, and in absolute agreement with each and every term of the offer.

Suppose the tree pruner has received your written offer and responds by saying "I accept your tree pruning offer for $750 provided I do not have to do the four palm trees around the swimming pool." This is a rejection of the offer since the acceptance is not a "mirror image" of the offer. The pruner changed one of the terms of the offer and is now proposing a **counter offer** back to you, the association manager. The counter offer is for $750 ("I will prune all of the palm trees except those around the swimming pool."). The Hubie Highlands Homeowner's Association is now the offeree and can accept or reject this counter offer.

Once a counter offer is made, it constitutes a rejection of the initial offer, which no longer exists.

An acceptance must be communicated to the offeror in order to show a present intention to contract with the offeror. If the offeror does not specify how the offer is to be accepted, then any reasonable mode under the circumstances may be used. Once again, communication might be by mail, in person, e-mail, fax, telephone call, or any other usual means. If the offeror does specify the manner in which the acceptance is to be made, then for the acceptance to be valid it must be made in the specified manner. For example, if a written offer states that it must be accepted in person, the mailing of a written acceptance does not form a contract.

An acceptance of an offer is normally effective when it has been sent.

Once again, this would be sending an acceptance letter through the mail slot at the post office, sending an e-mail or fax, communicating by telephone conversation or messenger, or any other usual means of communication. The drawback with this approach is that an acceptance may become lost and never received by the offeror. Therefore, there is a contract but the offeror does not know that. Consequently, it is within the power of the offeror to change the rule and make the acceptance of the offer effective to form the contract only when it has been received. A prudent offeror will also require that acceptance to be in writing to satisfy any potential proof problems.

E. CONTRACTUAL CAPACITY

As the association manager, you need to be aware that contracting with a minor (person under the age of 18) is extremely risky. Minors can normally enter into contracts, but have the ability to disaffirm (get out of) the contract while a minor or within a reasonable period of time after turning 18.

Any promise in a contract made by a minor can be disaffirmed.

Upon disaffirmance, the minor (or former minor) is entitled to get back everything given to the adult or merchant under the contract and must return that which was received (if it can be returned). For example, Gertrude sold her television to a minor. Months later, the minor dropped it and now it does not work. The minor can return the set and Gertrude must return the full purchase price. Therefore, as the manager, you may need to check the identification of a person to make sure they are at least 18 years of age before entering into a contract.

One exception might involve the **emancipated minor**. In California, a person under the age of 18 is emancipated if:

1. the person has entered into a valid marriage; or
2. the person is on active duty with the armed forces; or
3. the person has received a declaration of emancipation from the court.

Once a minor is emancipated, the minor's contracts are binding and enforceable just as though they were made as an adult.

F. CONSIDERATION

Every enforceable contract requires consideration.

In its simplest form, **CONSIDERATION** *means one person has promised to do or not to do something in return for which another person has promised to do or not to do something.* This is a typical bilateral contract. The tree pruner promised to prune the trees and the association promised to pay the money. Each person's promise was given in consideration for (in return for) the other person's promise.

Perhaps an easy way to understand the concept of consideration is that "In order to get something, you have to give up something." What did the association get in consideration of its promise to pay a tree pruner $750? The association received the tree pruner's promise to prune the trees. What did the tree pruner get in return for the promise to prune the palm trees? The tree pruner got the promise of the association to pay $750. Neither party was legally obligated for the promised performance prior to this bargain. Each party had to give up something by way of each party's promise in order to get the promise of the other party.

Promises made for actions that have already taken place are not enforceable because they lack consideration.

In other words, as the association manager, you notice that Maxine, one of the unit owners, has just completed washing all of the windows in the Hubie Highlands Homeowner's Association meeting hall. Maxine says that she noticed they needed to be washed and decided to help out and do the job. You are so impressed with her performance that you say "I will see that tomorrow you are paid $100 for your work because I am so impressed." You have a change of heart and refuse to pay. Is Maxine legally entitled to the money? No, there was no consideration to support your promise as the association manager. What did you get in consideration (in return for) the promise to pay Maxine? The answer is nothing, because Maxine had already performed the window cleaning act. The association did not promise to give up something ($100) in order to get something (washed windows) because the windows had already been washed.

G. UNLAWFUL ACTIONS

The following are activities which may occur on the development property and may pose serious concerns for you, as the manager.

1. Lotteries

In California, it is a misdemeanor to participate in a lottery.

But what is a lottery? California law states that "A **LOTTERY** *is any scheme for the disposal or distribution of property by chance, among persons who have paid or promise to*

pay any valuable consideration for the chance of obtaining such property or a portion of it,... whether called a lottery, raffle, gift-enterprise, or by whatever name the same may be known." In analyzing the above, if an activity has a prize, consideration, and chance, it is illegal. A major exception is the California state lottery, which contains those three elements but was passed by the voters and is legal.

For example, many of the owners are using the meeting facility to watch professional football games on the large screen television. A number of guests are invited and it is quite successful. The organizers of the event raise money to pay for the expensive food and beverage items consumed in large quantities by the attendees. This is done by selling raffle tickets for various prizes that the attendees donate for each week's event. Is there a prize? Yes, the donated items. Is there a chance? Yes, the winners are drawn out of a football helmet. Is there consideration? Yes, each person pays $1 for a raffle ticket. Is this an illegal activity on the development grounds? Yes, it is a misdemeanor. It may seem harmless and in good fun, but it still violates the law.

California recently revised the law on raffles and lotteries in response to demands for making such activities legal as fundraisers.

California law now allows eligible organizations to conduct a raffle if 90% of the gross receipts directly support beneficial or charitable purposes.

An eligible organization is a private, nonprofit, tax exempt organization having conducted business in California for at least one year and which is registered with the Department of Justice. This complex legislation contains restrictions on promoting the raffle, compensation paid for ticket sales, and annual filings with the Department of Justice. Does this section help the football group? No, the group cannot meet the requirements. Is this really a problem to worry about? Only if someone complains to local law enforcement that an illegal activity is taking place in the development.

2. Gambling and Betting

Additionally, California outlaws gambling and betting, so another illegal activity might be taking place if the attendees are betting on the outcome of the football games or have a "football pool" on the results. As the manager, you should seek the advice of the board of directors as to whether this activity should continue.

H. LICENSING STATUTES

California law requires licensing for many occupations, trades, and professions including, but not limited to, real estate brokers, architects, accountants, collection agencies, interior designers, medical personnel, cosmetologists, and alarm installers.

An examination, experience, education, or any combination of these may be required for obtaining a regulatory license.

A contract made by an unlicensed person is unenforceable against the other party of the contract if it is for professional services that require a license.

For example, in a planned development, a homeowner contracted with an unlicensed individual to build a screened porch on the back of the home. The homeowner had the plans drawn up and furnished all the materials and secured the applicable building permit. The contract with the unlicensed individual provided for building the screened porch, installing applicable wiring and plumbing, and making sure it passed its building inspections, in return for payment of $4,200. Even if the unlicensed person completes construction and it passes all inspections, the homeowner is not legally liable to pay the $4,200. The person can also be reported to the appropriate government officials for a citation for contracting without a license. Recovery may be successful for material, however, in this case, the homeowner supplied the materials. What the person doing the building should have done was to contract with the homeowner as the homeowner's employee for a specific wage per hour to do the project.

If there is no contract for a flat fee for the end result, the contracting license law is not applicable.

The problem with hiring the person as an employee is the requirement for workmen's compensation insurance and withholding of taxes, among others. More often than not, the owner would be unsuccessful in seeking return of any money paid for labor that had already taken place. The law provides that the unlicensed person cannot recover, nor can the other party recover against the unlicensed person for prior payments.

I. STATUTE OF FRAUDS

1. How it Works

California law provides that certain contracts are not enforceable in court unless they, or some note or memorandum thereof, are in writing and signed by the person being sued or by that person's agent. This is known as the **STATUTE OF FRAUDS**. The purpose of this statute is to insure that a fraud will not be committed on the courts by having either a plaintiff or defendant lie about the existence or nonexistence of a contract and dupe the court into believing their position. Therefore, in certain subject matter areas, legislation requires an enforceable contract be in writing and signed by the person being sued. In subject areas other than those requiring a written contract, verbal contracts are enforceable in court.

A prudent party will require that all contracts be in writing and signed.

The contract subject to the statute of frauds has to be in writing and signed at the time of the lawsuit, although it should have been signed when it was entered into. The following is a partial list of the subject matter areas under the statute of frauds which might be applicable to a common interest development:

1. An agreement that by its terms is not to be performed within a year from the making thereof.
2. Contracts for the sale of real property, or any interest therein, as well as leases over one year. An interest therein would include things like easements, restrictions on the use of the land, and agreements for gas, oil, or mineral leases.
3. Employment of a real estate broker to purchase or sell real estate or lease real estate for a period longer than one year.
4. An agreement by a purchaser of real property to pay an indebtedness secured by the property. Sometimes a purchaser of real property agrees to assume (take over) the existing indebtedness secured by the real property being purchased.
5. Contracts for the purchase and sale of goods at a price of $500 or more.

FOR EXAMPLE - SALE OF GOODS

The law provides that a contract for the sale of goods for the price of $500 or more is not enforceable by way of action or defense unless there is some writing to indicate that a contract for sale has been made between the parties and signed by the party against whom enforcement is sought.

For example, the board of directors has decided to replace outdoor furniture in the swimming pool and tennis court areas, giving specific directions and authorization to you, the manager, to make the purchase. You telephone an outdoor furniture company and order assorted outdoor furniture totaling $8,450. The furniture is in stock and delivery is guaranteed no later than two weeks from the date of the phone call. You are pleased because the furniture is an exceptional value considering its high quality and the price discount for these closeout items. The new line of outdoor furniture is considerably more expensive.

Unfortunately, the furniture does not arrive. You wait an additional week and call the company to see where the furniture is. The company spokesperson says that all of the closeout furniture has been sold and shipped and that, unfortunately, the Hubie Highlands' order probably went to someone who may have been willing to pay more money.

(continued)

Because of the immediate demand for the furniture, you place another order for comparable items with a different furniture company which are delivered within five days but cost $1,700 more. Has there been a breach of a verbal contract for the purchase of outdoor furniture? Yes, by the seller. Will Hubie Highlands be successful in a lawsuit against the breaching seller for the difference between the contract price and the replacement contract price? No, the contract involved a purchase of goods at a price of $500 or more and there is nothing in writing and signed by the party being sued, which is the seller. Had the purchase contract been put in writing and signed, the association would be successful in its lawsuit.

2. Exceptions

The statute of frauds is about proof of the existence of a contract in important subject matter areas.

If the parties have fully performed a verbal contract which comes under the statute of frauds, this executed verbal contract is binding. For example, in a verbal contract selling real estate, the buyer has paid the money and the seller has delivered the deed. The buyer then finds a better parcel and wants to return the deed and get the money back. The argument of the buyer is that the contract is not enforceable because it deals with real estate and it was not in writing and signed. Unfortunately for the buyer, the executed verbal contract for the purchase of real estate is good evidence to the court that the contract existed. Therefore, the statute of frauds is not applicable and the verbal contract is binding.

Part performance involving the transfer of an interest in real property will also remove the contract from the writing requirement of the statute of frauds.

For example, a buyer and seller have a verbal contract to purchase a vacant lot with the deed to be delivered upon full payment. The buyer has made a partial payment of the purchase price, has been allowed to take possession of the property, and start construction of a structure on the property, and has made several periodic payments toward the purchase price. The seller now refuses to fully perform the contract, citing that it involves the sale of real estate and is not in writing and signed. The buyer's possession has been actual, visible, notorious and exclusive. In other words, the buyer has acted like the owner of the property. As such, should the buyer be allowed to finish performance of the verbal contract and acquire the deed to the property? Yes. The buyer, by entering into possession of the property and starting the structure, has completed sufficient part performance to show a contract exists and satisfies the proof requirement under the statute of frauds.

J. MISTAKE

A mistake is an understanding that is not in agreement with the facts as they exist.

Generally, there are two types of mistakes: a mistake of fact and a mistake of law.

1. Mistake of Fact

A ***MISTAKE OF FACT*** *must be material (important) and not something trivial and insignificant whereby the party would have entered into the contract anyway.* Sometimes a major issue is whether or not the mistake of fact is material or trivial.

a. Mutual Mistake

A ***MUTUAL MISTAKE*** *occurs when both parties make the same mistake regarding a material fact.* This prevents a binding contract because the parties did not agree on the same thing (there is no "meeting of the minds"). If that is the case, the contract can be rescinded and the parties place each other back in the position they occupied before contracting.

b. Unilateral Mistake

There is no requirement that the mistake be mutual in order to rescind the contract. *Rescission is possible if only one party made a mistake, usually referred to as a* ***UNILATERAL MISTAKE***, but only in certain situations. As a general rule, if one party makes a mistake which causes that person to enter into the contract, and the other party did not make the same mistake, the parties are bound to the terms of the contract and there will be no rescission by the mistaken party.

It's easy to understand why recession for unilateral mistake is not often granted. If a contract can be rescinded solely on the basis of a person's mistake, anyone who wanted out of a contract would go to court, announce he or she had made a mistake, and seek to rescind the contract.

There are some exceptions where a party is allowed to rescind a contract based on a unilateral mistake. If the non-mistaken party knew that the other party to the contract had made a mistake, or, as a reasonable person standing in the shoes of an offeree, should know of the offeror's mistake, it would be unfair for the non-mistaken party to "snap up" an obviously erroneous offer and force the other person to perform the contract. Sometimes it is difficult to prove what the non-mistaken party knew, or, as a reasonable person, should have known.

c. Clerical or Computational Error

Depending on state law or court decisions, sometimes a party is allowed to rescind a contract based on a clerical or computational error. Generally the error must be material, resulting from simple carelessness or negligence, and have been discovered and communicated to the non-mistaken party before the non-mistaken party relied on the contract to his or her detriment.

d. Error in Judgment

Sometimes relief is refused for a contract entered into because of an error in judgment. An error in judgment is not a clerical or computational mistake. An ***ERROR IN JUDGMENT*** *is when, for example, the tree pruner offers to prune all of the trees on the Hubie Highlands property but forgot to include the cost of the rental of a bucket lift able to reach the necessary height.* This is not a computational error, as the numbers added up correctly and the association has accepted the offer. Is the tree pruner liable on the contract? Yes, if the pruner refuses to do the pruning for the contract price, the association can retain someone else to do the job, and if it costs the association more money, then sue the breaching pruner for the difference between the breached contract price and the new contract price.

2. Mistake of Law

Where both parties to a contract make substantially the same mistake as to what the law actually is, a ***MISTAKE OF LAW*** *has occurred which will permit rescission of the contract.* Where one party is aware the other party is making a mistake of law, the non-mistaken party has a duty to rectify the mistake or else rescission may be an appropriate remedy. This presents a real problem as to proof because of the difficulty the mistaken party will have proving that the other party knew the mistake was being made.

K. ACTUAL FRAUD

The person claiming to be a victim of "actual fraud" must show that a misrepresentation of a material (important) fact was made with knowledge of the misrepresentation and that the victim justifiably relied on the misrepresentation to his or her detriment.

California recognizes five types of actual fraud:

1. Intentional misrepresentation;
2. Negligent misrepresentation;
3. Suppression;
4. False promise; and
5. Any other act intended to deceive another person.

1. Intentional Misrepresentation

INTENTIONAL MISREPRESENTATION means that a statement was made knowing that it was false. In other words it was a lie to induce the other party to enter into the contract.

2. Negligent Misrepresentation

NEGLIGENT MISREPRESENTATION occurs when a positive statement was made, not knowing if it was true, and the other party relied on it. In other words, when the statement was made there was no basis for believing it was true. The statement may have been a guess but, nevertheless, it was a negligent misrepresentation.

3. Suppression

SUPPRESSION is when the truth of a condition is not easily discoverable through reasonable inspection or investigation. For example, there are no required disclosures if a private party wants to sell an automobile knowing that the transmission is going out. If the prospective purchaser does not ask about the transmission, the seller is not obligated to disclose any information. If the buyer purchases the car only to discover the transmission problem, the buyer should have checked the transmission condition before purchasing. There was no active concealment so this is not fraud. *ACTIVE CONCEALMENT takes place where the owner puts a "sludge" in the transmission to hide the shifting problem temporarily.* Also, if the buyer had asked if there were any problems with the transmission, the seller has the obligation to truthfully disclose the facts. There are a number of legally required disclosures regarding a real estate transaction. However, an unscrupulous seller can lie when filling out the disclosure forms and take the money and run before the fraud is discovered.

4. False Promise

A *FALSE PROMISE occurs at the time of entering into a contract when one person makes a promise about performing an obligation with absolutely no intention of performing it.* Once again proof is a problem, because of the difficulty the claiming party has in proving what the state of mind was at the time the other person made the statement.

5. Any Other Act Intended to Deceive

This is the legislature's way of allowing flexibility within the courts. The term "any other fact intended to deceive" gives the courts an opportunity to look at the facts of a case and, if a fact is bad enough but does not fit in with the other actual fraud items, the court can call it an "act to deceive."

The victim of actual fraud will generally have a choice as to whether to rescind the contract and be placed back in the position that he or she was in before the contract was entered into or leave the contract the way it is and seek damages for what it cost to remedy the fraud.

L. CONDITIONS

CONDITIONS *are provisions in the contract which determine the time for performance, the order of performance, or establish the circumstances under which a performance obligation begins or ends.*

Conditions are usually found when words such as "if," "when," "provided," "unless," "as soon as," and "upon the condition that" are used.

A performance obligation in a contract is conditional when the rights or duties of any party to the contract depend on the occurrence of an uncertain event. Conditions are either precedent, concurrent, or subsequent.

1. Condition Precedent

A **CONDITION PRECEDENT** *is one which is to be performed or occur before some right dependent on it accrues, or some act dependent on it is performed.* In other words, the condition has to occur before the happening of the next event. For example, the nursery company does not have to start planting the shrubs and landscaping until such time as the concrete walkways and planter boxes are installed and dry.

In a lawsuit, it is generally the plaintiff's burden to prove a condition precedent has occurred and the defendant has refused to perform.

2. Condition Subsequent

A **CONDITION SUBSEQUENT** *is one referring to a future event, upon the happening of which the obligation becomes no longer binding on the other party if the other party chooses to enforce the condition.* In other words, there is a binding obligation to perform that can be discharged by the occurrence of a condition in the future. For example, the tree pruner promises to have the palm trees pruned by 5 p.m. tomorrow evening provided it does not rain between now and then.

In a lawsuit, it is generally the defendant's burden to prove the occurrence of a condition subsequent which has discharged the defendant from performance.

3. Conditions Concurrent

CONDITIONS CONCURRENT are those which are mutually dependant and are to be performed at the same time. For example, the real estate sales contract calls for the seller to deliver the title to the property to the buyer at exactly the same time that the buyer will deliver the purchase price to the seller.

M. SATISFACTION CLAUSES

A contract may contain a *SATISFACTION CLAUSE that provides that one party's performance must be satisfactory to the other party, and if it is not, the other party does not have to perform.* The usual dispute is whether performance is "satisfactory." Typically, contracts containing a satisfaction clause are put into one of two categories. One category includes contracts involving the personal taste or judgment of a party, and the other category involves contracts which are not personal in nature and generally deal with mechanical operation, sometimes referred to as mechanical utility or operative fitness.

1. Judgment or Taste

If the satisfaction clause in a contract involves the taste or judgment of a party, that party's sole determination of his or her satisfaction is final, as long as the determination was made in good faith.

These contracts usually involve employment or creative services. For example, sometimes a person is hired and told by the employer that he or she can continue to work there as long as his or her performance is satisfactory. This is not an objective standard and is not recommended. Another example of a satisfaction clause might be found in a contract between an association and an artist for a painting of an association's entrance to be displayed in the meeting hall. The contract states that the painting must be satisfactory to both the president and secretary of the association before payment of any money to the artist. Obviously, if the president and secretary do not like the painting, they do not want to display it, nor pay for it. So long as the president and secretary are acting in good faith about their dislikes of the painting, they are protected from liability. On the other hand, if they realize the association is having financial difficulty and would be better off not buying the painting, and use the satisfaction clause as a reason to save money, they are not acting in good faith and are liable for the purchase price. Once again, the question becomes how the artist can prove the association is not acting in good faith.

2. Mechanical Utility or Operative Fitness

If the satisfaction clause in a contract involves mechanical utility or operative fitness, the standard of satisfaction is not the party's personal satisfaction, but whether performance would be satisfactory to a reasonable person.

Suppose an association has contracted for the installation of a new air conditioning system in the meeting hall and the contract contains a clause that says the air conditioning system "must operate satisfactorily." If there is a dispute over the operation of the equipment, the standard is what a reasonable person would think is satisfactory, not what the association thinks is satisfactory.

N. TIME FOR PERFORMANCE

Sometimes the contract specifies the time for performance. This specification can either be general, "by the end of the rainy season," or specific, "by 5 p.m. Thursday, March 17."

If no time is specified for the performance of an act in a contract, a reasonable time period is allowed.

What is reasonable to one person may not be reasonable to another. For example, say you, the association manager, contract with a tree pruner to prune the association palm trees for $750. You become upset when three days pass and the pruner has not returned to prune the trees. On the fourth day, the pruner comes with the equipment to prune the trees and you tell him that the association is canceling the contract because of the pruner's failure to perform. You state that the expectation was the pruner would prune the trees starting the next day. The pruner says there was no time in the contract for commencing nor completing performance, and that commencing performance four days later is perfectly reasonable. What is a reasonable period of time?

You should never enter into a contract without a specific time for performance because it allows for performance to be completed within a "reasonable" period of time—which is unknown.

O. FINAL AGREEMENT CLAUSE

A *FINAL AGREEMENT CLAUSE makes it clear that there are no other agreements between the parties, and that this agreement is final.* A contract may contain a clause similar to below:

> All understandings between the parties are incorporated in this agreement. The agreement terms are intended by the parties as a full, final, complete and exclusive expression of their agreement with respect to the subject matter contained herein, and may not be contradicted by evidence of any prior agreement or of a contemporaneous oral agreement.

In other words, evidence of the agreement may be shown only by the terms of the agreement. It is important to know that if there is something else agreed to by a party that is not stated in the written contract, then it is not enforceable. Therefore, if there is something important agreed to that is not in the written contract, it should be written in the contract before it is signed.

P. BREACH OF CONTRACT

With regard to the administration of an existing contract, as the manager, you need to formulate an action plan in the event of a breach of contract. Recall the previously mentioned breach of contract by the seller of the outdoor furniture. With any breach problem, as the manager, you must determine whether the breach is absolute or a distinct possibility. If it appears to be a distinct possibility, you should attempt to communicate with the other party and use friendly persuasion and explore every option to induce the party to complete contract performance. The association does not have to settle for anything less than it was entitled to receive under the contract. If the breach is absolute, then you need to report the breach to the person you answer to. Most likely, this person is one of the officers of the association or perhaps a committee.

A copy of the contract, any correspondence, and any other supporting documentation should be provided by the manager. It is wise for you, as the manager, to keep a "correspondence record," which means that you make written notations about the verbal conversation with the other contracting party immediately after it takes place. This record prevents future loss of memory issues. Also, you should consider a written confirmation letter after a verbal conversation with a contracting party. This communication does just what it says, it confirms the important matters agreed to in a verbal conversation and will hopefully prevent any misunderstandings or loss of memory issues. Once the matter is delivered to an officer, the matter is now out of your hands and those who are charged with making the appropriate decisions regarding a breach of contract will now make the determination as to what will happen next.

It is important to remember that once the association has entered into a binding contract with another party, the association cannot change its mind at a future date without exposure to potential legal liability.

With a binding contract, an association cannot, at a future date, decide to cancel the contract because it was not in the best interest of the association to enter into it in the first place, or circumstances have changed and it's best not to have to perform the contract. This is a breach of contract and the association has potential liability for damages to the non-breaching party. Perhaps the association will be lucky enough to unilaterally cancel a contract and the other party will merely let the matter fade away without seeking a legal remedy.

II. Contracting Through Agents

A. INTRODUCTION

The ultimate responsibility for conducting the affairs of an association lies with the owners, through the election of a board of directors.

Under the governing documents, the owners elect a board of directors to manage the association on their behalf. Usually, the board members are also owners of separate interests within the development. Since the board of directors is charged with the management of the association, the owners take a "watch and see" position with regard to the functioning of the association. If the membership is not happy with the way the board is running the association, the membership can take action to remove or elect new directors.

In broad terms, the board handles the major decision-making task for the association. The board may decide to run all aspects of the association or to delegate day-to-day management to an owner, a group of owners forming a management committee, hire an individual as an employee to be the association manager, or retain the services of an outside manager, either an individual or a company. Sometimes the governing documents of the association will establish how the association is to be managed. Whatever form management takes, assuming its not day-to-day management by the board of directors, your responsibility, as the manager, is to help implement the decisions of the board of directors. Those decisions may be general or specific in nature.

If the association retains management services independent from the owners, the board will be contracting with either a manager who is an employee of the association or an individual or management company that is retained by the association. In both of these situations, the association is entering into a "contract" with the provider of management services. In some states the provider of management services must make a disclosure to the board of directors regarding qualifications and background.

B. CONSIDERING OUTSIDE MANAGEMENT

When contemplating the need for management by someone other than those within the development, an association must consider the following.

1. Owner Apathy

It is not uncommon for the association to find that the owners are not interested in being involved in the business of running the association affairs. This could include owners living within the development or nonresident owners who rent out their units. Sometimes these nonresident owners have never lived within the development and only purchased the property on speculation as an investment. Other owners may have lived within the development but have since moved to another location. Of course, this may cause a conflict between the resident owners and the nonresident owners.

Nonresident owners, who have tenants in their units, are not particularly interested in having the association incur any expenses which might lead to a change in an assessment amount, since the purpose of the rental is to make money. Resident owners, on the other hand, might be interested in spending association money to "fix up" certain areas in a development to make them more aesthetically pleasing. An additional problem is, as the number of renters occupying units increases, the number of problems also increase. Sometimes renters do not have the same pride of ownership or share the same concerns as other unit owners. Problems often surface with the parking, use of the swimming pool or tennis courts, and use of the association meeting hall.

The quality of a living environment can be reduced by renters, who, as temporary tenants, do not share the same concerns as unit owners.

2. Outside Management Does Not Live There

Associations are run by a board of directors. This could be a relatively small group of individuals running a very large housing development. If a very active core of members places its favorites on the board of directors, that favoritism may be returned by the board doing things to benefit those who elected them. A board member may feel pressure to grant concessions to adjoining neighbors or friends in the development at the expense of owners that are not known personally, absentee owners, tenants, and new owners. Additionally, sometimes the board members take the "appeasement" position and, rather than engage in a conflict with some of the more expressive, vocal, and tenacious owners, will choose the easy route by giving concessions to avoid the conflict. These are the types of problems that a nonresident and outside manager can avoid.

Since an outside manager is a neutral party, it might be easier for that manager to convince or persuade individuals to do something in the best interest of a community without feeling pressure from the neighbors.

3. Nature of the Development

A small common interest development can probably be run by the owners, without the need for an outside manager. Very large developments may need permanent managers residing on-site, working full-time running the association's business. If the development has lots of amenities with governing documents imposing extensive maintenance and repair responsibilities on the association for the common areas, as well as the appropriate separate areas, this may be a project which is beyond the skill of a resident volunteer manager.

An experienced professional management company has the resources to completely run an association's affairs by using its own staff or related contractors.

MANAGEMENT OPTIONS – THE BOARD OF DIRECTORS CHOICE:

1. Through Officers
2. Volunteer Owners or Committee
3. Hire Employee for Association
4. Contract With Managing Agent (Person or Entity)

C. AGENTS FOR THE ASSOCIATION (CORPORATION)

In California, a nonprofit corporation must have a chairman of the board or a president or both, a secretary, a chief financial officer (treasurer) and such other officers with such titles and duties that shall be stated in the bylaws or determined by the board as may be necessary to enable it to sign instruments.

The president, or if there is no president, the chairman of the board, is the general manager and chief executive officer of the corporation, unless otherwise provided in the articles or bylaws.

Any number of offices may be held by the same person unless provided otherwise in the articles or bylaws.

Except as otherwise provided in the articles or bylaws, officers shall be chosen by the board and serve at the pleasure of the board, subject to any rights under a contract of employment. The officers are supposed to be in charge of carrying on the day-to-day business operations of the association. The powers and duties of each officer are generally set by the articles or bylaws of the corporation or by a board resolution.

Like the directors, the officers owe a fiduciary duty to the corporation and must always act in the best interest of the corporation by putting the corporation interests ahead of the personal interests of an officer.

Any contract or conveyance made in the name of the corporation which is authorized or ratified by the board, or is done within the scope of authority, actual or apparent, conferred by the board or within the agency power of the officer executing it, except as the board's authority is limited by law, binds the corporation. For example, the association president hires Roberta Chan to be the association manager.

If a party enters into a contract with an association, believing that the signing officers have the authority to do so, that contract is valid and binding.

Any contract, when signed by the chairman of the board, the president, any vice president, the secretary, an assistant secretary, the chief financial officer, or any assistant treasurer of the corporation is not invalidated as to the corporation by any lack of authority of the signing officers in the absence of actual knowledge on the part of the other person that the signing officers had no authority to sign the contract. For example, if a contract for tree trimming services is signed by the president and secretary of the association, that contract is binding on the corporation regardless of whether those signing lacked the authority to do so, unless the tree trimming service knew of the lack of authority to enter into the contract.

The board may delegate the management of the activities of the corporation to any person or persons, management company, or committee however composed, provided that the activities and affairs of the corporation are managed and all corporate powers are exercised under the ultimate direction of the board. In other words, the board can designate the authority to enter into contracts on behalf of the association to one of the above mentioned groups. However, the association is managed and all its powers are exercised under the ultimate direction of the board.

Since the association, as a corporation, is a separate legal entity and only exists on paper, the above information gives guidance as to who has the authority to bind the association to contracts. In other words, who is an agent for the association.

D. HUBIE HIGHLANDS EXAMPLE

The Hubie Highlands Homeowner's Association, through the actions of its chairman of the board and president, has hired Roberta Chan as its employee property manager to handle the day-to-day business of running the Association. Chan could have been retained as an independent contractor (managing agent). Among other things, the Association has given her the authority to act as an agent and bind the Association to contracts, within certain limits, with third persons. For example, under board direction, Chan contracted on behalf of the Association to have John Jurivick remove cracked tiles and install new ones in the swimming pool area. Therefore, there is a contract between Hubie Highlands Homeowner's Association and John Jurivick. When Jurivick has completed the project he will be paid with a check signed by the treasurer of the Association or Chan, if she has the authority to do so. If she does not have the authority to contract for the Association, she would take Jurivick's bid (offer) to the appropriate Association officer for a decision (see **Figure 11-1**).

Figure 11-1

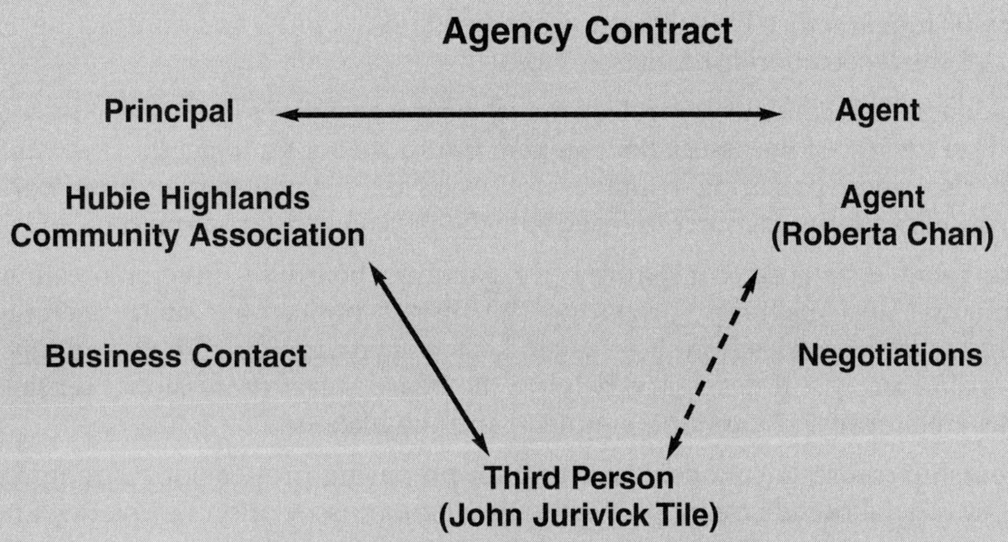

The Hubie Highlands Homeowner's Association currently has two full-time employees to work out of the Association office: a part time bookkeeper/secretary and a full-time handyman. Historically, the Hubie Highlands Homeowner's Association had been managed by a committee of owners appointed by the board of directors who handled the day-to-day activities on a volunteer basis with each committee member working part-time hours during the week.

The committee of volunteers that had been managing the Association did an adequate job, but lacked the consistency necessary to make it run as efficiently as possible. Sometimes volunteers would not show up for their hours of work, lacked enthusiasm, tried to sway everyone on the committee to their way of thinking, were not competent in some areas, and would generally burn out after a year or so on the committee. There was difficulty in finding replacements for the members who resigned from the committee.

E. TYPICAL DUTIES FOR A MANAGER

A contract with an association may provide that the manager will do the following:

1. Financial services consisting of collection of assessment payments from the members, handling collections for delinquent payments, preparing budgets, data sheets, accounting entries, and reports for the board of directors and the memberships, making sure that all funds collected are properly deposited in the bank and properly recorded in the accounting books.
2. Handle enforcement of association rules and regulations.

3. Provide for proper property maintenance, such as: inspection of the premises looking for areas that need repair and preventive maintenance, arranging for the repairs or maintenance by soliciting estimates and/or bids, and contracting on behalf of the association for those services.
4. Risk management, consisting of: reviewing all insurance policies for proper coverage in the best interest of the association, seeking insurance quotes to get the best value for the association, preparing insurance notices for the membership and the board, and working with the treasurer to make sure the premiums are paid on time.
5. Management assistance, consisting of: organizing board of director meetings and membership meetings, preparing the proper notices for such meetings, working with the association secretary to keep a current minute book, and other appropriate records, if necessary, helping the board select professional services such as an attorney, accountant, engineer, and the like.
6. Membership communications, consisting of: preparing proper notices required to be sent to the membership, preparing the regular association newsletter, and preparing any other notices or announcements deemed necessary.
7. Needed services, consisting of: lawn and shrubbery grooming services, maintenance of the security system, cleaning and servicing the swimming pool and tennis courts, and the like.

F. THE EMPLOYEE, THE AGENT, AND THE INDEPENDENT CONTRACTOR

In order to understand how an association is run, it is important to differentiate between employees, agents, and independent contractors. You may have been or currently are an employee. How is the determination made whether or not a person is an employee?

The most significant factor in determining whether a person is an employee is the right of another to control the details of the job, even if the right to control is not being exercised.

The association certainly has the right to exercise control over the activities of their two workers and of Roberta Chan. However, Chan is also an agent for the association with the power to contract on behalf of it with third persons like John Jurivick. In other words, ***EMPLOYEES*** *work for the employer*, while ***AGENTS*** *work for the employer and can contract on behalf of the principal (employer).*

INDEPENDENT CONTRACTORS *are hired by the employer to work "independently" and not under the direction and control of the employer as to the details of the work.* The contract is for the end result and the independent contractor works independently to achieve the result. Therefore, the independent contractor is not an employee. However, the independent contractor may be an agent for a principal. For example, a general contractor building a storage building in the development is an independent contractor and not an employee of the association, but may have the authority to purchase materials on behalf of the association.

If Pat is currently working as a shoe salesperson for a store in the shopping mall, is Pat an employee, or agent, or both? Pat is both an employee and an agent. Pat works under the direction and control of the store owner (employer) as to the details of the job and Pat also enters into contracts on behalf of the store with customers when they purchase shoes. The shoe contract is between the store and the customer and because Pat is an agent for the store Pat is not a party to the contract. Pat's authority to act on behalf of the store is limited to shoe sales. Pat's authority does not cover other areas of store operation, nor would a reasonable customer expect that a salesperson would have authority beyond shoe sales.

As we will see later with employer liability, determining whether a person is an employee or an independent contractor is very important.

G. CREATION OF THE AGENCY

Any person having capacity to contract may appoint an agent, and any person may be an agent. This means a principal must be over the age of eighteen, but an agent does not have the same age requirement.

Normally, the agency relationship is created by an express contract between the principal and the agent.

This contract may be oral or in writing, but in writing is preferred. Even without an express contract, agency can be implied from the words and conduct of the individuals, as well as the circumstances surrounding the activities of the parties. If there is an issue as to whether or not there is an agency, the court will decide that issue based on the facts.

1. Actual or Ostensible Agency

An agency is either actual or ostensible. An ***ACTUAL AGENCY*** *is created by the written or verbal contract between the principal and the agent.* An **OSTENSIBLE AGENCY**, *sometimes referred to as an apparent agency, is created by actions, or inactions, of the principal which cause a third person to believe another to be the agent of the principal when that is not the case.* This means the principal did or did not do something which caused a third person to believe another was the agent for the principal and, consequently, an agency exists.

Ostensible agency cannot be created by actions or representations of anyone other than the principal.

For example, the president is asked by Jurivick if Chan is the person to talk to about a replacement tile contract. The president says that Chan is that person and "whatever she says goes as far as the Association is concerned." It now appears to Jurivick that Chan can bind Hubie Highlands Homeowner's Association to a tile contract even though Chan does not have the authority to do so.

2. Agency By Ratification

An agency can also be created by ratification. ***RATIFICATION*** *takes place when the principal accepts the benefits of a transaction done by a person who is not the agent for the principal.* The principal thereby shows an intention to be bound by the transaction with the third person and entered into on the principal's behalf.

For ratification to take place, the person whose unauthorized action is being considered for ratification must have told the third person that he or she was acting as an agent for the principal.

For example, if an appliance store delivery person attempts delivery of a large screen television set allegedly purchased by you through your agent, you are not bound by the agreement since you do not have an agent. However, if this person represented to the appliance store that he or she was acting as your agent and you choose to keep the television set, then you have ratified the contract and must pay for it. The third party may cancel the transaction at any time prior to ratification since there is no contract with you until ratification takes place.

H. THE AGENT'S RELATIONSHIP WITH THE PRINCIPAL

An agent owes the highest degree of diligent and loyal service to the principal.

In general terms, it is said that the agent has a fiduciary duty to the principal. More specifically, the duties owed by an agent to the principal consist of a duty of care and a duty of loyalty.

1. Duty of Care

The duty of care requires the agent (Chan) to follow the instructions of the principal (Association) using reasonable care and skill in performance of the job.

Can an agent ever disobey the instruction of the principal? An agent can disobey instructions from the principal where it is clearly in the best interest of the principal that the agent should do so and there is no time to communicate with the principal for instructions. For example, a flash flood threatens the development and there is not time to have a board meeting. Chan contracts with a company for sandbagging for $5,800 and saves the development. Her agency contract forbids her from contracting for over $5,000. To save the development, she can disobey the instructions.

2. Duty of Loyalty

The duty of loyalty requires that an agent be loyal to the principal at all times.

Usually, this means obedience, accounting, and notification. An agent cannot compete against the principal in areas related to the agency unless they have agreed otherwise. Also, anything acquired by the agent as result of the agency belongs to the principal. For example, confidential information or customer lists acquired while the agent was working for the principal belongs to the principal.

Any secret profits or gifts that an agent acquires as a result of the agency can be recovered by the principal, unless they agree otherwise.

For example, Roberta Chan, representing the Hubie Highlands Homeowner's Association, purchased tennis nets and equipment from Tom's Tennis on behalf of the Association. The seller gave Chan an expensive wrist watch when the contract was signed. Chan can keep the wrist watch if a full disclosure of its acquisition is made to the Association and it permits Chan to keep it. If Chan keeps the wrist watch a secret and it is discovered, the Association can recover the wrist watch as well as terminate Chan's employment.

An agent cannot place his or her personal interest ahead of the principal's.

The agent must get permission from the principal prior to the purchasing of anything the principal is selling or buying anything the principal is buying. An agent must make a full and complete accounting of the affairs of the agency to the principal if requested. The agent must also inform the principal of any information acquired with regard to the agency.

FOR EXAMPLE - California Civil Code Section 2332

As against a principal, both principal and agent are deemed to have notice of whatever either has notice of, and ought, in good faith and the exercise of ordinary care and diligence, to communicate to the other.

This means whenever the agent learns about the agency, the principal instantaneously knows, when in fact, the principal might never be told by the agent.

I. DUTIES OF PRINCIPAL TO AGENT

If the agent is also an employee, the employer (principal) is obligated to the employee (agent) for all of the responsibilities provided in the California Labor Code. Additionally, the principal must indemnify the agent for cost and expenses incurred in performing the duties of the agency. *INDEMNIFICATION in this sense means to reimburse.* However, if the agent's actions were unauthorized, negligent, or willful the principal is under no duty to indemnify the agent.

J. THE RELATIONSHIP BETWEEN THE PRINCIPAL, THE THIRD PERSON, AND THE AGENT

The general rule is that a principal is never bound on an agreement with a third person unless the agent had authority to enter into the agreement.

There are three sources of an agent's authority: actual, ostensible, and ratification.

1. Actual Authority

ACTUAL AUTHORITY is that which the principal expressly gives the agent, or intentionally, or by want of ordinary care allows the agent to believe the agent has. This authority is usually expressed in the employment contract. How does the agent convince a third person of the agency? For example, when Roberta Chan arrives at Tom's Tennis to purchase the nets and equipment, Tom has two immediate concerns. One concern is verifying whether Chan is an agent for the Association (principal) and the other is whether Chan is authorized by the Association to purchase these items on its behalf. Usually, this can be satisfied by Tom communicating with the principal. Tom is not allowed to rely on statements about the agency made by Chan. When Chan enters into a valid contract on behalf of the principal for the purchase, it is also binding on Tom.

Actual authority also consists of any authority given to the agent by statute.

FOR EXAMPLE - California Civil Code § 2319(1)

An agent has the authority to do everything necessary or proper and usual, in the ordinary course of business, for effecting the purpose of the agency.

2. Ostensible Authority

OSTENSIBLE AUTHORITY of the agent, like ostensible agency, comes from actions or statements, or the lack thereof, made intentionally or carelessly by the principal causing a third person to believe that the agent has authority to act on behalf of the principal.

Ostensible authority is not created by actions or words of the "agent."

It can be created in either of two instances:

1. When a person purports to act as an agent for a principal when in fact the person is not an agent; or
2. When an agent purports to act on behalf of a principal but does not have the authority to contract in that particular subject matter area.

The principal becomes liable on the contract if the third person changed his or her position by relying upon the ostensible authority. When a principal titles someone as general manager, that conveys considerable ostensible authority. Through the eyes of third persons it certainly appears that the general manager would have authority to do all things reasonable and necessary for running that type of business. Therefore, general managers have considerable power to contract for the principal, even when actual authority does not exist.

For example, the Hubie Highlands Association authorizes Chan to buy grass seed and Chan calls on Karen's Nursery, having previously entered into several contracts with her to purchase seed. Is the Association bound to a contract through Karen for the purchase of grass seed and lawn fertilizer if the Association does not want the fertilizer? Chan had no actual authority to buy fertilizer, only seed. Nevertheless, the contract for fertilizer is binding between Karen and the Association. Karen may or may not let the Association cancel the fertilizer contract.

The general rule is that a principal is never bound by a contract where the agent (Chan) had no authority to act.

Since Chan had no actual authority to purchase fertilizer, why is the Hubie Highlands Association bound on the contract? Because Chan had ostensible authority to purchase fertilizer for the Association. The Association placed Chan in a position as viewed through the eyes of local merchants, to purchase landscape materials for Hubie Highlands and, therefore, because of previous dealings, Karen relied on the ostensible authority in selling the fertilizer. Chan has liability to the Association for any loss resulting from the purchase of the fertilizer and can be fired for breach of the employment contract.

If Chan purchased a water ski boat on behalf of the Association, is the principal bound? No, Chan has neither actual authority nor ostensible authority to purchase a water ski boat or any other item not related to running a development. Therefore, unless the Association ratifies the contract for the purchase of the ski boat, it is unenforceable. The seller of the ski boat should have verified Chan's authority with the principal before entering into the sales agreement.

3. Ratification

Even though the principal is not bound on a contract with the third person because of the lack of actual or ostensible authority, the principal can become liable on a contract by ratifying the unauthorized act. Ratification means the principal agrees to be liable for an unauthorized act.

For ratification to take place, the principal must have full knowledge of all of the material facts involved in the unauthorized act in order to make a determination whether to ratify it and form a contract or, in the alternative, return any benefit received to the third person.

If the principal did not have full knowledge of the material facts, the principal can later rescind the contract. Usually ratification will take place by acceptance of the benefit of the transaction by the principal or some confirmation of the contract sent by the principal. Additionally, the principal has to have the power to authorize the act at the time of ratification; you can't ratify something you could not have done in the first place.

K. UNDISCLOSED PRINCIPAL

In our material so far, the identity of the principal has been made known to the third person. *On occasion, the principal may wish to sell items or purchase items without third persons realizing the identity of the party with whom they are contracting. The principal becomes an* **UNDISCLOSED PRINCIPAL** and retains an agent to carry out the undisclosed principal's directions without telling the third person that a principal is involved. Obviously, the third person believes that he or she is contracting with the agent, not knowing the agent is acting for an undisclosed principal. Therefore, in the event of a breach of contract, the third person can hold either the agent or, upon discovery of the principal's identity, the principal liable for breach of contract. Since there can only be one contract, the third person must make an election sometime during the litigation so there will be a judgment against only one contracting party.

If the third person breaks the contract, the principal may become disclosed and sue to enforce the contract. However, a third person dealing with an undisclosed principal may deduct claims the third person has against the agent from any payments arising from the contract. This deduction arises from the belief that the third person is contracting with the individual who is not known to the third person to be an agent. All deductions are proper until such time as the third person receives notice of the agency.

L. THE RELATIONSHIP BETWEEN THE AGENT AND THE THIRD PERSON

When an agent performs an authorized act on behalf of the principal with a third person, the contract is between the principal and the third person.

The agent is not a party to that contract and, hence, not liable should either the principal or the third party breach the contract. When the agent purports to act on behalf of the principal, the third person receives a warranty from the agent that the agent does in fact have authority to act on behalf of the principal. If it turns out that the agent committed an act without authority and the principal is not bound on the contract, the third person can hold the agent liable for damages for breach of the warranty of authority.

It is important to realize that if you are an agent for a principal and are not sure of whether you have the authority to bind your principal, communicate with your principal to confirm the authority or lack thereof.

If you are unable to communicate with your principal, you must make it clear to the third person that you are not sure of your authority and will not warrant that you have the authority to bind the principal. As a practical matter, make sure that you get a written agreement from the third person to that effect.

An agent or employee is always liable for his or her own torts, for example negligence or fraud.

If the agent commits a fraud on the third person, the agent is liable to the third person whether or not the principal is liable. The principal can become liable for the fraud by either instructing the agent to commit the fraud or by ratification of the fraudulent act.

Generally, an agent is not liable for the torts of the principal unless the agent participates in the activity.

A principal may give false information to the agent that the agent reasonably believes to be true. If the agent makes representations to a third person of this false information, the agent is not liable to the third person because the statements were made reasonably believing them to be true. However, the principal is liable to the third person. On the other hand, if prior to contracting, the agent discovers that the statements are false, the agent must tell the third person. If the agent does not do so the agent is committing a fraud on the third person and is liable for damages.

M. TERMINATION OF THE AGENCY

1. Termination By Law

California law provides that an agency is terminated, as to every person having notice thereof, by any of the following:

1. The expiration of its term.
2. The extinction of its subject.
3. The death of the agent.
4. The agent's renunciation of the agency.
5. The incapacity of the agent to act as such.

If the agency is due to expire on November 15, the agency and the authority within it terminates on that date. If the agency is to sell a rare painting, the destruction of the painting or its sale terminates the agency. The agency terminates at the very instant of death of the agent. If the agent refuses to be employed as an agent or loses the capacity to act as an agent, the agency terminates at that moment. A temporary illness, injury, or disability does not, by itself, terminate the agency.

2. Termination By the Principal

Looking at termination from the principal's view, unless the power of an agent is coupled with an interest, the agency is terminated by revocation by the principal or the death or incapacity of the principal. However, there is a binding contract if a bona fide transaction was entered into through the agent with a third person acting without knowledge of the revocation, death, or incapacity of the principal.

In the event of death or incapacity, the contract binds the estate of the principal.

Regarding revocation, the employment contract is generally either one "at will" or "for a term." *If the employment contract is **AT WILL**, it can usually be terminated when the principal or the agent desires to do so.* No just cause is needed for termination; the agency ends, and usually, there is no liability for damages. *If the employment contract is **FOR A TERM**, the principal (employer) or the employee (agent) will have to show just cause for terminating the employment contract in order to avoid liability for damages.* Whether or not there was just cause, the authority to bind the principal is extinguished.

3. Notice of Termination

Let's assume an agent has been acting as such for many years and the employment contract terminates on May 12. At that moment, the authority to bind the principal to contracts is extinguished. Will the principal be bound on a usual contract with a third person entered into on behalf of the principal by the former agent on May 14? The answer is yes since the termination of the authority on May 12 is effective as to every person having notice thereof. Therefore, if the principal is worried about becoming bound on a contract entered into through a former agent, the principal must give notice of termination of authority to third persons. This is because the third person, having not received notice of the termination of the authority, is dealing with an ostensible agent. Nothing appears to the third person to have changed.

Individual (or actual) notices must be given to third parties where the third party had previously dealt with the agent on behalf of the principal or to third parties where the principal knows the agent had begun to negotiate.

In all other cases, the notice of termination will be effective if advertised in a newspaper of general circulation in the area where the agent conducted business on behalf of the principal.

The public notice of termination of authority in a newspaper is sometimes referred to as "constructive notice."

4. Power Coupled With an Interest

If an agent's power is coupled with an interest, the principal is unable to terminate the agency.

A ***POWER COUPLED WITH AN INTEREST*** *is one which is created for the benefit of the agent instead of the principal.* For example, a principal asked his agent to loan him $20,000. She is reluctant to do so because of the poor financial condition of the principal. The principal and the agent ultimately contract for the loan of $20,000 by the agent in exchange for which the agent is appointed as the exclusive agent to sell a rare painting owned by the principal for a minimum of $30,000. The contract provides that the sole source for repayment of the loan plus interest is from the proceeds of the sale of the painting. Additionally, the agent is to receive a fifteen percent commission on the sales price of the painting. This is a power coupled with an interest. The "interest" has to be something more than the compensation for services rendered by the agent; in this case the agent's fifteen percent commission. The "power coupled with an interest" is the agent's power to sell the painting as her sole means of recovering the principle and interest on the loan. Therefore, the principal's death, incapacity, or attempted revocation are ineffective to terminate her power to sell the painting.

N. PRINCIPAL'S LIABILITY FOR ACTS OF THE AGENT

A principal may be held liable for the acts of an agent under the following circumstances.

1. Principal's Wrongful Conduct

A principal is liable for wrongful acts committed by an agent transacting business for the principal if the principal authorized or ratified those acts.

For example, a principal intentionally misrepresents important information needed by the agent to transact business for the principal. The agent gives that information to a third person, not realizing that it is incorrect, and the third person relies on that information and suffers a loss. The principal, and not the agent, is responsible for the damages suffered by the third person. A principal is also liable if the principal ratifies a wrongful act by an agent.

2. Respondeat Superior

Every day members of our society commit wrongful acts, generally called **TORTS**. For example, you might be the victim of another person's fraud or physically harmed by their negligence or intentional acts. Obviously, the person who commits the tort is liable to you for the damages caused by that act. We will now consider when a principal is vicariously liable for the torts caused by the principal's agent.

The doctrine of "respondeat superior" holds the principal liable for the torts of employees/agents.

Certainly the employee is liable for his or her own torts, but why should the innocent principal also be liable? The California Supreme Court, in *Hinman v. Westinghouse Electric Company*, 2 Cal. 3d 956, 88 Cal.Rptr.188, 471 P.2d 988 (1970), quoted the eminent legal scholar Dean Prosser regarding the reason for the doctrine of respondeat superior:

> Although earlier authorities sought to justify the respondeat superior doctrine on such theories as "control" by the master of the servant, the masters "privilege" in being permitted to employ another, the third party's innocence in comparison to the master's selection of the servant, or the master's "deep pocket" to pay for the loss, the modern justification for vicarious liability is a rule of policy, a deliberate allocation of a risk. The losses caused by the torts of employees, which as a practical matter are sure to occur in the conduct of the employer's enterprise, are placed upon that enterprise itself, as a required cost of doing business. They are placed upon the employer because, having engaged in an enterprise which will, on the basis of past experience, involve harm to others through the torts of employees, and sought to profit by it, it is just he,

rather than the innocent injured plaintiff, should bear them; and because he is better able to absorb them, and to distribute them, through prices, rates or liability insurance, to the public, and so to shift them to society, to the community at large.

a. Requirements of Doctrine of Respondeat Superior

Under the doctrine of respondeat superior, a principal is liable for the torts committed by an agent if: 1) the agent is an employee; and 2) the agent committed the tort while acting in the course of employment.

The doctrine of respondeat superior holds the principal liable whether or not the agent violated expressed instructions or exceeded his or her authority.

The first requirement for a plaintiff to win a lawsuit under the doctrine respondeat superior is to prove that the individual causing the harm was an employee of the principal at the time of the event. The test for determining employment, mentioned earlier in the chapter, is the right of the employer to control the details of the job.

The second requirement is that the employee was acting within the course of his or her employment at the time of the event. The determination as to whether an employee committed a tort during the course of his employment turns on whether or not: 1) the act performed was either required or incident to his duty; or 2) the employee's misconduct could be reasonably foreseen by the employer in any event.

Generally, the issue is determining whether the agent was "on the job" performing the work he or she was hired to perform. However, sometimes it's not clear whether the agent was acting in the course of employment. Should the principal be liable if the agent was on the job at the time of the event but doing something for his or her personal benefit?

Generally, if the personal benefit activity is considered a "minor deviation" from the course and scope of employment, the principal is liable.

The principal is not liable if the personal benefit activity constitutes a "substantial departure" from the course and scope of the agent's employment. Who determines whether, under the facts, the activity of the agent was a substantial departure or a minor deviation? This is to be determined by the jury, unless the facts are undisputed and no conflicting inferences are possible, then the determination will be made by the judge. Note that at the time of the event causing harm to the plaintiff, the agent could be doing something completely for personal benefit, but, as long as it is a minor deviation, the principal has liability.

b. Employee Carelessness

Most situations will involve employee carelessness or negligence causing harm to someone's person or property. If respondeat superior applies, the employer (principal) is also liable to pay for the damages. The employee is liable to the employer for damages paid by the employer caused by the employee. Employers use insurance to protect against such liability. There is a problem if the claim exceeds the amount of the employer's insurance.

c. Employee Assaults

The principal is liable for intentional harm caused by the agent if the act is committed in the scope of employment.

The typical cases involve an agent's assault or fraud. An ***ASSAULT*** *is placing a person in immediate fear of bodily harm or offensive contact*. If the assault is in some way connected to the scope of employment and is motivated by the job rather than a completely independent personal act, the employer is liable for the harm caused by the assault.

d. Fraud

The principal will be liable for the fraudulent acts of an agent while acting in the course of employment, even though the principal was unaware of the fraudulent statements. Additionally, where the principal authorizes the fraudulent representations or is aware of the fraud and does nothing, the principal is liable.

If both the employer and employee are responsible to a victim for a loss suffered, the victim may sue both, but must ultimately elect to recover against only one of them.

O. EMPLOYER'S LIABILITY FOR ACTIONS OF INDEPENDENT CONTRACTORS

Historically, an employer was not liable for harm caused by the actions of an independent contractor or the employees of the independent contractor. However, over time, significant exceptions from the historic rule have been created. If the employer (association) is negligent or careless in checking out the qualifications of the independent contractor and the independent contractor is not competent and has a history of careless acts, the employer may be liable for injuries caused by the contractor's lack of skill or inability to act with reasonable care. Certainly this is something Chan should investigate before recommending an independent contractor.

If the independent contractor is following the directions, requirements, or plans of the employer and such conduct results in injury or damage to others or their property, the employer is liable.

On the other hand, if the plans, requirements, or directions are proper and, nevertheless, the independent contractor is careless in following those plans, the employer is not liable.

Also, an employer may be liable when employing an independent contractor to perform work which is inherently dangerous and, in so doing, someone else is injured. A major issue is determining what inherently dangerous work is.

If the employer has to pay for the actions of the independent contractor, the employer is entitled to indemnification from the independent contractor.

It makes good sense for the employer to have adequate insurance as well as verify the contractor's insurance. Keep in mind that if the harm or injury caused results from something other than the nature of the job, the employer is not liable. For example, if the independent contractor uses a defective lawnmower for the job which caused harm or damage, the employer would not be liable. If the independent contractor is negligent or careless, causing injury or damage to the independent contractor's employees, the employer is not liable.

III. Required Disclosures and Conduct for California CID Managers

In California's Davis-Stirling Act and the Business and Professions Code, there are required disclosures pertaining to common interest development managers.

A. BUSINESS AND PROFESSIONS CODE

1. Terms

A ***COMMON INTEREST DEVELOPMENT MANAGER*** *is an individual who, for compensation, or the expectation of compensation, provides or contracts to provide management or financial services, or represents himself or herself to act in the capacity of providing management or financial services to a community association.*

FINANCIAL SERVICES *are acts performed or offered to be performed for compensation for a community association including, but not limited to, the preparation of internal* *unaudited financial statements, internal accounting and bookkeeping functions, billing of assessments, and related services.*

***MANAGEMENT SERVICES** are acts performed or offered to be performed in an advisory capacity for a community association.* These include, but are not limited to, the following:

1. Administering or supervising the financial or common area assets of a community association or common interest development, at the direction of the community association's governing board.
2. Implementing resolutions and directives of the board of directors.
3. Implementing provisions of the governing documents.
4. Administering a community association's contracts, including insurance contracts.

A common interest development manager can contract to provide management services or financial services or both to the community association.

An individual who is a member of a business entity who acts as a principal on behalf of a company that provides the services of a common interest development manager is personally considered to be a common interest development manager.

B. ANNUAL DISCLOSURE

On or before September 1, 2003, and on an annual basis thereafter, a person who either provides or contemplates providing the services of a common interest development manager to a community association must disclose to the board of directors the following information:

1. Whether or not the manager has met the requirements to be called a certified common interest development manager. If so, the name, address, and telephone number of the association that certified the manager, along with the date of certification and the status of certification.
2. The location of his or her primary office.
3. Prior to entering into or renewing a contract with a community association, the manager must disclose to the board whether the fidelity insurance of the community manager or his or her employer covers the operating and reserve funds of the community association. This requirement cannot be construed to compel or require a community association or common interest development manager to require fidelity insurance.
4. The possession of an active real estate license, if applicable.

C. CERTIFIED CID MANAGER

The law provides that in order to be called a "certified" common interest development manager, the individual must meet certain educational and testing requirements.

A common interest development management firm cannot become a certified common interest development manager.

Listing oneself as "certified," or using any other term that implies or suggests certification without having met the legal requirements for certification, is an unfair business practice. It is also an unfair business practice to state or advertise that a person is certified, registered, or licensed by a governmental agency to perform the functions of a certified common interest development manager if he or she is not. Additionally, to state or advertise a registration number, unless required by law, is also an unfair business practice.

D. DAVIS-STIRLING ACT DISCLOSURES

1. Disclosure

Under the Davis-Stirling Act, a prospective managing agent of a common interest development must provide a written statement to the board of directors of the association as soon as practicable, but in no event more than 90 days before entering into a management agreement which shall contain all of the following information concerning the managing agent:

1. The names and business addresses of the owners or general partners of the managing agent. If a corporation, the names and business addresses of the directors and officers and shareholders holding greater than 10% of the shares of the corporation.
2. Current licenses held by the persons in paragraph 1 above, such as architectural design, construction, engineering, real estate, or accounting, which have been issued by the state. Regarding such a license, the statement must include: what license is held, the dates the license is valid, and the name of the licensee on the license. Additionally, current professional certifications or designations held by persons in paragraph 1 above, such as architectural design, construction, engineering, real property management, accounting, and including a professional common interest development manager. If any certification or designation is held the statement must state: 1) what the certification or designation is or what entity issued it; 2) the dates the certification or designation is valid; and 3) the names in which the certification or designation is held.
3. A ***MANAGING AGENT*** *is a person or entity who, for compensation or in expectation of compensation, exercises control over the assets of a common interest*

development. A managing agent does not include either a full-time employee of the association or any regulated financial institution operating within the normal course of its regulated business practice (California Civil Code Section 1363.1).

2. Managing Agent Handling Funds

In California, a managing agent of a common interest development who receives funds belonging to the association must deposit all such funds that are not placed into an escrow account with a bank, savings association, or credit union, or into an account under the control of the association, into a trust fund account maintained by the managing agent in a bank, savings association, or credit union in the state.

All funds deposited must be kept in a financial institution which is insured by the federal government and must be maintained there until dispersed in accordance with written instructions from the association.

At the written request of the board of directors, the funds received shall be deposited into an interest-bearing bank account in a bank, savings association, or credit union in the state, provided all of the following requirements are met:

1. The account is in the name of the managing agent as trustee for the association or in the name of the association.
2. All of the funds in the account are covered by insurance by an agency of the federal government.
3. The funds are kept separate, distinct, and apart from funds belonging to the managing agent or any other person or entity the managing agent holds funds in trust for, except that in very limited situations pursuant to state law the funds may be commingled.
4. The managing agent discloses to the board the nature of the account, how interest will be calculated and paid, whether service charges will be paid to the depository and by whom, and any notice requirements or penalties for withdraw of funds from the account.
5. No interest earned on funds in the account can go directly or indirectly to the benefit of the managing agent or his or her employees.

The managing agent shall maintain a separate record of the receipt and disposition of all funds deposited including any interest earned.

IV. Discrimination in Employment Contracts

The Equal Employment Opportunity Commission (EEOC) enforces Title VII of the Civil Rights Act, the Equal Pay Act of 1963, the Age Discrimination in Employment Act of 1967, the Rehabilitation Act of 1973 (Section 501 and 505), Titles I and V of the Americans with Disabilities Act of 1990, and the Civil Rights Act of 1991.

The United States Equal Employment Opportunity Commission (EEOC) has an excellent website which contains an enormous amount of material about discrimination in employment. The following material is based upon or duplicated from the website and provides basic or important information to consider when the association, managing agent, or management service company is hiring employees.

www.eeoc.gov
U.S. Equal Employment Opportunity Commission

A. AGE DISCRIMINATION IN EMPLOYMENT ACT

The *AGE DISCRIMINATION IN EMPLOYMENT ACT OF 1967 (ADEA) protects individuals who are 40 years of age or older from employment discrimination based on age.* These protections apply to both employees and job applicants. It is unlawful to discriminate against the person because of his or her age with respect of any term, condition, or privilege of employment, including hiring, firing, promotion, layoff, compensation, benefits, job assignments, and training. Additionally, it is unlawful to retaliate against an individual for opposing employment practices that discriminate based on age or for filing an age discrimination charge, testifying, or participating in any way in an investigation, proceeding, or litigation under the ADEA.

This act applies to employers with 20 or more employees, including governments, labor unions and employment agencies.

B. AMERICANS WITH DISABILITIES ACT OF 1990

The *AMERICANS WITH DISABILITIES ACT OF 1990 (ADA) prohibits private employers, with 15 or more employees, including governments, employment agencies, and labor unions, from discriminating against qualified individuals with disabilities in job application procedures, hiring, firing, advancement, compensation, job training, and other terms, conditions, and privileges of employment.* An individual with a disability is a person who:

1. has a physical or mental impairment that substantially limits one or more major life activities;

2. has a record of such an impairment; or
3. is regarding as having such an impairment.

A qualified applicant or employee with a disability is an individual who, with or without reasonable accommodation, can perform the central functions of the job in question. Reasonable accommodation may include, but is not limited to:

1. making existing facilities used by employees readily accessible to and usable by persons with disabilities;
2. job restructuring, modifying work schedules, reassignment to a vacant position;
3. acquiring or modifying equipment or devices adjusting or modifying examinations, training materials, or policies, and providing qualified readers or interpreters.

An employer is required to make a reasonable accommodation to the known disability of a qualified applicant or employee if it would not impose an undue hardship on the operation of the employer's business.

UNDUE HARDSHIP *is defined as an action requiring significant difficulty or expense when considered in light of factors such as an employers size, financial resources, and the nature and structure of its operation.* An employer is not required to lower quality or production standards to make an accommodation, nor is an employer obligated to provide personal use items such as glasses or hearing aids.

Employers may not ask job applicants about the existence, nature, or severity of a disability.

Applicants may be asked about their ability to perform specific job functions. A job offer may be conditioned on the results of a medical examination, but only if the examination is required for all entering employees in similar jobs.

Medical examinations of employees must be job-related and consistent with the employer's business needs.

Employees and applicants currently engaged in the illegal use of drugs are not covered by the ADA when an employer acts on the basis of such use. Tests for illegal drugs are not subject to the ADA's restrictions on medical examination. Employers may hold illegal drug users and alcoholics to the same performance standards as other employees.

Considering the above, when interviewing a prospective employee it would be advisable to ask about the person's abilities and not disabilities. Consider handing the employee a list of specific job tasks and ask the applicant how the applicant will complete or perform each task.

It is also unlawful to retaliate against an individual for imposing employment practices that discriminate based on disability or for filing an age discrimination charge, testifying, or participating in any way in an investigation, proceeding, or litigation under the ADA.

C. TITLE VII OF THE CIVIL RIGHTS ACT OF 1964

TITLE VII OF THE CIVIL RIGHTS ACT OF 1964 protects individuals against employment discrimination on the basis of race and color, as well as national origin, sex, and religion as well as an amendment for pregnancy. Title VII applies to employers with 15 or more employees, including state and local governments, as well as employment agencies, labor organizations, and the federal government. It is unlawful to retaliate against an individual for opposing employment practices that discriminate based on race or color, national origin, sex, religion, pregnancy, or for filing a discrimination charge, testifying, or participating in any way in an investigation, proceeding, or litigation under Title VII.

1. Race and Color Discrimination

It is unlawful to discriminate against any applicant or employee because of his or her race or color in regard to hiring, termination, promotion, compensation, job training, or any other term, condition, or privilege of employment. Title VII also prohibits employment decisions based on stereotypes and assumptions about abilities, traits, or the performance of individuals of certain racial groups. Title VII prohibits both intentional discrimination and neutral job policies that disproportionately exclude minorities and that are not job related. Equal employment opportunity cannot be denied because of marriage to or association with an individual of a different race, membership in or association with ethnic based organization or groups, or attendance or participation in schools or places of worship generally associated with certain minority groups.

Title VII violations include:

1. Discrimination on the basis of an immutable characteristic associated with race, such as skin color, hair texture, or certain facial features even though not all members of the race share the same characteristic. Also prohibited is discrimination on the basis of a condition that predominately affects one race unless the practice is job related and consistent with business necessity.
2. Harassment on the basis of race and/or color violates Title VII. Ethnic slurs, racial jokes, offensive or derogatory comments, or other verbal or physical conduct based on an individual's race or color constitutes unlawful harassment if the conduct creates an intimidating, hostile, or offensive working environment or interferes with the individual's work performance.

3. Title VII is violated where employees who belong to a protected group are segregated by physically isolating them from other employees or customer contact. Employers may not assign employees according to race or color. It is also illegal to exclude members from one group from particular positions or to group or categorize employees or jobs so that certain jobs are generally held by members of a certain protected group.
4. Requesting pre-employment information that discloses or tends to disclose an applicant's race strongly suggests that race will be used unlawfully as a basis for hiring.

2. Sex Discrimination

Title VII protects individuals against employment discrimination on the basis of sex. It is unlawful to discriminate against any employee or applicant for employment because of his or her sex in regard to hiring, termination, promotion, compensation, job training, or any other term, condition, or privilege of employment. It also prohibits employment decisions based on stereo types and assumptions about the abilities, traits, or performance of individuals on the basis of sex. Title VII prohibits both intentional discrimination and neutral job policies that proportionally exclude individuals on the basis of sex and that are not job related. Prohibited sex-based discrimination also covers:

1. Sexual harassment, which includes practices ranging from direct request for sexual favors to work place conditions that create a hostile environment or persons of either gender, including same sex harassment.
2. Discrimination is prohibited on the basis of pregnancy, child birth, and related medical conditions.
3. The Equal Pay Act of 1963 requires that men and women be given equal pay for equal work. The jobs need not be identical but they must be substantially equal. Title VII also prohibits compensation discrimination on the basis of sex. Unlike the Equal Pay Act, however, Title VII does not require that the claimant's job be substantially equal to that of a higher paid person of the opposite sex or require the claimant to work in the same establishment.

3. Sexual Harassment

Unwelcome sexual advances, request for sexual favors, and other verbal or physical conduct of a sexual nature constitute sexual harassment when this conduct explicitly or implicitly effects an individual's employment, unreasonably interferes with an individual's work performance, or creates and intimidating, hostile, or offensive work environment. Sexual harassment can occur in a variety of circumstances, including but not limited to the following:

1. The victim as well as the harasser may be a man or a women. The victim does not have to be of the opposite sex.

2. The harasser can be the victim's supervisor, an agent of the employer, an supervisor in another area, a co-worker, or a non-employee.
3. The victim does not have to be the person harassed. It could be anyone affected by the offensive conduct.
4. Unlawful sexual harassment may occur without economical injury to or discharge of the victim.
5. The harasser's conduct must be unwelcome.

It is helpful for the victim to inform the harasser directly that the conduct is unwelcome and must stop immediately. The victim should use any employer complaint process or grievance system. Employers should take steps to prevent sexual harassment from occurring. They should clearly communicate to employees that sexual harassment will not be tolerated. Employers should take immediate and appropriate action when an employee complains.

4. National Origin Discrimination

National origin discrimination means treating someone else less favorably because he or she comes from a particular place, because of his or her ethnicity or accent, or because it is believed that he or she has a particular ethnic background. National origin discrimination also means treating someone else less favorably at work because of marriage or association with someone of a particular nationality.

Violations include:

1. Title VII prohibits any employment decision, including recruitment, hiring, and firing or layoff, based on national origin.
2. Title VII prohibits offensive conduct, such as ethnic slurs, that creates a hostile work environment based on national origin. Employers are required to take appropriate steps to prevent and correct unlawful harassment. Likewise, employees are responsible for reporting harassment at an early state to prevent its escalation.
3. An employer may not base a decision on an employee's foreign accent unless the accent materially interferes with job performance. A fluency requirement, such as English, is only permissible if required for the effective performance of the position for which it is imposed. English-only rules must be adopted for nondiscriminatory reasons. An English-only rule may be used if it's needed to promote the safe or efficient operation of the employer's business.
4. Title VII and other anti-discriminatory laws prohibit discrimination against individuals employed in the United States, regardless of citizenship. However, relief may be limited if an individual does not have work authorization.

5. Pregnancy Discrimination

Discrimination on the basis of pregnancy, childbirth, or related medical conditions constitutes unlawful sex discrimination under Title VII. Women who are pregnant or affected by related conditions must be treated in the same manner as other applicants or employees with similar abilities or limitations.

Those protections include:

1. An employer cannot refuse to hire a pregnant woman because of her pregnancy, because of a pregnancy-related condition, or because of the prejudices of co-workers, clients, or customers.
2. An employer may not single out pregnancy-related conditions for special procedures to determine an employee's ability to work. If an employee is temporarily unable to perform her job due to pregnancy, the employer must treat her the same as any other temporarily disabled employee. Pregnant employees must be permitted to work as long as they are able to perform their jobs. If an employee has been absent from work as a result of a pregnancy-related condition and recovers, her employer may not require her to remain on leave until the baby's birth. An employer also may not have a rule that prohibits an employee from returning to work for a predetermined length of time after childbirth. Employers must hold open a job for a pregnancy-related absence the same length of time jobs are held open for employees on sick or disability leave.
3. Any health insurance provided by an employer must cover expenses for pregnancy-related conditions on the same basis as cost for other medical conditions. Pregnancy-related expenses should be reimbursed exactly as those incurred for other medical conditions. The amounts payable by the insurance provider can be limited only to the same extent as amounts payable for other conditions. No additional, increased, or larger deductible can be imposed.

Employers must provide the same level of health benefits for spouses of male employees as they do for spouses of female employees.

4. Pregnancy-related benefits cannot be limited to married employees. If an employer provides any benefits to workers on leave, the employer must provide the same benefits for those on leave for pregnancy-related conditions. Employees with pregnancy-related disabilities must be treated the same as other temporarily disabled employees for accrual and accrediting of seniority, vacation calculation, pay increases, and temporary disability benefits.

D. EQUAL PAY AND COMPENSATION DISCRIMINATION

The ***EQUAL PAY ACT*** *requires that men and women be given equal pay for equal work in the same establishment*. The jobs need not be identical, but they must be substantially equal.

It is job content, not job titles, that determines whether jobs are substantially equal.

Employers may not pay unequal wages to men and women who perform jobs that require substantially equal skill, effort, and responsibility, and that are performed under similar working conditions within the same establishment. Each of these factors is summarized as follows:

1. **Skill.** Measured by factors such as experience, ability, education, and training required to perform the job. The key issue is what skills are required for the job not what skills the individual employees may have.
2. **Effort.** The amount of physical or mental exertion needed to perform the job.
3. **Responsibility.** The degree of accountability required in performing the job.
4. **Working conditions.** This encompasses two factors: 1) physical surroundings like temperature, fumes, and ventilation; and 2) hazards.
5. **Establishment.** The prohibition against compensation discrimination under the EPA applies only to jobs within an establishment. An ***ESTABLISHMENT*** *is a distinct physical place of business rather than an entire business or enterprise consisting of several places of business*. However, in some circumstances, physically separate places of business will be treated as one establishment.

Pay differentials are permitted when they are based on seniority, merit, quantity or quality of production, or a factor other than sex.

These are known as ***AFFIRMATIVE DEFENSES***, and it is the employer's burden to prove that they apply. In correcting a pay differential, no employee's pay may be reduced. Instead, the pay of the lower paid employee must be increased. It is also unlawful to retaliate against an individual for opposing employment practices that discriminate based on compensation, or for filing a discrimination charge, testifying, or participating in any way in an investigation, proceeding, or litigation under the Equal Pay Act.

E. FILING A COMPLAINT WITH THE EEOC

Any individual who believes that his or her employment rights have been violated may file a charge of discrimination with the EEOC. All laws enforced by the EEOC, except the Equal Pay Act, require filing a charge with the EEOC before a private lawsuit may be filed in court. Although there are some exceptions, a charge usually must be filed within 180 days from the date of the alleged violation.

F. PROHIBITED DISCRIMINATION IN CALIFORNIA

California law provides that it is an unlawful employment practice, unless based on a bona fide occupational qualification, or, except where based on applicable security regulations established by the United States where the State of California:

> For an employer, because of the race, religious creed, color, national origin, ancestry, physical disability, mental disability, medical condition, marital status, sex, age, or sexual orientation of any person, to refuse to hire or employ the person or to refuse to select the person for a training program leading to employment, or to bar or discharge the person from employment or from a training program leading to employment, or to discriminate against the person in compensation or in terms, conditions, or privileges of employment.

It is also illegal for an employer to discriminate against or harass a female employee because of her pregnancy.

The California Department of Fair Employment and Housing, located at **www.dfeh.ca.gov**, contains useful employment information.

A person claiming to be the victim of an alleged unlawful practice may file a complaint with the Department of Fair Employment and Housing. With a few limited exceptions, no complaint may be filed after the expiration of one year from the date upon which the unlawful practice or refusal to cooperate occurred.

www.dfeh.ca.gov

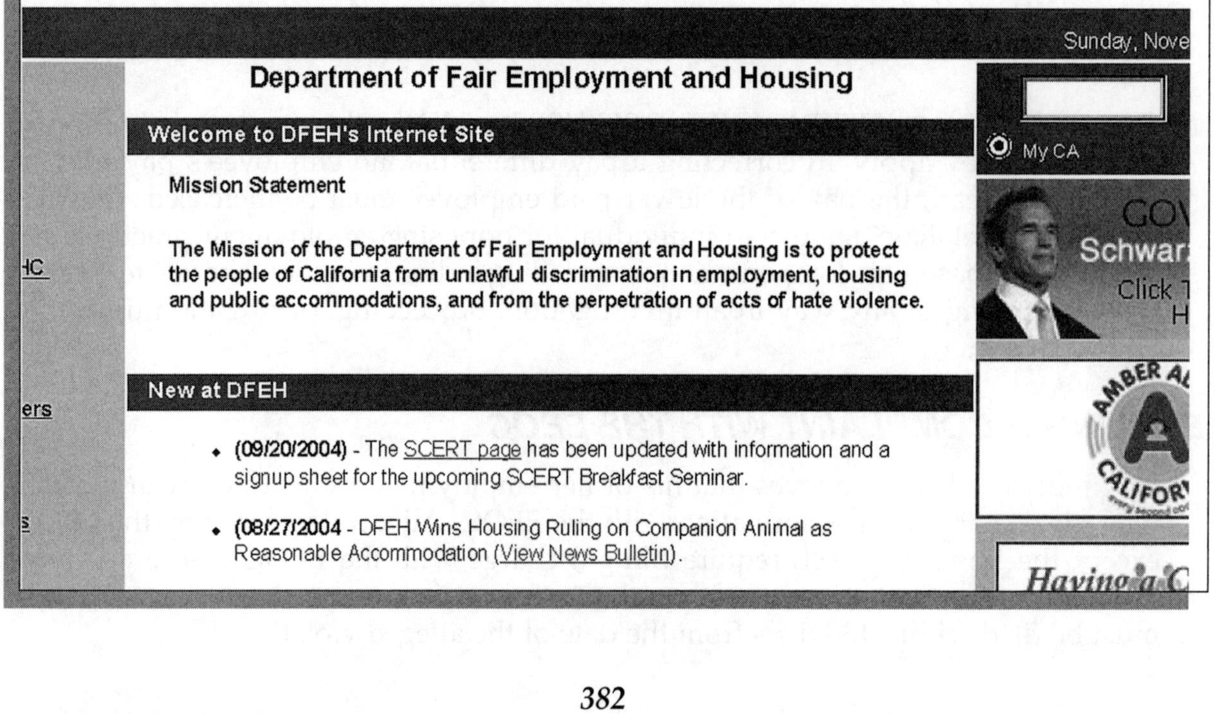

V. CHAPTER SUMMARY

An express contract is one in written or spoken words. An implied contract is one that arises from the conduct between the parties. A quasi contract is used by a court to prevent unjust enrichment by a defendant at the expense of the plaintiff. An executed contract has been fully performed. An executory contract means performance still remains. A bilateral contract generally arises from the exchange of one promise for another. A unilateral contract offer is a promise made in exchange for a possible performance of a future act.

An offeror makes an offer which is definite in its terms, shows a present intention to contract, and is communicated to the offeree. The offeree receives the offer. Acceptance means the offeree agrees to each and every term of the offer thereby forming a contract. An offer can terminate when the offeror revokes it, the offeree rejects it or proposes a counter offer, if the time period for the offer has expired, if the offeree or offeror becomes insane or dies, death or destruction of the subject matter of the offer, if the law changes and makes the subject matter of the offer illegal. An acceptance of an offer by the offeree forms a contract.

Generally, minors can enter into contracts but can disaffirm them while still a minor or within a reasonable period of time after turning 18. The minor is entitled to get back everything given under the contract and must give back what the minor received under the contract if it still exists.

Consideration means each party to the contract gave up something in order to get a promise or performance from the other party.

Illegal activities that may appear in the development would be illegal gambling or raffles.

California requires a license for engaging in certain occupations. If a person does not have a license, it is a misdemeanor and the person cannot collect for services rendered.

The statute of frauds requires that in order to enforce a contract in court it must be in writing and signed by the person being sued.

Sometimes parties choose not to perform their contract obligation because they decided they made a mistake.

A unilateral mistake generally does not allow a person out of a contract. Two exceptions would be a clerical error or the mistake was obvious to the offeree. In a mutual mistake, both parties make the same mistake and either party can rescind the contract. With the mistake of law, if both parties make the same mistake either can rescind the contract. Or if one party made the mistake the contract is binding unless the other party was aware of the mistake.

Actual fraud consists of intentional misrepresentation, negligent misrepresentation, suppression, false promise, and any other act intended to deceive the other person.

Conditions in a contract are either precedent, subsequent, or concurrent.

Satisfaction clauses are risky if the subject matter is a personal taste item or an item of judgment. A reasonable person's satisfaction is the standard for a contract involving mechanical utility or operative fitness.

Performance in a contract must be at any time standard set in the contract. If there is no time for performance set in the contract, it must be performed within a reasonable period of time.

A final agreement clause means that the parties sign a contract agreeing that every term of the bargain is stated in that contract. If a contract is broken, the victim normally determines the dollar loss caused by that breach and can hold the breaching party liable for money damages.

A common interest development manager carries two types of authority. One is the authority to enter into contracts on behalf of the association that has actually been given by the association (actual authority). The other is ostensible authority, which is what appears through the eyes of a reasonable outsider as the authority that a common interest development manager would have to bind the association to contracts.

As the association manager, you may lack authority to bind the association to any contracts. The manager's contract with the association might be to seek out, negotiate, prepare requests for proposals, accepts bids, and do other activities in order to receive the best offer from an outside party made to the association. You will then present the offer to the appropriate association individuals for acceptance, rejection, or the proposal of a counter offer. If this is the case, you must make it clear to the third party that you lack any authority to bind the association to a contract.

Through the eyes of the third person making an offer, it would certainly appear that you have the authority to enter into the contract on behalf of the association if you are the "association manager."

If this is not the case, it is important for you to tell the third person something to the effect that you manage day-to-day activities within the community but has no authority to enter into contracts binding the association. You should explain that you will be more than happy to convey an offer from the third person to the appropriate individual within the association for further action.

If, as the manager, you have some authority to enter into contracts on behalf of the association but lacks authority for other transactions, once again, this needs to be clear to the third person. Otherwise, the third person may reasonably believe that you have the authority to contract on behalf of the association.

If you do have some authority to enter into contracts on behalf of the association, he or she must correctly sign the contract to avoid any potential personal liability. Signing either of the two following ways should prevent personal liability exposure:

1. Hubie Highlands Homeowner's Association by (your name), Association manager; or
2. (Your name), Association manager, on behalf of Hubie Highlands Homeowner's Association.

As the manager, you should make sure that you have a good relationship with the treasurer, secretary, or whoever is signing checks on behalf of the association. The reason for this is, if you negotiated the contract between the association and the third party, when the third party submits a billing statement or invoice which isn't paid as soon as desired, the third party will start calling you to see where the payment is. These calls are not productive, sometimes embarrassing, and certainly cause friction, since you have no control over the payment.

You should be aware of contractors performing services or providing materials within the development. Unpaid contractors may place a mechanic's lien upon the property for which the labor or material were provided. California provides that, in a condominium project, no labor performed or services or materials furnished with the consent of, or at the request of, an owner or the owner's agent or contractor, shall be the basis for the filing of a lien against any other property of any other owner unless that owner has consented to or requested the performance of labor or furnishing the materials or services. Consent is deemed to have been duly given by the owner of any condominium in the case of emergency repairs thereto. Labor performed or services or materials furnished for the common areas, if authorized by the association, shall be deemed to be performed or furnished with the expressed consent of each condominium owner.

The owner of any condominium may remove a lien against the owner's condominium by payment to the lien holder of the fraction of the total sum secured by the lien which is attributable to his or her condominium.

It is very important to keep current on the areas involving discrimination and employment. Lack of knowledge may result in a mistake which can be very costly for the association and the manager. A periodic review of the Equal Employment Opportunity Commission (EEOC) website is a good idea. It is also important to note that many of the unlawful discriminatory practices apply to employers of 15 or more employees. This would appear to let small employers escape without liability for discriminatory conduct. However, state law may not have such a limitation. In any event, discriminatory practices in employment should not occur or be condoned. Attending workshops, seminars, or lectures on how to engage in lawful employment practices would be a good idea for key individuals to attend.

VI. REVIEW QUESTIONS

1. Maxine called Harold and agreed to purchase two 19-inch computer monitors for $200. Harold agreed to sell the monitors for that price and deliver them between noon and 1 p.m. This is an example of which of the following?

a. An implied contract
b. An express contract
c. A quasi contract
d. An invalid contract

2. Which of the following is not usually under the direct control of an employer?

a. An independent contractor
b. An employee
c. An employee who is an agent for the employer
d. All of the above are under the direct control of the employer

3. In California, a perspective managing agent must provide a written disclosure statement to the board as soon as practicable, but in no event more than how many days before entering into a management agreement?

a. 10 days
b. 30 days
c. 60 days
d. 90 days

4. When an agency by ratification is created, who does the ratifying?

a. The agent
b. The third person
c. The principal
d. All of the above

5. When is a unilateral contract formed?

a. When the offeror makes the offer in exchange for the act.
b. When the offeree accepts the offer by fully performing the requested act.
c. When the unilateral contract offer is put in writing and signed by both parties.
d. There is no such thing as a unilateral contract.

6. Ostensible agency is created by which of the following?

a. Actions or inactions of the agent
b. Actions or inactions of the principal
c. Actions or inactions of the third person
d. None of the above

7. When a contract is fully performed, it is said to be:

   a. executory.
   b. executed.
   c. ostensible.
   d. none of the above.

8. The fiduciary duty owed by an agent to the principal consists of a:

   a. duty of loyalty.
   b. duty of care.
   c. duty to inform the principal of information regarding the agency.
   d. all of the above are duties owed to the principal.

9. Maxine contracted to purchase two computer monitors from Harold. Harold is to deliver the monitors to Maxine's office. The contract did not specify the date for delivery. Therefore, Harold must deliver the monitors:

   a. within a reasonable time.
   b. within 48 hours.
   c. within 3 business days.
   d. within 10 business days.

10. A person under the age of 18 is emancipated if the person:

   a. has entered into a valid marriage.
   b. is on active duty with the armed forces.
   c. has received a court declaration of emancipation.
   d. All of the above.

ANSWERS: *1. b; 2. a; 3. d; 4. c; 5. b; 6. b; 7. b; 8. d; 9. a; 10. d*

ONE SINGER ISLAN
15 PENTHOUSE ESTAT
Sales Cente

CHAPTER 12

Sales and Leases, Fair Housing, and Insurance

I. Restrictions On Sales and Leases

A. INTRODUCTION

More than likely, the governing documents, typically the covenants, conditions, and restrictions (CC&Rs), will contain a provision regarding leasing of the units within the development.

FOR EXAMPLE – PLANNED DEVELOPMENT
Section 10A

Single-Family Dwelling Unit; Leases. Each Dwelling Unit shall be used as a residence for a single family and for no other purpose. No unit shall be leased or rented for less than six months, without prior written approval by the Association Board of Directors.

Chapter 12

CHAPTER OUTLINE

FOR EXAMPLE – CONDOMINIUM
11.1 Rental Units

11.2 No Transient Purposes. With the exception of a lender in possession of a unit following a default in a mortgage, a foreclosure proceeding or any deed or other arrangement in lieu of a foreclosure, no unit owner shall be permitted to lease a unit for hotel or transient purposes which is defined as renting for any period less than thirty days. The association through a board resolution may prohibit the leasing of any unit for a period for less than six months.

11.3 Entire Unit. No unit owner may lease less than the entire unit.

11.4 Written Leases. All leasing or rental agreements shall be in writing and be subject to this declaration, the articles of incorporation and the bylaws of the association, and the association rules and regulations and any default by the tenant in complying with these documents constitutes a default under the lease or rental agreement. The board shall be notified in advance of an owner's intention to rent or lease a unit and also notified of the names of all occupants of the unit being rented or leased.

B. STATE LEGISLATION

In California, legislation provides that any rule or regulation of an association that arbitrarily or unreasonably restricts an owner's ability to market his or her interest in a common interest development is void.

Recall, as covered in Chapter 10, a homeowner's association may not impose an assessment or fee in connection with the marketing of an owner's interest in an amount that exceeds the association's actual or direct cost. Additionally, the association may not

establish an exclusive relationship with a real estate broker through which the sale or marketing of an owner's interest in the development is required. The terms ***MARKET and MARKETING*** *mean the listing, advertising, or obtaining or providing access to show the owner's interest in the development*. In light of the above, consider the following issues:

1. Marketing his or her interest in the common interest development probably means the sale of the interest, where the owner is transferring title, as opposed to the leasing of the interest, where the owner is transferring possession.
2. The rule or regulation cannot be arbitrary or unreasonably restrict the owner's ability to market the interest. This implies that there can be reasonable restrictions on an owner's ability to market his or her interest. For example, a restriction that there can be no open houses after 7:00 p.m. might be considered reasonable. Arbitrary would mean that a restriction is being applied to one person selectively as opposed to others without any logical rationale. For example, if four previous owners were allowed open houses after 7:00 pm., why can't this owner have one?
3. Court decisions have established that recorded restrictions are presumed to be reasonable and the burden of proof is on the complaining party to show that they are unreasonable. The association needs to be careful, because even if it has a reasonable restraint, it must enforce that restraint in a reasonable and non-arbitrary manner. In order to assist in the effective and efficient running of a common interest development, consider the following:

FOR EXAMPLE – California Civil Code Section 1370

Any deed, declaration, or condominium plan for a common interest development shall be liberally construed to facilitate the operation of the common interest development, and its provisions shall be presumed to be independent and severable.

You may have encountered the term "restraints on alienation." Obviously, a ***RESTRAINT*** *would be some sort of restriction on the freedom of one's action.* ***ALIENATION****, a term that is not used very often, means the transfer of ownership or an interest in property from one person to another by any means.* Therefore, the transfer can be either an ownership interest (title) or a possessory interest in property which could be the leasing or renting of the unit. California has legislation covering this topic, which provides "conditions restraining alienation, when repugnant to the interest created, are void." The term ***REPUGNANT*** *normally means something that is repulsive, offensive, or disgusting, but it can also mean something which is inconsistent, illogical, or contradictory.*

If the restriction on sale or leasing is contained in unrecorded documents, such as bylaws or operating rules and regulations of the development, then the association has the burden of proving that the restriction is reasonable. Therefore, as the association manager, you need to check all of the governing documents to locate any provisions regarding restrictions on the sale or lease of separate interests.

Whether or not restrictions can be placed on units that are rented is a question of state law, provisions in the governing documents (whether recorded or not), and court decisions.

The following North Carolina case raises issues of importance to the association board and you, as the association manager.

Miesch v. Ocean Dunes Homeowner's Association, Inc.

120 N. C. App. 559, 464 S. E. 2d 64 (1995)
Edited Excerpts From the Opinion of Justice Martin

FACTS AND ISSUES:

Plaintiffs are the owners of a residential unit in Ocean Dunes Condominiums in North Carolina. The condominium consists of approximately 196 individual units, together with swimming pools, tennis courts, and various other recreational facilities and common areas. A majority of the units within the condominium are available for short-term rental, although some of the owners are permanent residents and do not rent their units.

The recorded declaration allows the common areas and facilities to be used by the owners of units for their use and the use of their immediate families, guests, or invitees and for all proper and normal purposes. The Association is a nonprofit corporation and has the power to make reasonable rules and regulations governing the use of the common areas and the power to levy and collect assessments against members to defray the common expenses of the condominium. The bylaws give the Association the power and duty to maintain, repair, replace, operate, and manage the common areas and facilities for the benefit of the members. Also the costs and expenses of doing so are "common expenses" shared by the unit owners.

The board of directors adopted a policy to charge a "user fee" to "short-term renters" of units within the condominium. Short-term renters are persons leasing units for less than 28 days. Payment of the fee is required in order for short-term renters to use the common areas and facilities. The fee is not charged to those renting for 28 days or more, to unit owners, or to non-paying guests or invitees of unit owners. The proceeds of the fee are used to pay Association employees who perform duties such as registering renters and guests, dispensing orientation packets and parking passes, informing renters about the facilities and area attractions, and providing security services to enforce the Association rules regarding the use of the common area and facilities.

(continued)

Plaintiffs rent their unit on a short-term basis. They filed this lawsuit seeking a declaratory judgment that the association has no power to adopt and enforce the user fee policy to collect the fees from any persons other than all of the owners of the units within the condominium. Plaintiffs also sought injunctive relief. The trial court concluded that the board of directors did not have the power to adopt and enforce the user fee, and declared that the user fee was invalid and unenforceable. The Association appealed.

DECISION AND REASONS:

The trial court found that the user fee creates two classes of owners for the purpose of collecting money for common expenses. The record shows that the fee is assessed only against short-term renters, and is used to defray common expenses. The fee amounts to an additional assessment for common expenses against invitees of only certain unit owners—those who lease their units to short-term renters. It is undisputed that all unit owners have the right to lease and/or permit the use of their units to third parties and permit the use of the common area and facilities by immediate family, guests, and invitees, and short-term renters. The user fee, however, selectively restricts the rights of those owners who lease to short-term renters by charging the renters for use of the common areas and facilities. The Association documents provide that common expenses might be assessed against the unit owners in proportion to their ownership interest. The user fee, however, attempts to defray common expenses by enforcing a fee for the use of the common areas and facilities against short-term renters, which is tantamount to an additional fee for common expenses being selectively and disproportionately enforced against invitees of only certain unit owners in violation of the Association's documents.

We recognize that the user fee restricts the express rights of unit owners who leased to short-term renters and is contrary to the provision of the Association documents. The general powers granted by the Association documents are not sufficient to impose the user fee. We also rule that there is no statutory authority in existence for defendant's right to charge a user fee. The condominium was created pursuant to the old Condominium Act. Subsequently, the General Assembly adopted a new Condominium Act. Some, but not all of the provisions of the new act remain applicable to old associations. The "official comment" explains the reason for not applying all new provisions to the old act:

...to make all provisions of this Act automatically apply to "old" condominiums might violate the constitutional prohibition of impairment of contracts. In addition, aside from the constitutional issue, automatic applicability of the entire Act almost certainly would unduly alter the legitimate expectations of some present unit owners and declarants.

The new act grants to condominiums associations the power to "impose and receive any payments, fees, or charges for the use, rental, or operation of the common elements other than limited common elements described in subsections...and for services provided to unit owners." This provision, however, was not made applicable to existing condominium associations. Therefore, we need not decide whether it would authorize the user fee at issue here.

If a "user fee" is necessary and desirable, the proper recourse is for the Association members to vote to amend the declaration and bylaws to permit such a fee. The decision of the trial court is affirmed.

The important points of the *Miesch* case for you, as the association manager, to consider are as follows:

1. Research and make sure the governing documents contain a provision that will allow the assessment of a fee or, for that matter, any other restrictions on renters of units within the community.
2. Research and confirm whether state law regulates the imposition of restrictions or fees on tenants within the community.
3. Follow legislation to see if any new changes are coming regarding renting of units and if necessary obtain membership approval for a position of reasonable restrictions or fees and impose those restrictions in a uniform, consistent, and non-arbitrary manner.

C. SIGNS – FOR SALE OR FOR RENT

In many of the governing documents of a homeowner's association, you can find restrictions on an owner's ability to post a sign on his or her property.

This can present a serious problem if it is a restraint on alienation when the owner is attempting to sell or lease a separate interest. Because of this, the legislature in California has decided to regulate such signs. Every provision which purports to prohibit or restrict the right to display on the owner's real property or real property owned by others with their consent, or both, signs which are reasonably located, in plain view of the public, of reasonable dimensions and design, and which do not adversely affect public safety, including traffic safety, and which advertise the property for sale, lease, or exchange, or advertise directions to the property, by the property owner or the owner's agent, is void as an unreasonable restraint on the power of alienation.

Such signs can advertise that the property is for sale, lease, or exchange by the owner or the owner's agent, direction to the property, the owner's or agent's name, and the owner's or agent's address and telephone number. Local governments have the power to limit or regulate the display or placement of a sign on a private or public right-of-way.

A "for sale" or "for rent" sign is deemed to be reasonable in dimension and design if it conforms to a local city or county ordinance that provides reasonable dimensions for such a sign.

D. ASSOCIATION COLLECTS FROM TENANT

Can the homeowner (community) association attempt to collect monies owed to it (by the owner) from an owner's tenant? The answer is yes.

AN EXAMPLE
11.9 - Rent to Association.

If a unit is rented by its owner, the board may collect, and the tenant or lessee shall pay over to the board, so much of the rent for such unit as is required to pay any amounts due the association from the owner. The renter or lessee shall not have the right to question payment over to the board, and such payment will discharge the renter's or lessee's duty of payment to the owner for rent.

The board can collect money owed by the property owner from the tenants, who can then deduct that amount from the rent they pay the owner.

E. DEALING WITH PROBLEM TENANTS

Recall the previously discussed provision that a default by a tenant in compliance with the declaration bylaws and association rules and regulations constituted a default under the lease or rental agreement. Assuming that the tenant has done so, what is the next step for you, as the manager, or the association board of directors? The next step would be to investigate any applicable state law that deals with eviction of tenants and, if required, give the proper notice to the defaulting tenants. The issue becomes: Who is going to give the notice? Since the tenant holds possession under the member's ownership interest, the member, as landlord, should give the tenant the notice. This makes it imperative that you, as the association manager, or appropriate individual, contact the member owner, advise the member owner of the conduct, and insist that the member take appropriate action against the tenant. Suppose a member refuses to do so? Can the association give the appropriate notice and/or institute eviction procedures against the tenant? This is a difficult position for the association unless the declaration authorizes the association to do so on the member's behalf. This would mean that the association names the owner as the plaintiff in an eviction proceeding, but is doing the litigation on behalf of the owner.

Eviction is a very complicated and tricky area for the association and it is advisable that, if problems occur with tenants of a member/owner, the association's attorney be contacted for immediate advice.

Additionally, if the problem has not occurred with tenants, this may be an appropriate time for you, as the association manager, and board of directors, to plan ahead by changing the appropriate governing documents to allow the association to deal with the tenants in the most efficient manner allowed by state law.

II. Federal Fair Housing Act

A. DISCRIMINATION

Under the federal Fair Housing Act as amended, it is unlawful to discriminate in the sale or rental of housing on the basis of race, color, religion, sex, familial status, national origin, or handicap.

The Fair Housing Act is a federal law, so it controls over conflicting state law (see **Figure 12-1 – Federal Non-Discrimination Poster**). If it does not conflict with state law, then the state law controls. Although it is unlikely that an association will engage in the sale or rental of units within a development, a general understanding of this important federal legislation is critical. The association may be involved in sale or rental of a unit should it acquire title, for example, a deed in lieu of foreclosure given to the association by a defaulting owner. Basically, regarding the above categories, it is unlawful:

1. To refuse to sell or rent after the making of a bona fide offer, or to refuse to negotiate for the sale or rental of, or otherwise make unavailable or deny, a dwelling to any person because of race, color, religion, sex, familial status, or national origin.
2. To discriminate against any person in the terms, conditions, or privileges of sale or rental of a dwelling, or in the provision of services or facilities in connection therewith, because of race, color, religion, sex, familial status, or national origin.
3. To make, print, or publish, or cause to be made, printed, or published any notice, statement, or advertisement, with respect to the sale or rental of a dwelling that indicates any preference, limitation, or discrimination based on race, color, religion, sex, handicap, familial status, or national origin, or an intention to make any such preference, intimidation, or discrimination.
4. To represent to any person because of race, color, religion, sex, handicap, familial status, or national origin that any dwelling is not available for inspection, sale, or rental when such dwelling is, in fact, so available.
5. For profit, to induce or attempt to induce, any person to sell or rent any dwelling by representations regarding the entry or prospective entry into the neighborhood of a person or persons of a particular race, color, religion, sex, handicap, familial status, or national origin.
6. To discriminate in the sale or rental, or otherwise make unavailable or deny, a dwelling to any buyer or renter because of handicap of: that buyer or renter; a person residing in or intending to reside in that dwelling after it is so sold, rented, or made available; or any person associated with that buyer or renter.
7. To discriminate against any person in the terms, conditions or privileges of sale or rental of a dwelling, or in the provision of services or facilities in connection with such dwelling, because of a handicap of: that person, or a person residing or intending to reside in that dwelling after it is so sold, rented, or made available, or any person associated with that person.

Figure 12-1

Equal Housing Lender

We Do Business In Accordance With The Federal Fair Housing Law

(Title VIII of the Civil Rights Act of 1968, as Amended by the Housing and Community Development Act of 1974)

IT IS ILLEGAL TO DISCRIMINATE AGAINST ANY PERSON BECAUSE OF RACE, COLOR, NATIONAL ORIGIN, RELIGION, SEX, FAMILIAL STATUS (including children under the age of 18 living with parents or legal custodians, pregnant women, and people securing custody of children under the age of 18), AND HANDICAP, TO:

- Deny a loan for the purpose of purchasing, constructing, improving, repairing or maintaining a dwelling or
- Discriminate in fixing of the amount, interest rate, duration, application procedures or other terms or conditions of such a loan.

IF YOU BELIEVE YOU HAVE BEEN DISCRIMINATED AGAINST, YOU MAY SEND A COMPLAINT TO:

U.S. DEPARTMENT OF HOUSING AND URBAN DEVELOPMENT
Assistant Secretary for Fair Housing and Equal Opportunity
Washington, D.C. 20410

or call your local HUD Area or Insuring Office.

The above detailed information describes unlawful conduct. Some definitions may be helpful in interpreting those provisions. ***FAMILIAL STATUS*** *means one or more individuals (who have not attained the age of 18 years) being domiciled with:*

1. *A parent or other person having legal custody of such individual or individuals; or*
2. *The designee of such parent or other person having such custody, with the written permission of such parent or other person.* The protection afforded against discrimination on the basis of familial status applies to any person who is pregnant or is in the process of securing legal custody of any individual who has not attained the age of 18 years.

A possible way of discriminating against families with children is by having a restriction on the total number of occupants in a unit.

If the purpose of the restriction is to discriminate against families with children, the activity is unlawful and the restriction is illegal. The Fair Housing Act does not limit the applicability of any reasonable local, state, or federal restriction regarding the maximum number of occupants permitted to occupy a dwelling. But, if challenged in the courts, there will be a careful examination by the court to determine whether the occupancy restriction has the effect of unreasonably excluding families with children. There must be some relationship between the size of the units and the number of occupants that makes reasonable sense.

In summary, an association cannot enforce covenants or restrictions that prevent families with children from buying or renting units within a development. Notice that the Fair Housing Act does not prevent discrimination on the basis of age provided that the person is over 18.

HANDICAP *means, with respect to a person:*

1. *a physical or mental impairment which substantially limits one or more of such person's major life activities;*
2. *a record of having such an impairment; or*
3. *being regarded as having such an impairment, but such term does not include current illegal use of, or addiction to, a controlled substance.*

Typically, a physical or mental impairment will include hearing, mobility, and visual impairments, chronic mental illness, chronic alcoholism, AIDs or AIDs-related complex, or mental retardation that substantially limits one or more major life activities. Major life activities consist of walking, talking, hearing, seeing, breathing, learning, performing manual tasks, and caring for oneself.

Federal law requires housing providers to make reasonable accommodations for persons with disabilities.

A ***REASONABLE ACCOMMODATION*** *is a change in rules, policies, practices, or services so that the person with a disability will have an equal opportunity for the use and the enjoyment of the residential unit or any common area.* The above mentioned preferential parking space for a mobility-impaired person would be such a reasonable accommodation. The federal law also allows persons with disabilities to make reasonable modifications regarding the unit. A ***REASONABLE MODIFICATION*** *is a structural change that is made to allow the person with disabilities the full enjoyment of the unit and related facilities.* These reasonable modifications are made at the resident's expense. For example, a reasonable modification would be allowing the person to install grab bars in the bathroom or installing a ramp for dwelling access.

Considering the handicapped, a policy of "no pets" must allow a visually impaired tenant to keep a guide dog.

Additionally, if the development offers ample, unassigned parking, it must honor a request from a mobility-impaired tenant or buyer for a reserved space near the unit if necessary to ensure that the individual can have access to the unit.

B. HOUSING FOR OLDER PERSONS

Congress has expressed its intent to preserve housing specifically designed to meet the needs of older persons. If the housing meets the definition under the FHA of "housing for older persons," it is exempt from the requirement of familial status, provided that it fits into one of the following categories:

1. It is occupied solely by persons who are 62 or older; or
2. It houses at least one person who is 55 or older in at least 80% of the occupied units, publishes and adheres to a policy that demonstrates intent to house persons who are 55 or older, and is able to produce verification of the ages of its residents through reliable surveys and affidavits; or
3. It has been determined by the Department of Housing and Urban Development (HUD) that the dwelling is specifically designed and operated for and occupied by elderly persons under a federal, state or local government program.

If the housing satisfies one of the three factors listed above, then it can legally exclude families with children. However, in the 55 or older housing, since at least 80% of the occupied units must have one person who is 55 or older, conceivably, other units (20% or less) could be rented to families with children.

If a person claims unlawful discriminatory practices, he or she must start a civil lawsuit no later than two years after the occurrence of the alleged discriminatory housing practice, or the termination of the alleged discriminatory housing practice (whichever is the later).

C. EXEMPTION FROM ILLEGAL DISCRIMINATION

None of the above discriminatory actions apply to any single-family house sold or rented by an owner, provided the owner does not own more than three single-family houses at any one time and, in the case of a sale, that the owner is not the most recent resident of the house prior to the sale and that this exemption applies only with respect to one sale in any twenty-four month period. Additionally, the house must be sold or rented without the use of any sales or rental facilities or services of any real estate broker or agent in the business of selling or renting resident dwellings, and without the publication, posting, or mailing of any advertisement or written notice which is unlawful as described above.

A second exemption from the above-mentioned unlawful conduct is rooms or units in dwellings containing living quarters intended to be occupied by no more than four families living independent of each other if the owner actually maintains and occupies one of the living quarters as a residence.

Each state may have its own fair housing laws in addition to the federal Fair Housing Act.

III. California Fair Employment and Housing Act

A. ILLEGAL DISCRIMINATION DEFINED

The legislature in California has declared that "the practice of discrimination because of race, color, religion, sex, marital status, national origin, ancestry, familial status, disability, or sexual orientation in housing accommodations is declared to be against public policy." The purpose of California's legislation is "to provide effective remedies that will eliminate these discriminatory practices." When based on any of the above characteristics, illegal discrimination is defined to include the following:

1. Refusal to sell, rent, or lease housing accommodations;
2. Refusal to negotiate for the sale, rental, or lease of housing accommodations;
3. Representation that a housing accommodation is not available for inspection, sale, or rental when that housing accommodation is in fact so available;
4. Any other denial or withholding of housing accommodations;
5. Includes provisions of inferior terms, conditions, privileges, facilities, or services in connection or with those housing accommodations;
6. Includes harassment in connection with those housing accommodations;
7. Includes the cancellation or termination of a sale or rental agreement;
8. Includes the provision of segregated or separated housing accommodations;

9. Includes the refusal to permit, at the expense of the disabled person, reasonable modifications of existing premises occupied or to be occupied by the disabled person, if the modifications may be necessary to afford the disabled person full enjoyment of the premises. However, in the case of a rental, the landlord may, where it is reasonable to do so, condition permission for a modification on the renter's agreeing to restore the interior of the premises to the condition that existed before the modification (other than for reasonable wear and tear); and
10. Includes refusal to make reasonable accommodations in rules, policies, practices or services when these accommodations may be necessary to afford a disabled person an equal opportunity to use and enjoy a dwelling.

However, discrimination **does not** include either of the following:

1. Refusal to rent or lease a portion of an owner-occupied single-family house to a person as a roomer or border living within the household, provided that no more than one roomer or border is to live within the household and the owner complies with the subdivision (c) of Section 12955, which prohibits discriminatory notices, statements and advertisements.
2. Where the sharing of living areas in a single-dwelling unit is involved, the use of words stating or tending to imply that the housing being advertised is available only to persons of one sex.

B. ILLEGAL DISCRIMINATORY ACTIVITIES

The above is a lengthy definition of types of illegal discrimination. The list below contains unlawful conduct in housing accommodations when the issue is race, color, religion, sex, sexual orientation, marital status, national origin, ancestry, familial status, or disability of a person. It is illegal:

1. For the owner of any housing accommodation to discriminate against or harass any person because of the above characteristics.
2. For the owner of any housing accommodation to make or cause to be made any written or oral inquiry concerning the above characteristics.
3. For any person to make, print, or publish, or cause to be made, printed, or published any notice, statement, or advertisement with respect to the sale or rental of a housing accommodation that indicates any preference, limitation, or discrimination based on the above characteristics. Or an intention to make any such preference, limitation or discrimination.
4. For any owner of a housing accommodation to harass, evict, or otherwise discriminate against any person in the sale or rental of housing accommodations when the owner's dominate purpose is retaliation against a person who has opposed practices unlawful under the law.

5. For any person to aid, abet, insight, compel, or coerce the doing of any of the acts or practices declared above to be unlawful.
6. For any person, for profit, to induce any person to sell or rent any dwelling by representations regarding the entry or perspective entry into the neighborhood of a person or persons who have the above characteristics.
7. To otherwise make unavailable or deny a dwelling based on discrimination because of race, color, religion, sex, sexual orientation, familial status, disability, or national origin.
8. Includes a perception that a person has any of those characteristics or that the person is associated with a person who has, or is perceived to have, any of those characteristics.

Under California law, no declaration or other governing document can include a restrictive covenant that is in violation of the above provisions.

Individuals who believe they have experienced housing discrimination can file a complaint with the Department of Fair Employment Housing (DFEH). Complaints must be filed within one year from the alleged discriminatory act. If they wish to bring their own lawsuit, they do not need a "right-to-sue" from the department and the lawsuit must be filed within two years of the alleged discrimination.

C. HOUSING FOR OLDER PERSONS

The above provisions relating to discrimination on the basis of familial status do not apply to housing for older persons. Housing for older persons means any one of the following:

1. Housing provided under any state or federal program that the Secretary of Housing and Urban Development determines is specifically designed and operated to assist elderly persons, as defined in the state or federal program.
2. Mobile home parks that meet the standards for housing for older persons as defined in the Federal Fair Housing Amendments Act of 1988 and implementing regulations.
3. Housing that meets the standards for senior housing under the California Unruh Civil Rights Act, except to the extent that those standards violate the prohibition of familial status discrimination and the Federal Fair Housing Amendments Act of 1988.

IV. California Unruh Civil Rights Act

A. INTRODUCTION

The Unruh Act prohibits a business establishment from discriminating in the sale or rental of housing based upon age.

This Act provides as follows:

> All persons within the jurisdiction within this state are free and equal, and no matter what their sex, race, color, religion, ancestry, national origin, disability, or medical condition are entitled to the full accommodations, advantages, facilities, privileges, or services in all business establishments of every kind whatsoever.

The California courts have determined that the Unruh Act covers common interest developments (CIDs).

However, where accommodations are designed to meet the physical and social needs of senior citizens, there may be established and preserved housing for senior citizens as provided under state law, unless that law has been preempted by the federal Fair Housing Amendments Act.

B. HOUSING FOR OLDER PERSONS

Under the Unruh Act, there are two exceptions from the prohibition against discrimination on the basis of age, although age is not mentioned, "familial status" eliminates age discrimination. One of the exemptions, like the FHA provisions, allows age discrimination when all residents are 62 years of age or older and where the housing accommodations are designed to meet the physical and social needs of senior citizens. The legislation has specific requirements for a design to meet physical and social needs of senior citizens, depending on when the structures were built and going through current construction, as well as compliance with all other applicable requirements for access and design that are imposed by law primarily related to access for persons with disabilities or handicaps.

The second exception is for residents 55 years of age or older who are in a senior citizen housing development. A ***SENIOR CITIZEN HOUSING DEVELOPMENT*** *is a residential development developed, substantially rehabilitated, or substantially renovated for senior citizens that has at least 35 dwelling units.* Like the above, the legislation provides for certain design and construction to meet the physical and social needs of the senior citizens depending on when the development is or was constructed.

The assumption here is that you, as the association manager, are managing a development which has already qualified under the appropriate design and construction law as meeting the physical and social needs of senior citizens. Therefore, managing a "62 and older" development primarily consists of making sure the residents meet the age criteria. Managing a "55 and older" development is more complex.

C. RESIDENTS NOT 55 AND OLDER

In an age 55 and older development, the law provides for others to occupy the premises who do not meet the age requirement.

1. Guests

The CC&Rs or other documents or written policy must permit temporary residency, as a guest of a senior citizen or qualified permanent resident, by a person of less than 55 years of age for periods of time, not less than 60 days in any year, that are specified in the CC&Rs or other documents or written policy.

2. Qualified Permanent Resident

A qualified permanent resident is a person who meets the following requirements:

a. He or she is residing with the senior citizen prior to the death, hospitalization, or other prolonged absence of, or dissolution of marriage with, the senior citizen;

b. He or she is 45 years of age or older, or was a spouse, cohabitant, or person providing primary physical or economic support to the senior citizen. A ***COHABITANT*** *refers to persons who live together as husband and wife, or persons who are domestic partners within the meaning of state law;* and

c. He or she is a disabled person or person with a disabling illness or injury who is a child or grandchild of the senior citizen or a qualified permanent resident who needs to live with the senior citizen because of the disabling condition, illness or injury. To meet the criteria of "disabled" or "disabling injury or illness" means satisfying the elaborate criteria defining those terms under state law. However, once the disabling condition ends, the board of directors may require the formerly disabled resident to leave the development upon receipt of six months written notice; or allow the person to remain a resident for up to one year.

The board of directors can take action to prohibit or terminate occupancy of a qualified permanent resident if the board finds, based on credible and objective evidence, that the person is likely to pose a significant threat to the health or safety of others that cannot be ameliorated (made better) by means of a reasonable accommodation; provided this action can only be taken after doing both of the following:

a. Providing reasonable notice to and an opportunity to be heard for the disabled person whose occupancy is being challenged and reasonable notice to the co-resident parent or grandparent of that person; and

b. Give due consideration to the relevant, credible, and objective information provided in the hearing. The evidence presented at the hearing is to be confidential and presented in a closed session (executive session) in order to preserve privacy of the affected person. The resident is entitled to have an attorney or other person to speak on his or her behalf or assist at the hearing.

Therefore, the above information shows how qualified permanent residents are entitled to continue to live in the senior development after certain events have occurred which would have prohibited them from living in the senior development on their own.

3. Permitted Healthcare Resident

Another category of individuals who can live in the senior citizen housing development are permitted healthcare residents. A ***PERMITTED HEALTHCARE RESIDENT*** *is a person hired to provide live-in, long-term, or terminal health care to a senior citizen, or a family member of the senior citizen providing that care.* The care provided by a permitted healthcare resident must be substantial in nature and must provide either assistance with necessary daily activities or medical treatment or both. The permitted healthcare resident is entitled to continue residency in the absence of the senior citizen from the dwelling unit only if both of the following are applicable:

a. The senior citizen became absent from the dwelling due to hospitalization or other necessary medical treatment and expects to return within 90 days; and

b. The absent senior citizen or an authorized representative submitted a written request to the board of directors stating the desire that the health care resident be allowed to remain until the senior citizen returns.

Upon a written request by the senior citizen or authorized agent, the board of directors has discretion to allow the healthcare resident to remain for longer than 90 days if it appears the senior citizen will return within a period of time not to exceed an additional 90 days. Obviously, if the senior citizen is moving into a convalescent hospital for a considerable length of time, the permitted healthcare resident will not be allowed to stay in the senior citizen housing development. The governing documents of the senior citizen housing development must allow a permitted healthcare resident to occupy a dwelling unit during the time the healthcare resident is actually providing live-in, long-term, or hospice health care to the senior citizen for compensation. Compensation may also include provisions of lodging and food in exchange for care.

4. Governing Documents For 55 and Over

The CC&Rs and other documents or written policy must set forth the limitations on occupancy, residency, or use on the basis of age.

Any limitation cannot be more exclusive than to require than one person in residence in each dwelling unit may be required to be a senior citizen and that each other resident in the same dwelling unit may be required to be a qualified permanent resident, a permitted healthcare resident, or a person under 55 years of age whose occupancy is permitted by being grandfathered into a senior citizen housing development by legislation. The limitation must at least require that the persons commencing occupancy include a senior citizen who intends to reside in the unit as a primary resident on a permanent basis. Considering the nature of others who may be residing in the development who are not 55 or older, it is understood that occupancy may result in less than all of the dwelling units being occupied by a senior citizen.

Because of a unique provision in the California legislation, the above material does not apply to California's Riverside County.

V. Manager's Journal (Fair Housing)

As a manager, you must at all times be able to verify the age of the residents within the development. This is certainly important because the FHA requires a demonstration that at least 80% of the units are occupied by at least one person who is 55 years of age or older. Therefore, even though that is not a requirement under the Unruh Act, it is important to make sure that the senior citizen housing development does not fall below the 80% occupancy requirement. Should it do so, it would lose its exemption from the FHA requirement against discrimination on the basis of familial status. Additionally, recall that the senior housing development must be able to produce verification of the ages of its residents through reliable surveys and affidavits. So in order to verify the age of the residents, you must consider some sort of reasonably reliable proof as to age. The use of a driver's license, birth certificate, valid state identification card, passport, or other documentation could be used to verify age.

As the association manager, you need to do the following regarding insurance:

1. Review each policy for a complete understanding of coverage. If there are any questions, check with the insurance agent to answer all appropriate questions to the your satisfaction.
2. Make certain that the distribution of the insurance summary and notice meets the time deadline. Additionally, keep a record sheet of a more complete summary of the policies. For example, make a list of the dates premiums are due, specifically what

items are excluded from coverage, what items are included in coverage, when a notice of claim needs to be filed, is arbitration mandatory for a dispute, and the like. Taking this document to meetings will avoid a situation where a board member or officer asks a questions about insurance coverage and you either don't know or can't remember.

3. As policies are set to expire, research the insurance market to make sure the association is getting the best coverage for each dollar spent. Factor in different deductible amounts which will vary the insurance costs and will provide the board with different options for saving association money.
4. Pay particular attention in the policies to see if association members are covered under the association's policy. For example, several of the guests held a dinner and dance party in the meeting hall. Due to something slippery on the floor, a member and a guest fell and both needed medical attention. Whose policy covers this injury?

VI. Davis-Stirling Requirements Regarding Disabilities (California Law)

A condominium owner may modify a unit, at the owner's expense, to facilitate access for persons who are visually handicapped, deaf, or physically disabled, or to alter conditions which could be hazardous to these persons.

These alterations may include modifications of the route from the public way to the door of the unit if the unit is on the ground floor or already accessible by an existing ramp or elevator. However, the right of modification is subject to the following conditions:

1. Modifications must be consistent to the applicable building code.
2. Modifications must be consistent with provision of the governing documents pertaining to safety or aesthetics.
3. Modifications outside the dwelling cannot prevent reasonable passage by other residents and must be removed by the owner if the unit is no longer occupied by the person requiring those modifications.
4. The owner must submit plans for the modifications to the association for review to determine whether the modifications comply with the governing documents or building code. The association cannot deny approval of the modifications without good cause.

VII. Remedies

A. FEDERAL HOUSING ADMINISTRATION (FHA)

An alleged violation of FHA provisions may be pursued by filing a petition with the Department of Housing and Urban Development (HUD) or the California Department of Fair Employment and Housing (DFEH).

In the alternative, instead of filing a petition with a government agency, a civil lawsuit can be filed in federal district court. Further, the United States Attorney General might determine that there is a consistent pattern of discriminatory practices and may file an action in federal district court pursuing the violations.

The statute of limitations for filing a petition with a government agency is no later than one year after the discriminatory practice has occurred or terminated.

If a civil litigation action is filed, the statute of limitations is two years after the discriminatory conduct has occurred or ended. The two-year time period is stopped during an administrative proceeding.

B. FAIR EMPLOYMENT AND HOUSING ACT (FEHA)

Under the Fair Employment and Housing Act, the petition may be filed with the Department of Fair Employment and Housing or file a civil action in the appropriate civil court.

C. UNRUH ACT

Under the Unruh Act, the person alleging a violation may bring a civil action in a California superior court. In the alternative, a petition can be filed under the provision of the Fair Employment and Housing Act.

Sporn v. Ocean Colony Condominium Association

173 F. Supp. 2d 244 (District Court New Jersey 2001)
Edited Excerpts From the Opinion of Justice Irenas

FACTS AND ISSUES:

Mr. Sporn suffers from severe spinal stenosis and is confined to a wheelchair. Plaintiff alleged that defendants failed to comply with their obligations under the FHA and New Jersey law to

(continued)

"reasonably accommodate" Mr. Sporn's handicap specifically, his request that he be provided with a handicapped parking space adjacent to a wheelchair-accessible entrance to the condominium. Mr. Sporn also alleged other violations. The pertinent portion of the FHA's definition of "discrimination" is: "A refusal to make reasonable accommodations in rules, policies, practices, or services, when such accommodations may be necessary to afford such person equal opportunity to use and enjoy a dwelling." Sporn sued the Ocean Colony Condominium Association for the alleged violation regarding reasonable accommodation and presently before this court is a Motion for Summary Judgment by the defendants.

DECISION AND REASONS:

Plaintiff's claim of denial of reasonable accommodations is without merit. While it is true that the FHA's reasonable accommodation requirements can and often will involve the imposition of some cost on a defendant, accommodation is required only where such measures may be necessary to afford such a handicapped person with equal opportunity to use and enjoy a dwelling and need only be reasonable. The FHA does not require accommodation wherever convenient or desired, but only where necessary.

It has been recognized on numerous occasions that the FHA may, in certain instances, entitle a handicapped tenant to a reserved parking space adjacent to a tenant's dwelling. Although plaintiffs have not offered any evidence of a specific nature of Mr. Sporn's handicap, or of the inadequacy of the parking arrangements that pre-existed his request for accommodation, defendants do not appear to challenge the necessity of plaintiff's accommodation, but instead focus on the reasonableness of the accommodations they attempted to provide.

In response to Sporn's requests for handicapped parking, the Association adopted a "Handicapped Parking Policy." This policy provided that handicapped parking spaces, which were defined as spaces closer to the condominium entrance, shall be provided to residents provided that any residents seeking such a space trade in their deeded parking space for an Association-owned space closer to the building entrance. On its face, this policy grants the same rights to the handicapped residents as it does to non-handicapped residents.

According to his own testimony, the problems that arose between the Association and Mr. Sporn began when Sporn demanded that he be provided a handicapped space, a proposal to which defendants agreed, but refused to give up his non-handicapped, deeded space as required by the Handicapped Parking Policy. When asked why he needed two spaces, Sporn did not offer any explanation related to his handicap, but instead, said "Because during the summer time we couldn't get any parking for any of our family that come down." These comments reveal that Sporn's request for "reasonable accommodation" was really a request for accommodation coupled with a demand for special treatment. The FHA only creates a right to a "reasonable accommodation," it does not create a right to an assigned handicapped space.

Accordingly, the court determines that the actions of the Association in negotiating with Mr. Sporn about the creation of a handicapped space, promulgating non-discriminatory handicapped parking regulations and offering handicapped space to Mr. Sporn several times, even after he rejected the Association's proposal constitutes a "reasonable accommodation" within the meaning of the FHA. Therefore, the motion for summary judgment made by the defendants was granted.

Shapiro v. Cadman Towers, Inc.

51 F. 3d 328 (Court of Appeals 2nd Circuit 1995)
Edited Excerpts From the Opinion of Circuit Judge Miner

FACTS AND ISSUES:

In 1990, Shapiro moved into a two-bedroom apartment in Cadman Towers. In the late 1970s, she was diagnosed as suffering from Multiple Sclerosis. At times, she suffers physical weakness, difficulty in walking, loss of balance and coordination, fatigue, and severe headaches. During good periods, she can walk without assistance; at other times, she needs a cane or a wheelchair. Shapiro also suffers from severe bladder problems resulting in incontinence. She presently catheterizes herself to relieve the buildup of urine. She moved into the Cadman Towers in 1990 and in 1992 acquired an automobile. Parking space in the Brooklyn Heights neighborhood is extremely scarce even though she had a "handicapped" sticker on her vehicle. She testified that the long delay in finding a parking space and walking to her building resulted in numerous urinary "accidents."

In her complex, there are more units than parking spaces. Parking in the building is approximately $90 a month, considerably less than the $275 charged by the closest commercial garage. Cadman Towers has adhered to a first-come/served policy when allocating parking spaces. An individual desiring a parking space puts their name on a waiting list. An applicant first waits for a space in one of the lots, and, after being assigned one in that location, becomes eligible to wait assignment of a space in the second lot. Each unit gets one space. However, six units have two parking spaces under a grandfathering arrangement, one elderly resident was permitted to have her son, who works nearby, use her parking space and three spaces were given without charge to certain building employees as part of their compensation.

Shapiro requested a parking spot in the second garage be made available to her immediately on account of her disability. The request was denied by the Board of Directors. The Board took the position that any duty under the Fair Housing Act to accommodate her disability did not come into play until she was awarded a parking space in the normal course. Once she became entitled to a parking space, then the building would attempt to reasonably accommodate her disability.

She filed a complaint with the Department of Housing and Urban Development, and after HUD issued a charge of discrimination, she elected to file a civil action in the district court. The United States also filed a complaint against Cadman Towers. The district court granted Shapiro's motion for a preliminary injunction finding that she would suffer irreparable harm absent injunction relief, because without a parking space she is subject to continued risk of injury, infection, and humiliation from her inability to walk distances and her incontinence. The court also noted the building could free up seven spaces by simply enforcing its own rules that each apartment should be allocated only one parking space and those spaces should go only to residents. Cadman Towers appealed.

(continued)

DECISION AND REASONS:

Pursuant to the FHA, Cadman Towers is required to make reasonable accommodations in its rules and practices so as to enable Shapiro to "use and enjoy a dwelling." As discussed above, without a nearby parking space, Shapiro is subject to risk of injury, infection, and humiliation each time she leaves the dwelling and each time she returns home. We agree with the district court that, under these circumstances, parking is a substantial factor in Shapiro's "use and enjoyment" of her dwelling. Thus, Cadman Towers can be required to incur reasonable costs to accommodate Shapiro's handicap, provided such accommodations do not pose an undue hardship or substantial burden. The district court found that Shapiro could be accommodated without displacing any existing tenants, because three parking spots are reserved for building personnel and these workers could park in a commercial garage. Moreover, the court found that one parking space was used by a person that did not live in the building.

These findings are well supported by the record and will not be disturbed on appeal. Accordingly, four parking spaces were available for handicapped individuals that would not impair the rights of other non-handicapped building residents. We also agree with the district court that this accommodation may involve some changes to Cadman Tower's present method of allocating parking spaces and may require it to incur some costs. We conclude that the district court did not abuse its discretion by requiring Cadman Towers to provide Shapiro with a parking space in its garage during this litigation. The order entered in the district court is affirmed.

VIII. Property and Liability Insurance

A. INTRODUCTION

Taking a broad point of view, ***PROPERTY AND LIABILITY INSURANCE*** *is essentially a plan to distribute the actual losses among a group of individuals bearing the same risk of an event by having the individuals contribute a small portion to a fund which will pay the unfortunate members of the group who suffer loss caused by the occurrence of the event.* Since the losses are sometimes more than one individual can bear, pooling of resources to cover the unfortunate individuals in the group who suffer the loss is the concept behind insurance.

In a common interest development, there are two primary groups that need to consider the use of insurance. One group is the homeowner's association (the corporation), composed of the individual members, the board of directors, the property manager, the employees that work for the association and, to a certain extent, those with whom the association contracts to provide services to the association, such as pool maintenance, grounds maintenance, tennis court resurfacing, and so on.

The other group consists of each individual owner, those within the owner's family, and individuals the owner invites onto his or her property, such as guests, appliance repair people, carpet layers, and so on. We will now consider each of these two groups and how insurance is an important consideration.

B. INDIVIDUAL OWNERS

Whether a home and lot owner in a planned development, or a unit owner in a condominium, each owner must decide on how to cover the risk of loss should something damage or destroy his or her property.

In considering insurance, the difference between real and personal property is important. ***REAL PROPERTY** in a planned development is the owner's home and lot on which it sits. The condominium owner's real property is somewhat less defined.* If the condominium owner owns the surfaces of the finished walls, floors and ceilings and everything contained therein, we might consider the structural items, such as walls, doors, and cabinets to be real property. Both owners, of course, own their ***PERSONAL PROPERTY** which is defined as everything which is not real property, within each of their dwellings.*

***RISK OF LOSS** is the probability that an event will occur which causes a loss of or damage to real or personal property of the owner.* Most of the time owners are concerned about replacing items which will cost a lot of money, when they do not have the funds available. This is balanced against the probability that an event will occur which will cause the loss. Basically, the owner must determine the likelihood of the loss of an item that he or she would want to replace, but could not afford to do so.

An owner can **self-insure** by having enough funds available so that in the event the loss should occur, the property can be immediately replaced by using his or her own funds. For most people this doesn't make a lot of sense because this seems like a lot of money sitting around waiting for something that is rather unlikely to occur when that money could be put to better use. In other words, if it is unlikely that your house will be struck by a flaming meteorite, then why would you have the replacement funds for your house kept available when the risk of loss is so small? On the other hand, the risk of loss of your toaster is less remote, but it's not very expensive to replace, so you will most likely decide that running the risk of loss yourself makes the most sense and a replacement fund or insurance does not.

1. Condominium Owner

One of the first things Gertrude needs to do upon purchasing her unit in Hubie Highlands is to consider the issue of insurance. Most of the time the declaration will mention insurance that the Homeowner's Association must provide for the protection of the common areas and, perhaps to a certain extent, protection for unit owners. When she purchased her unit, she received the summary of the

Homeowner Association's property, general liability, earthquake, flood, and fidelity insurance policies. Regardless of what people tell Gertrude or what the summary says, she should investigate for herself the exact language contained in the declaration, or other pertinent governing documents regarding insurance coverage. Some declarations are rather detailed regarding insurance coverage by the Association and the owners, others are rather general in terms. Gertrude needs to know what her ownership and insurance responsibilities are as stated in the governing documents. If she can determine the requirements for insurance by the Association, it may help her determine what she needs to cover with her condominium insurance.

She may find one of three types of association insurance policy coverage:

1. **Coverage that insures the building including walls, the roof, the floors, halls, stairwells, elevators, etc**. The Association's insurance does not cover anything inside the owner's unit such as carpeting, wall covering, floor covering, cabinets, appliances, interior walls, bathroom fixtures, wiring, plumbing, and attached light fixtures, to name a few. Therefore, in the event of a loss, the unit owner would be responsible for repairing or replacing all of those items inside the unit.
2. **Coverage that insures the structure as well as certain items inside the owner's unit**. Normally, these items will include cabinets, appliances, carpeting, wall covering, and may include others. Therefore, Gertrude is only responsible for insurance to cover her personal property inside the unit and any alterations or additions she made to the original structure. For example, if the Association's insurance covers the carpet in her unit and Gertrude has recently replaced it with very expensive carpeting, she may be responsible for insuring the difference between the coverage provided by the Association's insurance for basic carpet and the value of Gertrude's existing carpet.
3. **Coverage that insures the structure and the items listed in paragraph 2 above plus coverage for improvements and fixtures**. For example, the built-in entertainment center she added to the living room or the slate countertop will be covered. She should keep records of these improvements in a safe place outside of her unit.

Typically, the unit owner purchases adequate insurance to cover what needs to be covered depending on the Association's coverage mentioned above. For coverage of improvements, the policy may only provide for a percentage of the policy maximum. For example, Gertrude has an $80,000 policy on her personal property. If her improvements coverage is 25%, and the loss is total, she will receive a maximum payment of an additional $20,000 to cover her improvements.

Obviously, Gertrude needs to inventory everything she owns to determine what would be covered if her loss of personal property was a total loss. Her insurance may give her the option of covering her personal effects at **"replacement cost"** or replace them at **"actual cash value."** In other words, if she has a three-year-old 32-inch television, replacement cost coverage will buy her a brand new 32-inch television set with the same or similar features. If she has actual cost value coverage, the cost of replacing her existing 32-inch television set, minus the amount of depreciation for three years, will equal the value of the television set which the insurance company will pay. In other words, she will be replacing the television set that was lost with a like television set. For the small increase in cost, replacement cost coverage is a smart purchase for Gertrude.

Gertrude needs to know that the items of personal property that she is covering with her insurance are typically protected from loss or damage from a number of very specific or identified causes. If an item of personal property is lost or damaged by something other than a listed cause in the insurance policy, she will not be paid. For example, if the television set was destroyed by a fire in a corner of the condominium, it is a covered loss. If the reason the television does not work is because rats got into the television and destroyed the inside, that is not a covered loss. Therefore, Gertrude needs considerable time with an insurance agent to make sure she understands what is covered and what is not covered under an insurance policy. One thing she'll want to make sure of is whether property of a guest brought into the unit is covered under her policy. For example, one of her former teachers is visiting her and has her jewelry stolen by a thief. Is that covered under her condominium insurance? Gertrude may also discover that certain items of personal property will not be covered under a general condominium insurance policy. She may have certain items that are considered to be collectables or have a high dollar value that will require a special addendum to her insurance policy and/or an appraisal to cover those items. She also needs to carefully look at insurance coverage to see if it covers against damage to the personal property by flood or earthquake.

Again, Gertrude needs to keep an extensive list of each and every item she owns along with some type of photograph of it. If the item is unusual in its value she may need to get it appraised so she can get the proper insurance coverage. She will need to keep this list in a place outside of the unit for safe keeping. She will also need to adjust the list periodically to reflect the items she no longer has and her new acquisitions. Additionally, the value of certain items may have gone up over time and her insurance coverage should reflect that. She will also need to make a decision whether she wants to cover her property with earthquake and/or flood insurance.

Most insurance policies only provide earthquake and/or flood coverage at an additional cost.

In her insurance policy, Gertrude may also want to consider an ***INFLATION CLAUSE,*** *which automatically raises the dollar amount of insurance coverage based on an increase in an inflation or price index.* Should Gertrude experience a major loss to her unit, she may need to have another place to stay while her unit is being repaired. Gertrude needs to consider whether she needs ***LOSS OF USE*** *coverage in her policy, which will pay for her expenses if she needs to stay somewhere else.* Typically, the insurance company pays her expenses for a specific period of time, either at a specific dollar amount per day, or pays her actual costs that she incurred that day. In other words, the insurance company will pay her a flat rate of $300 for each day she remains away from her unit while it is being repaired, or she can submit expense claims and they will reimburse her for the actual expenses that it cost her to be out of her unit. The reimbursement will probably have a maximum amount per day.

Another type of coverage that is unique to condominium owners is ***LOSS ASSESSMENT COVERAGE,*** *which covers owners for assessments for certain kinds of losses that they must help pay for.* For example, someone is seriously injured at the swimming pool and receives a judgment against the Association which is in excess of the amount of insurance coverage. All of the owners are going to have to pay their proportionate share of the remaining dollar amount to the victim. Obviously, this is something that the owners may not have considered in shopping for insurance. Another area where this could occur would be major damage to one of the buildings in Hubie Highlands, but the insurance maximum is not enough to pay for the rebuilding of the building. Consequently, all the owners will be assessed for the deficiency. Loss assessment insurance will cover your risk for these types of assessments. Gertrude may find that there is a maximum assessment dollar amount that the insurance will cover per loss or perhaps she can purchase coverage in certain dollar increments. For example, she may pay a certain dollar amount for each $1,000 worth of coverage for a loss assessment.

Although it will probably be included in her condominium owner's policy, Gertrude will also need to consider ***PERSONAL LIABILITY INSURANCE,*** *which protects her if other people make a claim or bring a lawsuit against her for personal injury or property damage.*

Many companies start with maximum coverage of $100,000. For example, Gertrude was negligent in spilling a large pot of boiling water on the feet of a dinner guest. This insurance coverage may also pay for her legal fees in defending the claim and court costs. If an owner is conducting business out of the separate interest, the owner needs special coverage for the risks of this activity.

Coverage of medical expenses may also be of interest to condo owners.

Usually this is a set dollar amount per person who is injured and is typically provided with Gertrude's personal liability coverage. However, it can cover medical bills of people injured in her unit even though she was not at fault. For example, a dinner guest is using one of Gertrude's sharp knives to cut bread and accidentally slices the end of her finger. This coverage would pay the medical expenses of that individual up to the maximum amount of coverage. It normally does not cover medical expenses for Gertrude's family members that live with her.

Gertrude may also want to see whether her liability coverage will cover her if she is sued for damages caused by renters in her unit. For example, Gertrude tours Europe for six months and rents out her unit to tenants. The tenants engage in conduct which causes bodily injury or property damage to another person. That person sues and decides to name Gertrude as a defendant. Does Gertrude's liability insurance cover the legal costs and expenses of defending the suit as well as, even though unlikely, any judgment that may be entered against her?

Condo owners should check whether or not their liability policy covers damages caused by renters or to other units.

Sometimes damage extends beyond the owner's unit. For example, the hot water hose going from the spigot to the washing machine ruptures at night. By the time Gertrude discovers the damage in the morning, water has seeped through and caused damage to the unit below her. If Gertrude's unit is covered by her insurance, does her insurance also cover the damage to the unit below her? She will probably find that, since she was not at fault, the unit owner below may have to recover from his or her insurance.

Like most insurance policies, the condominium policy that Gertrude purchases will probably have losses that are excluded from coverage. Therefore, Gertrude needs to read very carefully the losses that are not insured against.

Most insurance policies have exclusions for earth movement, flood, or underground water damage, insect or animal damage, or damage caused by contamination or deterioration, intentional damage, and perhaps mold.

She will also have to pay her deductible amount on her property loss claims.

There is generally no deductible on liability coverage.

One other coverage of interest is ***OCCASIONAL WORKER COVERAGE****, which is normally automatically included in the basic condominium policy. It covers injuries to someone working on the separate interest*. For example, Gertrude hires a person to install new lights. The worker falls and is injured. This worker's compensation claim is covered in the owner's policy.

2. Planned Development Owner

An owner of a condominium has separate interest ownership in a unit, whereas in a planned development, an owner's separate interest usually includes both a house and a lot.

The insurance for an owner of a house and lot in a planned development is not much different than that of Gertrude's condominium. The only major difference is that the insurance policy will cover more real property when it's covering an entire house than it would cover in a condominium. Consideration might also be given to other items on the lot that may need insurance coverage.

C. INSURANCE FOR THE HOMEOWNER (COMMUNITY) ASSOCIATION

1. Fire and Other Damage

In Hubie Highlands, since there are several structures, the Homeowner's Association will probably look for a ***BLANKET INSURANCE POLICY**, which covers all of the structures on a property, including losses due to fire and lightning, with typical* **EXTENDED COVERAGE**, *which will cover losses from causes such as smoke, hail, wind, explosion, riots and civil commotion, falling objects, and water damage, to name a few*. In analyzing such an insurance policy, it is always wise to study the items that are excluded from coverage such as earthquake and flood. If those items are important to the Association, the Association needs to add the coverage. Recall from paragraph 1, 2, and 3 in the previous "Individual Owners" section (page 415) that the Association needs to decide which coverage is necessary. **Most of the time the governing documents, usually the declaration, will state the type of coverage required**.

Additional items of coverage might include weight of ice, snow, or sleet, theft, vandalism, malicious mischief, freezing, and accidental discharge or overflow of water. Most basic insurance coverage for real property does not include earthquake or flood damage. However, this insurance might be required by the governing documents or lending institutions. The coverage may be included as a separate policy at additional expense. The following case considers who is covered under the policy.

Adelman v. Associated International Insurance Company

90 Cal.App.4th 352, 108 Cal.Rptr.2d. 788 (App. 2 Dist. 2001)
Edited Excerpts From the Opinion of Justice Croskey

FACTS AND ISSUES:

Plaintiffs are the individual owners of condominium units within the Chateau Chamberay Condominium project in Los Angeles.

(continued)

The project is a multi-story common interest development within the meaning of the Davis-Stirling Common Interest Development Act. It is managed by the Chateau Chamberay Homeowner's Association (HOA). Associated International Insurance Company (AIIC) had issued to the HOA a homeowner's policy of property insurance which provided coverage for losses from various perils, including earthquake damage.

The policy covered the common areas of the project but did not extend coverage to the individual units owned by the plaintiffs. The policy was in effect on January 17, 1994, when the Northridge earthquake occurred. The project suffered substantial damage, including damage to the structure. Such damage as occurred to the project, including its common areas, was covered under AIIC's policy.

The HOA made a timely, proper, and documented claim under the policy seeking repair of the damage caused to the common areas of the project. AIIC failed to make such repairs or provide the funds required under the policy which were necessary to complete the repairs. As a result, the necessary repairs to the structure of the project were not made. Such structural repair had to be made before plaintiffs could commence or complete the repairs to their individual units. Indeed, the repair of the damage to the common areas was so necessarily intertwined with the repair of the individual units that the latter could not be accomplished without completion of the former.

The HOA filed an action against AIIC seeking damages for breach of contract and other theories of recovery. The HOA's breach of contract claim was submitted to binding arbitration and resulted in a judgment in favor of the HOA in the sum of $707,387.

Plaintiffs claim to have a personal economic interest in the prompt performance by AIIC of its obligation under the policy. They argue that the entire aim and purpose of that policy, although describing only the HOA has the "named insured," was the protection of the interest of the plaintiffs, who were not only the owners of the insured premises and the persons who would directly benefit from AIIC's performance, but also the parties who would be directly and immediately harmed by the failure of AIIC to render a timely and proper performance. Therefore, the plaintiffs seek damages for a delay and inability to make repair to their individual units, relocation costs, rental and storage expenses, and the diminution of the value of their units.

AIIC responded to the plaintiffs' complaint by filing a demurrer which was granted by the trial court. AIIC argued that the plaintiffs were attempting to recover under the policy and they had no standing (as non-insureds) to seek such a recovery. As individual unit owners, they had no standing to prosecute a claim which belonged solely to the HOA. The damage to the plaintiffs' individual interests in their units was not covered under the policy and AIIC had no liability therefore as it had not agreed to assume such a burden under the policy.

(continued)

DECISION AND REASONS

We believe plaintiffs have not alleged a basis for the imposition of a duty of care upon AIIC in its performance of the obligations due under the indemnity policy issued to the HOA. AIIC's demurrer was therefore properly sustained. Thus, we must affirm the order of dismissal entered by the trial court.

2. The Deductible

If a homeowner (community) association's coverage includes a deductible and there is a claim, the deductible will have to be absorbed by the association.

Either the association members have planned ahead and have an account with funds in it that can be used for a deductible if there is a claim, or the association will assess every owner a proportionate share of the deductible. If the association has an account, the issue becomes how much to keep in the account, since the association is unaware of a future claim amount.

The following case is of interest when an association decides to sue the insurance company on a denied claim.

Larkspur Isle Condominium Owner's Association, Inc. v. Farmers Insurance Group

31 Cal.App.4th 106, 37 Cal.Rptr.2d 3 (App. 1 Dist. 1994)
Edited Excerpts From the Opinion of Justice Corrigan

FACTS AND ISSUES:

Larkspur Isle is a complex of 186 units originally built in the early 1970s. The parties stipulated that water leakage began in 1972 and that asbestos was used in the original construction. Larkspur Isle Condominium Owner's Association Inc. (Association) admitted during discovery that it believed damage to asbestos ceiling materials occurred at various times between 1972 and the present. In May 1985, the Association sued the developers for defective construction. In August 1985, Farmers Insurance Group and its member company Truck Insurance Exchange (Truck) issued a one year policy under which the Association later made its claim. In 1986 or 1987, the Association learned of the potentially hazardous asbestos-containing material in the ceilings. The Association notified Truck of a possible claim in 1987, the claim was denied and the Association filed this lawsuit against Truck. At the time of trial, the Association sought recovery only for the cost of abating the asbestos-containing ceiling materials damaged by rain water leakage on the second-floor units and making related repairs. The jury found for the Association for $497,346. Truck appealed.

(continued)

DECISION AND REASONS:

The California Supreme Court has adopted the "manifestation rule" for allocating indemnity between successive first-party property insurers for progressive losses spanning multiple policy periods. Under that rule, liability for a progressive loss falls on the insurer on the risk at the time the loss manifests, i.e., at that point in time when appreciable damage occurs and is, or should be known, to the insured such that a reasonable insured would be aware that his or her notification duty under the policy has been triggered. The manifestation rule incorporates the loss-in-progress rule: the principle that an insurer cannot insure against a loss that is known or apparent to the insured.

Thus, under the manifestation, insurers whose policy terms commence after initial manifestation of the loss are not responsible for any potential claim relating to the previously discovered and manifested loss.

Truck argues the undisputed facts show that the condominiums experienced appreciable water damage before Truck issued its policy. The Association, without disputing there had been observable water damage well before the policy period, argues damage to the asbestos-containing ceiling materials is severable.

Water damage to one particular element of a ceiling, such as the asbestos-containing materials sprayed onto the drywall here, may not be separated out as a distinct loss where it proceeds from the same progressive destruction as earlier-discovered water damage. We conclude the evidence was insufficient to support the verdict, because the loss manifested prior to Truck's policy, and was thus, as a matter of law, an uninsurable loss in progress as to Truck. The judgment is reversed.

3. Homeowner Association's Personal Property

The homeowner association also needs to insure items of personal property from loss or damage.

In Hubie Highlands, this would include items such as tennis nets, tables, chairs, umbrellas, and towels at the swimming pool, large screen television and related equipment, tables, chairs, couches, and related cooking equipment in the Association meeting hall, and computers, photo copier, and related office equipment in the Association office. The Association needs to decide whether the coverage will be replacement cost or actual cash value. For example, the Association's two-year-old leather sofa is destroyed by a fire in the meeting center. It will currently cost $1,600 to replace it. Replacement cost coverage pays the association $1,600 for its replacement. Actual cash value will determine the life span of the sofa in years, and deduct from the $1,600 the amount of depreciation for the first two years and pay what remains. The missing amount to replace the leather sofa will have to come from the members. Additionally, any deductible will have to come from the members.

What is important for the members to realize is that, ultimately, a loss is paid for by the members, whether it be through insurance, a reserve account, or assessments.

Another important consideration for the Association is determining what types of losses and what types of items are excluded from policy coverage. For example, an excluded loss could be "earth movement" and an excluded item from a covered loss might be "glass breakage."

4. Lender Requirements

In a condominium development, the extent of insurance coverage on the structures is sometimes dictated by lenders who are financing either individual condominium purchases or the entire development. Oftentimes these lenders will require a blanket insurance policy that provides coverage for all of the real property located within the development. It is an awkward situation when a person wishes to purchase a condominium within the development but is having difficulty because the lender is not comfortable with the insurance coverage the association has on the structures.

FOR EXAMPLE – PLANNED DEVELOPMENT
13 A.

The Association shall keep all insurable improvements and fixtures of the common areas insured against loss or damage by fire for the full insurance replacement cost thereof, and may obtain insurance against such other hazards and casualties as the Association may deem desirable. The Association may also insure any other property, whether real or personal, owned by the Association against loss or damage by fire and such other hazards as the Association may deem desirable, with the Association as the owner and the beneficiary of such insurance.

The insurance coverage with respect to the common areas shall be written in the name of, and the proceeds thereof shall be payable to, the Association. Insurance proceeds shall be used by the Association for the repair or replacement of the property for which the insurance was carried. The Association shall continuously maintain in effect such casualty, flood, and liability insurance and a fidelity bond meeting the requirements for planned unit developments established by the Federal National Mortgage Association, the Government Mortgage Association, and the Federal Home Loan Mortgage Corporation, so long as any of which is a mortgagee or owner of a lot, dwelling unit or commercial unit in the development, except to the extent such coverage is not available or has been waived in writing by that organization, as applicable.

(continued)

FOR EXAMPLE – CONDOMINIUM
13 D.

The Association shall maintain, to the extent reasonably available, insurance against loss of personal property of the Association by fire, theft or other losses with a deductible provision as the board of directors deems advisable.

FOR EXAMPLE – CONDOMINIUM
13 F.

The Association shall maintain, to the extent reasonably available, property insurance on the condominium, which may, but need not, include equipment, improvements, and betterments, in a unit installed by the unit owners, insuring against all risk or direct physical loss commonly insured against. The total amount of insurance after application of any deductibles shall not be less than 100% of the actual cash value of the insured property at the time the insurance is purchased and at each renewal date, exclusive of land, excavations, foundations, and other items normally excluded from property policies.

5. Liability Insurance

LIABILITY INSURANCE *is used by the homeowner association to protect itself against financial loss caused from being held legally liable for bodily injury or death of another and/or for damage to or loss of the property of another.* Litigation is very expensive and having to pay a large judgment can be an enormous burden on an association. Therefore, the association needs adequate insurance to cover against potential liability claims. However, general liability policies may not cover all of the situations which could result in a financial loss to the association.

Another issue is ***ERRORS AND OMISSIONS INSURANCE****, which protects against losses resulting from negligent acts, errors, and omissions, or breach of any duty by the directors or officers of an association.* If an individual has exposure to liability for mistakes made while serving in a representative capacity, it is doubtful that the member will seek such a position. As was discussed in Chapter 3, the individual member may be protected by the business judgment rule, California legislation, and/or insurance. Individual board members or officers will probably have to purchase their own insurance policy to cover themselves. Sometimes the association will reimburse each person's insurance cost. A more difficult issue is where the owners own their separate interest and own, as tenants in common, the common areas with the association running the development as an unincorporated association.

6. California Approach

a. Director/Officer Protection

To limit the liability exposure of officers or directors of a homeowner (community) association, California has passed legislation to that effect which is summarized as follows:

> A volunteer officer or director of the community association is not personally liable for an amount in excess of the insurance coverage listed below, to any person who suffers injury, including, but not limited to, bodily injury, emotional distress, wrongful death, or property damage or a loss as a result of the tortious act or omission (probably negligence) of the director when:

1. The common interest development is exclusively residential.
2. The act was performed in the scope of the director's or officer's association duties.
3. The scope of the officer's or director's association duties shall include, but not be limited to, both of the following decisions: Whether to conduct an investigation of the common interest development for latent deficiencies prior to the expiration of the applicable statute of limitations; and whether to commence a civil action against the builder for defects in design or construction.
4. The act or omission was performed in good faith.
5. The act was not willful, wanton, or grossly negligent.
6. The officer or director is a volunteer, i.e. receiving no compensation for services rendered, however payment of actual expenses incurred does not effect the volunteer status.
7. An officer or director, who at the time of the act was a person who signed the declaration of restrictions for the development or who received compensation as an employee of the declarant. Compensation from a financial institution that purchased a separate interest at a foreclosure sale is not a volunteer.
8. The limitation of liability applies only to a volunteer officer or director who is a tenant of a separate interest in the common development or who owns no more than two separate interests.
9. At the time of the act the association had insurance that covered the general liability of the association and individual liability of officers and directors for negligent acts or omissions in the minimum amount of $500,000 if the development consist of 100 or fewer separate interests or $1,000,000 if the development has more than 100 separate interests.
10. The association's liability for its own negligent acts is not limited.

Basically, the above is designed to limit personal liability of individuals who hold positions as officers or directors of an association.

Under California law, an "association" means a nonprofit corporation or unincorporated association created for the purpose of managing a common interest development.

The liability protection only occurs when the above requirements are satisfied. Obviously, it is important that the association acquire and maintain coverage for the minimum amount of insurance required. If the claim is in excess of the minimum amounts of insurance, the individual officers and directors are protected from personal liability. However, nothing in the above is to be construed to limit the liability of the association for its negligent acts or omissions caused by an act or omission of an officer or director of the association. Therefore, it appears as though the association may have liability for dollar amounts in excess of the minimum coverage and should consider higher coverage to protect association assets.

Note that the protection is only for directors and officers. This may make owners somewhat skeptical about serving on an association committee that will end up making certain decisions regarding the association since a committee member is not protected.

Keep in mind that the protection for officers and directors is for liability in excess of the association's available insurance. It does not protect the officer or director from being sued.

Therefore, the association needs to make sure that officers and directors have insurance which will cover their legal defenses in the event they are sued. Additionally, if the lawsuit naming a director or officer deals with something other than bodily injury, wrongful death, emotional distress, or property damage, such as fraud, breach of contract, breach of the fiduciary duty owed to the association, etc, the officer and directors are not protected from liability. Obviously, it is imperative that the association communicate with an insurance agent who has in-depth knowledge regarding insurance for a common interest development.

In certain parts of the country, one major issue that might involve owners getting upset with the board of directors would be covering the development with earthquake insurance.

Earthquake insurance is expensive and may have a high deductible.

If the decision is to cover the property with insurance, some members will complain that, in light of the risk, it is wasted money. On the other hand, if the

board does not cover the development with earthquake insurance and an earthquake significantly damages the property, directors may be defendants in lawsuits because of a failure to cover the property with insurance.

A practical solution to the question of whether or not to insure against earthquake damage is to have the owners vote on whether or not they want that coverage. This removes the decision from the board of directors.

b. Owner Protection

Because of the problem regarding potential personal liability for claims involving common interest developments, where the common areas are not owned by an incorporated homeowner's association but owned in tenancy in common with the other owners, such as may be the case with a condominium, California lawmakers intervened with legislation which is summarized as follows:

> Any cause of action in tort against any owner of a separate interest arising solely by reason of an ownership interest as a tenant in common in the common area shall be brought only against the association and not against the individual owners of the separate interests, if both of the following conditions are met:
>
> 1. The association maintains, and has in effect for this cause of action, one or more policies of insurance which includes coverage for general liability of the association; and
> 2. That coverage is at least $2,000,000, if the common interest development consists of 100 or fewer separate interests, or $3,000,000 if there are more than 100 separate interests.

This legislation attempts to protect the separate interest of owners who are members of the association. The litigation can be brought only against the association and the question becomes what assets does the association own? Since the association may own very little, that probably explains why the minimum dollar coverage is significantly higher than mentioned in the previous section. Remember, these are minimum amounts and the association may desire higher coverage.

Members may be individually responsible by assessment, not personally, for an amount exceeding the insurance coverage.

Recall that members of incorporated associations are protected from personal liability by law. An incorporated association owning the common areas is the preferred approach in California, since the law provides that "A member of a corporation is not, as such, personally liable for the debts, liabilities, or obligations of the corporation." The Uniform Common Interest Ownership Act addresses the liability issue in a very simple manner. For example, in Minnesota, Section 3-111(b) of the Uniform Condominium Act, it provides that "No unit owner shall have tort liability arising out of ownership of the common elements provided that the association has liability insurance coverage on the occurrence in an amount not less than $1,000,000."

7. Fidelity Insurance

If the governing documents require coverage, or if the board determines it is in the best interest of the association, purchasing fidelity insurance offers protection against financial loss. This coverage may be already included in the association's general blanket policy. ***FIDELITY INSURANCE** covers losses experienced through the dishonest or fraudulent acts of employees who have access to association funds.* In the alternative, a bond could be posted for employees having such access rather than purchase the insurance. Once again, this is an area where checking with an insurance agent can offer some good suggestions. Certainly the amount of the insurance should cover at least several months of operating income plus an amount equal to or exceeding the accumulative balance contained in any reserve account or fund.

Good accounting practices and periodic reviews of the books and accounts should keep the risk of loss minimal.

8. Workmen's Compensation Insurance

Every employer needs to pay workmen's compensation insurance to cover employees.

Since who may or may not be an employee is subject to debate, it is probably a good idea for the association to acquire and maintain workmen's compensation insurance even if the association does not have, or does not think it has, an "employee" at that point in time. There may also be exposure to liability when contracting with outside sources to provide services on the property. It is important for you, as the manager, to make sure that those venders can produce a **certificate of insurance**. Also, the association may want to be named as additional insured on the vendor's policy. Having consistent workmen's compensation insurance will help the association if a vendor has let the insurance lapse and is performing services on development property when someone is injured or is an occasional worker.

Additionally, the association may discover that if it is using a management company to run the day-to-day affairs of the association, it may want to be listed as an additional insured on the association's current insurance policies. Finally, as the association manager, you should insist that somewhere in the association's insurance policies you are protected from lawsuit expenses and a possible judgment for making a mistake. If there is no coverage and you are an independent contractor, you need to get your own insurance. The association will want to verify the coverage for its own protection.

As a manager, you also need to be vigilant in determining if any of the owners are conducting a business out of their separate interest property. If so, the association may insist on the owner obtaining liability insurance covering that business operation and may want the association to be named as an additional insured. Also, remember that daycare centers must either have insurance or have their customers sign a liability waiver.

9. Insurance Notice Distribution

A summary of the association's property, general liability, and earthquake, flood, and fidelity insurance policies must be distributed within 60 days preceding the beginning of the association's fiscal year.

The summary must include all of the following information about each policy:

1. The name of the insured;
2. The type of the insurance;
3. The policy limits of the insurance; and
4. The amount of the deductible if any.

The association must, as soon as reasonably practical, notify the members by first-class mail if any of the above policies have lapsed, been cancelled, are not immediately renewed or replaced, or if there is a significant change, such as a reduction in coverage or limits or an increase in the deductible. If the association receives a notice of non-renewal for any of these policies, it must immediately notify the members if replacement coverage will not be in effect by the date the existing coverage will lapse. The association may meet its obligations to disclose the above information by making a copy of the policy declaration page and distributing it to the membership. In addition to the summary of the insurance policies, the following statement must appear in at least **ten-point bold face type**:

> "This summary of the Association's policy of insurance provides only certain information, as required by subdivision (e) of Section 1365 of the Civil Code, and should not be considered a substitute for the complete policy terms and conditions contained in the actual policies of insurance. Any Association member may, upon request and provision of reasonable notice, review the Association's insurance policies and, upon request and payment of reasonable duplication charges, obtain copies of those policies. Although the Association maintains the policies of insurance specified in the summary, the Association's policies of insurance may not cover your property, including personal property,

or real property improvements to or around your dwelling, or personal injuries, or other losses that occur within or around your dwelling. Even if a loss is covered, you may nevertheless be responsible for paying all or a portion of any deductible that applies. Association members should consult with their individual insurance broker or agent for appropriate additional coverage."

IX. CHAPTER SUMMARY

Most governing documents, typically the covenants, conditions, and restrictions (CC&Rs), will contain a provision regarding leasing of the units within the development. In California, any rule or regulation that arbitrarily or unreasonably restricts an owner's ability to market his or her interest in a CID is void. "Market" and "marketing" mean the listing, advertising, or obtaining or providing access to show the owner's interest in the development. This refers to "restraint on alienation." Restraint is some sort of restriction on the freedom of one's action. Alienation means the transfer of ownership or an interest in a property from one person to another, by any means. Whether or not restrictions can be placed on units that are rented is a question of state law, provision in the governing documents (whether recorded or not), and court decisions.

Many HOAs have governing documents with restrictions on an owner's ability to post a sign on his or her property. A "for sale" or "for rent" sign is reasonable in dimension and design if it conforms to a local city or county ordinance that provides reasonable dimensions for such a sign.

The board can collect money owed by the property owner from the tenants who can then deduct that amount from the rent they pay the owner. Evictions are tricky and expensive. It's best to contact an attorney for advice.

Under the federal Fair Housing Act, as amended, it is unlawful to discriminate in the sale or rental of housing on the basis of race, color, religion, sex, familial status, national origin, or handicap. Familial status means one or more individuals (under 18) living with a parent or legal custodian, a designee of parent or custodian, with their written permission. An association cannot enforce CC&Rs that prevent families with children from buying or renting units within a development. Handicap is a physical or mental impairment which substantially limits one or more of a person's major life activities, a record of having such an impairment, or being regarded as having such an impairment, but does not include current illegal use of or addiction to a controlled substance.

Federal law requires housing providers to make reasonable accommodations for persons with disabilities. A visually impaired tenant is allowed to keep a guide dog, even if the association has a no pets policy.

Each state may have its own fair housing laws in addition to the federal Fair Housing Act. The federal act takes precedence if in conflict with state laws.

The Unruh Civil Rights Act is a California law that prohibits a business from discriminating in the sale or rental of housing based upon age. The California courts have determined that the Unruh Act covers common interest developments.

A senior citizen housing development is a residential development developed, substantially rehabilitated, or substantially renovated for senior citizens that has at least 35 dwelling units. In an age 55-and-older development, the law provides for others to occupy the premises who do not meet the age requirement. This includes guests, qualified permanent residents (like a husband or wife), and permitted healthcare residents. A permitted healthcare resident is a person hired to provide long-term, live-in, or terminal health care to a senior citizen or family member of the senior citizen providing that care. The CC&Rs, other documents, or written policy must set for the limitations on occupancy, residency, or use on the basis of age.

According to the Davis-Stirling Common Interest Development Act in California, a condo owner may modify a unit, at the owner's expense, to facilitate access for persons who are visually handicapped, deaf, or physically disabled, or to alter conditions which could be hazardous to these persons.

The statute of limitations for filing a petition with a government agency is no later than one year after the discriminatory practice has occurred or terminated. An alleged violation of the FHA provision may be pursued by filing a petition with the Department of Housing and Urban Development (HUD), or the California Department of Fair Employment and Housing (DFEH). Petitions alleging a violation of the Fair Employment and Housing Act may be filed with the Department of Fair Employment and Housing, or by the filing of a civil action with the appropriate civil court. Under the Unruh Act, the petition may be filed under the FEHA or by bringing a civil action in a California superior court.

Property and liability insurance is a plan to distribute the actual loss among a group of individuals bearing the same risk of an event by having the individuals contribute a small portion to a fund, which will pay the unfortunate members of the group who suffer loss caused by the occurrence of the event. For insurance purposes, real property in a planned development is the owner's home and lot on which it sits. Condo owner's real property is somewhat less defined. Personal property is everything which is not real property in each dwelling. Risk of loss is the probability that an event will occur which causes a loss of, or damage to, the real or personal property of the owner.

Most insurance polices have exclusions for earth movement, flood, underground water damage, insect or animal damage, or damage caused by contamination or deterioration, intentional damage, and perhaps mold. Most insurance policies only provide earthquake and/or flood coverage at an additional cost.

An inflation clause automatically raises the dollar amount of insurance coverage based on an increase in an inflation or price index. Loss of use coverage in a policy pays for expenses if the insured needs to stay somewhere else. Loss assessment coverage covers the owners for assessments for certain kinds of losses that they must help pay for. Occasional worker coverage is for injuries to someone working on the separate interest. Personal liability insurance protects an owner if other people make a claim or bring a lawsuit against the insured for personal injury or property damage. There is generally no deductible on liability coverage. Condo owners should check as to whether their liability policy covers damages caused by renters or to other units.

A blanket insurance policy covers all of the structures on a property, including losses due to fire and lightning, with typical extended coverage, which will cover losses from causes such as smoke, hail, wind, explosion, riots and civil commotion, falling objects, and water damage. Most of the time, the governing documents, usually the declaration, will state the type of coverage required.

If an HOA's insurance requires the payment of a deductible upon a claim, that deductible is absorbed by the association, although ultimately the loss will be paid for by the members through insurance, a reserve account, or assessments. Liability insurance is used by the HOA to protect itself against financial loss caused by the bodily injury or death of another and/or for damage or loss of the property of another. Errors and omissions insurance protects against losses resulting from negligent acts, errors, and omissions, or breach of any duty by the directors or officers of an association. The protection for officers and directors is for liability in excess of the association's available insurance. It does not protect the officer or director from being sued.

Earthquake insurance can be expensive, so the owners should probably vote on whether they want this coverage.

Fidelity insurance covers losses experienced through the dishonest or fraudulent acts of employees who have access to association funds. Workmen's compensation insurance covers employees, and needs to be paid by every employer.

A summary of the association's property, general liability, and earthquake, flood, and fidelity insurance policies must be distributed within 60 days preceding the beginning of the association's fiscal year.

X. REVIEW QUESTIONS

1. Which of the following documents would most likely contain provisions regarding leasing of units within the development?

    a. The bylaws
    b. The articles
    c. The CC&Rs
    d. None of the above

2. Assessments coverage means:

    a. the owner has enough funds in a bank account to cover any association assessment.
    b. the owner agrees to cover any new assessment with a lien on the owner's property.
    c. the owner has insurance which, up to a specific dollar amount, will cover an increase in an assessment.
    d. assessment coverage is not a term covered in the book.

3. A rule that attempts to prohibit or limit an owner's ability to sell their ownership is often referred to as:

    a. a title transfer restriction.
    b. a restraint on resale.
    c. a restraint on alienation.
    d. a right of first refusal.

4. Which of the following causes for damage to a structure is not normally covered under a standard policy of insurance?

    a. Fire
    b. Wind
    c. Falling object
    d. Earthquake

5. The court, in *Miesch v. Ocean Dunes Homeowner's Association, Inc.*, concluded that the user fee policy was:

    a. binding and enforceable on all tenants.
    b. binding and enforceable only on short term tenants leasing units for less than 28 days.
    c. binding and enforceable only on tenants leasing units for more than 28 days.
    d. unenforceable in its current form.

6. California's legislation regarding "for sale" signs in a common interest development:

a. prohibits "for sale" signs within the development.
b. prohibits "for sale" signs within the development provided the association has passed a rule to that effect.
c. allows "for sale" signs within the development provided the signs meet reasonable requirements.
d. allows any type of "for sale" sign in the development provided it is on the owner's property.

7. An association may consider errors and omissions insurance to protect:

a. members of the board of directors.
b. officers of the association.
c. all owners in the association.
d. a and b are correct answers.

8. Under the Federal Fair Housing Act, it is unlawful to discriminate on all of the following factors, except:

a. religion.
b. familial status.
c. sex.
d. sexual preference.

9. The Federal Fair Housing Act covers:

a. only the sale of housing.
b. only the rental of housing.
c. both the sale and rental of housing.
d. both the sale and rental of all types of property including housing, commercial, industrial, commercial, and retail.

10. Eva has two children, Emile, age 16, and Florence, age 19. Does this grouping satisfy the definition for "familial status"?

a. No, because one child is 19.
b. Yes, because one child is not 18 and residing with a parent.
c. No, because both children have to be under 18 years of age.
d. Yes, because the age requirement for familial status for children is 21 years of age.

ANSWERS: *1. c; 2. c; 3. c; 4. d; 5. d; 6. c; 7. d; 8. d; 9. c; 10. b*

CHAPTER 13

Over-the-Air Reception Devices Rule

I. Introduction

Most common interest developments (CIDs) have a section in their governing documents, typically in the declaration, which some way restricts or prohibits the installation of television antennas, satellite dishes, and other types of antennas on a building or on a lot.

The purpose of the restriction is to provide a consistent and clean appearance within the development, which will maintain the desirability of the units and increase the property values. Obviously, this was a problem when satellite dishes could be six or more feet in diameter or when the neighbor became a ham radio operator and the roof of the house looked like the top of a conning tower on a aircraft carrier. It seemed as though every house had a different type or style of exterior roof-mounted television antenna, and occasionally a television antenna or radio antenna was mounted on a pole or mast instead of on the roof. By including the antenna restrictions in the recorded declaration, each buyer became aware of such restrictions and agreed to abide by them when purchasing in the development.

In some developments, television or radio reception was limited to antennas which could be installed within the attic, or, in some instances, the declaration allowed the

Chapter 13

CHAPTER OUTLINE

AN EXAMPLE
20.11 TELEVISION, CABLE, SATELLITE DISH

Subject to applicable law and the enforceable provisions of contracts, no television cables, no aerial, satellite dish or antennae shall be placed or erected upon any Unit, Common or Limited Common Element, or affixed in any manner to the exterior of any building or structure on the property unless expressly authorized by the Association Board.

installation of antennas or satellite dishes which could not be seen from adjoining property or public streets.

Subsequently, cable television and radio delivery became the preferred way to receive broadcasts. However, satellite broadcasts increased the demand for satellite dishes or other types of antennas that could receive satellite transmissions as an alternative to reception by cable. As a result of the restrictions and/or permits, with attached fees, common in local governments and community associations, along with the outright prohibition of antennas and satellite dishes, the federal government decided to regulate the entire field of reception devices. Congress directed, in **Section 207** of the **Telecommunications Act of 1996**, that the Federal Communications Commission (FCC) adopt an Over-the-Air Reception Devices Rule. This rule would cover governmental and non-governmental restrictions on a viewer's ability to receive video programming signals from direct broadcast satellites, multi-channel multi-point distribution (wireless cable) providers, and television broadcast stations. The Rule can be found at 47 Code of Federal Regulations Section 1.4000 (herein after "the Rule") and has been in effect since October 14, 1996. A copy of the Rule is provided at the end of this chapter.

Essentially, the ***OVER-THE-AIR RECEPTION DEVICES RULE*** *prohibits restrictions that impair the installation, maintenance, or use of antennas used to receive video programming by viewers*. The Rule covers video antennas, including direct-to-home satellite dishes that are less than one meter (39.37 inches) in diameter (or of any size in Alaska), TV antennas, and wireless cable antennas. Restrictions are unenforceable that:

1. unreasonably delay or prevent installation, maintenance, or use of reception devices;
2. unreasonably increase the cost of installation, maintenance, or use of reception devices; or
3. preclude reception of an acceptable quality signal.

The Rule applies to viewers who place antennas that are within the stated size limitations on property that they own or rent and that is within their exclusive control or use, including condominium owners, stock cooperative owners, apartment

development owners, and tenants who have an area where they have exclusive use, such as a balcony or patio, in which to install the antenna. The Rule also applies to single-family homes, townhomes, and manufactured homes. This Rule allows local governments, community associations, and landlords to enforce restrictions that do not unreasonably impair the installation, maintenance or use of permissible antennas, as well as enforce restrictions needed for safety or historic preservation. Additionally, it may be possible, under certain circumstances, to provide a central or common antenna which can be used instead of individual antennas.

> *"The Rule" does not apply to common areas that are owned by a community association, a landlord, or jointly by a condominium or cooperative owners. Restrictions on antennas installed in the common areas are enforceable against tenants or unit owners.*

II. Resolving Disputes

In this new, somewhat confusing, and certainly controversial area of regulation, there have been and will undoubtedly be more disputes between homeowner (community) associations and owners regarding the installation of antennas and satellite dishes. Typically, a dispute will arise when an association member seeks permission, according to the procedure in the declaration, for the installation of a reception device and the permission is denied by the association, or its appropriate committee, or the permission will be granted with various restrictions unacceptable to the owner. Or, in the alternative, the owner has not followed the proper procedure established in the declaration and has installed a satellite dish or antenna and the association seeks to have it removed.

How will these types of disputes be settled? If the owner believes a restriction in the declaration has been pre-empted by the FCC's rule, and the community association disagrees, either party may file a **Petition for Declaratory Ruling** with the Federal Communications Commission (herein after, "Commission") or a court of competent jurisdiction. It may be that the community association believes it can demonstrate a highly specialized or unusual situation for the imposing of prohibited restrictions and will seek a waiver of the Rule from the Commission.

In any event, when filing a petition with the Commission, no particular format is required. The petitioning party simply describes the facts of the situation including a copy of the restrictions of the association and any appropriate correspondence that has taken place. The Petition for a Declaratory Ruling or a waiver must be served on all interested parties. If the homeowner (community) association files a petition seeking a declaratory ruling that its restrictions are enforceable under the rule and is seeking to do so against a particular member, service must be made on that particular member.

The homeowner (community) association is not required to serve all other members of the association, but must provide constructive notice of the proceeding to other members whose interest may foreseeably be affected.

This constructive notice can be accomplished by placing notices in member mail boxes, placing a notice in the community association newsletter, or on the community association bulletin board. Proof of service of the petition, as well as proof of constructive notice of the petition, must be provided to the Commission.

In the alternative, if the member is challenging the community association's restriction, the member must serve the association. The member must include a proof of service with the petition, which is a statement showing that a copy of the petition was provided to the community association. The proof of service should give the name and address of the party served, the date served, and the method of service such as regular mail, certified mail, personal service, or otherwise. Typically, service on the incorporated community association will be made on the agent for service of process listed in the Articles of Incorporation.

While the Petition for Declaratory Ruling or waiver is pending with the Commission or a court, the restriction may not be enforced unless it is necessary for safety or historic preservation. Additionally, no fines or penalties, including attorney's fees, may be imposed by the restricting entity while the petition is pending.

If the Commission finds that the restriction is permissible, the member using the antenna will generally have at least 21 days in which to comply with the ruling before a fine or penalty is imposed.

III. Disputes Resolved By the Commission

In order that individual members, the board of directors of the association, and association managers have a better understanding of the Over-the-Air Reception Devices Rule, the following Federal Communication Commission rulings are provided. Since future conduct is guided by past conduct, in each of the following rulings the exact language of the restriction is stated. In light of the ruling regarding the specific language, other community associations and community association managers can take appropriate steps necessary to adjust the language of their particular restrictions to bring them into line with the Commission rulings or choose not to enforce their restrictions against members.

Each of the following rulings resulted from a petition filed before the Commission with the decision rendered by the Chief of the Cable Services Bureau.

Chapter 13

A. IN THE MATTER OF MICHAEL J. MACDONALD CSR 4922-0

October 14, 1997.

PETITION ISSUES

The petition was filed by MacDonald seeking a determination that the Architectural Control Committee Rules and Regulations adopted by the Savannah Lakes Village Property Owner's Association, Inc., which imposed certain restrictions on the installation and placement of antennas, are pre-empted by the Over-the-Air Reception Devices Rule and are unenforceable. Savannah filed a response opposing the petition. The following restrictions are at issue:

1. Only antennas of one meter or less in diameter are permissible.
2. An Architectural Control Committee permit is required before an antenna may be installed. There is a five-dollar fee for the permit.
3. Permit applications must include a plot plan showing proposed location and size of antenna, description of screening (if applicable), and certification of signal reception locations by a dealer or installer.
4. Installation must comply with building codes, screening, unobtrusive placement, painting, camouflage, or other reasonable means to insure safety and minimize the visual effect. Installation is preferred in the rear yard, not visible from the street, golf course or to neighbors, and ground mounted, as long as signal reception is not impaired.
5. Failure to have a permit or properly screen either propane tanks or satellite dishes may result in loss of privileges or use of property owner's association facilities.

In the opposition to the petition, Savannah states that a 1984 archeological survey of an area including Savannah Lakes Village identified a late Paleo-Indian archeological site in the area and asserts that the South Carolina State Historic Preservation Officer determined that this site was eligible for inclusion on the National Register of Historic Places.

DISCUSSION

The Rule places the burden of proof in proceedings on the entity seeking to enforce a restriction.

1. Historic preservation exemption.

The Rule provides that a restriction that otherwise would be prohibited is permissible if it is necessary to preserve an historic district listed or eligible for listing in the National Register of Historic Places. We find inadequate evidence to conclude that Savannah Lakes Village is, or is eligible to be, in the National Register of Historic Places. Furthermore, neither Savannah's antenna regulations nor its response to the Petition offers a sufficient connection between the restrictions it imposes on antennas and its concerns about preserving a Paleo-Indian site. In the absence of proof of listing or eligibility for listing, we conclude that this is not an historic district as defined in the Rule.

2. Permit requirement.

Savannah requires a five-dollar fee, which, while a relatively small amount, is an unreasonable expense because it is an unwarranted charge. Savannah also requires a certificate from the dealer or installer certifying that installation in a location other than preferred by Savannah is necessary to avoid impaired reception. Although Savannah's preference for ground-mounted installation in a rear yard not visible from the street may be a permissible preference, Savannah may not implement its preference by delaying installation while it determines whether to grant a permit. The approval procedures are time consuming and likely to deter potential antenna users. We conclude that they impose unreasonable delay in violation of the Rule. In addition, Savannah's certification requirement applies to antenna users who install antennas themselves, as well as to those who hire an installer. This requirement compels users to hire an installer for the purpose of certifying that the installation in a non-preferred location is necessary. We find that requiring an antenna user to hire an installer solely to provide a certificate is an unreasonable expense that violates the Rule.

3. Antenna size.

To the extent that the Savannah regulations prohibit installation of TVBS (television broadcast station) antennas larger than one meter in diameter, they are pre-empted because the Rule protects all TVBS antennas without a per se limitation on size or shape.

The one meter in diameter size limitation is on direct-to-home satellite dishes, not TVBS antennas.

4. Screening and camouflaging requirements.

Savannah's antenna regulation requires screening and camouflaging, which may impose unreasonable expense in some circumstances. While we agree that such requirements can be unreasonable, the Savannah regulation purportedly requires only "reasonable measures." There is no assertion that Savannah's implementation or enforcement of this requirement, thus far, has imposed unreasonable expense or delay or precluded acceptable quality reception. However, petitioner alleges that the screening and camouflaging requirements could add unreasonable costs or delay installation. We conclude that Savannah must specifically state that by "reasonable" it means those requirements that do not impose unreasonable expense or delay or preclude reception of an acceptable quality signal.

5. Loss of community privileges.

Savannah has offered no explanation or justification for this penalty, and we believe that penalties of this sort are likely to deter installation. Therefore, in the absence of any justification offered by the association, we cannot uphold the penalty.

CONCLUSION

We conclude, based on the record, that Savannah Lakes Village is not an historic district as defined in the Rule, and Savannah antenna regulations are not exempt from the Rule for reasons of historic preservation. We find that the prior approval requirement in Savannah's antenna regulation violates the Rule because it is likely to delay unreasonably the installation of antennas covered by the Rule. Moreover, the antenna regulation fails to provide adequately for exceptions to its placement preference and the screening/camouflaging requirements would impair installation, maintenance or use of antenna. We find that those provisions of the Savannah regulations pertaining to installation of antennas conflict with the Rule and are hereby pre-empted.

B. IN THE MATTER OF CS WIRELESS SYSTEMS, INC. CSR 4947-0

October 14, 1997.

PETITION ISSUES

Petitioner, CS Wireless Systems, Inc., filed a Petition for Declaratory Ruling seeking a determination that the covenants, conditions, and restrictions of the Property Owners of North Hampton Association, Inc., which restrict the use of externally mounted antennas are prohibited by the Rule. Petitioner is a wireless cable service provider serving more than 13,000 customers in the San Antonio, Texas, area. Petitioner states that specialized antennas are required to receive its wireless cable microwave signals which it transmits and which are dependent upon line-of-sight reception. North Hampton's restrictions provide:

1. No antenna or device of any type for receiving or transmitting signals (electronic or otherwise) shall be erected, constructed, placed, or permitted to remain on the exterior of any houses, garages, or buildings constructed on any lot; nor shall any free standing antenna of any style be permitted to remain on any lot. TV satellite reception disks shall be screened by a fence or other similar facility, so as to conceal them from view of any other lot or public street.

Petitioner contends that the Jermiers own a home in the North Hampton community and installed an antenna less than 12 feet above the peak of the roof, the minimum height necessary to obtain a line-of-sight signal. The North Hampton Association wrote a letter to the Jermiers notifying them that the installation was in violation of the rules.

CONCLUSION

We find that the North Hampton Association's covenants violate the Rule. The first sentence is an outright prohibition against the installation of externally-mounted antennas that is not justified on either safety or historic preservation grounds. Wireless cable antennas operate on line-of-sight contact with the transmitter or repeater and, given current technology, require an unobstructed view of the transmitter or repeater. North Hampton's outright prohibition violates the Rule because it prevents installation, maintenance, or use of the antennas and thereby, necessarily, precludes reception of an acceptable quality signal.

We also find that the second sentence of the North Hampton Association covenants appears to except "TV satellite reception disk" from the outright prohibition but, nevertheless, mandates screening of the dish to render it less visible. We note that mandatory screening of satellite dishes or other antennas would be permissible if the covenants provided for exceptions to the screening requirement in situations where screening would unreasonably delay installation, or unreasonably increase the cost of installation, maintenance, or use of the antenna, or preclude reception of an acceptable quality signal. However, as written, this section does not allow for exceptions to the screening requirement and is, therefore, prohibited by the Rule.

C. IN RE JORDAN E. LOURIE CSR 5185-0

June 18, 1998.

PETITION ISSUES

The restrictions at issue are from the Roxbury Run Village in Delaware County, New York, and provide:

> No exterior television or radio antenna of any sort shall be placed, allowed or maintained upon any portion of the improvements to be placed upon the property, nor upon any structure situated on the property.

Lourie owns a townhouse in Roxbury Run Village which is subject to the restrictions. Lourie proposed to install an eighteen-inch antenna on the chimney of his unit. Since the Association is obligated to maintain the entire exterior of any unit, it contends that any installation of any antenna would be prohibited. Subsequently, Lourie received a notice that the Association had adopted a resolution imposing a fine of $25 per day for the installation of any exterior appliance. Lourie and the Association arranged for a meeting to resolve the matter, but the Association informed Lourie that the issue of satellite antennas had been placed on the agenda of the upcoming annual membership meeting and that any meeting with Lourie must wait until after the membership meeting. The association contends that it has constantly prohibited the placing of objects on exterior walls because of a concern for being held responsible if any object attached should fall or blow off and injure someone. The Association also contends that the chimney surface is not within Lourie's exclusive use or control. The Association contends the chimney surface area is one which the Association controls and for which it holds responsibility for repair, replacement and maintenance.

CONCLUSION

Under the Rule, the Association, as the restricting entity, has the burden to show that its restrictions do not impair the installation, maintenance, or use of over-the-air reception antennas or that its restrictions qualify for either the safety or historic preservation exception to the rule. Lourie is the owner with exclusive use of the townhouse, including its chimney. As exclusive user of the chimney, Lourie's use of his dish clearly falls within the Rule. One need not physically occupy something to use it. The determination of exclusive use is not dependent on actual use. In any event, Lourie uses his chimney to form the outer surface of his flue. However, because the Association has responsibility for the chimney's maintenance, it can require Lourie to remove the dish temporarily if necessary to perform normal maintenance.

Furthermore, we do not believe it inappropriate for the Association to take reasonable steps to protect itself from liability stemming from the installation of the subject antenna, provided that indemnification is not used as an equivalent for prior approval. Lourie's chimney is not in a common area. The Association's written restrictions, and the implementation thereof with respect to Lourie, create an outright prohibition of antennas covered by the Rule. There was no evidence presented to show that the prohibition is necessary for valid safety or historic preservation reasons. The restrictions violate the Rule.

D. IN RE JASON PETERSON CSR 5115-0

February 4, 1998.

PETITION ISSUES

Association restriction Section 9.10 states:

> Without prior authorizations of the Board, no television. . . antennas, or satellite dishes of any sort shall be placed, allowed or maintained on the exterior of any Townhouse Unit. . .

Petitioner owns a townhouse in Geneva, Illinois, which is subject to the above restriction which is enforced by the Chesapeake Commons Homeowner's Association. Petitioner states he was told by the Association that installation of an 18-inch DBS satellite dish is prohibited and that upon installation of the dish the Association will have it removed and bill the petitioner for the expense. Petitioner further states that he was told that the only manner in which he could receive broadcast programming was via Cable TV.

CONCLUSION

We find that Chesapeake's written restrictions and the implementation thereof with respect to the petitioner create an outright prohibition of antennas covered by the Rule. By definition, restrictions and implementation such as present here impair the installation, maintenance, or use of covered antennas and are unenforceable.

E. IN THE MATTER OF JAMES SADLER CSR-5074-0

July 1, 1998.

PETITION ISSUES

The restrictions provide as follows:

> Except for any antenna installed by Declarant [the Association], no television or radio antenna or antenna of any sort, or any part thereof, shall extend outside of any Unit or be placed on or affixed to the exterior of any improvement herein.

James Sadler owns a townhome condominium subject to the regulations adopted by the Chatsworth Country Townhomes Association. Sadler wants to install a direct satellite broadcast dish on his townhome outside wall and inside the townhome's patio area. The dish is installed inside the condominium patio area and mounted on the exterior wall that separates the sliding glass doors exited to the patio and the first-floor windows overlooking the doors. The dish does not extend outside the patio area or above the ceiling of the first floor of the unit and will be installed on the wall with screws. Chatsworth requested that Sadler move the dish out of sight from the street. Sadler complied with the request by moving the dish below the walls surrounding the patio, but because he was unable to receive a signal in that new location, he moved the dish back to its current position above the walls surrounding the patio. Sadler does not own the condominium and has a letter from the owner stating he supports Sadler's request.

Sadler also objects to several guidelines regarding installation: The first one restricts the installation of satellite dishes to the roof in an area designated by the board and to the interior of the patio area but not attached to the fence post, walls of the building or other common area; second, a requirement that the dish not be visible from the street or any common area. Sadler contends that requiring him to move the dish to the roof imposes an unreasonable cost on him and an unreasonable risk that the dish could be stolen from the roof. Third, Sadler notes that a guideline requires that prior to installation of a dish, an application must be completed for approval describing the proposed location of the dish along with two sets of plans describing the work to be performed and the materials used and a copy of the contractor's license. Fourth, Sadler objects to the guidelines that require him to indemnify Chatsworth for liability if the dish is installed on the roof and further to reimburse the Association if the installation, maintenance or use of the dish on the roof damages

the roof. Further guidelines require the antenna user to pay the Association's contractor to inspect the installation after it is performed; the antenna user to hire a licensed contractor to install the dish if the City of Los Angeles requires one; the contractor to be insured; and the antenna user to provide the Association with copies of the contractor's worker's compensation and comprehensive general liability policies before the work begins.

The Association contends that the walls separating the condominium from the patio where the dish is installed is a common area and not an area of exclusive use. Condominium occupiers have exclusive use of the patio, but that piercing any of the building's exterior wall invades the common area. The Association also argues that Sadler is merely a tenant and does not have an ownership interest. The Association sent Sadler the following letter:

> To date, the Association has spent $1,016.50 in attorney's fees in an attempt to have Mr. Sadler move the satellite dish from the common area wall. Currently, Mr. Sadler's petition is pending with the FCC in Washington to obtain an order that he be permitted to maintain his satellite dish in its present location. If the Association must respond to the Petition, additional attorney's fees will be incurred.
>
> Pursuant to the CC&Rs and the Civil Code of California, the Association will be entitled to seek reimbursement of its attorneys' fees incurred to compel compliance with the Association's governing documents.

CONCLUSION

The Rule places the burden of demonstrating that the challenged restriction complies with the Rule on the party seeking to oppose the restriction. Although Sadler does not have an ownership in the property, the owner has given his consent to the installation of the dish. We see no distinction between the tenant and the owner for the purpose of this petition. We find that Sadler has exclusive use of the dwelling unit's exterior wall. The Condominium Plan Notes and the Condominium Plan Diagram demonstrate that the condominium owner owns the interior and exterior surfaces of the condominium's first floor wall facing the patio. We believe that the condominium dweller has the same rights of ownership and use in the patio area as within the condominium unit. No evidence has been presented that Sadler pierced the wall beyond the boundary of the condominium owner's ownership and use.

We find that requiring Sadler to move the dish to the roof will unreasonably increase the cost of installation to Sadler. Sadler's evidence was an installer's estimate that it could cost between $250 to $350 to move the dish from his patio to the roof. We agree with Sadler that the Association's prior approval requirement violates the Rule by imposing an unreasonable delay and expense if applied to the installation of devices on property over which the viewer has a direct or indirect ownership interest and exclusive use or control.

We do not believe it unreasonable to hold the antenna user liable for any personal or property damage caused by the installation, maintenance, or use of the antenna. Those provisions that require Sadler to indemnify the Association for liability arising from the installation, maintenance, and use of his dish on his patio area are reasonable and enforceable including reimbursing the Association for repairing damage to any common area caused by installation, maintenance or use of the dish in the patio area.

It is also a violation of the Rule to compel an antenna user to hire a contractor in order to certify that installation meets the Association's Guidelines as an unreasonable expense. If an antenna user installs a dish in an area that violates legitimate guidelines, then the Association may assess a penalty on the user at that time. These dishes are designed for the viewer to install and requiring a contractor is an unreasonable expense. Nevertheless, if a contractor is employed to install a dish, we believe that it is a reasonable requirement for the contractor to have insurance to pay for any personal injuries or structural damage to the property. However, the requirement that the viewer obtain and provide the Association with copies of the contractor's worker's compensation and general liability insurance policies is unreasonable because it places a burden on viewers who abide by the guidelines by using insured contractors.

With regard to attorney's fees, we believe that the threat of attorney's fees operates as a substantial deterrent to viewers exercising their rights to install a dish while such a restriction is under review and could therefore unreasonably prevent the installation of a dish. We find that assessing attorney's fees while a petition is pending is prohibited under the Rule.

F. IN RE JAY LUBLINER AND DEBORAH GALVIN, POTOMAC, MARYLAND CSR 4915-0, APPLICATION FOR REVIEW OF DECLARATORY RULING ISSUES BY THE CHIEF, CABLE SERVICES BUREAU

August 20, 1998.

REVIEW ISSUES

Potomac Ridge Homeowner's Association, Inc. filed an Application for Review of the previous decision by the FCC that the Association had failed to satisfy its burden of demonstrating that its covenants, conditions, and restrictions do not conflict with the standards set forth in the Commission's Over-the-Air Reception Devices Rule. Lubliner and Galvin installed an outdoor television antenna on the roof of their single-family home located in the Potomac Ridge subdivision in Montgomery County, Maryland. The Association's covenants prevent the use of any type of outdoor antenna. Lubliner had sought permission from the Association to install an outdoor antenna because he alleged that the aluminum siding on his house prevented him from receiving acceptable quality signals with an indoor antenna in the attic. The Association refused to allow the installation of an outdoor antenna.

Lubliner filed a petition and the decision of the Chief of the Cable Services Bureau concluded that the Association failed to meet its burden of proof that its prohibition of exterior antennas did not impair reception.

DECISION

The Association presented evidence of television broadcast signal strength tests conducted inside and outside other properties and argued Lubliner could receive an acceptable signal inside the house. The Bureau noted that one of the several indicators of the unreliability of the Association's signal measurements was a unit of measurement used. Specifically, the bureau found that the Association's use of "decibel"(dB) in the signal strength measurements appeared to be incorrect. Measurement expressed in dB are incorrect for the purpose of determining signal quality because they lacked the necessary point of reference. Measurements to be useable should have been expressed in decibels relative to one milliwatt (dBM). We agree with the Bureau that petitioners use of decibel, without a reference point, is insufficient in the present context because one cannot determine whether the measured signal is of sufficient strength to provide acceptable quality reception without reference to an objective standard for signal strength. Therefore, the test results were unreliable and not useable to demonstrate whether the Association's antenna restriction impairs Lubliner's television reception.

Moreover, if the test results show anything, they demonstrate that several of Lubliner's neighbors appear to be unable to receive at least one local television broadcast signal using antennas installed inside their homes. Our decision here rests on the Association's failure to show that Lubliner could receive an acceptable quality signal. The Association decided not to seek access to the Lubliner's home as part of its defense of its antenna restriction, and did not indicate in its test report if any of the homes where the test was conducted also had aluminum siding. If the Association had requested access to Lubliner's house for the purpose of performing reasonable signal quality test and Lubliner had refused access, then the Association might have a basis for a persuasive argument that it was prevented from effectively demonstrating that its restrictions do not preclude reception of an acceptable quality signal.

G. IN THE MATTER OF TRABUE CSR-4974-0

May, 1999.

PETITION ISSUES

Association Restrictions include:

1. Antennas

Prior approval of the Architectural Review Committee for an antenna that is designed to receive direct broadcast satellite service, including direct-to-home satellite services, that is one meter or less in diameter; or an antenna that is designed to receive video program services via multipoint distribution services, including multichannel multipoint distribution services, instructional television fixed services, and local multipoint distribution services, and that is one meter or less in diameter or diagonal measurement; or an antenna that is designed to receive television broadcast signals, is not required, provided it meets the following requirements:

a. Antennas and dishes shall be painted in a fashion that blends into the background against which they are mounted, provided such painting will not interfere with reception. Mounting materials, accessories, and cabling shall be painted in a fashion that blends into the background against which they are mounted.

The Trabues (petitioners) are homeowners in the Garden Lakes planned community, located in Avondale, Arizona. They challenged the above regulations. They allege that the Association cited them for erecting a direct broadcast satellite antenna without prior approval; that the Association instructed them to paint the entire apparatus the same color as the house; and that the Association sought to impose on them a fine of $50 per day. They argued that the Association's painting requirement is based on aesthetic concerns and is not necessarily for safety or historic preservation. Additionally, petitioners allege that painting the entire apparatus would be unreasonable as it can cost as much as 40 to 50 percent of the price of the dish and will void the warranty. Additionally, petitioners contend that not everyone who owns a satellite dish has been required to paint it, and that the Association does not require painting of other, arguably comparable items, such as telephone boxes and cable boxes, both of which are visible from sides of homes.

The Association contends that painting the antenna can be done for a minimal cost and it does not void the manufacturer's warranty. The Association furnished affidavits of two homeowners who have painted their satellite dishes to conform to the Association's requirements and have experienced no degradation or loss of signal. Additionally, the Association provided a statement from a local satellite dealer stating that a dish may be painted without losing the quality of the picture as long as non-metallic paint is used.

CONCLUSION

Although not prohibited in every case, here the Association's requirement goes beyond painting the dish itself to require the mounting materials, accessories, and cabling associated with the dish must also be painted. This part of the Association's requirement conflicts with evidence offered by the Association which states that certain parts of the antenna, including the cables, should not be painted. Voiding the manufacturer's warranty impairs maintenance and use by opposing unreasonable expense. We conclude, therefore, that the Association's painting requirement is preempted insofar as it applies to cables and other accessories the painting of which would void the warranty. As to the requirement to paint the dish, there is no evidence that such a requirement imposes unreasonable delay or precludes reception of an acceptable quality signal. The Association's management agent states that he is willing to pay for painting an antenna under certain circumstances. We find that the Association's requirement to paint the dish itself, as distinguished from the cables and accessories, does not appear to void this manufacturer's warranty. In addition, we interpret the Association's offer to paint the dish to apply to the petitioner's dish. The Association's requirement that the dish be painted does not impose an unreasonable expense or otherwise impair installation, maintenance or use of antennas covered by the Rule. The Association's requirement for prior approval is prohibited by the Rule because it can impose an unreasonable delay.

H. IN THE MATTER OF HOLLIDAY CSR 5399-0

October 8, 1999.

PETITION ISSUES

Association Restrictions, paragraph 11, includes:

> Architectural Design and Environmental Control. No building, fence, walls or other structure shall be erected, placed, or altered on any building lot in this Subdivision until the building plans, specifications and plot plan showing the location of such structures have been approved as to the conformity and harmony of external design with existing structures herein and as to the building with respect to topography and finished ground elevations by an Architectural and Environmental Control Committee.

The Hollidays seek a determination that the above provision as applicable to antennas and supporting structures is prohibited. Hollidays own a single-family dwelling in Indianapolis, Indiana and they have installed six masts in the rear of their lot which are secured to the ground by guy wires. There are five masts approximately thirty feet in height which are roughly even with their roofline, two of which simply provide support to another mast, and one ten foot mast. Petitioners have affixed five television antennas and three satellite dish antennas to these masts. The antennas provide reception for ten television sets, nine video cassette recorders, and seven satellite receivers. The Hollidays did not seek the Association's approval for installation of the antennas and supporting structures.

The Association states that although paragraph 11 does not address multiple antennas directly, it is the Association's policy to permit the installation of only one satellite dish that is one meter or less in diameter and one television antenna that extends no more than twelve feet above the roof line. Therefore, it would not approve the Holliday's installations even if they sought approval. The Association justifies its policy on general safety concerns and the need to retain the appearance and value of other homes in the neighborhood. The Association argues that the Rule speaks only of "an antenna" in the singular and nothing in the Rule dictates that an entity cannot impose reasonable restrictions on the number of antennas a party is permitted to erect.

CONCLUSION

We find that the Association's written restriction and its implementation thereof with respect to Holliday's antennas create an impermissible prior approval requirement for antennas covered by the Rule. The Commission has held that a requirement of prior authorization is prohibited unless it is justified by legitimate safety or historic preservation considerations. The Association's generalized reference to safety concerns contained in its response does not satisfy the Rule. An Association or other restricting entity cannot impose an arbitrary limit of a number of antennas a viewer may install provided they are necessary to receive the video programming available for reception in the viewer's viewing area. An Association may prohibit the installation of equipment that is merely duplicative and not necessary for the reception of video programming. However, the evidence in this proceeding does not contain sufficient information to enable us to determine whether it is necessary for the Hollidays to maintain five television antennas and three satellite dish antennas in order to receive the video programming available in their viewing area. The restriction is unenforceable.

I. IN THE MATTER OF ROBERTS CSR 5531-0

May, 2001.

PETITION ISSUES

The Association restriction provides:

> No television, radio, short wave, microwave, satellite or other antenna, pole, tower or dish shall be placed, constructed, or maintained upon any lot (including, but not limited to, upon the roof of exterior walls of living unit or other structure) unless: (i) the antenna, pole, tower, or dish is fully screened and not visible from neighboring property due to a parapet wall which conforms architecturally with the structure of the living unit or other structure; or (ii) the antenna, pole, tower, or dish is otherwise fully and attractively screened or not visible from neighboring property. Any means of screening or concealment shall be subject to the Architectural and Landscaping Guidelines adopted by the Committee and shall be subject to approval by the Committee in accordance with Article 4 of this Declaration.

The Roberts reside in a single-family home located in the Canada Vistas subdivision in Scottsdale, Arizona. They installed a multichannel multipoint distribution service antenna in an area within their exclusive use and control. Roberts argue that the present location of the antenna is the only site on the property where the required line-of-sight to receive an acceptable signal can be had which is supported by the video service provider. According to the Roberts, they applied for approval and the Association's Board of Directors denied the request. The Board stated that:

1. the antenna was for Internet service only;
2. there was no documentation to support the contention the antenna could not be relocated;
3. Roberts failed to submit a proposal for screening or camouflage; and
4. Roberts did not following the Association's prior approval procedure.

Roberts argue that the screening requirement represents an unreasonable increase in the cost of the antenna installation. The Association contends that the Roberts are not the owners of the property, that the screening requirement is legitimate and that the Roberts have not shown how it would be too expensive.

Sprint Corporation's manager of the Scottsdale area has verified that the antenna in question cannot get line-of-sight reception at the alternative location demanded by the Association. The manager stated that "It is impossible for Mr. Roberts to comply with the screening requirements and still receive a line-of-sight signal."

CONCLUSION

The Association's prior approval requirement compels potential antenna users who must install the antenna in a manner that requires screening or that is visible to first prepare and submit a detailed drawing or blueprint for the proposed screening or installation. The Federal Communication Commission has specifically concluded that requirements for approval by community associations might prove to be a disincentive for potential antenna users, effectively preventing access to the video programming signals that Congress sought to provide.

In this case, although the Association's preference for an installation that is not visible from neighboring properties may be a permissible preference, the Association may not implement its preference by delaying installation while its architectural committee examines the required screening proposal. These approval procedures are time-consuming and likely to deter potential users. The 1996 Act and the Rule require homeowner associations to enforce preferred placement provisions through methods that do not delay or hinder those who have a right to site their antennas at alternative locations. We note that the burden of demonstrating that the placement restrictions do not impair the installation, maintenance or use of antennas lies with the Association. Here, the Association has provided no evidence to meet this burden, even after it indicated that it would seek independent verification that the antenna could not be relocated. In this case neither a safety nor historic preservation justification for the Association's approval requirement exists. We conclude that the Association's prior approval requirement is prohibited by the Rule because it can impose an unreasonable delay. An antenna user need not be the owner of the property, nor have the owner's permission to install an antenna.

J. IN THE MATTER OF WOJCIKEWICZ CSR 6030-0

September 29, 2003.

PETITION ISSUES

Association restrictions in the Declaration:

Section 3.07 ALTERATIONS, ADDITIONS, OR IMPROVEMENTS TO HOMES AND HOME EXTERIORS: No additions, alterations, or improvements (including, without limitation, changes in the exterior color of a Home, construction of an out building, fence, awnings, antenna, satellite dish or similar improvements or changes in landscaping) shall be made to any Lot, Home, Home Exterior or any part of the Home which is visible from outside the Home by an Owner without the prior written consent of the Board in compliance with applicable Municipality ordinances.

Section 8.03 ANTENNAE: No television antenna, radio receiver, or transmitter or other similar device shall be attached to or installed on any portion of any Home Exterior or the Community Area.

Association Rules and Regulations:

SATELLITE/ANTENNA INSTALLATION: We strongly encourage satellite dishes to be professionally installed and located on the roof in a location approved by the Board. All dishes must be removed if the home is sold and the purchaser does not agree to maintain the satellite dish. Any damage done by or to the satellite dishes is the responsibility of the homeowner.

II. Installation Rules

A. Antenna Size and Type.

1. DBS/MDS antennas that are 24 inches or less in diameter may be installed. Antennas of any kind larger than 24 inches are prohibited.

B. Location

2. If acceptable quality signals may be received by placing antennas inside a dwelling unit, without unreasonable delay or unreasonable additional expense, then the outdoor installation is prohibited.

III. Installation

5. Antennas may not be mounted to the chimneys of any owner's unit due to the possible impairment to the integrity of that fixture.

V. Safety

1. Antennas shall be installed and secured in a manner that complies with all applicable city and state laws and regulations, and manufacturer's instructions. The owner, prior to the installation, shall provide the Association with a copy of any applicable governmental permit.

VI. Antenna Camouflaging

A. Antennas may not extend beyond the fence or above the roof line.

VII. Number of Antennas

A. No more than one antenna may be installed by an owner.

IX. Notification Process.

A. Any owner desiring to install an antenna must complete a notification form and submit it c/o the Association to the office. If the install is routine (conforms to all rules and restrictions set forth above), it may start immediately.

B. If the installation is other than routine for any reason, owners and Board must establish a mutual time to meet and discuss installation methods.

Wojcikewicz (Petitioner) resides in a townhome located in the Woodmere Townhomes Community. His home is an interior unit in a group of four adjoining townhomes. Petitioner contends that he owns his lot and townhome, including the roof, and has exclusive use of the roof. The Woodmere Townhome Association of Darien, Illinois, states that its restrictions prohibit only installation of antennas on common areas. The argument is that because the townhome roofs adjoin each other and are maintained and insured by the Association, the roofs are common area. Therefore, the Association contends that because the roof is a common area, the Rule does not apply and the commission does not have jurisdiction over antenna installation on petitioner's roof.

CONCLUSION

Roofs or exterior walls may be restricted access areas where residents are not granted exclusive or permanent possession, and the agreed-upon scope of physical possession is set forth in the lease or other controlling document. The petitioner owns his townhome. The Declaration for Woodmere Townhomes defines the home exterior as the ". . . roof, foundation, steps, footings, decks, outer surface of exterior walls and garage door of a Home." Additionally, the Declaration specifies that each owner shall have ". . . the exclusive right to use and enjoy the Owner's Home and Home exterior." Based on these documents we find that for the purposes of application of the Rule, petitioner has a property interest in the roof because it is expressly designated for his exclusive use. Although petitioner does not have exclusive control over his roof as a result of the easement granted to the Association to perform maintenance on the roof, we have previously ruled that the rights of third parties to enter and/or exercise control over the owner's exclusive-use area for such reasons as inspection or maintenance does not defeat the owner's rights under the Rule. The Association's easement to perform maintenance therefore does not defeat the petitioner's right to the exclusive use of this roof. Therefore, since the roof is not a common area, the Rule applies to the Association's restrictions on antenna located on this property.

We find that the written restrictions and implementations thereof with respect to petitioner's request to install his antenna on the roof create an impermissible prior approval requirement for antennas covered by the Rule. Aesthetic factors alone may not justify a prior approval process.

NOTIFICATION PROCESS

The Association's Section IX notification process is permissible only to the extent it constitutes a simple notification by an owner to the Association that he has installed or is about to install an antenna.

ANTENNA SIZE

The Association contends that because the petitioner's TV antenna is larger than one meter in diameter, it is not covered by the Rule. We find that petitioner's six-foot by eight-foot TV antenna is covered by the Rule. The Rule does not restrict the size of TV antennas designed to receive local television broadcast signals.

PLACEMENT PREFERENCES

Section II B.2. and Section VI.A. deal with placement of the antenna. Petitioner states that despite three different TV antennas in several locations in his attic and boosting a signal with an amplifier, he cannot receive an acceptable quality HDTV signal. We find that petitioner has the right to place his TV antenna on his roof or any other location that is within his exclusive use or control where he has a direct or indirect ownership or leasehold interest, and the Association has not met the burden to prove that installation on the preferred alternate location will provide an acceptable quality signal.

Section VII. A. is impermissible because the Federal Communication Commission has ruled that an Association may not impose an arbitrary limit on the number of antennas a viewer may install, provided they are necessary to receive the video programming available for reception in the viewer's viewing area.

Section V.1. violates the Rule because such requirements are unenforceable where there is nothing in the evidence to enable it to determine whether the code sections are safety related or whether they otherwise impair installation, maintenance or use under the Rule and because it is unnecessarily burdensome to require a homeowner to cull through all ordinances, laws, regulations, and industry standards to determine which ones apply.

Section III.5. is unenforceable because the Association has not satisfied its burden to justify a blanket prohibition of antenna installation on the chimney if such location is necessary for the petitioner to receive an acceptable quality signal.

K. IN THE MATTER OF BELL ATLANTIC VIDEO SERVICES COMPANY CSR 5398-0

April 26, 2000.

PETITION ISSUES

Association restrictions provide:

> No outside television aerial or radio antenna, or other aerial or antennae for either reception or transmission which may be viewed from the front yard of the Lot, or which projects above the roof ridge line, shall be maintained upon the Property of Lot, except as addressed by a Standing Resolution.

Standing Resolution:

> Whereas the size and placement of TV antennas and satellite reception dishes are subject to regulation and approval by the Meadow Community Services Association (MCSA) Environmental Preservation Committee (EPCOM).
>
> Whereas the EPCOM is authorized by the MCSA Declaration of Protective Covenants to adopt a Standing Resolution that permits the placement of such reception devices in locations other than on the rear roof surface of a home, is located in accordance with the guidelines of Standing Resolution adopted by the EPCOM.
>
> Now therefore be it resolved that TV satellite dishes/antennas may be located within the rear yard of any home, without the necessity of securing formal EPCOM approval provided that:
>
> 1. the dish/antenna diameter does not exceed 24 inches, and
> 2. the distance from the top of any pole-mounted dish/antenna to the ground beneath the dish shall not exceed 72 inches, and
> 3. subject to the above limitation as to dish size and height above the ground, such TV reception devices also may be located on any rear corner or rear wall surface of any home.

Bell Atlantic argues that MCSA violates the Rule by using two restrictions jointly to unreasonably delay or prevent Bell Atlantic's prospective clients at The Meadow from installing, maintaining, and using television and antenna satellite reception devices on their respective properties. Bell Atlantic professionally installed an 18-inch satellite dish and a broadcast antenna on resident Bradshaw's property and because of the multi-ridged structure of her roof and need for continued reception of the broadcast signals, it installed a reception device in a location and at a height other than the preferences in the restrictions. Bradshaw received a letter from the chairman of the EPCOM, requesting the satellite dish and antenna be removed and relocated to conform with the requirements of the Association's protective covenants and the standing resolution pertaining to TV dishes. If Bradshaw did not do so the MCSA would take further action.

CONCLUSION

A prior approval process is impermissible unless it is necessary for bona fide safety or historic preservation consideration. We find MCSA's prior approval requirement impermissible under the Rule. The satellite dish restriction violates the Rule because the Rule specifically allows the installation of satellite dishes of up to one meter (39.37 inches) in diameter or diagonal measurement. The Rule does not limit the size of a TVBS antenna that a user may install. Therefore, MCSA's restrictions are unenforceable because they effectively prohibit the installation of antennas that are protected by the Rule.

The preferences regarding size and height restrictions involving the placement preferences of the antennas would be in compliance with the Rule if they did not unreasonably delay installation, add unreasonably to the cost of installation, maintenance or use of an antenna, or impair the reception of an acceptable quality signal. In this case, however, placement preferences delay the installation, maintenance and use of the satellite dish-TVBS antenna combination that Bradshaw needs to receive the alternative video programming Bell Atlantic provides, add to Bradshaw's installation expenses, and impair signal reception. The requirement that antennas and dishes not be visible from the front yard and the height restrictions violate the Rule by establishing a per se bar to antennas that extend over the roof line and those installed in rear yards that exceeds the 72-inch height limitation.

L. IN THE MATTER OF FRANKFURT CSR-52380

February 7, 2001.

PETITION ISSUES

The following guidelines of the New Century Town Townhouse Association in Vernon Hills, Illinois are contested:

The following rules shall apply to devices covered by Section 207 of the Telecommunications Act of 1996 in the interest of promoting the safety and welfare of the Association:

1. Type of mountings permitted/prohibited.
   a. Freestanding on patio or deck-prohibited.
   b. Fence right/railing-prohibited.
   c. Siding mounted-permitted.
   d. Roof mounts-prohibited.
   e. Fireplace chimney mounted-prohibited.
   f. Balcony mounts on railing or deck-permitted.
   g. Pole mounted on detached footing-prohibited.

2. Height Restrictions
   a. DBS-not more than 12 feet above roof level.
   b. MMDS-not more than 12 feet above roof level.
   c. TVBS-not more than height limitations above roof level as specified in local BOCA Code.
   d. Devices are to generally be mounted so they are not visible from front of unit.
   e. Mounted devices shall only be as high as necessary above a structure surface to the device as required clear view of the transmitting signal antenna/satellite.

3. Size Restrictions.
   a. DBS-dish shall not exceed 1 meter (39.37 inches) in diameter.
   b. MMDS-dish shall not exceed 1 meter (39.37 inches) in diameter or diagonally.
   c. TVBS-antennas shall be limited in size pursuant to local BOCA code.

4. Location of Device.
   a. Rear of dwelling unit unless signal would be impaired.
   b. Device may be mounted on owner's side of firewall toward rear of unit.
   c. If rear of unit is not suitable, device shall be placed on side of dwelling unit.
   d. If rear and side of dwelling unit is not suitable, device shall only then be permitted in front of dwelling unit in a location as inconspicuous as possible.
   e. Device shall not interfere nor obstruct exterior maintenance responsibilities of the Association.
   f. Device shall not be located near power lines or other utilities, e.g. gas, water, etc.
   g. Device shall not extend beyond unit lot lines.
   h. Devices are prohibited on Association common property.

5. Installation.

   a. Device shall be grounded in accordance with N.E.C. and local codes.
   b. Device shall be installed in complete accordance with local codes and requirements. It shall be securely fastened as follows:

      1. Siding mounted devices shall be anchored securely to a wall stud with corrosive resistant fasteners.
      2. Mounting brackets and corrosive resistant fasteners (except those furnished with the antenna by its manufacturer) shall be painted to match the unit siding color. If desired the antenna and its factory furnished mounting materials (usually a medium grey color) may be painted to match the unit siding color. The goal of this painting requirement/permission is to help maintain the aesthetics of the community.
      3. All devices shall be able to withstand 50 mile per hour winds without failure.
      4. All devices shall exhibit UL (Underwriters Laboratory) label or equivalent.
      5. All devices shall comply with all ordinances, laws, regulations and industry standards.
      6. Any permits required shall be at owner's expense.
      7. All energy needed to operate said device shall be at owner's expense.
      8. No device shall impair the signals of other devices or any other type. . . .
      9. Owner is responsible for maintaining the paint or other finishes on the device and its, brackets, fasteners, or other associated hardware so they do not rust and weaken over time.
      10. For safety, all exterior wiring shall be neatly attached to the device and building structure and hidden from view as much as possible to prevent the wiring from coming loose and causing bodily injury or property damage. If practical, wiring shall be run internally to prevent U.V. deterioration and wind damage.

6. Removal.

   a. Should the device be removed, the owner shall restore premises to condition it was in prior to installation, wear and tear expected.

7. Architectural and/or Appearance Application.

   a. Owner shall submit an Architectural and/or Appearance Application to the Association prior to installation. Said Application shall be acted upon the Association no more than 30 days after receipt of a fully completed Application along with all required attachments.

8. Damage.

   a. Owner is responsible for any damage caused directly or indirectly by the device or installation thereof.

9. Severability.
    a. Should any provision of this Resolution be found to be unenforceable, all other provisions shall remain in full force and effect.

The New Century Town Townhouse Association's "Appearance or Architectural Change of Improvement Application" requires the homeowner to perform the following tasks in order to get prior approval for the installation of an antenna:

1. Submit a sketch of the antenna's installation; including its colors, construction materials and its location; a copy of the properties survey; and a legal description of the applicant's property;
2. Record the Application and supporting documents with the Recorder of Deed and/or Registrar of Torrens within 14 days after the Association approves the Application, to supply the Association with a copy of the recording documents, and to bear the recording costs;
3. Agree to obtain and comply with applicable building codes;
4. Agree to comply with the Association's declarations, bylaws, rules, and regulations regarding the antenna installation;
5. Agree to remove the antenna installation and bear the cost of such removal, or to have the Association remove the installation at the applicant's expense, if the installation interferes with the Association's maintenance responsibilities;
6. Indemnify the Association, its members, and agents from liability arising from the antenna installation;
7. Permit the Association access to the property for purposes of enforcing the application;
8. Agree that failure to comply with any of the Application's requirements may result in revocation of the approval for the antenna installation and that the applicant will remove the installation at his or her expense; and
9. Agree to permit the Association or enter the applicant's property in order to repair an antenna installation if the applicant does not repair the installation after 14 days written notice from the Association that the installation requires repair.

Petitioner Frankfurt asserts that the Guidelines impair the installation, maintenance, and use of a satellite dish on his townhome. Frankfurt argues that the Guidelines' provisions requiring prior approval unreasonably delays installation, requiring antennas to exhibit a UL label prevents the installation of an antenna because antennas do not bear this label, and requiring antennas to withstand 50 mph winds unreasonably increase the cost of installation. The Association states that Frankfurt improperly installed his satellite dish on his townhome's balcony railing by securing the dish with six thin straps of unknown material.

Additionally, the Association states that Frankfurt did not properly ground his satellite dish until the city's electrical inspector had twice found the dish did not meet grounding requirements of the local code. The Association requested that Frankfurt complete the application for installation and issued a complaint against him after he refused to do so. At the complaint hearing, Frankfurt declined to tell the board how the antenna was grounded, mounted and whether it could withstand winds of 50 mph. The Association found Frankfurt had installed the dish in an unsafe manner in violation of the Guidelines and fined him $1,000.

CONCLUSION

The Rule generally prohibits restrictions that impair the installation, maintenance and use of the reception device, however, the Rule also provides an exception for legitimate safety goals that serve a stated safety purpose. In order to satisfy this safety exception, the proponent of the safety restriction, in this case the Association, has the burden of demonstrating that the restriction satisfies four elements:

1. The legitimate safety objectives of the restriction must be clearly identified;
2. The restriction must be necessary to accomplish the safety objective;
3. The restriction must be no more burdensome to effect antenna users than is necessary to achieve the defined safety objectives; and
4. The restriction must not be discriminatory and should be applied to the extent practicable to other devices that are comparable in size and weight and pose a similar or greater safety risk as these antennas.

The legitimate safety objective must clearly be defined in either:

1. the text, preamble, or legislative history of the restriction; or
2. a separate document that is readily available to affected antenna users.

The statement in the Guidelines' preamble that they have been enacted in the "interest of promoting the safety and welfare of the Association" is a general statement of safety that fails to set forth the specific safety objectives of the individual Guidelines. However, where the safety objective of a particular restriction is clearly apparent on the face of the restriction, we can find that a safety objective is adequately defined.

1. The Guidelines require that an antenna user submit an "Architectural and/or Appearance Application" for prior approval before the antenna user may install an antenna. We find that the Application requirement does not meet the elements of a safety exception. The Association did not clearly define a legitimate safety objective for its application requirement. The Association argues a prior approval process is the only way to insure safety installation Guidelines are met before injuries or property damage occur. The Association requires the user to submit a brochure containing the antenna's specifications and installation instructions and a sketch demonstrating where the dish will be

installed. A legitimate method for achieving compliance with safety installation Guidelines would be for the Association to inspect the antenna installation after it has been installed. Requiring a homeowner to submit a sketch and a copy of the antenna manufacturer's brochure will not insure that a homeowner will install the antenna according to those documents. A legitimate restriction to insure compliance with the safety restrictions would be to require the antenna user to notify the Association that the antenna user is installing the antenna and to submit the antenna's brochure. After the installation, the Association could, if it desired, inspect the installation for compliance with the antenna brochure's installation instructions and the Guidelines. A sketch prepared pursuant to the Guidelines would not demonstrate compliance with the safety restrictions. The Application process also does not provide any standards by which the Association could review the Application. Finally, the 30-day waiting period for the processing of the Application is clearly unnecessarily burdensome. A review of two pieces of paper, the sketch and the antenna's brochure, by a technically qualified individual should not take 30 days.

2. We find that the Guideline's requirement that an antenna installation withstand 50 mph winds without becoming airborne is a clearly defined legitimate safety objective. The Association states that the homeowner may demonstrate that the antenna complies with this restriction simply by giving the Association a copy of the antenna's installation and specifications brochure. We find that this would not be a burdensome method for requiring compliance if the Association were to implement such a requirement. If the Association had included reference to a brochure as an acceptable means of compliance, then the wind load restriction would not have been unnecessarily burdensome. In the absence of this reference, an unnecessary burden is placed on the antenna user because the antenna user has no reasonable way to ascertain how to comply with the 50 mph restriction. As written, the wind load restriction appears calculated to deter any antenna installation rather than promote safety antenna installation. Therefore, the restriction was unnecessarily burdensome when it was enforced against Frankfurt.

3. We find that it is clearly apparent on the face of the grounding requirement that the requirement's legitimate safety objective is to prevent lightning from traveling into the building; thus the requirement is not invalid because the objection is not stated in the Guidelines. However, neither the grounding requirement nor the comments set forth in the specific requirements of the N.E.C. or of any applicable local codes are stated. Lacking that information, we cannot decide whether those sections clearly identify legitimate safety objections or whether the requirements to achieve those objectives are unreasonably burdensome. Thus, we cannot permit the Association to enforce the N.E.C. or the unspecified local codes.

4. The Guidelines require that the antenna be "installed in complete accordance with local codes and Requirements. And that the antenna "comply with all ordinances, laws, regulations and industry standards." It is unclear from the

Association's Guidelines which codes, laws, regulations, ordinances etc., an antenna user is required to obey. Because we have nothing to enable us to determine whether the code sections are safety related or whether they otherwise impair installation, maintenance or use, the Association cannot enforce them. Additionally, these requirements are unenforceable because it is unnecessarily burdensome to require a homeowner to cull through all ordinances, laws, regulations and industry standards to determine which ones apply.

5. Guideline 5.b4. requires all antennas to exhibit a "UL (Underwriters Laboratory) label or equivalent." However, the Association has not clearly defined a legitimate safety objective because it has not clarified the nature of the safety concern that would be addressed by a UL examination of the antenna. In other words, the Association has not shown how an examination of an antenna by UL is necessary to address a specific safety concern.
6. Guideline 5.b10. requires that exterior wiring be "hidden from view as much as possible in order to prevent such wiring from coming loose and causing bodily injury or property damage." We do not believe that keeping the wiring hidden from view will achieve a legitimate safety objective and that this requirement is likely designed merely to satisfy the Association's aesthetic preferences. Thus, we find that this Guideline does not have a legitimate safety objective. However, the Association may enforce this Guideline as a non-safety restriction in order to enforce its aesthetic references so long as the Guideline and its enforcement do not impair installation, maintenance, or use of the antenna.
7. Guideline 1 prohibits the installation of antennas on free standing mounts, poles, roofs, and chimneys. We find that the flat prohibition on these types of installations does not have a legitimate safety objective. The Association could require the antenna user to install a pole in concrete according to the antenna manufacturer's depth standards. The Association has not shown any legitimate safety objectives for the remaining installation prohibitions.
8. Guidelines 5.b.1 and 5.b.2 set forth requirements for securing and fastening antennas to their mounts. Because it is clear on the face of these requirements that they are designed to prevent antennas from detaching and possibly causing a safety hazard, we find that these requirements are enforceable under the Rule's safety exception.
9. Guideline 2 prohibits the installation of any antenna on a mast that exceeds 12 feet above the roof level. This requirement is prohibited because it sets a complete bar to antennas over 12 feet, and an antenna exceeding this height that does not pose any safety risk may be necessary for the antenna user to receive an acceptable quality signal.
10. Guideline 4's required locations for antenna installation permit the antenna user to install an antenna in alternative locations if the antenna signal would be impaired in the required locations. Nevertheless, this Guideline is unenforceable because requiring installation in the required locations may unreasonably delay or increase the cost of installation, maintenance or use of the antenna.

11. Requiring the applicant to fill out an approved Application with the Recorder of Deeds is not safety related and constitutes an impairment under the Rule.
12. Guideline 4.e requires that a device not obstruct the exterior maintenance responsibilities of the Association. Although an Association may have reasonable maintenance responsibilities that do not impair, if the Association were to use this Guideline in a manner that impaired an antenna user's use of the antenna, then the Guideline would be unenforceable. Thus, as written, Guideline 4.e does not impair; as implemented under particular circumstances, it may impair.

Since the application requirement, as stated above, is not enforceable and the wind load and grounding requirement as they are currently written are not enforceable against Frankfurt and since the Association has not shown that Frankfurt's antenna is not mounted in accordance with any of the Association's enforceable guidelines, the Association had no basis for accessing the fine against Frankfurt and such a fine is not enforceable.

CALIFORNIA CIVIL CODE SECTION 1376

§1376. Restrictions on installation or use of video or television antenna

(a) Any covenant, condition, or restriction contained in any deed, contract, security instrument, or other instrument affecting the transfer or sale of, or any interest in, a common interest development that effectively prohibits or restricts the installation or use of a video or television antenna, including a satellite dish, or that effectively prohibits or restricts the attachment of that antenna to a structure within that development where the antenna is not visible from any street or common area, except as otherwise prohibited or restricted by law, is void and unenforceable as to its application to the installation or use of a video or television antenna that has a diameter or diagonal measurement of 36 inches or less.

(b) This section shall not apply to any covenant, condition, or restriction, as described in subdivision (a), that imposes reasonable restrictions on the installation or use of a video or television antenna, including a satellite dish, that has a diameter or diagonal measurement of 36 inches or less. For purposes of this section, "reasonable restrictions" means those restrictions that do not significantly increase the cost of the video or television antenna system, including all related equipment, or significantly decrease its efficiency or performance and include all of the following:

(1) Requirements for application and notice to the association prior to the installation.

(continued)

(2) Requirement of the owner of a separate interest, as defined in Section 1351, to obtain the approval of the association for the installation of a video or television antenna that has a diameter or diagonal measurement of 36 inches or less on a separate interest owned by another.

(3) Provision for the maintenance, repair, or replacement of roofs or other building components.

(4) Requirements for installers of a video or television antenna to indemnify or reimburse the association or its members for loss or damage caused by the installation, maintenance, or use of a video or television antenna that has a diameter or diagonal measurement of 36 inches or less.

(c) Whenever approval is required for the installation or use of a video or television antenna, including a satellite dish, the application for approval shall be processed by the appropriate approving entity for the common interest development in the same manner as an application for approval of an architectural modification to the property, and the issuance of a decision on the application shall not be willfully delayed.

(d) In any action to enforce compliance with this section, the prevailing party shall be awarded reasonable attorney's fees.

IV. MANAGER'S JOURNAL

As you can tell from reading the Commission decisions, no associations have been very successful in limiting the installation and use of television antennas and satellite dishes. It is interesting that individual association members would file a petition with the Federal Communications Commission to enforce the legal rights under the Over-the-Air Reception Devices Rule. It is important that you, as an association manager, become familiar with the provisions of the Rule which follows and see how the Rule has been interpreted and challenged in the previous twelve decisions. It is necessary for you to review all association rules regarding installation, use, and maintenance of television antennas and satellite dishes as stated in association documents. If portions of the association rules conflict with the Federal Regulations it will be necessary for you, as the manager, to point this out to board members and propose a change in association regulations to bring them in conformity with the Rule. Also included is California's legislation on reception devices which predates the Rule. The manager may find legislation in other states as well. Whenever Civil Code Section 1376 is in conflict with the Rule, the Rule controls. If there is no conflict then that portion of Section 1376 applies in California. Thereafter, if you are a Californian, read Section 1376 carefully and match it with the Rule.

V. FCC: OVER-THE-AIR RECEPTION DEVICES RULE

www.fcc.gov/mb/facts/otard.html
Federal Communications Commission

Preemption of Restrictions on Placement of Direct Broadcast Satellite, Multichannel Multipoint Distribution Service, and Television Broadcast Antennas.

As directed by Congress in Section 207 of the Telecommunications Act of 1996, the Federal Communications Commission adopted the Over-the-Air Reception Devices Rule concerning governmental and nongovernmental restrictions on viewers' ability to receive video programming signals from direct broadcast satellites ("DBS"), multichannel multipoint distribution (wireless cable) providers ("MMDS"), and television broadcast stations ("TVBS").

The rule is cited as 47 C.F.R. Section 1.4000 and has been in effect since October 14, 1996. It prohibits restrictions that impair the installation, maintenance or use of antennas used to receive video programming. The rule applies to video antennas including direct-to- home satellite dishes that are less than one meter (39.37") in diameter (or of any size in Alaska), TV antennas, and wireless cable antennas. The rule prohibits most restrictions that: (1) unreasonably delay or prevent installation, maintenance or use; (2) unreasonably increase the cost of installation, maintenance or use; or (3) preclude reception of an acceptable quality signal.

Effective January 22, 1999, the Commission amended the Rule so that it also applies to rental property where the renter has an exclusive use area, such as a balcony or patio.

On October 25, 2000, the Commission further amended the Rule so that it applies to customer-end antennas that receive and transmit fixed wireless signals. This amendment became effective on May 25, 2001.

The Rule applies to viewers who place antennas that meet size limitations on property that they own or rent and that is within their exclusive use or control, including condominium owners and cooperative owners, and tenants who have an area where they have exclusive use, such as a balcony or patio, in which to install the antenna. The Rule applies to townhomes and manufactured homes, as well as to single-family homes.

The Rule allows local governments, community associations and landlords to enforce restrictions that do not impair the installation, maintenance or use of the types of antennas described above, as well as restrictions needed for safety or historic preservation. In addition, under some circumstances, the availability of a central or common antenna can be used by a community association or landlord to restrict the installation of individual antennas. In addition, the Rule does not apply to common areas that are owned by a landlord, a community association, or jointly by condominium or cooperative owners. Such common areas may include the roof or exterior wall of a multiple dwelling unit. Therefore, restrictions on antennas installed in or on such common areas are enforceable.

(continued)

This fact sheet provides general answers to questions that may arise about the implementation of the Rule, but is not the Rule itself. For further information or a copy of the Rule, call the Federal Communications Commission at 888-CALLFCC (toll free) or (202) 418-7096. The Rule is also available via the Internet by going to links to relevant Orders and the Rule.

Q: What types of antennas are covered by the Rule?

A: The Rule applies to the following types of video antennas:

(1) A "dish" antenna that is one meter (39.37") or less in diameter (or any size dish if located in Alaska) and is designed to receive direct broadcast satellite service, including direct-to-home satellite service, or to receive or transmit fixed wireless signals via satellite.

(2) An antenna that is one meter or less in diameter or diagonal measurement and is designed to receive video programming services via MMDS (wireless cable) or to receive or transmit fixed wireless signals other than via satellite.

(3) An antenna that is designed to receive local television broadcast signals. Masts higher than 12 feet above the roofline may be subject to local permitting requirements.

In addition, antennas covered by the Rule may be mounted on "masts" to reach the height needed to receive or transmit an acceptable quality signal (e.g. maintain line-of-sight contact with the transmitter or view the satellite). Masts higher than 12 feet above the roofline may be subject to local permitting requirements for safety purposes. Further, masts that extend beyond an exclusive use area may not be covered by this Rule.

Q: What are "fixed wireless signals"?

A: "Fixed wireless signals" are any commercial non-broadcast communications signals transmitted via wireless technology to and/or from a fixed customer location. Examples include wireless signals used to provide telephone service or high-speed Internet access to a fixed location. This definition does not include, among other things, AM/FM radio, amateur ("HAM") radio, Citizens Band ("CB") radio, and Digital Audio Radio Services ("DARS") signals.

Q: Does the Rule apply to hub or relay antennas?

A: The Rule applies to "customer-end antennas" which are antennas placed at a customer location for the purpose of providing service to customers at that location. The Rule does not cover antennas used to transmit signals to and/or receive signals from multiple customer locations.

Q: What types of restrictions are prohibited?

A: The Rule prohibits restrictions that impair a person's ability to install, maintain, or use an antenna covered by the Rule.

(continued)

The Rule applies to state or local laws or regulations, including zoning, land-use or building regulations, private covenants, homeowners' association rules, condominium or cooperative association restrictions, lease restrictions, or similar restrictions on property within the exclusive use or control of the antenna user where the user has an ownership or leasehold interest in the property. A restriction impairs if it: (1) unreasonably delays or prevents use of; (2) unreasonably increases the cost of; or (3) precludes a person from receiving or transmitting an acceptable quality signal from an antenna covered under the Rule. The Rule does not prohibit legitimate safety restrictions or restrictions designed to preserve designated or eligible historic or prehistoric properties, provided the restriction is no more burdensome than necessary to accomplish the safety or preservation purpose.

Q: What types of restrictions unreasonably delay or prevent viewers from using an antenna?

A: A local restriction that prohibits all antennas would prevent viewers from receiving signals, and is prohibited by the Commission's Rule. Procedural requirements can also unreasonably delay installation, maintenance or use of an antenna covered by this Rule. For example, local regulations that require a person to obtain a permit or approval prior to installation create unreasonable delay and are generally prohibited. Permits or prior approval necessary to serve a legitimate safety or historic preservation purpose may be permissible.

Q: What is an unreasonable expense?

A: Any requirement to pay a fee to the local authority for a permit to be allowed to install an antenna would be unreasonable because such permits are generally prohibited. It may also be unreasonable for a local government, community association or landlord to require a viewer to incur additional costs associated with installation. Things to consider in determining the reasonableness of any costs imposed include: (1) the cost of the equipment and services, and (2) whether there are similar requirements for comparable objects, such as air conditioning units or trash receptacles. For example, restrictions cannot require that expensive landscaping screen relatively unobtrusive DBS antennas. A requirement to paint an antenna so that it blends into the background against which it is mounted would likely be acceptable, provided it will not interfere with reception or impose unreasonable costs.

Q: What restrictions prevent a viewer from receiving an acceptable quality signal?

A: For antennas designed to receive analog signals, such as TVBS, a requirement that an antenna be located where reception would be impossible or substantially degraded is prohibited by the Rule. However, a regulation requiring that antennas be placed where they are not visible from the street would be permissible if this placement does not prevent reception of an acceptable quality signal or impose unreasonable expense or delay. For example, if installing an antenna in the rear of the house costs significantly more than installation on the side of the house, then such a requirement would be prohibited. If, however, installation in the rear of the house does not impose unreasonable expense or delay or preclude reception of an acceptable quality signal, then the restriction is permissible and the viewer must comply.

(continued)

The acceptable quality signal standard is different for devices designed to receive digital signals, such as DBS antennas, digital MMDS antennas, digital television ("DTV") antennas, and digital fixed wireless antennas. For a digital antenna to receive or transmit an acceptable quality signal, the antenna must be installed where it has an unobstructed, direct view of the satellite or other device from which signals are received or to which signals are to be transmitted. Unlike analog antennas, digital antennas, even in the presence of sufficient over-the-air signal strength, will at times provide no picture or sound unless they are placed and oriented properly.

Q: Are all restrictions prohibited?

A: No, many restrictions are permitted. Clearly-defined, legitimate safety restrictions are permitted even if they impair installation, maintenance or use provided they are necessary to protect public safety and are no more burdensome than necessary to ensure safety. Examples of valid safety restrictions include fire codes preventing people from installing antennas on fire escapes; restrictions requiring that a person not place an antenna within a certain distance from a power line; and installation requirements that describe the proper method to secure an antenna. The safety reason for the restriction must be written in the text, preamble or legislative history of the restriction, or in a document that is readily available to antenna users, so that a person wanting to install an antenna knows what restrictions apply. Safety restrictions cannot discriminate between objects that are comparable in size and weight and pose the same or a similar safety risk as the antenna that is being restricted.

Restrictions necessary for historic preservation may also be permitted even if they impair installation, maintenance or use of the antenna. To qualify for this exemption, the property may be any prehistoric or historic district, site, building, structure or object included in, or eligible for inclusion on, the National Register of Historic Places. In addition, restrictions necessary for historic preservation must be no more burdensome than necessary to accomplish the historic preservation goal. They must also be imposed and enforced in a non-discriminatory manner, as compared to other modern structures that are comparable in size and weight and to which local regulation would normally apply.

Q: How does the Rule apply to restrictions on radiofrequency (RF) exposure from antennas that have the capability to transmit signals?

A: All transmitters regulated by the Commission, including the customer-end fixed wireless antennas (either satellite or terrestrial) covered under the amended Rule, are required to meet the applicable Commission guidelines regarding RF exposure limits. The limits established in the guidelines are designed to protect the public health with a large margin of safety. These limits have been endorsed by federal health and safety agencies, such as the Environmental Protection Agency and the Food and Drug Administration. The Commission requires that providers of fixed wireless service exercise reasonable care to protect users and the public from RF exposure in excess of the Commission's limits. In addition, as a condition of invoking protection under the rule from government, landlord, and association restrictions, a provider of fixed wireless service must ensure that customer-end antennas are labeled to give notice of potential RF safety hazards posed by these antennas.

(continued)

It is recommended that antennas that both receive and transmit signals be installed by professional personnel to maximize effectiveness and minimize the possibility that the antenna will be placed in a location that is likely to expose subscribers or other persons to the transmit signal at close proximity and for an extended period of time. In general, associations, landlords, local governments and other restricting entities may not require professional installation for receive-only antennas, such as one-way DBS satellite dishes. However, local governments, associations, and property owners may require professional installation for transmitting antennas based on the safety exception to the rule. Such safety requirements must be: (1) clearly defined; (2) based on a legitimate safety objective (such as bona fide concerns about RF radiation) which is articulated in the restriction or readily available to antenna users; (3) applied in a non-discriminatory manner; and (4) no more burdensome than necessary to achieve the articulated objectives.

For additional information about the Commission's RF exposure limits, please visit **http://www.fcc.gov/oet/rfsafety** or call the RF Safety Information Line at **202-418-2464**.

Q: Whose antenna restrictions are prohibited?

A: The Rule applies to restrictions imposed by local governments, including zoning, land-use or building regulations; by homeowner, townhome, condominium or cooperative association rules, including deed restrictions, covenants, bylaws and similar restrictions; and by manufactured housing (mobile home) park owners and landlords, including lease restrictions. The Rule only applies to restrictions on property where the viewer has an ownership or leasehold interest and exclusive use or control.

Q: If I live in a condominium or an apartment building, does this Rule apply to me?

A: The Rule applies to antenna users who live in a multiple dwelling unit building, such as a condominium or apartment building, if the antenna user has an exclusive use area in which to install the antenna. "Exclusive use" means an area of the property that only you, and persons you permit, may enter and use to the exclusion of other residents. For example, your condominium or apartment may include a balcony, terrace, deck or patio that only you can use, and the Rule applies to these areas. The Rule does not apply to common areas, such as the roof, the hallways, the walkways or the exterior walls of a condominium or apartment building. Restrictions on antennas installed in these common areas are not covered by the Commission's Rule. For example, the Rule would not apply to prohibit restrictions that prevent drilling through the exterior wall of a condominium or rental unit.

Q: Does the Rule apply to condominiums or apartment buildings if the antenna is installed so that it hangs over or protrudes beyond the balcony railing or patio wall?

A: No. The Rule does not prohibit restrictions on antennas installed beyond the balcony or patio of a condominium or apartment unit if such installation is in, on, or over a common area. An antenna that extends out beyond the balcony or patio is usually considered to be in a common area that is not within the scope of the Rule.

(continued)

Therefore, the Rule does not apply to a condominium or rental apartment unit unless the antenna is installed wholly within the exclusive use area, such as the balcony or patio.

Q: Does the fact that management or the association has the right to enter these areas mean that the resident does not have exclusive use?

A: No. The fact that the building management or the association may enter an area for the purpose of inspection and/or repair does not mean that the resident does not have exclusive use of that area. Likewise, if the landlord or association regulates other uses of the exclusive use area (e.g., banning grills on balconies), that does not affect the viewer's rights under the Commission's Rule. This Rule permits persons to install antennas on property over which the person has either exclusive use or exclusive control. Note, too, that nothing in this Rule changes the landlord's or association's right to regulate use of exclusive use areas for other purposes. For example, if the lease prohibits antennas and flags on balconies, only the prohibition of antennas is eliminated by this Rule; flags would still be prohibited.

Q: Does the Rule apply to residents of rental property?

A: Yes. Effective January 22, 1999, renters may install antennas within their leasehold, which means inside the dwelling or on outdoor areas that are part of the tenant's leased space and which are under the exclusive use or control of the tenant. Typically, for apartments, these areas include balconies, balcony railings, and terraces. For rented single-family homes or manufactured homes which sit on rented property, these areas include the home itself and patios, yards, gardens or other similar areas. If renters do not have access to these outside areas, the tenant may install the antenna inside the rental unit. Renters are not required to obtain the consent of the landlord prior to installing an antenna in these areas. The Rule does not apply to common areas, such as the roof or the exterior walls of an apartment building. Generally, balconies or patios that are shared with other people or are accessible from other units are not considered to be exclusive use areas.

Q: Are there restrictions that may be placed on residents of rental property?

A: Yes. A restriction necessary to prevent damage to leased property may be reasonable. For example, tenants could be prohibited from drilling holes through exterior walls or through the roof. However, a restriction designed to prevent ordinary wear and tear (e.g., marks, scratches, and minor damage to carpets, walls and draperies) would likely not be reasonable provided the antenna is installed wholly within the antenna user's own exclusive use area.

In addition, rental property is subject to the same protection and exceptions to the Rule as owned property. Thus, a landlord may impose other types of restrictions that do not impair installation, maintenance or use under the Rule. The landlord may also impose restrictions necessary for safety or historic preservation.

(continued)

Q: If I live in a condominium, cooperative, or other type of residence where certain areas have been designated as "common," do these Rules apply to me?

A: The Rules apply to residents of these types of buildings, but the rules do not permit you to install an antenna on a common area, such as a walkway, hallway, community garden, exterior wall or the roof. However, you may install the antenna wholly within a balcony, deck, patio, or other area where you have exclusive use.

Drilling through an exterior wall, e.g. to run the cable from the patio into the unit, is generally not within the protection of the Rule because the exterior wall is generally a common element. You may wish to check with your retailer or installer for advice on how to install the antenna without drilling a hole. Alternatively, your landlord or association may grant permission for you to drill such a hole. The Commission's Rules generally do not cover installations if you drill through a common element.

Q: If my association, building management, landlord, or property owner provides a central antenna, may I install an individual antenna?

A: Generally, the availability of a central antenna may allow the association, landlord, property owner, or other management entity to restrict the installation by individuals of antennas otherwise protected by the Rule. Restrictions based on the availability of a central antenna will generally be permissible provided that: (1) the person receives the particular video programming or fixed wireless service that the person desires and could receive with an individual antenna covered under the Rule (e.g., the person would be entitled to receive service from a specific provider, not simply a provider selected by the association); (2) the signal quality of transmission to and from the person's home using the central antenna is as good as, or better than, than the quality the person could receive or transmit with an individual antenna covered by the Rule; (3) the costs associated with the use of the central antenna are not greater than the costs of installation, maintenance and use of an individual antenna covered under the Rule; and (4) the requirement to use the central antenna instead of an individual antenna does not unreasonably delay the viewer's ability to receive video programming or fixed wireless services.

Q: May the association, landlord, building management or property owner restrict the installation of an individual antenna because a central antenna will be available in the future?

A: It is not the intent of the Commission to deter or unreasonably delay the installation of individual antennas because a central antenna may become available. However, persons could be required to remove individual antennas once a central antenna is available if the cost of removal is paid by the landlord or association and the user is reimbursed for the value of the antenna. Further, an individual who wants video programming or fixed wireless services other than what is available through the central antenna should not be unreasonably delayed in obtaining the desired programming or services either through modifications to the central antenna, installation of an additional central antenna, or by using an individual antenna.

(continued)

Q: I live in a townhome community. Am I covered by the FCC Rule?

A: Yes. If you own the whole townhouse, including the walls and the roof and the land under the building, then the Rule applies just as it does for a single-family home, and you may be able to put the antenna on the roof, the exterior wall, the backyard or any other place that is part of what you own. If the townhouse is a condominium, then the Rule applies as it does for any other type of condominium, which means it applies only where you have an exclusive use area. If it is a condominium townhouse, you probably cannot use the roof, the chimney, or the exterior walls unless the condominium association gives you permission. You may want to check your ownership documents to determine what areas are owned by you or are reserved for your exclusive use.

Q: I live in a condominium with a balcony, but I cannot receive a signal from the satellite because my balcony faces north. Can I use the roof?

A: No. The roof of a condominium is generally a common area, not an area reserved for an individual's exclusive use. If the roof is a common area, you may not use it unless the condominium association gives you permission. The condominium is not obligated to provide a place for you to install an antenna if you do not have an exclusive use area.

Q: I live in a mobile home that I own but it is located in a park where I rent the lot. Am I covered by the FCC Rule?

A: Yes. The Rule applies if you install the antenna anywhere on the mobile or manufactured home that is owned by you. The Rule also applies to antennas installed on the lot or pad that you rent, as well as to other areas that are under your exclusive use and control. However, the Rule does not apply if you want to install the antenna in a common area or other area outside of what you rent.

Q: I want a conventional "stick" antenna to receive a distant over-the-air television signal. Does the Rule apply to me?

A: No. The Rule does not apply to television antennas used to receive a distant signal.

Q: I want to install an antenna for broadcast radio or amateur radio. Does the Rule apply to me?

A: No. The Rule does not apply to antennas used for AM/FM radio, amateur ("ham") radio, Citizen's Band ("CB") radio or Digital Audio Radio Services ("DARS").

Q: I want to install an antenna to access the Internet. Does the Rule apply to me?

A: Yes. Antennas designed to receive and/or transmit data services, including Internet access, are included in the Rule.

(continued)

Q: Does this mean that I can install an antenna that will be used for voice and data services even though it does not provide video transmissions?

A: Yes. The most recent amendment expands the Rule and permits you to install an antenna that will be used to transmit and/or receive voice and data services, except as noted above. The Rule will also continue to cover antennas used to receive video programming.

Q: I have already installed an antenna that is used solely for the purpose of receiving video programming. Am I affected by this amendment?

A: Persons who have already installed, or who plan to install, an antenna designed to receive only video programming are not affected by this amendment. The purpose of the amendment is to permit persons to install antennas that may be used for voice and data services, as well as for video programming services. The Rules concerning restrictions on the placement of video antennas will apply equally to antennas that are used for voice and data services.

Q: I'm a board member of a homeowner association, and we want to revise our restrictions so that they will comply with the FCC Rule. Do you have guidelines you can send me?

A: We do not have sample guidelines because every community is different. We can send you the Rule and the relevant orders, which will give you general guidance. (See list of documents at the end of this fact sheet.) Some communities have written restrictions that provide a prioritized list of placement preferences so that residents can see where the association wants them to install the antenna. The residents should comply with the placement preferences provided the preferred placement does not impose unreasonable delay or expense or preclude reception of an acceptable quality signal.

Q: What restrictions are permitted if the antenna must be on a very tall mast to get a signal?

A: If you have an exclusive use area that is covered by the Rule and need to put your antenna on a mast, the local government, community association or landlord may require you to apply for a permit for safety reasons if the mast extends more than 12 feet above the roofline. If you meet the safety requirements, the permit should be granted. Note that the Commission's Rule only applies to antennas and masts installed wholly within the antenna user's exclusive use area. Masts that extend beyond the exclusive use area are outside the scope of the Rule. For installations on single-family homes, the "exclusive use area" generally would be anywhere on the home or lot and the mast height provision is usually most relevant in these situations. For example, if a homeowner needs to install an antenna on a mast that is more than 12 feet taller than the roof of the home, the homeowners' association or local zoning authority may require a permit to ensure the safety of such an installation, but may not prohibit the installation unless there is no way to install it safely.

(continued)

On the other hand, if the owner of a condominium in a building with multiple dwelling units needs to put the antenna on a mast that extends beyond the balcony boundaries, such installation would generally be outside the scope and protection of the Rule, and the condominium association may impose any restrictions it wishes (including an outright prohibition) because the Commission rule does not apply in this situation.

Q: Does the Rule apply to commercial property or only residential property?

A: Nothing in the Rule excludes antennas installed on commercial property. The Rule applies to property used for commercial purposes in the same way it applies to residential property.

Q: What can a local government, association, or consumer do if there is a dispute over whether a particular restriction is valid?

A: Restrictions that impair installation, maintenance or use of the antennas covered by the Rule are preempted (unenforceable) unless they are no more burdensome than necessary for the articulated legitimate safety purpose or for preservation of a designated or eligible historic site or district. If a person believes a restriction is preempted, but the local government, community association, or landlord disagrees, either the person or the restricting entity may file a Petition for Declaratory Ruling with the FCC or a court of competent jurisdiction. We encourage parties to attempt to resolve disputes prior to filing a petition. Often calling the FCC for information about how the rule works and applies in a particular situation can help to resolve the dispute. If a local government, community association, or landlord acknowledges that its restriction impairs installation, maintenance, or use and is preempted under the rule but believes it can demonstrate "highly specialized or unusual" concerns, the restricting entity may apply to the Commission for a waiver of the Rule.

Q: What is the procedure for filing a petition or requesting a waiver at the Commission?

A: There is no special form for a petition. You may simply describe the facts, including the specific restriction(s) that you wish to challenge. If possible, attach a copy of the restriction(s) and any relevant correspondence. If this is not possible, be sure to include the exact language of the restriction in question with the petition. General or hypothetical questions about the application or interpretation of the Rule cannot be accepted as petitions.

Petitions for declaratory rulings and waivers must be served on all interested parties. For example, if a homeowners' association files a petition seeking a declaratory ruling that its restriction is not preempted and is seeking to enforce the restriction against a specific resident, service must be made on that specific resident. The homeowners' association will not be required to serve all other members of the association, but must provide reasonable, constructive notice of the proceeding to other residents whose interests foreseeably may be affected. This may be accomplished, for example, by placing notices in residents' mailboxes, by placing a notice on a community bulletin board, or by placing the notice in an association newsletter.

(continued)

If a local government seeks a declaratory ruling or a waiver from the Commission, the local government must take steps to afford reasonable, constructive notice to residents in its jurisdiction (e.g., by placing a notice in a local newspaper of general circulation). Proof of constructive notice must be provided with a petition. In this regard, the petitioner should provide a copy of the notice and an explanation of where the notice was placed and how many people the notice reasonably might have reached.

Finally, if a person files a petition or lawsuit challenging a local government's ordinance, an association's restriction, or a landlord's lease, the person must serve the local government, association or landlord, as appropriate. You must include a "proof of service" with your petition. Generally, the "proof of service" is a statement indicating that on the same day that your petition was sent to the Commission, you provided a copy of your petition (and any attachments) to the person or entity that is seeking to enforce the antenna restriction. The proof of service should give the name and address of the parties served, the date served, and the method of service used (e.g., regular mail, personal service, certified mail).

All allegations of fact contained in petitions and related pleadings before the Commission must be supported by an affidavit signed by one or more persons who have actual knowledge of such facts. You must send an original and two copies of the petition and all attachments to: Secretary, Federal Communications Commission, 445 12th Street, S.W., Washington, D.C. 20554, Attention: Media Bureau.

Q: Can I continue to use my antenna while the petition or waiver request is pending?

A: Yes, unless the restriction being challenged or for which a waiver is sought is necessary for reasons of safety or historic preservation. Otherwise, the restriction cannot be enforced while the petition is pending.

Q: Who is responsible for showing that a restriction is enforceable?

A: When a conflict arises about whether a restriction is valid, the local government, community association, property owner, or management entity that is trying to enforce the restriction has the burden of proving that the restriction is valid. This means that no matter who questions the validity of the restriction, the burden will always be on the entity seeking to enforce the restriction to prove that the restriction is permitted under the Rule or that it qualifies for a waiver.

Q: Can I be fined and required to remove my antenna immediately if the Commission determines that a restriction is valid?

A: If the Commission determines that the restriction is valid, you will have a minimum of 21 days to comply with this ruling. If you remove your antenna during this period, in most cases you cannot be fined. However, this 21-day grace period does not apply if the FCC Rule does not apply to your installation (for example, if the antenna is installed on a condominium general common element or hanging outside beyond an apartment balcony). If the FCC Rule does not apply at all in your case, the 21-day grace period does not apply.

(continued)

Q: Who do I call if my town, community association or landlord is enforcing an invalid restriction?

A: Call the Federal Communications Commission at (888) CALLFCC (888-225-5322), which is a toll-free number, or 202-418-7096, which is not toll-free. Some assistance may also be available from the direct broadcast satellite company, multichannel multipoint distribution service, television broadcast station, or fixed wireless company whose service is desired.

GUIDANCE ON FILING A PETITION

Q: What are the procedural requirements for filing a Petition for Declaratory Ruling or Waiver with the Commission?

A: There is no special form for a petition. You may simply describe the facts, including the specific restriction(s) that you wish to challenge. If possible, attach a copy of the restriction(s) and any relevant correspondence. If this is not possible, be sure to include the exact language of the restriction in question with the petition. General or hypothetical questions about the application or interpretation of the Rule cannot be accepted as petitions.

Petitions for declaratory rulings and waivers must be served on all interested parties. An entity seeking to impose or maintain a restriction must include with its petition a proof of service that it has served the affected residents. Similarly, an antenna user seeking to challenge the permissibility of a restriction must include with the petition a proof of service that the antenna user has served the restricting entity with a copy of the Petition.

If you are an antenna user, you must serve a copy of the Petition on the entity seeking to enforce the restriction (i.e., the local government, community association or landlord). If you are a local government, community association or landlord, you must serve a copy of the Petition on the residents in the community who currently have or wish to install antennas that will be affected by the restriction your Petition seeks to maintain. For example, if a homeowner's association files a petition seeking a declaratory ruling that its restriction is not preempted and is seeking to enforce the restriction against a specific resident, service must be made on that specific resident. The homeowner's association will not be required to serve all other members of the association, but must provide reasonable, constructive notice of the proceeding to other residents whose interests may foreseeably be affected. This may be accomplished, for example, by placing notices in residents' mailboxes, by placing a notice on a community bulletin board, or by placing the notice in an association newsletter. If a local government seeks a declaratory ruling or a waiver from the Commission, the local government must take steps to afford reasonable, constructive notice to residents in its jurisdiction (e.g., by placing a notice in a local newspaper of general circulation). Proof of constructive notice must be provided with a petition. In this regard, the petitioner should provide a copy of the notice and an explanation of where the notice was placed and how many people the notice might reasonably have reached.

(continued)

Finally, if a person files a petition or lawsuit challenging a local government's ordinance, an association's restriction, or a landlord's lease, the person must serve the local government, association or landlord, as appropriate. You must include a "proof of service" with your petition. Generally, the "proof of service" is a statement indicating that on the same day that your petition was sent to the Commission, you provided a copy of your petition (and any attachments) to the person or entity that is seeking to enforce the antenna restriction. The proof of service should give the name and address of the parties served, the date served, and the method of service used (e.g., regular mail, personal service, certified mail).

If you wish to file either a Petition for Declaratory Ruling or a Petition for Waiver pursuant to the Commission's Over-the-Air Reception Devices Rule (47 CFR Section 1.4000), you must file an original and two copies of your Petition on the following address:

Office of the Secretary
Federal Communications Commission
445 12th Street, S.W.
Washington, D.C. 20554
Attn: Media Bureau

Q: What are the substantive requirements for filing a petition for waiver or declaratory ruling?

A: To file a Petition for Waiver, follow the requirements in Section 1.4000(c) of the rule. The local government, community association or landlord requesting the waiver must demonstrate "local concerns of a highly specialized or unusual nature." The petition must also specify the restriction for which the waiver is sought, or the petition will not be considered.

To file a Petition for Declaratory Ruling, follow the requirements set forth in Section 1.4000(d) of the rule. Set out the restriction in question so that we can determine whether it is permissible or prohibited under the Rule. In a Petition for Declaratory Ruling, the burden of demonstrating that a particular restriction complies with the Rule is on the entity seeking to impose the restriction (e.g., the local government, community association or landlord).

We recommend that you include the language of the restriction in question, as well as a daytime telephone number, with your petition.

While a petition for declaratory ruling or waiver is pending with the Commission or a court, the restriction in question may not be enforced unless it is necessary for safety or historic preservation. No fines or penalties, including attorney's fees, may be imposed by the restricting entity while a petition is pending. If the restriction is found to be permissible, the antenna users subject to the Ruling will generally have at least 21 days in which to comply before a fine or penalty is imposed.

VI. CHAPTER SUMMARY

To keep appearances uniform and increase property values, most CIDs restrict or prohibit the installation of television antennas, satellite dishes, and other types of antennas on a building or lot within the community. This restriction is usually found in the declaration of the governing documents.

The federal government regulates the entire field of reception devices. Section 207 of the Telecommunications Act of 1996 deals with the Over-the-Air Reception Devices Rule, which prohibits restrictions that impair the installation, maintenance, or use of antennas used to receive video programming by viewers. It covers video antennas, including direct-to-home satellite dishes, that are less than one meter (39.37 inches) in diameter (or any size in Alaska), TV antennas, and wireless cable antennas.

The Over-the-Air Receptions Devices Rule (referred to as "the Rule") makes restrictions unenforceable if they:

1. unreasonably delay or prevent installation, maintenance, or use of reception devices;
2. unreasonably increase the cost of installation, maintenance, or use of reception devices; or
3. preclude reception of an acceptable quality signal.

"The Rule" does not apply to common areas that are owned by a community association, a landlord, or jointly by a condominium or cooperative owners. Restrictions on antennas installed in the common areas are enforceable against tenants or unit owners.

If an owner believes a restriction in the declaration has been pre-empted by the FCC's rule, and the community association disagrees, either party may file a Petition for Declaratory Ruling with the FCC (referred to as "the Commission") or in a court of competent jurisdiction.

The association must provide constructive notice of the proceedings to other members whose interest may foreseeably be affected. If the Commission finds that the restriction is permissible, the member using the antenna will generally have at least 21 days in which to comply with the ruling before a fine or penalty is imposed.

VII. REVIEW QUESTIONS

1. In this chapter, "the Rule" refers to which of the following?

   a. The Over-The-Air Broadcasting Rule
   b. The Over-The-Air Reception Devices Rule
   c. The Over-The-Air Standards and Practices Rule
   d. None of the above

2. Congress directed that the Federal Communications Commission adopt the Over-the-Air-Reception Devices Rule in Section 207 of the Telecommunications Act of:

   a. 1969.
   b. 1996.
   c. 1999.
   d. 2001.

3. The Rule covers:

   a. TV antennas.
   b. wireless cable antennas.
   c. satellite dishes.
   d. all of the above.

4. The Rule covers direct-to-home satellite dishes that are:

   a. more than one meter in diameter.
   b. less than one meter in diameter.
   c. of any size.
   d. considered discreet in size.

5. The Rule applies to:

   a. tenants in apartment complexes.
   b. condominium owners.
   c. homeowners in a planned development.
   d. all of the above.

6. If an association member believes that an association restriction regarding the installation of a satellite dish is contrary to the Rule, the member may file a Petition for Declaratory Ruling with:

   a. the Federal Communications Commission.
   b. a court of competent jurisdiction.
   c. either the Federal Communications Commission or a court of competent jurisdiction.
   d. none of the above.

7. An association restriction which would otherwise be prohibited under the Rule is permitted if:

a. the membership of the association unanimously voted for the restriction.
b. the restriction is necessary to preserve a pre-historic or historic district, included in, or eligible for inclusion on, the National Register of Historic Places.
c. the restriction satisfies the requirements of a clearly defined safety objective.
d. both b and c are correct answers.

8. *In the Matter of Michael J. MacDonald* involved an application for a permit from an architectural control committee along with a five-dollar fee for the permit for the installation of an antenna. The commission concluded:

a. the permit process was enforceable but the five-dollar fee was unenforceable.
b. the permit process was unenforceable as well as the five-dollar fee for the permit.
c. the architectural control committee permit process and the five-dollar fee were permissible.
d. none of the above are correct answers.

9. *In Re Jordan E. Lourie* involved a townhouse that Lourie owned and an 18-inch antenna he wanted to install on the chimney of his unit. The commission concluded that:

a. since the association is obligated to maintain the entire exterior of any unit, the installation of the antenna is prohibited.
b. Lourie could install the antenna on the chimney only if the installation is done by a licensed contractor.
c. since the chimney surface is not within Lourie's exclusive use or control the chimney is a "common area" and the antenna could not be installed.
d. Lourie is the owner of the unit with exclusive use of the townhouse, including its chimney, and Lourie can install the antenna.

10. Which of the following is true concerning the application of the Rule to renters who want to install an antenna?

a. The Rule covers antennas and renters are not required to have the consent of a landlord prior to installing an antenna.
b. Renters must have the landlord's permission before the installation of an antenna.
c. Renters must have the landlord's permission before installing a satellite dish but not a television antenna.
d. None of the above.

ANSWERS: 1. b; 2. b; 3. d; 4. b; 5. d; 6. c; 7. d; 8. b; 9. d; 10. a

CHAPTER 14

Law and the Courts

I. Introduction

Oliver Wendell Holmes, in his book *The Common Law*, stated that "[t]he law embodies the story of a nation's development through many centuries…" He further said that "[t]he substance of the law at any given time… corresponds... with what is then understood to be convenient, but its form and machinery… depend very much upon its past." Through Holmes we see that law is made up of the history and customs of a people. From this we can construe that a country with an emphasis on rule by law is one with a history of respect for order and one that undertakes to establish institutions that respect the customs of its people.

> *Therefore, we can conclude that law is a set of guidelines that help maintain order in a society.*

Chapter 14

CHAPTER OUTLINE

II. Sources of Law

There are four primary sources of law in America, including the following:

1. **Constitutional Law** – The supreme source of law is through constitutional provisions, as interpreted and implied.
2. **Statutory Law** – The largest source of law is the enactment and interpretation of statutes.

3. **Common Law and Judicial Decisions** – One of the first sources of law in the Anglo-saxon world, and still of major importance today, was the decisions of English courts.
4. **Administrative Regulations** – Finally, in today's modern complex society, the promulgation of rules and regulations by administrative agencies is a growing source of law. Of lesser importance are executive orders issued by the executive branch and also international treaties.

The source of the types of law could also be expressed as a form of the governmental structure established by the U.S. Constitution. Statutory laws emanate from the legislative branch. Common law, as well as the interpretation of constitutional law and statutory law, are made by the judicial branch. From the executive branch comes administrative law, executive orders, and international treaties (subject to confirmation by two-thirds of the Senators present when voting on the treaty).

A. CONSTITUTIONS

Since 1787, the U.S. Constitution has been the supreme law of the land.

All law in the United States must be consistent with the constitution to be enforced. The Constitution establishes a federation as our government structure with both a national government and independent state governments.

In addition to the federal constitution, the states have their own constitutions. In fact, twelve of the original thirteen states had written constitutions (some with Bill of Rights) before the enactment of the U. S. Constitution. These constitutions give the states a governmental structure that reflects our federal government. Each state has a legislature, an executive (usually referred to as the governor), and a judiciary.

B. STATUTORY LAW

The legislative branch provides the second source of law, that of statutory law.

In fact, this type of law is probably the most pervasive source of law in our country. In contrast with the common law, legislatures act in a proactive manner and attempt to remedy future problems. Each year legislatures add to the statutory laws of their states. These statutes are placed in codes that are compilations of statutes. In California, there were originally only four codes. Now, there are 29 different codes (see **Figure 14-1**).

When a law has been placed into one of the existing codes, that law has been "codified."

Figure 14-1

Listing of Current California Codes

Business and Professions Code	Fish and Game Code	Public Contract Code
Civil Code	Food and Agriculture Code	Public Resources Code
Code of Civil Procedure	Government Code	Public Utilities Code
Commercial Code (Uniform)	Harbors and Navigation Code	Revenue and Taxation Code
Corporations Code	Health and Safety Code	Streets and Highways Code
Education Code	Insurance Code	Unemployment Insurance Code
Elections Code	Labor Code	Vehicle Code
Evidence Code	Military and Veterans Code	Water Code
Family Code	Penal Code	Welfare and Institutions Code
Finance Code	Probate Code	

As our modern society has become more complex and commerce among the states has increased, there has been an increased effort at creating statutory laws that are uniform across the states. To help this process, the **National Conference of Commissioners on Uniform State Laws** was established. The Conference, established in 1892, has members from each state. The Conference meets annually and recommends laws where it believes uniformity would be of benefit. Recall the Uniform Common Interest Ownership Act and the Uniform Condominium Act mentioned in Chapter 1.

Another type of statutory law occurs at local levels. Both counties and cities enact statutory law as they pass ordinances with which its citizens must comply.

Dog leash laws, motor vehicle laws, laws forbidding skateboarding, and land use zoning laws are all examples of local statutory laws.

C. COMMON LAW

In early English history, the king was the primary source of law and the resolver of disputes. As time went on, the king appointed people to act on behalf of the sovereign when resolving disputes. These appointees ultimately form what we now know as the judicial branch. As these "judges" decided cases, they created the **common law**, meaning the laws were to be applied "commonly" throughout the realm. This is where many of the legal principles we have today had their origins. For example, contract law, tort law, and agency law all started as common law, although much of the common law has been codified.

Unlike its English origins, ***COMMON LAW*** *in the United States refers to state law, whereby a judge decides a case and announces the reasoning behind the ruling. These judge-made, or case laws, are then integrated into state law.*

The legal principle of ***STARE DECISIS***, *meaning to abide by, follow, or adhere to decided cases*, uses these forces as it guides judges in deciding the cases.

Stare decisis provides a degree of certainty and stability to society and makes the law predictable.

It accomplishes this by requiring lower court judges to abide by published supreme and appellate court decisions. These precedents are considered ***BINDING***, *meaning they are controlling of the dispute under current consideration by the judge*. Precedents are to be used when the facts of the case are similar to those in a published opinion.

Precedents are rarely overruled by the courts, unless dictated by a substantial shift in the viewpoint of society.

D. JUDICIAL STABILITY

As mentioned, the doctrine of *stare decisis* promotes stability in the law. Requiring courts to follow precedent leads to judicial stability because an individual or business can engage in conduct which was lawful in the past, with the expectations that it will be lawful in the present, as well as lawful in the future. When a precedent cannot be found to help resolve an existing dispute, the court will try to use a similar previous decision as a basis for a logical or rational extension of that decision. The court might also find some part of a previous decision that can be used by analogy to help resolve the current dispute. This concept of judicial stability lessens a court's necessity to develop new law or change existing law.

However, if judicial stability was always required, it would be difficult for the courts to develop law in new areas that were not in existence in the past, as well as dispense justice where fairness calls for the court to be flexible in rendering a decision. Sometimes, precedents or legislation deal with concepts or issues that are antiquated or obsolete in today's society and, therefore, must be changed.

Substantial justice might require that the court interpret the precedent in order to reach a proper or just result.

For example, if court litigation involves a written contract, the court may decide the case based on judicial stability and follow the exact language of the contract to decide the case. On the other hand, the facts of the dispute may require the courts to interpret the law in such a way that the terms of the contract must be modified or ignored to make sure that, through judicial flexibility, a fair and just result becomes the decision in the case. In the following case, the court could choose judicial stability, and enforce the terms of the contract, or judicial flexibility, and render a decision that voids or nullifies contract provisions.

Lemle v. Breeden

462 P.2d 470 (Supreme Court of Hawaii 1969)
Edited Excerpts From the Opinion of Justice Levinson

FACTS AND ISSUES:

Breeden owned a house located in the Diamond Head area of Honolulu. The house faced the water and was attractively landscaped. It consisted of several structures containing six bedrooms, six baths, a living room, kitchen, dining room, garage, and salt water swimming pool. It was constructed in a "Tahitian" style with a corrugated metal roof over which coconut leaves have been woven together to give it a "grass shack" effect. This Tahitian style is relatively open without screening on windows or doorways.

After moving to the United States, Breeden hired a real estate agent to rent the house. The agent showed the property to the plaintiff and his family, who were newcomers to Hawaii from New York, and told them the property was available for immediate occupancy and was fully furnished. An inspection of the property by the plaintiff showed no problems, and the plaintiff entered into a lease for approximately nine months, paying $1,190 to rent the property. The plaintiff, with his wife and four children, moved onto the premises, and that evening, it become abundantly clear that there were rats in the main dwelling and on the corrugated roof. They notified the agent, who had an exterminator set traps. During the next several nights, the rats continued to move about the dwelling, causing the family to sleep in the living room and move out after occupying the premises for three days.

The plaintiff sued for return of the $1,190, claiming the house was uninhabitable. Breeden claimed that the plaintiff was bound by the contract, had an opportunity to inspect the house, and the doctrine of *caveat emptor* (let the buyer beware) prevailed, and the lease was enforceable for its full term. Judgment was for the plaintiff. The defendant appealed.

DECISION AND REASONS:

At common law, when land was leased to a tenant, the law of property regarded the lease as equivalent to a sale of the premises for a term. The lessee acquired an estate in land and became both owner and occupier for that term subject to the ancient doctrine of *caveat emptor*.

At one time, the rule of *caveat emptor* in lease transactions may have had some basis in social practice, as well as in historical doctrine. Common law leases were customarily lengthy documents embodying the full expectations of the parties, and there was generally equal knowledge of the condition of the land by both landlord and tenant. The land itself would often yield the rents and the buildings were constructed simply, without modern conveniences, like wiring or plumbing.

(continued)

In modern society, however, where the vast majority of tenants do not reap the rent directly from the land, but bargain primarily for the right to enjoy the premises for living purposes, often signing standardized leases, as in this case, common law conceptions of a lease and the tenant's liability for rent are no longer viable.

Here the facts demonstrate the uninhabitability and unfitness of the premises for residential purposes. For three sleepless nights, the plaintiff and his family literally camped in the living room. They were unable to sleep in the proper quarters, or make use of the other facilities in the house, due to natural apprehension of the rats, which made noise scurrying about on the roof and invaded the house through the unscreened openings.

By adopting the view that a lease is essentially a contractual relationship with an implied warranty of habitability and fitness, a more consistent and responsive set of remedies are available for a tenant.

Each case must turn on its own facts. Here, there was sufficient evidence for the trier of fact to conclude that the breach was material and that the plaintiff's action in rescinding the rental agreement was justifiable. The plaintiff gave notice of rescission and vacated the premises after the landlord's early attempts to get rid of the rats failed. When the premises were vacated, they were not fit for use as a residence. Nor was there any assurance that the residence would become habitable within a reasonable time. We affirm the judgment for the plaintiff on the ground that there was a material breach of the implied warranty of habitability and fitness for the use intended which justified the plaintiff's rescinding the rental agreement and vacating the premises.

Here the Court exercised judicial flexibility and interpreted contract law in such a way that it included a "habitability and fitness" warranty to reflect contemporary housing issues.

E. ADMINISTRATIVE LAW

The industrial revolution brought many changes to societies around the world.

One change in the legal world was the need for a more proactive mechanism for regulating business activities. The common law may have brought stability, predictability, and certainty to business society, but its reactive nature proved too slow for correcting many social ills. Statutory law was able to fill in the gap initially, but as society became more complex, new societal problems appeared, generally referred to as market failures, that demanded more immediate action.

While the legislature is empowered to enact laws, it is up to the executive branch to interpret those laws, and the judicial branch to enforce those laws.

Congress realized that there was a need for more specialized oversight of various society functions. While the legislative branch is able to write broad flexible laws, there is a need for day-to-day administration of those laws through administrative agencies.

III. Classifications of Law

There are many ways in which law may be classified. The three basic classifications are:

1. substantive or procedural;
2. public or private; and
3. civil or criminal.

A. SUBSTANTIVE VERSUS PROCEDURAL

Substantive laws either grant individual legal rights or impose legal duties on them.

For example, laws that prohibit the possession of illegal substances, such as marijuana, are substantive in nature as they impose a duty on individuals to not possess those illegal substances.

Procedural laws enforce the rights or duties granted by the substantive laws by imposing on the government a procedural structure that must be followed when establishing or enforcing substantive laws.

For example, rules of civil procedure direct how a person takes a case through the court system.

B. PRIVATE OR PUBLIC

The body of law governing the interaction between individuals is considered ***PRIVATE LAW***. Contract law, property law, tort law, and business entity law are examples of laws that are private in nature. ***PUBLIC LAW*** *deals with how the government is organized and how it interacts with the people of the country.*

Constitutional law, criminal law, and administrative law are examples of public law.

C. CIVIL OR CRIMINAL

Civil law is concerned with how individuals interact with each other.

Most of the laws that will be discussed in this textbook are examples of civil law. The law of torts, contracts, agency, and business entities are not only examples of private law, they are also examples of civil law. ***CRIMINAL LAW**, on the other hand, is concerned with behavior that is considered unacceptable to society at large.* Government attempts to restrict behavior that disrupts the societal order are normally undertaken through criminal laws. The legislature identifies unacceptable behavior and then enacts a statutory law restricting and punishing that behavior.

D. LAW VERSUS EQUITY

Another classification is whether the legal cause of action (what the person bringing a lawsuit is alleging the other person did, as far as violating a legal right or failing to adhere to a legal duty) requires a legal remedy or an equitable remedy. *Where a person is seeking monetary damages, he or she is seeking a **LEGAL REMEDY**.* Sometimes monetary damages are not sufficient to remedy the wrong that has been committed. In those cases, a person seeks a remedy in equity. ***EQUITABLE REMEDIES** attempt to create fairness and justice for the person who has been harmed.*

Common equitable remedies include specific performance, rescission, restitution, injunction, and reformation.

***SPECIFIC PERFORMANCE** is used when a contract has been breached (broken) and the harmed person wants completion of the specific contract performance agreed to.* Usually, specific performance is given only where the item is unique, and money damages would not be adequate. ***RESCISSION** is used to cancel a contract due to some irregularity. After rescission, it is as if there had never been a contract.* ***RESTITUTION** is required, that is, placing the parties in their original positions, by having each side return to the other whatever had been transferred.* An ***INJUNCTION** is issued by a court to prohibit someone from doing an act or requiring them to do an act.* If a mistake has been made in the writing of a contract, so that the writing does not reflect the parties' intentions, a court will sometimes reform the terms to reflect the true intention of the parties. *When the courts correct the language of a contract, it is called **REFORMATION**.*

IV. Court Systems

Before a court may hear a dispute, it must have the power and authority to decide the case and to award the decision to the winning party.

When a court has the power and authority to decide a case, it is said to have "jurisdiction."

California, like all other states, has both federal and state courts operating within its boundaries. This dual system of courts requires us to have a basic understanding of each system to fully appreciate how disputes are settled through litigation. While the state courts are the primary place where most litigation takes place, more and more we see the influence of the federal judiciary.

A ***COURT*** *is a place where a dispute is heard and a determination rendered about the outcome of the dispute.* While Alternative Dispute Resolution (ADR) is growing in importance, the courts still implement the laws.

A. TYPES OF COURTS

In both the federal and state court systems, the courts are structured in three tiers.

The different tiers are the trial courts, the intermediate appellate courts, and the highest level appeals court. Each type of court performs a different function.

1. Trial Courts

The trial courts are where the facts of the case are determined and the appropriate legal rules are applied to resolve the dispute.

The plaintiff files the lawsuit and the defendant gets sued. If it is a jury trial, the jury is responsible for listening to the evidence presented in the courtroom, evaluating the credibility of the witnesses and evidence, then, by using its collective wisdom, determine what exactly happened in the dispute, and finally, after the judge instructs them on what law to apply, applies that law to the facts to reach a decision in the dispute. The judge decides whether the evidence may be admitted, the legal rules should apply, and instructs the jury as to what law they are to apply to the proven facts. *If the trial does not involve a jury, the judge performs his or her normal functions, as well as that of the jury. This type of trial is often referred to as a* ***BENCH TRIAL***.

Because trial courts are considered "courts of record," a verbatim record of the trial is maintained of all testimony and arguments presented to the court. *This record of the court's proceedings is normally transcribed by a* ***COURT REPORTER***. A major function of the record (transcript of proceedings) is for use by the appellate courts if an appeal of the trial court's decision is made. However, the parties to the litigation may agree to trial without keeping a record.

Within both the state and federal systems, there are courts with limited jurisdiction (a term to be discussed later) and general jurisdiction. *The courts with* ***LIMITED JURISDICTION*** *are restricted to hearing only certain types of cases*. The cases may be limited to a certain dollar amount or to a particular area of law. *Courts with* ***GENERAL JURISDICTION*** *have no restrictions placed on the types of disputes they may resolve.*

2. Appellate Courts

As you can imagine, some people are dissatisfied with the ruling by the trial court. Often, the losing or winning parties are not satisfied with the remedy they were awarded. If a party is not satisfied with the trial court's decision, they may appeal to the intermediate appellate courts, alleging a mistake of law was made. *The party making the appeal is called the **APPELLANT** and the party opposing the appeal is called the **APPELLEE** (sometimes **RESPONDENT**).*

The appellate court's primary function is to review the trial court's decision for errors in law.

The appellate court reviews the record of the trial court, reads briefs prepared by each party's attorney (these are written arguments), and may listen to oral arguments by the party's attorney. No new evidence is permitted in the appellate courts; only review of the evidence and arguments presented in the trial court. It is mandatory that the party object at the trial to any legal error to preserve it for potential appeal.

Any legal error not objected to in the trial court will not serve as grounds for a future appeal, and is waived.

If a party is not satisfied with the ruling in the intermediate appellate court, he or she may seek discretionary review by the highest appellate court. There is no right, either constitutional or legislative, to this appeal and the highest court may refuse to hear the appeal.

To seek review by the highest court, a party must petition for a hearing.

B. FEDERAL COURTS

Article III, Section 1 of the U.S. Constitution provides:

The judicial power of the United States shall be vested in one Supreme Court, and in such inferior courts as the Congress may from time to time ordain and establish.

This judicial power is limited in Article III, Section 2 of the U.S. Constitution to certain cases. The types of cases most often dealt with involve constitutional issues, federal laws, treaty provisions, disputes where the United States is itself a party, disputes among the individual states, and where citizens of different states are disputing cases with damages in excess of $75,000. Other types of cases limited to the federal courts are those involving certain foreign officials, and all cases involving admiralty and maritime jurisdiction.

1. Trial Courts

As was previously mentioned, the federal court system is a three tiered system (see **Figure 14-3**). In the first tier we find the trial courts. This tier consists of both general trial courts and specialized courts. *The general trial courts are known as the **UNITED STATES DISTRICT COURTS**.* In total, there are 94 U.S. District Courts. Some states only have one U.S. District Court, while others have more. For example, California has four District Courts within its borders (see **Figure 14-2**). Congress has also created specialized courts, such as the Tax Court, Bankruptcy Courts, the Court of International Trade, and the Court of Federal Claims.

Figure 14-2

U.S. District Courts in California

Northern District	San Francisco
Eastern District	Sacramento
Central District	Los Angeles
Southern District	San Diego

2. Subject Matter Jurisdiction

Before a case may be heard in the U.S. District Court, it is necessary that the court have subject matter jurisdiction over the case.

The federal courts obtain subject matter jurisdiction **if the dispute involves either a federal question or there is diversity of citizenship of the parties**. A federal question occurs whenever the dispute involves the U.S. Constitution, a federal statute, or a federal treaty. For example, under Title VII of the 1964 Civil Rights Act, sexual harassment is considered a form of gender discrimination. If an employee of a business entity believes he or she has been sexually harassed by one of his or her supervisors, and, after complaining about this supervisor's behavior, the company refused to stop the harassment, he or she could sue in federal district court for a violation of his or her Title VII rights. The lawsuit is brought in the U.S. District Court, since a federal law is allegedly being violated.

"Diversity of citizenship" gives the federal courts jurisdiction when the parties are citizens of different states and the amount in controversy is in excess of $75,000.

Figure 14-3

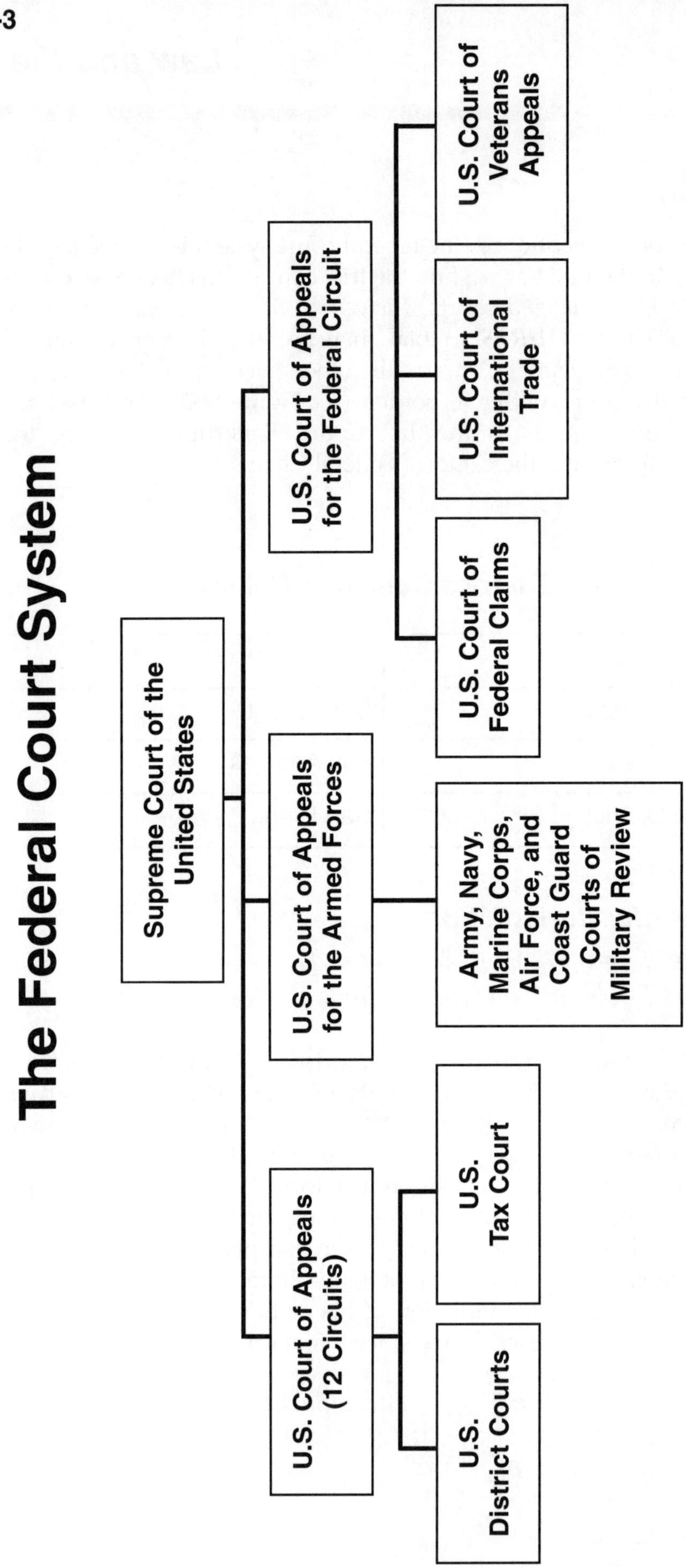
The Federal Court System
Supreme Court of the United States
U.S. Court of Appeals (12 Circuits)
U.S. Court of Appeals for the Armed Forces
U.S. Court of Appeals for the Federal Circuit
U.S. District Courts
U.S. Tax Court
Army, Navy, Marine Corps, Air Force, and Coast Guard Courts of Military Review
U.S. Court of Federal Claims
U.S. Court of International Trade
U.S. Court of Veterans Appeals

The concept behind diversity jurisdiction is to provide an out-of-state defendant with a neutral forum so that the bias of one state's citizens will not be used against an out-of-state defendant. For example, Pang, a citizen of Texas but on vacation in California, causes an automobile accident that injures Mary. As a result of these injuries, Mary must have her left leg amputated. If Mary files suit against Pang in a California state court, would the jury be biased against Pang as a Texas citizen? To remove this potential bias, diversity jurisdiction would permit the action to be heard in federal court, which may lessen any bias.

Federal courts have **EXCLUSIVE JURISDICTION** to hear certain cases such as admiralty, antitrust, bankruptcy, copyright and trademarks, federal crimes, patents, suits against the United States, and other specified crimes.

State and federal courts have **CONCURRENT JURISDICTION** to hear cases over which federal court does not have exclusive jurisdiction. A party may resort to either state or federal court.

What about corporations? In what state is a corporation a citizen?

When determining in what state a corporation is a citizen, we need to know the state in which it is incorporated and the state in which it has its principal place of business.

This is because a corporation can be a citizen of more than one state for diversity purposes. Therefore, if a corporation is incorporated in Nebraska but has its principal place of business in California, then it is a citizen of both Nebraska and California.

In the example above, could Mary have sued using the California state courts? The answer to that question is yes. Unless Congress has declared that disputes involving certain areas are to be tried in the federal court system, concurrent jurisdiction exists and the dispute may be brought in either federal or state courts. If Congress has declared exclusive jurisdiction over an area, then only the federal courts may hear the dispute. Bankruptcy is a good example of this; to file for bankruptcy a person must file in the U.S. Bankruptcy Court.

3. Appellate Courts

a. Court of Appeals

If one party is not satisfied with the result in the U.S. District Court, he or she may appeal to the U.S. Court of Appeals, alleging "mistakes of law" were made by the district court.

Congress has created eleven circuits for the nation, and each circuit has a court of appeals. California is located in the 9th Circuit. Congress has also created two other court of appeals, both of which are located in Washington, D.C. One is the Court of Appeals for the District of Columbia and the other is the Court of Appeals for the Federal Circuit, making a total of 13 court of appeals. The Court of Appeals for the District of Columbia hears appeals from the district court located in Washington, D.C. The Court of Appeals for the Federal Circuit hears appeals for patent, trademark, and copyright cases. It also hears cases from the U.S. Claims Court, cases from the U.S. Court of International Trade, and cases in which the United States itself in the defendant.

b. U.S. Supreme Court

The U.S. Constitution established the U.S. Supreme Court, and on February 2, 1790, it held its first public session.

The U.S. Supreme Court has both original and appellate jurisdiction, but its primary function is to serve as the last and final court for reviewing court cases from both the federal courts and certain state cases.

Reviews, however, are discretionary, and the U.S. Supreme Court normally does not have to review an appeal unless it wants to. If an appellant wants to have the U.S. Supreme Court review his or her case, the appellant must petition for a ***writ of certiorari***. Of the approximately 5,000 petitions the U.S. Supreme Court receives each year, only about 150 are actually granted by the court. Most of the cases accepted for review by the Supreme Court involve either important constitutional issues or interpretation of significant federal statutes.

The Supreme Court is comprised of a chief justice and eight associate justices (see **Figure 14-4**). The justices are appointed by the President of the United States and are subject to confirmation hearings in the United States Senate. Supreme Court Justices have a lifetime appointment with no set term limits or forced retirement age.

C. STATE COURTS

In most states the court systems are divided into trial courts, appellate courts, and a supreme court.

1. Trial Courts

This textbook cannot fully examine the judicial system of every state. Therefore, we focus here just on California's system by example.

Figure 14-4

Members of the Supreme Court of the United States - 2005 Term

Chief Justice:	William H. Rehnquist
Associate Justices:	Stephen G. Breyer
	Ruth Bader Ginsberg
	Anthony M. Kennedy
	Sandra Day O'Connor
	Antonin Scalia
	David H. Souter
	John Paul Stevens
	Clarence Thomas

Most states have similar court systems. In California, the trial courts are the county superior courts, with each of the 58 counties having a superior court. The jurisdiction of the superior court currently is divided into unlimited jurisdiction cases and limited jurisdiction cases. **Figure 14-5** shows the division.

Figure 14-5

Subject Matter Jurisdiction - Superior Court

Unlimited Cases	Limited Cases
1. Felonies 2. Civil Suits over $25,000 3. Probate (Wills and Estates) 4. Conservatorships of adults lacking mental abilities 5. Family Law Cases 6. Juvenile Matters 7. Guardianships of Minors 8. Injunctions or Writs 9. Appeals from Limited Cases	1. Misdemeanors 2. Civil Suits $25,000 or Less 3. Preliminary Hearings in Felony Cases 4. Traffic Matters 5. Small claims cases where damages sought are $5,000 or less

2. Appellate Courts

The superior court serves as the appellate court for appeals made from both small claims courts and limited jurisdiction case courts for the county in which those courts are located. This means that the superior is the lowest level appellate court in California.

Appeals from the superior court are taken to the intermediate appellate court, the Courts of Appeal. In total, there are six Appellate Districts that cover the state. Three-justice panels decide the cases heard by the Courts of Appeal. The justices are selected to serve on the panels through a rotation system to ensure the distribution of cases among the various justices. In order for people to read and use courts of appeal decisions, the decisions are published in a set of books called the *California Appellate Reports* (available on the Internet).

Not all decisions are published; however, opinions are published when a new legal rule is established, an issue of continuing public interest is involved, existing law is criticized, or the decision makes a significant contribution.

Figure 14-6 lists the different Courts of Appeal districts and the cities in which they are located.

Figure 14-6

Locations of California Courts of Appeal

Court of Appeal	Location
First Appellate District	San Francisco
Second Appellate District	Los Angeles and Ventura
Third Appellate District	Sacramento
Fourth Appellate District, Division One	San Diego
Fourth Appellate District, Division Two	Riverside
Fourth Appellate District, Division Three	Santa Ana
Fifth Appellate District	Fresno
Sixth Appellate District	San Jose

> **Are the Names Confusing?**
>
> You may have noticed that there is a difference between the names of the intermediate courts at the federal level and the state level. Maybe the following will help.
>
> **Federal Intermediate Courts:**
>
> In the federal system the intermediate courts are called the Court of Appeals.
>
> **California Intermediate Courts:**
>
> In the California system, the intermediate courts are called Courts of Appeal.

3. Supreme Court of California

As the state's highest court, the Supreme Court of California is the court of last resort for questions of state law. Its greatest function is to oversee the orderly development of law within the state.

The California Supreme Court does not have to grant review (except for automatic appeals of death penalty judgments). Parties wishing to appeal a decision by the Courts of Appeal must petition for review by the Supreme Court. In deciding whether to review the Courts of Appeal decision, the Supreme Court considers the importance of the case to securing uniform decisions across the state and whether the legal issues are of statewide concern.

A Supreme Court decision becomes the "law" for the entire state.

The decisions of the Supreme Court are issued in **written opinions**. These opinions are published in the *California Official Reports*. With the advent of the World Wide Web, the Supreme Court's opinions, and the opinions of the Courts of Appeal, that have been issued within the last sixty days, are available from the State of California Judicial Branch website.

www.courtinfo.ca.gov
State of California Judicial Branch

D. VENUE

Before filing a lawsuit, the plaintiff must make certain that he or she is filing the suit in a court with the "proper venue."

The California Court System

Supreme Court	One Chief Justice and six Associate Justices. May grant discretionary review of cases decided by the Courts of Appeal. Certain other cases, such as death penalty appeals, are appealed directly to this court. Justices are appointed by the Governor and confirmed by the Commission on Judicial Appointments. The appointments are confirmed by the public at the next general election. Justices also come before the voters at the end of their 12-year terms.
Courts of Appeal	Six Districts, 19 Divisions with 105 Justices. Panels of 3 Judges hear appeals from Superior Courts (except death penalty cases). They determine whether a trial court committed a legal error in handling the case.
Trial Courts	Four hundred court locations with 1,444 judges, 437 commissioners and referees. A judge and sometimes a jury hears witnesses testimony and other evidence and decides cases based on the relevant facts and law.

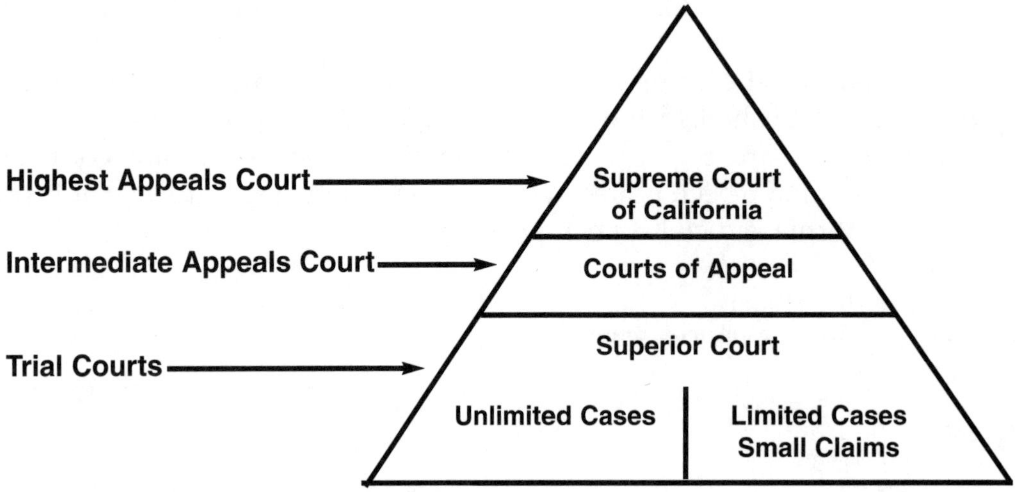

***VENUE** is defined in Black's Law Dictionary (1968) as: "A neighborhood; the neighborhood, place, or a county in which an injury is declared to have been done, or fact declared to have happened." **PROPER VENUE** means that the lawsuit will be heard by the court with jurisdiction in the geographic location closest to where the injury or event occurred.* For example, a business located in Tucson, Arizona, sold a new forklift to a business located in Irvine, California. A defect in the forklift caused an injury to the operator at the Irvine business. The local Superior Court in Irvine would be the proper venue for the case because the injured victim resides there, the event occurred at that location, the witnesses are most likely from that general vicinity, and medical services were rendered in Irvine.

1. Choice of Law and Choice of Forum

*Sometimes the parties to a contract specify that the law of a particular state or nation is the law that will apply in the event of a dispute regarding the contract (**CHOICE OF LAW**) and/or provide that in the event of litigation concerning the contract such litigation must be filed in a particular court (**CHOICE OF FORUM**).* For example, a choice of law clause might provide that in the event of a dispute regarding the contract, the law of the state of Nevada will be applied. The party drafting the contract does not have to be familiar with the laws in all other states because the other party to the contract agreed to that clause at the time of entering into the contract. Therefore, if a lawsuit was filed against the drafting party in Georgia, the Georgia court would apply Nevada law in resolving the dispute, even though the law of Georgia might be somewhat different. If the state law selected in the contract has a reasonable relationship to the nature of the contract and there is no overwhelmingly compelling reason why the court should not apply the law agreed to by the parties, the court will apply that law to the parties to the contract.

A contract may also provide that any lawsuit regarding the contract must be brought in a particular state or country. Of course, the tendency of the drafting party to the contract will be to require the lawsuit be brought in a forum convenient to the drafting party. This convenient forum requires less uncertainty regarding laws and courts in other locations, is close and convenient for the drafting party, and may, to a certain extent, enjoy the support of local citizens who may be on a jury.

As long as there is some reasonable basis for the selection of the forum, and the provision is not designed to discourage or prevent lawsuits by the non-drafting party, the forum selection clause is binding.

E. COURT PROCEDURES

Having decided on the proper court to bring your lawsuit, now you must get the suit started. California has established procedures that must be followed if you desire to have a court decide your matter. As we discuss the court procedures, we will divide the process into three stages. These stages represent the pretrial stage, the trial stage, and the post-trial stage.

1. Pretrial Stage - Pleadings

The pretrial stage is comprised of three components. During this stage the parties will file with the court various documents referred to as "the pleadings," possibly file certain motions challenging the other party's allegations, and both sides will undertake discovery to find out what evidence exists to support his or her claims.

*The **PLEADINGS** are documents that must be prepared and filed to start the lawsuit. The primary documents that make up the pleadings are the complaint, the answer, and often a cross-complaint and answer.* California has standardized the pleadings to simplify this process.

2. The Complaint

The complaint is filed by the person who believes he or she has a legal cause of action against another person and with its filing the lawsuit is started.

A filing fee must be paid to the court when the complaint is filed. A ***LEGAL CAUSE OF ACTION*** *means the person has had a legal right or duty violated by another person and has the ability to use the courts as a means to resolve the dispute.* The complaint must provide a **statement of facts** that shows a legal cause of action exists, and a demand for relief by the court. The complaint will be served upon the defendant with a summons that serves as notice to the defendant that he or she is being sued, why he or she is being sued, and when an answer must be given to the court.

In California, a defendant generally has 30 calendar days to file a written response with the court.

This written response will normally be either an answer or a demurrer (some jurisdictions call this a motion to dismiss), both of which will be discussed in more detail later.

3. Proper Jurisdiction

a. Subject Matter

In establishing that the court has proper jurisdiction over the case, the plaintiff must show that the court has subject matter jurisdiction, as was previously discussed.

b. Personal Jurisdiction

The plaintiff must also show that the court has jurisdiction over the person or property being sued. ***IN PERSONAM JURISDICTION*** *(jurisdiction over the* *person)* is obtained by serving a summons upon the defendant. The basis for this type of jurisdiction is on the defendant's legal existence, as well as presence or other conduct in the state. The overriding concern is that the defendant has had some minimal contact with the state that makes the exercise of jurisdiction reasonable in the forum state. Remember that a corporation is considered a citizen of a state if it was incorporated there or if its principal office is located in the state.

What happens if the defendant is not a resident of the forum state? In this California case, the plaintiff may use the state's long-arm statute to exercise personal jurisdiction. The object of the ***LONG-ARM STATUTE*** *is to permit the plaintiff to bring an out-of-state defendant into the state for the purposes of defending against the claims made by the plaintiff.* Normally, the defendant must have maintained "minimum contacts" with the state so that traditional notions of fair play and substantial justice are not offended. In the following case, *Ratcliffe v. Pedersen,* look at how the court analyzes whether or not to permit the use of long-arm jurisdiction.

Ratcliffe v. Pedersen

51 Cal. App. 3d 89, 123 Cal. Rptr.793 (App. 5 Dist. 1975)
Edited Excerpts From the Opinion of Justice Gargano

FACTS AND ISSUES:

Ratcliffe is a resident of the State of California. Pedersen is an importer of foreign-made motorcycles and a resident of the State of Idaho. Ratcliffe brought this action in the Superior Court of Tulare County for breach of contract and misrepresentation. The complaint, in two causes of action, alleged: 1. that Pedersen breached his oral agreement to make Ratcliffe the northern California distributor for Pedersen's imported "Wildcat" motorcycles; and 2. That Pedersen made numerous misrepresentations in connection with the distributorship.

Pedersen challenged the court's jurisdiction with a motion to quash service of summons. In a sworn statement, Pedersen claimed that he never had been a resident of California and that he never resided in this state or transacted any business with Ratcliffe.

At the conclusion of the hearing, the court granted Pedersen's motion to quash service of summons. Ratcliffe appealed.

(continued)

DECISION AND REASONS:

A California court may exercise jurisdiction over a nonresident defendant only within the perimeters of the due process clause of the United States Constitution as delineated by the decisions of the United States Supreme Court. Consequently, "[a] defendant not literally 'present' in the forum state may not be required to defend [himself] in that state's tribunal unless the 'quality and nature of the defendant's activity' in relation to the particular cause of action makes it fair to do so."

Stated in another manner, "... due process requires only that in order to subject a defendant to a judgment in personam, if he be not present within the territory of the forum, he have certain minimum contacts with it such that the maintenance of the suit does not offend 'traditional notions of fair play and substantial justice.'"

A distinction is made between a cause of action which has arisen out of or in connection with a defendant's forum-related economic activity and a cause of action which is entirely distinct from that activity. When the cause of action arises out of the forum-related economic activity, the forum state will entertain jurisdiction over the nonresident defendant; in fact, an isolated act of economic activity, such as the making and performance of a contract in the forum state, may be sufficient to accord the forum state jurisdiction over the defendant when the cause of action is related to that isolated act of economic activity; but where the cause of action is entirely distinct from the forum-related economic activity, the defendant cannot be sued in the forum state unless that economic activity has reached "... such extensive or wide-ranging proportions as to make the defendant sufficiently 'present' in the forum state ..." to support jurisdiction over him. ...

We turn to the court's order quashing service of summons with these constitutional principles in mind.

Pedersen cannot deny that he was carrying on economic activity in this state when the events described in Ratcliffe's complaint transpired; he was not only selling foreign-made motorcycles to Frank Wheeler, a Lancaster California resident, for resale in California and throughout the country, but the motorcycles were stored in a California warehouse and released to the California resident from the warehouse whenever Wheeler furnished appropriate letters of credit. Nor can Pedersen deny that his economic activity in this state had not reached "extensive or wide-ranging proportions" as during the period from 1970 to 1971, Pedersen sold Wheeler approximately 400 motorcycles, and these sales represented his entire motorcycle business.

We are not persuaded by Pedersen's argument that the causes of action alleged in the Ratcliffe's complaint were unrelated to Pedersen's economic activity within California. When seeking to invoke jurisdiction based upon minimum contacts, it is enough to show that the cause of action is "sufficiently connected" with the forum-related activity so that it cannot be said that the cause of action is "entirely distinct" from that activity. One test is to ascertain whether the economic activity put in motion the events which ultimately gave rise to the Ratcliffe's cause of action.

(continued)

Under this test, the cause of action is "sufficiently connected" with the defendant's forum-related activity whenever there is a causal connection between the two in the sense that the cause of action would not have arisen except for the economic activity. It seems very clear to us that the Ratcliffe's causes of action meet this test. It was Pedersen's economic activity in California which put in motion the events which gave rise to Ratcliffe's causes of action and, hence, there was a causal connection between the causes of action and Pedersen's economic activity.

Pedersen was importing large quantities of foreign-made motorcycles for resale in California and storing the vehicles in a California warehouse for delivery to Frank Wheeler on presentation of appropriate letters of credit; he also knew that Wheeler was setting up distributorships throughout the state to promote the sale of the vehicles to California residents.

We hold that the Superior Court of Tulare County has jurisdiction to entertain Ratcliffe's lawsuit under the "minimum contacts" rationale. When the above mentioned facts are viewed in light of California's interest in having the lawsuit tried here, it is not unreasonable to require Pedersen to defend in a California tribunal.

The order in favor of Pedersen is reversed.

Note that Pedersen now must defend the lawsuit in California and if Ratcliffe can not prove a contract with Pedersen or fraud, Pedersen will win.

c. In Rem Jurisdiction

"In Rem Jurisdiction" refers to a court's right to jurisdiction over a property, not a person.

Sometimes a "person" is not being sued. What if Bill discovers another person's name has appeared in the chain of title to his vacant lot? To determine ownership, he will bring a **quiet title action** to determine ownership, which is basically an action against the real estate, in the county where the lot is located. Since the lot and its ownership are the subject matter of the lawsuit, the court has in rem jurisdiction. For in rem jurisdiction, the property must be within the court's jurisdiction, but not necessarily the alleged owners of the property, and the property must be related to the plaintiff's cause of action.

Another type of legal action where in rem jurisdiction is appropriate would be probate proceedings, since the court is administering and distributing the deceased's property.

Where the legal action affects property and is a means to settle a personal claim by seizing the property because personal jurisdiction cannot be

acquired, "quasi in rem jurisdiction" is appropriate. For example, Abdul is a creditor of Harrison. Harrison refuses to pay the debt to Abdul even though payment is diligent. Abdul is unable to obtain personal jurisdiction over Harrison because Harrison is not a resident of California and it does not appear that Abdul can successfully obtain long-arm jurisdiction over Harrison to get a judgment. Abdul discovers that Harrison maintains a savings account in a California bank. Abdul can file a suit to attach the savings account and then have a court order that the seized account be used for the purposes of settling the debt. Since Abdul is actually suing the savings account, the jurisdiction is considered quasi in rem.

"Quasi In Rem Jurisdiction" refers to a court's jurisdiction over financial assets, such as a savings account.

4. The Answer

Once the complaint has been served on the defendant, the defendant may either answer the complaint or file a ***DEMURRER*** *(motion to dismiss the action)*. If the defendant fails to controvert every material allegation of the complaint or file a ***CROSS-COMPLAINT*** *(when the defendant counter sues the plaintiff)*, then the allegations are taken as true. Therefore, any allegations not denied will be considered as a truthful statement and relieve the plaintiff from the need to prove it at trial. Therefore, in the ***ANSWER****, the defendant will either admit or deny the allegations made by the plaintiff in the complaint*. Also, the defendant may assert defenses to the plaintiff's claims.

If the defendant fails to either file a motion challenging the plaintiff's complaint or an answer to the complaint, the plaintiff may ask that a default judgment be entered against the defendant. A ***DEFAULT JUDGMENT*** *means the defendant may not oppose the allegations in the complaint.*

It is also possible that the defendant may cross-complain against the plaintiff for damages the defendant has suffered. The **cross-complaint** operates much like the original plaintiff's complaint and forces the plaintiff to file an answer to the cross-complaint to respond to the allegations made by the defendant. For example, Lisa sues Robert claiming that Robert failed to deliver the toasters he had promised. When Robert filed his answer to Lisa's complaint, he included a cross-complaint, alleging that Lisa had never paid for toasters he delivered. By filing this cross-complaint, Robert is suing Lisa for the unpaid monies and she must then file an answer to his cross-complaint.

5. Pretrial Stage - Motions

a. Demurrer

A ***DEMURRER*** *to the plaintiff's complaint may be filed by the defendant instead of filing an answer. With this procedure, the defendant objects to the complaint because there are legal problems with the complaint that appear on the face of the pleading*. This objection may be because of improper jurisdiction of the subject matter or that the complaint fails to state a legal cause of action that will permit the court to grant relief. In ruling on the demurrer, the judge will take the facts as pleaded by the plaintiff to be true for the purposes of the motion and then decide if there is a legal claim that entitles the plaintiff to relief by the court. If the court sustains the demurrer, the lawsuit ends. However, if the court overrules the demurrer, then the defendant must answer the plaintiff's complaint.

Some argue against using demurrers because the courts will normally permit the plaintiff to amend the defective complaint if a demurrer is granted. By permitting the complaint to be amended, the court is giving the plaintiff a "more correct" shot at the defendant.

b. Motion to Quash Service of Summons

This motion claims that the court does not have proper jurisdiction because the service was defective (see *Ratcliffe v Pedersen*).

c. Venue Motion - Location

This motion challenges the trial court's location within the state.

d. Motion to Dismiss for Inconvenient Forum

This motion seeks to have the case tried in a state other than California.

e. Motion to Strike - Defects

A motion to strike challenges defects that were not subject to challenge by demurrer.

Two other motions may be made during the pretrial stage, but normally occur after discovery, to try and secure a judgment without a trial.

f. Motion for Judgment on the Pleadings

A motion for judgment on the pleadings may be made at any time during the trial process. In California, this motion operates like a demurrer without the time restrictions. A demurrer must be filed within thirty days of service while the motion for judgment on the pleadings does not face this restriction. The

same grounds for granting a demurrer are used by the court in determining whether to grant a motion for judgment on the pleadings. Basically, the legal sufficiency of the pleadings is challenged by using this motion.

There is no real difference between a judge sustaining a demurrer and granting a motion for judgment of the pleadings.

g. Motion for Summary Judgment

A ***MOTION FOR SUMMARY JUDGMENT*** *argues that there are no triable issues of fact and that a judgment may be rendered as a matter of law.* This motion is normally made after discovery because supporting evidence, such as declarations or affidavits, admissions, answers to interrogatories, and testimony obtained through depositions, are admissible and can be used by the court in making its ruling. If this motion is granted, the court decides there are no triable issues of fact in dispute for a jury to decide, and that the court, as a matter of law, can render the verdict.

6. Discovery

After the pleading phase has been completed, the parties begin the discovery process. In ***DISCOVERY,*** *the parties use various tools to help "discover" evidence that supports or hinders their claims and helps each side know the strengths and weaknesses of their cases.* The hope is that this knowledge will encourage each side to reach a settlement of the issues without having to go to trial, narrow the issue being litigated, or preserve what evidence exists so it is available for trial. The six basic methods of discovery are:

a. interrogatories
b. depositions
c. inspection of documents, tangible things, and places
d. physical and mental examinations
e. requests for admissions
f. exchanges of expert trial witness information

a. Interrogatories

INTERROGATORIES *are written questions submitted to the opposing party.* They are designed to find relevant information that will lead to admissible evidence.

Interrogatories may only be sent to the parties to the lawsuit and not witnesses.

These questions must be answered under oath in writing, and returned to the sending party.

b. Depositions

A *DEPOSITION is a written or oral statement made under oath, given before a trial, which is preserved in writing.* ***ORAL DEPOSITIONS*** *are more common and give an attorney the opportunity to ask questions of either the other party or other witnesses.* Obtaining information from non-parties must be done by the use of depositions. The questions must be answered under oath, and usually both parties' attorneys are present. The deposition must be stenographically recorded unless both parties otherwise agree or the court otherwise orders. The person recording the deposition also serves as the **deposition officer** who is authorized to administer the required oath. By testifying under oath, the witness is subject to the penalties of perjury if he or she is not truthful.

WRITTEN DEPOSITIONS *are much like interrogatories in that they are written questions that must be answered in writing, under oath, but they may be sent to witnesses who are not parties to the lawsuit.* Written depositions remove the need for the attorneys and the deponent to be in the same location at the same time. In other words, in an oral deposition both the attorneys and the deponent must be together in the same room for the deposition to take place. By using a written deposition, there is no need for the opposing attorney to be present when the questions are answered. In this respect, the written depositions operate like interrogatories.

c. Inspection of Documents, Tangible Things, and Places

This discovery tool permits pretrial inspection of relevant documents, tangible things, and places. What if Gertrude had an automobile accident and she is not certain who owns the automobile driven by the person who crashed into her? By demanding an inspection of the title document for the automobile involved in the crash, Gertrude can determine who is the automobile's legal owner. She may also want a mechanic to inspect the automobile and would then demand the automobile be made available. Additionally, actual entry into the premises of the other party may be allowed if such entry is relevant to gathering evidence.

d. Physical and Mental Examinations

What if you are involved in a lawsuit where the other party claims certain physical damages? Wouldn't you want to make certain that these physical damages are real? This discovery tool permits a physical examination if the physical condition is an issue in the lawsuit. If a person's mental condition is an issue to a lawsuit, the court may order a psychiatric examination.

e. Requests for Admissions (Yes or No)

Where the other methods of discovery are geared towards finding evidence to support the allegations made in the pleadings, ***REQUESTS FOR ADMISSIONS*** *are a means to compel the other party to admit factual information so time is not spent in discovering that information.* However, the other party can deny the fact and send you searching. These requests can be for admissions as to the genuineness of specified documents, or the truth of specified matters of fact, opinion relating to fact, or application of law to fact.

f. Exchange of Expert Trial Witness Information

As society has gotten more complex, so have lawsuits. As a result, the use of experts in trials has been growing. *A person is qualified to testify as an* ***EXPERT TRIAL WITNESS*** *if he or she has special knowledge, skill, experience, training, or education sufficient to qualify him or her as an expert on the subject to which his or her testimony relates.*

The person testifying as an expert must be found by the trial court judge to qualify as an expert.

To prove that he or she is an expert, the person may use any admissible evidence, including his or her own testimony, to qualify him or herself to the judge. When testifying, it is appropriate for the other party to question the expert about the compensation and expenses being paid to the expert witness. If the trial court judge wishes to limit the number of expert witnesses testifying at the trial, he or she may do so.

It is very important to determine what experts will be testifying and what their testimonies will be. A party to a lawsuit may obtain a list of the other party's expert trial witnesses, be furnished a copy of the experts' reports, and have the expert witness available for a deposition. If a party fails to provide the above, on objection of any party who has made a complete and timely compliance with this section, the trial court may exclude the expert testimony.

7. Trial Stage

a. Jury or Non-Jury Trial

After the pretrial stage is completed, the trial stage begins. **California Constitution Article I section 16** provides that a "trial by jury is an inviolate right and shall be secured to all, but in a civil cause three-fourths of the jury may render a verdict." It is not necessary for all trials to be tried in front of juries. If the parties agree, a court trial may be held without a jury. In a court trial, the judge serves as the **trier of fact**. The above cited section of the California Constitution further provides that a jury shall consist of 12 persons, unless the parties agree to a lesser number.

Not everybody can serve on a jury. To serve as a juror, a person must be at least 18 years of age, domiciled in California and be a resident of the jurisdiction in which the court is located, not have been convicted of a felony where their civil rights have not been restored, not be serving on a grand jury or other trial jury, not be subject to a conservatorship, and have sufficient knowledge of the English language. All persons selected for jury service must be selected at random from a source list maintained by the jury commissioner that is a representative cross section of the population served by the court. At least annually, the jury commissioner will create a master list of names to be used in selecting qualified jurors. From these lists, a jury panel is summoned to court to serve on a jury.

If you are summoned to court to serve as a juror, must you go? Yes!

If you to fail to respond to the summons, a court will compel you to attend. Further, after a court hearing, the court may find you in contempt of court, which is punishable by fine, incarceration, or both. If you are chosen to serve on a jury, are you paid for your time? Again, the answer is yes. In California, jurors are entitled to receive fifteen dollars per day and reimbursement of thirty-four cents per mile actually travelled in attending court as a juror after the first day. Some cities and counties have adopted higher juror fees, so you might be entitled to more than the state requirements.

Once the jury panel is in the courtroom, the following perjury acknowledgement and agreement must be obtained from the panel with each prospective juror answering "I do" to the judge: "Do you, and each of you, understand and agree that you will accurately and truthfully answer, under penalty of perjury, all questions propounded to you concerning your qualifications and competency to serve as a trial juror in the matter pending before this court; and that failure to do so may subject you to criminal prosecution?" The court clerk then randomly selects members from the jury panel to be seated and subjected to ***VOIR DIRE*** *(French for "to speak the truth")*. During *voir dire,* a potential juror is asked questions by the court and the attorneys in order to determine whether the person can be a fair and impartial juror. These questions may be in the form of a questionnaire that has been approved by the court and/or oral questions asked directly to the prospective juror.

What happens if, during *voir dire,* it is determined a person would not be a good juror due to a bias? Each side is permitted to challenge any prospective juror.

If it is determined that a prospective juror has an implied or an actual bias, they may be challenged "for cause" and excused from seating on the jury.

There is no limitation on how many jurors may be challenged for cause. What if no bias was discovered, but one of the parties simply does not believe the

person would be a good juror? Each side is permitted a certain number of ***PEREMPTORY CHALLENGES**, whereby a prospective juror may be dismissed for any reason except race or gender.* In a civil suit with only two parties, each side is permitted six peremptory challenges. After all the challenges have been made, the jury is sworn in and the trial itself begins.

b. Order of the Trial

California legislation establishes the order of proceedings for the trial.

1. **Opening Statements.** First, the plaintiff states the issue and his or her case. Second, the defendant may then state his or her defense, but the defendant may wait until after the plaintiff has put on his or her case.
2. **Case Presentation.** The plaintiff then presents his or her case by producing the evidence needed to prove the allegations made in the complaint. After that, the defendant opens his or her defense, if not done previously, followed by the presentation of evidence to support his or her defense.
3. **Rebuttal Evidence.** After the defendant is finished presenting his or her case, both the plaintiff and defendant may offer rebuttal evidence.
4. **Closing Arguments.** At the conclusion of the presentation of evidence, the plaintiff offers his or her closing arguments. The defendant then offers his or her closing argument. The plaintiff may then rebut points made in defendant's arguments.
5. **Jury Instructions.** The judge will then charge the jury by reading jury instructions that were previously prepared by the parties to the lawsuit and given to the judge. The jury instructions are statements of law and for civil trials are contained in a book entitled, *California Jury Instructions - Civil (BAJI).* The judge will instruct the jury on both procedural matters and substantive law. **Figure 14-7** is BAJI No.1.00, that is normally the first instruction given by the judge to the jury.

Figure 14-7

BAJI 1.00
RESPECTIVE DUTIES OF JUDGE AND JURY

Ladies and Gentlemen of the Jury:

It is now my duty to instruct you on the law that applies to this case. It is your duty to follow the law. As jurors, it is your duty to determine the effect and value of the evidence and to decide all questions of fact. You must not be influenced by sympathy, prejudice, or passion.

The jury instructions, based on the law disclosed by the pleadings, are to be prepared in advance by each side and given to the judge prior to the first witness being sworn in. Prior to argument, each side is to prepare jury instructions based on questions of law developed by the evidence and not disclosed by the pleadings. The judge then determines with which instructions he or she will charge the jury. The judge is permitted to modify the instructions submitted by the parties. These instructions, or charges, are given to the jury, informing them of the law they are to apply to the facts, as they determine the facts to be.

6. **Case Goes to the Jury for a Verdict.** If no motion for a ***DIRECTED VERDICT*** *(a judge's order to a jury to return a specified verdict, usually because one of the parties failed to prove its case)* was made, or if made and not granted, then the matter is given to the jury to determine the facts of the case and to apply the law as given to them in the jury instructions. The jury then renders its verdict in the case. A ***VERDICT*** *is how the jury pronounces upon the issues in the case in favor of either the plaintiff or defendant.*

8. Motions Made During the Trial

a. Motion for a Judgment of Nonsuit

After the plaintiff has completed his or her opening statement, or the presentation of his or her evidence in a trial by jury, the defendant may move for a judgment of nonsuit. A ***MOTION FOR JUDGMENT OF NONSUIT*** *attacks the sufficiency of the plaintiff's evidence and argues that no evidence was presented to support the pleadings.* If this motion is granted, it is considered adjudication upon the merits of the case, and the case is dismissed by the court finding for the defendant.

b. Motion for a Directed Verdict

After all parties have completed the presentation of all their evidence in a trial by jury, a motion for a directed verdict may be made. A ***MOTION FOR A DIRECTED VERDICT*** *asks the court to rule that there are no factual issues for the jury to consider.* Essentially, this motion is granted when no evidence was offered during the trial to support the claims or defenses made by the party opposing the motion. If the court grants the motion, the case is removed from the jury and the judge renders the verdict.

9. Post-Trial Motions

Two motions that may be made after the jury's verdict are a motion for a new trial and a motion for judgment notwithstanding the verdict.

a. Motion for a New Trial

The motion for a new trial should only be granted when the error complained of is prejudicial and results in a miscarriage of justice.

Examples of grounds for a new trail would be newly discovered evidence that could not have been discovered and produced for the trial with reasonable diligence, excessive or inadequate damages, and jury misconduct.

b. Motion for a Judgment Notwithstanding the Verdict

Here the jury has reached a verdict. A motion for a judgment from the judge notwithstanding the jury verdict is to be granted only if a motion for a directed verdict should have been granted had the motion been previously made. Therefore, if there is sufficient evidence to support the jury's verdict, the motion for a judgment notwithstanding the verdict should be denied.

10. Appeal

After the trial court's verdict has been rendered, either party may appeal the decision to the Courts of Appeal. However, an appeal from a limited action in superior court is taken to the appellate division of the superior court of the county in which the court is located. All other appeals are taken to the Courts of Appeal unless there is a direct appeal to the Supreme Court, such as a death penalty case.

The general basis for appeal is that a mistake of law was made by the trial court. Appellate courts do not review a trial court case for mistakes about facts.

The trial court is the proper place for making factual decisions and the appellate court is limited to reviewing the trial court proceeding for legal mistakes, abuse of discretion, or a lack of substantial evidence to support the verdict.

An appeal is taken by filing a **notice of appeal** with the clerk of the court from which the appeal is being made. The filing fee must be paid at this time, or within ten days if the notice of appeal was filed on the last day possible to appeal. The notice of appeal must be filed either within thirty days of the date the clerk mails the **notice of entry of judgment**, within thirty days of the date of service of the notice of entry of judgment, or within ninety days of the entry of judgment, whichever occurs first.

The clerk of the court will then transfer the record of the trial court to the appellate court. The record essentially contains all the material produced at the trial court that is relevant to the appeal. The pleadings, a transcript of the testimony given at the proceedings, the judge's rulings, and the verdict will be contained in the record. The attorneys for the parties will then present ***BRIEFS***, *which are legal arguments,* to the court. Oral hearings may take place depending on whether the attorneys believe it necessary. After the appellate court reviews the case, it will either ***AFFIRM*** *(agree with)* the lower court's ruling; ***REVERSE*** *(overturn)* the lower court's ruling; or ***REMAND*** *(send back)* for further trial court proceedings to be held in light of the appellate court's decision.

11. Enforcing the Judgment

By getting a judgment against the defendant, the plaintiff has a variety of collection tools available that were not available before getting the judgment. A judgment is not self-enforcing.

It is necessary for the winning party to seek collection of the judgment if the losing party refuses to pay.

The primary mechanism for collecting a monetary judgment is a writ of execution. A ***WRIT OF EXECUTION*** *is an order issued by the court clerk directing the levying officer, usually the sheriff of the county, to seize certain property of the losing party.* The order directs the sheriff to sell the seized property in order to satisfy the judgment that has been rendered against the losing party. It is also possible to obtain a lien on the losing party's property (both personal and real estate), take a portion of the debtor's wages, or take the judgment amount out of the debtor's bank account. With regard to the lien, the losing party's property serves as security for the winning party. For example, a judgment lien could be placed on a vacant lot owned by the losing party to hopefully guarantee that the winning party is paid the money owed under the judgment. If the property is sold before the judgment has been fully paid, money from its sale will be used to pay the judgment.

The process of collection is not an easy one and it is advisable to seek professional help when trying to collect on a judgment.

Judgments are good for ten years and can be renewed every ten years. The judgment amount earns interest at a rate of 10% per year.

It is important to know that certain practices are not permitted when trying to collect a judgment. Threatening to use physical force or threatening to file criminal charges is prohibited. It is also impermissible to harass an individual in trying to get payment. Harassment includes abuse of the telephone or similar means of communication. It is also inappropriate to improperly disclose certain aspects of the debt to others. Other prohibited practices include using false representations, initiating communication with debtor after request to send communications to debtor's attorney, and sending communications that simulate a legal or judicial process or falsely appears to be authorized by a governmental agency or attorney.

V. HOW TO FIND CALIFORNIA LEGISLATION

Figure 14-1 lists the Codes in California. If you wanted to read a Code section, how would you find it? The first, and easiest, way would be to start with a reference. You are told to read and summarize **Civil Code section 1360.5**. You can locate the "California Codes" in county law libraries, law school libraries, university libraries, and in many community college libraries as well as on the Internet.

www.leginfo.ca.gov/calaw.html
California Law

At the library, you will find approximately 200 volumes with the outside binder listing the code title and section numbers contained therein. The volumes are usually organized alphabetically. You locate the volumes labeled "Civil Code," and find the particular one with section 1360.5 within the range on numbers listed on the binding. Skimming through that particular volume, you will locate section 1360.5 and discover that an owner can, with limitations, keep one pet within a common interest development. Always look in the back of the code book, the "pocket part," to see if there have been any changes in a code section since the hardbound volume was printed. You will look up the section number in the same manner. If the section number is not in the pocket part, it remains the same. If it is in the pocket part, read carefully to see if there have been any changes.

The second way to find a code section would be to locate it by topic. You want to know if pets are allowed in a common interest development. At the end of all the code volumes is an index. You would look under common interest development which will send you to condominiums, then a subtopic of pets, to Civil Code section 1360.5; or look under pets, subtopic condominium for 1360.5

If you use the website, click on California law; check the Civil Code box and click search; then locate and click on 1358-1362.

VI. HOW TO FIND CALIFORNIA COURT DECISIONS

As was mentioned, court decisions are reported (written) in books. California Official Reports contains Supreme Court decisions starting with *The People v. Smith,* 1 Cal. 1 (1850). "Cal.", or sometimes "C.", refers to *California Official Reports.* The number to the left is the volume and the number to the right is the page number where the case starts, which is true of all the case books. The number in parenthesis, "(1850)" in this case, indicates the year the case was decided. The book title and volume number are on the binding. In 1934, after 220 volumes, the volumes start again with volume 1 containing cases decided in 1934 and continues through 71 volumes. This is known as the second series, which is noted on the book binding, and is usually cited as "Cal. 2d." The third series started with volume 1 containing cases decided in 1969 and lasted 54 volumes. It is usually cited as "Cal. 3d." The fourth series started again with volume 1 containing cases decided in 1991 and continues to this day. It is usually cited as "Cal. 4th."

California Official Appellate Reports contain the published Courts of Appeal decisions. It started with *The People v. Curtis 1,* Cal.App. 1 (1905). The "Cal.App.", or sometimes "C.A.", refers to *California Official Appellate Reports.* After 140 volumes, a second series was started in 1934, usually cited as "Cal. App. 2d," which ran for 276 volumes. In 1969, the third series started, "Cal.App. 3d," and it continued for 235 volumes. In 1991, the fourth series started, "Cal.App. 4th," which continues to this day. The year of the court decision is in the parenthesis and you may find the district number in front of the year (2nd Dist. 1993).

Decisions rendered by both the California Supreme Court and the California Courts of Appeal within the last sixty days can be found on the Internet.

www.courtinfo.ca.gov./opinions/
Supreme Court Opinions

These are referred to as "**Slip Opinions**" and have not been prepared for publication yet. These opinions are as the court filed them and are still subject to changes, such as editing and even rehearings granted by a reviewing court.

In 1960, an additional reporter series was added. This series is called the *California Reporter,* and is cited using "Cal.Rptr.", or sometimes "C. R." It contains both Supreme Court decisions and Courts of Appeal decisions from 1960 through the present. They are the same cases as found in *California Official Reports* and *California Official Appellate Reports.* The *California Reporter* is referred to as an unofficial reporter, and a second series was started in 1991 and is cited as "Cal.Rptr. 2d" (there is now also a 3rd series).

California cases can also be located in the *Pacific Reporter* regional series. The current series contains cases from fourteen other states. The original series, "Pac.", ended with volume 300 in 1931. The second series, "P. 2d", started and continues through today with over 960 volumes. In 1960, California Courts of Appeal decisions were dropped from the *Pacific Reporter.* Therefore, after 1960, only California Supreme Court decisions are in the *Pacific Reporter.* A typical citation for a California case would be: *Stop Youth Addiction, Inc. v. Lucky Stores,* 950 P. 2d 1086 (1998).

VII. HOW TO FIND COURT DECISIONS FROM OTHER STATES

Many other states have a reporter for that state and the published case is also included in a regional (also called sectional or geographic) reporter for that cluster of states:

The *Atlantic Reporter* covers: Connecticut, Delaware, Maine, Maryland, New Hampshire, New Jersey, Pennsylvania, Rhode Island, Vermont, and the District of Columbia [A.].

The *Pacific Reporter* covers: Alaska, Arizona, California, Colorado, Hawaii, Idaho, Kansas, Montana, Nevada, New Mexico, Oklahoma, Oregon, Utah, Washington, and Wyoming [P.].

The *Northeastern Reporter* covers: Illinois, Indiana, Massachusetts, New York, and Ohio [N.E.].

The *Southeaster Reporter* covers: Georgia, North Carolina, South Carolina, Virginia, and West Virginia [S.E.].

The *Northwestern Reporter* covers: Iowa, Michigan, Minnesota, Nebraska, North Dakota, South Dakota, and Wisconsin [N.W.].

The *Southwestern Reporter* covers: Arkansas, Kentucky, Missouri, Tennessee, and Texas [S.W.].

The *Southern Reporter* covers: Alabama, Florida, Louisiana, and Mississippi [So.].

For Example:

Hidden Harbour Estates v. Basso, 393 So. 2d 637 (Fla. Dist. Ct. App. 1981)

VIII. USING CALIFORNIA'S SMALL CLAIMS COURT

Because many of you, as well as the association you manage, will probably have disputes involving small amounts of money, we will look more closely at small claims courts in this section. Small claims court is designed as a fast, inexpensive and fair method of resolving small disputes. Small claims courts are found in many states, but for the purpose of example, we will focus on California.

1. Jurisdiction

What if you or the association you represent has a claim against someone for $2,000. Do you have to go to superior court with an attorney? The answer is no. You may file your claim in the small claims court if it is for $5,000 or less. In small claims court, no attorney may appear on behalf of either party, there is no right of appeal for a losing plaintiff, and you may not have a jury trial.

The small claims court has jurisdiction for the recovery of money where the demand does not exceed $5,000.

The plaintiff may waive any amount of damages over the $5,000 to give the small claims court jurisdiction. In other words, if the plaintiff's claim is for $5,300, the plaintiff can waive (forgive forever) $300 and seek only $5,000. This will give the small claims court jurisdiction. A person is limited to bringing only two claims per year to small claims court where the amount of each claim is over $2,500. The court may also grant equitable relief in the form of rescission, restitution, reformation, or specific performance in lieu of or in addition to money damages. We will now explore these remedies available to the plaintiff.

2. Damages - Money

In most cases, a plaintiff wants the defendant to pay money for the ***DAMAGES*** *(harm or injury)* caused. It may be $900 to: fix Gertrude's car because the defendant was negligent in backing into it at the tennis courts; repay a loan; compensate for fixing a computer; pay delinquent association assessment; or pay for damage to the association meeting hall caused by a negligent member. However, the plaintiff might seek a different remedy from the defendant.

3. Rescission and Restitution

Rescission and restitution means the plaintiff wants to *cancel a contract* ***(RESCISSION)*** and be returned to the *position occupied before entering into the contract* ***(RESTITUTION)***. For example, you may want to return a camera that was broken when you purchased it and it cannot be fixed. You want your money back. If the seller says no, you can sue to ***RESCIND*** *(cancel)* the contract and offer restitution (give back what you got—the camera) to get back what you gave (money).

4. Specific Performance

SPECIFIC PERFORMANCE *means the plaintiff asks the court to order that the defendant perform the contract exactly as promised.* For example, your sister contracted to sell you your great grandfather's painting of Mount Shasta for $900, she later changed her mind and refused to deliver it to you. Since there is no way a dollar value can be placed on an heirloom, you sue for specific performance seeking an order from the court that she deliver the painting to you and take your money.

5. Reformation

In ***REFORMATION***, *the plaintiff is asking the court to change something in a written contract which does not accurately reflect the true bargain of the parties.* For example, a provision, never agreed to by the parties, was inserted in the written contract by mistake. The plaintiff wants the court to remove the provision because the defendant wants to keep it in there.

6. Filing a Claim

All counties are required to provide an advisory service to assist people with free advice on small claims court. This advisory service is an excellent starting point for preparing your case. To begin the suit, the plaintiff files a claim under oath with the clerk of the small claims court. To file a claim with the small claims court, a fee of twenty dollars must be paid unless the plaintiff has filed over 12 claims in the preceding 12 months. If more than 12 claims have been filed, the fee is sixty dollars. The claim is filed using a claim form approved by the Judicial Council. The claim will include the name and address of the defendant if known, the

amount and/or the basis of the claim, and that the plaintiff has made a demand for payment from the defendant or a demand for one of the other remedies. The defendant has refused the demand, and that the plaintiff understands that the judgment will be conclusive and without a right of appeal.

7. Service of Process

Once the lawsuit is filed with the small claims court clerk, it is necessary to serve a copy of the plaintiff's claim and the order from the clerk directing the parties to appear at the time set for the hearing. Depending on the situation, there are a variety of ways the claim and order can be served, but the following may be the most common for an association or member to use:

a. **Mail.** The clerk of the small claims court can cause a copy of the claim and order to be mailed to the defendant by any form of mail providing for a return receipt. The service on the defendant is complete on the date the defendant signs the mail return receipt.

b. **Personal Service.** The plaintiff may cause a copy of the claim and order to be delivered to the defendant in person. Someone other than the plaintiff, and at least 18 years old, must do the service and fill out the form with a sworn statement as to how and when the service was completed.

c. **Substitute Service.** Without the need to attempt personal service on the defendant, the plaintiff can cause service (by someone at least 18 years old) of a copy of the claim and order by substituted service. ***SUBSTITUTE SERVICE*** *can be accomplished by leaving a copy of the claim and order during usual office hours at the defendant's office or, if no physical address is known, at the defendant's usual mailing address, other than a post office box, with the person who is apparently in charge thereof. He or she must then mail a copy of the claim and order by first-class mail, postage prepaid, to the person to be served at the place where the copy was left*. This allows service at a place of business where the defendant is unavailable, hiding, or out of the office or whatever facility is the usual mailing address (probably a residence).

The documents must be left with a person at least 18 years of age who must also be informed of the contents of the documents. In other words, the process server must tell the recipient that the documents consist of a claim against the defendant filed with the small claims court and the order provides the hearing date for resolution of the dispute. One of the more problematic issues may be the verification that the person who received the documents is 18 years of age or older. Additionally, it is important to mail the copy on the same day that the copies were left at the location. Service is deemed complete on the tenth day after the mailing. The above method deals with service on a corporation, which has forfeited its charter to do business, a joint stock company, and unincorporated association or partnership, or a public entity. That's why leaving it with a person will be deemed having served the defendant.

In the alternative, substitute service can be accomplished on a minor, conservator for the defendant, or a person authorized to receive service for the defendant by leaving a copy of the complaint and order at the defendant's dwelling house, usual place of abode, usual place of business, or usual mailing address other than a post office box. It must be left in the presence of a competent member of the household or a person apparently in charge of the office, place of business, or usual mailing address, who is at least 18 years of age and is informed of the contents of the complaint and order. Thereafter, a copy of the complaint and order must be mailed by first-class mail, postage prepaid, to the person who is to be served at the place where the copies were left. Again, service is deemed complete on the tenth day after the mailing.

Such service must be completed at least 15 days before the hearing date if the defendant resides in the county where the action is filed, or at least 20 days before the hearing date if the defendant resides outside the county.

Finally, if the owner of real property in California resides in another state and has no lawfully designated agent for service of process in California, process may be served by any of the methods described above if the claim relates to that property.

8. Cross-Claim

If the defendant has a claim against the plaintiff relating to the contract, transaction, matter, or event which is the subject of the plaintiff's claim, the defendant may cross-complain. If the cross-claim exceeds the jurisdictional limits of the small claims court, he or she may file the cross-claim with a court of competent jurisdiction and ask the small claims court to transfer the claim to that court. The small claims court, in deciding whether to transfer the claim, may render a judgment of the small claims case prior to the transfer, not render judgment and transfer the small claims case, or refuse to transfer the small claims case on the grounds that justice would not be served.

9. The Hearing

The actual hearing is informal, with the object being to dispense justice fairly and inexpensively. Each party has the right to present evidence by witnesses at the hearing. If the defendant fails to appear, the court may require the plaintiff to present evidence to prove his or her claim. As was previously stated, no party may be represented at the hearing by an attorney but you could use an attorney to help prepare your case. However, if an attorney is a party to a small claims case he or she may take part in the hearing.

While the small claims court's decision is final to the plaintiff on his or her claim, the defendant or a losing plaintiff on a cross-claim by the defendant, may appeal. The appeal is to the superior court's appellate department in the county where the

small claims court resides. An appeal is made by filing a notice of appeal with the clerk of the small claims court. The notice of appeal must be filed not later than thirty days after the clerk has delivered or mailed notice of entry of judgment to the parties. If the notice is not filed within the thirty-day period, the notice of appeal is ineffective for any purpose. The appealing party must pay the filing fee for the appeal.

10. An Appeal

The appeal to the superior court is a new hearing, and will be conducted in an informal manner; however, an attorney may now be used by either party. There is no right to pretrial discovery and there is no right to a jury trial by either party.

The judgment of the superior court after hearing the small claims court appeal is final and not appealable.

Where good cause has been shown, and where necessary to achieve substantial justice between the parties, the superior court appellate department may award a party an appeal reimbursement of attorney fees actually and reasonably incurred in connection with the appeal not exceeding $150, and loss of earnings and expenses of transportation and lodging actually and reasonably incurred in connection with the appeal not exceeding $150. If the superior court has found that the appeal was without substantial merit, and was not based on good faith but was intended to harass the other party, the court may increase those dollar amounts from $150 to an amount not exceeding $1,000.

IX. CHAPTER SUMMARY

A civilized nation respects the rule of law and has a fair and just system for resolving disputes.

Law is a set of guidelines that help maintain order in society. The four primary sources of law in America are: constitutional law, statutory law, common law, and administrative law.

The U.S. Constitution establishes the principle of separation of powers by dividing governmental functions into three branches of government. These branches are the legislative branch, the executive branch, and the judicial branch.

Statutory law is enacted by the legislatures and has the capability of being more proactive. State statutes are codified into state codes. Local legislative acts are called ordinances.

Stare decisis gives the common law a stable, predictable, and certain approach. Stare decisis helps provide for judicial stability, however, the courts can exercise judicial flexibility when circumstances demand flexibility due to fairness, or to ensure justice is rendered.

Common Law is based on judicial decisions rather than legislative action.

Administrative law provides a more day-to-day administration to certain societal problems. These administrative laws are mostly made within the executive branch.

Substantive law imposes legal rights or duties on people. Procedural laws govern how the substantive legal rights and duties are enforced.

Private law governs the interaction between individuals, while public law deals with how the government is organized and how the government interacts with its citizens.

Civil law involves the dealings between individuals, and criminal law involves the interaction between the individual and society.

Legal remedies are used when monetary (money) damages are appropriate. The more common equitable remedies are specific performance, rescission, injunction, reformation, and restitution and they are used when legal remedies are not appropriate for the situation.

Jurisdiction is the power and authority of a court to decide a case.

The federal courts are: United States District Courts, United States Court of Appeals, and the United States Supreme Court. Federal jurisdiction involves: constitutional issues, federal laws, treaties, lawsuits involving the U.S., disputes between states, and disputes between citizens of different states with damages in excess of $75,000.

The U.S. District Court is the trial court; the U.S. Court of Appeals consists of 13 circuits, with California in the 9th Circuit. The U.S. Supreme Court consists of 9 justices and has discretion as to whether or not it reviews a case.

The California courts are: Superior Court (Unlimited Jurisdiction Actions and Limited Jurisdiction Actions with the Small Claims Court), Courts of Appeal, and Supreme Court. The Courts of Appeal are located in six geographic districts in California.

The Supreme Court selects the cases it wants to hear, and its decisions become the law for the state.

The pleadings consist of a complaint (served with a summons), an answer to the complaint, and sometimes a cross-complaint and related answer.

Discovery consists of: interrogatories; depositions; inspection of documents, tangible things, and places; physical and mental examinations; requests for admissions; and exchanges of expert trial witness information.

During jury selection, a prospective juror can be dismissed for cause or by a peremptory challenge.

A motion for nonsuit argues that no evidence was presented to support the pleadings.

A motion for a directed verdict asks the judge to render a verdict since there was no evidence submitted to support the opposing parties contentions, and therefore, no need for a jury verdict.

Two post trial motions are a motion for a new trial and a motion for a judgment notwithstanding the verdict.

Appeals are taken from the Superior Court to the appropriate Court of Appeal; appeals from a limited action case are made to the Superior Court Appellate Department.

X. REVIEW QUESTIONS

1. A "bench trial" refers to:

   a. a jury trial.
   b. a trial by the judge.
   c. an imaginary line in the courtroom beyond which no one is allowed without permission of the judge.
   d. a proceeding before the California Supreme Court.

2. The legal principle of *stare decisis* means:

   a. to decide cases with a fair and open mind.
   b. to stare decisively into a witness'es eyes to determine if the witness is telling the truth or not.
   c. for a judge to decide a case based on a "gut reaction" rather than the weight of the evidence.
   d. to follow or adhere to previously decided Courts of Appeal and Supreme Court cases.

3. In England, judges decided cases and the decision became the:

   a. statutory law.
   b. common law.
   c. procedural law.
   d. historic law.

4. The case of *Lemle v. Breden*, involving rats in the residential dwelling, demonstrated:

   a. caveat emptor.
   b. stare decisis.
   c. contract interpretation.
   d. constitutional issues.

5. The "record" of a court means:

   a. the exact amount of time the trial took.
   b. the piece of paper that the jury writes its verdict on and hands to the judge.
   c. the number of cases determined by that court during a calendar year.
   d. the testimony recorded and transcribed by a court reporter.

6. The United States Supreme Court consists of a total of:

   a. 9 justices.
   b. 11 justices.
   c. 12 justices.
   d. 13 justices.

7. Which of the following is not an equitable remedy?
   - a. Money damages
   - b. Specific performance
   - c. An injunction
   - d. Rescission

8. Subject matter jurisdiction refers to:
   - a. the proper geographic place to file a lawsuit.
   - b. the authority of a court to decide a particular type of case.
   - c. the study of law.
   - d. all of the above.

9. An appellate court's primary function is to:
   - a. review the trial court's decision for error in law.
   - b. make sure that the trial court's decision regarding the facts of the case was correct.
   - c. allow the appealing parties to introduce new evidence to the appellate court hoping to change the lower court's decision.
   - d. all of the above.

10. A motion that is normally made after discovery is completed which argues that there are no triable issues of fact and that a judgment should be rendered now as a matter of law is a:
   - a. motion for summary judgment.
   - b. demurrer.
   - c. motion to strike.
   - d. motion to quash service.

ANSWERS: 1. b; 2. d; 3. b; 4. c; 5. d; 6. a; 7. a; 8. b; 9. a; 10. a

Law and the Courts

4 FT

CHAPTER 15

Alternative Dispute Resolution (ADR)

I. Introduction

Is the best method to settle a legal conflict to immediately take the person to court? This is the prevailing attitude among many people in the United States. Think about it. If you have been involved in an automobile accident where the other person was at fault, but did not admit to that fault, what did you immediately think about doing? "Sue the bastard" is not an uncommon reaction. But stop and think for a minute. How wise is it to immediately sue? What will be the costs of litigating this dispute? You will probably need to hire an attorney, who will either be paid by the hour worked, or will take a percentage of your final recovery. You will spend countless hours dealing with various matters, including having your deposition taken and possibly answering interrogatories; and what about the emotional costs?

A "deposition" is a written or oral statement admissible in court and considered testimony under oath. "Interrogatories" are formal questions asked to a witness, usually answered under oath.

Might there be a better method to resolving this dispute? The California Legislature has found that approaching dispute resolution from an adversarial position "can be unnecessarily costly, time-consuming, and complex when achieved through formal

Chapter 15

CHAPTER OUTLINE

court proceedings." It therefore encourages the parties to resolve their disputes without using the judicial process.

The legislature has encouraged the use of various alternative dispute resolution (ADR) procedures such as negotiation, mediation, and arbitration to resolve disputes in a more efficient and effective manner.

There are definite potential advantages to ADR when compared to litigation. Not all of these advantages will be present in every situation but in many cases the advantages are present. Among these advantages are:

1. **Speedier:** With the crowded court calendars, it may be years before the dispute is actually heard by the court.
2. **Less expensive:** As they say, "time is money." Taking less time reduces the expense of resolving the dispute. Normally there is ***LIMITED DISCOVERY****, which is the process of determining what evidence exists prior to trial.*
3. **Use of an expert as the decision maker:** In some of the ADR processes, the parties are able to select the decision maker by agreement. This gives them the opportunity to have an expert knowledgeable in the field making the decision.
4. **Proceedings are confidential:** Most of the ADR processes are private affairs and closed to the public. Negotiations and decisions are confidential and not available for public inspection unless the parties approve.
5. **Decisions are usually final and not appealable:** Some decisions reached through the ADR processes are final and binding upon the parties. This finality reduces the expense and time.
6. **Less formal:** ADR uses the parties themselves to determine how the process will run. The formalities of judicial procedures are not a normal aspect of many ADR processes.

ADR does not refer to any one type of procedure. Rather, it refers to the choices individuals have in resolving disputes.

We will discuss some of these procedures so you will be better prepared to resolve future disputes and be aware of the various alternatives to litigation that exist. Specifically, we will look at negotiation, mediation, early neutral evaluation, arbitration (both court-annexed and contractual), mini-trials, and private judging.

It is helpful to separate the types of ADR into non-adjudicative and adjudicative methods. The ***NON-ADJUDICATIVE METHODS*** *seek to have the parties resolve their disputes voluntarily. No binding decision made or required.* Sometimes the dispute resolution methods will involve a neutral third party to help the parties in reaching a resolution to the dispute. In ***ADJUDICATIVE METHODS****, a neutral third party is used but rather than* *just helping the parities reach a voluntary agreement, the neutral third party actually decides the result of the dispute.*

Types of ADR

Non-Adjudicative	Adjudicative
Negotiation	Judicial Arbitration
Mediation	Private Arbitration
Early Neutral Fact-Finding	Private Judging
Mini-Trials/Summary Trials	

II. Negotiation

The most commonly used method to resolve disputes is negotiation.

When parties voluntarily work out their differences and reach an acceptable solution to the dispute in a peaceful manner, a ***NEGOTIATION*** *has taken place.* In fact, simply deciding to use ADR requires the parties to negotiate with each other in reaching this determination. Suppose association member Kathy and you, the association manager, are in disagreement on payment for a broken window, missing blender and broken faucet after a party she had in the recreation center. She finally agrees to pay for the window and blender and the association will replace the faucet. You both now have successfully negotiated the dispute. Sometimes the parties (or association) may directly negotiate the solution, as just described, or they may use agents (such as attorneys, the board president, or perhaps the association manager) in reaching an acceptable solution. The Hubie Highlands Homeowner's Association, as a corporation, must use an agent to represent it. There are no formal requirements or procedures for how negotiations must take place but there are certain points one can consider in helping to ensure a successful negotiation occurs.

Many people see negotiation as a winner-take-all event. They only see winners and losers. Oftentimes this is because they are stuck on a position—what they want. In the recreational room situation, Kathy's position might be that she was absolutely not at fault; the window and faucet were already broken and the blender was never there. Therefore, the association must pay for the broken items and replace the blender. You may take offense at her position and claim she is responsible for everything even though you are not 100 percent sure of the room's condition at the time of the party.

A good approach to this dispute is to focus not on positions but rather on the underlying interests or needs. As the manager, your interests or needs might be to get the room fixed as quickly as possible since there is another party next weekend. Now, as you discuss the situation, you will more likely think of the costs of insisting on a position. It will take time to litigate and the attorney will cost money. It might be in the association's interest to seek a speedier and less costly resolution by agreeing to limit how much Kathy can escape paying. Determine the other side's interests by asking "why" that person wants what he or she asked for.

There are two types of negotiations: distributive and integrative.

A. DISTRIBUTIVE NEGOTIATION (Win-Lose)

***DISTRIBUTIVE NEGOTIATION** is often referred to as a "win-lose" situation.* When the parties are stuck on their positions, they are probably involved in distributive negotiations. The distributive negotiator does not think about the other party's situation. They focus on their personal situation and believe that either they win or they lose.

Essentially, distributive negotiation is a zero sum game, where a win occurs only by defeating the other party.

In the recreation room situation, it is probable that if there were distributive negotiating, it would lead to future litigation instead of a successful negotiation.

B. INTEGRATIVE NEGOTIATION (Win-Win)

The second type of negotiation, ***INTEGRATIVE NEGOTIATION**, takes place when the parties participate in joint problem solving.* The parties take a win-win attitude in trying to settle the dispute. The two parties don't focus on "their own" solution, but rather identify solutions that benefit each other. They do this by asking "why" the other party wants the solution suggested and developing options that will satisfy those interests or needs. In this way, they seek to mutually gain from the situation instead of defeating the other party.

Where the parties are concerned about the relationship between them, integrative negotiation offers the best method for negotiating a solution.

In either of these two types of negotiations the process is the same. Each negotiation will go through three stages. In the first stage, the parties prepare for the negotiations. The second stage involves the actual negotiations, and the third stage occurs when the negotiations conclude.

Negotiation Stages:
1. Preparation
2. Actual Negotiation
3. Conclusion of Negotiation

C. NEGOTIATION PREPARATION

Preparation is extremely important to ensure a successful negotiation.

It is at this stage that you must determine not only your goals, but also the goals of the other party. Search for facts that will influence the negotiations. Try and identify the arguments the other party will use against you and develop counter-arguments. In addition you should identify your interests and needs, as well as the interests and needs behind the other party's goals. How can you determine what the other party is thinking? While it is probably impossible to know with certainty what the other party's thoughts are, you can try to better understand them if you put yourself into their position. Think about the negotiations as if you were the other party. When you "stand in their shoes" you may see things differently and gain a better understanding of why they make the arguments they do.

Another key part of preparation is determining alternatives you would accept.

D. ACTUAL NEGOTIATIONS

In stage two, the actual negotiations, try to focus on interests not positions. Focus on needs rather than wants. The classic story used to illustrate this point is the two sisters fighting over an orange. Each wants the orange, but neither informs the other as to why she needs the orange. The simple solution is to split the orange in half and each gets only one-half of the orange if they only focus on their wants. If they share their needs, they would find out that one sister needs the orange to make orange juice and the other sister needs the peel to make an orange peel cake. Had they focused on each other's needs instead of wants, an integrative solution could have been reached.

It is also important to remove issues of the parties' personalities from the negotiations.

Don't personalize the situation, maintain the focus on issues. When actually negotiating remember to be an active listener! Don't interrupt the other party when they are talking. Listen to them and repeat in your own words what you heard them

Negotiation Stages

Preparation	● Gather factual information ● Learn about the other party ● Develop your goals and understand your interests/needs ● Determine other party's goals/interests/needs ● Develop your best agreement
Actual Negotiations	● Depersonalize and focus on issues, especially the other party's ● Actively listen ● Develop options for settlement ● Focus on agreement, not disagreement ● Avoid anger, count to ten, then respond ● Silence is golden
Concluding Negotiations	● Preserve relationship ● Let them save face; let them believe they won; be considerate in winning ● Deadlines can be effective ● Review and clarify the agreement ● Write down agreement and get signatures ● Review for yourself how negotiations went

say. As the negotiations proceed, emphasize agreements with the other party. Don't dwell on disagreements, keep the momentum going by seeking common ground with the other party. Negotiating when angry often leads to bad results, keep your cool and if necessary, take a time out from the negotiations. Remove yourself either mentally or physically from the negotiations so you can calm down and think more clearly. Finally, never forget that "silence is golden." Often, people get nervous when there is too much silence and they speak to avoid the awkward silence. In breaking the silence, they may say something they will regret. Use this to your advantage by staying quiet and letting the other person feel the awkward silence; make them speak to fill the quiet.

E. CONCLUDING NEGOTIATIONS

In most situations, you should be concerned about maintaining a positive relationship with the other party. After all, Kathy is an association member. You never know when you will need to negotiate with her again, and if you have "burned your bridges," the next time you negotiate with the person may not be a pleasant experience. When reaching an agreement, it can be wise to let the other party believe they won the negotiations. By letting them save face, you may win more than you anticipated, since they will be more positive about the experience. Remember that no one likes to be a loser! If the actual negotiations are dragging along, it is possible deadlines will cause the other party to move from their rigid position. Good options combined with deadlines often create the energy needed for a settlement to be reached.

Finally, if agreement has been reached, remember to review and clarify what you have agreed to. People's memories fail over time and it is best to memorialize the agreement in writing signed by all parties. That way, the agreement will serve as the memory of what was agreed to as opposed to each party's biased memory.

After all is said and done, whether an agreement has been reached or not, be certain you review your own performance during the negotiations.

What went right? What went wrong? How could it have gone better? Reviewing the negotiations and asking yourself questions such as these will allow you to improve your negotiation skills.

III. Mediation

Another non-adjudicative method of ADR is mediation.

Sometimes direct negotiations between the involved parties do not work out and it is helpful if a neutral third party helps the parties in their negotiations. ***MEDIATION*** *is, according to the legislature, "a process in which a neutral person (or persons) facilitates communication between the disputants to assist them in reaching a mutually acceptable agreement..."* The role of the neutral third party is to increase the lines of communication between the parties, not reach a resolution to the dispute for them. Mediation provides an opportunity for the parties to reach an acceptable solution and not to have a resolution imposed on them by an outside third party.

When the parties are highly interested in maintaining their relationship over the long term, mediation offers a process that is intended to resolve the dispute, but ensure the parties' relationship is minimally harmed.

A. JUDICIAL MEDIATION

Mediation may either be a ***JUDICIAL MEDIATION*** *(a lawsuit has been filed)* or a private mediation. Until recently, most mediations were private, which means the parties contractually agreed to utilize mediation to resolve their dispute. However, the concept of judicial arbitration began when the California Legislature authorized a pilot project in Los Angeles County "to encourage alternative dispute resolution methods in general, and mediation in particular." Judges, in counties that have elected to participate in the program, may order the parties to undertake mediation under this project, although the parties still maintain the right to proceed with litigation if the mediation is not successful.

B. PRIVATE MEDIATION

PRIVATE MEDIATION is where the parties contractually agree to use mediation as a method of resolving their dispute. If the parties want, they may include a mandatory mediation clause in a contract they are entering into. Then if a dispute arises out of the contract, the parties will have previously agreed to use mediation. A typical clause could be found in an association's covenants, conditions, and restrictions (CC&Rs).

AN EXAMPLE - 34.1 Policy-Mediation

The parties hope there will be no disputes arising out of their relationship. To that end, each commits to cooperate in good faith and to deal fairly in performing its duties under this Declaration in order to accomplish their mutual objectives and avoid disputes. But if a dispute arises, the parties agree to resolve all disputes by the following alternative dispute resolution process: (a) the parties will seek a fair and prompt negotiated resolution, but if this is not successful, (b) all disputes shall be resolved by binding arbitration, provided that during this process, (c) at the request of either party made not later than forty-five (45) days after the initial arbitration demand, the parties will attempt to resolve any dispute by non-binding mediation (but without delaying the arbitration hearing date). The parties confirm that by agreeing to this alternative dispute resolution process, they intend to give up their right to have any dispute decided in court by a judge or jury.

If the parties either did not include this type of clause in their contract or the dispute does not involve a contract issue, the parties may still stipulate to take the dispute to mediation. In this situation, one of the parties simply suggests to the other party that mediation be used in an attempt to resolve the dispute and the other party agrees.

C. ADVANTAGES OF MEDIATION

Because most legal disputes settle before litigation, mediation offers an excellent opportunity to reduce the costs of resolving the disputes.

According to the American Arbitration Association, disputes involving commercial matters are resolved with a written settlement agreement 85 percent of the time and personal injury matters conclude with a written settlement agreement 95 percent of the time. If a neutral third party can help the two disputants voluntarily settle the dispute, time, money, and emotional costs can be minimized.

There are many advantages of mediation. One is that mediation offers the parties the ability to reach a satisfactory agreement among themselves instead of having a resolution imposed upon them. If the parties are concerned about their relationship, mediation offers the ability to preserve rather than destroy it.

A distinct advantage of mediation is that the neutral third party provides a means of focusing on the real issues involved in the dispute from an objective viewpoint.

Where the parties are having a hard time getting around the personalities, such as when one party tries to "bully" the other party, the mediator offers a mechanism for the parties to communicate with each other by going through the mediator. This way, viable settlement alternatives may be developed that benefit both parties. Finally, as opposed to litigation, the parties maintain an active role in reaching a settlement of the dispute. This high degree of involvement leads to a higher degree of satisfaction among the disputants.

D. THE MEDIATOR

What is the function of the mediator? The ***MEDIATOR*** *facilitates the negotiations among the parties and is the neutral person who conducts a mediation*. Because the goal of a mediation is for the parties to voluntarily reach an agreement, the mediator works to improve the communication between the two parties and help each side focus on the issues instead of the other party's personality. The mediator does not use his or her authority to impose a result on the parties. In fact, the mediator does not possess this type of authority.

It is not uncommon for mediators to meet individually with each party in a caucus. The purpose of the ***CAUCUS*** *is to provide a mechanism for both parties to convey his or her issues and concerns to the mediator*. By meeting individually with each party, the mediator can spot weaknesses in communication and help increase the quality of interaction between the parties as they seek to satisfy their interests.

For a mediation to be successful, it is important that the mediator obtain information from the parties concerning the issues involved in the dispute.

Are there any special qualifications or requirements for a person to serve as a mediator? The answer to that question is no. The method of selection and the qualification of the mediator is determined by the parties. The parties will want a person experienced in successful mediation techniques to mediate the dispute. It might be useful to find a mediator who has experience in disputes involving common interest communities. Remember, it is up to the disputants to make the determination as to who shall mediate.

What about confidentiality of the mediation proceedings? To make for an effective alternative to litigation, the communications made during mediations sessions must be confidential. Obviously, people will be reluctant to disclose sensitive material if there is a chance the information may ultimately be used against them in future proceedings.

In California, what happens during a mediation is confidential, not subject to discovery, and disclosure is not required.

FOR EXAMPLE - California Evidence Code Sections 1119 and 1121

No evidence of anything said or any admission made or any writing prepared for the purpose of, in the course of, or pursuant to, a mediation or a mediation consultation is admissible or subject to discovery, and disclosure of the evidence cannot be compelled in any arbitration, administrative adjudication, civil action, or other non-criminal proceeding.

All communications, negotiations, or settlement discussions by and between participants in the course of a mediation or a mediation consultation shall remain confidential.

Neither a mediator or anyone else may submit to a court or other adjudicative body, and a court or other adjudicative body may not consider, any report, assessment, evaluation, recommendation, or finding of any kind by the mediator concerning a mediation conducted by the mediator, other than a report that is mandated by a court rule or other law and that states only whether an agreement was reached, unless all parties to the mediation expressly agreed otherwise in writing or orally (provided additional requirements are satisfied).

E. PROCESS OF MEDIATION

It can be helpful to think of mediation as having five stages.

1. Stage One - Mediation Process Started

In stage one, the parties start the mediation process. There is a dispute between the parties and mediation has been decided as a method to attempt reaching settlement. This is also the point when a mediator is selected. If a mediation service was referenced in the mediation clause, the mediation service's procedure will determine how the mediator is to be selected. If no mediation service is referenced, then the parties must agree upon who will mediate the dispute.

2. Stage Two - Opening Statement

In the second stage, the mediation starts and the mediator holds the opening session. The mediator will explain the process to the parties and guidelines will be established under which the mediation will be conducted. Normally, the parties will make their opening statements describing the situation from their perspective. The mediator will try to gain as much knowledge as possible about the facts surrounding the situation and start identifying the interests of each party.

3. Stage Three - Identify Interest and Needs

The third stage is where the mediator starts identifying the interests and needs of the parties. The mediator will probably caucus with the parties as he or she tries to determine the significance and priority of the interests of each party. Through questions, the mediator will try to help each party understand the other party's interests and needs and will focus on issues that the parties have in common and minimize the differences. The mediator may offer an objective evaluation of the case to help each party understand how the dispute looks to a neutral third party.

4. Stage Four - Mediated Negotiations

At the fourth stage the parties enter what can be called "mediated negotiations." Since mediation involves a voluntary agreement between the parties, they must negotiate the settlement. Because they are being assisted by the neutral third party at this stage in their negotiations, it is appropriate to think of it this way. During this stage the mediator keeps the parties focused on their interests and needs and tries to prevent the negotiations from becoming distributive in nature. The parties want to stay focused on jointly solving the dispute. The mediator will caucus with the parties and help them prioritize the issues involved in the negotiations. The parties develop the alternatives or options for settlement. Hopefully, they each have created a position that is reasonable for the situation at hand. The mediator may assist the parties in developing the alternatives, but usually mediators want the parties to develop their own settlement alternatives.

5. Stage Five - Conclusion

The fifth and final stage is the conclusion. Either the parties reach an agreement or they realize that a voluntary settlement is not possible in this situation. If an agreement has been reached, a signed written agreement should be produced. The mediator may have been drafting an agreement as the parties' positions evolved through the mediated negotiations. As the parties indicated common interests, the mediator normally uses these to begin the drafting of a final settlement agreement.

Mediations are not free. The parties must pay for the services of the mediator unless it is a judicial mediation.

Normally, the parties will share the costs of the mediation unless otherwise agreed. If the parties are using a mediation service, the organization usually charges a filing fee to set up the file and then an hourly charge for the actual mediation. These hourly fees compensate both the mediation service and the mediator. Some of the services will apply either all or part of the filing fee to the fees charged for arbitration if the dispute is not settled in mediation and the dispute goes to arbitration.

The Process of Mediation

Stage One: Starting Mediation

1. Deciding to use mediation.
2. Selecting the mediator.

Stage Two: Opening Session

1. Mediator explains process and establishes guidelines to be followed.
2. Parties make their opening statements.
3. Mediator determines facts surrounding dispute.
4. Mediator starts identifying parties' interests.

Stage Three: Identifying Issues

1. Mediator helps parties look beyond positions and focus on issues.
2. Mediator helps parties identify interests and needs.
3. Determine significance and priority of each interest.
4. Mediator develops strategy to help each party understand the other party's interests and needs.
5. Mediator may provide an objective evaluation of the case to help each party understand how the dispute looks to a neutral third party.

Stage Four: Mediated Negotiation

1. Parties start negotiating from the options they have developed.
2. The mediator may help create the options and alternatives.
3. Mediator may continue caucusing with the parties as the options are shared with the other party.

Stage Five: Conclusion

1. Either parties have reached an agreement or they recognize dispute cannot be voluntarily resolved.
2. If agreement has been reached, reduce the agreement to a signed writing.

IV. Early Neutral Evaluation (ENE)

Some courts use an ADR technique referred to as early neutral evaluation. ***EARLY NEUTRAL EVALUATION (ENE)*** *occurs when a judge assigns an evaluator to meet with the parties to a lawsuit and review the case.* The evaluator, normally an experienced attorney, will question the parties to determine if there is a possibility for settlement.

The evaluator attempts to get the parties to reach a settlement, but if no settlement can be reached, the evaluator writes an evaluation offering his or her assessment of the case. The evaluator will inform each party of how the evaluator "sees" the case and will offer his or her opinion about how the case may play out in court. Where liability is seen as a potential in the evaluator's eyes, he or she will provide the parties with an opinion as to what the damages might be awarded to the injured party. The evaluator's opinion is not binding on the parties. But once the parties review the evaluation, that review may cause one or both parties to settle immediately.

V. Mini-Trials

Sometimes, it is helpful if the principals to a dispute hear the evidence first hand. Especially in business disputes, it is common for management to turn the matter over to the attorneys and wait for the eventful litigation. In an attempt to reduce the expense of business litigation, the mini-trial has evolved.

The ***MINI-TRIAL*** *is a nonbinding ADR technique that closely resembles a court trial.* The parties select a neutral third party to advise the parties. In most cases, the parties have volunteered to use the mini-trial and agree to the procedural processes to be followed. These processes will specify how the mini-trial will be conducted and will address what type of "discovery" will be permitted. Normally, the extent of discovery is limited. At the mini-trial, the parties provide the neutral third party with the facts. The case as presented by each party reflects a summarized version of the facts. Attending the mini-trial are decision makers from each side. The idea is that upon hearing the facts for themselves, the decision makers will be more inclined to reach a settlement to the dispute.

At the conclusion of the mini-trial, the decision makers will meet to try and reach a settlement to the dispute. If no agreement is reached, the neutral third party will offer an opinion to the likely result if the parties desire. This will encourage the parties to settle or continue with litigation.

VI. Summary Jury Trial

A type of ADR technique that reflects the judicial process is the summary jury trial. *In a* ***SUMMARY JURY TRIAL****, the parties to a dispute agree to present a shortened case presentation to a mock jury. The jury serves in an advisory role to provide the parties an idea of how a real jury would rule.*

The summary jury trial proceeds much like a mini-trial, with a neutral third party acting as a judge and the people serving as a jury. The attorneys for each side present the case in a summarized fashion and then the jury deliberates on the verdict. Sometimes the members of the jury are not told their decision will only be advisory to the parties. This is to create a more real decision on the jury's part.

VII. Arbitration

Possibly the most well known of the various ADR techniques is arbitration.

In an ***ARBITRATION****, a neutral third party hears each side present the case from their viewpoint and then makes a decision regarding the results of the case.* This decision may be either binding or nonbinding. However, most private arbitrations are binding. In fact, in *Moncharsh v. Heily & Blase et al.*, 3 Cal. 4th 1, 10 Cal.Rptr.2d 183 (1992), the California Supreme Court stated that "it is a general rule that parties to a private arbitration impliedly agree that the arbitrator's decision will be both binding and final." If the decision is binding, the arbitrator's decision is final and not subject to appeal by either party as to the merits of the facts or law.

Due to the advantages of ADR that were discussed earlier, both the state of California and the federal government have passed legislation favoring arbitration. Congress expressed its strong support of arbitration by passing the **Federal Arbitration Act** (9 USCS Sections 1 et seq.). The California legislature, in 1961, enacted the **California Arbitration Act** (Code of Civil Procedure Sections 1280 et seq.). The courts have been very favorable in interpreting these acts when forced to determine if an agreement was made to arbitrate. However, these acts do have conflicting provisions as shown in the following case.

Basura v. U.S. Home Corporation

98 Cal. App. 4th 1205, 120 Cal. Rptr. 2d 328 (App. 2 Dist. 2002)
Edited Excerpts From the Opinion of Justice Klein

FACTS AND ISSUES

This litigations arises out of alleged design and construction defects in residential homes located in Palmdale. There are 48 plaintiffs and respondents in this action. The plaintiffs acquired their properties directly from U.S. Home Corporation (Home). The contracts between Home and buyers herein are from sales agreements for the conveyance of residential real property. Paragraph 14 states in relevant part: "By initialing in the space below, you are agreeing to have any dispute arising out of the matters included in the 'arbitration of disputes' provision decided by neutral arbitration as provided by California law and you are giving up any rights you might possess to have the dispute litigated in a court or jury trial." Ultimately the plaintiffs filed this action against Home. Subsequently Home filed a petition to compel arbitration of the plaintiffs' claims contending it had binding arbitration agreements with the plaintiffs.

(continued)

Plaintiffs' Contentions:

1. The arbitration clause was not enforceable if either party failed to initial it. Here 28 plaintiffs initialed the clause but Home did not initial it (with regard to the other 20 plaintiffs, they and Home initialed it).
2. California Code of Civil Procedure Section 1298.7 permits a purchaser to pursue a construction defect case in court even if the purchaser signed an agreement to convey real property containing an arbitration clause. Therefore all 48 plaintiffs can sue and avoid arbitration.
3. The Federal Arbitration Act (FAA) does not preempt California Code of Civil Procedure 1298.7 so as to make the California statute unavailable to all plaintiffs.

Contentions of Home:

1. The court is required to order the buyers to arbitrate the matter because all of the buyers had consented to arbitration by initialing the clause.
2. CCP Section 1298.7 is preempted by the FAA because the contracts at issue in this case involve interstate commerce.

The trial court denied the request of Home to compel arbitration by the 48 individuals who had bought homes from Home since: **1.** Home had failed to initial the arbitration clause on 28 of the contracts there was no arbitration agreement as to those 28 contracts; and **2.** CCP Section 1298.7 precludes compulsorily arbitration of construction defect lawsuits.

DECISION AND REASONS

The pertinent provision for this action is Section 1298.7, which states: "In the event an arbitration provision is included in a contract or agreement covered by this title [real estate], it shall not preclude or limit any right of action for bodily injury or wrongful death, or any right of action to which Section 337.1or 337.15 is applicable." Sections 337.1 and 337.15 pertained to litigation to recover damages for construction and design defects. In other words, the net effect of Section 1298.7 is to permit a purchaser to pursue a construction and design defect action against the developer in court, even if the purchaser signed an agreement to convey real property containing an arbitration clause.

Here, Section 1298.7 directly conflicts with Section 2 of the FAA. The United States Supreme Court held the FAA preempted a Montana statute declaring an arbitration clause unenforceable unless notice that the contract is subject to arbitration is typed on the first page of the contract in underlined capital letters. The Supreme Court noted Section 2 of the FAA provides that written provisions for arbitration "shall be valid, irrevocable, and enforceable, save upon the grounds as exist at law or in equity for the revocation of any contract." The high court affirmed its earlier rulings that the text of Section 2 declares that state law may be applied if that law arose to govern issues concerning the validity, revocability, and enforceability of contracts generally. Thus, generally acceptable contract defenses, such as fraud, duress, or unconscionability, may be applied to invalidate arbitration agreements without contravening Section 2.

(continued)

Courts may not, however, invalidate arbitration agreements under state laws applicable only to arbitration provisions. The plaintiffs do not allege any contract defense.

The FAA applies to a contract evidencing a transaction involving "interstate commerce". In the instant case, the declaration states the construction of the development project in Palmdale involved receipt and use of building materials and equipment such as GE Appliances, Merrilet Cabinets, Majestic Fireplaces, Alanco Windows, Carrier Heat & Air equipment, Progress Lighting, Delta plumbing, World Carpet and Armstrong flooring, which were manufactured and/or produced in states outside California and which were shipped to the job site in Palmdale. Also showing commerce across state lines, Home contracted with out-of-state design professionals, trade contractors, subcontractors and others; Home communicated by interstate mail and telephone without-of-state manufacturers, design professionals, trade contractors, subcontractors; and Home engaged in marketing and advertising activities throughout the country using interstate media.

The uncontroverted facts compel the conclusion that the agreements between Home and the plaintiffs involve interstate commerce. Therefore, the agreements are covered by the FAA. Accordingly, section 1298.7 cannot be utilized by plaintiffs to avoid the arbitration agreements.

Here, 28 of the plaintiffs obviously intended agreed to arbitration in that they initialed the arbitration clauses in their respective contracts. As for Home, in view of the fact it initialed the arbitration clauses in the contracts with the 20 other plaintiffs, it reasonably may be inferred that Home intended to be bound by arbitration across the board and that its failure to initial the arbitration clauses in each and every contract was simply due to clerical error. Therefore, the trial court is directed to conduct an evidentiary hearing and to make a factual determination as to whether Home intended to be bound by arbitration, notwithstanding its failure to initial the arbitration provisions with the 28 plaintiffs. If the court finds that Home so intended, it shall compel the 28 plaintiffs to arbitrate their claims.

A. COURT-ANNEXED ARBITRATION

In California, arbitrations may be either court-annexed or private. ***COURT-ANNEXED ARBITRATIONS*** *are where the court orders the case to arbitration.* In these situations, the arbitration is nonbinding and either party may ask for a ***TRIAL DE NOVO*** *(the trial proceeds as if the arbitration never took place).* In ***PRIVATE ARBITRATION****, the parties voluntarily agree to use arbitration to resolve the dispute.*

The California Legislature has declared that arbitrations should be both encouraged and required to help resolve small civil claims.

In superior court jurisdictions with eighteen or more judges, and in those jurisdictions with less than eighteen judges that provide for it by local rule, arbitration is mandated for use when the case involves less than fifty thousand dollars.

Each superior court may provide by local rule that all limited civil cases be submitted to arbitration. Court-annexed arbitrations may also occur where the parties stipulate to the use of arbitration regardless of the amount in controversy or upon the election of the plaintiff if the amount awarded will not exceed fifty thousand dollars.

While a court-annexed arbitration is not binding and the parties are entitled to a *trial de novo*, there are risks in not accepting the arbitrator's award. If a party seeks a *trial de novo* after a court-annexed arbitration and the ultimate judgement is not more favorable than what the arbitrator awarded, that party will be responsible for paying the costs incurred in bringing the matter to court, including any cost paid by the county to the arbitrator. Further, they will be unable to recover these costs from the other party.

B. PRIVATE ARBITRATION

There is no legal duty for parties to arbitrate disputes.

Therefore, the duty to arbitrate arises either from a statutory obligation or through a contract entered into between the parties. For a statutory obligation example, California Civil Code Section 1354 requires that for certain types of lawsuits brought to enforce conditions and restrictions it is a prerequisite to have served a Request for Resolution on the other party to the dispute in an attempt to resolve it through mediation or arbitration. There are some exceptions to the requirement, but the emphasis is on an attempt to legislate mandatory alternative dispute resolution prior to litigation. Enforcement of conditions and restrictions is covered in another chapter. If the duty to arbitrate has been created by contract, the parties either have an agreement to submit disputes to arbitration or, where there is no existing arbitration clause, the parties enter into an agreement to take an existing dispute to arbitration.

Giving up the right to litigate a dispute is a serious matter, and arbitration clauses should be knowingly executed.

Arbitration clauses should be written in such a manner that they stand out from the rest of the contract. In fact, some statutes require certain language and type size.

FOR EXAMPLE

California Code of Civil Procedure Section 1298 requires that when a contract for the sale of real estate or a listing agreement provides for arbitration, that provision must be clearly titled "ARBITRATON OF DISPUTES." If the arbitration provision is included in a printed contract, it must be set out in at least **8-POINT BOLD TYPE** or in contrasting red in at least 8-point type, and if it is included in a typed contract, it must be set out in capital letters.

(continued)

Then immediately above the line or space for the parties to indicate their assent or non-assent to the arbitration provision and immediately following the provision must appear the following in at least 10-point bold type if set out in a printed contract or 8-point type if in red or in capital letters if typed:

> "Notice: By initialing in the space below you are agreeing to have any dispute arising out of the matters included in the "arbitration of disputes' provision decided by neutral arbitration as provided by California law and you are giving up any rights you might possess to have the dispute litigated in a court or jury trial. By initialing in the space below you are giving up your judicial rights to discovery and appeal, unless those rights are specifically included in the "arbitration of disputes' provision. If you refuse to submit to arbitration after agreeing to this provision, you may be compelled to arbitrate under the authority of the California code of civil procedure. Your agreement to this arbitration provision is voluntary."
>
> "We have read and understand the foregoing and agree to submit disputes arising out of the matters included in the "arbitration of disputes' provision to neutral arbitration."

Where an arbitration clause has not been used, a submission agreement may be executed where the parties agree to take the dispute to arbitration.

In a private arbitration, the "arbitration clause" (or the submission agreement), establishes the scope of arbitration and the arbitrator's powers.

Extreme care should be taken to ensure all possible concerns are addressed by the submission agreement. To ensure that the parties' concerns are protected, it is common for an arbitration service to be used. There are many services available, some are profit organizations and others are nonprofit. These services provide procedures to be followed and when an arbitration clause references an arbitration service, those procedures determine exactly how the arbitration will be handled. An example of an arbitration service's rules is the American Arbitration Association's (AAA) "Commercial Arbitration Rules." These rules are available through the AAA's website or by writing to their offices to obtain a copy.

www.adr.org
American Arbitration Association

C. STARTING THE ARBITRATION

Either an arbitration agreement will be "self-executing" or will require a court order to start the process.

A ***SELF-EXECUTING ARBITRATION*** *clause provides a method for selecting the arbitrator, procedures for how the arbitration will be conducted, and a provision for continuing the arbitration if one party refuses to proceed.* Under a self-executing agreement, written notice is sent to the other party indicating arbitration is being sought under the agreement. The notice should contain what the dispute is about, the amount of damages, and what remedy is being sought. The party that receives the notice may then respond with a statement answering the demand.

If the agreement is not self-executing and the other party refuses to arbitrate after a demand to do so, then the court may be petitioned for an order compelling the other party to arbitrate the dispute. The petition must state the existence of a written agreement to arbitrate, that an actual dispute exists, and that the other party refuses to arbitrate. This petition must be served on the other party. A response is due within ten days of service within the state and within thirty days if served outside the state.

D. SELECTING THE ARBITRATOR

One of the advantages of arbitration is the ability of the parties to select the neutral third party deciding the case. If the arbitration clause includes the method of selecting the arbitrator, that is how the arbitrator will be selected. If not, the parties must mutually agree on who will arbitrate the matter. If no agreement can be reached, the parties may petition the court to appoint an arbitrator from a list of persons supplied jointly by the parties. If the arbitration clause referenced an arbitration service, the service's rules will be followed in selecting the arbitrator. Quite probably a "strike list" will be used by the arbitration service in selecting the arbitrator. A strike list works by the association sending a list of persons from the panel of neutrals maintained by the association to each party. The parties then "strike" from the list any unacceptable names. The list is then returned to the association where one of the acceptable names is selected to arbitrate the dispute.

Unless the arbitration agreement provides for more than one arbitrator, the arbitration will be by a single neutral arbitrator.

To ensure that the arbitrator is neutral, the person selected to be the arbitrator must disclose information that might cause the arbitrator to be biased in favor of one of the parties.

A party to the arbitration may disqualify the person selected on the basis of the disclosure if done within fifteen days after service of the disclosure statement. Each party has a right to disqualify one court-appointed arbitrator without cause and may petition the court to disqualify any subsequent appointee upon a showing of cause. Look at the following arbitration clause.

AN EXAMPLE - CONDOMINIUM - 35 Binding Arbitration

Any claim between or among any party subject to this Declaration (including without limitation, the Declarant, Association Board or officer, Unit Owners, or their employees or agents) arising out of or relating to this Declaration, a Unit or Units, the Condominium or the Association shall be determined by Arbitration in the country in which the Condominium is located commenced in accordance with the state arbitration code, provided, that the total award by a single arbitrator (as opposed to a majority of the arbitrators) shall not exceed $50,000, including interest, attorneys' fees, and costs. If any party demands a total award greater than $50,000, there shall be three (3) neutral arbitrators. If the parties cannot agree on the identity of the arbitrator(s) within ten days of the arbitration demand, the arbitrator(s) shall be selected by the administrator of the American Arbitration Association (AAA) office in the nearest city from its large, Complex Case Panel (or have similar professional credentials). Each arbitrator shall be an attorney with at least five years' experience in real estate law and shall reside in the county in which the Condominium is located or within a thirty mile radius of the Condominium address. Whether a claim is covered by the Article shall be determined by the arbitrator(s). All statutes of limitations which would otherwise be applicable shall apply to any arbitration proceeding hereunder.

What exactly does the arbitrator do? Of course, getting to the truth of the dispute is a primary goal of the arbitrator. The arbitrator will listen to the parties, their witnesses, review offered evidence, and then determine the facts of the dispute. After analyzing the facts, the arbitrator will render a decision. During the hearing, it is the arbitrator's responsibility to keep the hearing under control. Each side should be given the opportunity to present their evidence and arguments. The arbitrator has the sole power to decide what to admit into evidence.

To ensure the attendance of witnesses, the arbitrator is empowered to issue subpoenas. A ***SUBPOENA DUCES TECUM*** *(in this case, a writ issued at the request of one of the parties to an arbitration, which requires a witness to bring to the arbitration any relevant documents under the witness's control)* may be issued to compel the production of books, records, documents, and other evidence.

E. DISCOVERY

Normally discovery is limited in arbitrations. Discovery is covered in Chapter 14 (Law and the Courts). Discovery is limited to claims involving personal injury unless the arbitration agreement expressly provides for it.

If complete discovery is permitted, some of the benefits to arbitration may be lost. Both costs and time will increase if discovery is not limited.

F. FINAL DECISION

When the arbitrator has finished hearing the case, he or she will render the decision. *The arbitrator's decision is called the **AWARD***. The award must be in writing and signed by the arbitrator. Where the parties submitted questions to the arbitrator, the award must include a determination of those questions.

*Where the award is **BINDING**, it is considered a final judgment in the dispute*. Courts will not vacate an award unless the award was obtained through corruption, fraud, or other undue means. A court will also vacate an award if it can be shown that a party's rights were substantially prejudiced by misconduct of an arbitrator; an arbitrator exceeded the powers vested in him or her; refusing to postpone a hearing where there was sufficient cause; refusing to hear material evidence; or the arbitrator was corrupt. If an arbitrator has failed to disqualify himself or herself under the provisions applying to judges, the award may be vacated.

FOR EXAMPLE - CONDOMINIUM - 35 Arbitration Process

The arbitrator(s) shall take such steps as may be necessary to hold a private hearing within ninety days of the initial demand for arbitration and to conclude the hearing within three days; and the arbitrator(s) written decision shall be made not later than fourteen calendar days after the hearing. The parties have included these time limits in order to expedite the proceeding, but they are not jurisdictional, and the arbitrator(s) may for good cause afford or permit reasonable extensions or delays, which shall not affect the validity of the award. The written decision shall contain a brief statement of the claim(s) determined and the award made on each claim. In making the decision and award, the arbitrator(s) shall apply applicable substantive law. Absent fraud, collusion or willful misconduct by an arbitrator, the award and decision shall be final, and the judgment may be entered in any court having jurisdiction thereof. The arbitrator(s) may award injunctive relief or any other remedy available from a judge, including without limitation joinder of parties or consolidation of this arbitration with any other involving common issues of law or fact or which may promote judicial economy; but shall not have the power to award punitive or exemplary damages; or to award attorneys' fees and costs to the prevailing party. The decision and award of the arbitrator(s) need not be unanimous; rather, the decision and award of two arbitrators shall be final.

VIII. Private Judging

A growing trend in California is the use of private judging. With many of the courts overloaded with cases, some litigants are willing to seek a decision with the force of a superior court's decision but rendered through a quicker method than waiting for a court hearing. In California there are essentially two types of private judging. One is reference and the other is the use of temporary judges.

A. REFERENCE

A reference is like arbitration except the decision is appealable through the court system.

There may be a reference by agreement of the parties, by application of any party, or on the courts own motion. There are essentially two types of reference: general reference and special reference.

1. General Reference

A ***GENERAL REFERENCE*** *is where the referee tries any and all issues of the dispute.* The referee's decision stands as the decision of the court. Therefore, the referee's decision is final and appealable.

2. Special Reference

In a ***SPECIAL REFERENCE,*** *the referee addresses a specific question of fact.* The referee makes a recommendation to the court in a special reference and the referee's recommendation is not considered a decision of the court.

Where the reference has been imposed on the parties through the court's own motion or without all parties' consent, the reference is "special."

Who may serve as a referee? The only requirement is that the person be a resident of the county where the court is located. If the parties agree on who they want to serve as the referee, that person will be appointed by the court if the residency requirement is met. If the parties do not agree on a referee, the court must appoint a person. When the court makes the appointment, the parties are entitled to object to the person.

B. TEMPORARY JUDGING

The California Constitution in article VI, section 21 provides:

> On stipulation of the parties' litigant, the court may order a cause to be tried by a temporary judge who is a member of the State Bar, sworn and empowered to act until final determination of the cause.

To make use of this right, the dispute must be in litigation. The parties may then submit a written stipulation to the presiding judge naming the person being suggested for appointment, including their office address. The person named must take an oath of office and once that oath has been filed, the temporary judge is empowered with the same authority as a regular judge. The temporary judge must follow the rules of evidence and procedures as used in superior court. The decision rendered by the temporary judge is final and carries the same weight as if made by a permanent judge. The decision is not only final, but also appealable, just as a superior court decision would be.

How does private arbitration differ from the use of a temporary judge? An arbitrator does not need to take and file an oath like a temporary judge. Nor does an arbitrator have to follow rules of evidence or judicial procedures (unless required by the written arbitration agreement). Also an arbitrator only issues an award and not a final appealable judgment.

Normally, an arbitrator's award is not reviewable by the courts for errors of fact or law, but the decision issued by the temporary judge is subject to appeal on these issues.

IX. CHAPTER SUMMARY

Remember the following key points:

Before HOA members are allowed to file a claim in superior court, common interest developments in California are required to provide an ADR process and provide notice of such a process to its members.

Alternatives to litigation are generally speedier, less expensive, have the advantage of using an expert as the decision maker, the proceedings may remain confidential, the decisions are final and not appealable, and the procedure is less formal than the litigation.

Non-adjudicative methods include negotiation, mediation, early neutral fact finding, and mini- trials/summary trials. No binding decision is reached.

Adjudicative methods include judicial arbitration, private arbitration, and private judging. The decision is binding.

Distributive negotiation is a "win-lose" situation with one party defeating the other. Integrative negotiation is a "win-win" situation with both parties identifying solutions that benefit each other.

The negotiation process has three stages: preparation, actual negotiation, and conclusion of negotiation.

In mediation, a neutral party facilitates communication between the disputants to assist them in reaching an acceptable agreement. Mediations are judicial or private. The mediation process consists of starting the mediation, the opening session, identifying issues, mediated negotiation, and the conclusion.

In early neutral evaluation, a judge assigns an evaluator to help the parties reach an agreement, and if no agreement is reached, the evaluator writes an evaluation offering an assessment of how the case will play out in court.

In a mini-trial, the decision makers from each side of the dispute listen to a mini-trial of the case and try to reach a settlement. In a summary jury trial, the parties agree to present a shortened case to a mock jury and a jury decision will advise the parties in how the case would likely be decided.

Arbitration is generally binding and is either court-annexed or private.

References are private trials by court-appointed referees. References are general, in which the referee tries all issues of the dispute, or special, in which the referee tries only a specific issue. The decision is binding and appealable to the court. If the parties agree, a person may be sworn in as a temporary judge to decide the dispute.

X. REVIEW QUESTIONS

1. ADR stands for:

   a. administrative dispute reasoning.
   b. alternative dispute resolution.
   c. alternative directive renegotiations.
   d. administrative dispute resolution.

2. During negotiation, if the parties are concerned about maintaining a relationship after the negotiation has concluded, which of the following offers the best method for negotiating a solution?

   a. Distributive negotiation
   b. Integrative negotiation
   c. Win-lose negotiation
   d. Planning for litigation

3. Adjudicative alternative dispute resolution includes all of the following except:

   a. litigation.
   b. judicial arbitration.
   c. private arbitration.
   d. private judging.

4. In a non-adjudicative process, the parties:

   a. are bound by a judicial decision.
   b. resolve their disputes voluntarily.
   c. must agree to abide by a mediator's decision.
   d. have submitted their dispute to binding arbitration.

5. In a mediation process:

   a. a neutral person facilitates communication.
   b. a mutually acceptable agreement is the goal.
   c. the mediator should be a neutral third party.
   d. All of the above are correct answers.

6. The phrase "silence is golden" refers to:

   a. talk as much as you can during the negotiation process because this will prevent the other party from speaking and should insure your success.
   b. during awkward silence periods, keep your silence and make the other person speak and hopefully say something that you can use to your advantage.
   c. use only one or two word answers to questions and maintain your silence as much as possible during the negotiation.
   d. None of the above are correct answers.

7. Which of the following was not suggested as an element of the concluding stage of a negotiation?

a. Try to be considerate in winning.
b. Using deadlines can be an ineffective way of negotiating an agreement.
c. Review and clarify an agreement.
d. Put the agreement in written form and get signatures from all parties.

8. When a weaker party meets to convey issues to a mediator, it is done in:

a. "a caucus."
b. a registered letter.
c. in the judge's chamber.
d. None of the above are correct answers.

9. A neutral third party is helping two parties reach a solution to their disagreement. The two parties have agreed that the neutral third party will not impose a solution to the disagreement. What type of alternative dispute resolution is this?

a. Private judging
b. Negotiation
c. Reference
d. Mediation

10. In judicial mediation:

a. judges may order parties to undertake mediation.
b. parties can still litigate if mediation is not successful.
c. the judge acts as the mediator.
d. Both answers a and b above are correct.

ANSWERS: 1. *b*; 2. *b*; 3. *a*; 4. *b*; 5. *a*; 6. *b*; 7. *b*; 8. *a*; 9. *d*; 10. *d*

Living in a California

COMMON INTEREST DEVELOPMENT

August 2002

For information on common interest developments, go to the California Department of Real Estate website at:

www.dre.cahwnet.gov/cidinfo.htm

A

Acceptance. The indication by the offeree of agreement to the terms of the offer, which forms a contract.

Accrual Basis Accounting. System whereby an accountant records the impact of a business event as it occurs. When the business performs a service, makes a sale, or incurs an expense, the accountant enters the transaction onto the books, whether or not cash has been received or paid.

Active Concealment. Takes place, for example, when an owner puts a "sludge" in an automobile's transmission to hide a shifting problem temporarily.

Actual Agency. Created by the written or verbal contract between the principal and the agent.

Actual Authority. That which the principal expressly gives the agent.

Actual Fraud. A misrepresentation of a material (important) fact made with knowledge of the misrepresentation and upon which the victim relied on the to his or her detriment.

Actual Knowledge. With regards to restrictions, actual knowledge can be accomplished by recording the restrictions and making sure that the owner receives a copy of them prior to purchasing a unit.

Adjudicative Methods. A neutral third party is used but rather than just helping the parities reach a voluntary agreement, the neutral third party actually decides the result of the dispute. (Compare with **Nonadjudicative Methods**.)

Adult Day Program. Any community-based facility or program that provides care to persons 18 or older in need of personal services, supervision, or assistance essential for sustaining the activities of daily living or for the protection of these individuals on less than a 24-hour basis.

Affirm. Agree with.

Affirmative Defenses. Pay differentials permitted when they are based on seniority, merit, quantity or quality of production, or a factor other than sex.

Age Discrimination in Employment Act of 1967 (ADEA). Protects individuals who are 40 years of age or older from employment discrimination based on age.

Agent. Works for the employer (the principal) and can contract on behalf of the employer.

Airport-Influenced Area (Airport Referral Area). The area in which current or future airport-related noise, over flight, safety, or airspace protection may significantly affect land use or necessitate restrictions on those uses as determined by an airport land use commission.

Alienation. The transfer of ownership or an interest in property from one person to another by any means.

Alternative Dispute Resolution (ADR). The resolution of disputes by negotiation, mediation, and arbitration, other than by lawsuit in court.

Americans With Disabilities Act of 1990 (ADA). Prohibits private employers with 15 or more employees, including governments, employment agencies, and labor unions, from discriminating against qualified individuals with disabilities in job application procedures, hiring, firing, advancement, compensation, job training, and other terms, conditions, and privileges of employment.

Answer. The defendant either admits or denies the allegations made by the plaintiff in the complaint.

Appellate Courts. The primary function of these courts is to review trial courts' decisions for errors in law. The party making the appeal is called the **Appellant**, and the party opposing the appeal is called the **Appellee** (sometimes **Respondent**).

Arbitration. A neutral third party hears each side present the case from their viewpoint and then makes a decision regarding the results of the case.

Arbitration Clause (Submission Agreement). In a private arbitration, this agreement establishes the scope of arbitration and the arbitrator's powers.

Articles of Incorporation. The required written document necessary to be filed with the Secretary of State in order to form a corporation.

Assault. Placing a person in immediate fear of bodily harm or offensive contact.

Association. A nonprofit corporation or unincorporated association created for the purpose of managing a common interest development. Refers to a **homeowner association**, also called a **community association**.

At Will. An employment contract that can be terminated when the principal or the agent desires to do so. (Compare with **For a Term**.)

Award. The arbitrator's decision.

B

Bilateral Contract. One in which a promise is exchanged for another promise.

Binding. Previously decided court decisions (precedents) control the dispute under current consideration by the judge; also where the award in a arbitration is binding, it is considered a final judgment in the dispute.

Blanket Insurance Policy. Covers all of the structures on a property, including losses due to fire and lightning. (Compare with **Extended Coverage**.)

Blank Proxy. Allows the person to vote on behalf of an absent member however the person chooses to do so. (Also see **Proxy** and **Proxy Holder**.)

Board Members. Individuals who are elected by the members of the association to make up the board of directors.

Briefs. Legal arguments contained in documents filed with the court.

Budgeting. The process of identifying, gathering, summarizing, and communicating financial information about an organization's future activities.

Bureau of Labor Statistics. The federal agency that computes the **consumer price index**.

Business Judgment Rule. Immunizes directors and officers from liability as long as the corporation acted in good faith, and with an eye toward the best interest of the association as any reasonably prudent person would do.

Bylaws. Govern a homeowner association's internal affairs (rules and procedures) and how it functions.

C

Calendar Year. The year that ends on December 31. (Compare to **Fiscal Year**.)

California Supreme Court. At the state level, the court of last resort for questions of state law. Its greatest function is to oversee the orderly development of law within the state.

Caucus. Provides a mechanism for both parties to convey his or her issues and concerns to the **mediator**.

Choice of Forum. When the parties to a contract specify that, in the event of litigation concerning the contract, such litigation must be filed in a particular court.

Choice of Law. When the parties to a contract specify that the law of a particular state or nation is the law that will apply in the event of a dispute regarding the contract.

Civil Law. Concerned with how individuals interact with each other. (Compare with **Criminal Law**.)

Codified. When a law has been placed into one of the existing Codes or a new Code.

Cohabitant. Refers to persons who live together as husband and wife, or persons who are domestic partners within the meaning of state law

Common Area. Sometimes called the "common elements," it can be owned in common by the owners of the separate interests, or some portion of the common area owned by the owners of separate interests and the balance of the common area owned by the homeowner (community) association. Also see **Exclusive Use Common Area**.)

Common Interest Development Manager. An individual who, for compensation, or the expectation of compensation, provides or contracts to provide management or financial services, or represents himself or herself to act in the capacity of providing management or financial services to a community association.

Common Interest Development Open Meeting Act. Enacted to make certain that members of the association/corporation will receive notice of board meetings and have an opportunity to attend and to speak at the meetings.

Common Law. Based on judicial decisions rather than legislative action.

Community Apartment Project. A development where the owners own the entire project and each owner gets the right to occupy one of the apartments.

Community Care Facility. Any facility, place, or building that is maintained and operated to provide non-medical residential care, day treatment, adult daycare, or foster family agency services for children, adults, or children and adults, including, but not limited to, the physically handicapped, mentally impaired, incompetent persons, and abused and neglected children.

Community Treatment Facility. Provides mental health treatment services to children in a group setting and has the capacity to provide secure containment.

Complaint. Filed by the person who believes he or she has a legal cause of action against another person and with its filing the lawsuit is started.

Condition Precedent. One which is to be performed or occur before some right dependent on it accrues, or some act dependant on it is performed.

Condition Subsequent. One referring to a future event, upon the happening of which the obligation becomes no longer binding on the other party if the other party chooses to enforce the condition.

Conditions. Provisions in the contract which determine the time for performance, the order of performance, or establish the circumstances under which a performance obligation begins or ends.

Conditions Concurrent. Those performance conditions which are mutually dependant and are to be performed at the same time.

Condominium Unit. Consists of an undivided interest in common in a portion of the real property (common area) coupled with a separate interest in a space called a "unit"; The air space contained within and the surfaces of the perimeter walls, floors, ceiling, windows, and doors.

Consideration. One person promises to do or not to do something in return for which another person promises to do or not to do something.

Consumer Price Index. A measure of the average change over time in the prices paid by urban consumers for a market basket of consumer goods and services.

Court. A place where a dispute may be heard and a determination rendered regarding the outcome of that dispute. (Also see **Trial Courts** and **Appellate Courts**.)

Court-Ordered Arbitrations. Occurs when the court orders the case to arbitration.

Covenant. An agreement between two landowners regarding a promise of one landowner to either do or not do something with regard to the property owned by that landowner.

Covenants, Conditions, and Restrictions (CC&Rs). Adeclaration, usually recorded by a developer, to create a common plan of private restrictions for a subdivision.

Credit Bidding. The amount owed to the association as of the date of the sale can be bid thereby insuring that if there is another bidder for the property, the association will be certain to get all amounts that it is owed to date.

Criminal Law. Concerned with behavior that is considered unacceptable to society at large. (Compare with **Civil Law**.)

Cross-Complaint. When the defendant counter sues the plaintiff.

D

Damages. Harm or injury.

Davis-Stirling Common Interest Development Act. Provides that a common interest development means any of the following: 1) condominium project; 2) planned development; 3) stock cooperative; or 4) community apartment project. It requires that a common interest development must be managed by a community association, also referred to as a homeowner association (HOA). The association can either be incorporated or unincorporated.

Declaration. The recorded document that states whether the common interest development is a community project apartment, condominium project, planned development, stock cooperative, or a combination thereof, and additionally, establishes enforceable restrictions on the use or enjoyment of any portion of the common interest development. Also known as **Covenants and Restrictions (C&Rs)** and **Covenants, Conditions, and Restrictions (CC&Rs)**.

Declaratory Relief. A statement from the court declaring the rights and duties contained in a written instrument or contract which can include a determination of the validity of all or part of the instrument or contract or a question of construction or interpretation of the document.

Default Judgment. A ruling entered against a defendant who fails to answer a summons in a lawsuit.

Deflation. A decline in the general price level of goods and services that results in increased purchasing power of money. The opposite of **Inflation**.

Demurrer. A motion to dismiss the action. With this motion, the defendant is objecting to the complaint because there are legal problems with the complaint that appear on the face of the pleading.

Deposition. A written or oral statement made under oath, given before a trial, which is preserved in writing. **Oral Depositions** are more common than other forms of discovery and give an attorney the opportunity to ask questions of either the other party or other witnesses. **Written Depositions** are much like interrogatories in that they are written questions that must be answered in writing, under oath, but they may be sent to witnesses who are not parties to the lawsuit.

Directed Verdict. A judge's order to a jury to return a specified verdict, usually because one of the parties failed to prove its case. (Also see **Verdict**.)

Disclosure Regarding Real Estate Agency Relationships. An agent must disclose the nature of the agency relationship to all parties as soon as practical.

Discovery. The parties use various tools to help "discover" evidence that supports or hinders their claims and helps each side know the strengths and weaknesses of their cases.

Duty of Care. Requires the agent to follow the instructions of the principal using reasonable care and skill in performance of the job.

Duty of Loyalty. Requires that an agent be loyal to the principal at all times.

E

Early Neutral Evaluation (ENE). Occurs when a judge assigns an evaluator to meet with the parties to a lawsuit and review the case.

Elderly Residential Care Facility. A housing arrangement chosen voluntarily by persons 60 years or older where varying levels and intensities of care are provided based on varying needs.

Employee. Works for the employer.

Equal Employment Opportunity Commission (EEOC). Administers and enforces Title VII of the Civil Rights Act, the Equal Pay Act of 1963, the Age Discrimination in Employment Act of 1967, the Rehabilitation Act of 1973 (Section 501 and 505), Titles I and V of the Americans with Disabilities Act of 1990, and the Civil Rights Act of 1991.

Equal Pay Act. Requires that men and women be given equal pay for equal work in the same establishment.

Equitable Remedies. Attempt to create fairness and justice for the person who has been harmed. It grants specific relief, not damages. (Compare with **Legal Remedy**.)

Equitable Servitude. A covenant or restriction that can be enforceable against another if the other person had knowledge of it, even though it wasn't recorded.

Error in Judgment. This happens, for example, if the tree pruner offers to prune all of the trees on the property but forgot to include the cost of the rental of a bucket lift able to reach the necessary height.

Errors and Omissions Insurance. Protects against losses resulting from negligent acts, errors, and omissions, or breach of any duty by the directors or officers of an association.

Establishment. A physical place of business rather than an entire business or enterprise consisting of several places of business.

Estoppel. A defense used to prohibit someone from recanting a previous statement, approval, or position.

Executed Contract. A contract that has been fully performed by both parties.

Executory Contract. One in which performance remains to be completed by either one or both parties.

Exclusive Use Common Area. That portion of the common area designated by the declaration for the exclusive use of a separate interest owner, rather than all the separate interest owners.

Expert Trial Witness. A person who has special knowledge, skill, experience, training, or education sufficient to qualify him or her as an expert on the subject to which his or her testimony relates.

Express Contract. One in which the terms are stated in written or spoken words.

Extended Coverage. Will cover losses from causes such as smoke, hail, wind, explosion, riots and civil commotion, falling objects, and water damage, to name a few. (Compare with **Blanket Insurance Policy**.)

F

False Promise. Occurs at the time of entering into a contract when one person makes a promise about performing an obligation with absolutely no intention of performing it.

Family Daycare Home. One that regularly provides care, protection, and supervision for 14 or fewer children, in the provider's own home, for periods of less than 24 hours per day, while the parents or guardian are away.

Fair Housing Act. Makes it unlawful to discriminate in the sale or rental of housing on the basis of race, color, religion, sex, familial status, national origin, or handicap.

Familial Status. Means one or more individuals (who have not attained the age of 18 years) being domiciled with: 1) a parent or other person having legal custody of such individual or individuals; or 2) the designee of such parent or other person having such custody, with the written permission of such parent or other person.

Fidelity Insurance. Covers losses experienced through the dishonest or fraudulent acts of employees who have access to association funds.

Final Agreement Clause. Makes it clear that there are no other prior agreements between the parties, and that this agreement is final.

Financial Services. Acts performed or offered to be performed for compensation for a community association including, but not limited to, the preparation of internal unaudited financial statements, internal accounting and bookkeeping functions, billing of assessments, and related services.

First Sale Notice. A notice delivered to a perspective buyer in a common interest development converted from an existing dwelling listing defects in the unit or common areas.

Fiscal Year. The chosen or established year for accounting purposes. (Compare to **Calendar Year**.)

Fixed Wireless Signals. Any commercial non-broadcast communications signals transmitted via wireless technology to and/or from a fixed customer location.

For a Term. An employment contract where the principal (employer) or the employee (agent) will have to show just cause for terminating the employment contract in order to avoid liability for damages. (Compare with **At Will.**)

Foster Family Home. Provides 24-hour care for six or fewer foster children and is the residence of the foster parent or parents, including their family, and whose care the foster children have been placed.

H-J

Handicap. Means, with respect to a person: 1) a physical or mental impairment which substantially limits one or more of such person's major life activities; 2) a record of having such an impairment; or 3) being regarded as having such an impairment, but such term does not include current illegal use of, or addiction to, a controlled substance.

Implied Contract. One in which is not reduced to writing, but rather is based on conduct.

Improvement Expenses. For new items which will enhance the living environment and increase the value of the units.

Indemnification. To reimburse.

Inflation. An increase in the general price level of goods and services; alternatively, a decrease in purchasing power. The oposite of **deflation**.

Inflation Clause. Automatically raises the dollar amount of insurance coverage based on an increase in an inflation or price index.

Injunction. A court order that either stops conduct (**prohibitory injunction**) or requires conduct (**mandatory injunction**). (Also see **Preliminary Injunction.**) A type of **Equitable Remedy**.

Independent Contractor. Hired by the employer to work "independently" and not under the direction and control of the employer as to the details of the work.

In Personam Jurisdiction. Jurisdiction over the person.

In Rem Jurisdiction. Refers to a court's right to jurisdiction over a property, not a person.

Intentional Misrepresentation. A statement was made knowing that it was false. (Compare to **Negligent Misrepresentation.**)

Interrogatories. Written questions submitted to the opposing party.

Judicial Foreclosure. The sale of the property results from the filing of court papers and is a supervised sale by the court.

Jurisdiction. The court power and authority to decide a case.

L

Laches. The legal doctrine that a legal right or claim will not be enforced or allowed if a long delay in asserting the right or claim has prejudiced the adverse party (hurt the opponent) as a sort of "legal ambush."

Legal Cause of Action. A valid claim entitling plaintiff to relief because person has had a legal right or duty violated by another person and has the ability to use the courts as a means to resolve the dispute.

Legal Remedy. Monetary damages are sought. (Compare with **Equitable Remedies**.)

Liability Insurance. Used by the homeowner association to protect itself against financial loss caused from being held legally liable for bodily injury or death of another and/or for damage to or loss of the property of another.

Lien. A recorded document against the owner's property which makes the property security for the amount owed.

Long-Arm Statute. Permits the plaintiff to bring an out-of-state defendant into the state court for the purposes of defending against the claims made by the plaintiff.

Loss Assessment Coverage. Covers owners for assessments for certain kinds of losses that they must help pay for.

Loss of Use. Coverage in an insurance policy that pays for expenses if a person needs to stay somewhere else.

Lottery. Any scheme for the disposal or distribution of property by chance, among persons who have paid or promise to pay any valuable consideration for the chance of obtaining such property or a portion of it,... whether called a lottery, raffle, gift-enterprise, or by whatever name the same may be known."

M

Management Services. Acts performed or offered to be performed in an advisory capacity for a community association.

Manager's Report. A means by which for the common interest development manager can inform the members about the daily operation of the development since the last homeowner's meeting.

Managing Agent. A person or entity who, for compensation or in expectation of compensation, exercises control over the assets of a common interest development.

Market (Marketing). The listing, advertising, or obtaining or providing access to show the owner's interest in the development.

Mediation. A process in which a neutral person (or persons) facilitates communication between the disputants to assist them to reach an acceptable agreement. A **Judicial Mediation** occurs after a lawsuit has been filed. A **Private Mediation** occurs after the parties contractually agree to use mediation as a method of resolving their dispute.

Mediator. Facilitates the negotiations among the parties and is the neutral person who conducts a mediation.

Members of the Association. Consists of the owners of the separate interests in the common interest development.

Mini-Trial. A nonbinding ADR technique that simulates a court trial with respect to selected issues.

Mistake of Fact. A mistake about a fact that is material (important) to a transaction.

Mistake of Law. A mistake about the legal effect of a known fact or situation. This will permit rescission of the contract.

Motion. A call for action that is used to get a group to make a decision on a particular topic. Most motions are either a **Main Motion** or a **Secondary Motion**.

Motion for a Direct Verdict. Requires the court to rule that there are no factual issues for the jury to consider.

Motion for Judgment of Nonsuit. Attacks the sufficiency of the plaintiff's evidence and argues that no evidence was presented to support the pleadings.

Motion for Summary Judgment. Argues that there are no triable issues of fact and that a judgment may be rendered as a matter of law.

Mutual Mistake. Occurs when both parties make the same mistake regarding a material fact.

N

Natural Hazard Disclosure Statement. The seller, or his or her agent, is required to provide prospective buyers with this document if the property is located within one or more of the six specified natural zones.

Negligence. Conduct that falls below the standard of care that a reasonable person (in this case, a reasonable community association) would exercise under the circumstances; sometimes called carelessness or recklessness.

Negligent Misrepresentation. Occurs when a positive statement was made, not knowing if it was true, and the other party relied on it. (Compare to **Intentional Misrepresentation**.)

Negotiation. When parties voluntarily work out their differences and reach an acceptable solution to the dispute in a peaceful manner. **Distributive Negotiation** is often referred to as being a "win-lose" situation. **Integrative Negotiation** takes place when the parties participate in joint problem solving.

Non-Adjudicative Methods. Seek to have the parties resolve their disputes voluntarily and there is no binding decision made or required. (Compare with **Adjudicative Methods**.)

O

Occasional Worker Coverage. Is normally automatically included in the basic condominium policy. It covers injuries to someone working on the separate interest.

Offeree. The party who receives an offer from the offeror.

Offeror. The party who makes the offer to an offeree.

Operating Expenses. Deal with the normal day-to-day operation of the association.

Operating Rule. A regulation adopted by the board of directors that applies generally to management and operation of the development for the conduct of the business and affairs of the association.

Ostensible Agency. Sometimes referred to as an **Apparent Agency**, it is created by actions, or inactions, of the principal which cause a third person to believe another to be the agent of the principal when that is not the case.

Ostensible Authority. Like **Ostensible Agency**, comes from actions or statements, or the lack thereof, made intentionally or carelessly by the principal causing a third person to believe that the agent has authority to act on behalf of the principal.

Over-the-Air Reception Devices Rule. Prohibits restrictions that impair the installation, maintenance, or use of antennas used to receive video programming by viewers.

P

Permitted Healthcare Resident. A person hired to provide live-in, long-term, or terminal health care to a senior citizen, or a family member of the senior citizen providing that care.

Personal Liability Insurance. Protects an owner if other people make a claim or bring a lawsuit against him or her for personal injury or property damage.

Personal Property. All property which is not considered real property.

Planned Development. A subdivision where the owner owns a lot as a separate interest and the homeowner (community) association owns the remaining common areas.

Pleadings. Documents that must be prepared and filed to start the lawsuit. The primary documents that make up the pleadings are the **Complaint** and **Answer**.

Power Coupled With an Interest. One which is created for the benefit of the agent instead of the principal.

Peremptory Challenges. Jury selection procedure whereby a prospective juror may be dismissed for any reason except race or gender.

Preliminary Injunction. At a hearing, a preliminary injunction keeps the situation from changing pending the possible issuance of a **permanent injunction** (final injunction) after a trial.

Private Law. The body of law governing the interaction between individuals. (Compare with **Public Law**.)

Private Sale. A situation where it is not necessary for the association to file any court papers in order to sell the owner's property.

Procedural Laws. Enforce the rights or duties granted by the substantive laws by imposing on the government a procedural structure that must be followed when establishing or enforcing substantive laws. (Compare with **Substantive Laws**.)

Pro Forma Statement. A carefully formulated expression of predicted results.

Property and Liability Insurance. A plan to distribute the actual losses among a group of individuals bearing the same risk of an event by having the individuals contribute a small portion to a fund which will pay the unfortunate members of the group who suffer loss caused by the occurrence of the event.

Proper Venue. Means that the lawsuit will be heard by the court with jurisdiction in the geographic location closest to where the injury or event occurred. (Also see **Venue**.)

Proxy. A written authorization, signed by a member or the member's attorney in fact, giving another person or persons power to vote on behalf of such member. (Also see **Blank Proxy** and **Proxy Holder**.)

Proxy Holder. The person or persons to whom the proxy is given.

Proxy, Irrevocable. It cannot be recalled or withdrawn for the period specified in the proxy.

Proxy, Revocable. May vote on the item only if the proxy form sets forth the general nature of that item.

Public Law. Deals with how the government is organized and how it interacts with the people of the country. (Compare with **Private Law**.)

Q-R

Quasi Contract. One that is imposed by the courts to prevent unjust enrichment when the technical requirements of a contract have not been met.

Quorum. The necessary number of members which must be in attendance before a board of directors can legally conduct business.

Ratification. Takes place when the principal accepts the benefits of a transaction done by a person who is not the agent for the principal. The confirmation or adoption of a previous act done either by the party himself or by another.

Real Estate Transfer Disclosure Statement. Identifies items of value attached to the structure or land and states whether these items are operational. It also asks the seller to identify any structural or material defects.

Real Property. Generally thought of as the land, anything permanently attached to the land, anything appurtenant (something running with the land such as a recorded right-of-way to cross the land), and those things on the land which are considered to be immovable by law (such as a giant oak tree).

Reasonable Accommodation. A change in rules, policies, practices, or services so that the person with a disability will have an equal opportunity for the use and the enjoyment of the residential unit or any common area.

Reasonable Modification. A structural change that is made to allow the person with a disability the full enjoyment of the unit and related facilities.

Reference. Like arbitration, except the decision is appealable through the court system. **General Reference** is where the referee tries any and all issues of the dispute. With a **Special Reference**, the referee addresses a specific question of fact.

Reformation. When the courts correct the language of a contract because it does not accurately reflect the true bargain of the parties. A type of **Equitable Remedy**.

Remaining Life. The anticipated number of years the major component will continue to exist and serve its purpose.

Remand. Send back.

Repugnant. Normally means something that is repulsive, offensive or disgusting, but it can also mean something which is inconsistent, illogical or contradictory.

Requests for Admissions. A means to compel the other party to admit factual information so time is not spent in discovering that information. A form of discovery.

Rescind. Cancel.

Rescission. Used to cancel a contract due to some irregularity. After rescission, it is as if there had never been a contract. A type of **Equitable Remedy**.

Reserve Expenses. Deal with replacement of major components.

Reserve Study. An important planning document which will help the board in preparing for the financial longevity and success of the development.

Residential Care Facility. Provides for persons with "chronic life-threatening illness" which serves 6 or fewer persons who are 18 or older, emancipated minors, or family units is considered a residential use of the property and the use of property by a single family.

Residential Facility. Any family home, group care facility, or similar facility for 24-hour non-medical care of persons in need of personal services, supervision, or assistance essential for sustaining the activities of daily living or for the protection of the individual.

Respondeat Superior. A doctrine that the principal is liable for the torts of employees/agents. (Also see **Tort.**)

Restitution. Placing the parties in their original positions by having each side return to the other whatever had been transferred. A type of **Equitable Remedy** accompanying restitution.

Restraint. A restriction on the freedom of one's action.

Reverse. Overturn a court's decision.

Risk of Loss. The probability that an event will occur which causes a loss of or damage to real or personal property of the owner.

Roll Call Vote. The chairperson calls out the name of each individual member, and that member either answers with a "Yes" or "No" on the motion as the person's name is called.

Rule Change. The adoption, amendment, or repeal of an operating rule by the board of directors.

S

Satisfaction Clause. A contractual clause providing that one party's performance must be satisfactory to the other party, and if it is not, the other party does not have to perform.

Secret Ballot. A written vote without a person's name on the vote.

Self-Executing Arbitration Clause. Provides a method for selecting the arbitrator, procedures for how the arbitration will be conducted, and provides for continuing the arbitration if one party refuses to proceed.

Senior Citizen Housing Development. A residential development developed, substantially rehabilitated, or substantially renovated for senior citizens that has at least 35 dwelling units.

Separate Interest. The title or ownership interest acquired by a purchaser.

Signed. The placing of the member's name on the proxy (whether by manual signature, typewriting, telegraphing transmission, or otherwise) by the member or such member's attorney in fact. (See **Proxy**.)

Small Claims Court. In California, it has jurisdiction for the recovery of money where the demand does not exceed $5,000.

Small Family Home. Provides 24-hour care in the licensee's home for six or fewer foster children who have mental disorders or developmental or physical disabilities and who require special care and supervision as a result of their disabilities.

Social Rehabilitation Facility. Provides social rehabilitation services for not longer than 18 months in a group setting to adults recovering from mental illness who temporarily need assistance, guidance, or counseling.

Solar Easement. The right of receiving sunlight across real property of another for any solar energy system.

Specific Performance. Used when a contract has been breached (broken) and the harmed person wants completion of the specific contract performance agreed to. A type of **Equitable Remedy**.

Staggered Terms. A process whereby each year only a certain number of board members are up for election and each term exceeds a year which means that the entire board is never elected at one time.

Stare Decisis. To abide by, follow, or adhere to decided court cases.

Statute of Frauds. California law that makes certain contracts unenforceable in court unless they, or some note or memorandum thereof, are in writing, and are signed by the person being sued or by that person's agent.

Statute of Limitations. The period of time within which a person (plaintiff) must file a lawsuit against a defendant.

Stock Cooperative. A corporation which owns the entire property and each shareholder of the corporation has the right to occupy a residential unit in the development which is known as a separate interest.

Substantive Laws. Affect individuals by either granting them legal rights or imposing legal duties on them. (Compare with **Procedural Laws**.)

Substitute Service. Accomplished by leaving a copy of the claim and order during usual office hours at the defendant's office or, if no physical address is known, at the defendant's usual mailing address, other than a post office box, with the person who is apparently in charge thereof. He or she must then mail a copy of the claim and order by first-class mail, postage prepaid, to the person to be served at the place where the copy was left.

Summary Jury Trial. The parties to a dispute agree to present a shortened case presentation to a mock jury. The jury serves in an advisory role to provide the parties an idea of how a real jury would rule.

Subpoena Duces Tecum. A writ issued at the request of one of the parties to an arbitration. It requires a witness to bring to the arbitration any relevant documents under the witness's control.

Suppression. Occurs when the truth of a condition is not easily discoverable through reasonable inspection or investigation.

T

Therapeutic Day Service. Provides non-medical care, counseling, education or vocational support, or social rehabilitation services on less than a 24-hour basis to persons under 18 years who would otherwise be placed in foster care or are returning to families from foster care.

Title VII of the Civil Rights Act of 1964. Protects individuals against employment discrimination on the basis of race and color, as well as national origin, sex, and religion as well as an amendment for pregnancy.

Tort. Wrongful act. (Also see **Respondeat Superior**.)

Transitional Housing Placement Facility. Licensed to provide transitional housing opportunities to persons at least 16 years old and not more than 18 years old who are in out-of-home placement under county social services or probation supervision and are participating in an independent living program.

Transitional Shelter Care Facility. Any group care facility that provides for 24-hour non-medical care of persons under 18 years in need of personal services, supervision, or assistance essential for sustaining the activities of daily living or for the protection of the individual for up to 90 days.

Trial Courts. Where the facts of the case are determined and the appropriate legal rules are applied to resolve the dispute. (Compare with **Appellate Courts**.)

Trial de Novo. A form of appeal in which the appeals court holds a trial as if no prior trial had been held. A trial de novo is common on appeals from small claims court judgments.

Trustee's Sale. A public auction; the foreclosed property is sold to the highest bidder.

U

Undisclosed Principal. When the principal wishes to sell items or purchase items without third persons realizing the identity of the party with whom they are contracting, the principal is undisclosed.

Undue Hardship. An action requiring significant difficulty or expense when considered in light of factors such as an employers size, financial resources, and the nature and structure of its operation.

Unilateral Contract. An agreement to pay in exchange for performance, if the potential performer chooses to act. A unilateral contract is distinguished from a **bilateral** contract, which is an exchange of one promise for another.

Unilateral Mistake. If only one party made a mistake. Rescission of a contract is possible under this condition.

United States District Court. The general trial court at the federal level.

United States Supreme Court. Has both original and appellate jurisdiction, but its primary function is to serve as the last and final court for reviewing court cases from both the federal courts and certain state cases (relating to federal law).

V-W

Venue. A neighborhood; the neighborhood, place, or a county in which an injury is declared to have been done, or fact declared to have happened. (Also see **Proper Venue**.)

Verdict. The method the jury uses to pronounce upon the issues in the case in favor of either the plaintiff or defendant. (Also see **Directed Verdict**.)

Voir Dire. The questioning of prospective jurors by a judge and attorneys in court. Voir dire is used to determine if any juror is biased and/or cannot deal with the issues fairly, or if there is cause not to allow a juror to serve.

Voting Power. Defined under the corporation law to mean "the power to vote for the election of the directors at the time any determination of voting power is made and does not include the right to vote upon the happening of some condition or event which has not yet occurred."

Writ of Execution. An order issued by the court clerk directing the levying officer, usually the sheriff of the county, to seize certain property of the losing party.

A

Index

B

C

D

E

F

G

H

I

J

K

L

HOMEOWNER'S
ASSOCIATION
MEETING TONIGHT

P

Q

R

S

T

U

V

W

Textbooks From Educational Textbook Company

Sometimes our textbooks are hard to find!

If your bookstore does not carry our textbooks, send us a check or money order and we'll mail them to you with our 30-day money back guarantee.

Other Great Books from Educational Textbook Company:

California Real Estate Principles, 10th ed. (2nd Printing), by Huber	$65.00	_____
How To Pass The Real Estate Exam (850 Exam Questions), by Huber	$40.00	_____
California Real Estate Law, by Huber & Tyler	$50.00	_____
Real Estate Finance, by Huber & Messick	$50.00	_____
Real Estate Economics, by Huber, Messick, & Pivar	$50.00	_____
Real Estate Appraisal, by Huber, Messick, & Pivar	$50.00	_____
Mortgage Loan Brokering, by Huber & Pivar	$50.00	_____
Property Management, by Huber & Pivar	$50.00	_____
Escrow I: An Introduction, by Huber	$50.00	_____
California Real Estate Practice, by Huber & Lyons	$50.00	_____
Real Estate Computer Applications, by Grogan & Huber	$50.00	_____
Homeowner's Association Management, by Huber & Tyler	$50.00	_____
California Business Law, by Huber, Owens, & Tyler	$65.00	_____
Hubie's Power Prep CD – 100 Questions - Vol. 1, by Huber	$50.00	_____

Subtotal _____
Add shipping and handling @ $5.00 per book _____
Add California sales tax @ 8.25% _____
TOTAL _____

Allow 2-3 weeks for delivery

Name: ______________________________
Address: ______________________________
City, State, Zip: ______________________________
Phone: ______________________________

Check or money order: Educational Textbook Company, P.O. Box 3597, Covina, CA 91722

For faster results, order by credit card from the Glendale Community College Bookstore:

1-818-240-1000 x3024
1-818-242-1561 (Direct)
Check us out at: www.etcbooks.com